The Great
American History
Fact-Finder

The Great American History Fact-Finder

★ ★ ★

The Who, What, Where, When, and Why
of American History

Pam Cornelison AND Ted Yanak

Second Edition

UPDATED AND EXPANDED

HOUGHTON MIFFLIN COMPANY

Boston · New York

2004

Visit our Web site: www.houghtonmifflinbooks.com.

Library of Congress Cataloging-in-Publication Data
Cornelison, Pam.
The great American history fact-finder : the who, what, where,
when, and why of American history / Pam Cornelison and Ted Yanak
— 2nd ed., updated and expanded
p.   cm.
Yanak's name appears first on the earlier edition.
ISBN 0-618-43941-2
1. United States — History — Dictionaries. I. Yanak, Ted. II. Title.
E174.C67 2004
973'.03—dc22   2004047480

PRINTED IN THE UNITED STATES OF AMERICA

MP 10 9 8 7 6 5 4 3 2 1

Text art credits follow the index.

Again . . . To Our Children

AMY, HOLLY,
JONATHAN, KRISTEN,
TAMMY, TED

•

*and the thousands of others who
have touched our lives*

Contents

List of Maps and Tables

Maps

Tables

Preface

REVISED ... UPDATED ... EXPANDED. Much has happened since *The Great American History Fact-Finder* first appeared in 1993, and we are proud to present this new and current edition. Updated through the beginning of the new millennium, its additions include such topics as the dot com boom and bust, Clinton's impeachment, the events of September 11, and America's war on terrorism. Used as a handy reference, it continues to provide needed answers to complete an assignment, settle an argument, prepare for a test, or become a champion of trivia and information about the history of the United States.

The origins of *The Great American History Fact-Finder* date back forty years. We each began our teaching career many years ago with optimism and a bit of awe, inspired in part by the words of Henry Adams: "A teacher affects eternity; he never knows where his influence stops." Both of us, fascinated by American history, have felt a continuing urge to share with others events that have deeply moved us: the experience of standing before the somber expanse of the Vietnam War Memorial; the eerie presence of Abraham Lincoln's strength at the Lincoln Memorial; the sense of living history felt while walking the streets at Harpers Ferry or standing in the spot at Gettysburg where Lincoln delivered his famous address; the story of the Marquis de Lafayette who believed so fervently in America's Revolution that he named his children George Washington and Virginie and took tons of earth back to France with him so that he could be buried in American soil.

In working with young people—our country's future—we have been inspired by the words of Patrick Henry in 1775: "I know of no way of judging of the future but by the past"; and by those of Thomas Jefferson in 1784: "History, by apprizing [men] of the past, will enable them to judge of the future." As teachers, we are also aware of the importance of approaching history as a story well told. California curriculum guidelines tell us that "the story of the past should be lively and accurate as well as rich with controversies and forceful personalities. . . . teachers must never neglect the value of good story-telling as a source of motivation for the study of history." We are challenged to bring "students into close encounters with powerful ideas, great events, major issues, significant trends, and the contributions of important men and women."

In the course of our careers, we have looked for a reference book that could answer quickly a simple question, stimulate curiosity, and generate a broader interest leading to deeper research. We never found such a resource, which is why *The Great American History Fact-Finder* came into being. Here, in one compact volume, alphabetically arranged, approximately 2,200 entries provide concise summaries of people and events important in American history. Obviously, we could have included many times that number of entries without covering the subject completely. Rather than be exhaustive, however, we have tried to be accessible, to help students and general readers alike discover the answers to questions most frequently asked about our country's history. For those who would like to follow the course of complex careers and events, we indicate cross references to related entries with small capital letters and provide a thorough index; for those whose curiosity is piqued by our necessarily brief entries, we offer a list of suggested further reading.

We conceived *The Great American History Fact-Finder* to enlighten and entertain as well as to inform. Many entries describe military and political leaders and events, but many also cover prominent people and events in the worlds of business, art, sports, entertainment, medicine, and science, because they too have made our country what it is. In making the difficult selection from among this wealth of material, we have tried to consider in each case who or what has made the greatest impact on a given aspect of American history, and we have also tried to include the stories too often left out of history books—the stories of women, blacks, and other minority groups. Finally, although we have approached our subject seriously, we include wherever possible colorful anecdotes, notable quotations, and humor.

The process of writing this book has been exciting, stimulating, and humbling. We were excited by our research, as we constantly learned new things, became immersed in the stories and the people, and dug deeper and deeper to pursue and check our facts. We were stimulated by our talks with people: with victims of World War II internment; with AIDS volunteers; with families of members of the 442nd Infantry, the Japanese-American World War II army unit; with tour guides, teachers, and students, all of whom expressed enthusiasm for this book. We were humbled by constantly finding more to learn: new explanations, controversies, and contradictions. Each stage of the process seemed better than the last, and we loved every minute of it.

As Robert E. Lee said following the Civil War in 1866, "It is history that teaches us to hope." We hope that *The Great American History Fact-Finder* will convey the pleasure and excitement that we experienced in writing it. As classroom teachers who have studied and taught the history of our country for a combined seventy years, we look upon this book as our contribution, our legacy, to our students and to all lovers of American history.

This new edition was only achieved with the support and enthusiasm of our editorial team at Houghton Mifflin. We wish to extend warmest thanks to our editor, Gordon M. Hardy, Director of Electronic Publishing and General Reference. It was through his persistence and encouragement that this revised and updated edition came into being; his expertise, insights, and painstaking care at every step were most valuable. We are also very grateful to Judy Moore and Wendy Holt for their editorial support and assistance. Our gratitude to our many friends and relatives whose encouragement and support made this project such a rewarding experience, and to our readers, whose letters have warmed and illuminated us, is immeasurable.

And finally, we express our deepest appreciation to the many students whose enjoyment of history and learning has been the catalyst that brought this book into being.

PAM CORNELISON

TED YANAK

Entries

★ ★ ★ ★ ★ ★

A **Aaron, Hank** (Henry; 1934–), black baseball player for the Milwaukee (later Atlanta) Braves and the Milwaukee Brewers. In 1974, despite death threats meant to keep Aaron from surpassing the record of a white, he broke Babe Ruth's all-time home run record of 714. He ended his twenty-three-year career after the 1976 season with 755 home runs and eleven major league records and was elected to baseball's Hall of Fame in 1982.

AARP, a nonprofit, nonpartisan membership organization for people age fifty and older. Founded in 1958 by retired California educator Dr. Ethel Percy Andrus, AARP (formerly known as the American Association of Retired Persons), represents more than 35 million members. With the goal of enriching the experience of aging, the group focuses its efforts and resources in four areas: health and wellness, economic security and work, long-term care and independent living, and personal enrichment. AARP is an advocate on behalf of people over fifty for issues including: ensuring the long-term solvency of Social Security; protecting pensions; fighting age discrimination; prescription drug coverage in Medicare; patient protections in managed care and long-term care; antipredatory home-loan lending; and other protections for older consumers. AARP is active in every state, the District of Columbia, Puerto Rico, and the U.S. Virgin Islands. The organization publishes a monthly magazine, *AARP The Magazine* and a monthly newspaper, the *AARP Bulletin*.

Abbott, "Bud" (William; 1896–1974), and **Lou Costello** (Louis Cristillo; 1908–59), comedians. Masters of slapstick and wordplay, Abbott and Costello performed in vaudeville and on Broadway, radio, and television; they made a series of popular films during the 1940s, including *Buck Privates* (1941) and *Who Done It?* (1942). Especially funny was their famous routine "Who's on First?"

Abbott, George (1887–1995), actor, director, producer, screenwriter. Known as "Mr. Broadway," Abbott wrote, produced, and directed some of the most notable Broadway plays, including *The Pajama Game, A Funny Thing Happened on the Way to the Forum,* and *Damn Yankees.* Abbott's career began in 1913 after he studied playwriting at Harvard, and for the next eighty years his projects influenced the development of modern theater. Involved in over one hundred twenty productions, he won six Tony Awards and a Pulitzer Prize for *Fiorello!* In 1963, at the age of seventy-six, Abbott celebrated his fifty-year anniversary in show business by writing his autobiography, *Mister Abbott.* In 1965, New York's Adelphi Theater was renamed the George Abbott Theater in his honor. The careers of many people were boosted through their affiliation with Abbott, including Carol Burnett, Kirk Douglas, Gene Kelly, Shirley MacLaine, Jerome Robbins, and Leonard Bernstein. Abbott continued directing until just before his death at the age of 107. He stands as one of the most admired men in the history of Broadway.

ABC Powers, an alliance of the South American nations of Argentina, Brazil, and Chile. When the TAMPICO INCIDENT involving the arrest of American sailors in Mexico occurred in 1914, war threatened. The issue was settled peacefully through the intervention of the ABC POWERS at a conference held at Niagara Falls, Canada.

Abdul-Jabbar, Kareem (born Ferdinand Lewis Alcindor, Jr.; 1947–), basketball player. A former UCLA all-American, Abdul-Jabbar, who became a Muslim in college and changed his name in 1971, led his team to three NCAA championships before becoming an all-pro center with the Milwaukee Bucks and Los Angeles Lakers. At 7'1⅜" tall, Abdul-Jabbar was renowned for his "sky hook," a virtually unstoppable basketball shot. He was voted the league's most valuable player six times and retired in 1989, holding the National Basketball Association career scoring record.

Abernathy, Ralph (1926–90), black civil rights leader and Baptist minister. With MARTIN LUTHER KING, JR., Abernathy helped found the SOUTHERN CHRISTIAN LEADERSHIP CONFERENCE (SCLC) in 1957 and became its president following King's assassination. He served from 1968 to 1977 and led the "Poor People's March" on Washington, D.C., in May 1968 to dramatize the plight of the poor.

Abolitionists (c. 1800–65), individuals who worked to bring an end to slavery. During the late 1700s, several northern states possessed antislavery or manumission societies, which could not then muster widespread support, but their activities, and that of others, intensified during the 1800s. In 1831 WILLIAM LLOYD GARRISON promoted the freeing of slaves in his newspaper, the *Liberator.* He founded the American Anti-Slavery Society in 1833 and was joined by ex-slave FREDERICK DOUGLASS and many others, black and white. Early women's rights activists, including SARAH AND ANGELINA GRIMKÉ, LUCY STONE, SOJOURNER TRUTH, and LUCRETIA MOTT, played important roles. Abolitionists wrote books and pamphlets and delivered lectures denouncing slavery, petitioned Congress and state legislatures for PERSONAL LIBERTY LAWS, and argued their cause in the courts. As the movement grew, bitter opposition divided abolitionists, mostly in the North, and slaveholders, mostly in the South. The mob murder of abolitionist newspaper editor ELIJAH LOVEJOY in 1837 intensified the unrest.

As American settlers moved west, the issue of abolition became complicated by the question of the expansion of slavery into the territories and the admission of new states as free or slave. This led to the development of the FREE-SOIL PARTY in 1848, the REPUBLICAN PARTY in 1854, and the violent standoff in BLEEDING KANSAS in the mid-1850s between abolitionists and free-staters, on one hand, and advocates of slavery, on the other. HARRIET BEECHER STOWE's book, *Uncle Tom's Cabin* (1852), attacking the institution, conveyed the abolitionists' message to thousands of readers. In 1859 JOHN BROWN'S RAID of a government arsenal at Harpers Ferry to obtain weapons for a slave uprising sparked the fears of slaveholders in the South. The struggle between those wanting to abolish slavery or to stop its expansion and those asserting the right of a state to allow slavery escalated until the CIVIL WAR erupted in 1861.

The abolitionists triumphed when Abraham Lincoln issued the EMANCIPATION PROCLAMATION in 1863, freeing slaves in the rebellious states, and when the Thirteenth Amendment to the Constitution was adopted in 1865, abolishing slavery in the United States.

Abrams v. United States (1919), U.S. SUPREME COURT decision upholding the constitutionality of the SEDITION ACT (1918). The act made it a crime to speak out against the U.S. government or to express opposition to World War I. OLIVER WENDELL HOLMES, JR., dissented arguing that the Sedition Act was a violation of freedom of speech as guaranteed in the First Amendment of the U.S. CONSTITUTION.

Acheson, Dean (1893–1971), lawyer and statesman. Acheson, secretary of state (1949–53) under President HARRY S. TRUMAN, influenced U.S. foreign policy following WORLD WAR II. As a developer of the MARSHALL PLAN, he assisted in the economic recovery of Europe. He helped engineer the NORTH ATLANTIC TREATY ORGANIZATION (NATO), the TRUMAN DOCTRINE, and other policies aimed at containing communism, including U.S. military intervention in the KOREAN WAR (1950–53). Acheson received the Presidential Medal of Freedom in 1964 and the 1970 PULITZER PRIZE for history for his book *Present at the Creation: My Years in the State Department* (1969).

Act of Toleration (1649), law enacted in the colony of Maryland guaranteeing religious freedom for Christians. It established religious toleration for Protestants and Catholics, but excluded Jews.

Adams, Abigail (1744–1818), wife of JOHN ADAMS and mother of JOHN QUINCY ADAMS. Intelligent and lively, Adams was a capable manager of her household and the family farm during her husband's frequent absences on diplomatic missions. During his presidency, she was a distinguished first lady and the leading figure in the social life of the U.S. capital. Her letters to her husband, published by their grandson CHARLES FRANCIS ADAMS, demonstrate both her charm and her perspicacity; among other topics, they reveal her support of women's rights, opposition to SLAVERY, and shrewd political judgment.

Adams, Ansel (1902–84), landscape and nature photographer and conservationist. Adams is known for his sharp, detailed, dramatic black-and-white photographs of the American Southwest and the mountains and forests of the Sierra Nevada. He wrote instructional books and in 1946 established the first college photography department at the California School of Fine Arts (now the San Francisco Art Institute). He was a member of the Sierra Club and supported conservation policies.

Adams, Brooks (1848–1927), historian. Adams, the grandson of JOHN QUINCY ADAMS, the son of CHARLES FRANCIS ADAMS, and the brother of HENRY ADAMS, was a critic of capitalism and argued in *The Law of Civilization and Decay* (1895) that civilizations rise and fall in predictable patterns. In *America's Economic Supremacy* (1900) and *New Empire* (1902), he predicted that in fifty years the United States and Russia would be the only true powers in the world. Adams felt that his prediction of the collapse of modern Western Civilization was fulfilled by the U.S. entry into World War I (1917).

Adams, Charles Francis (1807–86), ambassador. Adams was a son of President JOHN QUINCY ADAMS. Appointed by President ABRAHAM LINCOLN as minister to Great Britain (1861–68) during the CIVIL WAR, Adams represented the Union cause, helping to prevent Great Britain from recognizing the Confederacy as an independent nation. In 1871 he represented the United States in the ALABAMA CLAIMS settlement. Adams, a pioneer in the editing of historical documents, edited and published the papers of his grandfather JOHN ADAMS and the correspondence of his grandmother ABIGAIL ADAMS.

Adams, Henry (1838–1918), educator and historian. Adams was a grandson of JOHN QUINCY ADAMS, a son of CHARLES FRANCIS ADAMS, and a brother of BROOKS ADAMS. A teacher of history at Harvard University and editor of the prestigious *North American Review* (1870–76), Adams won the 1919 PULITZER PRIZE for *The Education of Henry Adams* (1907), in which he wrote, "A teacher affects eternity; he can never tell where his influence stops." His nine-volume *History of the United States of America during the Administrations of Thomas Jefferson and James Madison* (1889–91) established his reputation and set scholarly standards for a generation of historians.

Adams, John (1735–1826), vice president (1789–97) under George Washington and second president of the United States (1797–1801). Born in Braintree, Massachusetts, and educated at Harvard, Adams taught school before becoming a leading Boston lawyer. Although he actively opposed the STAMP ACT as a violation of the unwritten British constitution, he demonstrated his sense of justice and his belief in due process by defending the British soldiers on trial for shooting citizens in the BOSTON MASSACRE. A delegate to the First and Second CONTINENTAL CONGRESSES, Adams was one of five men selected to prepare the DECLARATION OF INDEPENDENCE, which he signed. From 1778 to 1788 Adams performed diplomatic missions in France, the Netherlands, and England. He helped negotiate the TREATY OF PARIS (1783), marking British recognition of American independence, and served as the first U.S. minister to Great Britain (1785–88). Adams was a profound political thinker, who made major contributions to the theory and practice of constitutional government. He drafted the Massachusetts Constitution of 1780, which became a model for later state constitutions and the U.S. CONSTITUTION.

In 1789 Adams became the first vice president of the United States, later describing the post as "the most insignificant office that ever the invention of man contrived or his imagination conceived." As political parties began to form during his terms as vice president, Adams sided with the Federalists, becoming in 1796 the only president who was a member of the FEDERALIST PARTY. The government faced many problems during the aftermath of the French Revolution, as European warships attacked and seized American vessels. Adams sent three diplomats to France to work out a peace treaty; their mission was ended by the XYZ AFFAIR, rousing anger against France in the United States. To stop criticism of the government and the undeclared war with France (1798–1800), the Federalist Congress passed the unpopular ALIEN AND SEDI-

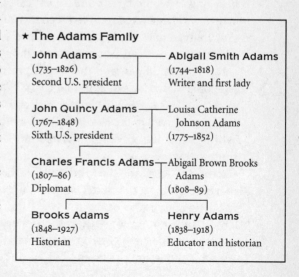

★ **The Adams Family**

John Adams (1735–1826) Second U.S. president	**Abigail Smith Adams** (1744–1818) Writer and first lady
John Quincy Adams (1767–1848) Sixth U.S. president	Louisa Catherine Johnson Adams (1775–1852)
Charles Francis Adams (1807–86) Diplomat	Abigail Brown Brooks Adams (1808–89)
Brooks Adams (1848–1927) Historian	**Henry Adams** (1838–1918) Educator and historian

TION ACTS; although Adams had little to do with the laws, their association with the Federalist party contributed to his defeat for reelection in 1800. Shortly before the end of his term, Adams appointed JOHN MARSHALL as chief justice as well as the MIDNIGHT JUDGES. In 1800 he became the first president to live in the WHITE HOUSE. Adams was the first chief executive whose son also served as president: JOHN QUINCY ADAMS became the sixth president in 1825.

Adams, John Quincy (1767–1848), sixth president of the United States (1825–29). Born to JOHN ADAMS and ABIGAIL ADAMS in Braintree, Massachusetts, Adams was immersed in politics at an early age. As a teenager, he traveled in Europe with his diplomat father and attended European schools. After graduating from Harvard, he served as minister to the Netherlands, Prussia, Russia, and Great Britain. He was chosen by the Federalists to fill a vacant U.S. Senate seat, but his failure to vote consistently along party lines and his opposition to the EMBARGO ACT (1807) resulted in his replacement. Adams was one of the American commissioners who negotiated the TREATY OF GHENT (1814) with the British, ending the War of 1812. As secretary of state under JAMES MONROE, Adams made an agreement with Great Britain for joint occupation of the Oregon Territory, negotiated the ADAMS-ONÍS TREATY (1819), resulting in the acquisition of Florida from Spain, and helped develop the MONROE DOCTRINE (1823).

In 1824 Adams became the first son of a president to be elected president himself. His administration was marked by controversy from the beginning. The ELECTION OF 1824 was thrown into the House of Representatives because none of the four candidates received the required majority of electoral votes, although Andrew Jackson received the most popular and electoral votes. The influential HENRY CLAY threw his support to Adams, believing he would be the one to best carry on Clay's AMERICAN SYSTEM. When Clay later was appointed secretary of state by Adams, Jackson partisans charged that a "corrupt bargain" had been made. As president, Adams advocated national construction of highways and canals, weather stations, and public buildings, and the establishment of a national university, but Jacksonian advocates of a limited central government blocked his proposals. He was defeated in his bid for reelection in 1828.

Adams served in the House of Representatives (1831–48) after leaving the White House, the only president to do so. During his years in the House he supported the Second BANK OF THE UNITED STATES and opposed the annexation of Texas and the Mexican War. His eight-year campaign on behalf of freedom of speech resulted in the House's repeal in 1844 of its GAG RULES restricting discussion of slavery.

Adams, Samuel (1722–1803), Revolutionary War leader. Adams, a Boston radical, gave voice to the colonial demand for independence through his speeches and writings. He opposed the SUGAR ACT (1764), the STAMP ACT

(1765), and the TOWNSHEND ACTS (1767), and helped organize the SONS OF LIBERTY (1765) and the COMMITTEES OF CORRESPONDENCE (1772–74). In 1773 Adams was one of the planners of the BOSTON TEA PARTY; when Britain responded by passing the INTOLERABLE ACTS (1774), he urged the boycott of British goods. He worked for the creation of the CONTINENTAL CONGRESS and served as a Massachusetts delegate to that body (1774–81); he signed the DECLARATION OF INDEPENDENCE in 1776. Although Adams at first opposed ratification of the Constitution (1788), he ultimately supported it in Massachusetts. Adams later succeeded John Hancock as governor of Massachusetts (1794–97).

Adams-Onís Treaty (1819), or Transcontinental Treaty, an agreement between the United States and Spain. The treaty provided for the cession of Florida to the United States for payment of $5 million and established the border between Spanish and American lands westward to the Pacific. Under its terms, the United States gave up its claim to Texas, and Spain gave up its claim to the Columbia River basin in the Oregon Territory. Ratified in 1821, the treaty was negotiated by Secretary of State JOHN QUINCY ADAMS and Luis de Onís, Spanish minister to the United States.

Addams, Jane (1860–1935), social worker, reformer, and peace activist. Addams helped found Hull House (1889) in Chicago, where immigrants and the homeless found shelter, education, and medical assistance. Her autobiography, *Twenty Years at Hull House* (1910), explained her philosophy of social reform. Her opposition to WORLD WAR I made her an unpopular figure for a time, but ultimately her quest for world peace won her both respect and the Nobel Peace Prize in 1931. Addams was also a strong advocate of women's rights and a prominent figure in the PROGRESSIVE MOVEMENT at the turn of the century.

Affirmative Action, the overall name given to policies to recruit and promote members of minority groups, women, handicapped people, and Vietnam War veterans. Supporters of affirmative action claim that it is necessary to remedy past discrimination against members of these groups. Opponents argue that the policy constitutes reverse discrimination against innocent members of groups that previously benefited from discrimination. The Supreme Court first addressed the issue in *Bakke* v. *Regents of University of*

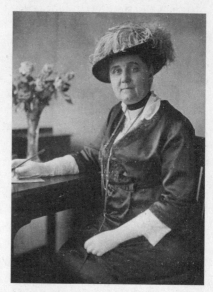

Jane Addams

California (1978). The Court's later decisions have explored issues arising out of affirmative action plans in hiring and promotion and in awarding of government contracts to minority contractors.

Afghanistan War (Oct. 7–Dec. 9, 2001), U.S. military action as part of President GEORGE W. BUSH'S WAR ON TERRORISM in response to the SEPTEMBER 11, 2001, TERRORIST ATTACKS. Called Operation Enduring Freedom and led by General TOMMY FRANKS, the purpose of the campaign was to target Osama bin Laden, suspected of planning and coordinating the September 11 attacks on the United States, and his terrorist network al-Qaeda, as well as the Taliban government of Afghanistan, which allegedly provided a safe climate for terrorist activities. Beginning on October 7, 2001, U.S. and British forces began daily air strikes of Taliban military installations and terrorist training camps. Assisted by Northern Alliance troops on the ground, who had been fighting the Taliban since their 1996 takeover, the Taliban regime fell two months after bombing began. However, pockets of fierce resistance remained, and the hunt for bin Laden and al-Qaeda members continued with U.S. troops maintaining a presence in the country into 2004.

AFL-CIO, acronym for AMERICAN FEDERATION OF LABOR–CONGRESS OF INDUSTRIAL ORGANIZATIONS. The AFL-CIO was created in 1955 through the merger of the two unions. GEORGE MEANY of the AFL and WALTER REUTHER of the CIO served, respectively, as the organization's first president and vice president. The union provides assistance for member unions in legal matters, government representation, and organizing work. It also assists in resolution of disputes and promotes desired legislation at both national and state levels. It has been the most conservative labor union of the twentieth century.

African Campaign (1940–43), military maneuvers in Africa during WORLD WAR II. In 1940, German forces tried to capture Egypt and the Suez Canal by controlling the North African coast. Led by Gen. Erwin Rommel ("the Desert Fox"), the Germans moved deep into Egypt before being stopped by the British. The United States landed forces in western North Africa in 1942. Caught between the British in the east and Americans in the west, the Germans in the region surrendered in 1943.

Agnew, Spiro (1918–96), vice president of the United States (1969–73) under RICHARD NIXON. An outspoken conservative and critic of the anti-Vietnam War movement, Agnew was the only vice president to resign from office while under criminal investigation, pleading "no contest" in October 1973 to charges of income tax evasion in 1967 while governor of Maryland (1966–68). The only other vice president who resigned from office was JOHN C. CALHOUN, who left to fill a Senate seat in 1832.

Agricultural Adjustment Act (1933), law passed by Congress to raise the prices of grain, milk, and other crops and to restore the purchasing power of American farmers to pre–World War I levels. The intent was to restrict production by giving a subsidy to farmers, who would then reduce the amount of staple crops they grew. By 1936 the farmers' share of the national income had increased substantially, but the law was declared unconstitutional by the Supreme Court in the case of *United States* v. *Butler* (1936). Further legislation by Congress restored some of the act's provisions, encouraging conservation, maintaining balanced prices, and establishing food reserves for periods of shortages.

Agricultural Revolution, changes in methods of farming and mechanization of agriculture that occurred after the Civil War, resulting in increased yields and making the United States the world's leading agricultural nation. Developments that brought about the revolution included improved methods of growing crops, the discovery that breeding could improve the quality of livestock, and the invention of new farm equipment. The introduction of such scientific methods as pest control, artificial fertilization, crop rotation, contour plowing, land reclamation, and irrigation contributed to improved crops. The revolutionary inventions included Eli Whitney's cotton gin (1793), Cyrus McCormick's harvesting machine, or reaper (1832), and John Deere's steel plow (1837), as well as cultivators, seed drills, and tractors. The machinery reduced the number of people needed to perform farm labor, initiating the population shift to the cities.

Agriculture, U.S. Department of (USDA) (1862), U.S. executive department, which serves farmers and consumers. Headed by the secretary of agriculture, a member of the president's cabinet, the USDA began as an agency to provide seed and information to farmers, and to help them receive a fair price for crops. Today its purpose is to help farmers in the areas of rural development, conservation, research, and education. It works to provide both reasonable incomes for farmers and fair prices for consumers. The department promotes nutrition education, inspects food, and runs the food stamp and school lunch programs.

AIDS (Acquired Immune Deficiency Syndrome), a viral disease that impairs the immune system of the human body, leaving it vulnerable to many disorders. The disease is thought to be caused by two similar viruses known as HIV (human immunodeficiency virus)-1 and HIV-2, transmitted by direct contamination of the bloodstream with infected body fluids. First recognized in 1981, AIDS has since reached global epidemic proportions. HIV/AIDS is the fastest growing threat to development today and a potential risk for national and regional security, as recognized by the United Nations Security Council in 2000. The World Health Organization (WHO) currently (2003) estimates 40 million adults and about 4 million children have been infected, the majority of them in Africa and Southeast Asia.

The social, political, and economic implications of the epidemic are far-reaching. In the first few years after its discovery, gay men in urban areas accounted for about two-thirds of all AIDS cases in adults. Since then, the disease has made inroads in other groups of the population. Close to half of the 5 million adults worldwide newly infected during 2002 have been women, whose children are then at risk of contracting or of being orphaned by the disease. Other social costs include extensive litigation; in the United States more cases have arisen from AIDS than from any other disease, with most stemming from discrimination against those with the disease. AIDS has become a political issue, as well, with numerous reports criticizing the failure of national leaders to address the impact of the disease and provide adequate funds for research, treatment, and public education.

The strains on the health care system are enormous and continue to increase. As the number of those infected increases and as new therapies extend and improve the quality of the lives of people with HIV and AIDS, the cost of care rises as well. The Centers for Disease Control (CDC) estimates that between 800,000 and 900,000 Americans currently are living with HIV. In the United States, researchers estimate that the cost of lifetime treatment for a person with HIV now averages about $155,000. Estimates are that 40,000 are infected yearly, resulting in an annualized cost of more than $6 billion. The cumulative cost of lifetime treatment increases by more than $6 billion yearly if the number of infections stays steady, as it has over the last decade. In the last five years alone, an estimated 200,000 people have been infected with HIV. Treating them over the rest of their lives will cost the nation $31 billion.

Research for a vaccine, effective treatment, and a cure continues, as do education efforts directed at preventing and demystifying the disease. Prominent citizens with HIV have helped in this effort. When basketball star MAGIC JOHNSON announced he had contracted the AIDS virus, the number of people requesting AIDS tests increased sharply.

Ailey, Alvin (1931–89), dancer and choreographer. Known for his theatrical, energetic dances that combine ballet, modern jazz, and African elements, Ailey was committed to the preservation of unique black cultural expression. After studying modern dance with Doris Humphrey, MARTHA GRAHAM, and Charles Weidman, Ailey formed his American Dance Theater in 1958 and served as its artistic director until 1980. The company began as a small, mostly black repertory company and grew to a large multiracial dance company that tours the world. Ailey was inspired by blues, spirituals, and gospel, creating seventy-nine ballets over his lifetime. His most popular and critically acclaimed work is *Revelations*.

Alabama (Heart of Dixie or Yellowhammer State) was admitted to the Union as the twenty-second state on December 14, 1819. (See maps, pages 540 and 541.) It seceded from the Union in 1861 to join the CONFEDERATE STATES OF AMERICA. Montgomery, the capital, was the site of the organization of the Confederacy and served as its first capital. Other major cities include Birmingham (center of the 1930s and 1940s southern labor movement), Montgomery, Mobile, and Huntsville. Alabama is the most industrialized state in the South, producing iron, steel, lumber products, and chemicals. Crops include soybeans, peanuts, and cotton. Several major civil rights actions took place in strongly segregated Alabama during the 1950s and 1960s, including the Montgomery bus boycott and the "Freedom March" from Selma to Montgomery. The largest space museum in the world, the Alabama Space and Rocket Center, is located in Huntsville, along with the National Aeronautics and Space Administration's Marshall Space Flight Center. The beaches and resorts along the gulf coast and the state's historic homes attract vacationers. Noted Alabamans include GEORGE WALLACE, HELEN KELLER, JESSE OWENS, WILLIE MAYS, HANK AARON, and SATCHEL PAIGE.

Alabama Claims (1872), legal dispute involving demands by the United States for reparations from Great Britain for shipping losses inflicted by British-built Confederate ships (called raiders), including *Alabama*, during the CIVIL WAR. The United States charged that British aid in building the raiders had violated international law and neutrality. An international tribunal convened in Geneva, Switzerland (1871–72), and awarded the United States $15.5 million. Diplomat CHARLES FRANCIS ADAMS represented the United States in the arbitrations.

Alamance, Battle of (May 16, 1771), revolt of about two thousand North Carolina colonial frontiersmen (called Regulators). Farmers rose up against heavy taxation, inadequate representation in the colonial assembly, and legislation that favored wealthy eastern planters. After three years of fighting, the colonial militia rushed the Regulators at Alamance Creek. The leaders were tried for treason, and some were executed.

Alamo, site of a battle during the war for Texas independence from Mexico. Located in the center of San Antonio, the structure, originally built as a Catholic mission, was

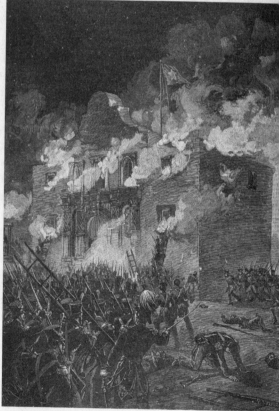

Alamo
An engraving showing the fall of the Alamo.

occasionally used for military purposes after about 1790. In opposing the TEXAS WAR FOR INDEPENDENCE (1835–36), Mexican Gen. Santa Anna and some 3,000 to 4,000 troops conducted a thirteen-day siege of the Alamo, where 187 Texans had retreated. From February 23 to March 6, 1836, the force led by William B. Travis and JIM BOWIE defended the fortress with limited supplies and ammunition. On March 6 the Mexicans stormed the fort and killed all defenders, including frontiersman DAVY CROCKETT. Women, children, and a black slave were spared. The heroic resistance of the defenders galvanized Texans. Six weeks later, led by SAM HOUSTON and shouting "Remember the Alamo!" they defeated Santa Anna at the BATTLE OF SAN JACINTO and won their independence.

Alaska (Land of the Midnight Sun) joined the Union as the forty-ninth state on January 3, 1959. (See maps, pages 540 and 541.) Alaska, the largest state in area (more than twice the size of Texas), is the smallest in population. It was acquired from Russia by Secretary of State WILLIAM H. SEWARD in the ALASKA PURCHASE of 1867. Alaska experienced booms in whaling, furs, and fishing, and a gold rush in 1896 when gold was discovered in the Klondike region of the Yukon. The highest mountain in North America is Mount McKinley (20,320 feet). The most populous cities are Anchorage and Fairbanks; Juneau, the capital, is the nation's largest city in area. Oil and gas are the main industries, followed by fishing, lumbering, fur raising, trapping, and tourism. The strongest earthquake in North American history struck near Anchorage on March 27, 1964, causing 117 deaths and over $500 million in damages.

Alaska Oil Spill (March 24, 1989), environmental disaster. Outward bound from Valdez, Alaska, the oil tanker *Exxon Valdez* struck an undersea reef in Prince William Sound and released nearly 11 million gallons (35,000 tons) of crude oil into the waters, the largest oil spill in U.S. history. The spill polluted beaches and endangered wildlife, and legal battles over responsibility for the spill continued into the 1990s.

Alaska Purchase (1867), treaty negotiated by Secretary of State WILLIAM H. SEWARD under which the United States purchased ALASKA from Russia for $7.2 million. The acquisition was made to eliminate Russian influence in the Western Hemisphere and to expand the U.S. territories. Many Americans, including the Radical Republicans, Seward's political opponents, derided the purchase, calling it "Seward's Icebox" and "Seward's Folly." Alaska at the time seemed to be only a great Arctic wasteland.

Albany Plan of Union (1754), first plan for uniting the colonies, proposed by BENJAMIN FRANKLIN at the Albany Congress. Delegates from seven colonies met in Albany, New York, with representatives of the Iroquois tribes to organize a common defense against the French at the onset of the FRENCH AND INDIAN WAR. Franklin's Albany Plan proposed a loose confederation of colonies with a representative grand council with power to levy taxes, raise troops, regulate Indian trade, and provide mutual defense. The crown-appointed council head would have final say about American affairs. To make his point, Franklin published in his *Pennsylvania Gazette* a sketch of a snake divided into eight pieces, each representing a colony, and entitled it "Join or Die." Although the congress adopted the Albany Plan, it was rejected by the colonial governments and by the British. It served as an important model for intercolonial union.

Albee, Edward (1928–), playwright. Albee achieved international stature with stage and screen productions of *Who's Afraid of Virginia Woolf?* (1962). Admired for his versatility, Albee won a Pulitzer Prize for the realistic drama *A Delicate Balance* (1966) and for the fantasy *Seascape* (1975). His early plays, often satirical social criticisms influenced by the "theater of the absurd," include *The Zoo Story* (1959) and *The Sandbox* (1960).

Albright, Madeleine (1937–), diplomat and U.S. secretary of state (1997–2000). Albright became the first female secretary of state and the highest-ranking female government official in U.S. history when she was appointed by President BILL CLINTON in 1997. Born in Prague, Czechoslovakia, she immigrated to the United States with her family in 1948. She studied at Wellesley College and earned a doctorate in political science from Columbia University. A Democrat, Albright was chief legislative assistant to Sen. EDMUND MUSKIE (1976–78) and a White House staff member (1978–81) during President JIMMY CARTER's administration, where she was responsible for foreign policy legislation. After an academic career as professor of international affairs at Georgetown University, Albright was serving as an adviser to Bill Clinton when the newly elected president appointed her to the United Nations in 1993. There she pressed for a more active U.S.

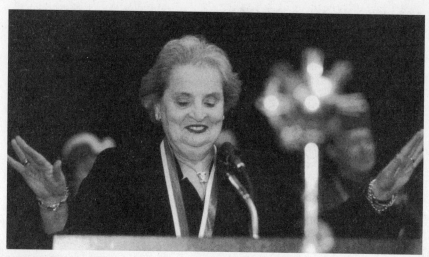

Madeleine Albright

presence. Albright was a major force in the negotiations for the expansion of NATO. She wrote her memoir, *Madam Secretary,* in 2003.

Alcoholics Anonymous (AA) (1935), worldwide organization formed by William Wilson ("Bill W.") and Robert Smith ("Dr. Bob") shortly after the repeal of Prohibition to help men and women overcome alcoholism and maintain sobriety. The only requirement for membership is the desire to stop drinking, which can be accomplished through a program called the Twelve Steps. Groups associated with AA include Al-Anon and Alateen, which support and educate families and friends of alcoholics.

Alcott, (Amos) Bronson (1799–1888), philosopher, educational reformer, and writer. Alcott in his writings and lectures advocated idealistic plans for schools and communities. His investments in failed projects caused his family to live in poverty; they included Temple School in Boston, a cooperative vegetarian community called Fruitlands, and Brook Farm, a cooperative experimental community. Alcott was a key member of the transcendentalist movement in American philosophy; his friends and colleagues included RALPH WALDO EMERSON, MARGARET FULLER, NATHANIEL HAWTHORNE, and HENRY DAVID THOREAU.

Alcott, Louisa May (1832–88), writer and suffragist. Daughter of Bronson Alcott, Louisa May Alcott worked as a Union nurse during the Civil War until her health suffered. She was active in the fight for women's right to vote and the temperance movement. Her books for children, including the semiautobiographical *Little Women* (1868), *Little Men* (1871), *Jo's Boys* (1886), and others, were immensely popular, providing much-needed income for her family. Many of her books are still read today, her character of the independent, ambitious Jo especially appealing to young girls.

Alden, John (1599–1687), colonist and leader of PLYMOUTH COLONY. A signer of the MAYFLOWER COMPACT, Alden served Plymouth as an assistant to the governor (1623–41, 1650–86), and as deputy governor (1664–65, 1667). His marriage to Priscilla Mullens inspired HENRY WADSWORTH LONGFELLOW's fictional poem, "The Courtship of Miles Standish" (1858). Descendants of Alden, Mullens, and their eleven children included Longfellow, WILLIAM CULLEN BRYANT, and JOHN QUINCY ADAMS.

Aldrin, "Buzz" (Edwin E., Jr.; 1930–), astronaut. In 1966, as pilot of *Gem-*

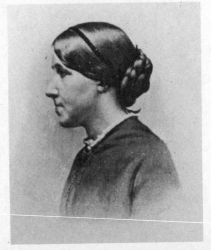

Louisa May Alcott

ini 12, Aldrin proved that people can work outside an orbiting vehicle by "walking" in space for several hours. On July 20, 1969, Aldrin and NEIL A. ARMSTRONG, the mission commander, landed on the moon in the *Apollo 11* lunar module; Armstrong preceded Aldrin in their historic walk on the moon. After retiring from the NATIONAL AERONAUTICS AND SPACE ADMINISTRATION (NASA) in 1971 and the U.S. Air Force in 1972, Aldrin entered private business and wrote an autobiography, *Return to Earth* (1973).

Alexander, Grover Cleveland (1887–1950), baseball player. A right-handed pitcher, Alexander set the major league record for shutouts by pitching sixteen runless games in 1916. He won thirty or more games in three consecutive seasons (1915, 1916, 1917) and is ranked third in lifetime pitching wins with 373, and second in career shutouts, with a total of 90. Alexander pitched 5,189 innings with the Philadelphia Phillies, the Chicago Cubs, and the St. Louis Cardinals from 1911 to 1929. He was inducted into the Hall of Fame in 1938.

Alger, Horatio (1832–99), writer. One of the most popular authors of his generation, Alger wrote more than one hundred "rags to riches" books for boys, all of them based on the theme that honesty, hard work, and virtue will always win out and be rewarded. *Ragged Dick* (1867), his first novel, set the pattern for those that followed.

Alien and Sedition Acts (1798), a series of four laws passed by a FEDERALIST-controlled Congress in anticipation of war with France during the administration of JOHN ADAMS. Designed to restrict the pro-French and antiwar activities of the Jeffersonian Republicans, three of the laws dealt with aliens (foreigners) and one with sedition (criticism of government officials and policy). Under the Alien Enemies Act (never repealed but amended) the president was authorized to imprison or deport citizens of enemy nations. The Alien Friends Act (never enforced and expired in 1800) permitted deportation of citizens of friendly nations. The Naturalization Act (repealed in 1802) increased the residency requirement for citizenship from five to fourteen years. The SEDITION ACT (expired in 1801) prohibited resistance to federal laws and criticism of the government. The Federalists designed the measures to expire at the end of Adams's term in 1801 and did not include Vice President THOMAS JEFFERSON in the list of federal officials protected from criticism. Opposing the Alien and Sedition Acts as a violation of freedom, Jefferson and JAMES MADISON challenged their constitutionality in their VIRGINIA AND KENTUCKY RESOLUTIONS (1798).

Ali, Muhammad (born Cassius Marcellus Clay; 1942–), boxer. Three-time world heavyweight boxing champion from 1964 to 1979, Ali, a flamboyant personality and self-promoter, achieved one of the sport's best records and recognition as one of the greatest boxers of all time. Known for proclaiming "I am the greatest" and for such colorful sayings as "I float like a butterfly and sting like a bee," Ali gained attention with his knockout predictions. His conversion to the Nation of Islam (also known as the Black Muslims) led to his refusal to be inducted into the army in 1967, citing religious reasons. After Ali was convicted of draft evasion, the World Boxing Association stripped him of his titles, but in 1970 the Supreme Court overturned his conviction. He defeated George Foreman in 1974 and regained his title. After his retirement in the late 1970s, he developed Parkinson's syndrome, which has restricted his activities.

Alinsky, Saul (1909–72), social reformer. Alinsky pioneered in community organization to help the poor. Among the groups he worked with were the Hispanics of California and black citizens of the ghettos in northern cities. He formed the Back-of-the-Yards program in 1938 and the Industrial Areas Foundation in 1940 to agitate for improvement in the stockyards area of Chicago. His book *Reveille for Radicals* (1946) is a classic manual on political activism.

Allen, Ethan (1738–89), leader of the GREEN MOUNTAIN BOYS and advocate of independence for VERMONT during the AMERICAN REVOLUTION. With the help of BENEDICT ARNOLD, he captured FORT TICONDEROGA from the British in 1775 in a surprise attack, an early victory for the Americans. An unsuccessful attempt to seize Montreal resulted in Allen's capture. Imprisoned until 1778, he wrote *A Narrative of Col. Ethan Allen's Captivity* (1779). Allen promoted Vermont statehood following his release. He also was known for his opposition to organized religion.

Allen, Frederick Lewis (1890–1954), editor and historian. Allen's best-known works are *Only Yesterday* (1931) and *Since Yesterday* (1940), informal histories of the United States during the 1920s and 1930s. Other works include *Lords of Creation* (1935), *The Great Pierpont Morgan* (1949), and *The Big Change* (1952), a synthesis of twentieth-century American history.

Allen, Gracie *See* GEORGE BURNS AND GRACIE ALLEN.

Allen, Paul G. (1953–), investor and philanthropist. Allen was born in Seattle, Washington, and in 1976 he cofounded Microsoft with BILL GATES. He served as head of research and new product development, remaining the company's chief technologist until he left in 1983. Named by the *Journal of Philanthropy* in 2003 as one of the top fifteen philanthropists in America, Allen creates and advances projects that change and improve the way people live. His six Paul G. Allen Foundations support ventures in the arts, health and human services, medical research, and technology in education. Allen owns the Seattle Seahawks NFL and Portland Trail Blazers NBA franchises. He is founder and chairman of Vulcan Inc., a business conglomerate.

Allen, Richard (1760–1831), black religious leader and reformer. The son of slaves, Allen bought his freedom in 1786, moved to Philadelphia, and worked to improve the plight of blacks in the postrevolutionary period. In 1787 he helped form the Free African Society, an organization to serve free blacks. Allen became a hero during the Philadelphia yellow fever epidemic of 1793, tending the sick with no thought of his own well-being. In 1794 he founded Mother Bethel, a black Methodist church, and five years later was ordained a minister in the Methodist church. In 1816 Allen founded and became first bishop of the African Methodist Episcopal Church, the first independent black Protestant denomination in the United States.

Allen, Steve (1921–2000), television and film entertainer, songwriter, and author. Allen was the originator and first host of the highly popular "Tonight Show" on NBC in 1954 and also starred in one of the most successful variety shows on television, "The Steve Allen Show." Allen composed hundreds of songs, appeared in motion pictures and television, and wrote over twenty books. His interest in political causes inspired his book *The Ground Is Our Table* (1966) about migrant labor.

Allen, Woody (Allen Stewart Konigsberg; 1935–), comic, author, actor, and film writer and director. After writing for television comedians and acquiring a following with his nightclub act, Allen began writing and directing plays and films. His film debut as an actor came in *What's New, Pussycat?* (1965), which he co-authored. Allen's works are bittersweet comedies, blending humor, romance, and philosophy, and focusing on contemporary fears and insecurities. Among Allen's other films are *Bananas* (1971), *Play It Again, Sam* (1972), *Annie Hall* (1977; won Academy Awards for best picture and for Allen as best director and best writer), *Manhattan* (1979), *Hannah and Her Sisters* (1986; won Academy Award for best screenplay), *Alice* (1990), *Mighty Aphrodite* (1995), *Hollywood Ending* (2002), and *Anything Else* (2003).

Alliance for Progress (1961), a U.S. foreign policy initiative in Latin America. The program was established by JOHN F. KENNEDY to help develop Latin American economies, thus reducing poverty and encouraging strong democratic (pro-American) governments. Despite initial successes, the program was ended during the 1970s after disappointing results.

Alliance with France, Treaty of (1778), a treaty between the United States and France, verifying French recognition of U.S. independence. Ratified by the CONTINENTAL CONGRESS, the treaty brought the benefits of economic and military assistance, provided for American aid to France in the event of English attack, and proposed that there would be no peace until England recognized the United States as an independent country.

Allied Powers, the name given to (1) the alliance of France, Russia, Great Britain, the United States, and nearly twenty other nations who opposed and defeated the Central Powers during WORLD WAR I, and (2) the nations that fought the Axis powers in WORLD WAR II, primarily the United States, Great Britain, France, the Soviet Union, China, Australia, and Canada.

Altgeld, John Peter (1847–1902), German-born reformer and governor of Illinois (1893–97). His defense of the rights of individuals against government power exposed Altgeld to extensive and unfair criticism. In 1893 he pardoned three anarchist leaders in the HAYMARKET AFFAIR of 1886, believing they had not received a fair trial. In 1894 he protested President Grover Cleveland's decision to send federal troops into Chicago during the PULLMAN STRIKE, charging interference in a state matter.

Amendment, in legislation, an addition to or change in a bill, existing law, or constitution. Article V of the U.S. CONSTITUTION specifies two ways by which it may be amended: (1) by a two-thirds vote of both houses of Congress; or (2) by a convention called at the request of two-thirds of the states. Amendments may become laws in two ways: (1) when ratified by the legislatures of three-fourths of the states (presently thirty-eight states); or (2) when ratified by conventions called for the purpose in three-fourths of the states. No amendment has been proposed by a national convention; all to date have been proposed by Congress and ratified by the states. The first ten amendments to the Constitution make up the BILL OF RIGHTS. For the text of all amendments to the U.S. Constitution and the date each was adopted, SEE APPENDIX.

America First Committee (1940–41), organization formed to oppose the entry of the United States into World War II. Its leaders, consisting of isolationists and other conservatives (including aviator CHARLES LINDBERGH), organized parades and rallies to encourage neutrality. After the Japanese attack on PEARL HARBOR, America First dissolved.

American Civil Liberties Union (ACLU) (1920), nonpartisan organization devoted to the defense of civil liberties as guaranteed in the U.S. Constitution. Its formation by a group that included JANE ADDAMS, ROGER BALDWIN, CLARENCE DARROW, JOHN DEWEY, and HELEN KELLER was in response to the post–World War I RED SCARE and Attorney General A. Mitchell Palmer's raids, which violated civil liberties. The ACLU has participated in hundreds of important cases, including the SCOPES TRIAL (1925) and *Brown* v. *Board of Education of Topeka* (1954). It provides lawyers and legal advice, gives testimony, advises government officials, and conducts educational programs. Its activities have been controversial because it defends civil liberties no matter how unpopular the person or group seeking protection may be.

American Colonization Society (1817), an organization formed for the purpose of returning free-born blacks and emancipated slaves to Africa, based on the belief that whites and African-Americans could not live together in peace. The society's founders included JAMES MADISON and JOHN MARSHALL. Land was purchased in 1821 for the settlement the next year of Monrovia (later Liberia) as an independent country on the west coast of Africa. Some twelve thousand blacks made the move by 1860. Although the society existed until 1912, opposition by abolitionists and blacks, who objected to its basic assumption regarding the separation of the races, caused the colonization movement to decline after 1840.

American Expeditionary Force (AEF), the American fighting force sent to Europe between June 1917 and November 1918 during WORLD WAR I. Commanded by Gen. John Pershing, more than 2 million Americans, called DOUGHBOYS, landed in Europe before the war ended.

American Federation of Labor (AFL) (1886), a federation of skilled craft and trade unions formed to improve wages and working conditions, shorten working hours, abolish child labor, and provide for collective bargaining. The AFL was founded by SAMUEL GOMPERS as the Federation of Organized Trades and Labor Unions (1881), but it was reorganized in 1886, with Gompers serving as president from 1886 to 1924 (except 1895). In 1935 JOHN L. LEWIS, dissatisfied with the organization of craft unions, led ten dissenting unions in the formation of the CONGRESS OF INDUSTRIAL ORGANIZATIONS (CIO), to operate within the AFL. The controversy arose from the difference between craft unions, organized by trade or specialty (e.g., cigar makers or plumbers) and industrial unions, which include all workers within a given industry regardless of their individual craft (e.g., mine workers or automobile workers). Their differing philosophies led to the expulsion of the CIO in 1936. The AFL and CIO operated separately until 1955, when they merged to form the AFL-CIO.

American Indian Movement (AIM) (1968), a civil rights organization established to work for equal rights and improved living conditions for Native Americans. Formed in Minneapolis to assist Indians at a local level, AIM spread to other cities, establishing chapters to work for better education, job programs, legal representation, and health care. To dramatize their cause, a group of AIM members in 1973 took over the town of Wounded Knee, South Dakota, the site of the 1890 massacre of over two hundred Sioux by the U.S. Cavalry. Other Indians occupied Alcatraz Island in San Francisco Bay to protest government seizure of Indian lands and restriction of Indian hunting and fishing rights. The demonstrations gained the Indians national attention but little public support. They also encountered much political opposition, and the group declined during the 1980s. Other groups, however, have sprung up to work toward the same ends.

American Legion (1919), association of veterans of American wars. Formed by a group of World War I officers, the American Legion is the world's largest veterans' organization. It promotes legislation concerning veterans' affairs and national security, provides help for disabled veterans, encourages child welfare and education programs, performs community service, and promotes patriotism.

American Party *See* KNOW-NOTHING PARTY.

American Red Cross (1881), society that works to relieve suffering from wars or national disasters. The International Red Cross was formed in 1864 under terms of the First Geneva (or Red Cross) Convention. Seventeen years later, largely through the efforts of CLARA BARTON, Congress ratified the treaty that established the American Red Cross Society. Its primary functions are to volunteer aid to armies in time of war and to provide relief in national and international disasters. Through the work and donations of over 10 million volunteers, the Red Cross provides health services that include research, first aid instruction, accident prevention programs, nutrition education, and the collection, processing, and distribution of blood for medical use without charge.

American Revolution (1775–83), also known as the American War of Independence, a rebellion of the THIRTEEN COLONIES against Great Britain. The causes of the Revolution were political, economic, cultural, and geographical.

Background Causes: Resentment among the colonists began in 1763 when England levied taxes to help pay for the FRENCH AND INDIAN WAR, giving colonists no voice in the decision, since they were unrepresented in Parliament. Britain also took steps to increase its control over the colonies and to enforce the often neglected NAVIGATION ACTS. The economic practice of mercantilism contributed to the belief that the colonies existed only to benefit the mother country. King George III issued the Proclamation of 1763, which prohibited American settlers from moving west beyond the Appalachian Mountains. In 1764 Parliament passed the SUGAR ACT, which levied taxes on molasses and sugar. Even more unpopular were the STAMP ACT (1765) directly taxing legal documents, licenses, bills of sale, and so on, and the QUARTERING ACT (1765), which required colonists to house British soldiers. Outraged colonists, who maintained that Parliament was violating the unwritten British constitution, asserted the principle of "no taxation without representation."

England repealed the Stamp Act in 1766 following the protests and a boycott encouraged by the Stamp Act Congress, but passed the DECLARATORY ACT (1766), asserting Parliament's and the king's legislative authority over the colonies. In 1767 the TOWNSHEND ACTS levied taxes on lead, paper, paint, glass, and tea. Again the colonists boycotted the goods, leading to the repeal of all the taxes except that on tea. On March 5, 1770, British troops fired into an unarmed rioting Boston mob, killing five men in what is known as the BOSTON MASSACRE. In 1773 the TEA ACT, favoring the East India Company, further aroused the colonists' anger. Under the leadership of SAMUEL ADAMS, colonists disguised as Indians staged the BOSTON TEA PARTY (1773), dumping 342 chests of tea into the harbor. Outraged, Parliament responded in March 1774 by closing the port of Boston to all trade and in May passing further Coercive Acts to punish the people of Boston and the colony of Massachusetts; the colonists called these the INTOLERABLE ACTS. COMMITTEES OF CORRESPONDENCE were organized by Patriots to exchange information among the colonies and coordinate resistance to British policies. The first CONTINENTAL CONGRESS met in September 1774 in Philadelphia to protest the Intolerable Acts and organize a new nonimportation agreement. Another Congress was planned for May 1775, but by then war had begun.

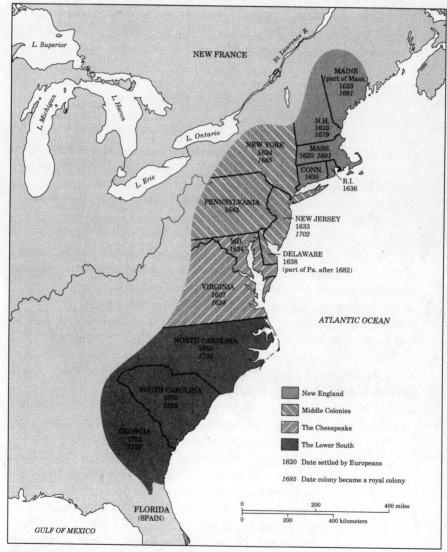

The American Colonies in the Eighteenth Century

Warfare: Upon hearing that colonists had a store of arms at Concord, Massachusetts, Governor General Thomas Gage sent troops to seize and destroy them. En route to Concord, at dawn on April 19, 1775, the British troops encountered a small group of militiamen at Lexington. Shots were fired with casualties on both sides. The British marched on to Concord, and heavy fighting broke out at the Concord Bridge. Seeing they were outnumbered, the redcoats began a hasty retreat to Boston. The American Revolution had begun.

The encounters at Lexington and Concord were followed by the capture of FORT TICONDEROGA (1775) and Crown Point (1775) in New York by BENEDICT ARNOLD and ETHAN ALLEN and the GREEN MOUNTAIN BOYS. The Second Continental Congress met in May and appointed GEORGE WASHINGTON commander in chief of the colonial forces. JOHN DICKINSON drafted the OLIVE BRANCH PETITION, sent to King George III, requesting that he seek a peaceful solution to the conflict; the king refused to receive the document and declared the colonists out of his allegiance and protection. The British won a costly victory in Boston at the BATTLE OF BUNKER HILL (Breed's Hill) (1775), suffering heavy casualties and winning the battle only after colonists ran out of ammunition. Henry Knox oversaw the transportation of heavy artillery from Fort Ticonderoga across Massachusetts to Dorchester Heights, south of Boston, where the cannons could command the city below. Brig. Gen. William Howe realized he could not hold the city, so he evacuated his troops to Canada on March 17.

In January 1776 THOMAS PAINE wrote his pamphlet *Common Sense,* jolting Americans to rally behind the cause of independence. On July 2, 1776, a declaration proposed in June by RICHARD HENRY LEE was presented to Congress, calling for independence. Congress adopted the DECLARATION OF INDEPENDENCE, drafted by THOMAS JEFFERSON, on July 4, 1776. By late 1776 General Howe had taken New York City and driven Washington and his small forces from Long Island and Manhattan and into New Jersey. Washington, taking a desperate chance, crossed the Delaware River and attacked the HESSIANS at Trenton, New Jersey, on Christmas Day, surprising and defeating them. This victory, along with another at Princeton, gave the Patriots new hope. At the end of the year, Paine's pamphlet *The Crisis* (1776) inspired the Patriots to continue their fight.

In the summer of 1777 Howe launched a campaign to seize Philadelphia. He captured the city, but the Continental Congress quickly moved to York. A British army moved south from Montreal to join British forces moving east from Lake Ontario and north from New York City. The armies were to meet in Albany, splitting New York in two, securing the Hudson Valley, and isolating New England from the rest of the colonies. Instead of moving north, Howe decided to take Philadelphia. Gen. JOHN BURGOYNE, moving

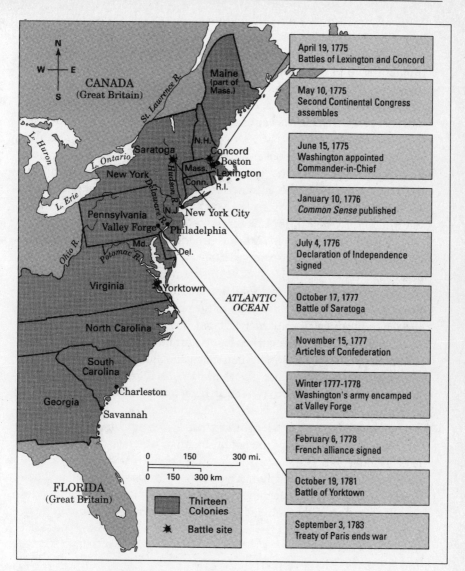

Major Events of the Revolutionary War, 1775–1783

south, sent a raiding party to gather supplies but was defeated by Patriot forces at the BATTLE OF BENNINGTON, Vermont. When Burgoyne's troops met a more powerful American army under HORATIO GATES and Benedict Arnold at the BATTLE OF SARATOGA, the British were decisively defeated. The American victory at Saratoga convinced the French that the Americans could win the war; agreeing to ally with the colonists, France entered the war against England. Driven from Philadelphia by Howe, Washington wintered at VALLEY FORGE (1777–78) where the German drillmaster BARON

FRIEDRICH VON STEUBEN whipped the American soldiers into a well-disciplined force.

The British changed their strategy in 1778 and moved into the South, expecting heavy Loyalist support. They captured Savannah, Georgia, and Charleston, South Carolina. The Americans, however, were victorious at King's Mountain, North Carolina, in 1780. In 1781 Gen. NATHANAEL GREENE and Gen. DANIEL MORGAN took charge of the American armies in the South. Gen. CHARLES CORNWALLIS and the British forces retreated to YORKTOWN, Virginia. French forces arrived at Rhode Island under Gen. Jean Rochambeau and the French fleet arrived under Adm. François DeGrasse, blockading the entrance to Chesapeake Bay. The armies of Washington, the MARQUIS DE LAFAYETTE, and Rochambeau marched south and began their siege of Yorktown on September 28, 1781. On October 17, Cornwallis surrendered. With the American victory at Yorktown, the British lost their desire to continue the war and negotiations for peace began.

Results: The United States sent BENJAMIN FRANKLIN, JOHN JAY, and JOHN ADAMS to negotiate the terms of the peace. By the TREATY OF PARIS (1783), Great Britain recognized the United States as an independent nation. The Great Lakes and Canadian border became the northern U.S. boundary, the Mississippi River the western boundary, and Spanish Florida the southern boundary. The treaty also gave Americans fishing rights off the Grand Banks of Newfoundland. An estimated 4,000 to 5,000 Americans died during the conflict, and British deaths totaled about 10,000.

American's Creed, The, the winning entry in a nationwide contest to write "the best summary of the political faith of America." Inspired by the nation's entry into World War I in 1917, the contest was designed to show the strength of America's values. The mayor of Baltimore offered a $1,000 prize, drawing about three thousand contestants. William Tyler Page of Maryland, a clerk in the House of Representatives, wrote the winning entry.

★ The American's Creed

I believe in the United States of America as a government of the people, by the people, for the people; whose just powers are derived from the consent of the governed; a democracy in a Republic; a sovereign Nation of many sovereign States; a perfect Union, one and inseparable; established upon those principles of freedom, equality, justice, and humanity for which American patriots sacrificed their lives and fortunes.

I therefore believe it is my duty to my country to love it; to support its Constitution; to obey its laws; to respect its flag; and to defend it against all enemies.

—WILLIAM TYLER PAGE

American System (March 30–31, 1824), plan for sectional cooperation advanced by Speaker of the House HENRY CLAY to strengthen nationalism during JAMES MONROE's administration. Designed to unite the nation economically and make it self-sufficient, the plan called for a national bank, a high tariff to protect American manufacturers from foreign competition, and internal improvements such as the construction of roads and canals to open up the West. Although Monroe questioned the power of the federal government to engage in these activities and Clay had trouble gathering support, Congress responded favorably, and an era of nationalism emerged.

American Woman Suffrage Association (AWSA) (1869), organization formed to work in individual states for women's suffrage. The AWSA, founded by abolitionists and women's rights activists such as LUCY STONE, her husband Henry Blackwell, and JULIA WARD HOWE, was more conservative than the NATIONAL WOMAN SUFFRAGE ASSOCIATION (NWSA), whose goal was a constitutional amendment giving women the right to vote. The groups also differed in their degree of support for black suffrage, the NWSA wanting to concentrate on securing the vote for women first. The two groups joined in 1890 to form the NATIONAL AMERICAN WOMAN SUFFRAGE ASSOCIATION.

Amistad Case (1841), U.S. Supreme Court case concerning a slave mutiny. In 1839 the U.S. Navy captured the Spanish slave ship *Amistad* near New London, Connecticut. Carrying fifty-three slaves, two Spanish planters, and crew, the ship had sailed from Cuba, a center for the slave trade, to deliver the slaves to a Caribbean plantation. The Africans seized the ship, killed the captain and the cook, and ordered the planters to sail to Africa. The planters tricked the slaves and headed north, eventually grounding the schooner near New London and resulting in its capture by the U.S. brig *Washington*. After the planters were freed, the Africans were imprisoned on charges of murder, which were later dismissed. The Africans continued to be held as the focus of the case turned to salvage claims and property rights when the planters demanded the ship and slave cargo be returned to them. President MARTIN VAN BUREN supported returning the Africans to Cuba. Northern abolitionists opposed this, taking up the Africans' cause and raising money to defend them. The case was taken to the U.S. District Court, which ruled that the slaves were being held illegally, and was then appealed to the Supreme Court. Former President JOHN QUINCY ADAMS defended the Africans and their right to regain their freedom. The Supreme Court decided in favor of the Africans, and twenty-five of them were returned to their homeland. The others died at sea or in prison while awaiting trial.

"Amos and Andy," radio characters of the 1920s, 1930s, and 1940s. Freeman Gosden and Charles Correll originated the "Amos and Andy" radio comedy show in 1928. Using a black dialect, they created other memorable characters such as "Kingfish," "Sapphire," and "Lightnin'." During the 1950s "Amos and Andy" appeared on television with black actors, but was criticized for its stereotyped portrayal of blacks.

Anarchism, the social, economic, and political philosophy that all forms of government interfere unfairly with individual liberty and should be abolished, to be replaced by free agreements and voluntary, cooperative, common ownership of property. Anarchists, whose philosophy dates back to ancient times, have resisted organized government by both nonviolent and terroristic means. Although anarchism never attracted a large following in the United States, anarchist activities surfaced sporadically in the late nineteenth and early twentieth centuries. A bombing at Haymarket Square during Chicago's McCormick Harvester Machine Company Strike of 1886 resulted in the arrest and conviction of eight anarchists who supported the strikers. Although no evidence ever linked them to the bombing, four were hanged. Following the murder of President William McKinley (1901) by anarchist LEON CZOLGOSZ, the U.S. government banned anarchists from entering the country, and states passed laws punishing the advocacy of anarchist beliefs. Foreign-born anarchist leaders were early targets of the RED SCARE. Alexander Berkman attempted to kill steel magnate HENRY CLAY FRICK in 1892; he and his ally EMMA GOLDMAN eventually were deported in 1919. During the 1920s the controversial SACCO-VANZETTI CASE resulted in the conviction and execution of two anarchists; their conviction was the result of prejudice against their views, which rendered their trial a mockery of justice. Anarchist activities declined after World War I.

Anderson, John B. (1922–), U.S. congressman from Illinois (1960–80) and independent presidential candidate (1980). During his twenty years in the House, Anderson served as chair of the House Republican Conference (1969–79). Moving during his career from a conservative to a moderate (and sometimes liberal) position on social and defense issues, Anderson sought the Republican presidential nomination in 1980. Realizing that his political views differed from many in his party, he ran as an independent against incumbent Democrat JIMMY CARTER and Republican challenger RONALD REAGAN. Anderson polled about 7 percent of the popular vote but received no electoral votes.

Anderson, Marian (1902–93), black singer. In a career affected by racism, Anderson became the first black soloist to sing with and become a permanent member of the Metropolitan Opera Company (1955) in New York City, and the first black to sing at the White House. In 1939 the DAUGHTERS OF THE AMERICAN REVOLUTION barred her from singing at Constitution Hall in Washington, D.C., because of her race. In protest, a group led by Eleanor Roosevelt and Interior Secretary Harold Ickes arranged for her to sing on the steps of the Lincoln Memorial on Easter, drawing over 75,000 people. Primarily a concert artist, Anderson's voice was distinguished for its range, richness, and clarity. She won the NAACP's SPINGARN MEDAL in 1939 and the United Nations' Peace Prize in 1977.

Anderson, Sherwood (1876–1941), author. Anderson's naturalistic works deal mostly with rebellion against contemporary industrial society and materialistic middle-class values. His first novel was *Windy McPherson's Son* (1916). *Winesburg, Ohio* (1919), a series of sketches of people in a small midwestern town, was his most important work. Other noted novels include *Marching Men* (1917), *Poor White* (1920), and *Dark Laughter* (1925). Other short story collections include *The Triumph of the Egg* (1921), *Horses and Men* (1923), and *Death in the Woods* (1933).

Andersonville, Georgia, site of a Confederate prisoner of war camp established in 1864 during the CIVIL WAR. Conditions at Andersonville were the worst of any prison camp on either side. Almost 50,000 Union prisoners passed through this prison; more than 12,000 died of disease, mistreatment, neglect, or malnutrition. Capt. Henry Wirz, in charge of the prison, was the only Confederate soldier to be tried and hanged for war crimes after the war.

André, John (1750–80), British major, a spy during the AMERICAN REVOLUTION. André and BENEDICT ARNOLD plotted to surrender the fort at West Point on the Hudson River to the British. After their plan was exposed, André was captured on his way to New York with secret papers in his boots and was later hanged.

Andros, Sir Edmund (1637–1714), British colonial governor of the colony of New York (1674–81), and governor of the Dominion of New England — New York, New Jersey, Connecticut, Rhode Island, Massachusetts, and New Hampshire — formed by James II (1686–88). Andros angered the colonists, who had governed themselves for decades, by restricting their liberties, abolishing their colonial charters, and increasing taxes. Resisting his despotic rule and his demand for Connecticut's charter (which gave people the right to govern themselves), the colonists hid their charter in the CHARTER OAK. Upon hearing that James II had been deposed, they imprisoned Andros and dissolved the Dominion. Andros was sent to England for trial, but he was released and served as royal governor of several other colonies.

Angel Island, the largest island in San Francisco Bay, called the ELLIS ISLAND of the West. Between 1836 and 1946 the island was an army base. A quarantine station built in 1888 served as a public health facility, checking arriving immigrants until 1946. During World War II Angel Island served as a major induction station, with some 87,000 soldiers passing through on their way to the Pacific front. In 1955 the island became part of the Golden Gate National Recreation Area.

Angelou, Maya (Marguerite Johnson; 1928–), novelist, poet, civil rights activist. Angelou gained wide recognition when she delivered her poem "On the Pulse of Morning" at the 1993 inauguration of President BILL

CLINTON. Born in St. Louis, Angelou chronicles her life in five autobiographies including her highly acclaimed first work of literature, *I Know Why the Caged Bird Sings* (1970). She has had a richly varied career as a dancer, nightclub singer, actress, director, composer, and teacher. She was active during the CIVIL RIGHTS MOVEMENT of the 1960s and earned a Pulitzer Prize nomination for her screenplay of *Georgia, Georgia* (1972). She won Grammy Awards for best spoken word albums *On the Pulse of Morning* (1994) and *A Song Flung up to Heaven* (2002).

Annapolis Convention (September 11–14, 1786), meeting in Annapolis, Maryland, of delegates of five states to discuss interstate commerce. Because of restrictions inherent in the ARTICLES OF CONFEDERATION, the Virginia legislature called an interstate conference to discuss uniform trade regulations. But with delegates representing only New York, New Jersey, Pennsylvania, Delaware, and Virginia, it was realized they could not deal with the interstate problem effectively. They then endorsed a report drafted by ALEXANDER HAMILTON with the assistance of JAMES MADISON that all states send representatives to a convention to be held in Philadelphia in 1787. The purpose of that meeting, later called the CONSTITUTIONAL CONVENTION, was to consider ways to strengthen the Articles of Confederation and thereby strengthen the Union.

Anson, Cap (Adrian; 1851–1922), baseball player. A powerful and influential figure in the world of professional baseball during the nineteenth century, Anson played twenty-seven seasons, the longest career of any major leaguer. When the National League (NL) formed in 1876, he joined its Chicago team, playing and managing until 1897. As a manager he led Chicago to five league championships. He led the NL in hitting three times and was the first man to get three thousand hits. Anson achieved a lifetime batting average of .339 (a record broken by TY COBB some twenty years later) and hit over .400 twice. He originated the concept of spring training and spread the game's popularity by participating in baseball tours around the world. At the same time, Anson was a bigot who would pull his team off the field rather than play against a team with a black player. His influence is often cited as a force in the unwritten rule that banned blacks from major league baseball until 1947. Anson was the first baseball player to write his autobiography, *A Ball Player's Career* (1900), and he holds the record of most errors by a first baseman in a season (58).

Anthony, Susan B. (1820–1906), suffragist and abolitionist. The daughter of a Quaker abolitionist, Anthony was a leader and lecturer in the women's rights movement of the nineteenth century. With ELIZABETH CADY STANTON, she cofounded the NATIONAL WOMAN SUFFRAGE ORGANIZATION (1869), advocating a constitutional amendment to give women the vote. (The Nineteenth Amendment became law in 1920, fourteen years after her death.) From 1892 to 1900 Anthony served as president of the NATIONAL

AMERICAN WOMAN SUFFRAGE ASSOCIATION. With Stanton, M. J. Gage, and I. H. Harper, she compiled and edited the *History of Woman Suffrage* (1881–1902).

Antietam, Battle of (September 17, 1862), engagement between Confederate forces under Gen. ROBERT E. LEE and Union forces under Gen. GEORGE B. McCLELLAN, Known as the Battle of Sharpsburg to Southerners, this was the bloodiest single day of the CIVIL WAR and led to Lee's withdrawal from Maryland. Lee invaded the North in the hope of gaining French and British recognition of the Confederacy. After a Union soldier found a copy of Lee's order outlining his plans at an abandoned camp, McClellan and his force of 70,000 men intercepted Lee at Sharpsburg, Maryland, on Antietam Creek. Because the Confederates were outnumbered nearly two to one, Lee's drive to the North was stopped. Although McClellan forced Lee's retreat to Virginia, the victory was not decisive because he failed to pursue Lee across the Potomac River. The North claimed victory, however, and Abraham Lincoln used the occasion to issue the preliminary EMANCIPATION PROCLAMATION five days later. Combined casualties totaled about 25,000 dead or wounded.

Antifederalists, loose alliance of politicians and citizens in 1787–88 who supported strong state governments and opposed ratification of the Constitution. Antifederalists agreed that the proposed Constitution would give the national government too much power. They felt that the state governments would become too weak and the national government too removed from local conditions, resulting in a loss of freedom. Some Antifederalists opposed the Constitution because it did not have a bill of rights; others, remembering their experience as British colonists, opposed the federal government's having the power to tax. Leading Antifederalists included PATRICK HENRY, GEORGE MASON, and JAMES MONROE of Virginia, SAMUEL ADAMS and ELBRIDGE GERRY of Massachusetts, Robert Yates and GEORGE CLINTON of New York, and Samuel Chase of Maryland. Despite their defeat, they prevailed in the matter of securing a set of amendments guaranteeing individual liberties; Congress framed the BILL OF RIGHTS in 1789, and all states had ratified them by 1791.

Anti-Masonic Party, the earliest third political party and the first to hold a national nominating convention (1831) and adopt a party platform. Organized in western New York in the 1820s to oppose Catholics, foreigners, and secret societies such as the Masons in politics, the movement spread through New England, the Mid-Atlantic states, and Ohio and Michigan. Their presidential candidate in the ELECTION OF 1832, William Wirt of Maryland, won only seven electoral votes. After 1832 the party declined and most of its members joined the WHIG PARTY.

Anti-Saloon League (1893), organization established to oppose the sale of alcoholic beverages. The league drew much of its membership from

churches and backed candidates solely on the basis of their views on temperance. Unlike other groups, the Anti-Saloon League worked with the
major political parties rather than backing the weak Prohibition party.
Wayne Wheeler was its leader for twenty-five years (1898–1927), helping to
draft both the Eighteenth Amendment and the Volstead Act. After Prohibition ended in 1933, the Anti-Saloon League lost its impetus.

Apollo Space Program, moon-landing project that met the goal set by
President John F. Kennedy on May 25, 1961, to land a man on the moon and
return him safely to earth by the end of the decade. Executed by the National Aeronautics and Space Administration (NASA), the Apollo
project experienced delays in research and through a tragic accident. On
January 27, 1967, during a routine test, a fire swept through the *Apollo* spacecraft, killing astronauts Virgil Grisson, Edward White, and Roger Chaf-
fee. On October 11, 1968, following several unmanned earth-orbit flights,
Apollo 7 made a 163-orbit flight carrying three astronauts. *Apollo 8* was the
first manned flight to leave earth orbit, achieve lunar orbit, and return to
earth. *Apollo 9* and *10* tested the lunar landing module in earth and lunar
orbits. *Apollo 11* was the first mission to carry out a moon landing; astronaut Neil Armstrong became the first human to walk on the moon. In
April 1970 the *Apollo 13* mission suffered a major accident when an explosion in the spacecraft damaged its life-support system. By reducing use of
electrical power, the three astronauts returned safely to earth. Subsequent
Apollo missions explored the lunar surface, with astronauts collecting
samples of moon rocks and installing instruments for scientific research.
The final flight was *Apollo 17* in December 1972.

Appleseed, Johnny *See* John Chapman.

**Appomattox Court House, Vir-
ginia,** site of the surrender on
April 9, 1865, of the Army of Northern Virginia commanded by Confederate Gen. Robert E. Lee to the
Army of the Potomac led by Union
Gen. Ulysses S. Grant, ending
the Civil War. The surrender took
place at the home of farmer Wilmer
McLean, one week after the fall
of Richmond and Petersburg. The
terms were quite generous. The
Confederate soldiers were to surrender their weapons; they were
given a day's rations and told they
could return to their homes and

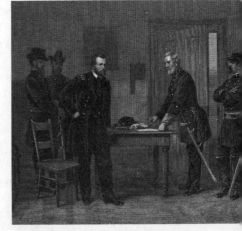

Appomattox Court House
*Lee surrendering to Grant, April 9, 1865, in
the court house at the town of Appomattox,
Virginia.*

keep any horses or mules they owned. Officers were allowed to keep their sidearms.

Arcaro, Eddie (George Edward; 1916–1997), jockey. In a career spanning thirty-one years, Arcaro won a record five Kentucky Derbies and became the first to win the Triple Crown — Kentucky Derby, Preakness, and Belmont Stakes — twice.

Arizona (Grand Canyon State), the last of the contiguous states to join the Union, became the forty-eighth state on February 14, 1912. (See maps, pages 540 and 541.) The Hopi village of Oraibi in the northeast part of the state is the oldest continuously inhabited town in the United States. Today the Indian population of Arizona is higher than that of any other state. The Spanish explored and ruled the area from the 1530s to the early 1800s, when it became part of Mexico. As a result of the MEXICAN WAR (1846–48), the United States annexed Arizona north of the Gila River and obtained the area south of the Gila through the GADSDEN PURCHASE (1853). Arizona was occupied by federal troops during the CIVIL WAR. After becoming a territory in 1863 the area was the scene of repeated conflicts between white settlers and Indians. The state grew slowly, but the development of irrigation systems made the soil rich and the advent of air conditioning made the climate bearable, so that it has become one of the nation's fastest growing areas. Major cities include Phoenix (the capital), Tucson, and Mesa. Magnificent deserts, mountains, plateaus, and the scenic wonders of the Painted Desert, Petrified Forest, and the Grand Canyon attract many visitors. Manufacturing, agriculture, and mining contribute to the state's wealth. Noted Arizonans include Stewart Udall, secretary of the interior, 1961–69; Representative Morris Udall, 1961–91; and BARRY GOLDWATER, former senator.

Arkansas (Land of Opportunity), joined the Union as the twenty-fifth state on June 15, 1836. (See maps, pages 540 and 541.) First settled by the Caddo, Osage, and Quapaw Indians, Arkansas was explored by Hernando de Soto of Spain in 1541, but Robert Cavelier, Sieur de La Salle, claimed the area for France in 1682. The land reverted to Spain in 1763, but France regained it in 1800. The United States bought Arkansas as part of the LOUISIANA PURCHASE (1803). Admitted as a slave state under terms of the MISSOURI COMPROMISE, Arkansas seceded from the Union in 1861, but rejoined it in 1868. A beautiful state of mountains, valleys, forests, and plains, Arkansas draws millions of visitors each year, attracted to its lakes, hot springs, historic sites, and the only active diamond mine in the United States, at Murfreesboro. Principal cities include Little Rock (the capital) and Fort Smith, an important manufacturing center. Service industries, manufacturing (including processed foods, electrical equipment, and paper products), and agriculture provide most of the state's income. Prominent Arkansans have included DOUGLAS MACARTHUR, "DIZZY" DEAN, J. WILLIAM FULBRIGHT, HATTIE CARAWAY, and BILL CLINTON.

Arledge, Roone, Jr. (1931–2002), television producer. Arledge was president of ABC Sports from 1968 to 1986. He introduced *Wide World of Sports, American Sportsman,* and *Monday Night Football.* Praised for his in-depth coverage of the 1964 Olympic Games in Tokyo, Arledge revolutionized sports coverage with the use of slow motion, instant replay, and the split screen. Arledge also created numerous feature news programs including *Nightline, 20/20, Prime Time Live,* and the Peabody Award winning Sunday news show *This Week.* He won over thirty Emmy Awards for his programming and was selected by *Life* magazine as one of the one hundred most important Americans of the twentieth century. He headed ABC News from 1977 until his death.

Arlington National Cemetery, Arlington, Virginia, since 1864 a burial ground for armed forces veterans and their dependents and those killed in battle. Located across the Potomac River from Washington, D.C., the land had been owned by the family of the wife of Gen. ROBERT E. LEE. It was confiscated by the Union during the CIVIL WAR. Its TOMB OF THE UNKNOWNS honors unidentified soldiers killed in World War I, World War II, the Korean War, and the Vietnam War. Among famous Americans buried at Arlington are Presidents JOHN F. KENNEDY and WILLIAM HOWARD TAFT.

Armstrong, Henry (Henry Jackson; 1912–88), boxer. Armstrong was the only fighter to hold three world titles simultaneously (1937–38) — the featherweight, welterweight, and lightweight titles.

Armstrong, Lance (1971–), national and world champion cyclist. Born in Plano, Texas, Armstrong won the U.S. amateur cycling championship in 1991 and turned pro in 1992, capturing ten titles by 1993. He won the Tour DuPont race twice (the first person to do so) with the largest margin of victory in the history of the race, and was considered to be the number one cyclist in the world. Diagnosed in 1996 with advanced testicular cancer, which had already spread to his brain and lungs, Armstrong was given a less-than-fifty-percent chance of survival. Following extensive treatment, he returned to cycling in 1998, becoming the first American to win the Tour de France four times and the fourth cyclist to win four consecutively. In one of the most stunning comebacks in the history of sport, he tied the world record by winning a fifth consecutive Tour title in 2003. Armstrong wrote his best-selling autobiography, *It's Not About the Bike: My Journey Back to Life* (2000) and *Every Second Counts* (2003). The Lance Armstrong foundation helps people to manage and survive cancer.

Armstrong, Louis (1901–71), jazz trumpet player and singer. Known as "Satchmo" (short for "satchel mouth"), Armstrong originated "scat," a type of improvised singing of meaningless syllables and sounds that became as well known as his trumpet solos. Much admired for his virtuoso performances with jazz groups during the 1920s, Armstrong led a big band during the 1930s and 1940s and performed in films. He became the first internationally famous jazz soloist through his world travels as a goodwill ambassador for the U.S. State Department.

Armstrong, Neil A. (1930–), astronaut and first man to walk on the moon. The *Apollo 11* lunar module *Eagle* landed on the moon on July 20, 1969, where Armstrong, the mission commander, and Col. EDWIN ALDRIN spent more than twenty hours on the surface. His first words as his feet touched the lunar dust became immortal: "That's one small step for man, one giant leap for mankind." Armstrong implanted an American flag, along with a plaque that read, "Here men from the planet Earth first set foot upon the moon July 1969 A.D. We came in peace for all mankind." After retiring from the National Aeronautics and Space Administration in 1971, Armstrong pursued teaching and private business ventures. He cochaired the presidential commission investigating the CHALLENGER DISASTER in 1986.

Arnold, Benedict (1741–1801), general during the AMERICAN REVOLUTION accused of treason. Originally a wealthy Connecticut merchant, Arnold joined in the war as head of a Connecticut militia company. He helped Ethan Allen seize FORT TICONDEROGA (1775) and led an unsuccessful expedition to capture Quebec (1776) during which he was severely wounded. In 1777 he helped defeat the British in the battle at SARATOGA, New York, although Gen. Horatio Gates received credit for the victory. Because Congress bypassed him and appointed five other soldiers to higher ranks, and because of pressure from his ambitious wife, Arnold grew embittered, which led him later to commit treason. In 1780 he conceived a plan to turn over West Point on the Hudson River to the British. The plan was discovered, however, and his accomplice, British Maj. JOHN ANDRÉ, was hanged as a spy. Arnold escaped behind British lines and spent the rest of his life in disgrace in Canada and England.

Arnold, Eddy (1918–), country western singer from the mid-1940s through the 1960s. Arnold first sang at the Grand Ole Opry with the Golden West Cowboys, earning the appellation "Tennessee Plowboy."

Arnold, Hap (Henry Harley; 1886–1950), leading advocate of military air power during the 1920s, 1930s, and 1940s along with Gen. BILLY MITCHELL. During WORLD WAR I Arnold organized and directed the air defense of the Panama Canal Zone. In WORLD WAR II he developed air power as both a strategic and a tactical weapon, directly commanding massive air strikes against Germany and Japan and initiating daylight bombing, which increased accuracy. In 1949 Arnold became the first soldier to receive the rank of general in the U.S. Air Force.

Aroostook War (1838–39), border conflict between Maine and New Brunswick over the Aroostook Valley. Because the boundary between Canada and Maine was never clearly defined under the terms of the TREATY OF PARIS (1783) following the American Revolution, a brief border war broke out when a group of Canadians entered the Aroostook Valley to claim land and jurisdiction. President MARTIN VAN BUREN sent Gen. WINFIELD SCOTT to the region to call a truce in March of 1839. In 1842 Secretary of State DANIEL WEBSTER of the United States and Lord Ashburton of Great Britain negotiated the settlement of the dispute through the WEBSTER-ASHBURTON TREATY.

Arthur, Chester Alan (1829–86), twenty-first president of the United States (1881–85). Born in Fairfield, Vermont, Arthur was educated at Union College in Schenectady, New York, before joining a New York City law firm in 1853. Attracting public attention for his defense of blacks, Arthur won a case in 1855 securing the rights of blacks to ride New York streetcars. He was collector of customs in the port of New York and a key ally of ROSCOE CONKLING. At the Republican National Convention in 1880, he worked for the nomination of Ulysses S. Grant for a third term as president. When this movement failed and James Garfield won the nomination, Arthur was chosen to run for vice president. In July 1881 Garfield was fatally wounded by CHARLES GUITEAU. When he died in September, Arthur became the fourth vice president to succeed to the presidency upon the death of a president. During his administration, known for its honesty and efficiency, he vetoed the CHINESE EXCLUSION ACT (1882) and strongly supported the PENDLE-TON ACT (1883), which created a civil service commission to regulate government hiring on a merit system basis. He had the WHITE HOUSE renovated, believing it should be a showplace for visiting dignitaries. Lack of strong support within his party and illness prevented Arthur from seriously seeking the presidential nomination in 1884.

Articles of Confederation (1781–88), the first constitution of the United States, informally adopted by the Second CONTINENTAL CONGRESS in 1777. A draft prepared by JOHN DICKINSON of Pennsylvania formed the foundation of the document ratified by the thirteen states in 1781. The Articles established a loose confederation of largely independent states with limited powers vested in the central government. It set up a national legislature called Congress, consisting of delegates from the states. Each state had one vote in Congress, regardless of its size or population. Reflecting the Americans' distrust of centralized authority, the Articles gave the central government no power to levy or collect taxes, regulate interstate commerce, or interfere with the states. There was no national executive and no supreme court. The few powers assigned to Congress included declaration of war and peace, maintenance of an army, and coinage of money. Amending the Articles required a unanimous vote of Congress. Because of its weaknesses, ALEXANDER HAMILTON and the other delegates to the ANNAPOLIS CONVENTION called for a convention to be held in Philadelphia, Pennsylvania, in 1787 to improve and amend the Articles. It was superseded by the CONSTITUTION in 1788. (SEE APPENDIX for the text of the Articles.)

Ashcan School, a group of painters formed in New York City in 1907. Also called "the Eight," it was led by Robert Henri and included William Glackens, JOHN SLOAN, George Luks, GEORGE BELLOWS, Ernest Lawson, and Maurice Prendergast. Strongly influenced by the realism of THOMAS EAKINS, these artists departed from the formal portraits and landscapes of the day, believing art should reflect the realities of modern urban life. Their scenes of streets, backyards, bars, beaches, and even ashcans earned them the epithet "Ashcan school." Many of its members helped organize the Armory Show in New York in 1913, a controversial exhibit of painting and sculpture that presented modern art to Americans for the first time.

Ashcroft, John (1942–), U.S. attorney general for President GEORGE W. BUSH (2002–). After graduating from Yale University and the University of Chicago, Ashcroft began his political career in 1973 as a Missouri auditor. He was elected twice as Missouri's attorney general and served as that state's governor from 1985 to 1993. He was elected to the U.S. Senate in 1994 but lost his reelection bid in 2000. Nominated by President Bush in 2000 to be U.S. attorney general, Ashcroft faced harsh questioning for his very conservative views on the death penalty, abortion, gay rights, and gun control, but was confirmed by the Senate. After the SEPTEMBER 11, 2001, TERRORIST ATTACKS, Ashcroft became a prominent figure in the U.S. "war on terror."

Ashe, Arthur (1943–93), tennis player. In 1968 Ashe became the first black to win the U.S. national men's singles championship and in 1975 the first to win the Wimbledon singles title. In 1992 he announced that he had contracted AIDS through a blood transfusion he received before the nation's blood supply was screened for the virus. Though he did not want to make his illness publicly known, he was forced to when newspaper editors warned him they had been tipped off about it and would run the story. This led to a nationwide debate about the right to privacy of public figures.

Assassination of Presidents, Four American presidents have died from assassins' bullets. In 1865 JOHN WILKES BOOTH killed ABRAHAM LINCOLN; CHARLES GUITEAU killed JAMES GARFIELD in 1881; and in 1901 LEON CZOLGOSZ killed WILLIAM MCKINLEY. JOHN F. KENNEDY was assassinated in 1963, allegedly by LEE HARVEY OSWALD. John W. Hinckley, Jr., shot RONALD REAGAN in 1981, but Reagan survived. Other assassination attempts have included attacks on ANDREW JACKSON, THEODORE ROOSEVELT (as an ex-president), FRANKLIN D. ROOSEVELT (as president-elect), HARRY S. TRUMAN, and GERALD FORD (twice).

Associated Press (AP), a cooperative nonprofit agency for gathering and distributing news stories and pictures. The Associated Press, which supplies about ten thousand newspapers, periodicals, and broadcasting stations throughout the world, originated in New York City in 1848 as the Harbor News Association. It was founded by six daily newspaper publishers to expedite news-gathering procedures. The group was reorganized in 1857 under the name of the New York Associated Press.

Assumption Plan (1790), proposal by Secretary of the Treasury ALEXANDER HAMILTON during George Washington's first term that the federal government assume war debts incurred by the separate states during the American Revolution. Hamilton argued that since the states' debts had resulted from their efforts to help the nation as a whole, they should be paid back by the federal government. The assumption of the debts would also reduce state taxes, thus making it easier for the federal government to exercise its newly acquired power of taxation. Opposition, led by Representative JAMES MADISON, came from states that had already begun to pay off their debts. A compromise between Hamilton and Madison, backed by Secretary of State THOMAS JEFFERSON allowed the bill to pass when Madison gave his support to the measure in return for Hamilton's support establishing the new national capital on the Potomac. Congress appropriated $21.5 million, obtained largely through federal taxes and loans from other countries, and paid off most of the debt by the early 1800s.

Astaire, Fred (Frederick Austerlitz; 1899–1987), actor and dancer. Astaire and his sister Adele danced together from 1906 to 1931. When Adele retired, he teamed with Ginger Rogers in 1933, and they became the most successful dance team in motion pictures. The skill, grace, elegance, and sophistication of Astaire's art and the originality, discipline, and perfection of his choreography became a trademark of his movies. His first film, *Flying Down to Rio* (1933), led to more than forty more movie musicals, including *The Gay Divorcee* (1934), *Top Hat* (1935), *Shall We Dance?* (1937), *The Barkleys of Broadway* (1949), *Daddy Long Legs* (1955), and *Funny Face* (1957).

Astor, John Jacob (1763–1848), German-born merchant, fur trader, and financier. Astor organized a lucrative fur trade with China and formed the American Fur Company (1808) to capitalize on the newly acquired lands of the Louisiana Purchase. In 1811 he built a trading post at the mouth of the Columbia River, naming it Astoria, a claim later used by the U.S. government to establish control over the OREGON TERRITORY. Astor invested his fur-trading profits in Manhattan real estate, becoming the wealthiest man in the country. When he died, he left an estate variously estimated at between $20 million and $40 million.

Atchison, David (1807–86), political leader. A proslavery leader and member of the U.S. Senate from Missouri, Atchison served as president pro tempore sixteen times between 1846 and 1854. Because of a unique occurrence, he is said by some historians to have served as president of the United States for one day — March 4, 1849. Inauguration day for Zachary Taylor fell on March 4, a Sunday, and Taylor decided not to take office until the following day. With the term of outgoing President JAMES K. POLK ending March 4, and by virtue of Atchison's senatorial position in the presidential succession, Atchison served as president for one day.

Atlanta Campaign (May 7–September 2, 1864), one of the last major military campaigns of the CIVIL WAR. Union Gen. WILLIAM TECUMSEH SHERMAN led more than 100,000 federal troops on a march from Chattanooga, Tennessee, to Atlanta, Georgia, as part of a drive to end the war. Sherman captured Atlanta in September and his troops burned a large part of the city to the ground in November. From Atlanta the Union armies followed with Sherman's March to the Sea, sweeping almost unopposed through Georgia to Savannah, living off the land since they had left their supply lines behind and destroying much of what they encountered. The Southerners' defeat in this campaign was a major disaster for the Confederacy.

Atlanta Compromise (September 18, 1885), statement of the views on race relations of black educator BOOKER T. WASHINGTON in a speech at the Cotton State Exposition. Washington proposed that blacks and whites both honor the separate-but-equal principle, urging that "in all things that are purely social, we can be as separate as the fingers, yet one as the hand in all things essential to mutual progress." This accommodationist policy almost endorsed segregation. It was his view that vocational education would give blacks the opportunity for economic security and that that was more valuable than social or political advantage. Although white leaders in both the North and the South responded favorably to Washington's policy, it disturbed black intellectuals such as W.E.B. Du BOIS, who believed that blacks should actively pursue civil rights and integration.

Atlantic Cable, a transatlantic telegraph cable on the floor of the ocean between Newfoundland and Ireland, laid in 1866 after twelve years of failed efforts. The project was planned and carried out by American financier CYRUS W. FIELD, who enlisted the aid of oceanographer Matthew Fontaine Maury and SAMUEL F. B. MORSE. By 1900, transatlantic telegraph cables numbered fifteen. In 1956 the first transatlantic telephone cable, which is still in operation, was laid from Newfoundland to Scotland.

Atlantic Charter (August 14, 1941), a joint statement of common objectives issued by President FRANKLIN D. ROOSEVELT of the United States and Prime Minister Winston Churchill of Great Britain prior to the U.S. entry into World War II. Designed to rally support for the war effort, it incorporated the aims of Roosevelt's FOUR FREEDOMS and set forth principles for postwar security. These included the abjuring of territorial aggression by the United States and England, the right of self-determination for all peoples, the right of freedom of the seas for all nations, and the establishment of an international system of security based on disarmament.

Atomic Bomb, powerful explosive weapon that derives its force from the sudden release of energy in a nuclear reaction called fission (or splitting) of the nuclei of such heavy elements as plutonium or uranium. In 1939, at the outset of WORLD WAR II, ALBERT EINSTEIN and other scientists suggested to President FRANKLIN D. ROOSEVELT that the United States develop such a device before the Germans, who were thought to be far advanced in research for such a weapon. The secret MANHATTAN PROJECT, under the direction of the U.S. Army, was begun in 1942. The first successful reactor was assembled at the University of Chicago by a team under physicist Enrico Fermi, who produced the first controlled chain reaction. This led to the construction of huge plants at Oak Ridge, Tennessee, and Hanford, Washington, to produce materials, and a laboratory at Los Alamos, New Mexico, headed by J. ROBERT OPPENHEIMER, to build the bomb. The first atomic bomb was tested successfully in 1945 at Alamogordo, New Mexico. The A-bomb was first dropped on HIROSHIMA, Japan, on August 6, 1945, by order of President HARRY S. TRUMAN and was followed by a second bomb dropped on Nagasaki, Japan, on August 9, 1945. The Japanese initiated surrender negotiations the next day.

Atomic Energy Commission (AEC) (1946), a federal agency established to regulate the development, production, and use of atomic power in the United States for both war and peace. Congress terminated the commission in 1974 and passed the Energy Reorganization Act, creating two new bodies, the Energy Research and Development Administration and the Nuclear Regulatory Commission to carry on and expand the functions of the AEC.

Attucks, Crispus (1723–70), a black sailor, the first of five colonists killed by British soldiers in the BOSTON MASSACRE.

Auden, W. H. (Wystan Hugh; 1907–73), British-born American poet. Achieving success in a variety of styles, Auden exerted a major influence on twentieth-century literature through his sonnets, free verse, critical essays, and plays. Settling in the United States in 1939, Auden became a U.S. citizen in 1946. His works, generally expressing a socialist viewpoint, often examine the moral problems of civilization. He wrote several symbolic and satiric verse plays including *The Dog Beneath the Skin* (1935) and *On the Frontier* (1938). His interest in religion, psychology, and politics is reflected in later poetic works such as *The Double Man* (1941) and the Pulitzer Prize-winning *The Age of Anxiety* (1948).

Audubon, John James (1785–1851), Haitian-born artist and naturalist. Audubon, the most famous of all nature painters in America, became a first-rate ornithologist through his early nineteenth-century paintings of all known species of American birds. His realistic, full-bodied drawings and paintings were first celebrated in England, where he published *Birds of America* (1827–38), containing 435 color engravings made from his watercolors by Robert Havell. Audubon wrote the five-volume *Ornithological Biography* (1831–39) in collaboration with Scottish naturalist

William MacGillivray. The naturalist and conservationist organization, the Audubon Society, memorializes his name.

Auerbach, Red (Arnold; 1917–), basketball coach and executive. Auerbach, the most successful coach in the history of the National Basketball Association (1946–66), rebuilt the last-place Boston Celtics into one of the most dominating teams in the history of professional sports. Led by BOB COUSY and BILL RUSSELL the Celtics won nine championships in ten years. After his retirement in 1966, Auerbach remained as the Celtics' general manager until 1984 and is now president of the organization.

Austin, Stephen (1793–1836), political leader. Austin carried out the plans of his father to colonize three hundred American families in Mexican-owned TEXAS, establishing the first authorized American settlement there in 1822. He became a Mexican citizen and administered the colony wisely, expanding his settlement by an additional nine hundred families. He was largely responsible for the law allowing slavery in Texas. Austin asked Mexico for a separate government for Texas in 1833. Falsely accused and imprisoned as a revolutionary, he returned to Texas in 1835 to find the citizens on the verge of revolt. Austin briefly commanded the Texas volunteers during the TEXAS WAR FOR INDEPENDENCE and sought support from the United States. After the LONE STAR REPUBLIC was established in 1836, SAM HOUSTON defeated Austin to become the first president of Texas. Austin served briefly as secretary of state of Texas before his death.

Autry, Gene (Orvon Gene; 1907–1998), singer, actor, songwriter, and business executive. Dubbed the "singing cowboy," Autry performed in over one hundred Hollywood westerns during the 1930s, 1940s, and 1950s. In the 1950s Autry became a businessman.

B **Bacon's Rebellion** (1676), an uprising of Virginia frontiersmen led by Nathaniel Bacon, a prosperous planter. It arose out of long-standing tensions between the colony's elite and its small farmers. The frontiersmen charged that Governor William Berkeley was failing to provide adequate protection to the planters against Indian raids. The governor fled the capital and JAMESTOWN was burned, but the movement collapsed when Bacon died, probably of dysentery, on October 26.

Baez, Joan (1941–), folksinger, composer, guitarist, and political activist. Baez, known for her strong, pure soprano voice and her straightforward renditions of folk ballads, became deeply involved in the civil rights and the anti-Vietnam War movements during the 1960s and 1970s. An advocate of nonviolence, she has written many songs protesting war, discrimination, and injustice.

Baker, James A. (1930–), politician. A Texas Republican, Baker served President GERALD FORD as undersecretary of commerce. As President RONALD

REAGAN's White House chief of staff and secretary of the treasury, he played an instrumental role in the revision of the federal tax system during the late 1980s. Baker served as secretary of state for President GEORGE H. W. BUSH (1989–92), achieving success in advancing Middle East peace negotiations. He was chief legal adviser for GEORGE W. BUSH during the ELECTION OF 2000 campaign and oversaw the Republican efforts in the recount of Florida's votes in that election.

Baker v. Carr (1962), a U.S. Supreme Court decision that ruled that Tennessee's legislature (as well as other states') had an unfair overrepresentation of rural districts. Chief Justice Earl Warren declared this to be a violation of the equal protection clause of the Fourteenth Amendment. The Court held that states must reapportion their election districts on the basis of population. By 1964 most states had reapportioned their legislatures along the lines of the one person, one vote doctrine. Later the courts applied this principle to U.S. congressional districts as well.

Bakke v. Regents of the University of California (1978), a Supreme Court case addressing the issues of AFFIRMATIVE ACTION policies. Claiming that he had been denied admission to the medical school at UC-Davis solely on the basis of his race, because, he said, his academic credentials were higher than those of some blacks who were admitted, Allan Bakke, a white man, charged that he was the victim of reverse discrimination. The decision revealed a deeply divided Court. Four justices, citing the 1964 Civil Rights Act, held in favor of Bakke. Four other justices held that the affirmative action admissions plan satisfied both the act and the equal protection clause of the Fourteenth Amendment. Justice Lewis F. Powell, the ninth justice, held that both the Constitution and the Civil Rights Act permitted schools to use race as a factor in admissions decisions, but that the UC-Davis plan was invalid because it made race the sole factor in the decision to reject Bakke. Thus, the Court's ruling upheld the general principle of affirmative action as a means of redressing past discrimination, but it did not dispel controversy over the principle.

Balanchine, George (Georgi Balanchivadze; 1904–83), Russian-born ballet dancer and choreographer. In 1934 Balanchine opened the School of American Ballet in New York City and pioneered an American "classic" tradition of dance. His influential ballet style combined classical Russian and exuberant athletic movements. Balanchine nurtured many of America's major dancers. In 1948 the school's performing company became the New York City Ballet, with Balanchine as its artistic director, a position he held until his death.

Baldwin, James (1924–87), author and spokesman for blacks. Baldwin became a major figure in contemporary American literature through his writings on sexual identity, racial tension, and discrimination in a white-dominated world. His many books, plays, and essays include *Go Tell It on* *the Mountain* (1953), *Notes of a Native Son* (1955), *Another Country* (1962), and *The Fire Next Time* (1963).

Baldwin, Roger N. (1884–1981), lawyer, reformer, and antiwar activist. Baldwin helped found the New York-based AMERICAN CIVIL LIBERTIES UNION (ACLU) in 1920 and served as its director until 1950. A supporter of the left during the 1920s and 1930s, he nevertheless removed Communists, including ELIZABETH GURLEY FLYNN, from the ACLU national board in 1940. President Jimmy Carter presented Baldwin with the Medal of Freedom in 1981.

Ball, Lucille (1911–89), actress and comedienne. Ball entertained audiences for over forty years in her more than fifty movies. "I Love Lucy," in which she starred with husband Desi Arnaz, was one of the most popular television comedies of all time, running from 1951 to 1957 and still in syndication. Though her persona on the show was that of zany housewife, she was in real life a shrewd businesswoman.

Ballinger-Pinchot Controversy (1909), a political conflict over conservation policies during the administration of William Howard Taft. Gifford Pinchot, chief of the Interior Department's Division of Forestry, accused Secretary of the Interior Richard A. Ballinger of abandoning the conservation policies of THEODORE ROOSEVELT by plundering and selling public lands. Taft sided with Ballinger and removed Pinchot from office. Although Ballinger later resigned, he and Taft were criticized for putting the interests of private industry over the good of the nation. Ballinger was later cleared by a congressional committee of any wrongdoing.

Baltimore Incident (1891), a diplomatic dispute that arose when the United States detained a ship carrying weapons from California to rebels in Chile, where a civil war was in progress. When the rebels came to power, their resentment over the U.S. action led to a mob attack on American sailors who were on shore leave from the *Baltimore* in Valparaiso, resulting in two deaths and seventeen injured. The United States demanded and received an apology and indemnity of $75,000 from Chile.

Bancroft, George (1800–91), first notable U.S. historian and diplomat. Bancroft's multivolume *History of the United States of America* (1834) recounted that history as a story of the triumph of American democracy and national unity under divine guidance. Bancroft served as secretary of the navy under James K. Polk and helped establish the U.S. Naval Academy at Annapolis. He later served as U.S. minister to Great Britain and Prussia.

Bank Holiday (March 6, 1933), an emergency measure by President Franklin D. Roosevelt, closing all U.S. banks. During the GREAT DEPRESSION, runs on the banks by depositors seeking their savings caused many banks to fail because they did not have enough cash on hand to meet the unexpected demand. When these banks failed, depositors lost their money, and depositors at other banks panicked and demanded their money. Following the holiday, which stopped this vicious cycle, FDR called Congress into special session. They passed the BANKING ACT of 1933, which set up government agencies to examine bank records, allow only those solvent to reopen, and regulate the banking system thereafter. By April 1, 1933, most of the nation's banks were operating and back to normal.

Banking Act (1933), established the FEDERAL DEPOSIT INSURANCE CORPORATION, which insured bank deposits. Passed during the early months of the NEW DEAL, it was intended to strengthen people's faith in banks and to stabilize the federal banking system. The amount insured is presently $100,000.

Banking Act (1935), reorganized the Federal Reserve Board and renamed it the Board of Governors of the Federal Reserve System. The FEDERAL DEPOSIT INSURANCE CORPORATION was made permanent and its powers concerning the control of credit were increased.

Bank of the United States (1791–1811), part of ALEXANDER HAMILTON's financial plan to get the new nation started on a strong economic basis. Congress established the First Bank of the United States in 1791 and chartered it for a twenty-year period. One-fifth of the Bank's stock was owned by the federal government and four-fifths by private business. The Bank had the power to issue bank notes redeemable for gold and silver, as well as to make loans and hold deposits. Because many people opposed the Bank, its charter was not renewed and it ceased operations in 1811.

Bank of the United States (1816–36), chartered for a twenty-year period and widely supported. Because of HENRY CLAY's political influence, its charter came up for renewal in 1832, becoming a major presidential campaign issue. Congress passed a bill to recharter the Second Bank but President ANDREW JACKSON vetoed it because he felt it favored the rich. Despite energetic lobbying by Bank president NICHOLAS BIDDLE, Congress failed to override his veto, and in 1836 the Second Bank of the United States ceased to function. It was reorganized as a private bank but went out of business in the wake of the panic of 1837.

Banneker, Benjamin (1731–1806), mathematician and scientist. Banneker, a free black man, gained early fame when he designed and constructed a striking clock of hand-carved wooden parts despite never having seen one. He was a successful farmer with only a few years of formal education who taught himself calculus and spherical trigonometry in order to construct a popular astronomical almanac (published annually from 1791 to 1797). ABOLITIONISTS cited his achievements as evidence of the intellectual equality of blacks, and Banneker himself argued the issue in letters to Thomas Jefferson.

Barbary Coast, the waterfront area of San Francisco during the California GOLD RUSH of 1849. The Barbary Coast attracted an unruly crowd of gamblers, con men, gangsters, prostitutes, and adventurers. Vigilante groups were organized to help suppress the lawlessness, which spread along the northern California coast.

Barbary Pirates, seamen from the Barbary States of North Africa (Algiers, Morocco, Tripolitania, and Tunis) who attacked ships of other nations in the Mediterranean Sea in the seventeenth and eighteenth centuries. These nations were expected to pay an annual tribute, or bribe, for safe passage; otherwise the Barbary pirates would seize ships and hold the crews for ransom. In 1801 President THOMAS JEFFERSON sent American ships and U.S. Marines to the coast of North Africa to put an end to the piracies. In 1815 the Barbary rulers agreed to abolish all demands for annual payments from and acts of piracy against the United States.

Barbed Wire, twisted steel wires with thornlike barbs used for fencing the open range in the West. Perfected and patented in 1874 by Joseph Glidden, barbed wire replaced wooden fences and shrubs throughout the GREAT PLAINS in the last quarter of the nineteenth century. Cattlemen opposed its use by homesteaders because it injured their livestock and closed the open range. Its use made possible the settlement of the frontier by thousands of small farmers.

Barkley, Alben W. (1877–1956), vice president of the United States (1949–53). Barkley, a Democrat, was elected on the ticket led by HARRY S. TRUMAN in 1948 and became the first vice president to sit on the National Security Council. He had served in the U.S. House of Representatives and the Senate for forty years. A strong supporter of the NEW DEAL, Barkley guided much important legislation through Congress.

Barnum, Phineas T. (1810–91), showman and businessman. Convinced of the unlimited gullibility of the public, Barnum made successful use of advertising and publicity stunts to promote his entertainments. In 1871 he opened a three-ring circus, the "Greatest Show on Earth," and ten years later combined forces with James Bailey, his chief competitor. Thus was created the famous Barnum and Bailey Circus, still in operation today.

Barry, John (1745–1803), naval commander during the AMERICAN REVOLUTION. Barry, as captain of the USS *Lexington,* captured the British ship of war *Edward* in the first naval victory of the Revolution. Later, as commander of the *Alliance,* he won many important naval victories over the British.

Barry, Rick (1944–), basketball player. As one of basketball's most gifted shooters, Barry is the only man to have led both the American Basketball Association and the National Basketball Association in scoring. Barry helped lead the Golden State Warriors to the championship in 1974–75.

Barrymore, theatrical family of two brothers and a sister. Ethel Barrymore (1879–1959), a much-admired beauty, appeared initially on Broadway in *Captain Jinks and the Horse Marines* (1901). She also acted in many films, including *Rasputin and the Empress* (1932) with her brothers and *None* *but the Lonely Heart* (1944), for which she won an Academy Award. John Barrymore (1882–1942) earned distinction for his performance of *Hamlet* (1922) on the stage. Dubbed "the Great Profile," he became a matinee idol during his years in motion pictures. His tumultuous personal life was the subject of much comment. Lionel Barrymore (1878–1954) won an Academy Award for his performance in *A Free Soul* (1931). He played Scrooge in annual radio broadcasts of Dickens's *A Christmas Carol* for many years and starred in the "Dr. Kildare" series in movies and on radio. Another notable role was that of Mr. Potter in Frank Capra's 1946 film, *It's a Wonderful Life.*

Bart, Black (Charles E. Boles; ?–?, active 1875–83), stagecoach robber who eluded Wells Fargo agents and California lawmen for eight years. Wearing a flour-sack mask, he robbed twenty-seven stages with a gun he later said was never loaded, and often left a hand-scrawled whimsical poem at the scene. Always polite, he tipped his hat to the ladies and never took their jewelry. Finally captured in San Francisco in 1883, he served four years in San Quentin and disappeared following his release in 1888.

Barton, Clara (1821–1912), founder of the AMERICAN RED CROSS. During the Civil War, Barton served as a nurse at the first Battle of Bull Run and later as superintendent of nurses for the Union army. In 1881 she organized the American Red Cross and was its president from 1882 until 1904. In 1898 Barton did distinguished relief work in Cuba during the Spanish-American War.

Baruch, Bernard (1870–1965), investor, economic and foreign policy adviser. Active in politics and public policy for more than sixty years, Baruch advised American presidents from Woodrow Wilson to John F. Kennedy. Baruch graduated from City College of New York in 1889 and began a career in finance. He secured a seat on the New York Stock Exchange, and through shrewd stock speculations he made a fortune by 1900. Baruch served as chairman of the War Industries Board during World War I and as an economic adviser during World War II. As a member of the United Nations Energy Commission, in 1946 he proposed the Baruch Plan, which would have placed all atomic energy and weapons under international control. Opposed by the Soviet Union, the plan was rejected.

Baseball, a game played by two teams of nine players each on a large field. The team scoring the most runs in nine innings wins the game. Probably derived from the English game of rounders or cricket, the first form of baseball was played in the United States during the 1800s. Historians refute the belief that ABNER DOUBLEDAY invented the game and give the credit to New York City sportswriter ALEXANDER CARTWRIGHT, who devised the rules of play and organized the Knickerbocker Base Ball Club of New York in 1845. The first organized game was played in Hoboken, New Jersey, on June 19, 1846, between the Knickerbockers and the New York Nine; the Nine won 21–3. The Civil War promoted growth of the game when troops played it during recreation periods.

The Cincinnati Red Stockings became the first professional team in 1869, and in 1876 the major leagues were formed when eight professional teams joined as the National League (NL). On April 22, 1876, Boston beat Philadelphia 6–5 in the first real major league game. By 1900 the NL consisted of the Boston Braves, Chicago Cubs, Cincinnati Reds, New York Giants, Philadelphia Phillies, Pittsburgh Pirates, Brooklyn Dodgers, and St. Louis Cardinals. The NL was joined in 1901 by the eight-team American League (AL), which in 1903 consisted of the Boston Red Sox, Washington Senators, Philadelphia Athletics, St. Louis Browns, Detroit Tigers, Cleveland Indians, Chicago White Sox, and New York Yankees. These sixteen teams played in the same cities for half a century.

In 1903 the first World Series took place between the champions of the two leagues. Baseball's popularity grew after 1900 to the extent that it is called the "national pastime," although the reputation of the game suffered in 1919 when eight Chicago White Sox players were banned from baseball for accepting bribes to lose the World Series against the Cincinnati Reds. The first All-Star Game was held in 1933 with the AL winning 4–2, and in 1935 Cincinnati introduced night baseball into the big leagues.

Baseball's color ban, which started in the 1880s, was broken in 1947 when JACKIE ROBINSON became the first black major league player, joining the Brooklyn Dodgers. The introduction of major league baseball on television in 1950 increased the sport's popularity. Presently the AL and the NL, each with fourteen teams equally divided into eastern and western divisions, play a 162-game schedule between April and September.

Basie, Count (William; 1904–84), pianist and band leader. Basie was given the nickname "Count" while working as a disk jockey. He formed his own jazz band in 1935 and performed in nightclubs, hotels, and theaters. His popularity earned him a recording contract. In 1951 Basie organized a new band for appearances in movies and television. His "One O'Clock Jump" is a jazz classic.

Basketball, a game played by two teams of five players each on a rectangular court, for a set period of time. Each team attempts to score points by shooting a ball through the opponent's basket, situated at either end of a court. The team scoring the most points wins the game. Created by Dr. JAMES NAISMITH in Springfield, Massachusetts, in 1891–92, to give athletes an indoor game to play in the winter, basketball has become immensely popular. Naismith's game was played with a soccer ball and two peach baskets, which were replaced with metal hoops and nets in the early 1990s.

The first college game took place in Iowa City, Iowa, in 1896, with the University of Chicago defeating the University of Iowa 15–12. In 1908 the National Collegiate Athletic Association (NCAA) was formed and set playing rules and eligibility standards. Collegiate basketball, played originally between teams in a local geographical area, expanded after 1934 when Notre Dame played New York University at Madison Square Garden; NCAA championships began in 1939. The national exposure to basketball on television following World War II increased attendance and interest in the sport.

The first professional game was played in Trenton, New Jersey, and the first professional league, consisting of teams from Philadelphia, New York, Brooklyn, and southern New Jersey, was the National League, formed in 1898. Numerous other leagues were organized, including the National Basketball League (NBL; 1937) and the Basketball Association of America (BAA; 1946), which merged in 1949 to form the National Basketball Association (NBA). The American Basketball Association (1967) merged with the NBA in 1976 to form the modern NBA, a league consisting of eastern and western conferences of twenty-seven teams.

Because early professional leagues were segregated, two all-black teams emerged during the 1930s, the New York Renaissance (the Rens) and the Harlem Globetrotters, who toured the country playing exhibition games. The first black player, Chuck Cooper from Duquesne University, joined the NBA in 1950 with the Boston Celtics, opening the sport to black players, who currently dominate the game.

Bataan, Battle of (April 9, 1942), a defeat of American military forces in the Pacific during WORLD WAR II. After the Japanese invaded the Philippines and attacked the island of Luzon, the outnumbered American forces under Gen. Jonathan Wainwright retreated to the Bataan Peninsula. The U.S. troops held out for three months before surrendering. The Japanese forced their prisoners to march the length of the peninsula under conditions of terrible hardship; this became known as the "Bataan death march." Bataan was liberated by Gen. DOUGLAS MACARTHUR and U.S. forces in 1945.

Baugh, Sammy (1914–), football player. One of the first successful passing quarterbacks, Baugh signed in 1937 with the Washington Redskins for $8,000, three times the salary of the next highest paid player. "Slingin' Sammy" was an accomplished punter, leading the Redskins to five division titles and two league championships during his sixteen seasons. He was elected to the pro football Hall of Fame in 1963.

Baum, L. Frank (1856–1919), writer. Baum created *The Wonderful Wizard of Oz* (1900), later a musical motion picture starring Ray Bolger, Jack Haley, Bert Lahr, Margaret Hamilton, and JUDY GARLAND. Baum wrote fourteen Oz books, which have become classics of children's literature.

Baylor, Elgin (1934–), basketball player. Baylor ranks among the top scorers and rebounders of the National Basketball Association. He and Los Angeles Lakers teammate JERRY WEST were the greatest scoring combination in the history of professional basketball.

Bay of Pigs (April 17, 1961), an invasion of Cuba by an anti-Castro Cuban exile force of about two thousand men. Organized and equipped by the U.S. CENTRAL INTELLIGENCE AGENCY and supported by the Eisenhower and Kennedy administrations, the exiled Cubans landed at the Bay of Pigs on the southern coast of Cuba. They hoped to spark a general revolt against Cuba's Communist government. Crushed by Fidel Castro's forces, most of the invaders were killed or captured. The failure was a political setback for President JOHN F. KENNEDY and the United States in Latin America and drove Castro even more firmly into the Soviet camp.

Beard, Charles A. (1874–1948), and Mary R. Beard (1876–1958), historians and social activists. The Beards wrote many books and articles on history and government both together and individually. To protest the erosion of academic freedom during World War I, Charles resigned as a professor at Columbia University and helped found the New School for Social Research in New York. His books argue that economic interests were the real reasons for the framing of the U.S. Constitution, the development of judicial review, and the rise of political parties. Although antifascist, he supported isolationism, criticizing Franklin D. Roosevelt's policies prior to World War II and opposing U.S. entry into that war. Mary was active in movements to help women workers and to obtain the vote for women. She wrote numerous books on the importance of writing and studying women's history and on viewing women as active agents in history, not merely as bystanders or helpmates for men.

Bear Flag Revolt (June 1846), American seizure of Sonoma, a Mexican stronghold in northern California, which resulted in the formation of the Republic of California. Without knowing that war had been declared between the United States and Mexico on May 13, a group of roving hunters and trappers, under the leadership of frontiersman William Ide, took over Mexico's headquarters at Sonoma. Ide and his followers proclaimed the "Republic of California" and created a flag displaying a grizzly bear facing a single red star and the words "California Republic." This action was followed by the conquest of California by JOHN C. FRÉMONT and his American forces during the Mexican War, resulting in the acquisition of California by the United States.

Beauregard, P.G.T. (1818–93), Confederate CIVIL WAR general. Assigned to Charleston, South Carolina, Beauregard gave the orders to fire on FORT SUMTER, which started the war, on April 12, 1861. His forces helped win the first Battle of BULL RUN. He also fought at SHILOH and defended Richmond and Petersburg at the end of the war.

Bechtel, Stephen Davison (1900–89), corporate executive, construction engineer. Bechtel took over his father's construction firm, W. A. Bechtel Co., and served as president from 1936 to 1960, building it into the world's largest construction and engineering firm. Specializing in large projects,

Bechtel supervised the construction of airports, ships, power plants, dams, factories, bridges, oil refineries, and hotels in 140 countries on seven continents. The Hoover Dam, the Trans-Arabia Pipeline, the San Francisco–Oakland Bay Bridge, the Alaska Pipeline, and the Bay Area Rapid Transit System (BART) are examples of Bechtel's projects. After the United States invaded Iraq in 2003, the Bechtel Corporation won a $680 million contract to repair Iraq's infrastructure.

Beckwourth, James (1798–1867), frontiersman, mountain man, and guide. The son of a white man and a mulatto slave woman, he was born legally a slave. His father took him to St. Louis, Missouri, where he was freed and grew up as a free man. Beckwourth worked at fur trading in the Rocky Mountains, married several Indian women over the years, and lived for eleven years with the Crow Indians under the name of Morning Star. As an army scout he discovered Beckwourth Pass, a route through the Sierra Nevada Mountains, in 1850. Thomas D. Bonner's book *The Life and Adventures of James P. Beckwourth, Mountaineer, Scout, Pioneer and Chief of the Crow Nation of Indians* (1856) chronicled his exploits.

Beecher, Henry Ward (1813–87), Protestant preacher and social reformer. At Plymouth Congregational Church in Brooklyn Beecher gained national recognition for his witty and eloquent sermons. Attracting large crowds, he preached against slavery and in support of women's suffrage. In the years following the Civil War, Beecher became the focus of a celebrated marital scandal in the Tilton divorce trial. HARRIET BEECHER STOWE was his sister.

Beecher's Bibles, name given to rifles provided to the antislavery forces during the bloodshed in Kansas in 1856. HENRY WARD BEECHER an abolitionist, raised money for the rifles, stating that the guns sent to equip the FREE-SOIL settlers moving to Kansas would be a stronger "moral" argument against proslavery men than the Bible.

Beiderbecke, Leon "Bix" (1903–31), jazz musician. Born in Iowa, Beiderbecke was a self-taught cornetist, pianist, and composer. Influenced by New Orleans jazz, he was the first white innovator of jazz. In his short career, he played with top bands including those of "King" Joe Oliver, Paul Whiteman, and LOUIS ARMSTRONG. His individualized style of jazz cornet playing influenced those who followed. He died at the age of twenty-eight from heavy drinking and illness.

Belafonte, Harry (1927–), singer. Belafonte, born in New York City of West Indian parents, spent part of his youth in the United States and part in Jamaica. He achieved international fame as a singer of Jamaican calypso and folk music with such hits as "Day-O," "Jamaica Farewell," "Man Smart, Woman Smarter," and "Brown Skin Girl." A civil rights leader in the 1950s and 1960s, Belafonte was instrumental in gathering performers to record *We Are the World* in 1985 to benefit starving Africans.

Belknap Scandal (1876), an allegation that William W. Belknap (1829–90), secretary of war under ULYSSES S. GRANT, accepted bribes from employees in the government Indian service. Impeachment proceedings were instituted in the House of Representatives, but Belknap resigned before the case could be tried.

Bell, Alexander Graham (1847–1922), scientist, inventor of the telephone, and educator. After years of experimenting with the transmission of sound through wire, Bell patented the first practical telephone in 1876 following the transmission of his famous message, "Mr. Watson, come here; I want you." The Bell Telephone Company was organized in 1877. Although litigation was instituted against Bell by others claiming to have invented the telephone earlier, the Supreme Court upheld his claim. Bell contributed significantly to the education of the deaf, establishing a school and founding the Alexander Graham Bell Association for the Deaf.

Bell, John (1796–1869), member of the HOUSE OF REPRESENTATIVES from Tennessee (1827–41) and SPEAKER (1834–35). In 1860 Bell was nominated for president by the CONSTITUTIONAL UNION PARTY, which carried only Kentucky, Tennessee, and Virginia. Although a southern slaveholder, Bell opposed the expansion of slavery into the territories in support of the preservation of the Union. But at the outbreak of the CIVIL WAR, when forced to choose, he supported the CONFEDERACY.

Bellamy, Edward (1850–98), author. Bellamy wrote *Looking Backward 2000–1887* (1888), a best-selling influential utopian novel picturing a society devoid of competition and private enterprise and populated by well-educated, happy, healthy people. Bellamy's ideas prompted the founding of clubs dedicated to his reforms and influenced the POPULIST PARTY platform in 1892. He founded the *New Nation*, a Boston weekly, in 1881.

Belleau Wood, Battle of (June 6–July 1, 1918), WORLD WAR I battle. The American Second Division Marines sought to support French troops by opening fire against the Germans in a forested area near the Marne River at Château-Thierry. In twenty days of fighting, the Americans suffered heavy casualties but claimed an important victory.

Bellow, Saul (1915–), writer. Bellow became the first novelist to win three National Book Awards with *The Adventures of Augie March* in 1953, *Herzog* in 1964, and *Mr. Sammler's Planet* in 1971. In 1976 he received both the PULITZER PRIZE for *Humboldt's Gift* and the Nobel Prize for literature. Bellow's novels and stories are noted for his skill in portraying the lives of intellectuals in postwar urban America and for his critical but sympathetic view of American Jewish life and his favorite city, Chicago.

Bellows, George (1882–1925), painter. Bellows, a leading American realist of the ASHCAN SCHOOL, produced "event" paintings such as *Stag at Sharkey's, Both Members of This Club,* and *Dempsey through the Ropes.* In 1909 at age twenty-seven, he was the youngest man to be elected to the National Academy of Design.

Benét, Stephen Vincent (1898–1943), writer and poet, whose work reflects his abiding interest in the history and folklore of America. *John Brown's Body* (1928), his epic poem about the Civil War, earned him the Pulitzer Prize for verse. His best-known short story, "The Devil and Daniel Webster" (1937), later became the subject of an opera, a play, and a film.

Benjamin, Judah P. (1811–84), lawyer and statesman. Elected to the U.S. Senate from Louisiana in 1852, Benjamin, who was Jewish, resigned in 1861 to become active in the Southern cause during the CIVIL WAR. JEFFERSON DAVIS appointed Benjamin attorney general of the CONFEDERATE STATES, and later as secretary of war and secretary of state. With the fall of Richmond, Benjamin escaped to England, where he practiced law.

Bennett, James Gordon, Sr. (1795–1872), editor and newspaper publisher. In 1935 Bennett founded the *New York Herald,* a daily newspaper that sold for a penny. Unique features of the paper included coverage of financial, sports, and society news, as well as national and international events. Bennett stationed correspondents at battlefields throughout the Civil War to provide firsthand coverage for his readers. The *Herald* was the first paper to use the telegraph as a means for getting news.

Bennington, Battle of (August 16, 1777), a small but important battle of the AMERICAN REVOLUTION, pitting British troops and HESSIANS under Gen. JOHN BURGOYNE against the GREEN MOUNTAIN BOYS of the Vermont countryside. Burgoyne's army needed supplies as they moved south from Canada into New York. He sent part of his troops to raid Bennington, Vermont, for the materials. Gen. John Stark learned that they were coming, gathered a formidable militia, and destroyed the invaders. This American victory reduced the size of the British army moving toward Albany, New York, and helped bring about the turning-point victory at SARATOGA.

Benny, Jack (Benjamin Kubelsky; 1894–1974), comedian. Following success in vaudeville and radio, Benny became a television star with his Emmy Award–winning show featuring Eddie "Rochester" Anderson, Dennis Day, and Mary Livingstone, his longtime partner and wife. Benny created an image that became an American institution: a miserly, vain, inept violinist who was forever thirty-nine years old.

Benton, Thomas Hart (1782–1858), politician. Originally the editor of the *Missouri Enquirer,* Benton became the first senator to be elected from Missouri when it became a state in 1821. Benton, a Democrat, supported expansionism and advocated gold over silver currency, which earned him the appellation "Old Bullion." Although he served in the Senate for thirty years, his support for the COMPROMISE OF 1850 led to his defeat for reelection. He was then elected to the House of Representatives (1853–55).

Benton, Thomas Hart (1889–1975), painter. As one of the leading artists of America's regionalist movement, or art based on small-town or rural scenes, Benton advocated a painting style that ignored foreign influence. He believed American art should present everyday subjects easily understood by ordinary people: subjects such as sharecroppers, black cotton pickers, politicians, gangsters, mountaineers, and scenes from small-town life. During the 1930s Benton was one of the most active muralists in the country. He was named for his great-uncle, Senator THOMAS HART BENTON of Missouri.

Bergen, Edgar (Bergren; 1903–78), entertainer. Bergen displayed his talent as a ventriloquist through his dummy, Charlie McCarthy. Beginning his career on the Chautauqua circuit, Bergen and McCarthy entertained in vaudeville, radio, films, and television. In 1938 they received a special wooden Academy Award for *A Letter of Introduction*. Upon Bergen's death, Charlie McCarthy was donated to the SMITHSONIAN. His daughter, Candice Bergen, has also had a notable acting career in films and television.

Berle, Milton (Berlinger; 1908–2002), comedian. Berle starred in Broadway productions, was featured in many motion pictures, and was a regular performer on radio. In 1948 he became a pioneer humorist in the new medium of television with his highly successful show, "The Texaco Star Theatre." "Uncle Miltie" was a favorite on early television.

Berlin, Irving (Israel Baline; 1888–1989), composer. Berlin composed music and lyrics for dozens of America's most popular songs, including "Easter Parade" and "White Christmas." One of his first hits, "Alexander's Ragtime Band," achieved immediate success in 1911. Berlin also wrote songs for Broadway musicals and motion pictures. Notable works include *This Is the Army* (1942), *Top Hat* (1935), and *Holiday Inn* (1942) In 1954 Congress presented him with a gold medal for composing "God Bless America."

Berlin Airlift (1948–49), a confrontation between East and West during the early years of the COLD WAR. When zones of occupation were set up after World War II, the city of Berlin, itself split between West and East, lay deep within Communist East Germany. Joseph Stalin in 1948 blockaded all surface traffic through East Germany into West Berlin, cutting off Western supplies of food and fuel in an effort to take over the whole city. The West, rather than concede the city to the Soviets or go to war over it, instituted an airlift to provide essential supplies. Every day for almost ten months, American and British cargo planes landed in West Berlin, sometimes as often as one per minute. The Berlin Airlift succeeded, and Stalin ended the blockade on May 17, 1949.

Berlin Wall (1961–89), a barrier built by East German soldiers and police to separate East and West Berlin and stop the exodus of refugees from Communist rule in East Germany. A barbed-wire fence, later replaced by a five-foot cement block wall topped with barbed wire and broken glass, made escape from East Berlin nearly impossible. Guards patrolled the wall with orders to "shoot to kill" anyone trying to scale it. To the surprise of the free world, in the wake of a citizens' revolt, the East German authorities with the tacit approval of Soviet ruler Mikhail Gorbachev allowed open traffic between East and West in November 1989 and the wall was dismantled (1989–90).

Bernstein, Carl *See* BOB WOODWARD AND CARL BERNSTEIN.

Bernstein, Leonard (1918–90), pianist, composer, and conductor. Bernstein conducted the New York Philharmonic from 1958 to 1969, greatly increasing the orchestra's prestige and reputation. In 1942 he conducted the famous Tanglewood orchestra in Massachusetts, which presented his first work, "Sonata for Clarinet and Piano." Bernstein, as a lecturer and conductor of a series of concerts for young people on television, was one of the most successful educators and popularizers of classical music in history. He wrote the scores for many Broadway musicals and motion pictures, including *On the Waterfront* (1954) and *West Side Story* (1957).

Berra, Yogi (Lawrence; 1925–), baseball player. An outstanding catcher for the New York Yankees and American League most valuable player three times, Berra was a fine hitter and consistent fielder. His modesty and congeniality made him a great favorite with baseball fans, as did his talent for such pithy comments as "It ain't over till it's over." He also managed pennant winners with the New York Yankees and the New York Mets and was elected to the baseball Hall of Fame in 1972.

Berry, Chuck (Charles; 1926–), rock musician and composer. Berry profoundly influenced early rock musicians of the late 1950s and early 1960s through his style and lyrics. He spent time in reform school and worked in an automobile plant before he became one of the first black rock stars. His first hit was "Maybellene" in 1955. Others included "Johnny B. Goode," "Sweet Little Sixteen," and "Rock and Roll Music."

Berry, Halle (1968–), actress. Berry won the academy award for best actress in 2002 for her performance in *Monster's Ball*, becoming the first African-American woman to do so. A former teenage beauty queen, she was first runner-up in the Miss U.S.A. competition in 1986. After finishing in the top five at the Miss World pageant, she worked as a model before being cast in television's *Living Dolls* in 1989. Her film career began with *Jungle Fever* (1991) and she had her first starring role as the superhero Storm in *X-Men* (2000).

Bethune, Mary McLeod (1875–1955), educator and civil rights leader. The fifteenth child of former slaves, Bethune established a school, now called Bethune-Cookman College, in Florida. Her work in education and to improve race relations brought her to national prominence. She served as director of the Division of Negro Affairs in the National Youth Administration during the New Deal and adviser to President Franklin D. Roosevelt.

She founded the National Council of Negro Women and served as vice president of the NATIONAL ASSOCIATION FOR THE ADVANCEMENT OF COLORED PEOPLE, whose SPINGARN MEDAL she received in 1935.

Biddle, Nicholas (1786–1844), banker. Biddle, member of a prominent Philadelphia family, attended the University of Pennsylvania at age ten and went on to become a poet, scholar, and banker. Appointed a director of the Second BANK OF THE UNITED STATES in 1819 by President James Monroe, he became the bank's president in 1822. Because of President ANDREW JACKSON's opposition, Congress did not recharter the national bank. Biddle remained president after the expiration of the federal charter in 1836, but the reorganized bank failed in the panic of 1837.

Bierce, Ambrose (1842–1914?), writer and journalist. Known for war stories and tales of the supernatural, Bierce's writing was influenced by his early poverty and serious Civil War experiences, as well as by EDGAR ALLAN POE and STEPHEN CRANE. After the war he worked for periodicals in San Francisco, where he became notorious for his acid wit and hair-trigger temper. He disappeared in Mexico in 1913 while covering Pancho Villa's campaigns for American newspapers, and his fate remains unknown. His book, *The Devil's Dictionary*, reflects his sardonic approach to life.

Bierstadt, Albert (1830–1902), landscape painter. As a later member of the HUDSON RIVER SCHOOL of painting, Bierstadt was one of the first artists to paint the vastness of the mountains and wilderness of the rugged American West. He traveled widely, making sketches and oil studies of nature that later provided the basis for many of his enormous canvases. Two of his works, *Discovery of the Hudson River* and *Settlement of California*, hang in the Capitol in Washington, D.C.

Big Five, the five great powers composing the Allies in WORLD WAR II. They, and their leaders, included Franklin D. Roosevelt of the United States, Winston Churchill of Great Britain, Joseph Stalin of the Soviet Union, Chiang Kai-shek of the Republic of China, and Charles de Gaulle of France. Since World War II the "Big Five" has referred to the five powers who were given permanent seats on the Security Council of the United Nations. They are the People's Republic of China, France, Great Britain, the Russian Federation, and the United States.

Big Four, four representatives at the Paris Peace Conference (1919) who negotiated the TREATY OF VERSAILLES, officially ending World War I. They were Woodrow Wilson of the United States, David Lloyd George of Great Britain, Georges Clemenceau of France, and Vittorio Orlando of Italy.

Big Stick Policy, name given to the foreign policy of President THEODORE ROOSEVELT. When faced with problems, he quoted an old African proverb, "Speak softly and carry a big stick, and you will go far." He applied this motto by sponsoring the establishment of a large U.S. Navy and by intervening in disputes regarding Alaska and Venezuela. He reshaped this policy as the Roosevelt Corollary.

Big Three, the three principal Allied leaders during World War II: Franklin Roosevelt of the United States, Winston Churchill of Great Britain, and Joseph Stalin of the Soviet Union.

Bill of Rights, the first ten amendments to the U.S. Constitution, which enumerate the fundamental liberties of U.S. citizens. The first bill of rights in America was the Virginia Declaration of Rights (1776), written by George Mason. It became a model for all later American bills of rights, including that in the U.S. Constitution, which was proposed by Congress in 1789 and ratified in 1791. See Appendix for the text of the Bill of Rights.

"Billy the Kid." See William Bonney.

Bingham, George Caleb (1811–79), painter and politician. Bingham's paintings depict natural landscape scenes, everyday frontier life, and political events. Some of his best-known paintings are *Jolly Flatboatmen, Raftsmen Playing Cards, Stump Speaking,* and *Verdict of the People.* Known as the "Missouri Artist," Bingham also painted portraits of government officials. Bingham served in the Missouri assembly and as the state's treasurer and fought for the Union as a general during the Civil War.

Bird, Larry (1956–), basketball player. Bird, an intense competitor, is considered one of the greatest forwards ever to play the game. A two-time college All-American at Indiana State, he signed with the Boston Celtics in 1979. Bird was one of only three players in NBA history to win most valuable

---

★ **Bill of Rights**

The Basic Protections Established by the Bill of Rights
For the complete text of the Bill of Rights, see Appendix.

First, the right to freedom of religion, speech, press, assembly, and petition
Second, the right to bear arms
Third, the right not to quarter soldier
Fourth, the right to protection from unreasonable searches and seizures
Fifth, the right to due process of law, including protection against self-incrimination
Sixth, the right, in criminal cases, to a jury trial, to confront witnesses, and to defense counsel
Seventh, the right, in civil cases, to a jury trial and to other legal protections
Eighth, the right to protection from unreasonable bail and cruel punishment
Ninth, other rights not specifically discussed in the Constitution
Tenth, the right of individuals or the states to powers not delegated to the United States by the Constitution

player honors for three consecutive seasons (1984–86). He retired from play in 1992, after winning the gold medal at the Barcelona Olympics as a member of the "Dream Team" with MAGIC JOHNSON and MICHAEL JORDAN. Bird was named to the NBA's fifty greatest players list in 1996. He came out of retirement in 1997 to coach the Indiana Pacers and a year later he was named NBA Coach of the Year and was elected to the Basketball Hall of Fame. He coached the Pacers for three seasons, stepping down at the end of the 2000 season. Bird joined the Pacers as president of basketball operations in 2003.

Birney, James (1792–1857), slaveholder who became an abolitionist. Birney served as an agent of the American Colonization Society, supporting political action to end slavery and settle freed slaves in Africa or the Caribbean. Presidential nominee for the LIBERTY PARTY in 1840 and 1844, he drew enough popular votes from Whig HENRY CLAY in New York to swing the state and the election in 1844 to Democrat JAMES K. POLK.

Black, Hugo L. (1886–1971), associate justice of the U.S. SUPREME COURT (1937–71). Black entered the U.S. Senate in 1927, where he became a noted progressive and supporter of Franklin D. Roosevelt's New Deal and 1937 Court-packing plans. Black was Roosevelt's first nominee to the Supreme Court, but after his confirmation a scandal erupted when it was discovered that during the 1920s Black had been a member of the Ku Klux Klan. In a radio speech defending himself, Black affirmed his dedication to the principles of democracy and the Bill of Rights. He became a leading liberal justice, known for his absolutist reading of the First Amendment clauses protecting freedom of religion, speech, and press, and advocacy of the "incorporation doctrine," which holds that the Fourteenth Amendment applies the Bill of Rights to limit the powers of state and local government.

Black Codes, laws passed by the legislatures of the southern states after the Civil War during RECONSTRUCTION in an attempt to regulate the activities of and place restrictions on the former slaves.

Black Friday (September 24, 1869), the day two financiers and stock speculators, JAY GOULD and JAMES FISK, attempted to corner the gold market. This created a serious stock market panic in New York City that pushed many Wall Street brokers and legitimate business firms into bankruptcy.

Black Hawk (1767–1838), Sauk Indian chief. Black Hawk struggled determinedly against the westward movement of the white settlers. During the WAR OF 1812 he aided the British against the Americans. In 1831 he led his tribes into Illinois to reclaim their homeland, leading to the BLACK HAWK WAR. Captured in 1832, Black Hawk was released to a reservation the following year. In 1833 he wrote his autobiography, a classic statement of Indian resentment of white settlers.

Black Hawk War (1832), conflict between the Sauk and Fox tribes and the United States. BLACK HAWK, chief of the Sauk and Fox Indians, tried to reclaim his tribal lands in Illinois from white settlers. In the ensuing war U.S. troops massacred most of the Indians. It was the final major Indian conflict in the Old Northwest Territory until the 1860s. (Abraham Lincoln served as a captain of volunteers during this war.)

Blacklist, a term describing efforts in the 1940s and 1950s to exclude from the entertainment industry writers, directors, and actors who had been members of the Communist party or organizations that the federal government labeled subversive. Many people could not find work for years because of the blacklist, which was maintained by film studios, television and radio stations, and private groups that lobbied the entertainment industry. Some managed to find work either by writing under false names or by having friends pose as the writers. Even though blacklisting ended in the 1950s and 1960s, the term passed into popular use to describe any list of people or organizations with whom one does not want to do business.

Black Muslims, members of a religious movement in the United States, which began in the 1930s. It encouraged and further developed the concept of black nationalism. Its most famous leader was MALCOLM X. Members reject Christianity, on the grounds that it is a religion of white people, and adopt the Islamic faith.

Black Power, a movement of militant black Americans that grew out of the civil rights crusade of the 1960s. Advocates of black power, like earlier black nationalists, called for independent political, social, economic, and cultural action and institutions for black people. The emphasis placed upon black culture, pride in the African heritage, and achievement was summed up in the motto "black is beautiful."

Black Republicans, a term applied by southern Democrats in the years before the Civil War to members of the REPUBLICAN PARTY. Those who used this term intended it to be an insult, hoping that white Americans who felt racial prejudice toward African-Americans would reject the Republicans as too sympathetic to the slaves' demands for liberty and equal rights. They continued to use this term during the RECONSTRUCTION period to label Republicans who favored legislation and other government action to help the freed slaves.

Black Union Troops, black soldiers, about 200,000 in number, who served in the Union forces during the CIVIL WAR. Encouraged by such abolitionists as Frederick Douglass to enlist, blacks composed about 12 percent of all Union soldiers. More than 38,000 died of wounds, disease, or sometimes execution when they were captured by Confederates. Twenty-three won the Medal of Honor for heroism. Although the men were forced to serve in segregated units, discriminated against in pay, assignments, and rank, the black troops were an important factor in the Union victory.

Black Warrior Incident (February 28, 1854), the seizure of an American merchant ship, *Black Warrior,* by Spanish authorities in Havana, Cuba, and the confiscation of its cargo. Southern Expansionists urged the United States to retaliate by going to war with Spain, but in 1855 the dispute was settled with Spain's apology and payment for damages.

Blackwell, Antoinette Brown (1825–1921), reformer and pioneer clergywoman. Although Blackwell earned a divinity degree, she was at first refused ordination because of her sex. As an active speaker and writer for women's rights, temperance, and abolition of slavery, she wrote many books and preached until the age of ninety as a Congregationalist pastor.

Blackwell, Elizabeth (1821–1910), first woman doctor in the United States. Blackwell, sister-in-law of ANTOINETTE BROWN BLACKWELL, spent her life working for the admission of women to the field of medicine. After teaching school for several years, she decided to become a physician in 1844. Refused admittance to twenty-nine medical schools, she studied privately until she was finally accepted by Geneva College in Geneva, New York. Blackwell opened the New York Infirmary for Women and Children, staffed by women; it was later expanded to include a medical school for women. During the Civil War she trained nurses for the Union army.

Blaine, James G. (1830–93), politician and statesman. Blaine helped shift the direction of the Republican party from its RECONSTRUCTION policies to conservative economic policies between 1877 and 1898. He represented Maine in the House of Representatives from 1863 to 1876, including six years as Speaker from 1869 to 1875. Blaine served in the Senate from 1876 until 1881, when he resigned to serve as secretary of state under President JAMES GARFIELD. In his second term as secretary of state (1889–92) under President BENJAMIN HARRISON, he pursued improved relations with Latin America and the annexation of the Hawaiian islands. A staunch supporter of western expansion, Blaine represented the United States in the first Pan-American Conference. Blaine unsuccessfully sought the Republican nomination for president in 1876, 1880, and 1892. His campaigns were hindered by charges of corruption in aiding a railroad deal, and his associations with politicians and big business earned him powerful enemies. He received the presidential nomination in the ELECTION OF 1884 but narrowly lost to GROVER CLEVELAND.

Blair Family, three influential statesmen during the 1800s. Francis Preston Blair (1791–1876), journalist and political leader, founded (1830) and edited the *Washington Globe* (which became the official organ of the Democratic party) and advised Andrew Jackson as a member of Jackson's KITCHEN CABINET. Blair started the *Congressional Globe* (later called the *Congressional Record*) to report the daily proceedings of Congress. Blair helped elect Lincoln to the presidency and served as his adviser, arranging the unsuccessful peace conference at HAMPTON ROADS in 1865. His son Francis Preston Blair, Jr. (1821–75) helped organize the FREE-SOIL PARTY in Missouri (1848) and ran for the vice presidency in 1868 as a Democrat with presidential nominee Horatio Seymour; they were defeated by Ulysses S. Grant. He later became a liberal Republican and served as a U.S. senator from Missouri (1871–73). Another son, Montgomery Blair (1813–83), represented DRED SCOTT before the Supreme Court in 1857 and served as postmaster general in Lincoln's administration. Blair House, the family mansion on Pennsylvania Avenue in Washington, D.C., was purchased by the federal government and is used to house guests of the United States.

Blanda, George (1927–), football player. Blanda, who was named "Player of the Year" in 1961 and 1970, played a record twenty-six seasons. He retired in 1975 at age forty-eight, the oldest man ever to play professional football, having set eleven offensive records including all-time scorer in pro football with 2,002 points. Blanda's scoring record was broken in 2000 by placekicker Gary Anderson of the Minnesota Vikings.

Bleeding Kansas (1854–60), the term used to describe the border war in KANSAS Territory between proslavery and antislavery settlers. Under the KANSAS-NEBRASKA ACT of 1854, the settlers of Kansas were to decide by POPULAR SOVEREIGNTY, or the vote of the people, whether Kansas would become a free or slave state. Violence broke out, touching off a civil war within the territory. Proslavery and antislavery groups created their own constitutions. That of the proslavery forces was called the Lecompton constitution, and it was ultimately defeated by the voters in 1858. After the death of more than two hundred people, Kansas was admitted to the Union under the Wyandotte constitution as a free state in 1861.

Blockade, the use of ships to cut off trade between a city or country and the rest of the world. The British tried to enforce a blockade against the United States during the WAR OF 1812. The most famous blockades in American history were the CIVIL WAR blockade of the South (covering the coast from Virginia to Texas) ordered by President Abraham Lincoln and the blockade of Cuba ordered by President John F. Kennedy during the CUBAN MISSILE CRISIS of 1962. The blockade of 1861–65 was a factor in the defeat of the Confederacy; the blockade of 1962 resulted in the Soviet Union's withdrawal of its missiles from Cuba.

Bloody Shirt, a term used by Democrats to describe the Republican party's charge in the years between the end of the Civil War and 1900 that the Democrats were to blame for the war and the assassination of Abraham Lincoln. The term comes from the phrase "waving the bloody shirt," which itself is a reference to the scene in Shakespeare's play *Julius Caesar* in which Mark Antony holds up the murdered Caesar's bloody toga to inflame the people of Rome against his assassins.

Bloomer, Amelia Jenks (1818–94), social reformer, temperance leader, and women's rights advocate. Bloomer was active in the dress-reform movement, protesting hoop skirts and other items of women's clothing that restricted their activities and injured their health. She invented and wore special trousers that were popularly called "bloomers." In 1849 she began a newspaper for women called *The Lily* in which she promoted her beliefs regarding social reforms, especially temperance.

Bly, Nellie (Elizabeth Cochrane Seaman; 1867?–1922), journalist. Bly took her pen name from Stephen Foster's song of the same name. A women's rights activist, she began her newspaper writing career at age eighteen. Known for her boldness and desire for firsthand experience in her writing, she once intentionally got herself arrested so she could write about treatment of women prisoners. In 1889 her newspaper sent her around the world to beat Jules Verne's *Around the World in Eighty Days* record; she made it in seventy-two days.

Bogart, Humphrey (1899–1957), actor. "Bogey" originally played minor roles in film comedies and westerns. He played the sinister Duke Mantee in *The Petrified Forest* on stage (1935) and in the movie (1936), and from then on he was a top box-office attraction. Well suited to the role of the tough guy who harbors sensitive feelings, he starred in *The Maltese Falcon* (1941), *Casablanca* (1942), and *The Big Sleep* (1946). Bogart won an Academy Award for his performance in *The African Queen* (1951). After his death, his 1940s films experienced a revival and are now considered classics. "Bogey" is one of film's most enduring legends and cult heroes.

Bonds, Barry (1964–), baseball player. The son of major league player Bobby Bonds, he began his career in 1986 with the Pittsburgh Pirates, then signed with the San Francisco Giants in 1992. He broke numerous baseball records, and is the only player in major league history to hit more than four hundred home runs and steal more than four hundred bases during his career. Bonds is the only major league player to win more than three Most Valuable Player awards; he holds the record of six MVP awards in the National League, the first player to win the honor in three consecutive years (2001, 2002, 2003). Bonds is only the fourth player to hit 600 or more home runs (672 as of May 2004), joining HANK AARON (755), BABE RUTH (714), and WILLIE MAYS (660). In 2002 he set baseball's major league record for home

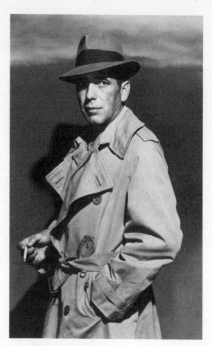

Humphrey Bogart

runs in one season with seventy-three, breaking the record of seventy set by Mark McGwire in 1998.

Bonney, William (1859–81), frontier outlaw. Known as "Billy the Kid," an infamous gunfighter, Bonney reportedly killed his first man at age twelve. His career of cattle stealing and murder ended in 1881 when Sheriff Pat Garrett cornered and shot him in New Mexico.

Bonnie and Clyde, gangsters during the 1930s. Bonnie Parker (1910–34) and Clyde Barrow (1909–34) roamed the Southwest, robbing banks and killing at least twelve persons, nine of whom were law officers. They courted publicity and, despite their outlaw status, became folk heroes to the depression-ridden readers who followed their exploits in the press. They were killed by Louisiana lawmen after eluding capture for two years.

Bonus Army, a group of unemployed World War I veterans who demonstrated during the GREAT DEPRESSION. The Bonus Law of 1924 had given every veteran a certificate payable in 1945, but the veterans wanted the bonus immediately. In June 1932, about 15,000 of them and their families marched on Washington, D.C., in a futile effort to pressure the Senate into passing a bill to grant immediate payments. President HERBERT HOOVER called upon Gen. DOUGLAS MACARTHUR and federal troops to disperse the Bonus Army and drive them out of the capital. The use of armed troops against unarmed men, women, and children shocked the nation.

Boom Towns, settlements that suddenly spring up or increase in size as the result of the discovery of a vital resource, such as gold, silver, or oil. In the nineteenth-century West, promoters fostered such booms to bring new settlers to their towns to buy land and work mines. If the mines did not produce the wealth the promoters promised, the settlers and workers left and the towns quickly died, becoming ghost towns.

Boone, Daniel (1734–1820), frontiersman. A pioneer in the early years of the new nation, Boone explored and settled Kentucky. His Wilderness Road wound through the Appalachians, serving as the main route to the West for many years. In 1775 Boone chose a site near the Kentucky River to build Boonesboro, which grew into the principal settlement of the region. Boone became a major symbol of the rugged frontiersman.

Booth, Edwin (1833–93), actor. Booth charmed theater audiences across America during the mid-1800s. The foremost American actor of his day, he was famous in England and the United States for his roles in Shakespeare's tragedies. He retired from the stage following the assassination of President Abraham Lincoln by his brother, JOHN WILKES BOOTH, but later returned to reestablish his reputation.

Booth, John Wilkes (1838–65), actor and assassin of ABRAHAM LINCOLN. The brother of EDWIN BOOTH, John performed successfully as a Shakespearean actor. As a Southern sympathizer during the CIVIL WAR, he was a member of the company of troops that seized JOHN BROWN at HARPERS

FERRY. Booth organized a plot to assassinate Vice President Andrew Johnson, Secretary of State William Seward, and Gen. Ulysses S. Grant, as well as Lincoln. Booth assassinated the president during a performance of *Our American Cousin* at Ford's Theater on April 14, 1865. Leaping from the balcony to the stage, Booth broke his leg but escaped. Federal troops found him hiding in a barn in Virginia, where he was shot and killed. Many of the other conspirators, though they botched their parts in the plot or did not even try, were also executed after a military trial.

Borah, William (1865–1940), politician. Borah was a prominent criminal and corporation lawyer in Idaho when he became involved in Republican politics. In 1906, he was elected to the U.S. Senate, where he was to remain for the rest of his life. A Progressive Republican, he was considered a political maverick, noted for his independent stands. He led campaigns for the sixteenth (collection of a federal income tax) and seventeenth (popular election of senators) amendments, but opposed the LEAGUE OF NATIONS and became a strong isolationist. He was largely responsible for the Washington Disarmament Conference (1921) and the KELLOGG-BRIAND PACT (1928). Bills sponsored by Borah created the DEPARTMENT OF LABOR and the Children's Bureau; he also helped uncover scandals in the administration of WARREN G. HARDING. Noted for his integrity, Borah was mentioned as a candidate for president, but his independence and the fact that Idaho had few electoral votes worked against him.

Borden, Lizzie (1860–1927), the subject of one of the most celebrated cases in American criminal history. Throughout her life Borden was active in church and temperance affairs in her hometown of Fall River, Massachusetts. There was much dissension within her family, and in 1892, at the age of thirty-two, she was charged with the ax murders of her father and stepmother. Although she was acquitted, the public ostracized her, and a chant, begun shortly after the murders, persisted: "Lizzie Borden took an ax / and gave her mother forty whacks / and when she saw what she had done / she gave her father forty-one." The case has inspired plays, books, a ballet, an opera, and a musical revue.

Border Ruffians, Missouri residents who in the 1850s entered the territory of KANSAS to ensure that it would become a slave state. At a time when antislavery forces were working to make Kansas a free state, the "border ruffians" voted fraudulently in Kansas elections and sought to intimidate the antislavery people through violence. Federal troops finally intervened to halt the lawlessness.

Border States, the slave states of DELAWARE, KENTUCKY, MARYLAND, and MISSOURI, which lay on the border between the North and South during the CIVIL WAR. These states had economic interests in the North, but slavery tied them to the South. Nevertheless, because of President Abraham Lincoln's prompt action in sending federal troops into these states, they remained with the Union at the outbreak of the war. When Virginia seceded from the Union, fifty Unionist counties in the western portion broke with the state and in 1863 joined the Union as WEST VIRGINIA, bringing the total of border states to five.

Borglum, Gutzon (1871–1941), sculptor. The MOUNT RUSHMORE NATIONAL MEMORIAL in South Dakota's Black Hills is Borglum's greatest achievement. The immense carvings of George Washington, Thomas Jefferson, Theodore Roosevelt, and Abraham Lincoln were begun in 1927. Utilizing dynamite and special drills, Borglum worked on the project until his death. It was completed by his son, Lincoln. In 1916 Borglum began work on a huge Confederate memorial to be carved into the face of Stone Mountain in Georgia. Financial disputes halted the project and it was not completed until 1970. Borglum sculpted many public monuments, including the head of Lincoln in the Capitol Rotunda in Washington, D.C.

Boston Massacre (March 5, 1770), a street incident between an angry crowd and a group of British soldiers. The Bostonians taunted the soldiers and threatened them with snowballs, stones, and clubs. Despite Capt. William Preston's efforts to prevent bloodshed, a shot was fired; the panicky soldiers then shot point-blank into the crowd, killing five. Preston and his men were

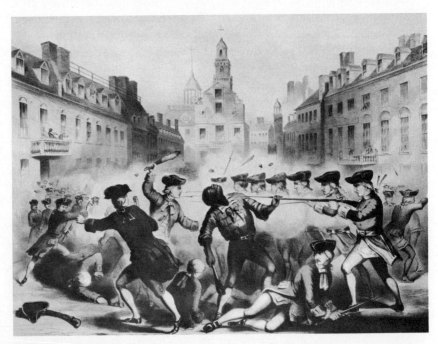

Boston Massacre
A print showing the American version of events during what came to be called the Boston Massacre.

acquitted of murder in a trial in which they were represented by Patriot lawyer John Adams, though two soldiers were convicted of lesser crimes. Revolutionary leaders used the incident to warn the colonies of the British threat to the colonists' liberties, and the massacre was viewed as the first battle of what became the AMERICAN REVOLUTION.

Boston News-letter, the first regularly published newspaper in the American colonies. Established in 1704 by John Campbell, the *News-letter* was the only newspaper in the colonies from 1704 to 1719. The first colonial newspaper to carry an illustration, it ceased publication in 1776.

Boston Police Strike (1919), a strike that took place in the Massachusetts capital because the police commissioner refused to recognize a policemen's union. Governor CALVIN COOLIDGE initially refused to intercede, but finally called out the state militia to maintain order in the city, declaring "There is no right to strike against the public safety by anybody, anywhere, anytime." Coolidge's breaking of the strike made him a national figure.

Boston Port Bill *See* INTOLERABLE ACTS.

Boston Tea Party (December 16, 1773), a midnight raid against British tea ships in Boston Harbor. A group of colonists, organized by Samuel Adams, disguised themselves as Mohawk Indians and raided ships belonging to Britain's East India Tea Company. They dumped the cargoes overboard to protest a British tax on tea imposed by Parliament in which they were not represented. The British then passed the INTOLERABLE ACTS to punish the colonists, especially the people of Boston. The Boston Tea Party was one of the events that led to the AMERICAN REVOLUTION.

Bounty-jumpers, men who collected a bounty for enlisting in the Union army but then deserted, during the CIVIL WAR. Under the Conscription Law (1863), men seeking to avoid compulsory military service could pay an individual a bounty of $300 to serve in their place. Some men enlisted and deserted as many as twenty or thirty times.

Bourbons, white southerners who gained control of their state governments at the end of RECONSTRUCTION in order to restore white supremacist rule. Their opponents called them Bourbons after the reactionary kings of France. Also called Redeemers, they were mostly conservative Democrats who aligned themselves with the industrial Republicans of the North to exploit the natural resources of the South for personal gain.

Bourke-White, Margaret (1904–71), photographer. Bourke-White created memorable photo-essays on World War II, the Korean War, Mahatma Gandhi and India's independence movement, and U.S. and Soviet factory workers. HENRY LUCE brought her to New York in 1929 to work as a photographer for his new *Fortune* magazine and later for *Life* magazine. Bourke-White collaborated with ERSKINE CALDWELL (later her husband) on *You Have Seen Their Faces* (1937), a book documenting the plight of southern blacks, and on *Say! Is This the U.S.A.?* (1941), a survey of life in America. The first official woman photojournalist during World War II, she recorded her experiences in *Dear Fatherland, Rest Quietly* (1946).

Bowie, Jim (1796?–1836), frontiersman. A hero of the Texas war for independence, Bowie fought and was killed, with a small force of defenders, at the ALAMO, a mission in San Antonio, Texas, besieged by a large force of Mexicans. He is credited with the invention of the bowie knife.

Boxer Rebellion (1900), antiforeign uprising in northern China. A secret society of Chinese rebels known as boxers formed a movement against the spread of Western influence in China. They attacked foreigners; killed Chinese Christians; and burned houses, schools, and churches. An international military force under the direction of the United States and all major European powers responded by crushing the uprising.

Boyd, Belle (1843–1900), Confederate spy during the CIVIL WAR. Boyd, using secret codes, supplied the Southern armies with information about the movement of Union troops. She was known for her romantic involvement with her informants. Captured and released three times, she wrote a book about her adventures, *Belle Boyd in Camp and Prison.*

Braddock, Edward (1695–1755), commander of British forces in America in 1754. General Braddock led British and colonial troops in an expedition against the French at Fort Duquesne during the FRENCH AND INDIAN WAR. Most of the troops, including Braddock, were killed in an ambush. Young GEORGE WASHINGTON, a member of this expedition, managed to organize the survivors and lead the retreat to safety.

Bradford, William (1590–1657), PILGRIM leader. After sailing to America on the *Mayflower* in 1620, Bradford was instrumental in writing the MAYFLOWER COMPACT. He helped select the site for the Plymouth colony and served as governor for over thirty years. He wrote a famous account, *Of Plymouth Plantation, 1620–47,* which is still in print.

Bradley, Bill (1943–), politician and basketball player. Bradley served in the U.S. Senate from New Jersey as a Democrat (1978–95). He gained recognition as an expert on energy conservation and an advocate for civil rights. A supporter of tax reform, he cosponsored the Bradley-Gephardt fair tax bill and ran an unsuccessful bid for the 2000 Democratic presidential nomination. A three-time All-American at Princeton, he studied two years at Oxford, England, as a Rhodes scholar and then signed with the New York Knickerbockers. Bradley played nine years, retired in 1977, and was elected to basketball's Hall of Fame in 1982. He has authored three nonfiction books, *Life on the Run* (1976), *Time Present, Time Past: A Memoir* (1995), and *Values of the Game* (1998).

Bradley, Omar (1893–1981), World War II general. As one of the most respected Allied commanders of WORLD WAR II, Bradley led U.S. forces in the North Africa, Sicily, and Normandy invasions. He commanded the

Twelfth Army Group, the largest fighting force ever gathered under one leader, from 1944 until the end of the war. Bradley was loved by those he commanded for his awareness of and concern for the ordinary soldier. From 1949 to 1953 he served as chairman of the Joint Chiefs of Staff, and in this capacity he supported President Harry S. Truman in relieving Douglas MacArthur as supreme Allied commander in Korea.

Bradley, Thomas (1917–98), politician. Elected the first black mayor of Los Angeles in 1973, Bradley has served five terms, more than any other mayor in the city's history. The son of a Texas sharecropper, Bradley graduated from the University of California, Los Angeles, and served on the Los Angeles police force from 1940 to 1962 before he entered politics. He was an unsuccessful Democratic candidate for the governorship of California in 1982 and 1986. Bradley received the NAACP's SPINGARN MEDAL in 1985 for his work in law and public service.

Bradshaw, Terry (1948–), football player. As quarterback for the Pittsburgh Steelers, Bradshaw achieved what no other pro football quarterback had done: he won four Super Bowls in six years. He shared *Sports Illustrated's* "Sportsman of the Year" title in 1979 with Willie Stargel. In 1984 he retired to become a television analyst for pro football games.

Bradstreet, Anne (1612?–72), Puritan poet. Born in England, Bradstreet traveled to America with her husband as part of JOHN WINTHROP's party, becoming one of the earliest settlers on Massachusetts Bay. She wrote the first book of poems published in America, *The Tenth Muse Lately Sprung Up in America,* in 1650.

Brady Handgun Violence Prevention Act (Brady Bill) (1993). The Brady Act created a five-day federal waiting period between filing the permit to purchase a gun and the actual purchase. This time gives officials the chance to investigate purchasers with possible criminal infractions. President Reagan initially opposed the bill, saying waiting periods should be imposed by states. President GEORGE H. W. BUSH held a similar position and presented an obstacle to its passage by linking it to his own crime bill. In late 1992, gun control became a key issue in the presidential campaign. In order to prompt a vote on the Brady Bill and to force the presidential candidates to take a position on it, Gun Control, Inc. mounted an effort to split the Brady Bill from the crime bill. Bill Clinton endorsed it and President Bush said nothing. When Clinton was elected president, the gun control movement had a supporter in the White House for the first time. The bill was passed by both houses of Congress in 1993 and signed by President BILL CLINTON in 1993, becoming law in 1994. In 1998 the waiting period was replaced by a mandatory, computerized national instant-check system that provides criminal background checks on all firearm purchasers, not just those buying handguns. The act was named for James Brady, the White House press secretary for President RONALD REAGAN, who was shot in the head and permanently disabled during an assassination attempt on Reagan in 1981. Brady and his wife, Sarah, were key supporters of the legislation.

Brady, Mathew B. (1823?–96), photographer. Brady earned recognition for his photographic record of the Civil War. Traveling with the Union army, he and his assistants covered the battlefields at Bull Run, Gettysburg, Antietam, Fredericksburg, and Petersburg, bringing home to viewers of the photographs the horrors of war. Brady also gained distinction for his portraits of famous persons, published in 1850 as *The Gallery of Illustrious Americans*. More than a third of the one hundred known photographs of Abraham Lincoln are credited to Brady.

Bragg, Braxton (1817–76), Confederate CIVIL WAR general. After serving with distinction in the Mexican War, Bragg took command of the Southern forces in Florida in 1861. His success at the BATTLE OF SHILOH earned him the command of the Army of Tennessee. In 1863 Bragg won at the BATTLE OF CHICKAMAUGA, but many did not think he used his advantage wisely. Two months later, he was defeated at MISSIONARY RIDGE. He resigned his command to serve as military adviser to Confederate President Jefferson Davis.

Brain Trust, close advisers of President FRANKLIN D. ROOSEVELT during the early days of his first term. The group, consisting mostly of college professors, suggested policies that influenced NEW DEAL legislation. They included Adolph A. Berle, HARRY L. HOPKINS, Raymond Moley, FELIX FRANKFURTER, and Rexford G. Tugwell.

Brandeis, Louis D. (1856–1941), lawyer and jurist. Brandeis graduated from Harvard Law School with the most brilliant record of any student in its history and became a successful attorney in Boston. In the late 1890s and 1900s he built a reputation as "the people's lawyer" by championing the public interest and refusing to take fees in such cases. Brandeis was an adviser to President Woodrow Wilson, who named him to the SUPREME COURT in 1916. Brandeis survived a bitter confirmation battle to become the first Jewish member of the Court. He served with distinction for twenty-three years, writing eloquent dissents with Justice Oliver Wendell Holmes, Jr., on issues such as freedom of speech and the right of privacy.

Brando, Marlon (1924–), actor. Brando received critical acclaim in 1947 with his stage interpretation of Stanley Kowalski in *A Streetcar Named Desire*, a role he re-created in the motion picture in 1951. He starred in *Viva Zapata* (1952), *The Wild One* (1953), and *Julius Caesar* (1953), among other films, and won the Academy Award for his performances in *On the Waterfront* (1954) and *The Godfather* (1972). He has also been active in social causes, such as improving conditions for American Indians.

Brandywine, Battle of (September 11, 1777), AMERICAN REVOLUTION conflict. The Americans, under Gen. George Washington, were defeated and forced to retreat by the British and HESSIANS, under Gen. Sir William

Howe, at Brandywine Creek, Pennsylvania. This victory enabled Howe to occupy Philadelphia with no opposition.

Brant, Chief Joseph (1742–1807), Mohawk Indian chief. Educated in Connecticut and a member of the Anglican church, Brant and his tribe fought on the side of the British in the American Revolution and were largely responsible for the CHERRY VALLEY MASSACRE in 1778. Britain awarded him a land grant in Canada following the war.

Bread Basket Colonies, a popular name for the Middle Colonies (Delaware, New Jersey, New York, and Pennsylvania). Due to a favorable climate, large farms grew wheat, corn, and other grains in abundance.

Breckinridge, John C. (1821–75), vice president of the United States (1857–61) under President James Buchanan, at thirty-five, the youngest ever to hold the post. Nominated by the southern Democrats for president in 1860, Breckinridge was defeated by Abraham Lincoln. Following his election to the U.S. Senate in 1861, he went over to the Confederacy, which caused his expulsion from Congress. As a general in the Confederate army, he fought at SHILOH, Vicksburg, Stones River, and CHICKAMAUGA. Jefferson Davis appointed him Confederate secretary of war in 1865.

Brennan, William, Jr. (1906–97), Supreme Court justice. Although Brennan was a Democrat, Republican president Dwight D. Eisenhower named him to the U.S. SUPREME COURT in 1956 because of his distinguished record. Considered a liberal, he defended civil liberties and the Bill of Rights, but often acted as a mediator between his conservative and liberal colleagues. Brennan's retirement in 1990 completed one of the longest periods of tenure on the Court, thirty-four years.

Brice, Fanny (Fannie Borach; 1891–1951), singer and comedienne. Brice achieved fame in the 1920s and 1930s as a performer on stage and in radio and motion pictures. Her most famous radio character was "Baby Snooks," a big-mouthed brat. *Funny Girl,* the Broadway musical and movie, portrayed her life.

Bridger, Jim (1804–81), mountain man. As a hunter, trapper, fur trader, and guide, Bridger scouted the western frontier for the U.S. government and discovered the Great Salt Lake in Utah. He helped map the OREGON TRAIL and, along with his partner, Louis Vasquez, established Fort Bridger in Wyoming. His fine geographical knowledge helped in the planning of overland stage routes.

Brinkley, David *See* CHET HUNTLEY AND DAVID BRINKLEY.

Brokaw, Tom (1940–), network news anchor. Brokaw joined NBC in 1966. From 1973 to 1976 he was NBC's White House correspondent and from 1976 to 1981 he hosted the morning program *Today.* In 1983 Brokaw became anchor and managing editor of *NBC Nightly News with Tom Brokaw.* He has covered every presidential election since 1968. In 1998 Brokaw wrote his first book, *The Greatest Generation,* an account of the generation of Americans born in the 1920s who came of age during the GREAT DEPRESSION, fought in WORLD WAR II, and went on to build postwar America. His next two books, *The Greatest Generation Speaks* (1999) and *An Album of Memories* (2001), continued the stories of that same generation. Brokaw announced that he planned to retire after the 2004 election.

Brooke, Edward (1919–), politician. As a liberal Republican who was elected Massachusetts state attorney general in 1962 and 1964, Brooke exposed widespread political corruption in the state government. In 1966 he became the first black to be elected to the U.S. Senate since Reconstruction and won reelection in 1972. He was defeated in 1978 by Paul Tsongas.

Brown, Dee (1908–), author. Brown wrote novels about the Wild West, including *They Went That-a-Way* (1960), *Creek Mary's Blood* (1980), and *Killdeer Mountain* (1983). His greatest success was his nonfiction work, *Bury My Heart at Wounded Knee* (1971), which describes the plight of the Plains Indians.

Brown, Jim (1936–), football player and actor. Signed by the Cleveland Browns in 1957, Brown led the National Football League in rushing eight times. He was elected to the professional football Hall of Fame in 1971. After retirement from football in 1966, he embarked on a career as a motion picture actor. He appeared in seventeen films, his best known being *The Dirty Dozen*. Brown also became an outspoken black activist.

Brown, John (1800–59), ABOLITIONIST. A man of burning religious faith, Brown joined the battle against slavery in BLEEDING KANSAS and achieved national notoriety with his participation in the POTTAWATOMIE MASSACRE. Aided by his followers, he led a raid on an arsenal at HARPERS FERRY, Virginia, in 1859. He planned to distribute the weapons to slaves to enable them to revolt against their masters. Captured by troops led by Col. Robert E. Lee in the course of the raid, Brown was put on trial, found guilty, and hanged. His execution made him a martyr to many Northerners, but Southerners and moderate Northerners looked upon him as a madman. Ralph Waldo Emerson's "John Brown's Body" was set to the tune of "The Battle Hymn of the Republic" and became a popular Union Civil War song.

Brown* v. *Board of Education of Topeka (1954), a decision by the U.S. SUPREME COURT of five cases challenging segregation laws requiring separate public schools for whites and blacks, a landmark of American constitutional history, and a symbol for the cause of civil rights. The case took its name from the lawsuit brought on behalf of Linda Brown, a pupil enrolled in the Topeka, Kansas, school system. Chief Justice EARL WARREN wrote for a unanimous Court that the doctrine of "separate but equal" first stated in *PLESSY* v. *FERGUSON* (1896) violated the equal protection clause of the Fourteenth Amendment (though the Court did not specifically overrule *Plessy*). THURGOOD MARSHALL led the legal team that won *Brown*.

Brubeck, Dave (1920–), jazz pianist and composer. Brubeck mixed jazz with his strong classical background and came up with the rich, new sound of progressive jazz. His quartet made concert tours throughout the world. Popular recordings include *Jazz Goes to College* and *Time Out*.

Bruce, Blanche K. (1841–98), black political leader during Reconstruction. Born a slave in Farmville, Virginia, Bruce left his master to found Missouri's first school for blacks. Following two years at Oberlin College, he moved to Mississippi and became a successful planter and educator. In 1874 he was elected to the U.S. Senate, where he worked for civil rights for minority groups. Bruce was the first black to serve a full term in the Senate, but the end of RECONSTRUCTION and the return of white supremacists to power prevented his reelection in 1882.

Bryan, William Jennings (1860–1925), politician. Called the "Boy Orator" for his skills as a public speaker, Bryan served in the U.S. House of Representatives from 1891 to 1895, where he advocated the free coinage of silver at a fixed rate with gold of 16:1. When he was nominated for president by the DEMOCRATIC and POPULIST parties in 1896, his Cross of Gold speech at the Chicago convention earned him national fame. He lost the election but was nominated again by the Democrats in 1900 and 1908 and was defeated each time. Bryan served as secretary of state from 1913 to 1915 under Woodrow Wilson, but resigned in protest over America's involvement in World War I. A Christian fundamentalist, Bryan was the prosecuting attorney at the SCOPES TRIAL in 1925. He died shortly after the trial ended.

Bryant, William Cullen (1794–1878), poet and editor, who wrote of the spiritual significance of nature. "Thanatopsis," a meditation on the meaning of death, is his best-known poem. In 1829 he became editor and part owner of the *New York Evening Post*. As a liberal newspaper editor and abolitionist, he broke with the Democratic party and became one of the founders of the Republican party in 1854.

Buchanan, James (1791–1868), fifteenth president of the United States (1857–61). Born near Mercersburg, Pennsylvania, Buchanan graduated from Dickinson College. He served in the U.S. House of Representatives (1820–31), as U.S. minister to Russia and England, in the U.S. Senate (1835–45), and as secretary of state for James K. Polk (1845–49). In 1854 he joined in writing the OSTEND MANIFESTO. In 1856 he received the Democratic presidential nomination, defeating Republican John C. Frémont and the candidate of the American party, former president MILLARD FILLMORE. As sectional tensions over slavery increased, he tried unsuccessfully to keep peace between the North and South. During Buchanan's term the Supreme Court handed down the *DRED SCOTT* DECISION, John Brown's raid occurred, and South Carolina seceded. He took no action (for which he was reviled at the time and afterward), only forestalling hostilities until

Abraham Lincoln was inaugurated. Buchanan was the only bachelor to hold the office of president.

Buck, Pearl S. (1892–1973), author. Born in West Virginia, Buck grew up with her missionary parents in China. The spirit and lives of the Chinese people inspired many of her novels and essays. *The Good Earth* (1931) won the Pulitzer Prize in 1932, and Buck received the Nobel Prize for literature in 1938. Her works promoted greater understanding between the peoples of the East and West.

Buckley, William F., Jr. (1925–), editor, author, and television personality. Buckley, a Roman Catholic and strong proponent of CONSERVATISM, founded the *National Review* in 1955, a weekly journal of conservative opinion, and produced a syndicated newspaper column, "On the Right." He hosted "Firing Line," a weekly television program featuring debates between himself and leading liberals, and wrote many books, including *Up from Liberalism* (1959), and a popular series of spy novels.

Budge, Don (1915–), tennis player. In 1938 Budge won the singles titles in the Australian, French, British, and U.S. championships. This was the first grand slam sweep in tennis.

Buell, Don Carlos (1818–98), Union CIVIL WAR leader. Given command of the Union Army of the Ohio, Buell assisted the Union victory at SHILOH. Though victorious at Perryville, he allowed Gen. BRAXTON BRAGG to retreat. Because of Buell's indecisiveness, President Abraham Lincoln relieved him from command, and he resigned from the army.

Buena Vista, Battle of (February 22–23, 1847), an American victory in northern Mexico during the MEXICAN WAR. Gen. ZACHARY TAYLOR, with devoted troops, defeated Santa Anna's larger army.

Bulfinch, Charles (1763–1844), architect and sculptor. Born in Boston to a wealthy family and graduated from Harvard, Bulfinch introduced the Federal style to the United States. He traveled throughout Europe where he studied classical designs and was advised by THOMAS JEFFERSON. Bulfinch was involved in planning much of old Boston, designing the old Massachusetts State House, New South Church, Massachusetts General Hospital, and many homes on Beacon Hill. From 1817 to 1830, Bulfinch succeeded BENJAMIN LATROBE and WILLIAM THORNTON as architect of the Capitol in Washington, D.C., where he constructed the central section, including the rotunda and the original dome.

Bulge, Battle of the (1944), the last German offensive of WORLD WAR II on the western front. The German forces under Gen. Karl von Rundstedt broke through the line of Allied troops in Belgium and penetrated more than forty miles before American troops, reinforced by Gen. GEORGE PATTON's Third Army, stopped them. The Allied counterattack wiped out the bulge (the forty-mile-wide and sixty-mile-deep German penetration), resulting in some 40,000 American and 220,000 German casualties. The remaining German forces retreated.

Bull Moose Party *See* PROGRESSIVE PARTY.

Bull Run (First battle; July 21, 1861), the first major engagement of the CIVIL WAR, known in the Confederacy as the Battle of Manassas. Confederate and Union troops met at Bull Run Creek (or Manassas Junction) about twenty-five miles southwest of Washington, D.C. Many Northerners, including congressmen, went to observe what they thought would be a glorious Union victory ending the Civil War almost before it began. The Northern army, led by Gen. Irvin McDowell, was routed by the Southerners, led by Gen. P.G.T. BEAUREGARD and Gen. THOMAS "STONEWALL" JACKSON. (It was Jackson's determined stand at this battle that earned him his nickname.) The Union troops and civilian observers beat a hasty retreat to Washington, D.C., and Confederate troops failed to pursue them.

Bull Run (Second battle; August 29–30, 1862). Near the first Bull Run fields in Virginia, Union troops, under Gen. John Pope, attacked Gen. THOMAS "STONEWALL" JACKSON and outnumbered Confederate troops, who were reinforced by ROBERT E. LEE and JAMES LONGSTREET. The Confederates made a brilliant charge, forcing the Union troops again to retreat, ensuring a victory for the South.

Bunche, Ralph (1904–71), scholar, diplomat, and civil rights advocate. For his mediation of an armistice between Jews and Arabs during the 1948–49 Arab-Israeli Wars, Bunche won the Nobel Peace Prize in 1950, the first black to do so. A brilliant student and scholar with a Ph.D. from Harvard, he taught at Howard University, engaged in important scholarly activities, worked with the State Department, and was a strong civil rights activist all his life. He served as under secretary general in the UNITED NATIONS from 1955 to 1971, directing peacekeeping missions in several regions. Bunche was given the NAACP's SPINGARN MEDAL and America's highest civilian award, the Medal of Freedom.

Bunker Hill, Battle of (June 17, 1775), an early but misnamed military engagement of the AMERICAN REVOLUTION, actually fought on Breed's Hill. British regulars under Gen. Sir William Howe attempted to dislodge from the hill about 1,200 colonial troops under Col. William Prescott. Three times the British charged the Patriots, suffering heavy losses, and twice they retreated; on the third attempt the Americans retired because of lack of ammunition. The British lost 1,054 men and the colonists 449 in this bloodiest battle of the Revolution. Seen as a moral victory for the Americans, it inspired them to fight on for independence. Prescott's order in this battle became famous: "Don't fire till you see the whites of their eyes!"

Buntline, Ned (1823–86), adventurer and author. Buntline, the pen name of Edward Zane Judson, wrote over four hundred dime novels about the Wild

West. Much of his material came from his colorful and adventurous life, which included Indian fights, a murder trial, a near-hanging by an angry mob, and a dishonorable discharge from the army during the Civil War. After meeting WILLIAM CODY, Buntline coined the name "Buffalo Bill" and wrote books on his life.

Burbank, Luther (1849–1926), horticulturist. During his career as an American plant breeder in California, Burbank taught himself the techniques of plant crossing and hybridization, resulting in the development of hundreds of new varieties of fruits, flowers, trees, and vegetables, among them the Shasta daisy and the Burbank potato.

Burger, Warren E. (1907–95), fifteenth chief justice of the United States (1969–86). Dwight D. Eisenhower appointed Burger to the U.S. Court of Appeals for the District of Columbia in 1955, where he served until 1969 when Richard Nixon appointed him chief justice. Burger believed in strict constructionism and took a moderately conservative position on the bench. He upheld the death penalty, urged some limits on the rights of defendants, and restricted access to legal abortions. Burger retired in 1986 and headed the commission to celebrate the two-hundredth anniversary of the Constitution in 1987.

Burgoyne, John (1722–92), British general in the AMERICAN REVOLUTION, known as "Gentleman Johnny." Burgoyne commanded the northern army with the goal of invading the colonies from Canada. Followed by a crowd of peddlers, wives, and children, his cumbersome army was defeated in the battle of Freeman's Farm. He captured FORT TICONDEROGA, but this was followed by severe losses of his HESSIANS at the BATTLE OF BENNINGTON. After battles at SARATOGA, New York, Burgoyne surrendered to Gen. HORATIO GATES on October 17, 1777. This event is considered to be the turning point of the American Revolution because it convinced France to become America's ally.

Burlingame Treaty (1868), an agreement between the United States and China that allowed unlimited voluntary Chinese immigration and permitted the Chinese to live and travel in the United States. In return, the United States promised not to intervene in Chinese domestic affairs. Thousands of Chinese came to the United States and worked as farmers in California and as laborers on the construction of the TRANSCONTINENTAL RAILROAD.

Burns, George (Nathan Birnbaum; 1896–1996), and **Gracie Allen** (1906?–64), comedy entertainers. One of the most successful husband-and-wife comedy teams on stage, radio, television, and films, Burns and Allen started in vaudeville in the 1920s. Their act featured a daffy, scatterbrained wife and her long-suffering but understanding husband. Their television program ran from 1950 to 1958. Following Allen's death, Burns became a solo entertainer, winning an Academy Award for his role in *The Sunshine Boys* (1975). He continued to appear in films and television in his nineties.

Burns, Ken (1953–), documentary filmmaker. Burns has produced several acclaimed historical and biographical documentaries for television and film. Known for his style of using narration, original prints, and photos, Burns selects projects that are uniquely American. His landmark Emmy-winning series *The Civil War* (1991) was the highest-rated series in the history of public television. Other award-winning titles include *The Brooklyn Bridge* (1981), *The Statue of Liberty* (1985), *Baseball* (1994), *The West* (1996), *Thomas Jefferson* (1997), and *Jazz* (2001).

Burnside, Ambrose (1824–81), Union commander during the CIVIL WAR. Burnside's Army of the Potomac was defeated at the BATTLE OF FREDER-ICKSBURG. Although victorious during the WILDERNESS CAMPAIGN under Gen. Ulysses S. Grant, he again met defeat at PETERSBURG and re-signed from the army in 1865 with an undistinguished record. Following the war Burnside served as governor of Rhode Island from 1866 to 1869 and in the U.S. Senate from 1875 until his death. Many men copied his side whiskers, called "burnsides" or "sideburns."

Burr, Aaron (1756–1836), vice president (1801–05), politician, and adventurer. A Continental Army officer during the American Revolution, Burr after the war became an attorney and politician in New York, where he helped organize the DEMOCRATIC-REPUBLICAN PARTY and became a senator. Burr was Thomas Jefferson's running mate in the presidential ELECTION OF 1800. Owing to a quirk in the electoral college system, Burr and Jefferson defeated the Federalist ticket but tied for the presidency. The House of Representatives cast thirty-five ballots before electing Jefferson president. Jefferson and his allies distrusted Burr thereafter, and disappointed Vice President Burr began to move toward an alliance with the Federalists. Burr's long-time adversary ALEXANDER HAMILTON begged Federalists not to support Burr against Jefferson in 1800 and helped defeat Burr in his 1804 bid to become governor of New York. Burr seized on a pretext to challenge Hamilton to a duel and on July 11, 1804, shot Hamilton dead. Burr fled south to escape indictments for murder. Dropped from the Republican ticket in 1804, he traveled to the Southwest. Rumors spread that he was planning to seize the western territories and Mexico to build an empire for himself. Jefferson in 1807 ordered Burr's arrest and trial for treason. Burr was acquitted in a trial presided over by Chief Justice John Marshall. (JONATHAN DAYTON was the actual author of the letter that was the principal evidence against him.)

Bush, George H. W. (1924–), forty-first president of the United States (1989–93). Born in Milton, Massachusetts, into a political family, Bush served as a pilot during World War II and was shot down in the Pacific; he won the Distinguished Flying Cross. Elected to the U.S. House of Representatives in 1966 and 1968 from Texas, Bush was twice defeated in attempts to win election to the U.S. Senate. He served as ambassador to the United

Nations under Richard M. Nixon and as Republican National Committee chairman, and was appointed by Gerald R. Ford to be U.S. liaison officer to China and director of the Central Intelligence Agency. Defeated by Ronald Reagan for the 1980 Republican presidential nomination, Bush served two terms as vice president under Reagan. Bush and his running mate, DAN QUAYLE, defeated their Democratic opponents, Michael Dukakis and Lloyd Bentsen, in the presidential ELECTION OF 1988. President Bush was noted for his interest in foreign and military affairs. He sent American forces to Panama in 1989 to oust the government of Gen. Manuel Noriega and in 1990–91 ordered American forces to Saudi Arabia to take part in an international effort to pressure Iraq into withdrawing from Kuwait, which Iraq had invaded in August. In January 1991 Bush persuaded Congress to authorize military action against Iraq; the PERSIAN GULF WAR resulted in a catastrophic defeat for Iraq, though the nation's leader, Saddam Hussein, remained in power. Despite his high reputation as an architect of foreign policy, Bush received harsh criticism for his supposed lack of interest in domestic policy and his perceived insensitivity to the plight of ordinary Americans during the recession of 1990–92, an accusation heightened after the Los Angeles riot in April 1992. In the 1992 presidential election, Bush and Quayle faced Democratic candidate Bill Clinton and his running mate Al Gore, following a campaign that focused on issues of the economy and experience; Bush lost by a wide margin of the electoral vote.

Bush, George W. (1946–), forty-third president of the United States (2001–). Born in New Haven, Connecticut, Bush is the eldest son of President GEORGE H. W. BUSH. He grew up in Midland and Houston, Texas, where his father was involved in the oil business. Following graduation from Phillips Andover Academy and Yale, he returned to Texas to fulfill his military service requirement with the Texas Air National Guard (1968–73). He earned an MBA degree from Harvard Business School and worked in the oil industry until 1986. At age forty, Bush reached a turning point in his life, swearing off alcohol and renewing his Christian faith. In 1994 he became governor of Texas, upsetting

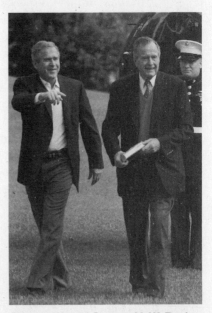

George W. and George H. W. Bush
President George W. Bush (left) and former President George H. W. Bush arriving from Camp David.

popular incumbent Ann Richards, and he became the first Texas governor to be elected to consecutive four-year terms. In the ELECTION OF 2000, with former Secretary of Defense RICHARD CHENEY as his running mate, Bush campaigned as a "compassionate conservative," winning one of the closest elections in American history. He lost the popular vote but defeated the Democratic ticket of Vice President AL GORE, JR. and Senator JOSEPH LIEBERMAN by only five electoral votes when Florida's electoral votes were awarded to him in a controversial Supreme Court decision. As president, Bush has faced numerous challenges, including terrorist attacks, recession, a WAR ON TERRORISM, and the AFGHANISTAN and IRAQ WARS. In the aftermath of the SEPTEMBER 11 TERRORIST ATTACKS in 2001, Bush implemented a series of measures to battle future acts of terror. These included the creation of a DEPARTMENT OF HOMELAND SECURITY, a Terrorism Information Awareness Program, and the U.S.A. PATRIOT ACT. While polls indicated strong public support for the Bush administration's counterterrorism initiatives, concerns were raised that many of the measures jeopardized civil liberties. After asserting that Iraqi dictator Saddam Hussein possessed forbidden "weapons of mass destruction," Bush authorized a full-scale invasion of Iraq in 2003, overthrowing the Hussein regime. Numerous allies and others protested the war because the United Nations did not authorize the attack. Bush came under further criticism when months of searching for Iraq's weapons of mass destruction produced no hard evidence. Allegations that the existence of these weapons was exaggerated to justify the war persisted. Bush is the second U.S. president to be the son of a president. JOHN QUINCY ADAMS was the first.

Butler, Benjamin F. (1818–93), Union CIVIL WAR general and politician. In 1862 Butler led the land forces supporting Adm. DAVID FARRAGUT's assault on New Orleans and became Louisiana's military governor. As commander he responded to civilian insults to occupying forces with controversial rules, including the infamous Woman Order no. 28, which stated that any disrespect shown by any female toward his men would be used as evidence of her being "a woman of the town plying her avocation," and she would be treated accordingly. This order provoked outrage and was the cause of his removal from New Orleans by Gen. Ulysses S. Grant. After the war Butler served in the U.S. House of Representatives as a Republican, where he helped enact Radical RECONSTRUCTION and managed the impeachment trial of President Andrew Johnson. Later as a Democrat, Butler served as governor of Massachusetts (1882–84) and in 1884 was the presidential candidate of the GREENBACK, or Anti-Monopoly, party.

Byrd, Richard (1888–1957), naval officer, aviator, and polar explorer. In 1926 Byrd made the first flight over the North Pole, for which he and copilot Floyd Bennett won the Congressional Medal of Honor. Byrd was also awarded the Distinguished Service Medal and was promoted to commander. He conducted expeditions to the Antarctic (1928–30) and made the first flight over the South Pole with Bernt Balchen on November 29, 1929, earning promotion to rear admiral.

Byrnes, James F. (1879–1972), politician. Active for nearly fifty years, Byrnes served in the U.S. House of Representatives as a Democrat from South Carolina (1911–25) and in the U.S. Senate (1931–41). He was appointed to the U.S. Supreme Court by Franklin D. Roosevelt in 1941 but resigned the following year to become director of the Office of Economic Stabilization and the Office of War Mobilization in 1944. Named secretary of state by Harry S. Truman in 1945, Byrnes opposed postwar Soviet expansion and participated in the decision to use the atom bomb. Byrnes resigned in 1947, denouncing the Fair Deal as socialistic; he returned to South Carolina where he was governor from 1951 to 1955, resisting efforts to integrate the state's schools and public facilities.

 Cabinet, the heads of the fourteen executive departments of the federal government (State, Treasury, Defense, Justice, Agriculture, Interior, Commerce, Labor, Health and Human Services, Housing and Urban Development, Transportation, Energy, Education, and Veterans). The name is derived from the British custom of referring to the prime minister and the heads of departments as the "cabinet." Although the term appears nowhere in the Constitution, President George Washington began the custom of regular consultation with his cabinet in 1789. Modern presidents seldom use the cabinet for the purposes that Washington had in mind. Cabinet members are nominated by the president and approved or rejected by the Senate. Once in office, members of the cabinet may be dismissed by the president without Senate consent.

Cable Act (September 22, 1922), stipulates that a foreign woman who marries a U.S. citizen does not automatically become a citizen, but must go through the process of naturalization. In addition, a woman who is an American citizen does not lose her citizenship if she marries a foreigner unless she chooses to renounce it.

Cage, John (1912–92), composer. Cage, the first major figure of modern experimental music, pioneered the use of silence in music. His innovative and controversial works incorporate unusual sounds from traditional instruments and specially "prepared" instruments, as well as sounds from the environment. His compositions include "Sonatas and Interludes" (1946–48), "Imaginary Landscapes, No. 4" (1951), "Water Music" (1952), and "Variations V" (1965).

Cagney, James (1899–1986), actor. Cagney appeared in more than sixty films, usually as a tough guy or gangster. One of the greatest stars of Hollywood's Golden Age, Cagney became an overnight sensation with his performance in *The Public Enemy* (1931). He received an Oscar for his portrayal of GEORGE M. COHAN in the 1942 musical *Yankee Doodle Dandy.*

Cairo Conference (1943), a meeting during WORLD WAR II in Cairo, Egypt, of Franklin D. Roosevelt of the United States, Winston Churchill of Great Britain, and Chiang Kai-shek of China. These Allied leaders agreed on military plans to defeat Japan and the terms of the Japanese surrender. Japan was to lose all islands and territories in the Pacific that it had seized since 1914, including Manchuria, Formosa, and Korea.

Calamity Jane (Martha Jane Burke; 1852–1903), frontierswoman. Known for dressing and acting like a man in her buckskin suits and wide-brimmed hats, Calamity Jane was an expert marksman, mule skinner, and railroad worker. She scouted for Gen. GEORGE ARMSTRONG CUSTER and was a companion of "WILD BILL" HICKOK. The origin of her nickname is uncertain; it may have derived from her skill with a gun or from her hard-luck experiences.

Calder, Alexander (1898–1976), sculptor and inventor of the mobile. Trained as an engineer before he turned to art, Calder made use of steel wires and connecting rods to create fanciful and elegant metal sculptures in motion. His innovative mobiles gained him recognition at exhibitions throughout the world. Calder's other works include stabiles (which, though stationary, change as the spectator moves around them), paintings, jewelry, toys, stage sets, and illustrations for children's books.

Caldwell, Erskine (1903–87), author, known for his realistic fiction and nonfiction about social injustice in the southern United States. Caldwell's best-selling works include *Tobacco Road* (1932), which in 1933 was adapted into a play that ran for over seven years on Broadway, and *God's Little Acre* (1933). He collaborated with photographer MARGARET BOURKE-WHITE, later his wife, on *You Have Seen Their Faces* (1937), a documentary about the plight of southern blacks.

Calhoun, John C. (1782–1850), politician and public official. Beginning his career as a member of the House of Representatives from South Carolina (1811–17), Calhoun was a leader of the WAR HAWKS, who advocated war with Great Britain. He was secretary of war under James Monroe and secretary of state under John Tyler, but he was best known for his service in the Senate. Elected in 1824 as John Quincy Adams's vice president, he was re-elected with Andrew Jackson in 1828. In 1832 he wrote the South Carolina Exposition and Protest, calling the TARIFF OF ABOMINATIONS unconstitutional and justifying the state's claimed power of nullification. Perhaps the most eminent and profound theorist of STATES' RIGHTS, Calhoun resigned from the vice presidency in 1832 (the first to resign the office) to accept re-election to the Senate from his home state. He served there until his death.

California (Golden State) became, on September 9, 1850, the thirty-first state in the Union. (See maps, pages 540 and 541.) Although Spanish explorer

Juan Cabrillo is credited with first exploring the area in 1542, Spanish settlement did not flourish until Franciscan friar JUNÍPERO SERRA established the first mission at San Diego in 1769. The twenty-one missions of the California mission chain became centers for farming and ranching, drawing large Indian populations. In 1822 California became a province of Mexico. The first group of U.S. settlers arrived via wagon train from Missouri in 1841, and in 1846, as a result of the BEAR FLAG REVOLT, California was ceded to the United States. It joined the Union as part of the COMPROMISE OF 1850. Thousands of people joined the GOLD RUSH to the state following the discovery of gold in 1848 at John Sutter's sawmill in Coloma.

For a century after that, between 1860 and 1960, California's population nearly doubled on the average of once every twenty years, and by 1970 it had become the nation's most populous state. California, though predominantly white, has, among the fifty states, the largest populations of American Indians, Chinese, Filipinos, Hispanics, Japanese, Koreans, and Vietnamese, and the second largest populations of blacks and Asian Indians. Major cities include Los Angeles, San Diego, San Jose, San Francisco, and Sacramento, the capital.

Its scenic wonders include Sequoia and Yosemite National Parks, Death Valley (282 feet below sea level), Mount Whitney (the highest point in the United States), and Lake Tahoe, one of the deepest lakes in the United States. The San Andreas fault, a break in the earth that runs near the California coast, causes earthquakes. The 1906 earthquake wreaked enormous damage in San Francisco, and in 1989 another caused heavy damage in the San Francisco Bay Area. California leads the nation in electronics, aerospace, and agriculture, especially fruits and vegetables. Tourism has become a leading industry with Hollywood, Disneyland, the San Diego Zoo, Carmel, and Monterey as some of the attractions. Noted Californians have included RICHARD M. NIXON, JOHN MUIR, JACK LONDON, EARL WARREN, and TED WILLIAMS.

Calloway, Cab (1907–94), jazz musician. Calloway became a nationally known performer when his band succeeded DUKE ELLINGTON's orchestra at Harlem's Cotton Club in 1931. Known for his unique style and flamboyant presentations, he used scat, substituting syllables like "hi-de-ho" for actual words. "Minnie the Moocher" became Calloway's trademark song. Calloway also appeared in several films including *Stormy Weather* (1943) and *Porgy and Bess* (1959). He compiled the *Hepster's Dictionary* (1938), the so-called jive language reference for audiences and musicians.

Cameron, Simon (1799–1889), politician. A U.S. senator from Pennsylvania for eighteen years (1845–49, 1857–61, 1867–77), Cameron established and controlled the Republican party machine there. In 1860, as Pennsylvania's favorite son candidate for the presidential nomination at the Republican National Convention in Chicago, he threw his support to ABRAHAM

LINCOLN. Appointed secretary of war, Cameron embarrassed Lincoln by his corrupt methods of negotiating army contracts. Removed from his post by Lincoln in 1862, Cameron was censured by the House of Representatives. Lincoln then appointed him minister to Russia, but he resigned the same year, later returning to the Senate.

Camp, Walter (1859–1925), football authority. As Yale University's athletic director and football coach, Camp selected the first annual All-American football team in 1889 from outstanding college players throughout the nation. He worked on the Intercollegiate Football Rules Committee, helping to change the game into modern U.S. football. Camp wrote numerous books on sports, especially football, and in 1917 moved to Washington, D.C., to organize classes in physical fitness for senior government officials.

Campanella, Roy (1921–93), baseball player. A great catcher for the Brooklyn Dodgers of the 1940s and 1950s, Campanella in 1969 became the second black baseball player to be selected for the Hall of Fame. Named the National League's most valuable player three times, he set records for a major league catcher in 1953 by hitting 41 home runs and 142 runs batted in. His career came to a tragic end in January 1958 when an automobile accident left him a quadriplegic.

Camp David Accords, an agreement resulting from discussions between President Anwar el-Sadat of Egypt and Prime Minister Menachem Begin of Israel in 1978. The talks, initiated and hosted by President JIMMY CARTER at Camp David, the presidential retreat in Maryland, ended with Israel agreeing to withdraw from the Sinai and granting autonomy to the Gaza Strip and the West Bank. Egypt and Israel also agreed to a peace treaty, which was signed on March 26, 1979. Begin and Sadat received the Nobel Peace Prize for these negotiations.

Cannon, Joseph (1836–1926), Speaker of the House (1903–11). Known as "Uncle Joe," Cannon exercised dictatorial powers in his role as SPEAKER. The political "revolution of 1910," led by GEORGE NORRIS and "CHAMP" CLARK, stripped the Speaker of the right to be on the powerful Rules Committee and the right to appoint other committees of the House. After the revolt, Cannon was defeated for reelection in 1912. He returned in 1914 to serve as a member of the U.S. House of Representatives, ending with a career total of forty-six years.

Cantor, Eddie (Edward Iskowitz; 1892–1964), entertainer. A star of vaudeville, motion pictures, radio, and television, Cantor charmed audiences with his singing and energetic comedy routines. He received a special Academy Award for distinguished service to the motion picture industry in 1956 and supported many charities and causes.

Capital of the United States, the city where the seat of government of the American nation is located. (The Capitol is the building that houses the Congress.) During and after the American Revolution, the Continental

Congress made its home in Philadelphia, Baltimore, Lancaster, Princeton, York, Annapolis, and Trenton. From 1784 through 1790 New York City was the seat of government. The Framers of the Constitution included a clause granting the capital of the nation a permanent home in a district ten miles square, to be called the District of Columbia. Disputes over its location divided the nation in 1789–90, as cities competed for this rich prize. The COMPROMISE OF 1790 ended the dispute by moving the seat of government to Philadelphia for ten years and then to a permanent site on the banks of the Potomac River. The city was renamed Washington in 1800, following the death of George Washington, who chose the site in 1792.

Capone, Al (Alphonse; 1899–1947), gangster. During PROHIBITION, Capone became a gang boss and, posing as a used furniture dealer, terrorized the competition to corner the market on bootleg whiskey. He controlled gambling, prostitution, and dance halls in Chicago. Gang warfare reached its peak in 1929 with Capone's "St. Valentine's Day Massacre" of a rival gang. In 1931 Capone was indicted for income tax evasion and was convicted, fined, and sent to Alcatraz prison. He was released in 1939.

Capote, Truman (Truman Persons; 1924–84), author. Capote wrote stage, television, and screen plays, documentaries, novels, and short stories, many of which center on the struggles of lonely people in the South. His best-known works include *Other Voices, Other Rooms* (1948), *The Grass Harp* (1951), and *Breakfast at Tiffany's* (1958). His semifictional novel, *In Cold Blood* (1966), about a grisly murder, developed a new genre in which the writer reports an actual event, drawing freely on fictional techniques and figuring prominently in the narrative.

Capper-Volstead Act (February 18, 1922), an act that exempted agricultural cooperatives from federal antitrust laws. It authorized farmer associations to form voluntary cooperatives for the producing, handling, and marketing of agricultural products. It was also known as the Cooperative Marketing Act.

Capra, Frank (1897–1991), motion picture director. During the 1930s Capra won Academy Awards for directing *It Happened One Night* (1934), *Mr. Deeds Goes to Town* (1936), and *You Can't Take It with You* (1938). His production and direction of the highly acclaimed film series *Why We Fight* during World War II earned a Distinguished Service Medal. In the 1940s his best movies were *Arsenic and Old Lace* and *It's a Wonderful Life*. Capra also made a notable series of educational films on science for television during the 1950s.

Caraway, Hattie (1878–1950), the first woman to be elected to the U.S. SENATE. Appointed by the governor of Arkansas in 1931 to fill her deceased husband's unexpired term, Caraway, a Democrat, was later elected and served to 1945. She was the first woman to chair a Senate committee and in 1943 the first woman to preside over a Senate session.

Cardozo, Benjamin Nathan (1870–1938), jurist. The shy, reclusive Cardozo was one of the greatest members of New York State's highest court, the Court of Appeals. Cardozo wrote many opinions that reformed doctrines of tort and contract law. He also wrote classic works of jurisprudence arguing that judges and lawmakers should be more responsive to social and technological change. In 1932 President Herbert Hoover named Cardozo to the U.S. SUPREME COURT. Cardozo became a leading member of the liberal bloc of justices, endorsing creative uses of government power to solve social problems so long as they remained within constitutional limits.

Carlton, Steve (1944–), baseball player. Carlton became the first and only left-handed pitcher to win four Cy Young Awards and to surpass three thousand strikeouts in a career. Winning over three hundred games while playing mostly for the St. Louis Cardinals and Philadelphia Phillies, he amassed over four thousand strikeouts, placing him second on the all-time major league list.

Carmichael, Hoagy (1899–1981), songwriter and musician. Although educated as a lawyer, Carmichael was a self-taught musician and composer. After his friend BIX BEIDERBECKE recorded his song, "Riverboat Shuffle," Carmichael went on to compose some of America's most popular songs, including "Stardust" and "Georgia on My Mind." While working in Hollywood he became a character actor, appearing in more than twenty films. In 1951 he won an Oscar for his song "In the Cool, Cool, Cool of the Evening."

Carmichael, Stokely (1941–98), black political activist. A field organizer for the STUDENT NONVIOLENT COORDINATING COMMITTEE in Mississippi, Carmichael became its head in 1966 and gained national attention with his promotion of the concept of BLACK POWER. He called for a racial revolution in the United States, urging blacks to seek control of their own lives and to reject white values. He aligned himself with the Black Panther party, but later resigned because of agreements it made with whites. He remained a strong black nationalist. Moving to Guinea in 1969, he changed his name to Kwame Touré and worked for the Pan-African movement.

Carnegie, Andrew (1835–1919), philanthropist and industrialist. Carnegie, a poor immigrant from Scotland, became one of the richest men in the world. In 1899 he established the Carnegie Steel Corporation by buying and consolidating many smaller steel mills. A strike at his HOMESTEAD, Pennsylvania, plant in 1892 turned into one of the bloodiest labor disputes in American history when he brought in Pinkerton guards, strikebreakers, and state militiamen to confront the workers. In 1901 his firm became one of the largest steel companies in the world when it joined with the U.S. Steel Corporation. Carnegie wrote "The Gospel of Wealth" (1889) and his *Autobiography* (1920), and used his enormous wealth to benefit humanity, establishing over 2,500 libraries in the United States and contributing generously to public education. He established the Carnegie Endowment for World Peace in 1910.

Caroline Affair (1837), a dispute between the United States and Great Britain during an uprising in Canada. The *Caroline,* an American ship engaged in carrying supplies to the Canadian rebels, was destroyed in American waters by Canadian troops. Great Britain ignored the protests of President Martin Van Buren, causing strain between the two countries. An apology later came from England as part of the WEBSTER-ASHBURTON TREATY of 1842.

Carothers, Wallace (1896–1937), chemist. Carothers left a teaching career at Harvard for research at the DuPont Company. In 1931 he developed neoprene, the first synthetic rubber. In 1938 he developed nylon, never realizing how it would revolutionize industry and consumer goods. Suffering from depression and failing health, Carothers committed suicide at age forty-one.

Carpetbaggers, northern businessmen, teachers, FREEDMEN'S BUREAU agents, and politicians who came into the South during RECONSTRUCTION following the Civil War to invest in businesses and land in the devastated region or to work with the emancipated slaves. Because former Confederate officeholders and soldiers could not vote or hold office, carpetbaggers joined with SCALAWAGS (native southern Unionists) to benefit politically from the new governments. They were much resented at the time by the defeated southerners for their working to establish social and political justice among the freed slaves, as well as for the corruption that followed in the wake of some of their efforts, particularly in railroad building. But recent researchers have looked upon their work with blacks as praiseworthy and have shown that they did much to help rebuild the South's economy and put needed reforms, such as public school systems, into place before their dominance ended in 1877. Their name is derived from the suitcases made of carpeting in which they carried their belongings.

Carrier, Willis (1876–1950), engineer and inventor. Considered the father of modern air conditioning, Carrier designed the first machine to control humidity in 1902, only one year after he graduated from Cornell University. In 1915 he and six friends formed the Carrier Engineering Corporation, where he pioneered the design and safe manufacture of refrigeration machines to cool large spaces. Carrier's company continues to be a world leader in cooling systems.

Carroll, Charles (1737–1832), Patriot and public official. At the request of the Continental Congress in 1776, Carroll accompanied a delegation to Canada that included Samuel Chase, JOHN CARROLL, and BENJAMIN FRANKLIN. Their mission was to obtain aid for the American colonists during the Revolution, but the attempt failed. Carroll later represented Maryland in the U.S. Senate. His death marked the passing of the last surviving signer of the Declaration of Independence. JOHN CARROLL and DANIEL CARROLL were his cousins.

Carroll, Daniel (1730–96), statesman. Carroll signed both the Articles of Confederation and the U.S. Constitution. In 1789 he represented Maryland as a member of the first U.S. House of Representatives and later served as commissioner of the District of Columbia. He was the brother of JOHN CARROLL and cousin of CHARLES CARROLL.

Carroll, John (1735–1815), first Roman Catholic bishop of the United States. Carroll founded Georgetown University in 1791 and planned and built the first major Catholic cathedral in the United States, located in Baltimore. Carroll became an archbishop in 1808.

Carson, Johnny (1925–), television entertainer. Carson, as host of "The Tonight Show" from 1962 to 1992, became the most successful nighttime personality in the history of television. Carson's sharp, clever monologues and his easy style of interviewing guests earned him high ratings and a consistent following that made him one of America's best-paid television entertainers. He was also noted for his acerbic political comments in his monologues.

Carson, Kit (Christopher; 1809–68), guide, frontiersman, and Indian agent. Carson acted as a guide for John C. Frémont on three western expeditions and during the Mexican War served with Gen. Stephen Kearny and Frémont in California. He became an Indian agent in 1854 and after visiting Washington, D.C., discovered he was a national hero because of his exploits. Appointed a colonel during the Civil War, Carson was assigned to New Mexico, where he battled Indians who had resisted incursions by white settlers for many years.

Carson, Rachel (1907–64), marine biologist and author. Carson wrote about the relation of all living things to nature in a way notable for its scientific soundness and the beauty of its language. Her 1951 best-seller, *The Sea around Us*, describes the characteristics and history of the sea. The publication of her final book in 1962, *Silent Spring*, caused widespread alarm

---

★ **Rachel Carson**
An excerpt from *Silent Spring*

The "control of nature" is a phrase conceived in arrogance, born of the Neanderthal age of biology and philosophy, when it was supposed that nature exists for the convenience of man. The concepts and practices of applied entomology for the most part date from that Stone Age of science. It is our alarming misfortune that so primitive a science has armed itself with the most modern and terrible weapons, and that in turning them against the insects it has also turned them against the earth.

with its claims that the use of chemicals was permanently harming the ecological balance in the world. The book aroused public concern about the use of pesticides, prompting government studies and helping inaugurate the modern environmental movement.

Carter, Jimmy (James Earl; 1924–), thirty-ninth president of the United States (1977–81). Born in Plains, Georgia, Carter graduated from the U.S. Naval Academy in 1946 and worked on the naval nuclear reactor project until 1953. In 1970 he was elected governor of Georgia and in 1974 launched his campaign for the 1976 Democratic presidential nomination. Carter slowly built a national identity through grass-roots campaigning, establishing himself as a spokesman for the common people. The Democratic party nominated him on the first ballot in 1976; he narrowly defeated the incumbent Republican president GERALD FORD. Notable achievements during his one term as president include the stressing of human rights, the establishment of a national energy policy, a new Panama Canal treaty, and the CAMP DAVID ACCORDS establishing peace between Egypt and Israel. He ordered an attempt to rescue U.S. hostages in Iran in 1980, which was unsuccessful; the ongoing hostage crisis was a contributing factor in his defeat for reelection in 1980. The Republican nominee, RONALD REAGAN, won the presidential election in a landslide and escalated the military buildup begun by Carter. In the years following his presidency, Carter enjoyed high acclaim for his humanitarian and peacemaking efforts. He has been involved in a variety of human rights and charitable causes through his Habitat for Humanity and the Carter Center, and in 2002 he won the Nobel Peace Prize for his human rights and mediation work.

Cartier, Jacques (1491–1557), French explorer of North America. In 1535 Cartier discovered the St. Lawrence River and explored it as far as present-day Montreal, Quebec. He made three voyages searching for the Northwest Passage and staked claims to the St. Lawrence region for France.

Cartwright, Alexander (1820–92), sportsman. Cartwright rather than ABNER DOUBLEDAY is now given credit for inventing the game of baseball. Doubleday had been thought to have invented the game in 1839 as a schoolboy in Cooperstown, New York, but lack of documentation led to doubts about the story; sports historians have confirmed that Doubleday was twenty years old and at West Point in 1839. In 1845 Cartwright started the first baseball team, the Knickerbocker Base Ball Club of New York, and wrote a set of rules first used in a game between the Knickerbockers and the New York Nine at Hoboken on June 19, 1846. These rules, amended in 1848 and 1854, formed the basis of today's game.

Carver, George Washington (1864–1943), black botanist and teacher at Tuskegee Institute in Alabama. To help southern farmers, Carver urged them to cultivate crops other than cotton. His experiments resulted in many new uses for soybeans, sweet potatoes, and especially peanuts. Carver also developed improved methods of farming with crop diversification and artificial fertilization. In 1940 he established the Carver Foundation for continuing research in agriculture.

Carver, John (1576–1621), the first governor of Plymouth Colony in present-day Massachusetts. Carver, a wealthy merchant, helped the Pilgrims acquire their charter and arrange their expedition to the New World. In London, with the aid of other merchants, he chartered the *Mayflower* and sailed from England in 1620. He helped select the site for the landing at Plymouth and was elected governor under the

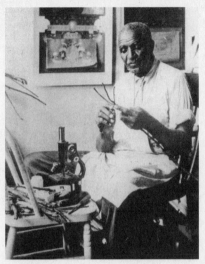

George Washington Carver
Carver working at his microscope.

MAYFLOWER COMPACT on November 21, 1620. He made a peace treaty with the Indian chief Massasoit, which stayed in effect for many years.

Cary, Mary Shadd (1823–93), black teacher and journalist. Born free in Delaware, Cary attended school in Pennsylvania because Delaware refused to educate blacks. After teaching in and establishing schools for blacks in Delaware, New York, and Pennsylvania, Cary started a school in Windsor, Ontario, for the large community of blacks who had escaped to Canada prior to the Civil War. The first black woman to edit a newspaper in North America, she founded the *Provincial Freeman* in 1853, a newspaper for the fugitive slaves. Cary campaigned for woman suffrage and at age sixty received a law degree from Howard University.

Casablanca Conference (January 1943), a meeting during WORLD WAR II in Morocco between President Franklin D. Roosevelt of the United States and Prime Minister Winston Churchill of Great Britain. The men planned the Allied military strategy following the North African campaign and decided to demand unconditional surrender from the Axis powers.

Cash, Johnny (1932–2003), singer, songwriter, musician. Cash's booming baritone voice and acoustic guitar led him to be an icon of American country music in a career spanning more than four decades with songs such as "I Walk the Line" (1956) and "Ring of Fire" (1963). Cash recorded more than 1,500 songs, and his success crossed well over onto the pop scene with 48 singles on Billboard's pop charts, rivaling both the Rolling Stones and the Beach Boys. Called "The Man in Black," he became famous for his image as an outlaw figure and identified with the downtrodden, often performing free concerts for prisoners. Cash won eleven Grammys and is the only artist to be elected to the Rock and Roll Hall of Fame, the Songwriters' Hall of Fame, and the Country Western Hall of Fame.

Cass, Lewis (1782–1866), politician. Cass represented Michigan in the U.S. Senate (1845–57), where he avidly supported the concept of America's MANIFEST DESTINY and proposed the doctrine of POPULAR SOVEREIGNTY (the people deciding whether a territory should be free or slave). In 1848 Cass won the DEMOCRATIC nomination for president but lost to the WHIG candidate, Gen. Zachary Taylor. He served as governor of Michigan Territory from 1813 to 1831, as secretary of war under President Andrew Jackson, and as secretary of state under President James Buchanan.

Cassatt, Mary (1844–1926), painter. As one of the foremost painters of the nineteenth century, Cassatt lived in France for many years, where she exhibited her paintings with the French impressionists, the only American to be so distinguished. Influenced by Degas (her teacher and friend) and Manet, Cassatt's impressionist paintings feature women as the main subject. Her best-known works portray the theme of mother and child in everyday activities.

Cather, Willa (1873–1947), novelist. The hardships and spirit of the pioneers settling the West provided the inspiration and themes for many of Cather's short stories and novels. She taught school, wrote short stories, and edited *McClure's Magazine,* all the time developing the graceful style she is noted for. Her best-known works include *O Pioneers!* (1913), *Death Comes for the Archbishop* (1927), and *My Ántonia* (1918). She won a Pulitzer Prize for her novel *One of Ours* (1922). Many of her books are heralded today as classics.

Catlin, George (1796–1872), painter and author known for his studies of American Indians. His fascination with Indians resulted in his living among several tribes, making sketches, engravings, and paintings, and taking notes on their lives. His illustrated books aroused interest in Indian culture among easterners and created a reliable record that is still useful.

Catt, Carrie Chapman (1859–1947), reformer and peace advocate. Elected to succeed SUSAN B. ANTHONY as president of the NATIONAL AMERICAN WOMAN SUFFRAGE ASSOCIATION in 1900, Catt served until 1904 and again from 1915 to 1920. In 1915 she directed the final massive drive for a constitutional amendment allowing women to vote and lobbied successfully for the ratification of the Nineteenth Amendment in 1920. She founded the League of Women Voters and helped establish the Women's Peace party during World War I.

Catton, Bruce (1899–1978), historian of the Civil War. Catton's three-volume history of the Army of the Potomac — *Mr. Lincoln's Army, Glory Road,* and *A Stillness at Appomattox* (1951–53) — won both the National Book Award and the Pulitzer Prize in 1954. He combined an excellent writing style with careful research in diaries, letters, and other documents of the time. His works include *This Hallowed Ground* (1956), *The Coming Fury,*

Terrible Swift Sword, and *Never Call Retreat.* (The last three, published from 1961 to 1965, are a second trilogy.) Catton served as editor of *American Heritage* magazine from 1954 to 1959.

Central Intelligence Agency (CIA) (1947), an agency responsible for obtaining political, military, and economic information from around the world. Congress created the CIA at the request of President Harry S. Truman to centralize the gathering of information deemed relevant to national security. The activities of the CIA are secret but are supervised by the NATIONAL SECURITY COUNCIL, and its director is responsible to the president. The CIA has access to advanced technology for its collection of intelligence, enabling it to monitor clandestine operations. Many of its activities have aroused much controversy: its role in domestic surveillance of U.S. citizens, in supporting rebel movements against governments of other countries, and in conducting various secret operations in Vietnam, the Mideast, and Latin America. Its critics charge that its methods and goals have been inconsistent with American democratic principles; its defenders counter that these methods are necessary to carry out its mission.

***Challenger* Disaster,** an accident that occurred on January 28, 1986, moments after lift-off at Cape Canaveral, Florida. The space shuttle *Challenger* exploded, killing all aboard, including a New Hampshire schoolteacher, Christa McAuliffe, the first private citizen chosen for a space flight. The other crew members were Comm. Francis "Dick" Scobee, Comm. Michael J. Smith, Dr. Judith A. Resnik, Dr. Ronald E. McNair, Lt. Col. Ellison S. Onizuka, and Gregory B. Jarvis. An investigation identified the failure of a seal on a solid-fuel booster rocket as the cause of the explosion, and a report was issued criticizing NASA for a long history of managerial and engineering mistakes. This tragedy slowed the work of the United States in the field of space exploration.

Chamberlain, Joshua Lawrence (1828–1914), military leader and educator. Educated at Bowdoin and later Bangor Theological Seminary, Chamberlain taught modern languages at Bowdoin and knew little of soldiering when he joined the Maine Volunteer Infantry. However, he saw much of the CIVIL WAR, including twenty-four battles and numerous skirmishes. He was wounded several times and had several horses shot out from under him. He led his regiment in defense of Little Round Top at GETTYSBURG and was honored with a CONGRESSIONAL MEDAL OF HONOR. Chamberlain was chosen by General ULYSSES S. GRANT to receive the formal surrender of Confederate forces at APPOMATTOX COURT HOUSE in 1865. Returning as a war hero, Chamberlain was elected to four terms as governor of Maine (1866–70). He then returned to Bowdoin where he taught and served as president (1870–83).

Chamberlain, Wilt (1936–99), basketball player. Chamberlain holds records as one of the leading scorers and rebounders in the National Basketball

Association's history. The NBA's most valuable player four times, in 1961–62 he scored over 4,000 points, averaging 50.4 points a game. On March 2, 1962, he scored 100 points in a single game. Chamberlain, who stood seven feet one inch, played for the Philadelphia/San Francisco Warriors, the Philadelphia 76ers, and the Los Angeles Lakers. He was much admired for his status as a superior black athlete.

Chambers, Whittaker *See* HISS CASE.

Champlain, Samuel de (1567–1635), French explorer. Called the "Father of New France," Champlain explored the St. Lawrence River Valley region in 1603, establishing Quebec as the first permanent settlement in New France in 1608. The first European to reach Lake Champlain, which he named for himself, he served as governor of the Quebec colony from 1633 to 1635.

Chancellorsville, Battle of (May 2–4, 1863), a major military engagement between the Union forces led by Gen. JOSEPH HOOKER and the Confederate forces led by Gen. ROBERT E. LEE during the CIVIL WAR. Fought near Chancellorsville, Virginia, the battle resulted in a remarkable defeat of the Northern army at the hands of outnumbered Southern troops. Confederate Gen. Thomas "STONEWALL" JACKSON, Lee's close military adviser, was accidentally shot by his own troops following the battle and died shortly after.

Chandler, Raymond (1888–1959), writer whose detective novels set a new literary standard for mystery fiction. Chandler's first book, *The Big Sleep* (1939), became a classic in the genre. Philip Marlowe, a tough, complex, and intriguing detective, appears in many of his stories, which are set in Los Angeles and convey a dark undercurrent of corruption. Several of his most popular mysteries, including *Farewell My Lovely* (1940), *The Lady in the Lake* (1943), and *The Long Goodbye* (1953), were made into motion pictures.

Chaney, Lon (1883–1930), actor. Chaney, the son of deaf-mute parents, starred in silent films including *The Miracle Man* (1919), *The Hunchback of Notre Dame* (1923), and *The Phantom of the Opera* (1925). He became known as the "man of a thousand faces" for his mastery of the art of elaborate movie makeup and played a wide variety of villainous roles in more than 150 films. His son, Lon Chaney, Jr., carried on the tradition; his most famous role was the Wolf Man.

Chaplin, Charles (1889–1977), film actor. Following his discovery by Mack Sennett in 1912, Chaplin, who was born in London and had an impoverished childhood, gained stardom and wealth as an actor, director, and producer during the era of silent comedies. He displayed his comic genius and versatility in such classic films as *The Tramp* (1915), *Easy Street* (1917), *The Gold Rush* (1925), and *City Lights* (1931). He formed United Artists Studios in 1918 with D. W. Griffith, Mary Pickford, and Douglas Fairbanks. He was highly criticized in the United States in the 1940s and early 1950s for his left-wing political beliefs, and while he was abroad he was banned from reentering the country. His film work after the advent of the talkies never lived up to his earlier performances, and he appeared in his last film, *Limelight*, in 1953. Chaplin was finally readmitted to the United States in 1972 to receive an honorary Academy Award for his unique contributions to cinematic art.

Chapman, John (1774–1845), pioneer planter of the frontier and basis for the legendary character of Johnny Appleseed. Chapman encouraged the establishment of orchards by planting apple saplings throughout the Midwest and distributing apple seeds to settlers moving west. He collected seeds from cider presses in Pennsylvania and exchanged them for food and clothing during his travels.

Charles, Ray (1932–2004), singer. Blinded at age six and an orphan, Charles formed a rhythm and blues trio in the 1940s and achieved success with his recording of *I Got a Woman* in 1956. An accomplished pianist, Charles skillfully mixes the sounds of country, gospel, blues, and soul music. Other hit songs have included "Georgia on My Mind," "Ruby," "Hit the Road, Jack," "Yesterday," and a unique rendition of "America the Beautiful."

Charter, a document issued by a government or ruler to an individual or group defining rights and privileges or powers. The king of England granted charters to the founders of the American colonies during the 1600s as a way of distributing lands. Charters usually conferred at least some rights of self-government on the colonists. The documents often became the focus of political disputes between colonists and officials appointed by the Crown. They also were sources and models for state constitutions adopted by the Americans in 1776.

Charter Oak, a hollow oak tree in Hartford, Connecticut, which was the secret hiding place of the colony's original charter from the king of England (1662). The colonists were given a new charter in 1687, but they were unwilling to give up their old one. According to legend, they displayed their independent spirit by refusing to turn it over, hiding it instead in the "charter oak."

Chase, Salmon P. (1808–73), antislavery activist, public official, and chief justice of the SUPREME COURT (1864–73). Before the Civil War, Chase, a prominent abolitionist, served in the U.S. Senate and became the first Republican governor of Ohio, but failed to win the Republican presidential nomination in 1860. President Abraham Lincoln named Chase secretary of the treasury; in that post, Chase maintained national credit, raised money to finance the Union army in the war and to meet war debts, and helped organize the national banking system in 1863. To remove the ambitious Chase as a competitor in the 1864 presidential election, Lincoln named him chief justice of the United States. As chief justice, Chase presided over the 1868 impeachment trial of President Andrew Johnson.

Château-Thierry, Battle of (June 3–4, 1918), an important military engagement in France during WORLD WAR I. The Allied forces broke an advance by the Germans and prevented them from crossing the Marne on their way to Paris, thus winning an important victory.

Chattanooga, Battle of (November 23–25, 1863). Following the Battle of Vicksburg in the CIVIL WAR, Union troops, under the command of Gen. ULYSSES S. GRANT moving eastward, encountered Confederate troops led by Gen. BRAXTON BRAGG at Chattanooga, Tennessee. The Union forces won a victory, and the Confederate forces retreated to winter quarters at Dalton, Georgia. Chattanooga was a strategic site for the North because it was a railroad and transportation center for the Confederate states.

Chautauqua Movement, a group of organized adult education centers begun during the 1870s for Bible study and recreation. The first meeting took place during the summer of 1874 at Lake Chautauqua, New York. By the end of the nineteenth century the program had spread throughout the United States and Canada and had expanded to include a variety of educational and farm studies. Also sponsored were weekly lectures, forums, and concerts.

Chavez, Cesar (1927–93), agricultural labor leader and symbolic Chicano leader. Chavez, a Mexican-American migrant farm worker, was a spokesman for the improvement of working conditions for his fellow farm workers. In 1962 he established the National Farm Workers Association, later named the United Farm Workers, in California and led a successful national boycott of table grapes in the effort to achieve recognition of the union. He consistently advocated nonviolent methods for achieving justice and equality — once, in 1968, fasting for twenty-five days to protest increasing violence in the struggle for union recognition.

Checks and Balances, a phrase describing a key feature of the form of government authorized by the CONSTITUTION. Under the system of checks and balances, separate institutions share key powers of government. For example, the president shares appointment power with the Senate; Congress shares its lawmaking power with the president. Each institution also has the power to block other institutions' actions; for example, the president can veto laws passed by Congress, but Congress can override the veto (by a two-thirds vote) to repass the laws, and the federal courts can hold actions by the legislative or executive branches unconstitutional. As James Madison wrote in the FEDERALIST

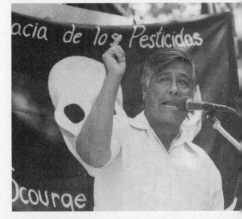

Cesar Chavez
Chavez at a rally marking the twentieth anniversary of the Delano grape strike.

PAPERS, each official of government has "the necessary institutional means and personal motives" to resist other institutions. The doctrine of checks and balances complements the doctrine of separation of powers.

Cheney, Richard (1941–), vice president of the United States (2001–) under GEORGE W. BUSH. Cheney served as White House Chief of Staff for President GERALD FORD from 1974 to the end of his administration in January, 1976. Elected to the House of Representatives from Wyoming in 1978, he was reelected five times. He became the Republican Conference Chairman in 1987 and served on the House Intelligence Committee, where he was a leading defender of the White House during the IRAN-CONTRA hearings. In 1989, Cheney became House Republican whip but was soon appointed secretary of defense by President GEORGE H. W. BUSH. With COLIN POWELL, Cheney codirected the Allied effort during the 1991 PERSIAN GULF WAR, raising his profile worldwide. As vice president, Cheney was one of the leading supporters of the 2003 IRAQ WAR.

Chennault, Claire (1890–1958), pilot and general during WORLD WAR II. After serving in the U.S. Army Air Service from 1918 to 1937, Chennault organized Gen. Chiang Kai-shek's air force during the second Sino-Japanese War. In 1941 he assembled an American volunteer group, the Flying Tigers, to support China in its war against the Japanese invaders. After the United States entered World War II, Chennault was recalled into American service and headed the air task forces in China.

Cherry Valley Massacre (November 11, 1778), a raid on American colonists during the AMERICAN REVOLUTION by British Tories in Cherry Valley, New York. Joining the Tories were Mohawk Indians under the leadership of JOSEPH BRANT. About forty people were killed, the town was burned to the ground, and livestock was confiscated. About seventy people were taken prisoner but released within a few days.

Chesapeake-Leopard Incident (June 22, 1807), a dispute between Great Britain and the United States. An English warship, the *Leopard*, opened fire on an American frigate, the *Chesapeake*, off Hampton Roads, Virginia, killing or wounding several American sailors. The British seized, or impressed, four men from the *Chesapeake*, maintaining that they were deserters. Following negotiations, the British disavowed the action and returned the surviving American seamen. Because the British refused to stop their policy of IMPRESSMENT, however, this incident was used by the WAR HAWKS to promote the WAR OF 1812 with England.

Chesnutt, Charles Waddell (1858–1932), fiction writer. Born to former slaves in Ohio, Chesnutt worked as a teacher before becoming a lawyer in 1887. While practicing law, he began publishing short stories in various magazines including *Atlantic Monthly*. His first novel, *The House Behind the Cedars* (1900) dealt with the attempt of a young black girl to pass for white. His novels concerned racial themes from a black viewpoint.

Only late in his career was he recognized as a prominent African-American author.

Chessman, Caryl (1921–60), criminal on San Quentin's death row for twelve years. In 1948 Chessman's arrest as the Los Angeles "Red-Light Bandit" led to his conviction on rape and kidnapping charges. While imprisoned he wrote *Cell 2455, Death Row* (1954) and *Trial by Ordeal* (1955), which attracted the attention of opponents of capital punishment. He received eight stays of execution, citing his lengthy stay on death row as excessive punishment. After his appeals were exhausted, Chessman was executed in the gas chamber on May 2, 1960.

Chickamauga, Battle of (1863), a military engagement during the CIVIL WAR. A Confederate army led by Gen. BRAXTON BRAGG attacked a Union army led by Gen. WILLIAM ROSECRANS at Chickamauga Creek, Georgia. The Confederates inflicted serious losses on the Union forces, causing them to retreat into Chattanooga. Gen. GEORGE THOMAS and his forces saved the remaining Union troops with their stubborn defense against the Confederates.

Chief Justice of the United States, the presiding member of the U.S. SUPREME COURT and the highest-ranking member of the federal judiciary. Like other federal judges, the chief justice is nominated by the president with the advice and consent of the Senate. His duties include assigning the writing of majority opinions ("the opinion of the Court") in cases when he votes with the majority (if the chief justice dissents, the associate justice in the majority who has seniority assigns the majority opinion). He also presides over the federal judiciary and helps make rules for the judicial system's handling of cases. His ceremonial duties include swearing in the president on Inauguration Day.

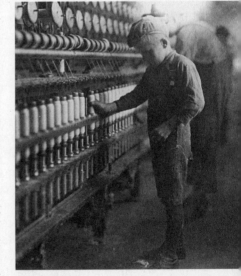

Child Labor, the use of children as workers in factories, farms, or other places of employment. The practice was common in the United States beginning in the 1700s and continuing until after World War I. Children as young as five worked long hours for low wages and under dangerous conditions. In 1916 the first federal child labor law was passed. Called the Keating-Owen Act, it prohibited the shipment of products made with child labor, but the

Child Labor
A young boy working in a textile mill in 1908.

Supreme Court ruled it unconstitutional in 1918. In 1924 a child labor amendment to the Constitution was approved by the Congress but was not ratified by the required three-fourths of the states. In 1938 Congress passed the FAIR LABOR STANDARDS ACT, which abolished child labor in interstate industries. Today all states have laws regulating the employment of children.

Children's Aid Society, an organization founded in 1853 by Charles Loring Brace to help orphaned, destitute, and homeless children in New York City. The society pioneered the placement of children in foster and adoptive homes rather than institutions. From 1854 to 1929 the Children's Aid Society sent more than 100,000 children on "orphan trains" from the slums of New York City to new homes in the West.

Chinese Exclusion Act (1882), a law prohibiting Chinese immigrant laborers from entering the United States for ten years after its enactment, and denying citizenship to Chinese nationals. The act was renewed for ten-year periods until World War II, when China became an ally with the United States against Japan. Chinese immigrants are now admitted under the quota system and are eligible for U.S. citizenship by naturalization.

Chisholm, Shirley (1924–), the first black woman to be elected to the U.S. Congress. A Democrat, Chisholm served in the U.S. House of Representatives from 1969 to 1983 and ran unsuccessfully for the presidential nomination in 1972. A reformer and educational specialist, Chisholm worked for women's rights, day care, environmental protection, and an end to the Vietnam War. She spoke out against the seniority system in Congress.

Chisholm Trail, a cattle trail stretching from San Antonio, Texas, to the railroad center at Abilene, Kansas. The trail, named for the half-Cherokee Indian trader Jesse Chisholm (1806–68), was developed during the late 1860s as one of the routes for the "long drive" of Texas cattle. Cowboys drove their herds along the trail from the open range to railroad shipping towns. The route declined in importance with the construction of railroads into Texas, which provided cheaper transportation to the livestock markets.

Chopin, Kate (1851–1904), author. Chopin's two collections, *Bayou Folk* (1894) and *A Night in Acadie* (1897), include a number of her more than one hundred short stories. She wrote realistically of the Cajun and Creole people of Louisiana and contributed to children's magazines and literary journals. Although Chopin was one of the first female authors to write honestly about women's feelings, her best-known novel, *The Awakening* (1899), dealt too openly with the subject of a woman's sexuality for most critics of the time, and she gave up writing because of their hostile criticism.

Church, Frederick Edwin (1826–1900), landscape painter. Church painted enormous panoramic landscapes with meticulous scientific detail. His paintings, flooded with light and brilliant color, feature mountains of

North and South America, vivid sunsets, and lush wilderness. A leading member of the HUDSON RIVER SCHOOL, Church was the only official pupil of the school's founder, THOMAS COLE.

Cibola, Seven Cities of, seven legendary cities in what is now the southwestern part of the United States. Indians related stories to Spanish explorers about seven cities that contained gold and jewels. FRANCISCO CORONADO led an expedition to locate the cities for Spain but found only small Indian villages containing nothing of value to him.

Circular Letter, a means used by eighteenth-century politicians to spread their views on public issues. The most famous was a 1767 letter issued by the Massachusetts legislature to other colonial assemblies in response to the TOWNSHEND ACTS. The letter urged that the colonists act together to resist taxation without representation in the British Parliament.

Civilian Conservation Corps (CCC) (1933), a NEW DEAL agency created to relieve unemployment among young men during the GREAT DEPRESSION. Workers in the CCC promoted soil conservation, planted millions of trees, constructed small dams, cleared forest fire hazards, and undertook irrigation projects. By 1942, when it was disbanded, some 3 million men had received work in the program.

Civil Liberties, basic rights guaranteed to all citizens under the BILL OF RIGHTS, such as freedom of speech, religion, and the press, and the rights to meet in peaceful assembly and to petition the government. They also guarantee the right to a jury trial and reasonable bail and proscribe cruel and unusual punishments and the loss of life, liberty, and property without due process of law. Many cases involving civil liberties have reached the U.S. Supreme Court, including those dealing with prayer in public schools, refusal to salute the flag, and burning the flag. The AMERICAN CIVIL LIBERTIES UNION (ACLU), a nonpartisan organization, defends the civil liberties of any U.S. citizen.

Civil Liberties Act (1988), legislation that redressed the grievous injustices endured by more than 110,000 victims of JAPANESE-AMERICAN INTERNMENT during World War II. Congress apologized for the wartime mistreatment of these Americans and appropriated $20,000 as compensation to each person still alive who had been interned.

Civil Rights Legislation, laws forbidding discrimination on the basis of race, religion, age, or sex. The Civil Rights Act of 1866 declared that blacks were citizens and had the same rights as white citizens. The Civil Rights Act of 1875 guaranteed equal rights for blacks in public places. In 1883 the Supreme Court ruled that the states could not deny blacks their civil rights, but that Congress had no jurisdiction over social rights. In 1957 an act set up a Civil Rights Commission to protect the right of blacks to vote, especially in the southern states. The Civil Rights Act of 1964 prohibited discrimination in voting, education, hiring and promotion of workers, and access to hotels, restaurants, theaters, and other public facilities. In March 1988 Congress overrode President Ronald Reagan's veto of the Civil Rights Restoration Act of 1987. The legislation extended antibias laws to entire institutions, making them subject to loss of federal funds if they were found to discriminate on the basis of race, sex, age, or physical handicap in *any* of their programs, not just those receiving federal funds.

Civil Service Reform, a movement to replace the SPOILS SYSTEM with a merit system, which gained momentum after the CIVIL WAR. Representative Thomas A. Jenckes of Rhode Island introduced reform legislation in Congress in 1865, but his bill failed to pass. The demands for reform became more vocal after the political scandals of the GRANT administration and the corruption of the GILDED AGE. GEORGE CURTIS organized the Civil Service Reform League in 1871. In 1883 Congress passed the first comprehensive national reform program, called the PENDLETON ACT, establishing the Civil Service Commission and a list of classified civil service jobs.

Civil War (1861–65), the conflict between the Northern states (the Union) and the eleven Southern states that seceded from the Union and were organized as the CONFEDERATE STATES OF AMERICA. It is also known as the War between the States, the War of Secession, and the War of the Rebellion.

Background and Causes: Dissension had been brewing between the North and South long before the first shots were fired on Fort Sumter, a

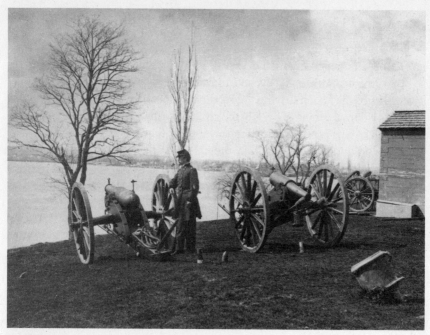

Civil War
A general stands watch at a Washington, D.C., arsenal.

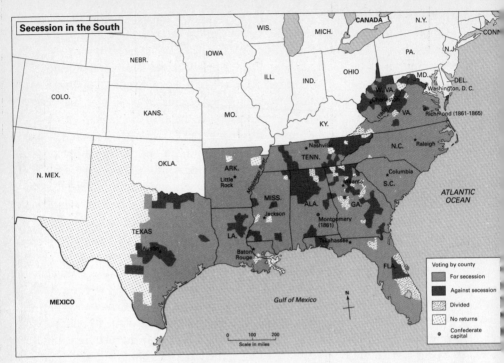

Secession in the South (by county)

Union military post in Charleston, South Carolina, on April 12, 1861. Most historians agree that the war had several causes:

1. Sectionalism entailed a variety of divergent opinions and practices regarding economics, ideals and morals, and ways of life. These sectional differences had been driving the North and South further and further apart since colonial times. The North, an industrializing society, favored the growth of cities and depended more on trade than agriculture. Northerners tended to oppose slavery and favored high tariffs to protect their products from foreign competition. The South had established a rural way of life based on plantations and supported by an agricultural economy and slave labor. Southerners relied on imports as well as exports of their products, especially cotton, and therefore wanted to keep tariffs low.

2. The chief cause of the war was the differences over slavery and its extension into the territories. The MISSOURI COMPROMISE (1820), the COMPROMISE OF 1850, and other political maneuvers delayed civil war for years but were ultimately unsuccessful in effecting a peaceful solution. Antislavery sentiment in the North was fueled by HARRIET BEECHER STOWE's publication of *UNCLE TOM'S CABIN* (1852) attacking the institution of slavery; the KANSAS-NEBRASKA ACT (1954), which repealed the Missouri Compromise and stated that settlers themselves under the

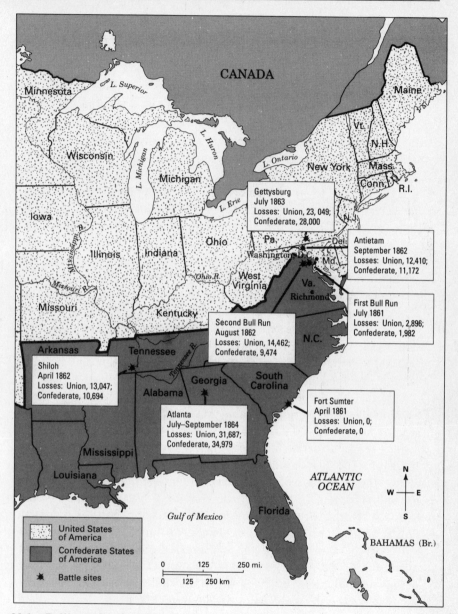

Gettysburg
July 1863
Losses: Union, 23, 049;
Confederate, 28,000

Antietam
September 1862
Losses: Union, 12,410;
Confederate, 11,172

First Bull Run
July 1861
Losses: Union, 2,896;
Confederate, 1,982

Second Bull Run
August 1862
Losses: Union, 14,462;
Confederate, 9,474

Shiloh
April 1862
Losses: Union, 13,047;
Confederate, 10,694

Atlanta
July–September 1864
Losses: Union, 31,687;
Confederate, 34,979

Fort Sumter
April 1861
Losses: Union, 0;
Confederate, 0

United States
of America

Confederate States
of America

Battle sites

0   125   250 mi.
0   125   250 km

Major Battles of the Civil War

doctrine of POPULAR SOVEREIGNTY should decide whether their territory
would be slave or free; and the *DRED SCOTT* decision (1857), which in effect
prohibited any opposition to the extension of slavery in the territories.
In turn, JOHN BROWN's raid on Harpers Ferry (1859) and the growth of
the REPUBLICAN PARTY, which considered slavery evil and opposed its

extension into western territories, angered Southerners. Their leaders urged that the South secede from the Union if the Republican ABRAHAM LINCOLN won the presidential ELECTION OF 1860.

3. The subject of secession was a third cause of the war. States' rights were at issue, with the South contending that because the states had joined the Union voluntarily, they had the right to secede and the federal government could not deny this right. Unionists disagreed, asserting that the Union of the states was permanent and inviolable. Abraham Lincoln summed up the feeling of Unionists when he said, "The Union is older than any of the states, and in fact, it created the states."

It is important to note that not all Southerners supported secession, and the election of 1860 illustrates this point. The DEMOCRATIC PARTY was ripped apart by the widening differences between the North and South. At the party convention in Charleston, the Democrats split over the issues, with Southerners calling for the protection of slavery in the territories and Northerners supporting popular sovereignty. The Republicans at their convention called for limiting the extension of slavery, and another party, the CONSTITUTIONAL UNION PARTY, favored compromise and moderation. Radicals known as "fire-eaters" in the South stepped up their calls for secession. Moderates in the South wanted to preserve the Union and work within it to compromise the differences. But in the end, Lincoln's Republican victory tipped the scales throughout the South.

Sure that his election meant the ruin of slavery, seven states — South Carolina, Georgia, Florida, Alabama, Mississippi, Louisiana, and Texas — seceded from the Union and in a convention in Montgomery, Alabama, formed the Confederate States of America in February 1861. They chose JEFFERSON DAVIS as president and ALEXANDER H. STEPHENS as vice president. When Lincoln sent ships carrying supplies to provision the federal fort at Fort Sumter, Confederate leaders ordered Gen. P.G.T. BEAUREGARD to attack before their arrival. After a day and a half of battle, Union Maj. Robert Anderson surrendered. Lincoln's call on April 15 for 75,000 troops to put down the insurrection in the South caused anger and defiance in the states of the Upper South and led Virginia, North Carolina, Tennessee, and Arkansas to withdraw from the Union and join the Confederacy. (The status of the border slave states of Delaware, Maryland, Kentucky, and Missouri remained ambiguous throughout the war. They did not secede and join the Confederacy, but substantial numbers of their citizens sympathized with the South. Raids and incursions by both sides took place in these states, especially Kentucky and Missouri, in efforts to win them for one side or the other.) A blockade of Southern ports was proclaimed and the Civil War began.

Warfare: Twenty-three northern states with a population of 22 million opposed eleven southern states with a population of 9.5 million, of whom

3.5 million were slaves. One of the Confederates' major military objectives was to capture Washington, D.C., the nation's capital, then to negotiate for peace, return the capital to the Union, and be left alone as an independent country. The South also hoped to be recognized by England as an independent nation. The Union's plan included (1) a blockade of the South to prevent Southern trade with foreign countries, especially England; (2) the control of the Mississippi River and New Orleans, thus dividing the Confederate states; and (3) the capture of Richmond, the Confederate capital, thus demoralizing the Confederate states and forcing a surrender.

Both the North, with the goal of reuniting the country, and the South, with the goal of remaining independent, were led by noted commanders. Virginia's secession proved to be advantageous to the Southerners, for it gave them ROBERT E. LEE to serve as commanding general of the Confederate forces. Gen. THOMAS J. "STONEWALL" JACKSON played a key role in early Confederate victories. As the war progressed, Gen. WILLIAM TECUMSEH SHERMAN and ULYSSES S. GRANT helped lead the Union armies to victory.

The North, confidently expecting a quick end to the war, launched a drive for Richmond under Gen. Irvin McDowell. The first major land battle of the war occurred at Bull Run, or Manassas as it was called in the South, an important railway center twenty-five miles southwest of Washington. (The North named battles after nearby water areas and the South named them after nearby towns.) Sightseers and picnickers, in anticipation of a day of victory and celebration, rode out from Washington to view the battle. The battle of BULL RUN (July 21), the only large-scale engagement of 1861, began well for the Federals but ended with a Confederate victory. It was here that Stonewall Jackson earned his appellation. The defeat was a shock to the Northerners, and Lincoln called up a real army of 500,000 volunteers prepared to serve for three years.

Although Washington and Richmond were only a hundred miles apart, the maneuvers and battles spanned almost four years. Early in 1862 Southern troops surprised Grant's army at Pittsburg Landing, Tennessee, at the BATTLE OF SHILOH (April 6–7), named for a church near the battlefield. Grant forced a Southern retreat, but not before serious losses were suffered on both sides. Richmond was not threatened seriously until the spring of 1862, when Northern Gen. GEORGE B. MCCLELLAN's PENINSULAR CAMPAIGN aimed at taking the city ended in defeat in the SEVEN DAYS' BATTLES (June). The Confederates won a second decisive victory at the Second Battle of Bull Run (August 29, 1862), pushing Northern troops again back to Washington.

The Confederate's invasion at Antietam, Maryland (September 17, 1862), was the bloodiest single day of the war, with over 23,000 men killed or wounded. The battle's importance lay in its ending Lee's first invasion of the

North. Because he retreated, the North claimed a Union victory. This discouraged European recognition of the Confederacy and prompted Lincoln to issue the preliminary EMANCIPATION PROCLAMATION (September 22) promising freedom to slaves held in the Confederacy.

The turning-point battle, the second and last invasion of the North, took place at GETTYSBURG, Pennsylvania (July 1–3, 1863). In this three-day battle, 23,000 Union men and 28,000 Confederates were killed, wounded, or missing; the victory went to the North. This ended the Confederate invasion and began its gradual military decline. Under Grant, the Union was also conducting a successful forty-eight-day siege of VICKSBURG (May 18–July 4, 1863). The South's loss of the city gave the North control of the Mississippi River, splitting the Confederacy and isolating its western areas. Confederate initiatives in Tennessee also failed.

Appointed commander of all the Union armies, Grant launched a plan in the spring of 1864 to attack the Confederacy on all fronts. Sherman captured and burned Atlanta in September and led the infamous March to the Sea through Georgia. Ordering his troops to wage "total war," destroying not only men but factories, farms, and livestock, Sherman changed the rules of fighting in hopes of making absolutely clear to the South the utter futility of continuing the war. At the same time, Grant himself, in pursuit of Lee in Virginia, conducted his WILDERNESS CAMPAIGN in May and June of 1864, leading to a bloody victory at COLD HARBOR. The enormous losses forced Grant to change his tactics. His Army of the Potomac moved to capture Petersburg, which controlled the rail lines to Richmond, in an effort to seal the capital off from outside support. After a nine-month siege of Petersburg led to the Union's taking the town, Lee evacuated Richmond and surrendered to Grant at APPOMATTOX COURT HOUSE, Virginia. Terms of the surrender were made on April 9, 1865. Less than a week later, Lincoln was dead, shot by assassin JOHN WILKES BOOTH, a Southern sympathizer.

Results: The costs of the Civil War were immense in both lives and dollars. Nearly as many Americans died in the Civil War as have died in all wars the United States has fought — approximately 620,000. The North lost about 360,000 troops. Although figures for the Confederacy are uncertain, an estimated one-fourth of its soldiers were killed. Many of the deaths were caused by disease, which was rampant among the troops and in the prison camps.

The Civil War left the South devastated, with its livestock, farms, factories, and railroads destroyed. Military operations tore up huge land areas, and the labor system ended in chaos. Thousands of civilians were refugees in areas far from home. Towns and cities lay in ruins. It was well into the twentieth century before the South fully recovered from the economic effects of the war.

Despite its destructiveness, the Civil War spurred industrial development in the North, promoting the petroleum, steel, food-processing, and manufacturing industries. The Northern victory established conclusively that a centralized federal government had precedence over states' rights, settling the question of secession once and for all. Finally, it brought about the abolition of slavery and freed some 4 million slaves. The meanings of that freedom, however, although assured by constitutional amendments, remain at issue to this day.

Clark, "Champ" (James Beauchamp; 1850–1921), Speaker of the House (1911–19). Elected as a Democratic representative from Missouri in 1892, Clark later served as minority leader and helped lead the revolt against the strong rule of Speaker JOSEPH CANNON in 1910. Replacing Cannon as Speaker of the House, Clark helped restore prestige to the position. In 1912 he was a leading contender for the Democratic presidential nomination and led on the first fourteen ballots, but lost to Woodrow Wilson.

Clark, Dick (1929–), television producer and disc jockey. With a career spanning fifty years, Clark's projects have included teen dance shows, television specials, daytime game shows, and feature films. Clark hosted *American Bandstand* (1957–87), the first network television series devoted to rock and roll and the longest running musical program in television history. He helped promote the careers of many artists of the fifties including Chubby Checker, Jerry Lee Lewis, and BUDDY HOLLY. Known as America's Oldest Teenager, Clark is known for his youthful appearance, but his efficient business sense and perception into the interests of American culture have been keys to his success.

Clark, George Rogers (1752–1818), frontiersman and military leader in the AMERICAN REVOLUTION. In 1778 Clark captured the British forts of Kaskaskia, Cahokia, and Vincennes in the West, which was then the area between the Ohio and Mississippi rivers. His military victories provided the basis for the American claims to the Mississippi River when the TREATY OF PARIS was signed in 1783. He was the elder brother of WILLIAM CLARK of the Lewis and Clark Expedition.

Clark, Kenneth Bancroft (1914–), educator, psychologist, and civil rights leader. Born in the Panama Canal Zone, Clark was reared in Harlem, New York City, received his Ph.D. at Columbia, and taught at City College of New York. He won national recognition for his work with emotionally disturbed ghetto children. His report on the psychological impact of racial segregation (1950) was an influential factor in the 1954 U.S. Supreme Court decision banning segregation in public schools. In his studies Clark had come to the conclusion that segregation was bad for all children, black and white. Some of his most important publications include *Prejudice and Your Child* (1955), *Dark Ghetto: Dilemmas of Social Power* (1965), *Pathos of Power* (1975), and *King, Malcolm, Baldwin: Three Interviews* (1984).

Clark, Mark (1896–1984), U.S. Army general. Clark graduated from West Point in 1917 and served in France during WORLD WAR I. During WORLD WAR II, he worked with the Free French forces in the invasion of North Africa. Clark commanded the Fifth Army during the invasion of Italy, capturing Salerno and Rome. He then served in Austria and the Far East. He was appointed commander in chief of the United Nations forces in Korea when he relieved Gen. MATTHEW RIDGEWAY in 1952, serving until the end of the KOREAN WAR in 1953.

Clark, William (1770–1838), soldier and explorer. In 1803, at the request of President Thomas Jefferson, Clark joined MERIWETHER LEWIS to lead an expedition to the Far West to explore the region and search for a land route to the Pacific. The LEWIS AND CLARK EXPEDITION lasted over two years, collecting enormous amounts of information about the territory included in the LOUISIANA PURCHASE. Clark served as governor of Missouri Territory from 1813 to 1821. He was the younger brother of GEORGE ROGERS CLARK.

Clay, Henry (1777–1852), Speaker of the House (1811–14, 1815–20, 1823–25). Although leader of the WAR HAWKS in Congress who urged war against England in 1812, Clay helped negotiate the peace and signed the TREATY OF GHENT in 1814. Known as the "Great Compromiser," Clay, who came from the border state of Kentucky, helped negotiate the MISSOURI COMPROMISE in 1820, the COMPROMISE TARIFF in 1833, and the COMPROMISE OF 1850. His repeated efforts to settle disputes over slavery through compromise delayed civil war but ultimately failed. Clay served as secretary of state under John Quincy Adams, as Speaker of the House of Representatives, and as an influential member of the U.S. Senate. Historians rank him one of the five great U.S. senators of all time. Clay, who made five attempts to receive the presidential nomination of the National Republican party (later Whig party), captured it three times but lost to John Quincy Adams in the ELECTION OF 1824, Andrew Jackson in the ELECTION OF 1832, and James K. Polk in the ELECTION OF 1844.

Clayton Anti-Trust Act (October 15, 1914), a law intended to plug loopholes in the SHERMAN ANTI-TRUST ACT of 1890 and to more clearly define unfair business practices. The act prohibited price discrimination and interlocking directorates for the purpose of eliminating competition. It recognized the legality of boycotts and strikes and stated that unions were not monopolies under the antitrust laws.

Cleaver, Eldridge (1935–98), black activist. While in prison, Cleaver wrote the powerful best-seller, *Soul on Ice* (1968), which deals with black attitudes toward American society. He joined the Black Panther party and in 1968 became the Peace and Freedom party's candidate for president. In 1969, faced with charges of attempted murder because of a shoot-out with Oakland police, he began an exile that lasted seven years. Cleaver became a conservative "born again" Christian and returned to the United States in 1975, touring the country for evangelical reasons while on probation. He wrote his autobiography, *Soul on Fire,* in 1978.

Clemens, Roger (1962–), baseball player. Clemens owns the strikeout record for a single nine-inning game by making twenty strikeouts in a game between the Boston Red Sox and the Seattle Mariners in 1986. He matched his own record ten years later in 1996 in a game between the Red Sox and Detroit. Called the "Rocket Man" for his fastball and strikeout ability, he won the Cy Young Award six times while playing for Boston, Toronto, and the New York Yankees (1986, 1987, 1991, 1997, 1998, 2001), an all-time record. He won World Series rings with the Yankees in 1999 and 2000, and in 2003 Clemens achieved his 300th career win and 4,000th career strikeout, the first player in baseball history to record both milestones in the same game. He stands behind NOLAN RYAN and STEVE CARLTON as only the third player to ever record 4,000 strikeouts.

Clemens, Samuel L. (Mark Twain; 1835–1910), humorist and author. A master of American literature, Clemens wrote in a colloquial, earthy style, inspired by the experiences of his childhood along the Mississippi River and his travels and lectures throughout the world. His humorous and satirical works present a realistic picture of nineteenth-century life but also carry universal implications that have lifted his best works into the realm of classic literature. Taking his pseudonym "Mark Twain" from the cry of a sailor calling out the shallows from the bow of a Mississippi riverboat, Clemens led a wandering life. He piloted a riverboat and worked as a newspaper reporter in Virginia City, Nevada, and San Francisco, California, before moving to Hartford, Connecticut, where he wrote most of his books. He published his first notable work, "The Celebrated Jumping Frog of Calaveras County," in 1865. This was followed by such classics as *Roughing It* (1872), *The Adventures of Tom Sawyer* (1876), *The Prince and the Pauper* (1882), *Life on the Mississippi* (1883), *The Adventures of Huckleberry Finn* (1884), and *A Connecticut Yankee in King Arthur's Court* (1889).

Clemente, Roberto (1934–72), baseball player. Clemente, one of the greatest outfielders in baseball history, played for the Pittsburgh Pirates for seventeen years and won the league's batting title four times, compiling a .317 lifetime average. He died in a plane crash in 1972 while carrying relief aid to victims of an earthquake in Nicaragua. Authorities waived the five-year waiting period and in 1973 elected him to the baseball Hall of Fame.

Cleveland, Grover (1837–1908), twenty-second and twenty-fourth president of the United States (1885–89 and 1893–97). Cleveland, the only president to be elected to two nonconsecutive terms, was born in Caldwell, New Jersey. He was admitted to the bar in 1859. Following his election as mayor of Buffalo, New York, in 1881, he became governor of New York in 1882. As the Democratic party nominee for president, he defeated Republican James

G. Blaine in a vicious campaign in the ELECTION OF 1884. The first Democratic president after the Civil War, Cleveland provided a quiet, honest civil service reform-type government during his term of office. But the ELECTION OF 1888 resulted in his defeat by Republican Benjamin Harrison. Harrison won a majority of electoral votes, though Cleveland had more popular votes. In 1892 Cleveland again won the Democratic nomination and this time defeated Harrison's reelection attempt. In his second term as president, Cleveland forced the repeal of the SHERMAN SILVER PURCHASE ACT, sent federal troops to subdue the PULLMAN RAILROAD STRIKE, and tried to lower the tariff.

Clinton, Bill (William; 1946–), forty-second president of the United States (1993–2001). After earning a degree in international affairs from Georgetown in 1968, Clinton attended Oxford University as a Rhodes scholar and Yale University Law School. In 1978, at age thirty-two, Clinton became governor of Arkansas, the youngest governor in the nation since Harold Stassen (Minnesota) forty years earlier. As governor (1979–81, 1983–93), Clinton attracted national attention for his innovative program to upgrade the state's educational system. As the Democratic nominee for the presidency in the ELECTION OF 1992, Clinton, with running mate AL GORE,

faced the incumbent Republican GEORGE H. W. BUSH. Calling for change in government and pledging to improve the economy, Clinton won the election by a wide margin of the electoral vote.

During his first term Clinton signed the Family and Medical Leave Act of 1993 requiring employers to allow unpaid medical leaves for family emergencies. An attempt to create a comprehensive health care system under a plan developed by first lady HILLARY RODHAM CLINTON failed to gain sufficient support. A long, steady growth in the economy and a deficit-reduction plan led to his reelection to a second term in 1996 by a comfortable margin over Republican senator ROBERT DOLE and H. ROSS PEROT. American prosperity and economic expansion continued, but beginning in 1998 during the course

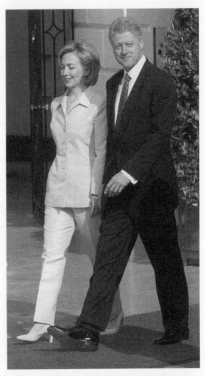

Hillary Rodham Clinton and Bill Clinton

of a sexual harassment lawsuit filed by a former Arkansas state employee, Clinton was accused of lying to a federal grand jury about his relationship with former White House intern Monica Lewinsky. This led to the disclosure of a two-year affair with the intern, which Clinton vigorously denied until faced with conclusive DNA evidence. On December 19, 1998, William Jefferson Clinton became only the second president (after ANDREW JOHNSON in 1868) to be impeached by the House of Representatives, charged with perjury and obstruction of justice. He was tried and acquitted by the Senate on February 12, 1999, allowing him to complete his second term. In the meantime, Clinton dealt with continued problems with Iraq and, together with Prime Minister Tony Blair, pushed for NATO intervention in Serbia. Also in 1999, in conjunction with a Republican-controlled Congress, Clinton balanced the federal budget for the first time since 1969.

Clinton, DeWitt (1769–1828), politician. As governor of New York (1817–23), Clinton worked to construct the ERIE CANAL; "Clinton's ditch" opened in 1825. Clinton served in the U.S. Senate from New York in 1802 and proposed the Twelfth Amendment, which revised the electoral college. As mayor of New York City he opened its first public school. The Federalist candidate in the presidential ELECTION OF 1812, Clinton lost the election to James Madison.

Clinton, George (1739–1812), brigadier general during the American Revolution and vice president of the United States (1805–12) under two presidents, Thomas Jefferson and James Madison. John C. Calhoun was the only other vice president to serve with two presidents. Earlier, as the first governor of New York, Clinton set another record by being reelected six times (1775–95, 1801–04). Because of his strong distrust of a powerful central government, he opposed the adoption of the U.S. Constitution.

Clinton, Hillary Rodham (1947–), first lady of the United States (1993–2001), lawyer, and politician. Educated at Wellesley and Yale, Clinton became a successful lawyer. As the wife of President BILL CLINTON, she took an active political role, leading a task force on national health care reform. The ensuing legislation failed in Congress, however. A child advocate, she chaired the Children's Defense Fund and authored *It Takes a Village: And Other Lessons Children Teach Us* (1997). In 2000 she was elected to the United States Senate from New York, becoming the first-ever first lady to win elected office. A book of her memoirs, *Living History* (2003), was an immediate best-seller.

Coal Strike (May 12, 1902), a major strike called by the United Mine Workers union to gain recognition, a nine-hour day, and a salary increase. After several months, President Theodore Roosevelt forced an end to the strike by threatening to operate the mines with federal troops. Workers, who resumed their jobs when the union won, were granted a wage increase, union recognition, and a shorter workday.

Cobb, Ty (1886–1961), baseball player. Considered by most experts to be the greatest hitter of all time, Cobb had the highest lifetime batting average of .367. As an original inductee into the Hall of Fame in 1936, Cobb outpolled all other baseball players, including Babe Ruth. He won twelve batting titles and in three seasons hit above .400. Called "the Georgia Peach," Cobb played for the Detroit Tigers and the Philadelphia Athletics. His temper, meanness, and aggressiveness, both on and off the field, made him generally disliked by his teammates.

Cochise (1815–74), chief of the Apache Indians of Arizona. Cochise, noted for his courage, fighting ability, and integrity in honoring treaties, maintained peaceful relations with white settlers until he was falsely accused of kidnapping a white child in 1861. Following his capture Cochise escaped and embarked on a series of raids and skirmishes against white settlers. A new treaty was negotiated by Gen. Oliver Howard in 1872, and Cochise retired to a reservation, where he died in 1874.

Code Talkers, Native Americans who transmitted secret messages based on their native languages during wartime. Lacking secure battlefield voice communication during WORLD WAR I, the U.S. Army employed Choctaws to encode voice communications, using their native language. The practice was expanded during WORLD WAR II to include Comanche, Navajo, and others. Navajo code talkers in the U.S. Marine Corps took part in every Marine assault in the Pacific between 1942 and 1945, and their codes were never broken.

Cody, "Buffalo Bill" (William; 1846–1917), frontiersman and showman. During the construction of the Kansas Pacific Railroad, Cody killed more than 4,000 buffalo to supply meat for railroad workers. He rode for the Pony Express and scouted for the Union army during the Civil War. As an army scout he met NED BUNTLINE, who wrote a series of dime novels on "Buffalo Bill." Cody's career as an entertainer expanded in 1883 when he organized the highly successful "Buffalo Bill's Wild West Show," featuring ANNIE OAKLEY.

Coercive Acts *See* INTOLERABLE ACTS.

Cohan, George M. (1878–1942), composer, actor, and producer. During Cohan's lifetime, he wrote more than forty plays and musicals, and produced, directed, and starred in most of them. Extremely patriotic, he stirred up audiences with his flag-waving enthusiasm. In 1904 he produced *Little Johnny Jones,* which featured "Give My Regards to Broadway" and "I'm a Yankee Doodle Dandy." In 1906 he composed "You're a Grand Old Flag" and in 1917 a song honoring the AMERICAN EXPEDITIONARY FORCE titled "Over There." Congress presented Cohan with a special medal of honor in 1940 for these two songs.

Cold Harbor, Battle of (June 1–2, 1864), major battle of the CIVIL WAR. Launching a drive toward Richmond as part of the Wilderness campaign,

Union Gen. ULYSSES S. GRANT, led about 50,000 troops in attack against about 30,000 Confederate defenders led by Gen. ROBERT E. LEE along a three-mile line, just north of Richmond. More than 12,000 Union soldiers were killed or wounded, 6,000 within the first hour. Southern losses numbered approximately 1,500.

Cold War, a term coined to describe the hostility between the United States and the Soviet Union from 1945 through 1989 — a hostility that never escalated into a shooting war. The cold war was rooted in the differences between the two nations' political and economic systems, because of both nations' status as nuclear superpowers, and because the leaders of each believed that the other was bent on world conquest. Beginning with the failure of the two former allies to agree on the postwar restructuring of Europe and the Soviet Union's imposition of Communist governments on the nations of Eastern Europe, the cold war developed into a worldwide conflict waged through "proxies" such as North and South Korea, East and West Germany, and North and South Vietnam. Notable events in the cold war include the 1960 U-2 INCIDENT the 1961 BAY OF PIGS invasion and BERLIN AIRLIFT crisis, and the 1962 CUBAN MISSILE CRISIS. The cold war ended between 1989, with the fall of the Berlin Wall, and 1991, with the collapse of a military coup against Soviet President Mikhail Gorbachev.

Cole, Nat "King" (Nathaniel Adams Coles; 1919–65), singer. Because of his soft, mellow tones, Cole became a top romantic singer during the 1940s and 1950s. He worked originally as a jazz pianist in nightclubs and vaudeville with the King Cole Trio. He later became the first black man to have his own radio and television series. Some of his best songs included "Mona Lisa," "Too Young," and "Nature Boy."

Cole, Thomas (1801–48), landscape painter. Cole founded the HUDSON RIVER SCHOOL to promote the painting of romantic wilderness scenes by American artists. Forests, mountains, and rivers of the American Northeast are subjects of Cole's works.

Colfax, Schuyler (1823–85), vice president of the United States (1869–73). Colfax worked as editor of the *St. Joseph Valley Register* in Indiana for eighteen years and was active in Whig politics. He became a Republican in 1854 and was elected to the House of Representatives, where he served as Speaker from 1863 to 1869. Elected with Ulysses S. Grant in 1868, Colfax became involved with the CRÉDIT MOBILIER scandal, which ended his political career.

Collins, Michael (1930–), astronaut. Pilot of *Apollo 11*'s command module *Columbia*, Collins flew on the first manned lunar landing mission in 1969 with NEIL ARMSTRONG and "BUZZ" ALDRIN. His first space mission was in 1966 as pilot of *Gemini 10*, when he walked in space at what was then a record altitude of 475 miles.

Colorado (Centennial State), organized as a territory in 1861, was admitted into the Union as the thirty-eighth state on August 1, 1876. (See maps, pages 540 and 541.) Important cities include Denver, the capital, Colorado Springs, home of the Air Force Academy, and Pueblo. The Rocky Mountains cover much of the state, providing attractions such as Pike's Peak, Rocky Mountain, Mesa Verde, and Dinosaur national parks. Tourism and skiing are important industries, with Aspen, Steamboat Springs, and Vail being world-famous skiing resorts. The leading industries are mining, manufacturing, and agriculture, including cattle and sheep herding. Noted personalities from Colorado include JACK DEMPSEY and BYRON WHITE.

Colt, Samuel (1814–62), inventor of the repeating pistol, patented in 1835. Called the "six-shooter," the gun became the first practical revolver for rapid firing of bullets. Colt established a manufacturing business and supplied a large number of guns to the U.S. Army during the Mexican and Civil wars.

Coltrane, John (1928–67), jazz saxophonist, composer. Coltrane began his career touring with jazz greats Earl Bostic, Bud Powell, and DIZZY GILLESPIE, but developed his own sound while working with the MILES DAVIS Quintet. He gained wide respect and fame for his mellow, stylistic innovations, influencing modern jazz during the 1960s and beyond.

Columbia **Disaster,** an accident that occurred on February 1, 2003, about fifteen minutes before the space shuttle *Columbia*'s scheduled landing at the Kennedy Space Center in Florida. The *Columbia* disintegrated about forty miles above the earth, killing all seven astronauts aboard: Commander Richard D. Husband; pilot William C. McCool; payload commander Michael P. Anderson; mission specialists David M. Brown, Kalpana Chawla, and Laurel Clark; and Israel's first astronaut, Ilan Ramon. Witnesses reported debris falling from the sky from California to Louisiana. An investigation found that upon takeoff, foam insulation broke off a pylon connecting the shuttle to its main fuel tank, gouging a hole in the shuttle's left wing that allowed super hot gas to penetrate the wing during reentry. The oldest of NASA's shuttle fleet, the *Columbia* was first launched in 1981. It was on its twenty-eighth mission.

Columbine High School Massacre (April 20, 1999), a planned shooting rampage at Columbine High School in Littleton, Colorado. The gunmen, Columbine seniors Eric Harris (18) and Dylan Klebold (17), entered their high school armed with four guns, several knives, and numerous exploding devices. They succeeded in delivering 188 shots on a shooting spree that killed twelve students and a teacher and wounded twenty-one others before killing themselves. According to their writings and videotapes, the gunmen had been planning the attack for over a year. Subsequent investigations found that the boys had been obsessed with death and violence and had expressed racist and anti-Christian prejudices, but no specific explanation for the shootings was uncovered. The weapons used by the shooters were illegally obtained by adults who knowingly violated laws and were later prosecuted and sentenced to prison. The incident was the subject of the 2001 Academy Award–winning documentary *Bowling for Columbine*, directed by Michael Moore, which investigated gun violence in the United States.

Columbus, Christopher (1451–1506), Genoese explorer who sailed under the aegis of the Spanish Crown. Columbus "discovered" America for Europeans while trying to find a water route west to Asia. In 1492 he sailed with three ships, the *Niña*, the *Pinta*, and the *Santa María*, landing in the Bahamas, perhaps on the island of San Salvador. His next three expeditions explored Cuba, Haiti, Puerto Rico, Jamaica, Trinidad, Honduras, and Panama. Columbus received a royal welcome in Spain following his first voyage and was at first made governor of the land he had discovered and was promised rich rewards. But his rule and that of those ruling in his absence was inept and often cruel. And as explorers following him began to realize the extent of the new lands, the Spanish monarchs reneged on many of their promises to him. Never realizing the full significance of his accomplishments, Columbus died a disappointed man.

Commager, Henry Steele (1902–1998), historian and educator, distinguished for his elegant and direct writing and for his commitment to democratic values and liberal policies. Commager taught at New York University, Columbia University, and Amherst College, retiring in 1991. His most influential book, *The Growth of the American Republic* (written with Samuel Eliot Morison), appeared in 1930; the seventh edition was published in 1980. Commager was a pioneer of the editing and publishing of anthologies of source materials of the American historical record, and his *Documents of American History* (1934, 8th ed. 1968) is a standard reference for historians. *The American Mind* (1950), *The American Character* (1970), and *The Empire of Reason* (1977) are landmark studies of American intellectual history. In 1993 Commager wrote *Commager on Tocqueville*, a new interpretation of Alexis de Tocqueville's *Democracy in America*. Also a prolific essayist, Commager wrote for numerous newspapers and magazines including *Saturday Review, Atlantic*, the *New Republic*, and the *New York Times Magazine*.

Commerce, Department of, one of the executive departments of the federal government. Its objectives include the promotion of domestic and foreign commerce and the encouragement of the growth of American industries. Originally part of the Department of Commerce and Labor, Commerce became a separate department in 1913. The Bureau of Patents and Trademarks, the Bureau of the Census, and the Weather Bureau are part of the Commerce Department.

Committee to Re-elect the President (CREEP) *See* WATERGATE.

Committee on Public Information (CPI) (1917), a committee formed by President Woodrow Wilson to launch a propaganda campaign to gain public support for American participation in WORLD WAR I. The CPI was headed by GEORGE CREEL, a progressive journalist. Many of the patriotic posters and pamphlets were exaggerated depictions of German deeds, some of them invented altogether. The program became a campaign of political warfare against Germany and its allies.

Committees of Correspondence (1764), groups of Patriots organized before the AMERICAN REVOLUTION to exchange information regarding British actions in the colonies. At the urging of SAMUEL ADAMS, the first committee was formed in Boston, with others following later. The Committees of Correspondence provided a network for molding public opinion and spreading propaganda against Great Britain.

Common Cause (1970), nonpartisan citizen's organization and lobby. Common Cause was established by John W. Gardner, former secretary of Health, Education, and Welfare. One of its original goals was to end the war in VIETNAM and streamline progressive changes in problems dealing with poverty, consumer fraud, civil rights, and ecology. The organization supports numerous liberal political reforms, including campaign finance, nuclear control agreements, and government ethics and accountability. It monitors congressional meetings and lobbyists on both federal and state levels.

Compact Theory, the theory that the U.S. Constitution was an agreement between the sovereign states creating a federal government of limited powers with the states retaining all other powers. The states could decide if and when the compact was broken. The theory was first expressed in the VIRGINIA AND KENTUCKY RESOLUTIONS and is a key component of the STATES' RIGHTS DOCTRINE and the doctrine of NULLIFICATION; it also asserts a state's right to secede from the Union. JOHN C. CALHOUN was a leading exponent of the compact theory.

Compromise of 1790, an agreement brokered by then Secretary of State THOMAS JEFFERSON, with the tacit approval of President GEORGE WASHINGTON, between Secretary of the Treasury ALEXANDER HAMILTON and Representative JAMES MADISON, under which Madison agreed to provide votes in the House for Hamilton's fiscal programs in return for Hamilton's agreement and that of his allies in the House and the Senate to move the capital from New York to Philadelphia for ten years and then to a permanent home on the banks of the Potomac.

Compromise of 1850, a series of acts through which Congress hoped to solve the dispute between abolitionists in the North and slaveholders in the South over the question of slavery in the territories gained in the Mexican

War. DANIEL WEBSTER, HENRY CLAY, and STEPHEN A. DOUGLAS supported the compromise; JOHN C. CALHOUN led the opposition. To appease the antislavery forces, the slave trade was prohibited in the District of Columbia, and California joined the Union as a free state. To satisfy the South, a stricter Fugitive Slave Law was enacted, making it easier to recover runaway slaves. The remainder of the land obtained from Mexico would be organized as the Utah and New Mexico territories, where slavery would be determined in each by POPULAR SOVEREIGNTY. The Compromise of 1850 helped delay civil war for about ten years.

Compromise of 1877, bargain settling the disputed presidential ELECTION OF 1876. Democratic candidate SAMUEL J. TILDEN led in popular and electoral (184–165) votes over his Republican opponent, RUTHERFORD B. HAYES. But corruption, fraud, and violence in three southern states and problems in Oregon left twenty electoral votes in question. Congress appointed a fifteen-member electoral commission to settle the issue. By a vote of eight to seven, Hayes received all twenty votes and became president, 185–184. Southern Democrats were furious but agreed to let Hayes take office peacefully if in return he agreed to pull all federal troops from the southern states. The troops were removed in 1877, ending the RECONSTRUCTION era and depriving the freed blacks of federal protection.

Compromise Tariff (1833), act sponsored by HENRY CLAY to appease the southern states who opposed any type of protective tariff. South Carolina's nullification of the tariff of 1832 and its threat to secede from the Union prompted its passage. It provided that the rates be progressively reduced until 1842, when they would be approximately the same as they were in 1816. The Compromise Tariff brought about South Carolina's repeal of its ordinance of nullification.

Comstock Lode, several large veins of silver and gold discovered in 1859–60 in Nevada, where Virginia City now stands. Named for Henry Comstock, one of the discoverers, the lode yielded almost $300 million worth of precious metals, becoming the richest lode of its size in U.S. history.

Concord, Battle of (April 19, 1775), the second clash of the AMERICAN REVOLUTION between the Patriots and the British. Because of unrest following the passage of the INTOLERABLE ACTS, British troops were sent to capture SAMUEL ADAMS and JOHN HANCOCK, and to destroy military supplies at Concord, Massachusetts. Already alerted to news of the mission by PAUL REVERE, Samuel Prescott, and William Dawes, Hancock and Adams escaped and the Patriots were ready. At the village green at Lexington, a skirmish occurred and eight MINUTEMEN were killed. A clash at the Concord Bridge resulted in casualties on both sides. The British were turned away and retreated to Boston. By the time they reached Charlestown, they had suffered 273 casualties, about three times as many as the colonists. War existed even before the Second Continental Congress had met or independence had been declared.

Conestoga Wagons, large, horse-drawn, four-wheeled wagons used by the pioneers migrating westward. Also called covered wagons or prairie schooners, they were developed in the Conestoga River valley in Lancaster County, Pennsylvania, around 1750. Many wagons were assembled to form a wagon train, led by a wagon master and guide, for the trip to California and Oregon Territory.

Confederate Constitution (1861–65), drawn up in the first capital of the CONFEDERATE STATES OF AMERICA, Montgomery, Alabama, after the secession of southern states from the Union. Modeled after the U.S. Constitution, the document included a few significant differences. The president served for one six-year term, and the powers of the central government were greatly limited. The Constitution prohibited tariffs, allowed cabinet members to be members of Congress, and banned the importation of slaves.

Confederate States of America (Confederacy), Organized in February 1861, the Confederacy consisted of eleven states that seceded from the Union: Alabama, Arkansas, Florida, Georgia, Louisiana, Mississippi, North Carolina, South Carolina, Tennessee, Texas, and Virginia. JEFFERSON DAVIS became president and ALEXANDER H. STEPHENS vice president. The Confederacy ended with the end of the CIVIL WAR.

Congressional Medal of Honor, the highest military award granted for courage in action at the risk of life beyond the call of duty, established by Congress in 1862.

Congress of Industrial Organizations (CIO), an association of labor unions. Originally formed as the Committee for Industrial Organization in 1935 by John L. Lewis to unionize both skilled and nonskilled workers, the organization grew rapidly and split away from the AMERICAN FEDERATION OF LABOR (AFL) in 1938, becoming the CIO. The CIO continued to grow with the objective of organizing mass-production industries in the United States. It fell short in organizing the South in the 1940s, and grew bureaucratic and conservative in the same era. In 1955 it joined with the AFL to form the AFL-CIO.

Congress of Racial Equality (CORE), a civil rights organization that promotes quality education as well as economic and political opportunities for blacks. Founded in 1942, CORE seeks ways to enable black communities to control their local services. During the 1960s the group, advocating nonviolence, sponsored FREEDOM RIDES in the South and cosponsored the March on Washington.

Congress of the United States, the institution of the American government entrusted by Article I of the Constitution with legislative powers. It has two chambers — the SENATE and the HOUSE OF REPRESENTATIVES.

Its powers include lawmaking and investigation. A bill (proposed law) must be adopted by a majority of the House and of the Senate and be signed by the president before it becomes a law; if the president vetoes the bill, the House and the Senate may repass it over his veto by a two-thirds vote in each chamber. Each chamber determines its own rules and procedures; both the House and the Senate use committees to carry on their business, as well as internal party organizations divided between the majority and the minority parties. The Constitution stipulates that Congress must meet every January. The vice president of the United States presides over the Senate and the Speaker of the House presides over the House of Representatives.

Conkling, Roscoe (1829–88), politician. A senator from New York, Conkling became the leader of the STALWARTS, or conservative wing, of the REPUBLICAN PARTY after 1876. A presidential hopeful that year, Conkling lost the nomination to Rutherford B. Hayes.

Connecticut (Constitution State) entered the Union on January 9, 1788, as the fifth state. (See maps, pages 540 and 541.) Connecticut's largest cities include Hartford (the capital), Bridgeport, and New Haven, the home of Yale University. Connecticut is a national leader in the manufacturing of metal goods. Agriculture, including tobacco, and tourism are important industries. Mystic Seaport, a re-creation of a New England coastal village of the 1800s, features old whaling vessels. The world's first nuclear-powered submarine, *Nautilus,* was built at Groton in 1954. The oldest daily newspaper in the United States is the *Hartford Courant,* which started in 1764. Noted personalities from Connecticut include inventor ELI WHITNEY and Chief Justice OLIVER ELLSWORTH.

Connolly, Maureen (1934–69), tennis player. By age sixteen, Connolly had won more than fifty championships and was the youngest woman (until Tracy Austin in 1979) to win the national women's single championship. In 1953 "Little Mo," as she was called by the press, became one of only a few players to win the Grand Slam. After being named woman athlete of the year for 1952–53, Connolly suffered a crushed leg in a horse-riding accident, cutting short her career at age nineteen.

Conscription *See* DRAFT.

Conservation Movement, a policy designed to preserve the nation's natural resources. The movement gathered strength at the beginning of the twentieth century largely through the efforts of President THEODORE ROOSEVELT, GIFFORD PINCHOT, and JOHN MUIR. The development of national parks, flood control, reforestation, and preservation of minerals, soil, water, and wildlife are objectives of federal and state planning. President FRANKLIN ROOSEVELT's, legislation did much to further the conservation movement through the creation of the CIVILIAN CONSERVATION CORPS. The movement was the precursor of the modern ecology movement.

Conservatism, a political philosophy that emphasizes tradition, tending to oppose change and preserve established institutions and values. A conservative is usually moderate and cautious, and skeptical of government involvement in social and economic programs. Some conservatives in the 1960s to the 1980s, however, were more accepting of "big government" intervention in such matters as defense and many issues of morality. Conservatism, contrasted with LIBERALISM, has tended to be associated in the twentieth century with the REPUBLICAN PARTY.

Constitution, U.S., the document that establishes the form of the national government and defines the rights and liberties of the American people. Written in 1787 by the CONSTITUTIONAL CONVENTION and adopted in 1787–88, the Constitution went into effect on March 4, 1789, after ratification by nine states. It is the oldest written constitution in the world. It creates a federal government of three branches — legislative, executive, and judicial; separates powers among these branches and establishes a system of checks and balances among them; and defines the distribution of power between the federal government and the states. As the supreme law of the land, it is regularly interpreted by federal and state courts in cases involving individual rights and the powers of government. The actual Constitution is housed in the National Archives in Washington, D.C. For the complete text of the Constitution, SEE APPENDIX.

Constitutional Convention (1787), a meeting at the State House (now INDEPENDENCE HALL) in Philadelphia of delegates from twelve of the thirteen states, which resulted in the framing of the U.S. CONSTITUTION. Originally proposed by the 1786 ANNAPOLIS CONVENTION and called by the CONTINENTAL CONGRESS for the sole purpose of revising the ARTICLES OF CONFEDERATION, the delegates to the convention scrapped the Articles and instead decided to frame an entirely new charter of government. Meeting in secret, the delegates (thirty to forty at any one time; fifty-five total) deliberated for four months. GEORGE WASHINGTON presided over the convention. JAMES MADISON drafted the VIRGINIA PLAN that was the basis of the convention's work, and kept a private journal of the debates that is a major document of American constitutional thought. Other key delegates included ROGER SHERMAN, BENJAMIN FRANKLIN, GOUVERNEUR MORRIS (who wrote the final version of the Constitution), WILLIAM PATERSON, JOHN RUTLEDGE, Hugh Williamson, GEORGE MASON, and JAMES WILSON.

Constitutional Union Party, a political party organized during the presidential CAMPAIGN OF 1860. It nominated Senator JOHN BELL of Tennessee for president and EDWARD EVERETT of Massachusetts for vice president. Its platform called for obedience to the U.S. Constitution, preservation of the Union, and enforcement of federal laws. The party, composed mostly of WHIGS, ignored the burning issue of slavery, hoping resolution of the issue could be accomplished within the Union. It drew thirty-nine electoral votes from the border states of Kentucky, Tennessee, and Virginia, and over 500,000 popular votes, but disappeared with the advent of the Civil War.

Continental Army, the military force organized by the Second Continental Congress with GEORGE WASHINGTON as commander in chief. Also known as the Patriot or Colonial army, it defeated the British during the AMERICAN REVOLUTION, despite problems of lack of money, shortages of equipment and transportation, desertions, brief enlistment periods, the spread of disease, and inadequate food, clothing, and supplies.

Continental Congresses, two gatherings of delegates during the colonial period. The First Continental Congress met in Philadelphia in 1774 and included representatives from all the colonies except Georgia. It adopted a Declaration of Rights and Grievances, which it sent to Parliament. It also organized the Continental Association to boycott English goods and called for a second congress if King George III did not act upon its demands. The Second Continental Congress met in 1775. It organized the CONTINENTAL ARMY and appointed GEORGE WASHINGTON commander in chief. It adopted the DECLARATION OF INDEPENDENCE on July 4, 1776, and began to frame the ARTICLES OF CONFEDERATION. It assumed the responsibility of directing the war and served as the government for the colonies from 1781 to 1789.

Contract with America (1994–95), Republican-led plan during the Clinton administration. Developed and promoted by then House of Representatives minority leader NEWT GINGRICH during the congressional election campaigns of 1994, the Contract with America, endorsed by more than 300 Republican congressional candidates, championed several reforms including a balanced budget amendment, limitations on welfare benefits, a line-item veto, a middle-class tax cut, and term limits for members of Congress. Gingrich, assuming the role of Speaker in 1995, brought all provisions of the contract to a floor vote in the House of Representatives in the first 100 days of the new Congress. The House approved all but one of the provisions (the proposed constitutional amendment on congressional term limits). However, bitter contentions with Democratic president BILL CLINTON, along with Senate opposition to items like the balanced-budget amendment and the line-item veto, prevented enactment of most of the plan.

Conway Cabal (1777), a conspiracy to remove Gen. GEORGE WASHINGTON from command of the Continental army during the AMERICAN REVOLUTION after defeats at BRANDYWINE and GERMANTOWN. Gen. Thomas Conway wrote to Congress and Gen. HORATIO GATES, who coveted the post of commander in chief, criticizing Washington's ability and leadership. Following the revelation of the plot, Conway resigned and both he and Gates wrote letters of apology to Washington for the incident.

Cooke, Jay (1821–1905), financier. In 1861 Cooke began a banking house, Jay Cooke and Company, which helped finance the Union effort during the Civil War by selling government bonds nationwide. His company failed in 1873 after investing heavily in the construction of the Northern Pacific Railway. Cooke repaid his creditors and acquired a new fortune through investments in silver mining.

Coolidge, (John) Calvin (1872–1933), thirtieth president of the United States (1923–29). Born in Plymouth, Vermont, Coolidge graduated from Amherst College in 1895. He entered Republican politics and rose steadily in the ranks. After three terms as lieutenant governor, he became governor of Massachusetts in 1918. The BOSTON POLICE STRIKE of 1919 brought him national attention, and in 1920 he was selected as WARREN G. HARDING's running mate. In 1923 Harding died, and Coolidge became president. He was reelected in 1924 because of prosperity, his popularity, and his quiet, honest, frugal manner. A strong supporter of private enterprise, he stated, "The business of America is business," and encouraged the stock market boom of the 1920s. He did not seek the nomination in 1928, stating, "I do not choose to run," though many historians believe that he hoped to be drafted by the 1928 Republican convention. He retired to write his autobiography and articles on public issues.

Cooper, Gary (1901–61), film actor. Good-looking, lanky, laconic, and unpretentious, Cooper played the all-American male, becoming a "hero" to millions of movie viewers. He played major roles in such films as *The Virginian* (1929), *Beau Geste* (1939), *Meet John Doe* (1941), *Mr. Deeds Goes to Town* (1936), *Pride of the Yankees* (1942), and *For Whom the Bell Tolls* (1943). Cooper received Academy Awards for best actor in *Sergeant York* (1941) and *High Noon* (1953).

Cooper, James Fenimore (1789–1851), novelist and social critic. Cooper is best known for *The Leatherstocking Tales,* a set of five novels about American frontiersman Natty Bumppo that includes *The Deerslayer* (1841) and *The Last of the Mohicans* (1826). Cooper was the first author to seriously portray American scenes and characters. After serving in the U.S. Navy he wrote *The Pilot* (1823), the first American novel about the sea.

Cooper, Peter (1791–1883), inventor, manufacturer, and philanthropist. Cooper built the first steam-driven locomotive, called Tom Thumb, for the Baltimore and Ohio Railroad in 1830 and eventually contributed to the development of the American iron industry. His wealth enabled him to finance much of Cyrus Field's undersea ATLANTIC CABLE. Cooper supported many political and social reforms after the Civil War. The GREENBACK PARTY nominated him for president in the ELECTION OF 1876, at age eighty-five. He also founded Cooper Union (1859), offering free courses in science and art.

Copland, Aaron (1900–90), composer, pianist, and conductor. Copland, one of the most important writers of twentieth-century music and a life-long liberal, promoted through his compositions the idea that all music — not just popular songs — should be accessible to the people. He frequently used American themes and rhythms in his serious works. Copland won the Pulitzer Prize for "Appalachian Spring" (1945) and an Academy Award for his music for *The Heiress* (1949).

Copley, John Singleton (1738–1815), portrait painter. Copley's portraits of such men as John Hancock, Paul Revere, and Samuel Adams were much ad-mired throughout New England and in Europe. At the urging of BENJAMIN WEST, Copley moved to London in 1774, where he painted many histori-cal works. His paintings are characterized by brilliant color, texture, and realism.

Copperheads, a group of Northern Democrats who opposed the CIVIL WAR and wanted an immediate peace settlement. Also called Peace Dem-ocrats, Copperheads argued that it was not worth the cost in human lives to force the Confederacy to surrender. They organized secret societies to per-suade Union soldiers to desert, and they assisted in the escape of Confederate prisoners. Some even smuggled guns and ammunition into the South. Copperheads wore the head of Liberty from the copper cent as a symbol, but their name — a term of abuse applied to them by Republicans — comes from the poisonous snakes that strike without warning.

Coral Sea, Battle of (May 4–8, 1942), a naval battle in the Pacific during WORLD WAR II, which blocked Japan's push southeast toward Australia. The Japanese and American forces fought a four-day battle in which only aircraft launched from aircraft carriers did the fighting; one ship did not fire at another. This air battle was one of the turning points of World War II.

Corbin, Margaret (1751–1800), heroine of the AMERICAN REVOLUTION. The Battle of Fort Washington (now Manhattan) in 1776 found Corbin at her husband's side, cooking for the men of the regiment. Upon the death of her husband by enemy fire, she took his place at the cannon until severely wounded. She was one of the first women in the United States to receive a military pension. A monument in her honor stands at West Point, where she is buried.

Cornwallis, Charles (1738–1805), British general of the AMERICAN REVO-LUTION. Cornwallis helped capture New York in 1776 and in 1780 directed the British southern campaign. Following his defeat of Gen. NATHANIEL GREENE at the Battle of GUILFORD COURT HOUSE, he moved into Virginia, where a French fleet and French and American troops surrounded him at YORKTOWN on October 19, 1781, forcing his surrender and ending the Revolution.

Coronado, Francisco (1510–54), Spanish explorer of the American Southwest and discoverer of the Grand Canyon. Coronado searched for the legendary SEVEN CITIES OF CIBOLA after hearing reports that these cities were rich in gold but found only poor Pueblo Indians. He also explored as far as present-day Kansas in search of gold and silver, but again without success. He finally became discouraged and returned to Mexico.

Corporate Responsibility Act (Sarbanes-Oxley Act) (2002), legislation passed in response to accounting irregularities and corporate fraud scandals at industry giants such as ENRON and WORLDCOM. These scandals contributed to steep drops in the stock market by 2002. The act imposes significant new changes in both auditing practices and corporate responsibility and strengthens criminal penalties for violations of securities laws. It attempts to increase investor confidence by setting in place numerous provisions, including the stiffening of standards for auditing firms and public accountants, as well as restricting the services that they can offer. It requires a rotation of audit partners and limits the hiring practices of publicly traded companies.

Corregidor, a rocky island at the entrance to Manila Bay in the Philippines. Sometimes called "Gibraltar of the Pacific," the island fell to the Japanese May 6, 1942, following a long siege against American and Filipino troops during WORLD WAR II. The surrender ended organized resistance in the Philippines until the United States freed the island of Luzon in 1945. Today Corregidor is a World War II memorial battlefield park.

Corrupt Bargain *See* JOHN QUINCY ADAMS.

Cosby, Bill (1937–), comedian and performer. Cosby became television's first black actor to star in a dramatic series ("I Spy" with Robert Culp, 1965–68). "The Bill Cosby Show" and "The Cosby Show" were other television successes. His credits include participation in public television's educational programs for children, performances in films, the production of many comedy records, and the winning of both Emmy and Grammy awards. Cosby is one of America's wealthiest and most popular entertainers.

Cotton, John (1585–1652), Puritan clergyman and leading member of the Congregationalist church in America. Facing persecution for his Puritan views in England, Cotton immigrated to Boston in 1633, where he became a respected leader. Believing in a close partnership between church and state, Cotton supported strict Puritanism and engaged in controversies involving ROGER WILLIAMS and ANNE HUTCHINSON, which resulted in their banishment from the MASSACHUSETTS BAY COLONY.

Cotton Gin, a machine invented by ELI WHITNEY in 1793 that separated seeds from cotton fiber. Before its invention, it took one person a full day to pick the seeds from a pound of cotton. The gin made it profitable to grow cotton (thus increasing demand for slaves) because it was easy to make, inexpensive, and enabled a person to process fifty pounds of cotton a day.

Coughlin, Father Charles (1891–1979), Roman Catholic priest and radio broadcaster. Coughlin spoke to millions in his weekly radio programs, which began in 1926 as sermons for the Shrine of the Little Flower church in Michigan, but later became tirades on political issues. Originally an admirer of Franklin D. Roosevelt, he turned against him and made bitter attacks on him and his policies. He became an anti-Semitic extremist in the 1930s, expressing sympathy for European fascists. Popular for a while, he gradually lost his followers. In 1942 the Roman Catholic Church ordered him to cease his political activities, and he became a parish priest.

Court-Packing Plan (1937), a proposal by President FRANKLIN D. ROO-SEVELT to reorganize the SUPREME COURT. Frustrated by a series of Court decisions striking down many New Deal laws as unconstitutional, Roosevelt argued that the justices were "nine old men" who were overworked and needed help. He proposed to nominate up to six new justices — one new justice for every justice over seventy who did not retire. The plan outraged FDR's opponents, who rejected the plan as an attempt to overturn the constitutional system of CHECKS AND BALANCES. They charged that he was seeking to become a dictator by destroying the only institution of government that did not bend to his will. Even his supporters divided over the plan, which Congress ultimately rejected after Chief Justice CHARLES EVANS HUGHES proved that the Court was not overworked and declared that the proposal would make the Court more inefficient.

Cousy, Bob (1928–), basketball player. Cousy, a great play-making guard, starred thirteen seasons for the Boston Celtics of the National Basketball Association. His ball handling and dazzling passing earned him the nickname of basketball's "Houdini of the Hardwood." One of the most exciting players in basketball history, he sparked the Boston Celtics to six NBA championships. He won the most valuable player award in 1957.

Cowpens, Battle of (1781), a confrontation during the AMERICAN REVOLU-TION at Cowpens, South Carolina. This brilliant victory for the American colonists, led by Daniel Morgan, almost completely destroyed the British forces.

Cox, Archibald C. (1912–2004), legal scholar and public official. Cox taught at Harvard Law School beginning in 1946. He was solicitor general in the Kennedy administration from 1961 to 1965, arguing many cases before the U.S. Supreme Court. In May 1973, as the WATERGATE scandal unfolded, President RICHARD M. NIXON named ELLIOT RICHARDSON as his new attorney general, and Richardson named Cox as special prosecutor in the Watergate case. When Cox tried to obtain secret presidential tape recordings for use in his investigation, Nixon refused, citing EXECUTIVE PRIVI-LEGE. In October 1973 Nixon ordered Cox not to seek the tapes, but Cox defied the order. Nixon then ordered Richardson to fire Cox, but Richardson refused and resigned his office, as did his second-in-command, William

Ruckelshaus. Solicitor General Robert H. Bork fired Cox, but a federal district court later ruled the firing illegal. Cox became a national hero and symbol of integrity for his role in the Watergate investigations.

Cox, James M. (1870–1957), politician. As governor of Ohio, Cox ran for president on the Democratic ticket in the ELECTION OF 1920 with running mate FRANKLIN D. ROOSEVELT. They defended the Treaty of Versailles and the League of Nations, but suffered a landslide defeat by Republicans WARREN G. HARDING and CALVIN COOLIDGE. This was the first election in which women had the right to vote throughout the country.

Coxey, Jacob (1854–1951), leader of "Coxey's Army." To dramatize the plight of the jobless and seek relief from the federal government, Coxey led a group of unemployed workers from Ohio to Washington, D.C. The march on Washington took place in 1894, in the depth of the depression that followed the financial panic of 1893. When Coxey's Army reached Washington, they were dispersed by the police and Coxey was arrested for trespassing on the Capitol lawn. Eventually he helped persuade Congress to pass legislation to help the unemployed.

Cozzens, James Gould (1903–78), author. Cozzens wrote realistic, detailed novels about moral conflicts and idealism among upper-class people. He first attracted critical attention with his novella *S. S. San Pedro* (1931). *Guard of Honor* (1948), about his World War II experiences, won the Pulitzer Prize for fiction in 1949. Other novels include *The Last Adam* (1933), *Men and Brethren* (1936), and the best-selling *By Love Possessed* (1957).

Crandall, Prudence (1803–90), educator and abolitionist. A Connecticut teacher, Crandall established the first school for black girls in New England. Canterbury Female Boarding School for white girls, formed in 1831, closed because of community opposition following the admission of one black girl. After reopening the school with twenty black girls, Crandall was arrested for breaking a state law that forbade education of blacks who did not come from Connecticut. Although Crandall was convicted, a higher court reversed the decision. Local mob reaction, however, ultimately closed the school for good.

Crane, Hart (Harold; 1899–1932), poet. Crane published his first volume of verse, *White Buildings*, in 1926. Inspired by Walt Whitman, he broke with his contemporaries and sought a spiritual affirmation of American life. He wrote *The Bridge* (1930), which used the Brooklyn Bridge as a complex symbol of the creative power of human beings and the meaning of life in America. Crane, who spent much time traveling, took his own life while on a ship to the United States from Mexico.

Crane, Stephen (1871–1900), author. Crane's powerful novel about the Civil War, *The Red Badge of Courage* (1895), as well as his earlier novel *Maggie: A Girl of the Streets* (1893), set new standards of realistic, unflinching depictions of American life in fiction. Crane died of tuberculosis when he was only twenty-eight, but in his brief life he proved himself an accomplished writer of novels, short stories, and poetry.

Crawford, Joan (Lucille LeSueur; 1908–77), actress. Crawford starred in over fifty films. Starting as the personification of 1920s flappers in such films as *Our Dancing Daughters,* she became noted for her portrayal of strong, assertive women in films like *The Women* (1939) and *Mildred Pierce* (1945; for which she won an Academy Award). She became the first woman director on the board of the Pepsi-Cola Company following the death of her husband, who was its director, in 1959.

Crawford, William (1772–1834), politician. In the ELECTION OF 1824 Crawford was picked as the presidential nominee by the Democratic-Republican caucus in Congress. Because he suffered a crippling stroke, his campaign stalled; in the contested election, JOHN QUINCY ADAMS was chosen by the House of Representatives. Crawford served in the U.S. Senate from Georgia, as minister to France, as secretary of war, and as secretary of the treasury.

Crazy Horse (1842?–77), chief of the Oglala tribe of the Sioux Indians. Joining ranks with SITTING BULL, Crazy Horse led his forces over Gen. George Crook at the Battle of the Rosebud on June 17, 1866. They then surrounded Col. GEORGE ARMSTRONG CUSTER at the Little Bighorn River in Montana, resulting in the death of Custer and all his men in what became popularly known as "Custer's Last Stand." Crazy Horse was pursued by Col. Nelson Miles and surrendered in Nebraska on September 5. He was stabbed to death when he resisted being locked up in a guardhouse after his arrest.

Crazy Horse Memorial, unfinished sculpture honoring Oglala Sioux Chief CRAZY HORSE and all Native Americans. Currently under construction at Thunderhead Mountain near Custer, South Dakota, the memorial will be the largest statue in the world. When finished, the mountain carving "in the round" will be 641 feet long by 563 feet high. Work began in 1948 by American sculptor Korczak Ziolkowski at the invitation of Lakota Chief Henry Standing Bear, and it continues under the direction of the Crazy Horse Memorial Foundation.

Crédit Mobilier, a construction company organized in 1864 by a few important stockholders to build the Union Pacific Railroad. The company bribed congressmen by selling them shares of stock at half the market value in return for favorable legislation regarding public land grants. Exposed in 1873 during the Grant administration, the unraveling Crédit Mobilier scandal revealed that Congressman Oakes Ames had distributed such stock to Vice President SCHUYLER COLFAX and Congressman HENRY WILSON. Also implicated were Speaker of the House James G. Blaine and Representative JAMES A. GARFIELD, both of whom denied the charges.

Creel, George (1876–1953), journalist. Appointed by President Woodrow Wilson to head the COMMITTEE ON PUBLIC INFORMATION from 1917 to 1919. Creel served, in effect, as U.S. minister of propaganda during World

War I, depicting the United States as the champion of justice and liberty. Creel mobilized public support for liberty loans and the war effort.

Crichton, Michael (1942–), writer, filmmaker. After graduating from Harvard Medical School, Crichton began his writing career. Called the father of the techno-thriller, he writes books that explore scientific themes, including *The Andromeda Strain* (1969), *Jurassic Park* (1990), and *Prey* (2002). Twelve of his books have been made into films. As creator and coexecutive producer of the television drama *ER*, Crichton is the only person to have the number one book, movie, and TV show simultaneously. He wrote and directed *Westworld* (1973), the first feature film to employ computer-generated special effects. Crichton has won numerous awards for his writing and film work, and in 2000 he was honored by having a newly discovered species of dinosaur named in his honor (Bienosaurus crichtoni).

Crittenden Compromise (December 18, 1860), a proposal by Senator John Crittenden of Kentucky to the U.S. Senate to keep the South from leaving the Union. Consisting of six constitutional amendments, the compromise extended the MISSOURI COMPROMISE line across the country to the Pacific Coast and allowed slavery south of that line. It also denied Congress the right to abolish slavery. Opposed by President-elect Abraham Lincoln, it was defeated in committee.

Crockett, Davy (1786–1836), frontiersman, soldier, and U.S. congressman from Tennessee. Crockett was a teller of tall tales, who became something of a folk hero. After moving to Texas, he joined the defenders of the ALAMO, where he was killed.

Cronkite, Walter (1916–), journalist and television reporter. As anchor of the CBS evening news from 1962 to 1981, Cronkite became the world's most widely seen newsman. He served as a war correspondent in Europe during World War II and provided ongoing coverage of the Vietnam War. His twenty-four consecutive hours of coverage of the *Apollo 11* landing on the moon and his extensive knowledge of the space program earned him the title of "honorary astronaut," bestowed by the astronaut corps.

Crosby, Bing (Harry; 1904–77), singer and film actor. Radio brought Crosby great popularity in the 1930s. He entertained G.I.s during World War II and starred in many movies. In 1944 he received an Academy Award for best actor in *Going My Way*. During Crosby's five-decade career he sold more than 30 million records, including one of the all-time classics, "White Christmas."

Cuban Missile Crisis (October 22–November 20, 1962), a confrontation between the United States and the Soviet Union regarding Soviet leader Nikita Khrushchev's placement of missiles in Cuba. The United States found evidence of missile bases capable of launching nuclear attacks on American cities and protested to the United Nations. President JOHN F. KENNEDY ordered a quarantine, or blockade, of military equipment being shipped to Cuba and persuaded the Soviet Union to remove all offensive weapons from the island. This confrontation was the most crucial conflict between the two superpowers during the COLD WAR and is considered to have been the closest brush with nuclear warfare in the 1960s.

Cuffe, Paul (1759–1817), black sea captain and philanthropist. Cuffe, a Quaker, was active in obtaining legal rights and privileges for blacks. It was through his efforts that they received the right to vote in Massachusetts in 1783. The son of an African-born slave and a Nantucket Indian woman, Cuffe earned a fortune from whaling and sea trade. He advocated the colonization of American blacks in Africa, using his own ship to finance their resettlement in 1815.

Cumberland Road, a nineteenth-century surfaced route to the West. Originally known as the National Road, it was authorized by Thomas Jefferson. Construction began in 1811 at Cumberland, Maryland; the road extended to Wheeling, West Virginia, by 1818 and to Vandalia, Illinois, by 1850. It was built on solid stone foundation with a gravel topping, but delays associated with the War of 1812, sectionalism, and lack of commitment affected its completion. Today it is known as U.S. Route 40, and its sturdy stone bridges still carry traffic.

Cummings, E. E. (Edward Estlin; 1894–1962), popular but controversial poet, painter, and playwright. Cummings's poetry features unconventional use of words, grammar, and spelling. He dropped punctuation and capital letters, even in his name (e e cummings), and arranged his poems in patterns on the page. His themes range from positive appreciations of life, love, and joy to bitter satire.

Cuomo, Mario (1932–), politician and liberal spokesman. Elected the first Italian-American governor of the state of New York in 1982, Cuomo was reelected in 1986 by the greatest margin in the history of New York's gubernatorial races. He won a third term in 1990. His eloquent keynote speech at the 1984 Democratic National Convention in San Francisco brought him national prominence, and he is often mentioned as a possible presidential candidate.

Curley, James M. (1874–1958), politician. Curley, best known for the four terms he served as the mayor of Boston (1914–18, 1922–26, 1930–34, 1946–50), enjoyed particular popularity among Boston's Irish immigrants. He also served in the U.S. House of Representatives (1911–14, 1943–47) and as governor of Massachusetts (1935–37). While mayor, he spent five months in federal prison after a conviction for mail fraud; President Harry S. Truman pardoned him in 1950. Curley's colorful political career, which spanned half a century, provided the inspiration for the novel *The Last Hurrah* (1956) by Edwin O'Connor.

Currier and Ives, a firm of American lithographers that published colored etchings representing American rural life during the middle and late 1800s.

Partners Nathaniel Currier (1813–88) and James Ives (1824–95) produced over 4,000 pictures, becoming America's most popular makers of hand-colored prints. Their work also appeared in *Harper's Weekly*.

Curtis, Charles (1860–1936), thirty-first vice president of the United States under HERBERT HOOVER (1929–33). A member of the House of Representatives for fourteen years and the U.S. Senate for twenty-one years, Curtis served as Senate majority leader and a member of the Senate Rules Committee. In 1928 Curtis, of Indian descent, was a favorite son nominee for president from Kansas at the Republican convention, but was selected as running mate for Herbert Hoover, instead. The Hoover-Curtis ticket defeated the Democrats, headed by AL SMITH. Hoover and Curtis were renominated in 1932 but lost to FRANKLIN D. ROOSEVELT.

Curtis, George W. (1824–92), author, editor, and reformer. Curtis served as editor of *Harper's* magazine, for which he wrote the "Easy Chair" column, and as political editor of *Harper's Weekly*. One of the founders of the Republican party, he was chairman of the National Civil Service Reform League (1865).

Cushing, Caleb (1800–79), lawyer and statesman. While serving as the first American envoy to China in 1843–45, Cushing negotiated the TREATY OF WANGHIA (1844), the first treaty opening Chinese ports to trade with the United States. Cushing served in the House of Representatives (1835–43) as a Whig, as attorney general (1853–57) as a Democrat appointed by President Franklin Pierce, and as U.S. minister to Spain (1874–77). Cushing acted as senior counsel for the United States in the settlement of the ALABAMA CLAIMS dispute (1871–72).

Custer, George Armstrong (1839–76), Civil War general and Indian fighter. Custer fought at the first Battle of BULL RUN and served with Gen. George B. McClellan in the PENINSULAR CAMPAIGN during the Civil War. After years of attacking and destroying the Plains Indians, Custer in 1876 was sent to the Little Bighorn River in Montana. Here he launched a surprise attack on Sioux Indians led by CRAZY HORSE and SITTING BULL. Unaware of the Sioux's superior strength, Custer and some 250 men were surrounded and killed in a battle lasting only a few hours. "Custer's Last Stand," as it came to be known, was the army's worst defeat in the western campaigns of the Indian wars.

Czolgosz, Leon (1873–1901), assassin of President WILLIAM McKINLEY. An anarchist, Czolgosz shot the president twice during a reception at the Pan-American Exposition in Buffalo, New York, September 6, 1901. He had concealed his revolver in a bandage and fired from only two feet away. His six-page confession said he wanted to change the government. McKinley died a week later from infection in one of the wounds. Czolgosz was electrocuted in Auburn, New York, on October 29, 1901.

D **Daley, Richard J.** (1902–76), politician. Daley served as mayor of Chicago for six terms beginning in 1955 and was Cook County Democratic chairman. He played an important role in national politics through his leadership of the Illinois Democratic delegation. One of the last of the big-city machine politicians, he promoted public works and expanded municipal services. A clash between Chicago police and anti-Vietnam War demonstrators during the 1968 Democratic National Convention seriously marred his national image and affected the remainder of his political career. His son, Richard M. Daley, was elected mayor of Chicago in 1989.

Dallas, George M. (1792–1864), vice president of the United States (1845–49). A Democrat, Dallas served in the U.S. Senate, and as minister to Russia and Great Britain. He persuaded Great Britain to renounce its claim to the right to search vessels on the high seas. The city of Dallas, Texas, was named for him.

Dana, Charles (1819–97), editor and public official. Dana served as managing editor of the *New York Tribune* and editor-owner of the *New York Sun*. His human interest stories and editorials were aimed at making newspapers more readable. He also served as an assistant secretary of war; his book *Recollections of the Civil War* (1898) recorded his observations from the front.

Dana, Richard Henry (1815–82), author. Dana recounted the experiences of his sea voyages to California via Cape Horn (1834–36) in his classic book, *Two Years before the Mast* (1840). Dana also helped form the antislavery FREE-SOIL PARTY.

Dandridge, Dorothy (1923–65), actress. A child star and member of the singing and dancing Dandridge Sisters, Dorothy Dandridge's early roles were stereotypical black female parts, but her singing ability brought her popularity in nightclubs around the country. Dandridge was the first African-American woman to be nominated for a Best Actress Oscar for her performance in *Carmen Jones* (1954). Other films included *Island in the Sun* (1957) and *Porgy and Bess* (1959), for which she won a Golden Globe award. Despite her success, she had to fight hard for leading roles at a time when they were seldom available to black women. Her life was plagued by failed marriages and addictions to drugs and alcohol, and she died from an overdose of antidepression medication.

Dare, Virginia (1587–?), the first white English child born in the New World. She was the daughter of settlers of the LOST COLONY OF ROANOKE Island off the North Carolina coast. Dare disappeared with other members of the settlement after supply ships returned to England.

Darrow, Clarence (1857–1938), lawyer. Noted for his willingness to represent unpopular clients and his talent for innovative legal arguments,

Darrow was the most famous lawyer of his time. He became a national figure in 1894, when he defended EUGENE DEBS against a charge of conspiracy in the PULLMAN STRIKE. For fifteen years, Darrow devoted himself to labor causes before turning to criminal law. In 1924 his eloquent two-day condemnation of capital punishment saved "thrill killers" NATHAN LEOPOLD and RICHARD LOEB from the death penalty. He is best remembered for his role in the SCOPES TRIAL of 1925, when he defended Tennessee schoolteacher John Scopes against a charge of violating state law by teaching evolution in a public school. His relentless questioning of prosecutor WILLIAM JENNINGS BRYAN, a fundamentalist, reflected Darrow's free-thinking, humane outlook on questions of faith and freedom of belief.

Dartmouth College v. Woodward (1819), a landmark U.S. SUPREME COURT decision in which Chief Justice JOHN MARSHALL ruled that the charters of business corporations are contracts and are guaranteed under the U.S. Constitution. The Court held that, because states may not interfere with the obligations of a contract, the state of New Hampshire acted illegally when it changed the provisions of Dartmouth's charter without the consent of the college. A graduate of the school, DANIEL WEBSTER argued on behalf of Dartmouth College.

Daughters of the American Revolution (DAR), a patriotic organization founded in Washington, D.C., in 1890. Its members are women descended from participants in the American Revolution. A generally conservative organization, its goal is to keep alive the memory of the members' ancestors and to encourage patriotic service and good citizenship. The DAR aroused controversy in the 1930s when the group refused to permit MARIAN ANDERSON to sing in its hall because she was black.

Davis, Angela (1944–), black political activist and scholar. Dismissed as a professor of philosophy at UCLA in 1970 for her radical views, Davis was accused but acquitted of conspiracy and murder charges, and returned to teaching and writing. She ran as the vice-presidential candidate on the Communist party ticket in 1980 and 1984.

Davis, Benjamin Oliver (1877–1970), first African-American general in the U.S. Army (1940–48). A graduate of Howard University, Davis served in the SPANISH-AMERICAN WAR before enlisting in the regular army in 1899. During the next forty years he served in Liberia, the Philippines, and as an instructor of military science at Tuskegee Institute. Every assignment he received was designed to avoid his being put in charge of white troops or officers. During WORLD WAR II he was appointed to the Committee on Negro Troop Policies (1942) where he helped to solve racial incidents. Davis was awarded the Distinguished Service Medal for his efforts to ease racial tensions and end discrimination in the armed forces. His retirement marked fifty years of service in the U.S. Army.

Davis, Benjamin Oliver, Jr. (1912–2002), first African-American general in the U.S. Air Force (1954–70). Davis attended West Point, graduating in 1936. The only African-American at the academy, he had no roommate and was shunned by many white cadets, who would only speak to him in the line of duty. As a combat pilot during WORLD WAR II, Davis led the fabled all-black Tuskegee Airmen and is credited with playing a major role in prompting the integration of the armed services following the war. After retiring from the Air Force in 1970, he was named director of civil aviation security in the U.S. Department of Transportation. In that post he supervised the federal sky marshal program, devising and coordinating measures that effectively ended a wave of aircraft hijackings in the United States. In 1971, he was named assistant secretary of transportation (1971–75).

Davis, Bette (Ruth; 1908–90), actress. Davis starred in over eighty films and acted on stage and in television. Her first major role was in *Of Human Bondage* (1934). She won Academy Awards for *Dangerous* (1935) and *Jezebel* (1938). One of her most memorable films was the classic *All about Eve* (1950). She was noted in Hollywood for her independence and her spirited fights for good roles.

Davis, David (1815–86), jurist and politician. As leader of the Lincoln forces at the Republican convention in 1860, Davis helped secure the nomination of Abraham Lincoln for the presidency. Lincoln appointed Davis to the Supreme Court in 1862. His most important act on the Court was his opinion in the 1866 case *Ex parte Milligan*, in which the justices ruled that military courts could not try civilians for civil offenses when the civil courts are in operation. He was the one independent member of the fifteen-member special commission named by Congress to sort out the disputed ELECTION OF 1876; the other members were equally split between Democrats and Republicans. The Republican-dominated Illinois legislature elected Davis to the Senate as part of a Republican plan to remove him from the commission; his successor voted with the Republicans to give the election to RUTHERFORD B. HAYES over SAMUEL J. TILDEN.

Davis, Gray (Joseph Graham Davis, Jr.; 1942–), politician. After graduating from Stanford University and the Columbia University Law School, Davis was an army captain in the VIETNAM WAR. Active in Democratic California politics, he held various offices in state government before winning the governorship in 1998. He maintained his popularity during his first two years in office, with a booming economy and strong support for education. Although his approval ratings began to sink due to the state's energy crisis, he was reelected in 2002. However, when the state's deficit escalated to a record $38 billion, Davis's popularity and credibility plunged to such low levels that in 2003 he became the first governor in the state's history to face a recall election. In an election that included 135 candidates on the ballot, voters ousted Davis and elected former bodybuilder-actor-businessman

ARNOLD SCHWARZENEGGER to be the next governor. It is only the second time in U.S. history that a sitting governor has been recalled, the first being North Dakota governor Lynn Frazier in 1921.

Davis, Jefferson (1808–89), president of the CONFEDERATE STATES OF AMERICA (1861–65). Davis, a Mississippian, served in the U.S. House of Representatives (1845–46), in the Mexican War, in the U.S. Senate (1847–51), and as secretary of war (1853–57). Davis, who had a prickly personality and took offense easily, was criticized for the centralizing tendencies of his policies, for his conduct of the war, and for failing to gain foreign aid and recognition for the Confederacy. Captured after the war as he tried to flee, he was charged with treason and imprisoned for two years, but was never brought to trial. His book *The Rise and Fall of the Confederate Government* (1881) offers his rationale for the Confederacy and for his policies.

Davis, John W. (1873–1955), politician and lawyer. A dark horse candidate for the Democratic nomination for president in 1924, Davis was a compromise choice when Alfred Smith and William McAdoo were still deadlocked after 103 ballots. Davis was soundly defeated by the incumbent, Calvin Coolidge. Davis served in the U.S. House of Representatives from West Virginia, as U.S. solicitor general, and as ambassador to Great Britain. One of America's great lawyers, he argued over a hundred cases before the U.S. Supreme Court, the last being his defense of South Carolina's system of segregation in *Brown* v. *Board of Education of Topeka* (1954).

Davis, Miles (1926–91), black composer and trumpeter. Davis, with an innovative, unique style and wide musical range, was known for elegant solos of jazz and rock melodies. He played with CHARLIE PARKER, Billy Eckstine, JOHN COLTRANE, and Herbie Hancock. In the 1940s and 1950s Davis pioneered new styles such as cool jazz and fusion, and later explored contemporary pop and hip hop. Albums such as *'Round About Midnight* (1955) and *Birth of the Cool* (1959) became classics.

Davis, Sammy, Jr. (1925–90), black entertainer. Davis, who was blind in one eye, began in show business at the age of four as a singer and dancer in a family act. His sixty-year career included many television appearances, Broadway musicals, and motion pictures. His personal popularity and his skills as a dancer, actor, and singer made him much sought after as an entertainer.

Dawes, Charles (1865–1951), diplomat, politician, and financier. Working for the Allied Reparations Commission, Dawes drew up the DAWES PLAN to help Germany pay for its WORLD WAR I damages, earning him the 1925 Nobel Peace Prize. Dawes served as Calvin Coolidge's vice president from 1925 to 1929.

Dawes Plan (1924), a plan of reparation payments following WORLD WAR I, drawn up by CHARLES DAWES, head of the Allied Reparations Commission. The most important provision of this plan — included because

Germany had defaulted on its reparations payments — allowed for significant American loans to Germany, which made that country's payments to
the Allies possible. The plan was replaced by the Young Plan in 1929.

Dawes Severalty Act (February 8, 1887), a law whereby Indian tribes lost
legal standing and their land was divided among tribal members. In
exchange for renouncing their tribal holdings, Indians were to become
full citizens and to receive 160 acres for a family, 80 acres for an individual,
after the expiration of a twenty-five-year federal trust. Intended to speed
assimilation of Indians into mainstream America, the act only undermined
tribal cultures, reduced the total amount of land owned by Indians (after al-
lotments were made, remaining land was offered for public sale), and led to
further deprivation and suffering among Native Americans. All Indians
were granted citizenship in 1924. The Dawes Act was reversed in 1934 with
passage of the Indian Reorganization Act, which promoted Indians' traditional tribal cultures and their autonomy.

Day, Dorothy (1897–1980), Roman Catholic journalist and social reformer.
A socialist and supporter of the Industrial Workers of the World, Day spent
most of her life caring for the sick and the poor, believing that helping the
needy was true Christianity. She cofounded the *Catholic Worker* (1933), a
monthly newspaper to promote social reform, and established dozens of
shelters for the poor and homeless throughout the country.

Dayton, Jonathan (1760–1824), political leader. As a soldier in the American
Revolution he saw action in New York and New Jersey. In 1787, at age
twenty-six, Dayton was the youngest delegate to the Constitutional Con-
vention and thus the youngest signer of the Constitution. Elected to the
House of Representatives from New Jersey, he served two terms as Speaker.
Dayton also served in the U.S. Senate. The city of Dayton, Ohio, was named
for him. In 1982 historians editing the AARON BURR papers determined
Dayton was the actual author of the principal piece of evidence against
Burr in his trial for treason — a letter purportedly by Burr sketching a plan
for molding an empire in western United States and Mexico.

D-Day (June 6, 1944), the day of the combined Allied forces invasion at
Normandy, under Gen. DWIGHT D. EISENHOWER, of German-occupied
France in WORLD WAR II. It established a long-awaited second front and
marked the beginning of the last stage of the war in Europe. The scope of
the invasion and logistics involved were unprecedented; it was the largest
amphibious landing in history. (See image, next page.)

Dean, "Dizzy" (Jerome; 1911–74), baseball player. Pitching for the St. Louis
Cardinals, Dean was selected most valuable player in the National League in
1934 when he won thirty games. He also pitched for the Chicago Cubs and
following his retirement became a baseball broadcaster. He was inducted
into the Hall of Fame in 1953. Dean was noted for his sense of humor and
his fairness toward black athletes.

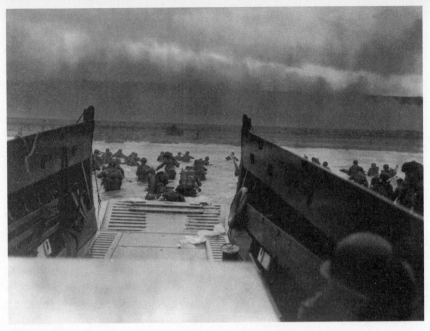

D-Day
*American soldiers storming a Normandy beach during the D-Day invasion of France,
June 6, 1944.*

Dean, James (1931–55), actor. Dean starred in three box-office hits, *Rebel
without a Cause* (1955), *East of Eden* (1955), and *Giant* (1956). He personified
the American youth of the mid-1950s with his emotional, moody portrayals
of troubled and rebellious young men. After his tragic death at age twenty-
four in an automobile crash, he became a legend and cult hero.

Dean, John (1938–), chief legal counsel to RICHARD NIXON. Dean's testimony before a Senate investigating committee in 1973 implicated Nixon and
other top officials in the WATERGATE cover-up. Admitting to his own
wrongdoings, Dean left office, was disbarred, and served a brief time in
prison before writing best-selling books about his role in the scandal, *Blind
Ambition* (1976) and *Lost Honor* (1982).

Deane, Silas (1737–89), diplomat. Deane was sent to France during the
AMERICAN REVOLUTION to acquire military and financial aid. He helped
enlist the services of European soldiers DeKalb, Lafayette, Pulaski, and Von
Steuben for the United States. Along with Benjamin Franklin and Arthur
Lee, he arranged for the TREATY OF ALLIANCE with France in 1778. Later
accused of treason and disloyalty, Deane was vindicated before he died
under mysterious circumstances while in exile in Europe.

Debs, Eugene (1855–1926), political and labor leader who led the PULLMAN
STRIKE in 1894. Debs, a leader of the Socialist Democratic party, changed to

the Socialist party in 1900 and was its presidential candidate five times. A pacifist, Debs spoke in opposition to involvement in World War I, which led to his conviction under the SEDITION ACT in 1918 and a ten-year prison sentence. In 1920, while in jail, he polled nearly a million votes as the Socialist presidential candidate. He was pardoned and was released from prison by President Warren G. Harding in 1921.

De Busschere, David (1940–2003), basketball player. One of the few athletes to play two professional sports, De Busschere played baseball for the Chicago White Sox and basketball for the Detroit Pistons and the New York Knickerbockers. At age twenty-four, he became the youngest player-coach in the NBA. In 1996, he was selected by the NBA as one of the fifty best basketball players ever.

Decatur, Stephen (1779–1820), naval officer who served in the undeclared naval war with France and the war with the Barbary pirates. During the WAR OF 1812 Decatur commanded the USS *United States* and the USS *President,* winning notable victories over the British. In 1815 he commanded U.S. ships sailing to Algeria and put a final end to tribute being paid to the Barbary pirates by foreign nations. He was killed by James Barron in a duel on May 22, 1820.

Declaration of Independence (July 4, 1776), the document in which the American colonists declared their independence from Great Britain. A committee of delegates from the colonies was selected to write the declaration at the Second CONTINENTAL CONGRESS. They included JOHN ADAMS, BENJAMIN FRANKLIN, THOMAS JEFFERSON, ROBERT R. LIVINGSTON, and ROGER SHERMAN. Most of the text was the work of Jefferson. It consists of three parts. The first lists the unalienable rights of people, including the power to change a government that denies them their rights. The second section lists abuses by the British government. The final part is

---

★ **Declaration of Independence**

An excerpt from the Declaration of Independence, July 4, 1776
For the complete text, SEE APPENDIX.

We hold these truths to be self-evident: that all men are created equal; that they are endowed by their Creator with certain unalienable rights; that among these are life, liberty, and the pursuit of happiness; that, to secure these rights, governments are instituted among men, deriving their just powers from the consent of the governed; that whenever any form of government becomes destructive of these ends, it is the right of the people to alter or to abolish it, and to institute new government, laying its foundations on such principles, and organizing its powers in such form, as to them shall seem most likely to effect their safety and happiness.

the declaration that the colonies are free and independent states. After approval by the Congress, it was signed by JOHN HANCOCK as president of the Congress and fifty-five members. The original document is now housed at the National Archives in Washington, D.C. (For the complete text, SEE APPENDIX.)

Declaratory Act (March 18, 1766), an act passed by the British Parliament after repeal of the STAMP ACT. The act stated that the king and Parliament had the right and power to make laws that were binding on the colonies "in all cases whatsoever," even though American colonists were unrepresented in Parliament.

Deere, John (1804–86), inventor and manufacturer. Deere in 1837 invented the first steel plow in the United States. His manufacturing business, established in 1839, was turning out over ten thousand plows per year by 1857. In 1868 Deere & Company began manufacturing cultivators and other agricultural implements, becoming one of the industry leaders.

Deerfield Massacre (February 28–29, 1704), an attack on Deerfield, Massachusetts, by Indians from Canada. The town was mostly destroyed by fire, and over a third of its three hundred inhabitants were captured and taken to Canada.

Defense, Department of, one of the fourteen cabinet departments of the executive branch of the U.S. government. The defense Department was formed as a result of World War II when American policymakers realized the importance of a united defense for the nation's safety. In 1947 Congress passed the National Security Act, establishing a Department of Defense, headed by a secretary, who is a member of the cabinet. The Joint Chiefs of Staff coordinate the operations of the three service branches and advise the president on military and defense matters. The major functions of the Defense Department are to plan for the defense of the nation, recruit and train personnel, and develop new weapons. The department includes a space command unit, which is responsible for shuttle flights carrying military cargoes and for antisatellite warfare. The department's operations have been financed by steadily increasing budgets since 1949 and have become part of a growing military-industrial complex.

DeForest, Lee (1873–1961), inventor. DeForest pioneered developments in wireless telegraphy, radio, a movie sound system, the phonograph, television, telephone, and radar. He developed the triode electron tube, called the audion, that revolutionized the fields of electronics and communications.

Delany, Martin R. (1812–85), black physician, author, social reformer. Born of free black parents, Delany studied both law and medicine at Harvard, but spent most of his life fighting discrimination and slavery. He worked for the UNDERGROUND RAILROAD and with FREDERICK DOUGLASS on the abolitionist newspaper, the *North Star*. Delany campaigned for the establishment of a black nation in Africa, but the CIVIL WAR interrupted the plans.

When he lobbied for an all-black army unit led by black officers, President ABRAHAM LINCOLN appointed him the first black major in the Union Army. He served as a judge in South Carolina during RECONSTRUCTION.

Delaware (First State), the first state to ratify the U.S. Constitution on December 7, 1787. (See maps, pages 540 and 541.) Delaware is the forty-ninth state in size but is the location of the headquarters of many large companies owing to its flexible corporation statutes. Wilmington, the only large city, is called "the Chemical Capital of the World" because it houses the research laboratories of several major chemical companies. Dover is the capital. Industries include manufacturing, canning, fishing, and agriculture. The region the state occupies was discovered by Henry Hudson in 1609. A noted resident of Delaware was JOHN DICKINSON.

DeLôme Letter (February 9, 1898), letter written by the Spanish minister to the United States to a friend in Cuba. He described President William McKinley as "weak" and a "cheap politician." Stolen and published in the *New York Journal*, the letter caused DeLôme's resignation. The incident was used as propaganda and was one of the factors that turned American public opinion against Spain, helping to bring about the Spanish-American War that year.

De Mille, Agnes (1909?–93), dancer, choreographer, and author. After touring Europe and the United States as a dancer, de Mille joined the American Ballet Theatre as a choreographer in 1940. Her best-known ballets include *Rodeo* (1942) and *Fall River Legend* (1948). De Mille received national acclaim for her innovative choreography of the hit Broadway musicals *Oklahoma!* (1943), *Carousel* (1945), *Brigadoon* (1947), and *Paint Your Wagon* (1951), in which she pioneered the technique of blending dance, story, and music into a unified work. De Mille's books include *To a Young Dancer* (1962), *Book of the Dance* (1963), and *Martha Graham* (1991), as well as several autobiographies, including *Where Wings Grow* (1978).

DeMille, Cecil B. (1881–1959), film producer and director. After moving to Hollywood in 1913, deMille established himself as an innovator in filmmaking. He was noted for his spectacular biblical and historical films, such as *The Ten Commandments* (1956) and *The King of Kings* (1927), which were immensely popular. He received an Academy Award in 1952 for his circus film, *The Greatest Show on Earth*.

Democracy, a form of government in which the people rule. In a direct democracy, such as the ancient Greek city-state of Athens, the people rule directly, voting on all public measures. In a representative democracy, such as the United States, the fifty states, and local governments, the people entrust the powers of government to representatives whom they elect in free and open elections. Many historians regard colonial agreements such as the MAYFLOWER COMPACT of 1620 and the FUNDAMENTAL ORDERS OF CONNECTICUT of 1638 as roots of American democracy.

Democratic Party, one of the two major American political parties. The nation's oldest, the party dates to 1828 and ANDREW JACKSON's presidential organization. Democrats have won twenty of the forty-four presidential elections they engaged in. Since the 1930s the party has drawn its support from immigrants, unions, blue-collar workers, educators, and blacks, as well as white southerners before the civil rights movement. The political symbol of the party is the donkey, which evolved from its use by Jackson when his opponents called him a "jackass" during the 1828 election campaign.

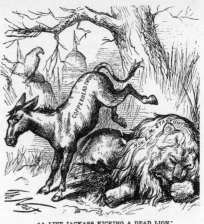

"A LIVE JACKASS KICKING A DEAD LION"
And such a Lion! and such a Jackass!

Democratic Party
The first representation — in a cartoon by Thomas Nast — of the Democratic emblem.

Democratic-Republican Party (1792–1824), a party created in opposition to the FEDERALIST PARTY — specifically, to the Washington administration's fiscal policies and pro-British foreign policy. Organized by James Madison and Thomas Jefferson with the aid of George Clinton and Aaron Burr, the Democratic-Republicans brought together former Antifederalists and moderate Federalists. They wanted weaker federal government, with most power assigned to the states, an economic policy favoring agriculture, and a foreign policy favoring the French Revolution. In the ELECTION OF 1796 Thomas Jefferson was their candidate against Federalist John Adams; Adams was elected president and Jefferson, vice president. In 1800 Jefferson and the Democratic-Republicans defeated Adams and the Federalists, who also lost control of Congress. After the disintegration of the Federalist party in 1816, the Democratic-Republicans divided into several groups. They, and the former Federalists, became the short-lived National Republican party, the WHIG PARTY, and the DEMOCRATIC PARTY. The Democratic-Republicans called themselves Republicans after Jefferson's election and are still sometimes referred to as the first Republican party, but it bears no relation to the present Republican party.

Dempsey, Jack (William; 1895–1983), boxer. Known as the "Manassa Mauler," Dempsey was heavyweight boxing champion of the world for seven years. In 1926 he lost the crown in a ten-round decision to Gene Tunney and lost the rematch because of the "long count" (so called because of a delay in starting the count when Dempsey did not immediately go to a neutral corner). Known for his dangerous left hook and his killer instinct,

Dempsey was voted the greatest fighter of the first half of the twentieth century by the Associated Press in 1950.

Deseret, a provisional state formed by the MORMONS in 1849. *Deseret* means "honeybee" in *The Book of Mormon,* symbolizing the hard work the Mormons had to exert for their settlement near Salt Lake, as well as the persecution they had undergone while moving westward in search of a homeland. After the United States obtained the territory they settled in by the treaty ending the Mexican War, the Mormons organized the State of Deseret and asked to be admitted to the Union. Congress rejected the request, mainly because polygamy, a practice of the Mormon faith at that time, had not been outlawed in the proposed state. Utah Territory was created instead.

De Soto, Hernando (1500?–42), Spanish explorer and adventurer. While searching for gold, De Soto led one of the earliest European expeditions to sight the Mississippi River (May 1541). He continued his unsuccessful search for gold on either side of the river but died of fever during the expedition. His body was committed to the waters of the Mississippi.

DeVoto, Bernard (1897–1955), writer. A versatile and controversial author of history books and novels, DeVoto wrote the Pulitzer Prize-winning *Across the Wide Missouri* (1947) and *Mark Twain's America* (1932). He also wrote popular serial novels under the name of John August about the exploration and settlement of the American West.

Dewey, George (1837–1917), naval commander. Dewey became a national hero during the Spanish-American War in 1898 when his fleet soundly defeated the Spanish in Manila Harbor in the Philippines. He was named admiral of the navy, the highest rank ever held by an American naval officer, and helped establish the United States as a major Pacific power with his victory.

Dewey, John (1859–1952), philosopher and educator. A leader of the philosophical movement called "pragmatism," Dewey influenced twentieth-century thought through his prolific writings on philosophy, education, art, and politics. As an educator at several universities (including nearly thirty years at Columbia), Dewey promoted progressive educational reform. He emphasized active problem solving and a curriculum including student interests. A defender of civil rights and progressive causes, Dewey served as president of the American Psychological Association, the American Philosophical Society, and the American Association of University Professors, which he helped found. His works include *The School and Society* (1899), *Freedom and Culture* (1939), and *Art as Experience* (1934).

Dewey, Thomas (1902–71), lawyer and public official. Dewey ran as the Republican candidate for president in the ELECTION OF 1944 but lost to Franklin D. Roosevelt. In the ELECTION OF 1948, he appeared to be a sure winner. But his defeat by Harry Truman was the greatest presidential upset in American history. Dewey made his reputation as a prosecuting attorney in New York and served three terms as the state's governor.

Dickey, James (1923–97), poet, novelist, and critic. Known chiefly for his works dealing with the survival of men against nature, Dickey gained national attention with his best-selling novel *Deliverance* (1970; film, 1972) about men in the South braving the elements on a white-water canoe adventure. He won the National Book Award for poetry in 1966 for *Buckdancer's Choice* (1965) and served as a consultant of poetry for the Library of Congress from 1966 to 1968.

Dickinson, Anna Elizabeth (1842–1932), orator. Dickinson attracted large crowds during the Civil War with her orations condemning slavery. She began speaking at age eighteen at a time when women orators were rare and became known as the North's "Joan of Arc." After the war she continued to campaign for the rights of women and blacks.

Dickinson, Emily (1830–86), poet. Dickinson lived most of her life as a recluse, seldom seeing anyone other than her immediate family and close friends. Her lyrics, chiefly concerned with immortality, love, nature, and death are notable for their simple, precise language, fresh imagery, variety of meter, and occasional whimsical humor. She wrote over 1,700 poems, most of which were not published until after she died. She is now considered to be one of the most gifted poets in American literature.

Dickinson, John (1732–1808), colonial Patriot and author. Dickinson wrote a series of newspaper articles against British taxation that were published in *Letters from a Farmer in Pennsylvania* (1768). The essays earned him the title "Penman of the Revolution." He also wrote the OLIVE BRANCH PETITION (1775). Dickinson represented Delaware at the 1787 CONSTITUTIONAL CONVENTION and played an important role in drafting the Constitution.

Dillinger, John (1902–34), bank robber. One of America's most wanted criminals, Dillinger led his gang in numerous bank robberies, eluding the police by making dramatic escapes. He was gunned down in Chicago by FBI agents after being betrayed by a lady friend.

DiMaggio, Joe (1914–99), baseball player. "Joltin' Joe" set a major league baseball record, hitting in fifty-six consecutive games during the 1941 season. The center fielder for the New York Yankees for thirteen years, he compiled a lifetime batting average of .325 and was named most valuable player three times. Called "the Yankee Clipper," he became a New York idol and succeeded Babe Ruth as baseball's superstar.

Dirksen, Everett M. (1896–1969), politician. Dirksen, a Republican from Illinois, served in the U.S. House of Representatives from 1933 to 1948 and in the Senate from 1950 to 1969. As Senate minority leader and a conservative, he was known for his powerful oratory. Dirksen played an important role in the enactment of the 1964 Civil Rights Act.

Discovery of America. The idea that Europeans "discovered" America in 1492 has been a basic assumption of American history, but it would be more accurate to say that Columbus's voyages led to the "first permanent arrival of Europeans in the Western Hemisphere." Millions of people and dozens of cultures thrived in this half of the globe long before Europeans came. All discoveries of America were accidental. In prehistoric times, the ancestors of American Indians migrated from Asia via a then-existing land bridge across the Bering Strait; they were probably hunters following herds of animals or mariners fishing for sea mammals. Their migrations continued southward down the continents, with various peoples adapting to new environments as necessary. A second group, Norwegian sailors called Vikings, probably reached America about the year 1000. Viking sagas suggest that Leif Ericson or his son was the first European to set foot on the North American continent at a place the Norsemen called Vinland, which may have been south of Newfoundland, though its site is the subject of controversy. Repeated fights with natives, called Skraelings, ended their visits around 1010. Almost five hundred years later in Europe, a new spirit of curiosity was sparked by the Renaissance and trade with the distant Indies and China. CHRISTOPHER COLUMBUS, a Genoese sailor seeking a new route to the East Indies, sailed west across the Atlantic Ocean, finding land probably at what he called San Salvador on October 12, 1492. News of his voyage opened the door to an age of exploration, with other Europeans following in search of riches. The name "America" was given to the continents in 1507 by the German geographer Martin Waldseemüller, who derived the term from the name of Italian explorer Amerigo Vespucci (1454–1512). When writing about his own travels to the New World in 1499, Vespucci claimed to be the first to recognize that the Americas were continents previously unknown by Europeans.

Disney, Walt (1901–66), cartoonist and motion picture producer. Disney pioneered the production of animated cartoons, introducing such characters as Mickey Mouse, Donald Duck, and Pluto. His first full-length animated feature was *Snow White and the Seven Dwarfs* (1937), followed by *Fantasia* (1940) and *Bambi* (1942), among others. Disney also produced family live-action films such as *Treasure Island* (1950) and *Swiss Family Robinson* (1960). Disney himself received twenty-nine Academy Awards for his films. He also enjoyed television success with "The Wonderful World of Disney" and "The Mickey Mouse Club." Disneyland, his dream amusement park, opened in California in 1955 and a second park, Disney World, opened in Florida in 1972, six years after his death.

Divine, Father (George Baker; 1880?–1965), black religious leader. In 1919 Father Divine founded the Peace Mission Movement, a nonsectarian interracial church organization that worked to end poverty and racial discrimination. Its headquarters were in Harlem, New York. Father Divine, considered to be the Messiah by many, attracted a huge following, especially in the Northeast during the Great Depression.

Dix, Dorothea (1802–87), social reformer. Dix gained worldwide respect for her efforts to win humane treatment for the insane. As a schoolteacher and humanitarian, she also started campaigns for civilized treatment and housing of prison inmates. She served as superintendent of U.S. Army nurses during the Civil War. Because of her work many states established publicly supported asylums for the mentally ill and abandoned the practice of chaining prisoners.

Dixie, a popular term used to refer to the South, particularly as a land of slaves and plantations before the Civil War. The song "Dixie" was composed in 1859 by entertainer David D. Emmett and became a popular marching song of the Confederate army during the war. Ironically, Emmett was a New Yorker who opposed secession.

Dixiecrat Party, another name for the States' Rights Democratic party. Southern Democrats broke away during the presidential campaign of 1948 to oppose their party's civil rights plank. They nominated J. STROM THURMOND for president and Fielding L. Wright for vice president. The party received thirty-nine electoral votes from southern states.

Doby, Larry (1924–2003), baseball player. Doby was the first black baseball player to play in the American League (AL), and the second in the major leagues. He was also the second black manager in the major leagues (with the Chicago White Sox), following FRANK ROBINSON. He joined the Cleveland Indians in 1947, eleven weeks after JACKIE ROBINSON broke the color barrier. Doby helped the Indians win the WORLD SERIES against the Boston Braves in 1948. He was a seven-time AL all-star during his thirteen years in the majors. Doby also played for the Detroit Tigers and was inducted into the Hall of Fame in 1998.

Dole, Elizabeth (1936–), politician. A Republican senator from North Carolina, Elizabeth Dole is a former secretary of transportation (1983–87) and secretary of labor (1989–90). From 1991 to 1998, Dole was head of the American Red Cross. She unsuccessfully sought the Republican presidential nomination in 1999. In 2002 Dole won the Senate seat of retiring North Carolina senator Jesse Helms. She has been married to ROBERT DOLE, former senator from Kansas, since 1975.

Dole, Robert (1923–), politician and Republican presidential nominee in 1996. Dole served in the U.S. Army during World War II, was twice decorated for heroism, but was severely wounded in the closing days of the war. After three years of convalescence, he was discharged with the rank of captain. He served in the Kansas Legislature and the U.S. House of Representatives before being elected to the Senate in 1968, rising to Senate minority, then majority leader. Dole was the Republican candidate for vice president in the ELECTION OF 1976 and for president in the ELECTION OF 1996. He resigned from the Senate in 1996 during his unsuccessful presidential race against President BILL CLINTON.

Dole, Sanford (1844–1926), lawyer and political leader in the Hawaiian Islands. Dole owned vast pineapple and sugar cane plantations in Hawaii and worked to protect his huge business interests there. An associate justice on the Hawaiian Supreme Court, he helped lead a revolution in Hawaii for a government that was more democratic but also represented the interests of the white elite. Queen Liliuokalani was deposed, and Dole became president of the provisional government in 1893. He served as president of the Republic of Hawaii from 1894 to 1898 and first governor of the territory of Hawaii from 1900 to 1903.

Dollar Diplomacy, U.S. foreign policy in the early 1900s of using American diplomatic influence to protect American investments in Latin America and Asia and encourage more stable governments. The policy, begun under President Theodore Roosevelt, was expanded by President William Howard Taft from 1909 to 1913. Woodrow Wilson repudiated the policy when he became president.

Donner Party (1846–47), one of the many groups of pioneers that met with disaster on the route west. Led by George and Jacob Donner, the party was marooned by early blizzards while trying to cross the Sierra Nevada. To survive, they constructed crude shelters and resorted to eating mice, their animals, leather clothing, and finally even their own dead. About half of the party survived and made it to California. Donner Pass is named for them.

Donovan, "Wild Bill" (William J., 1883–1959), lawyer, intelligence officer, and diplomat. Donovan won the Congressional Medal of Honor for service in World War I and served as assistant U.S. attorney general (1925–29). Under Franklin D. Roosevelt, he organized and directed the Office of Strategic Services (OSS) (1942–45), which was the forerunner of the CENTRAL INTELLIGENCE AGENCY. Donovan was mentor to generations of American intelligence professionals.

Dooley, Thomas (1927–61), physician to the people of Southeast Asia. As a medical officer in the U.S. Naval Reserve, Dooley volunteered for service on a ship moving refugees from North to South Vietnam, where he established refugee camps. After resigning from the navy he organized a private medical mission in northern Laos. In 1957 he founded Medico (Medical International Corporation) and set up hospitals in Cambodia, Laos, and Vietnam. Dooley wrote *Deliver Us From Evil* (1956), *The Edge of Tomorrow* (1958), and *The Night They Burned the Mountain* (1960) about his experiences, contributing the royalties to his medical work. He was posthumously awarded the Congressional Medal of Honor for his humanitarian work after his death from cancer at age thirty-four.

Doolittle, James (1896–1993), soldier and airman. Doolittle earned the Congressional Medal of Honor for leading air raids on Tokyo, Japan, with sixteen B-25 bombers during WORLD WAR II. These daring raids in 1942 greatly boosted the morale of the U.S. fighting forces. Doolittle was an expert in the field of military navigation and tactical bombing.

Dorr's Rebellion (1842), a movement led by Thomas W. Dorr for constitutional reform in Rhode Island. Attempting without success to persuade the conservative legislature to call a constitutional convention to revise the state's form of government, Dorr and his supporters decided to invoke the right of revolution recognized in the Declaration of Independence. They organized and elected their own convention, wrote a new constitution, and elected Dorr governor. The conservatives, angered by the Dorrites, called their own convention, wrote a conservative new constitution, and elected their own state government. Eventually, in a largely bloodless civil war, the conservatives prevailed, and the Dorrites were prosecuted for treason against the state. In *Luther* v. *Borden* (1845), Chief Justice Roger B. Taney held that conflicts between actions of the two governments of the state were "political questions" that the Court could not and would not resolve.

Dorsey, Jimmy (1904–57), and **Tommy Dorsey** (1905–56), musicians. The Dorsey brothers formed one of the nation's most popular dance bands in 1933 during the big-band era. Jimmy played the saxophone and Tommy the trombone. In 1935 they separated to form their own bands and were highly successful with Jimmy's big hits of "Amapola" and "So Rare" and Tommy's "Marie" and "I'll Never Smile Again." In 1953 they joined again, calling themselves "the Fabulous Dorseys."

Dos Passos, John (1896–1970), novelist. Dos Passos's books are characterized by their realistic depiction of American life. His best-known work, the *U.S.A.* trilogy, includes *The 42nd Parallel* (1930), *1919* (1932), and *The Big Money* (1936). They focus on the failed possibilities and deterioration of culture he believed took place during the first three decades of the twentieth century.

Dot-Com Boom and Bust, phenomenon of the late 1990s and into the first years of the new decade. By 1996, approximately 45 million people were using the Internet, about 30 million of those in the United States and Canada. Forty-four percent of U.S. households owned a personal computer, and 14 million of them were online. By 1999 the number of U.S. Internet users reached more than 75 million. Between 1995 and 2000, startup companies developed almost overnight and were seen as having the potential to grow at extraordinarily rapid rates. There was a burst of new technology during this period, with particular emphasis on its applications to the Internet and telecommunication. "E-commerce" became the new buzzword as Internet shopping rapidly spread, and there seemed to be a dot-com address for just about everything imaginable, leading to a frenzy of investments in Internet technical stocks. Favorable economic and financial conditions (such as corporate profits, stock prices, and interest rates) were instrumental in supporting the boom, but just as quickly as it grew, it burst in mid 2000 through 2001 as investment spending plunged. Stock indexes dropped and thousands of dot-coms were forced to close their doors. Some say that spending on Internet and telecommunication projects got ahead of itself, and an erosion of business practices combined with uncertainties such as terrorism and war contributed to lack of confidence among investors. The dot-com collapse has changed the fortunes of many, but a few established companies including Amazon.com and eBay.com have come through successfully, appearing to have a potential for long-term survival.

Doubleday, Abner (1819–93), soldier and sports figure. As a general in the Union army, Doubleday was with the troops at FORT SUMTER who returned the first shot fired by the Confederates in 1861 to start the CIVIL WAR. He was in several major battles, including Gettysburg in 1863. Doubleday is often erroneously credited as the originator of baseball. Doubleday Field in Cooperstown, New York, is named in his honor.

Doughboy, name given to American soldiers during WORLD WAR I. The name may have come from the large brass buttons on the uniforms of Union soldiers in the Civil War; they were said to resemble doughboys, a flour dumpling cooked in soup. The name was used by soldiers in France because they resented being called "Sammies" and "Teddies."

Doughfaces, the name given to northerners, chiefly northern Democrats, who allied themselves with proslavery southern Democrats before the Civil War. Prominent doughfaces included Presidents FRANKLIN PIERCE and JAMES BUCHANAN.

Douglas, Stephen A. (1813–61), politician. Known as the "Little Giant" because of his short stature but outstanding oratory, Douglas, an Illinois Democrat, served in the U.S. House of Representatives and in 1846 was elected U.S. Senator. He sponsored the KANSAS-NEBRASKA ACT in 1854, which included the idea of POPULAR SOVEREIGNTY. In the Illinois Senate election of 1858 he took part in a series of seven famous debates against Republican ABRAHAM LINCOLN, focusing on the extension of slavery. The state legislature chose Douglas for the Senate seat, but the debates made Lincoln a national political figure. In 1860 the Democratic party split three ways over the issue of slavery. The northern faction chose Douglas as its candidate, JOHN C. BRECKINRIDGE became the southerners' candidate, and old-line Unionists rallied behind JOHN BELL's Constitutional Union ticket. Republican Lincoln was elected. Douglas supported Lincoln's actions until his sudden death the next spring.

Douglas, William O. (1898–1980), jurist. Douglas, a leading member of the legal realist movement, taught law at Columbia and Yale, until President Franklin D. Roosevelt named him to the U.S. Supreme Court in 1939.

During his thirty-six years on the Court (the longest period served by any justice), Douglas became known for his erratic brilliance, his absolutist view of the Bill of Rights, and his championing of conservation and environmental causes. An aloof, cantankerous, and difficult man, Douglas was a world traveler and prolific author. Right-wing Republicans, led by House minority leader Gerald R. Ford, tried unsuccessfully to impeach Douglas in 1970. Douglas retired from the Court after suffering a severe stroke in 1975. In his last years, he wrote two volumes of memoirs, *Go East, Young Man* (1974) and *The Court Years* (1980).

Douglass, Frederick (1818–95), an escaped slave who became a prominent abolitionist. Douglass escaped from Baltimore, Maryland, and settled in New Bedford, Massachusetts, where he worked as a chimney sweep and laborer. A celebrated orator, he spoke tirelessly for the antislavery cause. To elude slave-catchers, he fled to England, bought his freedom, and returned to Massachusetts, where he founded the abolitionist newspaper *The North Star*. During the Civil War Douglass helped recruit black troops into the Union army (his own son served in the first black regiment) and was an adviser to Abraham Lincoln. After Reconstruction he served as American minister to Haiti.

Doves, people who oppose war, named after the traditional bird of peace. The term came into popular use during the VIETNAM WAR to describe opponents of the war, who called for withdrawal of American troops, as contrasted with Hawks, who wanted a military solution to the conflict.

Dow, Charles (1851–1902), editor and economist. During his early career Dow wrote for several major newspapers on financial and economic topics. In 1882 he organized Dow Jones & Company with Edward D. Jones. They turned out a newsletter for Wall Street financiers, which became the *Wall Street Journal* in 1889. As editor, Dow established the *Journal* as an influential, authoritative publication. He developed a sophisticated method of analyzing market trends known as the Dow-Jones averages.

Draft (also called conscription), a system to secure troops for service in the armed forces. Men were first drafted for national military service during the Civil War, first by the Confederacy in 1862 and then by the Union in 1863 when volunteers proved inadequate. Because the Conscription Act of 1863 was inequitable — it allowed a person to hire a substitute to serve in his place — it resulted in DRAFT RIOTS in New York City.

Compulsory service was next invoked during World War I with the Selective Service Act of 1917, which delivered almost 3 million men to the armed forces, as compared to about 1 million volunteers. The draft was discontinued after the armistice in 1918, and the United States maintained only voluntary forces until 1940. The draft was reinstated with the Selective Training and Service Act of 1940, the first peacetime U.S. draft, requiring all men from twenty-one to thirty-six years of age to register. The Selective

Service System was established in that year to administer the draft. The act was amended several times to prepare for World War II. During the war the draft supplied more than 10 million men.

The Selective Service System, amended after the war to require eighteen months' service, was allowed to expire on March 31, 1947, and for a year there was no draft. But when the armed forces declined to well below the 2 million men desired by the Department of Defense, Congress enacted the Selective Service Act of 1948, requiring twenty-one months' service of non-veterans and single men between nineteen and twenty-six. It was due to expire on June 30, 1950, but when North Korea invaded South Korea that month, Congress extended it until July 1951. The act was amended several times thereafter. About 2 million men were drafted for the Korean War (1950–53). From 1965 to 1973, during America's heavy involvement in the Vietnam War, about 1.7 million men were drafted.

Early in 1973 when the draft law expired, the government turned to an all-volunteer force. To stimulate volunteering, pay and benefits were improved. The Selective Service System was retained, however. Legislation in 1980 and 1981 required all men to register for the draft when they reach the age of eighteen, thus assuring the government of a list of men who can be inducted in the event of a national emergency.

Draft Riots, disturbances in many parts of the country during the summer of 1863, shortly after the Emancipation Proclamation went into effect. The draft riots protested against military service laws that allowed called-up men to hire a substitute or purchase an exemption by paying $300 to the government. The poor could not afford this, and their resentment culminated in riots, the worst of which occurred in New York City. The riot lasted from July 13 to 18, 1863, resulting in burned buildings (including an orphanage for black children) and the killing and wounding of hundreds of people, mostly innocent African-Americans.

Drake, Edwin (1819–80), petroleum entrepreneur. Drake was the first man in the world to employ the method of drilling to secure oil. In 1859 he drilled the first successful oil well in the United States near Titusville, Pennsylvania.

Dred Scott **Decision** (1857), a ruling by the SUPREME COURT that the justices hoped would settle the question of slavery once and for all. Dred Scott, a slave, was taken by his owner from Missouri, a slave state, to Illinois, a free state, and later to Wisconsin Territory, where slavery was prohibited. When he returned to Missouri, Scott claimed that his residence on free soil had made him a free man. Writing for the majority, Chief Justice ROGER B. TANEY ruled that the original intent of the Framers of the Constitution was (1) that black men and women had no rights that whites were bound to respect, (2) that they could not become citizens of the United States, and (3) that Congress had no power to exclude slavery from any part of U.S.

territory, thus striking down the MISSOURI COMPROMISE as unconstitutional. The decision was denounced throughout the North and West, and exacerbated public controversy over slavery. Meanwhile, Scott was freed by the trustees for his owner, who had gone insane; becoming a porter in a St. Louis hotel, Scott died in 1858.

Dreiser, Theodore (1871–1945), journalist and author, who was the greatest realist novelist of his time. He is noted for his focus on the less savory aspects of American life. *An American Tragedy* (1925), one of Dreiser's major novels, was based on a notorious murder case. It was later adapted as a Broadway play and a movie. His interest in socialism is reflected in several books of the 1920s through the 1940s. Dreiser, a prolific writer, also wrote plays, poetry, short stories, and memoirs.

Drew, Charles Richard (1904–50), black surgeon and medical researcher. Drew made an immense contribution to modern medicine when he established that blood plasma could replace whole blood in transfusions. In 1941 he resigned as director of the AMERICAN RED CROSS blood bank program to protest its policy of segregating blood donations. He was awarded the NAACP's SPINGARN MEDAL in 1944. Drew died in a North Carolina hospital where he was taken after a car crash. A myth, still in circulation, sprang up after his death that he had been refused admittance to a white hospital and had bled to death in a segregated hospital, which, one version had it, lacked blood plasma. Several black doctors with him at the time disputed this story, and black scholars since have established its falsity. Drew died despite excellent treatment he received at a white hospital.

Du Bois, W.E.B. (1868–1963), black historian and civil rights activist. Du Bois helped found the Niagara civil rights movement (1905) and the NATIONAL ASSOCIATION FOR THE ADVANCEMENT OF COLORED PEOPLE (NAACP; 1909) and was awarded the 1920 SPINGARN MEDAL for his efforts on behalf of independence for African colonies. He edited *The Crisis* for the NAACP for many years. Du Bois was the first black to earn a Ph.D. from Harvard University and also studied abroad. In his classic work, *Souls of Black Folk* (1903), Du Bois argued that to achieve racial equality college-educated blacks must speak out and fight for equal rights. His vigorous debates with BOOKER T. WASHINGTON about the best ways for African-Americans to pursue equality attracted national attention from African-Americans and whites alike. Du Bois became increasingly unhappy over racism in the United States, joined the Communist party, and moved to Ghana in 1961.

Due Process of Law, a phrase appearing in the Fifth and Fourteenth Amendments of the U.S. Constitution, both of which forbid the taking of "life, liberty, or property without due process of law." The Supreme Court has interpreted due process of law — a phrase that some trace back to the

Magna Carta — to mean fundamental fairness, not merely the mechanical observance of empty legal forms.

Dukakis, Michael (1933–), politician. The son of a Greek immigrant, Dukakis graduated from Swarthmore College and Harvard Law School and served in the Massachusetts House of Representatives from 1963 to 1970. He was elected governor in 1974, lost in 1978, but was reelected in 1982 and 1986. Dukakis ran as the Democratic presidential nominee in the ELECTION OF 1988. Although he was known as an effective politician and problem solver, he ran a lackluster campaign and was defeated by Vice President GEORGE H. W. BUSH.

Dulles, Allen (1893–1969), diplomat and government official. Dulles served the U.S. government in many posts. He worked in the Office of Strategic Services during WORLD WAR II and during the cold war was appointed director of the CENTRAL INTELLIGENCE AGENCY. His involvement in the BAY OF PIGS invasion, which resulted in failure, prompted his resignation. He was the younger brother of JOHN FOSTER DULLES.

Dulles, John Foster (1888–1959), lawyer and statesman. A leading Wall Street lawyer and moderate Republican, Dulles helped in the formation of the United Nations and served briefly in the U.S. Senate, filling an unexpired term. He earned praise for his development of the Japanese peace treaty in 1951. As secretary of state under DWIGHT D. EISENHOWER, Dulles was a major force in the formation of U.S. COLD WAR policy and author of the EISENHOWER DOCTRINE and the tactic of brinksmanship.

Dunbar, Paul Laurence (1872–1906), black writer and poet. Born to escaped slaves, Dunbar wrote about the experiences and emotions of black Americans. His poems, published in newspapers and magazines, were in great demand, as were his poetry readings on lecture tours. He published twelve books, but his collections of poems were the most successful. *Majors and Minors* (1895), which treated black themes with pathos and humor, established his reputation. Other collections of poetry, using folk materials, included *Lyrics of Lowly Life* (1896) and *Lyrics of Sunshine and Shadow* (1905).

Duncan, Isadora (1878–1927), dancer and choreographer. A controversial but influential dancer, Duncan's style was inspired by the art of ancient Greece. Often costumed in long flowing robes, she danced barefoot. An avant-gardist and admirer of the Russian Revolution, she founded dance schools for children in Europe and was a forerunner of modern dance.

Dunne, Finley Peter (1867–1936), humorist and journalist. Dunne edited three Chicago newspapers before he was thirty. His fictional character of Mr. Martin Dooley, a witty American-Irish Roman Catholic bartender who explains to customer Hennessy the current events of the day, became extremely popular. Dunne's biting and raucous commentary, written in broad Irish dialect, criticized American foreign policy and domestic social conditions in over seven hundred newspaper sketches between 1893 and 1919. His books include *Mr. Dooley in Peace and War* (1898) and *Mr. Dooley's Philosophy* (1900).

du Pont, family of Delaware industrialists of French descent. Pierre-Samuel du Pont de Nemours (1739–1817), an expert on economics, fled to America after the French Revolution. At the request of President Thomas Jefferson, he prepared a national education plan, which, though never adopted in America, was used in France. One son, Victor Marie (1767–1827), became a director of the Bank of the United States, Philadelphia. His other son, Eleuthère Irénée (1771–1834), established a gunpowder factory in 1802 near Wilmington, Delaware, the beginning of the present-day du Pont Company. Among Eleuthère's successors were his son Henry (1812–89), who expanded the company and led its development of high-power explosives in 1880, and his grandson Henry Algernon (1838–1926), who won a Medal of Honor in the Civil War. Eleuthère's great-grandsons, Thomas Coleman (1863–1930), Pierre Samuel (1870–1954), and Alfred I (1864–1935), reorganized, modernized, and expanded the company, as it diversified into development of chemicals and chemical products.

Durand, Asher B. (1796–1886), painter and engraver. Durand established his reputation with his engraving of John Trumbull's painting *The Signing of the Declaration of Independence* in 1823. A member of the HUDSON RIVER SCHOOL, he painted realistic landscapes of New England, as well as portraits. Durand also designed bank notes and served as president of the National Academy of Design from 1845 to 1861.

Durant, Will (William James; 1885–1981), historian and philosopher. Durant taught Latin and French at Seton Hall while studying for the priesthood. Disillusioned, he left and began writing and lecturing on philosophy. *The Story of Philosophy* (1926) became a best-seller. He devoted many years of his life, from 1935 to 1976, to the eleven-volume *The Story of Civilization*. The last five volumes were written with his wife, Ariel (Ida Kaufman; 1898–1981). The tenth volume, *Rousseau and Revolution,* won them a Pulitzer Prize in 1968.

Dust Bowl, the southern part of the Great Plains plagued by frequent dust storms, particularly during the 1930s. These storms, resulting from drought and unwise farming methods, caused severe environmental damage to areas of Kansas, Nebraska, Texas, Oklahoma, and New Mexico. John Steinbeck's classic novel *The Grapes of Wrath* (1939) depicts the plight of the "Okies" — migrant farmers fleeing the dust bowl.

Dylan, Bob (Robert Zimmerman; 1941–), musician. Dylan, influential in the 1960s as a singer and composer, took his name from poet Dylan Thomas. He is especially noted for his folk and social protest songs, such as "The Times They Are A-Changin' " and "Blowin' in the Wind."

E **Eagleton, Thomas** (1929–), politician. Eagleton, a U.S. senator and Democrat from Missouri, is the only man nominated at a national convention for the vice presidency to resign his candidacy. He resigned twelve days following his nomination in 1972 when the news media disclosed that he had received shock treatments for emotional exhaustion and depression. R. Sargent Shriver replaced Eagleton, who continued to serve in the Senate until 1987.

Eakins, Thomas (1844–1916), painter and sculptor. Although Eakins achieved little notice during his lifetime, he eventually was recognized as a major American artist. He painted with great attention to detail, often using photographs to achieve scientific accuracy in his study of the human body. Among Eakins's subjects were people of all walks of life in realistic situations.

Earhart, Amelia (1897–1937), aviator and feminist. In 1932 Earhart became the first woman to fly the Atlantic Ocean alone and the first woman to earn the Distinguished Flying Cross. Her accomplishments inspired many women. Earhart, who was a strong feminist, served as a career counselor for women at Purdue University. Earhart disappeared July 2, 1937, while attempting a flight around the world with her navigator, Fred Noonan. Their plane vanished in the central Pacific Ocean and was never recovered.

Early, Jubal (1816–94), Confederate general. Although Early objected to Virginia's secession, he immediately joined the Confederate ranks at the outbreak of the CIVIL WAR. He fought at the First Battle of BULL RUN, ANTIETAM, FREDERICKSBURG, and CHANCELLORSVILLE. He led a raid on Washington, D.C., in 1864 but could not take the city. Following their retreat to the Shenandoah Valley in March 1865, Early's troops suffered a defeat by Gen. PHILIP H. SHERIDAN and Union cavalrymen. Noted for his crusty manner, Early spent much time after the war recording and defending his version of the Confederate experience.

Earp, Wyatt (1848–1929), gunslinger, gambler, and peace officer in America's early West. Earp worked as a buffalo hunter and lawman in Missouri and Kansas before moving to Tombstone, Arizona. There he won mythic fame for the "gunfight at the OK Corral," when he and two of his brothers, along with "Doc" Holliday,

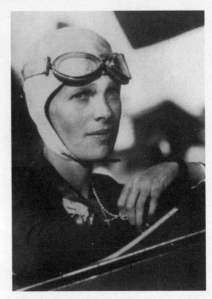

Amelia Earhart

forced a showdown with the notorious Clanton gang on October 26, 1881. All of the gang, except one Clanton and a companion, were shot dead.

Eastman, George (1854–1932), inventor, manufacturer, and philanthropist. Eastman revolutionized the art of photography, perfecting roll films and light cameras, including the hand-held Kodak. He formed the Eastman-Kodak Company in 1892, and by utilizing innovative low-cost techniques and large-scale production, the company became the largest of its kind in the world. It was the first company in the United States to introduce an employee profit-sharing system. Eastman contributed millions of dollars to schools and institutions.

Eaton Affair (1831), incident during ANDREW JACKSON's administration involving his cabinet members and their wives. The 1829 marriage of Secretary of War John Eaton to Peggy O'Neale caused friction in Washington society. O'Neale, wife of a ship's purser, had shocked Washington with her involvement with Eaton before her husband's death; the Eatons' wedding failed to quiet the scandal. The cabinet wives, led by Mrs. John C. Calhoun, considered her socially unacceptable; Jackson and Secretary of State Martin Van Buren supported her. Finally Van Buren, to cut through the mess, resigned and other cabinet members followed suit, giving Jackson the chance to reorganize his cabinet. Van Buren's graciousness toward Mrs. Eaton eventually led to Jackson's selection of him as his running mate in 1832 and to Van Buren's succession as head of the Democratic party.

Eddy, Mary Baker (1821–1910), founder of the Christian Science religion. A lifelong search for the principle of Jesus' healings led Eddy to turn to the Bible following a life-threatening accident in 1866. Her immediate recovery convinced her that disease is an illusion and resulted in her discovery of Christian Science (1870) and her publication of *Science and Health with Key to the Scriptures* (1875), her major work on theology and healing. The religion holds that God, Spirit, is the only power and reality, and that man's perfection is real and demonstrable. Spiritual healing is an important aspect of its teachings. Eddy founded The First Church of Christ, Scientist, in Boston, in 1879, and the *Christian Science Monitor* in 1908.

Ederle, Gertrude (1906–2003) swimmer. In 1926, at the age of nineteen, Ederle became the first woman to swim the English Channel. Strong seas forced her to swim thirty-five miles to cover the twenty-one miles from near Calais, France, to Dover, England. But she broke the previous

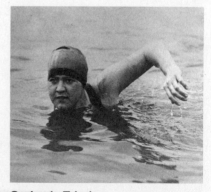

Gertrude Ederle

record by two hours, swimming it in a little over fourteen hours.

Edison, Thomas (1847–1931), inventor. Edison, known as the "Wizard of Menlo Park," changed the world by inventing the incandescent electric lamp, the phonograph, and the motion picture projector. He also developed the world's first electric power station. In his lifetime Edison, who said that genius is "1 percent inspiration and 99 percent perspiration," obtained patents for more than a thousand inventions.

Edmonds, Sarah (1841–98), Union soldier during the CIVIL WAR. Disguised as "Frank Thompson," Edmonds fought at the First Battle of Bull Run and Fredericksburg. As a woman she spied on Confederate troops. Although many other women served with Union troops in disguise, Edmonds was one of the few to be recognized for her role and the only woman to be granted a veteran's pension by Congress.

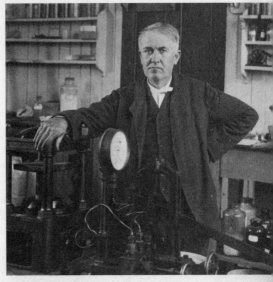

Thomas Edison
Edison in his East Orange, New Jersey, laboratory, ca. 1901.

Education, Department of, an agency of the federal government formed to administer programs intended to promote educational opportunities. The department began in 1867 as a federal agency and in 1953 became part of the Department of Health, Education, and Welfare. In 1979 HEW split and Education became a separate executive department. The secretary of education, a member of the cabinet, is the president's chief adviser on educational matters.

Edwards, Jonathan (1703–58), clergyman. As a philosophical theologian and revivalist in Puritan New England, Edwards exerted profound influence on colonial beliefs through his sermons. His preachings contributed to a movement called the GREAT AWAKENING with its emphasis on personal redemption through faith.

Ehrlichman, John (1925–99), presidential assistant for domestic affairs in the Nixon administration. Ehrlichman was an active participant in the WATERGATE SCANDAL and cover-up. His indictment and conviction in 1974 resulted in his serving eighteen months in an Arizona prison camp. He wrote the political novels *The Company* (1976) and *The Whole Truth* (1979).

Einstein, Albert (1879–1955), physicist. Einstein, born in Germany and living in Switzerland, published three papers in 1905 that revolutionized science. These papers explained the photoelectric effect, Brownian motion, and the theory of relativity. The latter presented the equation $E = mc^2$ — the energy in matter equals its mass multiplied by the square of the velocity of light — a formula that anticipated the splitting of the atom and the release of atomic energy thirty-five years later. He received the Nobel Prize for physics in 1921. Einstein, who was Jewish, fled Nazi Europe in 1933 and accepted a post at the Institute for Advanced Studies at Princeton, where he remained for the rest of his life. Although a pacifist, Einstein in 1939 was troubled by the course of the war in Europe and wrote a letter to Franklin D. Roosevelt, explaining the possibility of building an ATOMIC BOMB and warning that the Nazis might be developing such a device. This led to the Manhattan Project and the production of a bomb in 1945. After the war, Einstein's role as a public figure and peace activist helped shape popular ideas of scientists and scientific genius.

Eisenhower Doctrine (1957), a policy formulated by Secretary of State JOHN FOSTER DULLES to maintain U.S. interests in the Middle East. Approved by Congress in 1957, the doctrine pledged U.S. financial and military aid to Middle Eastern countries resisting Communist expansion. The policy was applied when U.S. Marines landed in Lebanon in 1958 at the request of the Lebanese government to restore order there.

Eisenhower, Dwight D. (1890–1969), thirty-fourth president of the United States (1953–61) and supreme commander of Allied forces in Europe during WORLD WAR II. Eisenhower led the U.S. invasion of North Africa and the D-DAY invasion of France. As president Eisenhower ended the KOREAN WAR with an armistice. Although initially reluctant to deal with civil rights matters, he ultimately enforced the Brown decision by sending troops to Little Rock, Arkansas, to back the desegregation of a school there. He also hesitated to condemn McCarthyism but in the end gave tacit approval to the senator's censure. He approved two huge transportation projects: the St. Lawrence Seaway and the Federal Highway Act of 1956 authorizing the interstate system. Alaska and Hawaii were admitted into the Union during Eisenhower's term. When he left office, his farewell address and most famous speech warned against the growth of the military-industrial complex.

Elastic Clause, the last paragraph of Article I, Section 8, of the U.S. CONSTITUTION, giving Congress the power to "make all laws which shall be necessary and proper" for carrying out the powers and purposes of the Constitution. So named because it can be used to expand the powers of Congress to fit appropriate situations, the elastic clause has provided a flexibility that has made frequent amendment of the Constitution unnecessary.

Elections, Presidential. For results of elections, SEE TABLE. Accounts of the issues and events in each election follow below.

The Process: Article II of the Constitution, modified by the Twelfth Amendment, specifies how the president and vice president are to be selected. Rejecting proposals that the chief executive be elected by Congress, by direct popular election, or by state legislatures, the Constitutional Convention of 1787 compromised on a form of indirect popular election. Each state was to choose, in any way its legislature determined, electors equal to the number of its members in Congress. Comprising what was to be called the electoral college, these electors met in their own states and voted for two persons on the same ballot. The person receiving the majority became president; the runner-up took the position of vice president. In the event of a tie or lack of a majority, the House of Representatives would decide, with each state casting one vote. If no candidate had a majority, the House would choose from the five leading contenders.

Because no distinction was made between ballots for president and vice president, the emergence of national political parties and the development of slates created confusion in the electoral system. A tie between Thomas Jefferson and Aaron Burr in the ELECTION OF 1800 sent the decision to the House of Representatives and led to the Twelfth Amendment to the Constitution (ratified in 1804) providing that electors cast separate votes for president and vice president. If no presidential candidate receives a majority of electoral votes, the House selects from the top three contenders, with each state casting one vote and a majority required to win. If no vice presidential candidate receives a majority, the Senate chooses from the two highest contenders, with each senator casting one vote and a majority required to win.

Election of 1789: After presiding over the Constitutional Convention in 1787, George Washington became associated with the new government and people took it for granted that he would be chosen as the first president. Although reluctant to run, Washington was finally convinced to do so by Alexander Hamilton and other leaders. The first presidential election was held in January 1789, and Washington, running unopposed, was unanimously selected, receiving all sixty-nine votes of the electoral college. Fearing a tie because most Federalists favored John Adams for vice president, Hamilton arranged that a number of votes be deflected from Adams to avoid an embarrassment to Washington, thus assuring him the presidency.

Election of 1792: The major difficulty in the second election was persuading Washington to seek reelection. Wanting to retire, Washington complained of old age and the criticisms of his administration by Democratic-Republicans. He was disturbed by a split within the government generated by the rise of political parties, and he attempted to discourage their growth. James Madison, Thomas Jefferson, and others finally convinced him that only he could hold the government together. The Democratic-Republicans, supporting Jefferson's ideas of a strict interpretation of the Constitution, favored George Clinton, governor of New York, as vice president. The Federalists, supporting the ideas of Alexander Hamilton and a stronger national government, advocated the reelection of John Adams, who won.

Election of 1796: By refusing to run for a third term, Washington set a precedent for two terms, which lasted until 1940. The election of 1796 was the first contested presidential race between political parties, the FED-ERALISTS led by Vice President John Adams and the DEMOCRATIC-REPUBLICANS led by Thomas Jefferson. The candidates of both parties were nominated by the first congressional caucus, a procedure that continued until 1828. The Federalists favored a strong central government and northern commercial interests. The Democratic-Republicans favored states' rights and southern agrarian interests, and opposed the JAY TREATY with Britain. The Federalists felt the agreement was essential to prevent a potentially devastating war with England. To gain southern support, the Federalists selected Thomas Pinckney of South Carolina as a vice-presidential candidate. But because the electors cast two votes for president, and because eleven Federalist electors in New Hampshire failed to give their votes to Pinckney (their party's vice-presidential nominee), Jefferson became vice president. This election resulted in the only instance in which a president and vice president were not of the same party.

Election of 1800: The election of 1800 involved the first peaceful transfer of power between political parties and marked the first of two instances in which the president was elected by the House of Representatives. The Democratic-Republicans, led by Thomas Jefferson, succeeded the Federalists, led by incumbent President John Adams. The system did not provide for separate ballots for president and vice president, and when each Democratic-Republican elector cast one vote for Jefferson and the other for Aaron Burr, a tie resulted. The election for president was thrown into the House, where each state received one vote. The House, still controlled by a partisan Federalist majority, was to decide the presidency, even though the incoming House was controlled by the other party. In all, there were 106 members in the House — 58 Federalists and 48 Democratic-Republicans, and if each member had cast one ballot, Burr would have been elected president. On the first ballot, Jefferson received the votes of eight states, one short of a majority of the sixteen states in the Union at the time. Six states backed Burr, but the representatives of Vermont and Maryland were equally divided, so their states lost their votes. On the first day, February 11, 1801, nineteen tie ballots were cast. A total of thirty-six ballots were taken before the House broke the deadlock. On February 17 Vermont and Maryland switched their support to Jefferson, and Delaware and South Carolina withdrew their support from Burr, casting blank votes. The final results were ten states for Jefferson and four for Burr. Thus Jefferson was elected the third president and Burr automatically became vice president. The Jefferson-Burr deadlock proved that the method of electoral voting was inefficient and resulted in the Twelfth Amendment, by which each elector casts one vote for president and the other for vice president.

Election of 1804: The Twelfth Amendment, passed in 1804, provided for separate electoral ballots for president and vice president for the first time. The Republicans, led by incumbent President Thomas Jefferson, won a landslide victory over the Federalists, led by Charles C. Pinckney. Jefferson was helped by his popular purchase of the Louisiana Territory in 1803, his reduction of federal government spending, and the nation's sense of prosperity. The only opposition occurred in New England. Federalists, regarding the LOUISIANA PURCHASE as a threat to New England's power and influence, plotted to enlist Vice President Burr to lead a secession of New York and New England from the Union. The Federalists alienated many voters and became discredited.

Election of 1808: Jefferson refused to run for a third term, reinforcing the precedent established by Washington. The Democratic-Republican congressional caucus nominated James Madison for president and Vice President George Clinton as his running mate, while the Federalists chose Charles C. Pinckney and Rufus King. Madison won the election easily and Clinton, receiving six electoral votes from his home state of New York for president, easily defeated King. The key issue of the election was the EMBARGO ACT OF 1807, imposed by President Jefferson, which had damaged the U.S. economy, especially the northeastern merchants and shipping industry. The economic problems briefly revived the Federalists, especially in New England. The embargo was repealed just prior to Jefferson's departure from office.

Election of 1812: The congressional caucus renominated Democratic-Republican Madison for president and chose Elbridge Gerry for vice president. The Federalists selected the lieutenant governor of New York, DeWitt Clinton, and Jared Ingersoll. The WAR OF 1812, declared by Madison five months earlier, was the key issue. Opposition to the war with Great Britain centered in New England and the Federalist-controlled commercial northeastern states. A vote for Madison meant a vote for war; a vote for Clinton, a vote for peace. Another issue was the challenge by Clinton supporters of Virginia's control of the presidency, called the Virginia Dynasty, which they charged favored agrarian over commercial states. The southern and western states strongly supported Madison. This was the last presidential election in which the Federalist party was a significant participant.

Election of 1816: Although James Monroe, Madison's chosen successor, barely won the nomination in the Democratic-Republican congressional caucus over William Crawford, secretary of war (with a vote of 65–54), he easily defeated the Federalists led by Rufus King. During the campaign the New England Federalists held a meeting, the HARTFORD CONVENTION, to consider secession. The signing of the TREATY OF GHENT in 1814 ending the War of 1812 ushered in a period of nationalism. The growth of the economy, the establishment of a standing army, the imposition of a protective tariff, the founding of the Second BANK OF THE UNITED STATES, and internal improvements including a system of roads and canals — all contributed to an ERA OF GOOD FEELINGS. Opposition from Federalists made them seem almost unpatriotic.

Election of 1820: Monroe ran unopposed and the Democratic-Republicans faced no organized opposition for reelection in 1820 because of peace and prosperity. Despite the suffering engendered by the panic of 1819 and sectional differences over the spread of slavery in the territories, Monroe won the presidency almost unanimously. Only one presidential elector, William Plumer of New Hampshire, refused to vote for him, later explaining that he had voted against Monroe because he thought he was incompetent. The Federalists had ceased to exist by the time of this election.

Election of 1824: After Monroe's retirement in 1824, the Democratic-Republican party became divided and selected sectional and favorite-son candidates. Although there were many contenders, four dominated: Secretary of State John Quincy Adams of Massachusetts, Speaker of the House Henry Clay of Kentucky, Secretary of the Treasury William Crawford of Georgia, and the War of 1812 hero Andrew Jackson of Tennessee. Crawford won the nomination of the party's congressional caucus, but a majority of the states chose electors by popular votes and nominations by congressional caucuses were discredited. A severe illness hampered Crawford's candidacy. No candidate received a majority of electoral votes, thereby throwing the election into the House of Representatives to choose from the top three candidates, with each state receiving one vote. The fourth-place candidate, House Speaker Henry Clay, threw his support to Adams, who was elected president by a vote of 13 to 11 on the first ballot. Adams then named Clay secretary of state, leading to allegations by Jackson and his supporters that a "corrupt bargain" had been struck. John C. Calhoun was elected vice president with a majority of the electoral votes. The key issues included the personalities of the candidates, all four of whom ran on the same ticket, and the growth of sectionalism. Adams became the first president to take office with a minority of popular votes.

Election of 1828: This election reestablished the two-party political system in the United States. The name "Democrat" was used for the first time in this campaign, marking the formal beginning of the DEMOCRATIC PARTY. Andrew Jackson and the Democrats easily won an overwhelming victory over incumbent Adams and the National Republicans. John C. Calhoun was reelected vice president. Jackson's Democratic party developed an efficient national political organization, but Adams's National Republicans lacked local organization. The 1828 presidential campaign was one of the dirtiest in the history of the United States. Both parties circulated false or exaggerated rumors about the opposition. Jackson and his supporters charged that the House of Representatives had ignored the will of the people by denying him the presidency in 1824 even though he had been the leader in popular and electoral votes. They reminded voters of Adams's "corrupt bargain" with Henry Clay. Jackson was denounced as a violent frontier barbarian, and his family was verbally attacked. Jackson was also criticized for brutality during the SEMINOLE WARS in Florida. The candidates' personalities were thrown into contrast: Adams, "the decadent aristocrat" and Jackson, "the common democratic man."

Election of 1832: The ANTI-MASONIC PARTY, the first third party in American politics, emerged out of growing hostility toward secret societies, particularly the Masons. This party held the first national presidential nominating convention. The other two parties followed the Anti-Masons' lead, so that all the presidential candidates of the major political parties were nominated by national conventions instead of the discredited party caucuses. Key issues in the campaign were the SPOILS SYSTEM, the tariff, and the AMERICAN SYSTEM of internal improvements paid for by the federal government. Andrew Jackson's veto of the rechartering of the BANK OF THE UNITED STATES became the major issue. Although he managed to close the bank and further antagonized his enemies by investing in state institutions called PET BANKS, Jackson won an overwhelming victory. In South Carolina, nullificationists cast their electoral votes for John Floyd.

Election of 1836: The Democratic party gave the presidential nomination to Andrew Jackson's hand-picked choice, Vice President Martin Van Buren, and chose Richard M. Johnson as running mate. The WHIG PARTY ran three candidates who were strong in different parts of the country, hoping their combined electoral votes would throw the election into the House of Representatives where they could defeat the Democrats, but their strategy failed. The Whigs accused the Democrats of abolitionism, increasing sectional tensions, and usurpation of power, but the election was basically a referendum on Andrew Jackson. In South Carolina the nullificationists cast their votes for Willie Mangum. In the vice-presidential race, no candidate won a majority of electoral votes so the decision was sent to the Senate. Johnson defeated Francis Granger of New York by a vote of 33–16, thus becoming the first and only man to be chosen vice president by the Senate.

Election of 1840: This election is considered by many historians as the first modern political campaign because of its use of imagery and advertising. The Whigs bypassed their perennial leader Henry Clay and chose war hero and Indian fighter William Henry Harrison, with John Tyler as his running mate. Despite the unpopularity of Martin Van Buren, who was blamed by many for the economic problems associated with the panic of 1837, the Democrats again backed him as a candidate. Incumbent Vice President Richard M. Johnson failed to gain renomination because of his unpopularity. The Democrats chose no vice-presidential candidate, leaving the selection to each state. Thus, Van Buren became the first and only presidential candidate to seek election without a running mate. This was a campaign of antics, not issues. Boisterous campaigning employed slogans like "Tippecanoe and Tyler Too" and "Van, Van, Van / Van is a used-up man." Torchlight parades, wild singing, mass meetings, and much hoopla abounded. More campaign songs were written for Harrison than any other president. Harrison, though of wealthy origins, was portrayed by the Whigs as the "log cabin, hard cider candidate" and Van Buren as the well-to-do aristocrat with no interest in issues of unemployment and depression. Modern politicking had made its appearance and Harrison won by a landslide. His inaugural address was the longest delivered by any president — longer than all four of Franklin D. Roosevelt's addresses put together. He contracted a cold on his inaugural day, which developed into pneumonia, and died after one month in office.

Election of 1844: Expansionism and slavery were the major issues of the election of 1844. The idea of MANIFEST DESTINY was very popular, especially in the South and West. Although John Tyler, who succeeded to the presidency following Harrison's death in 1841, wanted the nomination, he became the first president not to receive nomination for a second term. Instead, the Whigs chose antiexpansionist Henry Clay for president. Former president Martin Van Buren was the leading candidate for the Democratic nomination, but because Van Buren opposed the annexation of Texas and the expansion of slavery, the Democrats picked the first dark horse, James K. Polk, who promised to bring Texas and Oregon into the Union. Silas Wright of New York was the almost unanimous choice for the vice-presidential nomination, but he refused to run out of respect for Van Buren. Pennsylvania lawyer George M. Dallas was chosen as a compromise running mate to appease Van Buren supporters. The LIBERTY PARTY renominated James G. Birney of Michigan for president, who deflected enough votes from Clay to make Polk the winner.

Election of 1848: Democratic President James K. Polk did not seek a second term, so his party nominated Senator Lewis Cass of Michigan. Cass sponsored the idea of POPULAR SOVEREIGNTY, which would allow the settlers of a territory to decide whether to become a free or slave state. Antislavery groups, dissatisfied with Cass, helped form the FREE-SOIL PARTY, advocating prohibition of the extension of slavery, and chose former president Martin Van Buren as their candidate. Although the Free-Soilers won no electoral votes, they drew enough support from Cass in Massachusetts and New York to give Mexican war hero Zachary Taylor and the Whig party a victory. The Free-Soil campaign helped lead to the creation of the REPUBLICAN PARTY in 1854, committed to the principle of free soil. Taylor died in 1850 and Millard Fillmore became the second vice president to succeed to the presidency because of the death of an incumbent.

Election of 1852: When Fillmore became president, he promptly endorsed the COMPROMISE OF 1850, which admitted California as a free state and provided that all other territories acquired from Mexico would be free of slavery restrictions. The Whigs, divided over the slavery issue, rejected Fillmore and Secretary of State Daniel Webster, and nominated Gen. Winfield Scott who supported the FUGITIVE SLAVE LAWS. The Democrats, also split over the issue of slavery, selected dark horse candidate Franklin Pierce of New Hampshire after forty-nine ballots. Free-Soil "Conscience" Whigs opposed the spread of slavery and "Cotton" Whigs encouraged its spread. Unity among Democrats and disunity among the Whigs led to Pierce's election.

Election of 1856: The campaign of 1856 centered around BLEEDING KANSAS and the concept of popular sovereignty. The violence that followed the KANSAS-NEBRASKA ACT changed the political system. The Whig party had died and the Republican party, backing a free-labor society, had been created in 1854. The Democrats chose former secretary of state James Buchanan of Pennsylvania, who had been out of the country during the debate over the Kansas-Nebraska Act and had taken no stand on it. Buchanan's running mate, JOHN C. BRECKINRIDGE, became the youngest man ever to serve as vice president. Even though Buchanan won the election, Republican candidate John C. Frémont and American, or KNOW-NOTHING PARTY candidate Millard Fillmore combined received more popular votes. The Republican party's showing alarmed the South.

Election of 1860: The election of 1860 led to the secession of southern states and the Civil War. Senator William H. Seward of New York was considered the leading Republican candidate but was seen as too fervent an abolitionist, and Abraham Lincoln won the nomination on the third ballot. Senator Hannibal Hamlin of Maine was chosen as his running mate. The Republicans opposed the extension of slavery into the territories and favored a homestead act and a tariff. The Democratic convention met in Charleston, South Carolina, but could not agree on a candidate; many southern delegates bolted. Reconvening in Baltimore, Maryland, the party formally split. The northern Democrats chose Senator Stephen A. Douglas of Illinois for president. The convention left the selection of the vice-presidential candidate to a caucus of the remaining southern delegates, who chose Benjamin Fitzpatrick of Alabama. Shortly after the convention, Fitzpatrick declined the nomination, and for the first time, a national committee had to fill a vacancy on a national ticket. Chosen unanimously was the former governor of Georgia, Herschel V. Johnson. The southern Democrats convened separately and nominated Vice President John Breckinridge of Kentucky for president. The Constitutional Union party was formed by ex-Whigs and Know-Nothings who chose Senator John Bell of Tennessee for president. Their platform embraced preservation of the Constitution and the Union as they existed, ignoring the controversial and divisive issues. The Deep South states of South Carolina, Alabama, Georgia, Louisiana, Florida, Mississippi, and Texas seceded from the Union when they learned that Lincoln had been elected. Later four states from the Upper South — Virginia, North Carolina, Tennessee, and Arkansas — joined the Confederacy.

Election of 1864: This election took place as the CIVIL WAR raged. RADICAL REPUBLICANS, afraid of defeat, talked of replacing Lincoln with a more overtly antislavery man, such as Salmon P. Chase, secretary of the treasury, or Gens. John C. Frémont or Benjamin F. Butler, but Lincoln prevailed. The Republican party appeared on the ballot as the National UNION PARTY and selected Tennessee military governor and pro-war Democrat Andrew Johnson as Lincoln's new running mate. The Democrats nominated Gen. George B. McClellan for president and Representative George Pendleton of Ohio as vice president to run on a peace platform. Lincoln won easily, largely because of Union victories in the field and his release of many Union soldiers to go home on furlough, allowing them to vote. Lincoln's campaign slogan was "Don't swap horses in midstream."

Election of 1868: RECONSTRUCTION policy in the aftermath of the Civil War was the key issue of the 1868 campaign. The Republicans rallied behind the most successful Union general of the war, Ulysses S. Grant, and chose Schuyler Colfax, Speaker of the House, as his running mate. Horatio Seymour, governor of New York, selected as the Democrats' standard-bearer, criticized the Republican's Reconstruction program and objected to their granting of rights to the freed slaves. The Republicans were skeptical of the wartime patriotism of the Democrats. The former slaves contributed to the Republican victory, with many of them exercising their right to vote for the first time.

Election of 1872: Horace Greeley, *New York Tribune* editor, was the choice of the Liberal Republicans; the Democrats endorsed him for the sake of expediency. Greeley ran on a platform of civil service reform and an end to Reconstruction. Grant, the Republican incumbent, also supported civil service reform and protection of the rights of the ex-slaves. Grant won the largest Republican popular majority of the century. Greeley died after the election but before the meeting of the presidential electors, and his votes were distributed among several Democratic candidates.

Election of 1876: The nation had tired of Reconstruction policies that kept federal troops in the South and the scandals that had occurred during Grant's administration. The economic depression that followed the panic of 1873 further troubled the Republican party. The Republicans nominated Rutherford B. Hayes, governor of Ohio, as a reform candidate. His Democratic opponent, Governor Samuel J. Tilden of New York, also promised change. Tilden won the popular vote majority but fell one vote short of the electoral majority of 185 needed to win. Hayes took 165 electoral votes. Twenty votes were disputed — nineteen from three states that still had Reconstruction governments (South Carolina, Louisiana, and Florida), and one from Oregon. Republican officials in the three southern states charged that racist electoral rules were used to take the black vote away from Hayes. The parties submitted two differing sets of electoral returns from these states and each claimed victory. Congress, split along party lines, was unable to decide the issue impartially. To determine the authenticity of the disputed returns, a fifteen-member electoral commission made up of ten congressmen and five U.S. Supreme Court justices was set up. The commission, composed of eight Republicans and seven Democrats, voted strictly along party lines, awarding the disputed votes and the presidency to Hayes. In return for a peaceful inauguration, the Republicans removed all federal troops from the southern states in what is known as the COMPROMISE OF 1877, which ended Reconstruction.

Election of 1880: Hayes did not seek reelection. The Republican party was divided between the STALWARTS led by New York Senator Roscoe Conkling, who supported Ulysses S. Grant for president, and the HALF-BREEDS, followers of Representative James G. Blaine. Ex-president Grant, out of office for four years, led on the first thirty-five ballots. On the thirty-sixth, a compromise candidate was selected, Representative James Garfield of Ohio. The Democrats selected Gen. Winfield Scott Hancock, a noncontroversial candidate. Both parties endorsed civil service reform, pensions for veterans, and exclusion of Chinese immigrants. Though the campaign lacked major issues, there was an extremely high voter turnout, resulting in Garfield's winning one of the closest elections in American history.

Election of 1884: This election gave the country the first Democratic president since before the Civil War. The Republican party split into three groups: the MUGWUMPS, who opposed government graft; the Stalwarts, who supported Grant for a third term; and the Half-Breeds, who were moderate reformers. James G. Blaine, nominated by the Republicans, was opposed by New York's Democratic governor, Grover Cleveland. In a campaign noted for mudslinging, Blaine alienated many voters, especially in New York when he did not dispute a statement by Rev. Samuel Burchard accusing the Democrats of "rum, Romanism, and rebellion." New York went for Cleveland, giving him the presidency.

Election of 1888: The Democrats renominated Grover Cleveland and selected Allen Thurman as his running mate to replace Thomas Hendricks, who had died in office. The Republicans chose Benjamin Harrison, a Civil War hero and grandson of William Henry Harrison. Although Cleveland received over 90,000 more popular votes than Harrison, he lost the election in the electoral college. The Republicans became the party of high tariffs, with the Democrats urging lower rates. Corruption characterized the campaign, in which votes were bought and deals were struck. The GRAND ARMY OF THE REPUBLIC, a society of northern Civil War veterans, was an important political force in the Republican party, which opposed President Cleveland after he vetoed veteran pension legislation and decided to return Confederate battle flags to the South.

Election of 1892: This election pitted Republican Benjamin Harrison against Grover Cleveland once again, with the People's, or POPULIST, party candidate Gen. James Weaver running for the first time. The major issue was the tariff, which had been raised by the Republicans in 1890. The Republicans continued to support high rates, and the Democrats advocated a tariff for revenue only. The Populists advocated government ownership of railroads. Cleveland avenged his defeat of 1888 and became the only president to be elected to nonconsecutive terms of office.

Election of 1896: The Democratic party, which absorbed Populist ideas, nominated William Jennings Bryan, who was opposed by Governor William McKinley of Ohio. The Democrats endorsed the "free and unlimited coinage of both silver and gold at the . . . ratio of 16 to 1." Bryan, an ex-congressman from Nebraska, based his campaign on his famous "Cross of Gold" speech, presented at the Democratic National Convention in Chicago. Emotionally proclaiming, "You shall not crucify mankind upon a cross of gold," he won the support of the delegates and campaigned across the country. McKinley conducted a front-porch campaign at home but acquired extensive financial backing from big business and manufacturers who helped portray Bryan and the Populists as radicals. In a campaign orchestrated by Mark Hanna of Ohio, the Republican organization raised large amounts of money, some from wealthy Democrats, to send speakers and pamphlets throughout the country. They outspent the Democrats by nearly twelve to one. The Democrats lacked funds and organization. "Gold Democrats," who refused to support the free-silver platform, formed the National Democratic party and nominated Senator John M. Palmer of Illinois for president. McKinley carried all the northern industrial states in winning the presidency.

Election of 1900: William Jennings Bryan campaigned as an anti-imperialist, condemning acquisition of the territories occupied as a result of the Spanish-American War and continued his crusade for the free coinage of silver. William McKinley did not actively campaign but had the support of big business and promoted a protective tariff. Owing to existing prosperity McKinley was easily reelected. Less than a year later, McKinley was assassinated and Vice President Theodore Roosevelt became the youngest man to serve as president of the United States.

Election of 1904: Roosevelt ran as a progressive liberal Republican, while Democratic candidate Alton B. Parker, a New York judge with backing from Wall Street, attacked Roosevelt for his antitrust policies and his acceptance of contributions from big business. Roosevelt won easily, largely because of his personal popularity, losing only the thirteen states in the South to the Democrats. For vice president the Democrats chose former West Virginia senator Henry G. Davis who, at age eighty, was the oldest candidate ever put on a national ticket by a major party.

Election of 1908: Roosevelt declined to seek another term and the Republicans chose Secretary of War and Roosevelt's personal choice, William Howard Taft. The Democrats chose William Jennings Bryan for the third time. The major campaign issue was Roosevelt and his reforms, which Taft promised to carry out. Backed by big business, Taft easily won the election.

Election of 1912: Roosevelt, angry over Taft's turn toward conservatism and failure to carry out Roosevelt's reform policies, challenged Taft for the Republican nomination. Taft won, and Roosevelt bolted the convention to form the PROGRESSIVE, or BULL MOOSE PARTY with himself as presidential nominee. The Democratic party nominated Woodrow Wilson, governor of New Jersey, on the forty-sixth ballot. Nicholas Murray Butler replaced James Sherman as the Republican nominee for vice president on October 30, 1912, following Sherman's death. The campaign turned on Roosevelt's NEW NATIONALISM, which called for a government with strong regulatory powers, and Wilson's NEW FREEDOM, which proposed antimonopoly policies and a return to small-scale business. Wilson, in winning, became the first Democratic president since Grover Cleveland. Given the combined vote of Roosevelt and Taft, the Republicans would have defeated the Democrats if the party had not split.

Election of 1916: Roosevelt refused a nomination by the Progressive party in an effort to reunify the Republicans. The Democrats' campaign emphasized Wilson's program of domestic reform and the fact that he had kept the United States out of the war in Europe. Charles Evans Hughes, ex-governor of New York, had left the U.S. Supreme Court to challenge Wilson on the Republican ticket, and he received the support of Irish- and German-Americans who openly opposed aid to Great Britain. Wilson was reelected by winning California. The electoral vote was the closest since 1876, with a margin of only twenty-three votes.

Election of 1920: In this first election in which women could vote and in which returns were broadcast by radio, the Republicans, led by Warren G. Harding, won an overwhelming victory. The Democrats nominated Governor James M. Cox of Ohio for president and Assistant Secretary of the Navy Franklin D. Roosevelt for vice president. After a period of progressive leadership, the Republican party returned to a more conservative position. The campaign revolved around America's isolationism following WORLD WAR I and the question of U.S. membership in the LEAGUE OF NATIONS. Many Americans, weary of the constraints of war and world problems, turned inward to domestic matters. The election was a repudiation of Wilson's progressivism and involvement in international affairs, and an endorsement of Harding's promise for a "return to normalcy." Conducting a front-porch campaign from his home in Marion, Ohio, Harding took all the electoral votes outside the South except Tennessee for a decisive victory, while Socialist party candidate Eugene V. Debs received over 900,000 popular votes while serving a federal prison sentence for opposing the war. Harding died in 1923 and Calvin Coolidge, sworn in by his father, a justice of the peace, became the sixth vice president to succeed to the presidency because of the death of the incumbent.

Election of 1924: After succeeding Harding in 1923, Coolidge, riding on a wave of prosperity and using the slogan "Keep Cool with Coolidge," easily won reelection. Ex-governor Frank Lowdon of Illinois led on the first ballot for vice president, even though he had publicly stated he would not accept the nomination. He received a majority of the vote on the second roll call, but when he refused, the convention turned to former budget director Charles G. Dawes. Dissatisfied members of both parties — reformers, farmers, and laborers — formed a third party, the PROGRESSIVE PARTY, and nominated Robert La Follette for president. The party's platform called for higher taxes on the wealthy, the end of child labor, and direct election of the president by popular vote. The Democrats split over leading candidates Alfred E. Smith (supported by eastern big-city politicians) and William McAdoo (backed by southern members of the Ku Klux Klan and western rural forces). After six days and 103 ballots, the Democrats chose a dark horse candidate, conservative John W. Davis of West Virginia, a well-known Wall Street lawyer, and as his running mate Governor Charles W. Bryan, brother of William Jennings Bryan. All Democratic votes came from the South. La Follette captured only the votes from his home state of Wisconsin.

Election of 1928: Coolidge announced, "I do not choose to run for president in 1928," although he hoped to be drafted by the Republican convention. The Republicans, however, turned to Secretary of Commerce Herbert Hoover, promising "a chicken in every pot and a car in every garage." Democrats nominated the governor of New York, "Happy Warrior" Alfred E. Smith. The two major issues were PROHIBITION and religion. Smith, a wet and a Roman Catholic, favored repeal of the Eighteenth Amendment and modification of liquor laws, while Hoover, a dry and a Protestant, opposed repeal of Prohibition and advocated full enforcement. Hoover won a large victory, partly because the country was prosperous. For the first time since Reconstruction, the Democratic hold on the "Solid South" was broken by the Republicans, but the Democrats carried the nation's twelve largest cities. This support by urban America marked the start of a major political shift in the country.

Election of 1932: The Republicans renominated Hoover, and the Democrats, confident of victory after the STOCK MARKET CRASH and the onset of the GREAT DEPRESSION, nominated Franklin D. Roosevelt, governor of New York. Setting a precedent, Roosevelt became the first nominee to make an acceptance speech at the convention. He promised a NEW DEAL for the American people, especially the "forgotten man at the bottom of the economic pyramid." The Democratic platform called for a reduction in federal spending and the repeal of Prohibition, but the major issue was how to get out of the depression. Roosevelt's eloquence and personality were enhanced by the fact that candidates campaigned on the radio for the first time. Roosevelt won a landslide victory, and the Democrats also took control of both houses of Congress.

Election of 1936: Roosevelt was renominated by the Democrats without opposition. The Republicans, strongly opposing the New Deal and "big government," nominated Alfred M. Landon, governor of Kansas. Eighty percent of the newspapers endorsed the Republican party, which was also supported by conservative Democrats including Alfred E. Smith. Big business accused FDR of destroying the nation's individualism and threatening its freedom, but he put together a coalition of intellectuals, blue-collar workers, southern farmers, and urban minority voters, including a huge number of blacks who shifted to the Democratic party. Roosevelt won in another landslide; Landon won only the states of Maine and Vermont.

Election of 1940: The Democratic party broke the tradition started by George Washington and nominated Roosevelt for a third consecutive term. Secretary of Agriculture Henry A. Wallace was chosen as the vice-presidential candidate over John Nance Garner, two-term vice president who no longer agreed with FDR's policies. The Republicans chose Wendell L. Willkie, a former Democrat and liberal internationalist businessman, to lead what had been a conservative isolationist party, because the major issue in 1940 was the overshadowing threat of World War II. The third-term issue was exploited by the Republicans using the slogan, "Washington wouldn't, Grant couldn't, Roosevelt shouldn't; no third term." Both candidates pledged to keep the country out of war. Roosevelt won the election handily and became the first president elected to a third term.

Election of 1944: With the country well into WORLD WAR II, Roosevelt decided to run for a fourth term in 1944. Because Democratic party regulars disliked Wallace because of his perceived radicalism, they persuaded FDR to replace him with Harry S. Truman, senator from Missouri. The Republicans chose Thomas E. Dewey over Willkie. Roosevelt himself was the major issue; his health was questionable, and his stand on communism and his competence as an administrator were challenged. Whether any person should serve four terms as president also became an issue. But with the war still raging, Democrats used the slogan, "Don't change horses in midstream," and FDR won easily for a fourth time. On April 12, 1945, he died of a cerebral hemorrhage, and after serving about one month as vice president, Truman was sworn in as president of the United States.

Election of 1948: Truman was nominated by the Democrats for president, but the Democrats split when a strong civil rights plank was included in the platform. Conservative southern Democrats bolted and, forming the States' Rights Democratic party, called the DIXIECRAT PARTY, nominated South Carolina Governor Strom Thurmond for president. Henry A. Wallace also left the Democrats, becoming the left-wing PROGRESSIVE PARTY candidate and badly hurting Truman's chances for reelection. The Republicans renominated Thomas E. Dewey. All newspapers and public opinion polls showed Dewey far ahead and predicted a Republican victory. Truman did not give up, however; he conducted a whistle-stop train campaign across the United States, criticizing the "do-nothing, good-for-nothing" Republican-controlled Congress. Dewey, believing he would win easily, all but stopped campaigning and thus "snapped defeat out of the jaws of victory." In the biggest political upset in American history and a stunning personal victory, Harry S. Truman was reelected president.

Election of 1952: The Republican party nominated the enormously popular World War II hero Dwight D. Eisenhower for president over "Mr. Republican" Senator Robert A. Taft of Ohio. Truman declined to run for reelection, so the Democrats selected Adlai E. Stevenson, governor of Illinois. The major issues included the ending of the KOREAN WAR, corruption in government, an inflationary economy, and a perceived communist threat. The Republicans used the slogan "I Like Ike" (Eisenhower). A scandal regarding use of campaign funds almost caused Republican vice-presidential candidate Richard M. Nixon to lose his place on the ticket. Declaring his innocence, Nixon appealed to the emotions of the public in a televised speech featuring his wife's "Republican cloth coat" and his little dog "Checkers," thus remaining on the slate. Eisenhower won by a huge landslide, the largest in American history.

Election of 1956: Despite medical problems during his first term (a heart attack and abdominal surgery), Eisenhower was nominated again by the Republicans, as was Stevenson by the Democrats. Republicans claimed credit for the country's prosperity and peace. The major issue of the campaign was foreign policy. Stevenson wanted to end the draft and halt nuclear testing. Near the end of the campaign, the Suez Canal crisis occurred, and Americans voted against change, reelecting Ike by overwhelming numbers.

Election of 1960: The Republicans nominated Vice President Richard M. Nixon of California. Unable to persuade guaranteed vote-getter Governor Nelson Rockefeller of New York to share the ticket, Nixon selected U.N. ambassador Henry Cabot Lodge, Jr. The Democrats chose Senator John F.

Kennedy of Massachusetts, who selected majority leader Senator Lyndon B. Johnson of Texas as his running mate. A bitter and hard-fought campaign included major issues of loss of national prestige, youth versus experience, inflation, and a "missile gap" between the United States and the Soviet Union. Although Kennedy was a Roman Catholic, and religion influenced a number of votes, it was not a major issue. Nixon originally led in the polls, but two factors helped Kennedy close the gap: Nixon's unwise pledge to campaign in all fifty states, which exhausted him both physically and financially, and more important, the first television debate between the two. The "great debates" allowed JFK to display his charisma and narrow the polls almost overnight. Kennedy won, becoming the first Catholic and youngest man, at age forty-three, elected to the presidency. On November 22, 1963, Kennedy became the fourth president to be assassinated, and Johnson became the eighth vice president to succeed to the presidency because of the death of an incumbent.

Election of 1964: The Democrats nominated liberal President Johnson, and the Republicans nominated conservative Senator Barry Goldwater of Arizona. The campaign was conducted in the middle of the escalating VIETNAM WAR. Goldwater said that North Vietnam should be constantly bombed and questioned the Social Security system. The Democrats adopted a social reform platform, with Johnson campaigning as a "candidate of peace" against the "militaristic candidate" Goldwater. The Republicans said they offered "a choice, not an echo." After a campaign featuring mudslinging and negative advertising, Johnson won overwhelmingly.

Election of 1968: President Johnson's announcement that he would not seek reelection stunned the nation following his surprisingly narrow victory over Senator Eugene McCarthy of Minnesota, an anti-Vietnam War candidate, in the New Hampshire Democratic primary. Vice President Hubert H. Humphrey announced his candidacy, supporting most of LBJ's policies. Senator Robert Kennedy of New York announced his intention to run as an antiwar candidate, and he and McCarthy challenged each other in Democratic primaries across the country, with Kennedy losing only in Oregon. In June, hours after winning the California primary, Kennedy was shot to death. Humphrey won the Democratic nomination at the convention in Chicago. The party was split over the war in Vietnam, and violence and bloodshed occurred in the streets of Chicago between antiwar protesters and the police. The Republicans, meeting in Miami, more peacefully rejected the liberal challenge of Nelson Rockefeller and the conservative challenge of Ronald Reagan, and the delegates nominated the moderate Richard M. Nixon as their standard-bearer, with running mate Spiro T. Agnew. The American Independent party nominated segregationist George Wallace, governor of Alabama, for president and Air Force Gen. Curtis LeMay for vice president, who proposed using nuclear weapons in

Vietnam. The major issues were the war, civil rights, "law and order," and the federal deficit. Nixon campaigned on the premise that he had a "secret plan" to end the war. The polls originally showed Nixon far ahead because of the bitter division within the Democratic party. Humphrey slowly closed the gap and late in the campaign announced that he would seek to end American involvement in Vietnam. But it was too late for him to overcome Nixon, who won.

Election of 1972: The Republicans renominated Nixon, and the Democrats, still split over the war in Vietnam, chose liberal Senator George McGovern of South Dakota for president and Senator Thomas Eagleton of Missouri for vice president. Eagleton resigned from the ticket after it was disclosed that he had once received electric shock treatments and other psychiatric help. The National Democratic Committee replaced Eagleton with R. Sargent Shriver, director of the Peace Corps. The major issues included the possibility of peace in Vietnam, the economy, and government spending. The Republicans, united because of prosperity, used the slogans "Four More Years" and "Nixon, Now More Than Ever." They accused McGovern of being the candidate of "acid, abortion, and amnesty." The Democrats lost in one of the greatest landslides in America's history, with McGovern winning only Massachusetts and Washington, D.C.

Vice President Spiro Agnew resigned from office in October 1973 amid charges of corruption. Under the Twenty-fifth Amendment, President Nixon nominated minority leader of the House of Representatives Gerald Ford for vice president. Ford's confirmation by both houses of Congress took place in December 1973. Then in August 1974 Nixon became the first president to resign from office after the House Judiciary Committee voted three articles of impeachment because of Nixon's involvement in a cover-up of a break-in at the Democratic party headquarters in the WATERGATE apartment and office complex. Vice President Ford was sworn in as president and nominated Governor Nelson Rockefeller for vice president. Congress confirmed his appointment in September 1974.

Election of 1976: The Democrats nominated former governor of Georgia Jimmy Carter. Despite a spirited challenge from conservative governor of California Ronald Reagan, the Republicans chose President Ford. Carter ran as an outsider, independent of the Washington, D.C., establishment. The major issue was the Watergate scandal and the disgrace Republicans had brought on the presidency. Also of importance was Ford's pardon of Nixon for any crimes he might have committed during the Watergate affair. Carter won a narrow victory, and both houses of Congress and the presidency were controlled by the Democrats.

Election of 1980: Senator Edward Kennedy of Massachusetts opposed President Carter in ten primaries, but Carter easily won the Democratic nomination. The Republicans chose former governor of California Ronald

Reagan for president and his principal rival in the primaries, GEORGE H. W. BUSH, for vice president. Liberal Republican John B. Anderson, representative from Illinois, ran on an independent ticket with the former Democratic governor of Wisconsin, Patrick J. Lucey, as vice president. The major issues included the economy, inflation, growing government spending, an energy shortage, and Carter's inability to free the U.S. hostages in Iran. Reagan, with his pledges to cut taxes, increase defense spending, and balance the federal budget, won a landslide victory, as the polls had predicted.

Election of 1984: The Republicans renominated President Reagan and the Democrats chose former vice president Walter Mondale, who had survived challenges from the Reverend Jesse Jackson and Senator Gary Hart of Colorado. Representative Geraldine Ferraro of New York became the first woman nominated by a major party for vice president when the Democrats selected her as Mondale's running mate. The major issues included the growing national debt, inflation, the need for new taxes, and heavy defense spending. Peace and prosperity ensured a Reagan victory, with the Republicans painting Mondale as a candidate of "special interests." Fifty-six percent of women voting chose Reagan-Bush over Mondale-Ferraro. The Republicans won another landslide victory, with Mondale winning only Washington, D.C., and his home state of Minnesota.

Election of 1988: Vice President GEORGE H. W. BUSH won the Republican nomination over numerous rivals in the primaries, including Senator Robert Dole of Kansas. In a somewhat surprising selection he picked an obscure conservative, Senator Dan Quayle of Indiana, for vice president. The Democrats nominated Massachusetts governor Michael Dukakis after he had won most of the primaries, defeating Jesse Jackson and Gary Hart. Hart withdrew from the race following disclosure of a personal scandal. Dukakis chose Lloyd Bentsen of Texas for vice president, hoping to repeat the 1960 winning combination of Kennedy (Massachusetts) and Johnson (Texas). The campaign was marred by mudslinging and controversial television advertisements. Bush fought back from an early-summer Dukakis lead with attacks on Dukakis's liberalism and the campaign promise, "Read my lips, no new taxes." He accused Dukakis of being soft on criminals because of a rape committed by Willie Horton while on prison furlough during Dukakis's term in office. Other major issues included abortion, the IRAN-CONTRA AFFAIR, and the question of Dan Quayle's competency to become vice president, a heartbeat away from the presidency. The Republicans won, partly because of continued prosperity and partly because of a lackluster Democratic campaign.

Election of 1992: Persistent economic recession gave Republican President GEORGE H. W. BUSH a 33 percent job-approval rate in 1992, but he and Vice President Dan Quayle won nomination despite a primary challenge from conservative news analyst Patrick Buchanan. The Democratic race —narrowed from five candidates to an uneven contest between Arkansas governor BILL CLINTON and former California governor Jerry Brown — went to Clinton, who chose AL GORE, JR., of Tennessee, as his running mate. H. Ross Perot, a Texas billionaire who had never held public office, created political havoc by running as an independent after grass roots efforts put his name on the ballot in all fifty states. His sudden mid-campaign withdrawal eroded his support, but returning in October, he won respect for his dedication to issues such as the deficit. His running mate was retired Vice Admiral James B. Stockdale, a much decorated former Navy fighter pilot and Vietnam War POW.

With Clinton's lead in the polls threatening the Republicans' twelve-year hold on the White House, Bush turned to Secretary of State James Baker to head his campaign, and increased attacks on Clinton's character. Clinton and Gore traveled by bus through Middle America, promoting their well-received platform for change. Perot's call for middle-class tax increases was made palatable by his folksy, straight-shooting manner and his use of millions of his own money to present his views in long television messages. After a debate over the debates, when Clinton accepted and Bush rejected formats proposed by a bipartisan commission, the presidential candidates met for three debates and the vice presidential candidates for one. Despite sharp exchanges over candidates' economic policies and trustworthiness and partly due to public demand and Perot's influence, the debates gained large audiences and high marks for seriously addressing the issue. The election went to the Clinton-Gore ticket, with a challenge to move America forward and out of economic recession.

Election of 1996: During the spring of 1996, President BILL CLINTON's popularity was rising as the United States enjoyed an increasing economic boom. Clinton and Gore were renominated for the Democratic ticket. The Republicans nominated former Kansas senator (and majority leader) ROBERT DOLE for president and ex-Representative and secretary of housing and urban development, JACK KEMP for vice president. With the economy growing and few foreign crises, the Republicans fought an uphill battle against the Democratic incumbents. ROSS PEROT again entered the race as a third-party candidate for the new Reform party, denouncing big government, budget deficits, campaign finance practices, and the existing two-party system. Televised debates featured only Dole and Clinton.

Dole faced an "age factor" (he was seventy-three). Although he offered experience and tax cuts, Clinton-Gore offered the voters continuing "peace and prosperity." Bill Clinton became one of only three Democratic presidents to be reelected during the twentieth century (joining WOODROW WILSON and FRANKLIN ROOSEVELT).

(*continued on page 176*)

Year	Number of States in Union	Candidates	Parties	Popular Vote		Electoral Vote
				Total Votes	%	
1789	11	**George Washington** (VA)	No party			69
		John Adams (MA)	designations			34
		Others				35
1792	15	**George Washington** (VA)	No party			132
		John Adams (MA)	designations			77
		George Clinton (NY)				50
		Thomas Jefferson (VA)				4
		Aaron Burr (NY)				1
1796	16	**John Adams** (MA)	Federalist			71
		Thomas Jefferson (VA)	Democratic-Republican			68
		Thomas Pinckney (SC)	Federalist			59
		Aaron Burr (NY)	Democratic-Republican			30
		Others				48
1800	16	**Thomas Jefferson** (VA)	Democratic-Republican			73
		Aaron Burr (NY)	Democratic-Republican			73
		John Adams (MA)	Federalist			65
		Charles C. Pinckney (SC)	Federalist			64
		John Jay (NY)	Federalist			1
1804	17	**Thomas Jefferson** (VA) and George Clinton (NY)	Democratic-Republican			162 162
		Charles C. Pinckney (SC) and Rufus King (NY)	Federalist			14 14
1808	17	**James Madison** (VA) and George Clinton (NY)	Democratic-Republican			122 113
		Charles C. Pinckney (SC) and Rufus King (NY)	Federalist			47 47
		George Clinton (NY)	Democratic-Republican			6
1812	18	**James Madison** (VA) and Elbridge Gerry (MA)	Democratic-Republican			128 131
		DeWitt Clinton (NY) and Jared Ingersoll (PA)	Federalist			89 86
1816	19	**James Monroe** (VA) and Daniel Tompkins (NY)	Democratic-Republican			183 183
		Rufus King (NY) and John Howard (MD)	Federalist			34 22
1820	24	**James Monroe** (VA) and Daniel Tompkins (NY)	Democratic-Republican			231 218
		John Quincy Adams (MA)	Democratic-Republican			1
1824	24	**John Quincy Adams** (MA)	Democratic-Republican	113,122	30.92	84
		Andrew Jackson (TN)	Democratic-Republican	151,271	41.34	99

Year	Number of States in Union	Candidates	Parties	Popular Vote Total Votes	%	Electoral Vote
1824 (*cont.*)		William H. Crawford (GA)	Democratic-Republican	40,856	11.17	41
		Henry Clay (KY)	Democratic-Republican	47,531	12.99	37
		Other		13,053	3.57	—

(As no candidate received a majority of electoral votes, the election was decided by the House of Representatives. John C. Calhoun ran unopposed for and was elected as vice president.)

Year	Number of States in Union	Candidates	Parties	Popular Vote Total Votes	%	Electoral Vote
1828	24	**Andrew Jackson** (TN) and John C. Calhoun (SC)	Democratic	642,553	55.97	178 171
		John Quincy Adams (MA) and Richard Rush (PA)	National-Republican	500,897	43.63	83 83
		Other		4,568	0.40	—
1832	24	**Andrew Jackson** (TN) and Martin Van Buren (NY)	Democratic	701,780	54.23	219 189
		Henry Clay (KY) and John Sergeant (PA)	National-Republican	484,205	37.42	49 49
		John Floyd (VA) and Henry Lee (MA)	Independent	N/A	N/A	11 11
		William Wirt (MD) and Amos Ellmaker (PA)	Anti-Masonic	100,715	7.78	7 7
		Other		7,273	0.56	—
1836	26	**Martin Van Buren** (NY) and Richard M. Johnson (KY)	Democratic	764,176	50.83	170 147
		William H. Harrison (OH)	Whig	550,816	36.63	73
		Hugh L. White (TN)	Whig	146,107	9.72	26
		Daniel Webster (MA)	Whig	41,201	2.74	14
		W. P. Mangum (NC)	Independent	N/A		11
		Other		1,234	0.08	—
1840	26	**William H. Harrison** (OH) and John Tyler (VA)	Whig	1,275,390	52.88	234
		Martin Van Buren (NY)	Democratic	1,128,854	46.81	60
		James G. Birney (NY)	Liberty	6,797	0.28	—
		Other		767	0.03	—
1844	26	**James K. Polk** (TN) and George M. Dallas (PA)	Democratic	1,339,494	49.54	170
		Henry Clay (KY) and Theodore Frelinghuysen (NJ)	Whig	1,300,004	48.08	105
		James G. Birney (NY)	Liberty	62,103	2.30	—
		Other		2,058	0.08	—
1848	30	**Zachary Taylor** (LA) and Millard Fillmore (NY)	Whig	1,361,393	47.28	163
		Lewis Cass (MI) and William O. Butler (KY)	Democratic	1,223,460	42.49	127
		Martin Van Buren (NY) and Charles Francis Adams (MA)	Free-Soil	291,501	10.12	—
		Other		2,830	0.10	—
1852	31	**Franklin Pierce** (NH) and William King (AL)	Democratic	1,607,510	50.84	254
		Winfield Scott (VA) and William A. Graham (NC)	Whig	1,386,942	43.87	42

Year	Number of States in Union	Candidates	Parties	Popular Vote		Electoral Vote
				Total Votes	%	
1852 (*cont.*)		John P. Hale (NH) and George Washington Julian (IN)	Free-Soil	155,210	4.91	—
		Other		12,168	0.38	—
1856	31	**James Buchanan** (PA) and John C. Breckinridge (KY)	Democratic	1,836,072	45.28	174
		John C. Frémont (CA) and William L. Dayton (NJ)	Republican	1,342,345	33.11	114
		Millard Fillmore (NY) and Andrew J. Donelson (TN)	American (Know-Nothing)	873,053	21.53	8
		Other		3,177	0.08	—
1860	33	**Abraham Lincoln** (IL) and Hannibal Hamlin (ME)	Republican	1,865,908	39.82	180
		Stephen A. Douglas (IL) and Herschel V. Johnson (GA)	Democratic	1,380,202	29.46	12
		John C. Breckinridge (KY) and Joseph Lane (OR)	Southern Democratic	848,019	18.09	72
		John Bell (TN) and Edward Everett (MA)	Constitutional Union	590,901	12.61	39
		Other		531	0.01	—
1864	36	**Abraham Lincoln** (IL) and Andrew Johnson (TN)	Republican	2,218,388	55.02	212
		George B. McClellan (NY) and George Pendleton (OH)	Democratic	1,812,807	44.96	21
		Other		692	0.02	—
1868	37	**Ulysses S. Grant** (OH) and Schuyler Colfax (IN)	Republican	3,013,650	52.66	214
		Horatio Seymour (NY) and Francis P. Blair (MO)	Democratic	2,708,744	47.3	80
		Other		46	—	—
1872	37	**Ulysses S. Grant** (OH) and Henry Wilson (MA)	Republican	3,598,235	55.63	286
		Horace Greeley (NY) and Benjamin Gratz Brown (MO)	Democratic, Liberal Republican	2,834,761	43.83	
		Charles O'Conor (NY) and John Quincy Adams II (MA)	"Straight" Democratic	18,602	0.29	—
		Other		16,081	0.25	—

(Greeley died shortly after the popular election and before the meeting of the presidential electors. The electors supporting him divided their 66 votes among minor candidates.)

Year	Number of States in Union	Candidates	Parties	Popular Vote		Electoral Vote
1876	38	**Rutherford B. Hayes** (OH) and William A. Wheeler (NY)	Republican	4,034,311	47.95	185
		Samuel J. Tilden (NY) and Thomas Hendrix (IN)	Democratic	4,288,546	50.97	184
		Peter Cooper (NY)	Greenback	75,973	0.90	—
		Other		14,271	0.17	—
1880	38	**James A. Garfield** (OH) and Chester A. Arthur (NY)	Republican	4,446,158	48.27	214
		Winfield S. Hancock (PA) and William English (IN)	Democratic	4,444,260	48.25	155
		James B. Weaver (IA) and Benjamin J. Chambers (TX)	Greenback-Labor	305,997	3.32	—
		Other		14,005	0.15	—

Year	Number of States in Union	Candidates	Parties	Popular Vote		Electoral Vote
				Total Votes	%	
1884	38	**Grover Cleveland** (NY) and Thomas A. Hendricks (IN)	Democratic	4,874,621	48.50	219
		James G. Blaine (ME) and John A. Logan (IL)	Republican	4,848,936	48.25	182
		Benjamin F. Butler (MA)	Greenback-Labor	175,096	1.74	—
		John P. St. John (KS)	Prohibition	147,482	1.47	—
		Other		3,619	0.04	—
1888	38	**Benjamin Harrison** (N) and Levi P. Morton (NY)	Republican	5,443,892	47.82	233
		Grover Cleveland (NY) and Allen G. Thurman (OH)	Democratic	5,534,488	48.62	168
		Clinton B. Fisk (NJ)	Prohibition	249,813	2.19	—
		Alson J. Streeter (IL)	Union Labor	146,602	1.29	—
		Other		8,519	0.07	—
1892	44	**Grover Cleveland** (NY) and Adlai E. Stevenson (IL)	Democratic	5,551,883	46.05	277
		Benjamin Harrison (IN) and Whitelaw Reid (NY)	Republican	5,179,244	42.96	145
		James B. Weaver (IA) and James G. Field (VA)	Populist	1,024,280	8.50	22
		John Bidwell (CA)	Prohibition	270,770	2.25	—
		Other		29,920	0.25	—
1896	45	**William McKinley** (OH) and Garrett Hobart (VA)	Republican	7,108,480	51.01	271
		William Jennings Bryan (NE) and Arthur Sewall (ME)	Democratic	6,511,495	46.73	176 149
		William Jennings Bryan (endorsed) and Thomas E. Watson (GA)	Populist			—
		John M. Palmer (IL)	National Democratic	133,435	0.96	—
		Joshua Levering (MD)	Prohibition	125,072	0.90	—
		Other		57,256	0.41	—
1900	45	**William McKinley** (OH) and Theodore Roosevelt (NY)	Republican	7,218,039	51.67	292
		William Jennings Bryan (NE) and Adlai E. Stevenson (IL)	Democratic, Populist	6,358,345	45.51	155
		John C. Woolley (IL)	Prohibition	209,004	1.50	—
		Eugene V. Debs (IN)	Socialist	86,935	0.62	—
		Other		98,147	0.70	—
1904	45	**Theodore Roosevelt** (NY) and Charles Fairbanks (IN)	Republican	7,626,593	56.41	336
		Alton B. Parker (NY) and Henry G. Davis (WV)	Democratic	5,082,898	37.60	140
		Eugene V. Debs (IN)	Socialist	402,489	2.98	—
		Silas C. Swallow (PA)	Prohibition	258,596	1.91	—
		Other		148,388	1.10	—
1908	46	**William H. Taft** (OH) and James Sherman (NY)	Republican	7,676,258	51.58	321
		William Jennings Bryan (NE) and John W. Kern (IN)	Democratic	6,406,801	43.05	162

Year	Number of States in Union	Candidates	Parties	Popular Vote		Electoral Vote
				Total Votes	%	
1908 (*cont.*)		Eugene V. Debs (IN)	Socialist	420,380	2.82	—
		Eugene W. Chafin (IL)	Prohibition	252,821	1.70	—
		Other		126,474	0.85	—
1912	48	**Woodrow Wilson** (NJ) and Thomas Marshall (IN)	Democratic	6,293,152	41.84	435
		Theodore Roosevelt (NY) and Hiram Johnson (CA)	Progressive	4,119,207	27.39	88
		William Howard Taft (OH) and James Sherman (NY)	Republican	3,486,333	23.18	8
		Eugene V. Debs (IN)	Socialist	900,369	5.99	—
		Other		241,902	1.61	—
1916	48	**Woodrow Wilson** (NJ) and Thomas Marshall (IN)	Democratic	9,126,300	49.24	277
		Charles Evans Hughes (NY) and Charles W. Fairbanks (IN)	Republican	8,546,789	46.11	254
		A. L. Benson (NY)	Socialist	589,924	3.18	—
		James Hanly (IN)	Prohibition	221,030	1.19	—
		Other		50,979	0.28	—
1920	48	**Warren G. Harding** (OH) and Calvin Coolidge (MA)	Republican	16,133,314	60.30	404
		James M. Cox (OH) and Franklin D. Roosevelt (NY)	Democratic	9,140,884	34.17	127
		Eugene V. Debs (IN)	Socialist	913,664	3.42	—
		Parley P. Christensen (UT)	Farmer Labor	264,540	0.99	—
		Other		301,384	1.13	—
1924	48	**Calvin Coolidge** (MA) and Charles Dawes (OH)	Republican	15,717,553	54.00	382
		John W. Davis (NY) and Charles W. Bryan (NE)	Democratic	8,386,169	28.84	136
		Robert M. La Follette (WI) and Burton K. Wheeler (MT)	Progressive	4,814,050	16.56	13
		Other		158,187	0.55	—
1928	48	**Herbert C. Hoover** (CA) and Charles Curtis (KS)	Republican	21,411,991	58.20	444
		Alfred E. Smith (NY) and Joseph Robison (AR)	Democratic	15,000,185	40.77	87
		Norman M. Thomas (NY)	Socialist	266,453	0.72	—
		William Foster (IL)	Communist	48,170	0.13	—
		Other		63,565	0.17	—
1932	48	**Franklin D. Roosevelt** (NY) and John Nance Garner (TX)	Democratic	22,825,016	57.42	472
		Herbert C. Hoover (CA) and Charles Curtis (KS)	Republican	15,758,397	39.64	59
		Norman M. Thomas (NY)	Socialist	883,990	2.22	—
		William Foster (IL)	Communist	102,221	0.26	—
		Other		179,758	0.45	—
1936	48	**Franklin D. Roosevelt** (NY) and John Nance Garner (TX)	Democratic	27,747,636	60.79	523
		Alfred M. Landon (KS) and Frank Knox (IL)	Republican	16,679,543	36.54	8
		William Lemke (ND)	Union	892,492	1.96	—
		Norman M. Thomas (NY)	Socialist	187,785	0.41	—
		Other		134,874	0.30	—

Year	Number of States in Union	Candidates	Parties	Popular Vote Total Votes	%	Electoral Vote
1940	48	**Franklin D. Roosevelt** (NY) and Henry A. Wallace (IA)	Democratic	27,263,448	54.70	449
		Wendell L. Willkie (IN) and Charles NcNary (OR)	Republican	22,336,260	44.82	82
		Norman M. Thomas (NY)	Socialist	116,827	0.23	—
		Roger W. Babson (MA)	Prohibition	58,685	0.12	—
		Other		65,223	0.13	—
1944	48	**Franklin D. Roosevelt** (NY) and Harry S. Truman (MO)	Democratic	25,611,936	53.39	432
		Thomas E. Dewey (NY) and John W. Bricker (OH)	Republican	22,013,372	45.89	99
		Norman Thomas (NY)	Socialist	79,100	0.16	—
		Claude A. Watson (CA)	Prohibition	74,733	0.16	—
		Other		195,778	0.41	—
1948	48	**Harry S. Truman** (MO) and Alben Barkley (KY)	Democratic	24,105,587	49.51	303
		Thomas E. Dewey (NY) and Earl Warren (CA)	Republican	21,970,017	45.12	189
		J. Strom Thurmond (SC) and Fielding Wright (MS)	State's Rights Democratic	1,169,134	2.40	39
		Henry A. Wallace (IA) and Glen Taylor (ID)	Progressive	1,157,057	2.38	—
		Other		290,647	0.60	—
1952	48	**Dwight D. Eisenhower** (KS) and Richard M. Nixon (CA)	Republican	33,936,137	55.13	442
		Adlai E. Stevenson (IL) and John Sparkman (AL)	Democratic	27,314,649	44.38	89
		Vincent Hallinan (CA)	Progressive	140,416	0.23	—
		Stuart Hamblen (CA)	Prohibition	73,413	0.12	—
		Other		86,503	0.14	—
1956	48	**Dwight D. Eisenhower** (KS) and Richard M. Nixon (CA)	Republican	35,585,245	57.37	457
		Adlai E. Stevenson (IL) and Estes Kefauver (TN)	Democratic	26,030,172	41.97	73
		T. Coleman Andrews (VA)	Constitution States' Rights	108,055	0.17	—
		Eric Hass (NY)	Socialist Labor	44,300	0.07	—
		Other		257,600	0.42	
1960	50	**John F. Kennedy** (MA) and Lyndon Johnson (TX)	Democratic	34,221,344	49.72	303
		Richard M. Nixon (CA) and Henry Cabot Lodge (MA)	Republican	34,106,671	49.55	219
		Eric Hass (NY)	Socialist Labor	47,522	0.07	—
		Other		337,175	0.48	—
		Unpledged (MS)		116,248	0.17	—
1964	50	**Lyndon B. Johnson** (TX) and Hubert Humphrey (MN)	Democratic	43,126,584	61.05	486
		Barry M. Goldwater (AZ) and William Miller (NY)	Republican	27,177,838	38.47	52
		Eric Hass (NY)	Socialist Labor	45,187	0.06	—
		Clifton DeBerry (NY)	Socialist Workers	32,701	0.05	—
		Other		258,794	0.37	—

Year	Number of States in Union	Candidates	Parties	Popular Vote Total Votes	Popular Vote %	Electoral Vote
1968	50	**Richard M. Nixon** (CA) and Spiro T. Agnew (MD)	Republican	31,785,148	43.42	301
		Hubert H. Humphrey (MN) and Edmund Muskie (ME)	Democratic	31,274,503	42.72	191
		George C. Wallace (AL) and Curtis LeMay (OH)	American Independent	9,901,151	13.53	46
		Henning A. Blomen (MA)	Socialist Labor	52,591	0.07	—
		Other		189,977	0.20	—
1972	50	**Richard M. Nixon** (CA) and Spiro T. Agnew (MD)	Republican	47,170,179	60.69	520
		George S. McGovern (SD) and R. Sargent Shriver (MD)	Democratic	29,171,791	37.53	17
		John G. Schmitz (CA)	American	1,090,673	1.40	—
		Benjamin Spock (CT)	People's	78,751	0.10	—
		Other		216,196	0.28	—
1976	50	**Jimmy Carter** (GA) and Walter Mondale (MN)	Democratic	40,830,763	50.06	297
		Gerald R. Ford (MI) and Robert Dole (KS)	Republican	39,147,793	48.00	240
		Eugene McCarthy (MN)	Independent	756,691	0.93	—
		Roger MacBride (VA)	Libertarian	173,011	0.21	—
		Other		647,631	0.79	—
1980	50	**Ronald Reagan** (CA) and George Bush (TX)	Republican	43,901,812	50.75	489
		Jimmy Carter (GA) and Walter Mondale (MN)	Democratic	35,483,820	41.02	49
		John B. Anderson (IL) and Patrick J. Lucey (WI)	Independent	5,719,722	6.61	
		Ed Clark (CA)	Libertarian	921,188	1.06	—
		Other		486,754	0.56	—
1984	50	**Ronald Reagan** (CA) and George Bush (TX)	Republican	54,450,603	58.78	525
		Walter Mondale (MN) and Geraldine Ferraro (NY)	Democratic	37,573,671	40.56	13
		David Bergland (CA)	Libertarian	227,949	0.25	—
		Other		570,343	0.61	—
1988	50	**George Bush** (TX) and Dan Quayle (IN)	Republican	48,881,011	53.37	426
		Michael Dukakis (MA) and Lloyd Bentsen (TX)	Democratic	41,828,350	45.67	111
		Ron Paul (TX)	Libertarian	431,499	0.47	—
		Lenora Fulani (NY)	New Alliance	218,159	0.24	—
		Other			0.25	—
1992	50	**Bill Clinton** (AR) and Al Gore, Jr. (TN)	Democratic	43,688,67	42.97	370
		George Bush (TX) and Dan Quayle (IN)	Republican	38,109,410	37.49	168
		Ross Perot (TX) and James B. Stockdale (CA)	Independent	19,089,432	18.78	—
		Andre Marrou (TX)	Libertarian	278,528	00.27	—
		Other		494,633	00.49	—
1996	50	**Bill Clinton** (AR) and Al Gore, Jr. (TN)	Democrat	47,401,185	49.2	379

Year	Number of States in Union	Candidates	Parties	Popular Vote Total Votes	%	Electoral Vote
1996 (*cont.*)		Bob Dole (KS) and Jack Kemp (NY)	Republican	39,197,469	40.71	159
		Ross Perot (TX) and Pat Choate (DC)	Reform	8,085,294	8.40	
		Other		1,590,616	1.62	
2000	50	**George W. Bush** (TX) and Dick Cheney (WY)	Republican	50,456,002	47.87	271
		Al Gore, Jr. (TN) and Joe Lieberman (CT)	Democrat	50,999,897	48.38	266
		Ralph Nader (DC)	Green	2,882,955	2.74	
		Patrick Buchanan (DC)	Reform	448,895	.42	
		Harry Browne (TN)	Libertarian	384,431	.36	
		Other		232,920	.20	

Note: one Gore electoral vote from Washington, D.C., abstained as a protest of the district's status

(*continued from page 168*)

Election of 2000: The election of 2000 was one of the closest, most protracted, and most controversial in the history of the United States. The Republican ticket of Texas governor GEORGE W. BUSH and RICHARD CHENEY defeated the Democratic slate of Vice President AL GORE, JR. and Senator JOSEPH LIEBERMAN. The election ended in a statistical tie, and its outcome was in doubt throughout a five-week recount battle until the U.S. Supreme Court made a decision that gave Bush-Cheney the win.

On voting day, November 7, 2000, the state of Florida, with twenty-five electoral votes, became the key to the presidency. The Florida vote was extremely close, and confusion arose due to outdated machine voting systems and charges of voter intimidation. When an automatic machine re-count of ballots gave Bush a lead of only 327 votes out of nearly 6 million cast, a full hand recount was ordered.

After five weeks of legal battles, the U.S. Supreme Court ruled by a five-to-four vote to stop the recount in Florida. This in effect handed Bush Florida's electoral college votes by a margin of 537 popular votes. On December 13, the day after the Supreme Court's decision, Gore conceded to Bush. In this election, Bush became the first chief executive since BENJAMIN HARRISON in 1888 to win in the electoral college while failing to finish first in the popular vote nationwide.

A number of third parties were involved in the presidential bid in the 2000 election, including the Green Party, which ran consumer advocate RALPH NADER, the Libertarian Harry Browne, and the Reform party, which ran conservative commentator Pat Buchanan. Although taking no electoral votes, they garnered about 4 million popular votes, possibly affecting the outcome of the race between the leading candidates in some states.

Electoral College, a group of people from each state chosen by the voters every four years to elect the president and vice president of the United States. The electoral college system is provided for under the U.S. Constitution, which states that the president and vice president are elected directly by an electoral college and only indirectly by the voters. The number of electors for each state equals the number of representatives and senators in Congress from that state. Each state has a different group of electors for each presidential candidate. The candidate who receives the popular vote majority of each state receives all of its electoral votes. Under the Twelfth Amendment, electors vote by separate ballot for president and vice president. The people vote in November, the electors vote in December at their state capitals, and the ballots are counted officially at a joint session of Congress in January.

In most elections, a candidate who wins the popular vote will also receive the majority of the electoral votes, but there have been four exceptions. In the ELECTIONS OF 1824, 1876, 1888, and 2000, the presidents who won the elections did so by winning fewer popular votes than their opponents, but more electoral votes. Today, a candidate must receive 270 of the 538 electoral votes to win an election. In cases where no candidate wins a majority of electoral votes, the decision goes to the HOUSE OF REPRESENTATIVES, which then selects the president by a majority vote of the states, with the representation of each state having one vote. The House decided the ELECTION OF 1800 and the ELECTION OF 1824.

Eliot, T. S. (Thomas Stearns; 1888–1965), playwright, critic, and poet. Born in St. Louis, Missouri, and educated at Harvard, Eliot in 1915 became an expatriate, living in London as a teacher, writer, and editor. In 1927 he became a British subject, describing himself as royalist in politics, Anglo-Catholic in religion, and classicist in literature. His influential poetry broke new ground both in subject matter and form. *The Love Song of J. Alfred Prufrock* (1917) and *The Waste Land* (1922) harshly criticized contemporary society. Lighter and religious in tone were *Ash Wednesday* (1930) and *The Four Quartets* (1935–42). Eliot also wrote the verse dramas *Murder in the Cathedral* (1935) and *The Cocktail Party* (1950). He won the Nobel Prize for literature in 1948.

Elkins Act (1903), sponsored by President Theodore Roosevelt, provided for the regulation of interstate railroads. The act forbade rebates or other rate reductions to shipping companies. Railroads were not allowed to offer rates different from the published rates.

Ellington, Duke (Edward Kennedy Ellington; 1899–1974), composer and bandleader. A creative improviser of big-band jazz music, Ellington's orchestras performed worldwide over his fifty-year career. Some of his classics include "Satin Doll," "Don't Get around Much Anymore," "Mood Indigo," and his theme, "Take the A Train." Ellington received the 1959 SPINGARN MEDAL and the 1969 Presidential Medal of Freedom.

Ellis Island, in New York Harbor near the Statue of Liberty, served as the site of the chief U.S. immigration station from 1892 to 1954. During that time, an estimated 17 million immigrants were processed before their entry into the country. Ellis Island is now part of the Statue of Liberty National Monument.

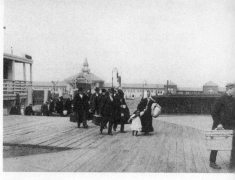

Ellis Island
Immigrants landing at Ellis Island, ca. 1900.

Ellison, Ralph W. (1914–94), black writer. Originally a student of music at Tuskegee Institute, Ellison moved to New York to pursue interests in photography, jazz, and art. His friendship with novelist RICHARD WRIGHT directed his energies toward writing. Ellison published *Invisible Man* in 1952, an extraordinary novel of the black experience in America that anticipated the civil rights struggle and established him as a major writer. He lectured widely on black American culture and creative writing.

Ellsworth, Oliver (1745–1807), jurist and diplomat. Ellsworth served as a delegate to the Continental Congress and as a member of the Constitutional Convention. He played an important role in drafting the GREAT COMPROMISE for the U.S. Constitution. A Federalist U.S. senator from Connecticut, he was instrumental in drafting the Judiciary Act of 1789, which established a system of lower federal courts. Ellis served as the third chief justice of the U.S. Supreme Court, from 1796 to 1800.

Emancipation Proclamation (1863), a military order issued by Abraham Lincoln during the Civil War that declared all slaves in states fighting against the Union to be free after January 1, 1863. Slaves in the border states were not affected. The proclamation allowed blacks to enlist in the Union army, thus strengthening the North's forces. The Thirteenth Amendment to the U.S. Constitution extended this decree. The proclamation also weakened the possibility of aid for the Confederacy from England because a majority of the British people opposed slavery.

Embargo Act (1807), a law passed by Congress preventing exports from American ports, thus keeping American ships from leaving and in effect prohibiting imports by foreign ships since they would have to depart empty. President Thomas Jefferson requested the action in response to the CHESAPEAKE-LEOPARD INCIDENT in which a British ship attacked an American naval vessel. His intent was to put pressure on rivals Great Britain and France by depriving them of goods and American trade. But the embargo backfired when the profits of American merchants plummeted. Highly unpopular, the embargo was repealed by Congress in 1809 and was replaced by the Non-Intercourse Act.

Emerson, Ralph Waldo (1803–82), essayist, lecturer, poet, philosopher, and abolitionist. Emerson's philosophy, known as transcendentalism, affected much of the thought and literature of the late nineteenth century. Through essays and lectures he taught that people must learn from their experiences in life, that they must look for the God-given power within themselves. In

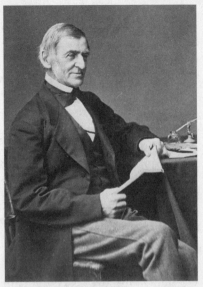

Ralph Waldo Emerson

his essay "Self-Reliance" (1841), he emphasizes optimism and the importance of the individual, encouraging people to rely on themselves and their own judgment.

Energy, Department of, an executive department of the U.S. government that works to meet the nation's energy needs. Established in 1977, the department develops and coordinates national energy policies and conservation programs. It also investigates and promotes new sources of energy and new ways to save existing supplies. The secretary of energy, a member of the president's cabinet, heads the department.

Engel* v. *Vitale (1962), a U.S. Supreme Court decision, also known as the Regents' Prayer Case, which held that required recitation of a prayer written by a state agency for use in public schools violates the freedom of religion portion of the First Amendment.

Enron Bankruptcy (2001), the largest corporate failure in the history of the United States at the time. (In 2002, the bankruptcy of WorldCom surpassed that of Enron.) Enron Corporation, an energy trading and communications company based in Houston, Texas, formed in 1985 when Houston Natural Gas merged with InterNorth, a natural gas company based in Omaha, Nebraska. It began as a small natural gas pipeline company, and within ten years it was named America's Most Innovative Company by *Fortune* magazine, retaining the title for five consecutive years. A series of scandals involving irregular accounting practices revealed hidden losses and misleading financial statements, as well as questionable campaign contributions, securities fraud, manipulation of natural gas prices, and rumors of bribery. Enron's stock price declined during 2001 from eighty-five dollars to thirty cents, and the corporation collapsed. Negative fallout continued when thousands of employees lost their pensions while Enron executives made fortunes by selling their stock shares. Enron filed for bankruptcy on December 2, 2001. Enron's collapse led to the CORPORATE RESPONSIBILITY ACT of 2002. The Justice Department's investigation of Enron's collapse continues, and it has resulted in numerous charges and arrests. The public accounting firm of Arthur Andersen, one of the nation's largest, collapsed after both the firm and some of its employees were convicted of obstruction of justice in their association with Enron.

Enumerated Powers, the precept that a government may exercise only those powers that are stated in its constitution. Congress is bound by Article I, Section 8, which enumerates what its powers may be, though it can rely on the ELASTIC CLAUSE to exercise powers not specifically granted as long as it does so to achieve goals specified in the Constitution.

Environmental Protection Agency (EPA), an agency of the federal government that oversees the environment. Established in 1970, the EPA monitors the quality of air and water and conducts programs dealing with hazardous and toxic wastes, and excessive radiation.

E Pluribus Unum, the motto of the great seal of the United States. From a Latin poem, it means "out of many, one." The motto, selected in 1776, refers to the formation of one nation from many colonies. It appears on every U.S. coin, as required by law.

Equal Rights Amendment (ERA), an amendment to the U.S. Constitution first proposed by National Woman's party leader ALICE PAUL in 1923. In its most recent form, it reads, "Equality of rights under the law shall not be denied or abridged by the United States or any state on account of sex." Passed by Congress in 1972, the amendment never took effect. Although the deadline for its ratification was extended to June 30, 1982, it failed to be ratified by the legislatures of three-fourths of the states, as required. Thirty-five of the needed thirty-eight states ratified it.

Era of Good Feelings, the period from around 1817 to 1825 when political party rivalries were minimal and peace and a strong spirit of nationalism prevailed in the country, at least on the surface. JAMES MONROE was president and the only political party was the DEMOCRATIC-REPUBLICAN PARTY. Literature and technology flourished during this period.

Ericcson, John (1803–99), inventor and engineer. Ericcson invented and patented the screw propeller for moving ships through water. He designed and built the ironclad *Monitor* for the Union navy during the Civil War.

Erie Canal (1825), a waterway connecting Buffalo on Lake Erie to Albany on the Hudson River, thus providing a water route from the Great Lakes to the Atlantic Ocean. Built by the state of New York through the efforts of Governor DeWitt Clinton, the Erie Canal made it possible to move manufactured goods inexpensively and more quickly. Originally ridiculed as "Clinton's ditch," it cut shipping costs, which reduced selling prices of goods. The canal became a rallying point for those advocating governmental power to make internal improvements.

Ervin, Sam J. (1896–1985), politician. Ervin served as a state legislator and justice of the North Carolina Supreme Court before being elected to the U.S. Senate in 1954. He served on the Senate committee that recommended censure of Senator JOSEPH McCARTHY in 1954. A conservative Democrat and constitutional expert, Ervin spent his twenty-year career in the Senate siding alternately with liberals and conservatives. He supported the VIETNAM WAR and opposed civil rights legislation in the 1960s, the EQUAL RIGHTS AMENDMENT in the 1970s, and the right for eighteen-year-olds to vote, but he was a strong defender of individual liberties. He became a household name at age seventy-six when he headed the Senate WATERGATE committee investigation that led to the resignation of President RICHARD NIXON. Ervin rejected Nixon's pleas of executive privilege, demanding that all information be turned over to Congress for study. Known for his folksy wit and charm, Ervin wrote three books: *The Whole Truth: The Watergate Conspiracy* (1980), *Humor of a Country Lawyer* (1983), and *Preserving the Constitution! The Autobiography of Senator Sam Ervin* (1984).

Erving, Julius (Dr. J; 1950–), basketball player. "Dr. J" won the most valuable player award three times playing for the Virginia Squires, the New York Nets, and the Philadelphia 76ers, and he led the league in scoring three times. Erving, a six-foot-seven-inch forward known for his jumping ability and slam-dunk shots, retired in 1987.

Escobedo* v. *Illinois (1964), a Supreme Court ruling that extended constitutional protection of the rights of anyone accused of a crime. Danny Escobedo, who was not permitted to consult with a lawyer upon his arrest for murder, was convicted on the basis of his interrogation by police without a lawyer present. The Supreme Court reversed the conviction, stating that the Sixth Amendment to the Constitution provides that accused persons have a right to advice from counsel in order to protect themselves against self-incrimination as provided in the Fifth Amendment.

Espionage Act (June 15, 1917), a law enacted by Congress in reaction to war hysteria. It made it a crime to help enemy nations or to interfere with the draft, and it allowed the postmaster general to censor mail that he thought might be treasonable. An amendment to the act, called the SEDITION ACT (May 16, 1918), extended its scope dramatically to include "disloyal" speech.

Esposito, Phil (1942–), Canadian-born U.S. hockey player. Esposito, the second leading scorer in National Hockey League history and the league's most valuable player in 1969 and 1974, played for the Chicago Black Hawks, Boston Bruins, and New York Rangers. He was the first player to exceed

100 points in a single season and won five scoring championships, including 152 points in 1970–71. With Esposito, the Bruins won two Stanley Cups. He retired as a player in 1981.

Evarts, William M. (1818–1901), lawyer and public official. Evarts, as a lawyer, handled many important trials. He represented the federal government in 1867, prosecuting JEFFERSON DAVIS for treason, and successfully defended ANDREW JOHNSON during his impeachment trial in 1868. He represented the United States in the arbitration of the ALABAMA CLAIMS against Great Britain. Evarts also served as attorney general, secretary of state, and U.S. senator from New York. As founder and president of the New York City Bar Association, Evarts led efforts for law reform and helped expose the TWEED RING.

Everett, Edward (1794–1865), clergyman, statesman, and orator. As the featured speaker in Gettysburg on November 19, 1863, Everett's two-hour oration preceded Abraham Lincoln's two-minute GETTYSBURG ADDRESS. His political career included service as a congressman, governor of Massachusetts, U.S. minister to England, secretary of state for Millard Fillmore, and a U.S. senator. His candidacy for vice president for the CONSTITUTIONAL UNION PARTY in the ELECTION OF 1860 ended in defeat.

Evers, Medgar (1925–63), civil rights leader. Evers received posthumously the 1963 SPINGARN MEDAL from the NAACP for his work as a civil rights activist. As the first field secretary for the NAACP in Mississippi he worked to register blacks to vote and helped organize economic boycotts. Killed by a sniper's shot a few hours after John F. Kennedy had made a national speech on civil rights, Evers was buried with full honors in Arlington National Cemetery.

Evert, Chris (1954–), tennis champion. Beginning her professional career at age sixteen, Evert won 157 singles championships, more than any other player, male or female. She dominated six U.S. singles championships, won three Wimbledon titles, seven French Open titles, and two Australian championships. After competing in more than 1,400 career matches and winning more than 90 percent of them, she retired in 1989, acknowledged as one of the best women players of all time.

Executive Privilege, the claim by the president of the United States of a right to refuse to testify, to refuse his subordinates permission to testify, or to refuse to provide evidence when sought by a court or a committee of Congress. Executive privilege is a doctrine of the law of evidence, like the attorney-client or priest-penitent privileges. First asserted during the Washington administration, executive privilege is based on the idea that the president must preserve the confidentiality of executive branch discussions so that he may receive the most candid advice possible. Opponents of the privilege argue that it is a cloak for executive misconduct. In *United States* v. *Nixon,* the Supreme Court recognized executive privilege but held that it is not absolute; courts can review each case to determine whether the assertion of privilege is justified or not.

Expansionists, Americans who believed that all of North and South America, as well as the islands of the Pacific, would eventually become part of the United States. Prior to the War of 1812, expansionists were called WAR HAWKS. Later, the concept of MANIFEST DESTINY embodied the idea of territorial expansion. IMPERIALISM refers to the idea of territorial expansion overseas.

Ex Post Facto Law, a law imposing penalties for an act committed before the law was passed and that was legal at the time. As provided in Article I, Section 9, of the U.S. Constitution, an ex post facto law is unconstitutional. The Constitution also prevents states from passing such laws.

F **Factory System,** a system of manufacturing introduced by the INDUSTRIAL REVOLUTION of the eighteenth and nineteenth centuries. Instead of goods being handmade by artisans in their homes and workshops, they were made by workers gathered under one roof — the factory. They sold their time for an hourly wage rather than their individually finished pieces. Plants used large, complex machinery operated by skilled and semiskilled workers. SAMUEL SLATER established the first U.S. textile mill, or factory, in 1791 at Pawtucket, Rhode Island.

Fairbanks, Charles W. (1852–1918), twenty-sixth vice president of the United States under Theodore Roosevelt (1905–09). Fairbanks was elected to the U.S. Senate from Indiana in 1897 and 1902. Although he hoped to receive the Republican presidential nomination in 1908, his inability to get along with Roosevelt provoked the president to support William Howard Taft. In 1916 Fairbanks accepted the vice-presidential nomination with Charles Evans Hughes, but they were defeated by Woodrow Wilson and Thomas R. Marshall.

Fairbanks, Douglas (born Julius Ullman; 1883–1939), actor. As a dashing adventure hero, Fairbanks starred in the silent classics *The Three Musketeers* (1921), *The Mark of Zorro* (1920), and *Robin Hood* (1922). He was a co-founder of United Artists in 1919 and the first president of the Academy of Motion Picture Arts and Sciences.

Fair Deal, the domestic policy of HARRY S. TRUMAN's second administration. The Fair Deal aimed to extend the New Deal program, introducing legislation for civil rights, fair housing, national health programs, and federal aid to farmers and education. Most bills were blocked by Congress, but the Social Security program was expanded.

Fair Labor Standards Act (June 25, 1938), a law establishing a minimum wage and a maximum workweek for employees engaged in interstate industries. Also known as the Wages and Hours Act, it abolished child labor and established time-and-a-half pay for overtime work. The law has been amended many times since its enactment.

Fall, Albert (1861–1944), politician. Fall was the first cabinet official to be found guilty of a felony while in office. Appointed secretary of the interior by Warren G. Harding, Fall resigned in 1923 because of his involvement in the TEAPOT DOME SCANDAL. He had taken $300,000 in bribes from oil men for illegal leases on public lands.

Fallen Timbers, Battle of (August 20, 1794), a major American victory over the Indian Confederacy in the Northwest Territory led by Gen. "Mad" ANTHONY WAYNE. The battle, which resulted in the defeat of a combined force of 1,500 Indians, ended a twenty-year period of warfare.

Farm Bloc, a group of midwestern senators and representatives in Congress, both Democrats and Republicans, who seek legislation to aid farmers. The farm bloc, an informal group in existence since World War I, tries to relieve agricultural distress, particularly in the Midwest.

Farm Credit Administration (FCA) (1933), a government agency that supervises and coordinates the cooperative Farm Credit System. Formed under the Farm Credit Act of 1933 as part of the NEW DEAL, the FCA gave aid to struggling farmers by coordinating loans during the GREAT DEPRESSION. The FCA continues to provide credit to farmers, ranchers, and agricultural organizations.

Farmer, Fannie Merritt (1857–1915), cooking expert. Farmer published the first real American cookbook, *The Boston Cooking-School Cook Book,* in 1896. Revised more than twenty times and renamed *The Fannie Farmer Cookbook,* it includes sections on entertaining, home management, and etiquette.

Farmer-Labor Party, political party organized around 1918 by former members of the PROGRESSIVE PARTY with the support of some midwestern farmer and labor groups. Its platform called for government ownership of public utilities, help for farmers, and improved labor conditions. Following the party's dissolution in 1924, its members supported ROBERT M. LA FOLLETTE, the Progressive party's candidate for president. It was successful at the state level in Minnesota, merging with the Democratic party.

Farmers' Alliance, association of farmers organized in the 1870s and 1880s to seek regulation of railroad and public utilities rates and to create cooperative marketing arrangements to eliminate middlemen. By 1890, at the peak of its power, the Farmers' Alliance had over 750,000 members, most of them supporting the POPULIST PARTY in 1892.

Farragut, David G. (1801–70), Hispanic-American Union naval officer during the CIVIL WAR. Farragut, who had entered the navy as a midshipman at the age of nine, gave the North an important victory when he captured New Orleans without bloodshed in 1862. Two years later he led a Union fleet in an assault on Mobile Bay; when warned about enemy torpedoes, he reportedly responded, "Damn the torpedoes! Full speed ahead!" The Confederates surrendered, ensuring Farragut's victory. Congress established the rank of admiral especially for him in 1866.

Faulkner, William (1897–1962), novelist. Faulkner gained international recognition as one of the great modern writers with his novels about rural and small-town life in his home state of Mississippi. His writing explored the traditions and decay of the South and its inability to adjust to modern life following the Civil War, but carried universal implications. Some of his best-known works include *The Sound and the Fury* (1924), *Light in August* (1932), and *Absalom, Absalom!* (1936). He received the 1949 Nobel Prize for literature and Pulitzer Prizes for *A Fable* in 1954 and *The Reivers* in 1962.

Favorite Sons, candidates put into nomination for president by their states' national party conventions to gain recognition and name exposure. If they do not receive support from other state delegations, favorite sons usually throw their support to another candidate or drop out in return for future political favors.

Federal Aviation Administration (FAA), a government agency for regulating and promoting air transportation, formed in 1958. It manages air traffic and certifies aircraft, airports, and pilots. In 1967 it became part of the Department of Transportation.

Federal Bureau of Investigation (FBI), the chief investigative branch of the Department of Justice. Established in 1908 and reorganized in 1924, the FBI investigates more than 180 kinds of federal crimes, including kidnapping, espionage, hijacking, treason, and theft involving interstate commerce. It conducts security clearances and houses the nation's largest collection of crime statistics in its National Crime Information Center. Its director is appointed by the president with Senate approval. Longtime director J. EDGAR HOOVER, who served as head from 1924 to 1972, greatly increased the scope and duties of the bureau and engaged in controversial activities, targeting for investigation those he considered "subversive." After Hoover's death, Congress and the attorney general issued new guidelines to prevent future abuse by the agency.

Following the SEPTEMBER 11, 2001, TERRORIST ATTACKS, the responsibilities of the FBI were broadened following criticism that the agency failed to act properly on information prior to the attacks. Under the leadership of Attorney General JOHN ASHCROFT, the bureau is being transformed into an agency dedicated to the prevention of terrorism, while remaining committed to other important national security and law enforcement responsibilities. It has increased its analytic and surveillance capabilities, improved law enforcement coordination and information sharing, and updated its information technology systems. The FBI manages the Foreign Terrorist Tracking Task Force (FTTTF) to identify potential terrorists attempting to enter or remain in the United States and to help dismantle terrorist networks worldwide.

Federal Communications Commission (FCC), a government agency that regulates interstate and foreign communications by radio, television, wire, and cable. Established by the Communications Act of 1934, the FCC has seven members appointed by the president and approved by the Senate.

Federal Deposit Insurance Corporation (FDIC), an agency of the government that insures deposit accounts in commercial banks. The FDIC was created by the Banking Act of 1933 in response to the Great Depression, when many banks failed. All national banks are required to belong to the FDIC and most state banks are volunteer members. The FDIC functioned well until the late 1980s when a burgeoning series of bank failures led to a crisis requiring that billions of tax dollars be pumped into the FDIC.

Federal Emergency Relief Act (May 12, 1933), an act that created the Federal Emergency Relief Administration. Part of the NEW DEAL, the FERA provided relief for the needy and unemployed by giving direct aid to the states. It received an initial fund of $500 million from the Reconstruction Finance Corporation for crisis relief. When Congress passed the Social Security Act of 1935, the work of the agency was completed.

Federalism, a system in which political power is divided between the national government and state governments, assigning the central government sovereign powers on federal matters and reserving to state governments powers over state and local matters.

Federalist Papers, a series of eighty-five essays written to New York City newspapers by Alexander Hamilton, James Madison, and John Jay during 1787–88. The letters, written under the pen name "Publius," explained and defended the U.S. CONSTITUTION, urging its ratification. Published in book form in 1788 as *The Federalist,* they have been widely respected for their authoritative analysis of the Constitution.

Federalist Party, one of the first political organizations in the United States. Key members Alexander Hamilton, John Adams, John Jay, and John Marshall supported manufactures, a protective tariff, and assumption of state debts. They favored a strong national government, a broad interpretation of the Constitution, and a sound financial policy based on industrialization, commerce, and urbanization. The party opposed the states' rights and agriculturist views of the DEMOCRATIC-REPUBLICANS led by Thomas Jefferson. John Adams was the only Federalist president. The party dissolved after the HARTFORD CONVENTION at the end of the War of 1812.

Federal Reserve System (1913), the central banking system of the United States established under the Federal Reserve Act of 1913, sometimes called the Glass-Owen bill. The most important job of the system, also known as the Fed, is to manage the country's supply of money. The president appoints a Federal Reserve Board of seven members to staggered terms of fourteen years to supervise the conduct of the banks in the Federal Reserve System. The act divided the nation into twelve districts, each with a Federal Reserve bank; the banks are located in Dallas, San Francisco, Boston, New York City, Philadelphia, Richmond, Atlanta, Cleveland, Chicago, St. Louis, Minneapolis, and Kansas City, Missouri.

Federal Trade Commission (FTC), a government agency established in 1914 to prevent unfair business practices and to maintain a competitive economy. The FTC controls radio and television advertising and regulates labeling and packaging. Its five commissioners, appointed by the president and subject to Senate approval, serve for seven-year terms.

Feiffer, Jules (1929–), political and social cartoonist who developed the syndicated cartoon "Feiffer" in 1956. Known for his clever style and simple drawings, Feiffer usually creates cartoons that involve a few characters conveying social and political commentary. Feiffer has opposed the war in Vietnam, conservative policies, and the nuclear arms buildup. He won the 1986 Pulitzer Prize for political cartooning.

Feminist Movement. The modern feminist movement in the United States has its roots in the nineteenth-century women's rights movement. Reform efforts by such activists as LUCRETIA MOTT, ELIZABETH CADY STANTON, SUSAN B. ANTHONY, Sarah Fuller, and the GRIMKÉ SISTERS were directed over the century at a variety of targets: women's right to speak in public, to own property in their own name after marriage, to receive a college education, to vote, to enter such professions as medicine and the ministry, to participate in public life on an equal footing with men.

Many of these women received their first political experience in other reform movements, such as temperance and, especially, abolitionism. Insights gained in those struggles were applied to their own situation. Mott and Stanton, for example, who called the first WOMEN'S RIGHTS CONVENTION in Seneca Falls, New York, in 1848, had met at an antislavery convention in London in 1840. Women's rights advocates often worked in tandem with such abolitionists as WILLIAM LLOYD GARRISON and FREDERICK DOUGLASS. They lectured, wrote pamphlets and books, petitioned lawmakers, and held annual conventions.

Gradually some of their goals were realized: Married Women's Property Acts were enacted in all states between 1839 and 1895; increasing numbers of women's colleges were founded and some existing institutions opened their doors to women; ELIZABETH BLACKWELL and ANTOINETTE BROWN BLACKWELL breached the barriers in medicine and the ministry. But it was not until 1920 that women received the vote with passage of the Nineteenth Amendment; and the drive for an EQUAL RIGHTS AMENDMENT, first proposed in 1923 by the National Woman's party and sought again in the 1980s, never succeeded.

Social forces were at play in the quest for equality: women, for example, were welcome in the workplace during both world wars when their labor was needed, but when peace came, they were expected to return to the home. The modern feminist movement opened in the 1960s and is often said to have been sparked by the publication of BETTY FRIEDAN's *The Feminine Mystique,* which addressed that expectation after World War II: women's greatest fulfillment, it was said again, was to be found in domesticity, but many women were discontented with their lives as wives and mothers only. (For a quotation from Friedan's book, see page 201.) And once again, feminism was influenced by the drive for black equality. The civil rights movement of the 1950s and 1960s culminated in the Civil Rights Act of 1964, which, among other things, prohibited employment discrimination on the basis of sex, race, religion, and national origin.

The modern movement, conducted by women such as GLORIA STEINEM, Eleanor Smeal, and Barbara Ehrenreich, among many others, and by groups like the NATIONAL ORGANIZATION FOR WOMEN, continued the drive for equality in the workplace, the professions, elective office, sports — in short, in all areas of life. Measurable progress was made, but feminist theorists, who ranged from moderates to radicals in their approach, agreed that much remained to be done. At issue still were the problems of sexual abuse of women, the right to abortion, women's promotions into top positions, equal pay scales, and the like.

Ferber, Edna (1887–1968), writer. Ferber wrote about the colorful American life of the 1800s in such novels as *So Big* (1925 Pulitzer Prize), *Show Boat* (1926), *Saratoga Trunk* (1941), and *Giant* (1952). With George S. Kaufman she wrote the Broadway hits *The Royal Family* (1927), *Dinner at Eight* (1932), and *Stage Door* (1936).

Fermi, Enrico (1901–54), physicist. A central figure in the Manhattan Project to build the first ATOMIC BOMB, Fermi first conducted experiments on radioactivity that won him the 1938 Nobel Prize for physics. He designed the first atomic piles and in 1942 produced the first nuclear chain reaction in an installation at the University of Chicago.

Ferraro, Geraldine (1935–), politician. Chosen by presidential candidate Walter Mondale as his running mate in the 1984 election, Ferraro was the first woman vice-presidential candidate of a major political party. Elected to the House of Representatives from a conservative New York district in 1978 and reelected twice, Ferraro, a liberal Democrat and Roman Catholic, sponsored women's economic equality legislation, supported the EQUAL RIGHTS AMENDMENT, and held a pro-choice view on abortion.

Fessenden, William P. (1806–69), politician. A U.S. senator from Maine, Fessenden helped found the Republican party during the 1850s. He served as secretary of the treasury under Abraham Lincoln and then returned to the Senate, where he opposed the Tenure of Office Act. Fessenden was one of the seven Republican senators who voted against removing President Andrew Johnson from office during his impeachment trial; this vote ended his political career.

Field, family of merchandisers, publishers, and philanthropists. Marshall Field I (1834–1908) established Marshall Field and Co., a world-famous Chicago dry goods store. He pioneered the use of vertical integration in a store's manufacturing, wholesaling, retailing, and shipping its own goods. Responsible for many merchandising innovations, Field was among the first to mark prices on merchandise, extend credit, allow returns or exchanges of goods for dissatisfied customers, and set up an in-store restaurant. Field contributed large sums to the University of Chicago and the Field Museum of Natural History in Chicago. His grandson, Marshall Field III (1893–1956), founded the *Chicago Sun* in 1941. After purchasing control of the *Chicago Daily Times* in 1947, he merged them to form the *Chicago Sun-Times* (1948). His son Marshall Field IV (1916–65) bought the *Chicago Daily News* in 1959 and served as editor and publisher of both the *Sun-Times* and the *Daily News*. His son Marshall Field V (1941–) was publisher of the *Sun-Times* from 1969 to 1980 and of the *Daily News* from 1969 until it ceased publication in 1978.

Field, Cyrus (1819–92), businessman and financier. Field planned and engineered the first telegraph cable across the Atlantic Ocean between the United States and Great Britain. After four abortive attempts, Field succeeded in 1866, creating a nearly immediate communications link between the two continents. He later promoted the installation of undersea cables across the Pacific to Asia and Australia.

Field, Stephen J. (1816–99), jurist. Field settled in California in 1849. Elected to the state legislature in 1850, he played a leading role in setting up the state's civil and criminal codes and later served on the state supreme court. Appointed to the U.S. Supreme Court by Abraham Lincoln in 1863, Field served on the bench for thirty-four years. Noted for his dissenting opinions, his decisions were important in the development of constitutional law. He was a leading spokesman for laissez-faire jurisprudence — the idea that law should not interfere with market forces.

Fields, W. C. (William Claude Dukenfield; 1879–1946), comedian. Known for his rasping voice, bulbous nose, cantankerous wit, and superb comedic talent, Fields played rascals in such comedies as *The Bank Dick* (1940), *My Little Chickadee* (1940), *Never Give a Sucker an Even Break* (1941), and *You Can't Cheat an Honest Man* (1939). His epitaph reads, "On the whole, I'd rather be in Philadelphia" (the town of his birth).

Filibuster, Congressional, a parliamentary device used in the U.S. Senate. A speaker holds the floor by continually talking, making it impossible for the Senate to continue with its business. Filibustering is used to prevent the passage of a particular bill. A tradition of unlimited debate exists in the

Senate, but it can be stopped by invoking the cloture (closure) rule, which limits debate to one hour per senator.

Filibustering Expeditions, armed expeditions launched during the mid-nineteenth century by groups of American adventurers trying to seize control of countries in Central America. The pirating expeditions were not authorized or supported by the U.S. government.

Fillmore, Millard (1800–74), thirteenth president of the United States (1850–53). Born in Locke, New York, Fillmore, a Whig, served in the House of Representatives. After his election to the vice presidency in 1848, Fillmore became the second vice president to succeed to the presidency, when Zachary Taylor died in 1850. During his administration, he supported and signed into law the COMPROMISE OF 1850, which helped delay the Civil War. Fillmore's strong support of the FUGITIVE SLAVE LAW gained him southern support but alienated northerners, so the Whigs did not nominate him in 1852. In 1856 the KNOW-NOTHING and WHIG parties nominated him for president, but he lost to Democrat James Buchanan.

Fireside Chats, weekly radio broadcasts by President FRANKLIN D. ROOSEVELT during the 1930s. In these informal talks the president shared the problems he and the country faced, as well as how he planned to deal with them. These chats contributed to FDR's popularity and gained support for his programs by making people feel that he was speaking directly to them on a personal level.

Firestone, Harvey (1868–1938), industrialist. Firestone founded and served as president of the Firestone Tire & Rubber Company in Akron, Ohio. He pioneered the manufacture of nonskid tire treads and low-pressure balloon tires; his company became the principal supplier of tires to the Ford Motor Company. To assure sources of supply, Firestone encouraged American support of countries producing rubber.

Fish, Hamilton (1808–93), politician and diplomat. Fish served in the House of Representatives (1843–45), as governor of New York (1849–51), and in the U.S. Senate (1851–57). He was appointed secretary of state by President ULYSSES S. GRANT and negotiated the Treaty of Washington (1871), thus settling the *ALABAMA* CLAIMS dispute with Great Britain. Fish also limited expansionism to ensure neutrality toward Spain and Cuba. His negotiations with Spain over the death of two U.S. sailors helped prevent the incident from escalating into war.

Fisk, James, Jr. (1834–72), businessman, financier, and speculator. Fisk, along with JAY GOULD, helped cause the stock market crash in 1869 known as BLACK FRIDAY. Fisk and Gould made millions and ruined many innocent investors when they tried to corner the gold market. Fisk was also involved in stock manipulation to control ship lines, as well as a struggle for control of the Erie Railroad, causing its ruin. Throughout his career and amidst many scandals, he flaunted his high-living style. He was shot in a quarrel at age thirty-seven.

Fitch, John (1743–98), inventor and engineer. Fitch designed the first practical steamboat in the United States in 1787. His boat featured a series of paddles propelled by a steam engine. Although two others followed in 1788 and 1790, he was not able to evoke enough passenger demand to make his boats profitable, and his financial backers abandoned the venture. It remained for ROBERT FULTON to build the first commercially viable steamer in 1807.

Fitzgerald, Ella (1918–96), black jazz singer. Fitzgerald gained world stature with popular recordings of sophisticated songs by Cole Porter, George Gershwin, and others. Known for a clear, pure vocal tone, she has recorded many jazz classics, such as *A Tisket A Tasket* (1938). In all, Fitzgerald sold more than 40 million albums and won thirteen Grammy Awards, more than any other jazz musician.

Fitzgerald, F. Scott (Francis; 1896–1940), novelist. Fitzgerald's books convey the essence of the ROARING TWENTIES. He and his wife, Zelda, lived an extravagant, glittering life, often reflected in his works. Noted novels include *This Side of Paradise* (1920), *The Beautiful and the Damned* (1922), *Tender Is the Night* (1934), and *The Great Gatsby* (1925), his masterpiece. Suffering from acute depression and alcoholism, Fitzgerald spent his last years writing scripts in Hollywood. He died of a heart attack before completing *The Last Tycoon*.

Five Civilized Nations, the name given by whites to the Chickasaw, Choctaw, Cherokee, Creek, and Seminole Indian tribes in southeastern United States. The Removal Act of 1830 forcibly moved the tribes to Indian Territory (present-day Oklahoma). The Cherokees were rounded up by troops and sent on a forced march, called the TRAIL OF TEARS, to Tennessee and Indian Territory in bitter weather; a quarter of the people died en route. The tribes were deemed "civilized" by whites because, while in the Southeast, they adopted European customs in an effort to coexist with whites. The Cherokees, for example, developed a written alphabet and published newspapers and books.

Flanagan, Father Edward Joseph (1886–1948), Roman Catholic priest. Guided by the belief that "there is no such thing as a bad boy," Father Flanagan in 1917 founded Boy's Town, a shelter for homeless boys, in Omaha, Nebraska. Boy's Town successfully rehabilitated underprivileged and delinquent youth. Father Flanagan's story was recounted in the film *Boy's Town* (1938), starring Spencer Tracy.

Fletcher* v. *Peck (1810), a U.S. SUPREME COURT case in which, for the first time, the Court declared a state law unconstitutional. The decision was the first step in establishing the supremacy of the Constitution and federal laws over state governments and laws. The Georgia legislature had given land grants to private speculators in return for bribes. The next legislature revoked the grants, but some of the original grants had already been sold. Chief Justice John Marshall held that the original grants were still valid because the Constitution prohibits any state from violating a contract.

Flexner, Abraham (1866–1959), educator. An authority on higher education, Flexner issued a report in 1910 called *Medical Education in the U.S. and Canada,* which recommended reforms in medical training. Flexner advocated progressive education and promoted changes in curricula and teaching methods. In 1930 he founded the Institute for Advanced Study at Princeton, becoming its first director.

Florida (Sunshine State), the twenty-seventh state to join the Union, March 3, 1845. (See maps, pages 540 and 541.) Florida, the southernmost state in the continental United States, was discovered by JUAN PONCE DE LEÓN, who claimed it for Spain and named it Florida, meaning "feast of flowers." During the next three hundred years, Florida was ceded to England, recaptured by Spain, and then turned over to the United States as part of the ADAMS-ONÍS TREATY in 1819. St. Augustine, founded in 1565, is the oldest permanent city in the country. Major cities include Tallahassee, the capital, Jacksonville, Miami (with a large Cuban-American population), Orlando, and Tampa-St. Petersburg. Florida, which has experienced several real estate booms and busts, is one of the fastest growing states, with tourism an important industry. Attractions include the warm climate, beautiful beaches, the Cape Canaveral space center, and Disney World. The Everglades National Park, which was one of the largest swamp areas in the world, is a nature preserve, though now badly damaged by environmental degradation. In addition to tourism, a leading industry is the growing of citrus fruits, tomatoes, melons, strawberries, and corn. In August 1992 southern Florida was devastated by Hurricane Andrew, the costliest natural disaster in the history of the United States. Famous Floridians include SIDNEY POITIER, CHRIS EVERT, and Marjorie Kinnan Rawlings.

Flynn, Elizabeth Gurley (1890–1964), political activist. Noted for her stirring oratory in the defense of the rights of labor, Flynn became active in the INDUSTRIAL WORKERS OF THE WORLD (IWW) in 1906. In 1920, reacting to the post-World War I red scare, she helped form the AMERICAN CIVIL LIBERTIES UNION (ACLU). In 1937 she joined the Communist party, later becoming its first woman leader. (The ACLU board ousted her in 1940 because of her Communist associations but reinstated her in 1976.) Flynn spent two years in prison (1955–57) under the SMITH ACT for advocating the overthrow of the U.S. government.

Fonda, Henry (1905–82), actor. Fonda won an Academy Award for best actor, playing opposite KATHARINE HEPBURN, in *On Golden Pond* in 1981. Following his film debut in 1935, he starred in *Young Mr. Lincoln* (1939), *The*

Grapes of Wrath (1940), and *The Ox-Bow Incident* (1943), among others. He portrayed idealistic heroes in many films, including *Advise and Consent* (1961), *Twelve Angry Men* (1956), and *The Best Man* (1964). Fonda also starred on Broadway in *The Caine Mutiny Court Martial, Clarence Darrow, First Monday in October,* and *Mr. Roberts,* a role he re-created in film.

Football, game played by two opposing teams of eleven players each who attempt to score points by running, passing, and kicking an inflated oval ball over the opposing team's goal line at either end of the rectangular playing field. The team possessing the ball is the offensive team, which must gain ten yards in four downs or yield possession to the defensive team, which attempts to keep the offense from scoring.

Football originated in the United States in the late nineteenth century, developed from England's soccer and rugby games. In the first intercollegiate game, Rutgers defeated Princeton 6 goals to 4 in 1869 at New Brunswick, New Jersey. The most influential figure in modernizing the game was WALTER CAMP of Yale University. In 1889 he and sportswriter Caspar Whitney selected the first All-American team, which showcases the best college players in the country. The roughness of the game caused serious injuries and deaths (eighteen players died in 1905 alone), prompting President Theodore Roosevelt to urge changes in the rules to avoid banning the game. The result was the formation of the National Collegiate Athletic Association in 1908, which set playing rules for the sport. According to some historians, the first forward pass was thrown in 1906 in a Wesleyan University game against Yale, eventually revolutionizing football.

The American Professional Football Association was founded in 1920 in Canton, Ohio, with JIM THORPE serving as its first president and superstar. In 1921 the league changed its name to the National Football League (NFL) but did not attract much attention until it signed RED GRANGE and other college stars. The first professional championship game took place in 1933, when the Chicago Bears defeated the New York Giants 23–21. By 1946 increased attendance warranted the establishment of a second league, the All-American Conference (AAC), which lasted four years; the two leagues merged in 1950. In 1960 the American Football League (AFL) was founded, and survived because of money received from television.

In 1970 the NFL's sixteen teams combined with the AFL's ten teams to form the National Football League. Today's twenty-eight-team NFL, divided into the American Football Conference and the National Football Conference with three divisions each, plays a regular season schedule of sixteen games. The final winners of the playoffs in each conference meet in the Super Bowl to determine the world champions. The Green Bay Packers defeated the Kansas City Chiefs 35–10 in the first Super Bowl in 1967.

Foraker Act (April 12, 1900), an act establishing a government for the U.S. territory of PUERTO RICO, which had been acquired following the

Spanish-American War. The governor of the island and an executive council were appointed by the president of the United States. The upper house of the legislature consisted of the eleven council members, while the lower house, the assembly, was elected by popular vote. The governor had veto power over all legislative acts. The Foraker Act was amended by the Jones Act of 1917, providing U.S. citizenship to Puerto Ricans and a greater measure of self-government.

Force Act (Bill) (January 16, 1833), a bill passed by Congress in response to South Carolina's passage of an ordinance of nullification protesting the TARIFF OF ABOMINATIONS in 1828. Although the act gave President Andrew Jackson the power to use the armed forces to execute the laws of the United States, the use of force was not necessary because South Carolina accepted Senator Henry Clay's COMPROMISE TARIFF OF 1833, which gradually lowered the rates of the tax.

Ford, Gerald R. (Leslie King, Jr.; 1913–), thirty-eighth president of the United States (1974–77). Born in Omaha, Nebraska, Ford grew up in Grand Rapids, Michigan. He played football at the University of Michigan and served in the navy during World War II. Elected to the House of Representatives in 1948, Ford became minority leader in 1965 and was a Republican party faithful. Following the resignation of Vice President SPIRO AGNEW, RICHARD M. NIXON, with congressional approval, chose Ford as vice president under the provisions of the Twenty-fifth Amendment to the Constitution. When Nixon resigned in August 1974, Ford became president, declaring, "Our long national nightmare is over," a reference to the WATERGATE scandal. One month after taking office, he granted Nixon a blanket pardon, an action that provoked widespread criticism and damaged his credibility. A conservative, he opposed governmental intervention in domestic matters and tried to reduce federal spending. Ford survived two assassination attempts in September 1975. In 1976 he edged out Ronald Reagan for the Republican presidential nomination, but lost the November election to Jimmy Carter by a very narrow margin. In 2003, Gerald Ford became the fourth former president to reach the age of ninety. The others were JOHN ADAMS, HERBERT HOOVER, and RONALD REAGAN.

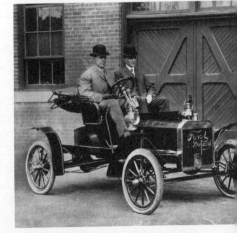

Henry Ford
Ford (right) seated in a 1905 Ford Model N.

Ford, Henry (1863–1947), automobile manufacturer. Ford built his first car in 1896 and formed the Ford

Motor Company in 1903. By 1909 he had worked out a system for mass producing the Model T using the assembly line and standardized parts. His production techniques drastically reduced the price of cars, and this, coupled with his decision in 1914 to pay his workers five dollars a day at a time when wages averaged eleven dollars a week, brought the purchase of a car within reach of average wage earners. Thus, he, more than any other single person, revolutionized transportation. By 1929 Ford was one of the largest manufacturers of cars in the world. Politically active, Ford opposed U.S. intervention in both world wars and ran unsuccessfully for the U.S. Senate in 1918. In 1936 he and his son Edsel established the Ford Foundation, which makes substantial grants to schools and colleges. Offsetting his mechanical genius were his anti-Semitism and his violent opposition to unions. As he aged, he became increasingly autocratic, refusing to make necessary changes in his company to arrest its precipitous decline. His family finally prevailed upon him to turn the company over to his grandson, Henry Ford II, two years before his death.

Ford, John (Sean Aloysius O'Feeney; 1895–1973), motion picture director. Ford, regarded by most film historians as the greatest American film director, made over a hundred pictures in his sixty-year career, including many westerns. He was the first director to win four Academy Awards. They were for *The Informer* (1935), *The Grapes of Wrath* (1939), *How Green Was My Valley* (1941), and *The Quiet Man* (1952). Ford received the Presidential Medal of Freedom shortly before his death. He was also the first person to be given the American Film Institute's Lifetime Achievement Award.

Forrest, Nathan Bedford (1821–77), Confederate general during the CIVIL WAR. Forrest led a famous cavalry unit responsible for many Southern victories, including a raid at Fort Pillow, Tennessee, in which he ordered the execution of scores of black defenders. Historians agree that he was one of the best strategists of the war. During Reconstruction, Forrest helped organize the KU KLUX KLAN and served as its first Grand Wizard.

Fortas, Abe (1910–82), lawyer and jurist. Fortas worked in the New Deal and practiced law in Washington. His most famous case was *GIDEON V. WAINWRIGHT*, in which he successfully represented Clarence Gideon. Lyndon Johnson appointed Fortas associate justice on the U.S. Supreme Court in 1965. He was named to replace Earl Warren in 1968 as chief justice, but the Senate hearings aroused controversy, and Johnson withdrew Fortas's name at his request. In 1969 questions arose about his acceptance of a fee from a foundation under investigation by the federal government, and he resigned from the Court.

Fort Donelson, Battle of (February 6, 1862), an early military engagement of the CIVIL WAR. The Confederates controlled the fort, located in Tennessee on the Cumberland River. In 1862 Union Gen. ULYSSES S. GRANT led a siege of the fort and forced an unconditional surrender of the thirteen thousand Confederate troops. This act made Grant a hero and earned him the nickname "Unconditional Surrender Grant."

Forten, James (1766–1842), black businessman and social reformer. Born of free black parents, Forten served during the American Revolution as a powder boy on an American ship. He returned to Philadelphia in 1786 and became involved in the ABOLITIONIST movement. At the same time he was apprenticed to a sail maker and purchased the business twelve years later. During the War of 1812 Forten recruited a force of 2,500 blacks to protect Philadelphia from a British attack. By 1832 he had accumulated a fortune from the sail-making business and supported WILLIAM LLOYD GARRISON and the American Anti-Slavery Society, which met frequently in his home. His daughter, Charlotte Forten, was prominent in the Female Anti-Slavery Society and published poetry in Garrison's *Liberator*.

Fort Henry, Battle of (February 6, 1862), a CIVIL WAR battle for control of a military fortification on the Tennessee River held by Confederate troops. Its capture by Union forces led by Gen. ULYSSES S. GRANT and Comm. Andrew Foote helped the North gain control of the Mississippi valley and split the Confederacy.

Fort Sumter (April 12, 1861), the site of the first shots of the CIVIL WAR. After the election of Abraham Lincoln in 1860, South Carolina seceded and demanded the surrender of Fort Sumter, a federal fort located in Charleston Harbor. Lincoln refused to let its commander, Maj. Robert Anderson, surrender and notified South Carolina of his intention to send supplies to the fort. Confederate general P.G.T. BEAUREGARD then opened fire, bombarding the fort for two days. On April 14 Anderson, out of supplies, surrendered. Lincoln, realizing there was no turning back, called for volunteers to serve in the Union army.

Fort Ticonderoga, a colonial fort located on Lake Champlain. During the AMERICAN REVOLUTION, Fort Ticonderoga fell to ETHAN ALLEN and the Green Mountain Boys, who were joined by BENEDICT ARNOLD in a surprise attack on May 10, 1775, which resulted in a British surrender. In 1777 the British, under Gen. John Burgoyne, recaptured the fort on their way south, just before their surrender at the Battle of Saratoga.

Forty-niners, adventurers and gold-seekers who went to California in 1849 after hearing of the discovery of gold at Sutter's mill in 1848. Forty-niners came from the eastern United States and from all parts of the world. Most traveled in covered wagons across the plains, but many came by water around Cape Horn, which took six months. Others went by ship to the Isthmus of Panama, crossed over the isthmus, and continued on to California by boat. The forty-niners dramatically increased the population of California, displacing many smaller Native American groups and hastening the admittance of the state into the Union.

Foster, Stephen (1826–64), composer. Foster wrote the words and music for more than two hundred songs, including "Away Down South" and "Oh! Susanna," a favorite of settlers heading west. Other Foster classics include "Old Folks at Home," "My Old Kentucky Home," "Nelly Bly," "Old Black Joe," and "Beautiful Dreamer." Ironically, his songs were inspired by southern life, though Foster had little firsthand knowledge of the South.

Founding Fathers, a term first used by President Warren G. Harding to describe the statesmen of the Revolutionary period who established the principles on which the U.S. government is based. They drafted and signed the Declaration of Independence and the U.S. Constitution.

Four Freedoms, the four principles President Franklin D. Roosevelt considered to be essential for world peace: freedom of speech, freedom of religion, freedom from want, and freedom from fear. The president spoke of the four freedoms in a 1941 address in which he called on Americans to support those who were fighting in World War II. "Freedom from fear and want" was also mentioned in the ATLANTIC CHARTER.

442nd Infantry, Japanese-American unit in World War II. Composed of all volunteers, the 442nd fought in the Italian campaign and became the most decorated unit in American military history. Awards to the 442nd included 3,600 Purple Hearts, 810 Bronze Stars, 342 Silver Stars, 47 Distinguished Service Crosses, and 17 Legion of Merits. One unit in the 442nd liberated Dachau at the end of the war.

Fourteen Points (1918), guidelines for peace proposed to Congress by WOODROW WILSON at the end of WORLD WAR I. The proposals included the abolition of secret alliances, freedom of the seas, a reduction of arms, self-determination for all countries and peoples, and the establishment of a LEAGUE OF NATIONS to promote world peace. The Fourteen Points were accepted by Germany and formed the basis of the armistice, but by the time of the Paris Peace Conference in 1919, many had to be compromised because of resistance by the leaders of France, Great Britain, and Italy. The fourteenth point, regarding the League of Nations, became part of the TREATY OF VERSAILLES, which was never ratified by the U.S. Senate.

Foxx, Jimmie (1907–67), baseball player. A powerful first baseman for the Philadelphia A's and Boston Red Sox, Foxx hit 534 home runs and compiled a .325 career batting average. Foxx, known as "Double X," was named the American League's most valuable player three times and hit the third highest home runs per season with 58 in 1932. He became a member of the Hall of Fame in 1951.

Frankfurter, Felix (1882–1965), jurist and adviser to Presidents Woodrow Wilson and Franklin D. Roosevelt. In 1920 Frankfurter helped found the American Civil Liberties Union and was active in the defense of Sacco and

Vanzetti in the mid-1920s. Appointed to the U.S. Supreme Court in 1939, Frankfurter advocated judicial self-restraint, a legal philosophy that urges judges not to write their personal views into the law. Frankfurter's views were popular among liberals when they urged courts not to strike down federal and state laws regulating the economy; they were unpopular when seen as obstacles to judicial decisions protecting individual liberties. He was vital to the Court's unanimous decision in the 1954 school desegregation case, *Brown* v. *Board of Education of Topeka.* He retired in 1962 because of ill health.

Franklin, Aretha (1942–), singer. Born in Memphis, Franklin sang with her sisters at their father's Baptist church, making her first recording at age fourteen. During the 1960s and 1970s, her popular recordings blended gospel, pop, rock, and rhythm and blues, and earned her the nickname, Queen of Soul. Franklin has more million-selling singles than any other female recording star and won fifteen Grammy awards. "Respect" became her signature song. On January 3, 1987, Franklin became the first woman to be inducted into the Rock and Roll Hall of Fame.

Franklin, Benjamin (1706–90), author, scientist, philosopher, and statesman. Franklin published *Poor Richard's Almanack* (1732–37) and the *Pennsylvania Gazette* (1729–48). He organized the American Philosophical Society and improved the postal service while he served as deputy postmaster general for the colonies. As a scientist and inventor he experimented with electricity, devised the lightning rod, created the Franklin stove, and developed bifocals. His significant contributions as a statesman included the ALBANY PLAN in 1754; in 1766 he helped convince the British Parliament to repeal the STAMP ACT. Franklin, who was a member of the Second CONTINENTAL CONGRESS, served on the committee to draft the DECLARATION OF INDEPENDENCE. He then became the first American minister to France during the AMERICAN REVOLUTION and successfully acquired French aid against Great Britain. He helped negotiate the TREATY OF PARIS with Great Britain in 1781–83. As a Pennsylvania delegate to the CONSTITUTIONAL CONVENTION in 1787, he served as a calming influence and broker of compromise between the large and small states and the free and slave states. Franklin was the only person

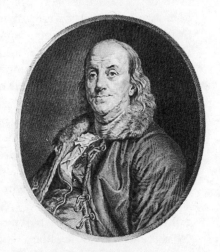

Benjamin Franklin

to sign all four of the great documents of the period: the Declaration of Independence, the Treaty of Alliance with France, the Treaty of Paris with Britain, and the U.S. Constitution.

Franklin, State of, an area in what is now eastern Tennessee and was formerly part of North Carolina, which was organized between 1784 and 1788 and named for Benjamin Franklin. Although unable to acquire congressional recognition, the area functioned as a state for four years. Its inhabitants framed and adopted a state constitution, elected John Sevier governor, passed laws, and collected taxes. North Carolina regained control of the area in 1788 and ceded it to Tennessee in 1796.

Franks, Tommy (1945–), commander in chief Central Command during U.S.–led AFGHANISTAN and IRAQ WARS. General Franks led the attack on the Taliban in Afghanistan in response to the SEPTEMBER 11, 2001 ATTACKS on the WORLD TRADE CENTER and the PENTAGON. After leading the invasion of Iraq and the overthrow of Saddam Hussein's regime, General Franks retired in July 2003.

Fredericksburg, Battle of (December 13, 1862), major battle of the CIVIL WAR in Virginia. Union forces led by the reckless general AMBROSE BURNSIDE attacked Confederate forces led by ROBERT E. LEE. The Union troops were repulsed, and a great slaughter ensued; they retreated two days later, giving the South an important victory. The Union lost over 12,000 soldiers compared to 5,000 casualties among the Southern troops.

Freedmen's Bureau (1865), an agency established by Congress at the end of the Civil War to provide food, clothing, shelter, education, and employment for the newly freed slaves. During its brief existence the bureau spent over $17 million and started over four thousand schools for black children. Gen. OLIVER O. HOWARD served as its first commissioner.

Freedom Riders, black and white college students, ministers, and others who rode interstate buses to test enforcement of a desegregation law. The rides took place during the civil rights movement in the summer of 1961. The freedom riders were brutally attacked by mobs of southern

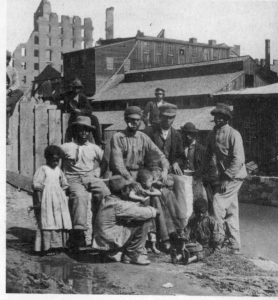

Freedmen's Bureau
A group of freedmen, Richmond, Virginia.

whites and received little or no protection from local police officials or the FBI.

Freeport Doctrine, a policy set forth by Senator STEPHEN A. DOUGLAS during the LINCOLN-DOUGLAS DEBATES in 1858 at Freeport, Illinois. In 1857 the Supreme Court had ruled, in the *DRED SCOTT* DECISION, that the people of a territory could not exclude slavery. Douglas argued that they could do so by adopting appropriate legislation. Slavery could not exist, he said, unless backed by "local police regulations." His argument helped him politically in the North but hurt him in the slave states.

Free-Soil Party (1848–54), a political party organized to oppose the spread of slavery into the territories acquired from Mexico. The party consisted of former LIBERTY PARTY members and antislavery DEMOCRATS and WHIGS. In the ELECTION OF 1848 they chose MARTIN VAN BUREN as their presidential candidate and CHARLES FRANCIS ADAMS as vice president. They drew enough votes from the Democratic candidate, LEWIS CASS, to make possible the election of the Whig candidate, ZACHARY TAYLOR. The party's slogan was, "Free soil, free speech, free labor, and free men." In 1854 the party dissolved, and many of its members joined the new REPUBLICAN PARTY.

Frémont, John C. (1813–90), adventurer, soldier, and political leader. During the Mexican War, Frémont participated in the BEAR FLAG REVOLT, which established the Bear Flag Republic. His involvement in a quarrel with Gen. STEPHEN KEARNY resulted in a court-martial and conviction for insubordination, but he later received a pardon from James K. Polk. Frémont served as one of California's first two senators, elected in 1850. In the ELECTION OF 1856, using the slogan "Free soil, free speech, free men, Frémont," he ran unsuccessfully as the first presidential candidate of the new REPUBLICAN PARTY. During the Civil War, Frémont commanded the Western Department. He later lost a fortune in a railroad venture and served as governor of Arizona Territory.

French and Indian War (1754–63), the American phase of Europe's Seven Years' War, a series of battles between Great Britain and the colonists against the French and their Indian allies. Highlights of the war included the defeat and death of Gen. Edward Braddock at Fort Duquesne (1755); the capture of Louisburg by Gen. Sir Jeffrey Amherst (1758); the British victories at FORT TICONDEROGA and Crown Point, and at Quebec, where both the British and French commanders, James Wolfe and the Marquis de Montcalm, were killed (1759); and the conquest of Montreal. Under the terms of the TREATY OF PARIS ending the war (1763), France lost its colonial possessions, and the French empire in North America came to an end.

French, Daniel Chester (1850–1931), sculptor. French's Minute Man statue for a memorial of the American Revolution in the town of Concord, Massachusetts, resulted in numerous commissions for public monuments.

His most famous work is the seated figure of Abraham Lincoln at the Lincoln Memorial in Washington, D.C.

Freneau, Philip (1752–1832), poet and journalist. Freneau earned the appellation "Poet of the American Revolution" for his anti-British poetry. He wrote *The British Prison-Ship* (1781) while imprisoned by the British aboard a privateer. Other works include *The Rising Glory of America* (1772) and *The American Village* (1772). His lyrical, imaginative poems about nature include "The Wild Honeysuckle" (1786) and "The Indian Burying Ground" (1788). After the war Freneau became editor of the *National Gazette* newspaper, supporting Thomas Jefferson and James Madison and opposing the FEDERALISTS' foreign and economic policies.

Frick, Henry C. (1849–1919), industrialist. Frick played a leading role in the creation of the Carnegie Steel Corporation in 1882. He was instrumental in breaking the union involved in the HOMESTEAD STRIKE in 1892. Frick helped negotiate the merger and formation of U.S. Steel in 1901 and became its director. Upon his death his home in New York City became the Frick Museum, for which he left $15 million and his art treasures.

Friedan, Betty (Betty Goldstein; 1921–), feminist leader and author. As a suburban housewife, Friedan in 1963 wrote *The Feminine Mystique*, which analyzed the role of women in American society and sparked the modern FEMINIST MOVEMENT. She founded the National Organization for Women in 1966 and served as its president. In 1971 she cofounded the National Women's Political Caucus, which encourages women to seek political office. She wrote another book in 1981, *The Second Stage*, further exploring women's lives.

Frost, Robert (1874–1963), poet. Frost found the inspiration for much of his poetry in the New England countryside and its way of life. Noted for their plain language, commonsense wisdom, and symbolism, Frost's poems received Pulitzer Prizes in 1924, 1931, 1937, and 1943. Honored works include *New Hampshire* (1923), *Collected Poems* (1930), *A Further Range* (1937), and

---

★ **Betty Friedan**

The opening passage of *The Feminine Mystique* (1963)

The problem lay buried, unspoken, for many years in the minds of American women. It was a strange stirring, a sense of dissatisfaction, a yearning that women suffered in the middle of the twentieth century in the United States. Each suburban wife struggled with it alone. As she made the beds, shopped for groceries, matched slipcover material, ate peanut butter sandwiches with her children, chauffeured Cub Scouts and Brownies, lay beside her husband at night — she was afraid to ask even of herself the silent question — "Is this all?"

A Witness Tree (1943). Frost's career received its greatest public recognition when, unable to read his inaugural poem in the bright sunlight he recited his older poem "The Gift Outright" at the inauguration of President John F. Kennedy in 1961.

Fugitive Slave Laws, laws that helped slave owners recover runaway slaves. The first law, passed in 1793, was unsatisfactory to slave owners because of lack of enforcement. In order to gain southern support for the COMPROMISE OF 1850, a provision for a stricter fugitive slave law was included, which allowed federal agents to arrest runaways anywhere in the United States and return them to their owners. The law became a major target of antislavery forces, who sought to smuggle escaped slaves to Canada via the UNDERGROUND RAILROAD and to pass PERSONAL LIBERTY LAWS.

Fulbright, J. William (1905–95), politician. Fulbright sponsored the Fulbright Act in 1946, which promoted cultural exchange for students and teachers by providing funds for study abroad. A Democrat from Arkansas, he served in the House of Representatives and in the Senate from 1945 to 1975. Although a conservative in domestic matters, Fulbright, as chairman of the Foreign Relations Committee (1959–74), took liberal positions in world affairs, criticizing U.S. involvement in Vietnam.

Fuller, Buckminster (1895–1983), inventor, architect, designer, engineer, and futurist. Fuller developed the geodesic dome, a light prefabricated enclosure constructed of numerous adjoining tetrahedrons.

Fuller, Margaret (Margaret Fuller Ossoli; 1810–50), journalist, women's rights activist, and critic. Fuller's major book, *Women in the Nineteenth Century* (1845), is a pioneering work on the right of women to be independent. Fuller served as editor of the *Dial*, a respected transcendentalist magazine, and became the first female journalist working for a major newspaper when she joined the staff of Horace Greeley's *New York Tribune* in 1844. Greeley sent her to Europe in 1846 to cover the revolutions unfolding there, making her one of the first foreign correspondents for an American newspaper. While in Italy, she married a revolutionary, Giovanni Ossoli, bore a son, and joined the movement for a free Roman republic. When that cause failed, the family set out for America, but all three perished when their ship sank off the coast of Fire Island.

Fuller, Melville Weston (1833–1910), chief justice of the United States Supreme Court (1888–1910). Fuller was a prominent lawyer in Chicago before Grover Cleveland appointed him chief justice. His Court declared the national income tax unconstitutional in *Pollock* v. *Farmers' Loan and Trust Company* (1895). (As a result, the Sixteenth Amendment was passed, permitting the government to levy the tax.) Fuller led the campaign for the Judiciary Act of 1891, which created federal circuit courts to lessen the Court's workload. He also served as a member of the Court of International Arbitration in The Hague from 1900 to 1910.

Fulton, Robert (1765–1815), inventor and artist. At the urging of ROBERT P. LIVINGSTON, the American minister to France, Fulton built the first commercially successful steamboat, *Clermont,* in 1807. Fulton also contributed to the development of the submarine with the launching of *Nautilus,* built in France, in 1800. He achieved success as a landscape and portrait painter, studying in England under BENJAMIN WEST.

Fundamental Orders of Connecticut (1639), the first written constitution in North America. Adopted by the residents of Hartford, Windsor, and Wethersfield, it was largely the work of THOMAS HOOKER, a Puritan clergyman. A plan for self-government of the colony, the orders put the welfare of the community above that of the individual, providing for the election of a governor, six assistants, and a legislative assembly to make laws.

G

Gable, Clark (1901–60), actor. As Hollywood's top box-office attraction for many years, Gable became known as "the King." He won an Academy Award for his performance in the comedy *It Happened One Night* (1934), which established him as the leading romantic star in movies. Gable's most famous role, as Rhett Butler in *Gone With the Wind* (1939), seemed to many to reflect his off-screen personality.

Gabriel's Rebellion *See* GABRIEL PROSSER.

Gadsden Purchase (December 30, 1853), a strip of land in the southwestern part of the United States acquired from Mexico for $10 million. Arranged by James Gadsden, U.S. minister to Mexico, the land was purchased to facilitate a direct railroad route to southern California.

Gag Rules (1836), a series of resolutions introduced by JOHN C. CALHOUN in the Senate and rejected there but passed in the House of Representatives forbidding the reading of antislavery petitions in Congress. JOHN QUINCY ADAMS repeatedly delivered speeches against the rules, arguing they denied the people the rights to free speech and to petition the government. The gag rules were repealed in 1844.

Galbraith, John Kenneth (1908–), economist. Born in Canada, Galbraith immigrated to the United States in 1931, first studying at Berkeley and later teaching economics at Harvard. He served as deputy head of the Office of Price Administration during WORLD WAR II and became an adviser to postwar administrations in Germany and Japan. A friend of President JOHN F. KENNEDY, Galbraith served as U.S. ambassador to India from 1961 to 1963. He advocated government spending to stimulate the economy and emphasized the power and ability of large, powerful corporations. He authored numerous books including *The Affluent Society* (1958) and *The Good Society* (1996).

Gallatin, Albert (1761–1849), public official and financier. A Swiss immigrant, Gallatin settled in Pennsylvania, where he played a major role in organizing the DEMOCRATIC-REPUBLICAN PARTY. As secretary of the treasury under Thomas Jefferson and James Madison, he helped to reduce spending and to begin paying off the national debt. He was also a key figure in the negotiations of the TREATY OF GHENT (1814) ending the War of 1812.

Galloway, Joseph (1731?–1803), lawyer, colonial official, and Loyalist. Galloway, a Pennsylvania delegate to the First CONTINENTAL CONGRESS in 1774, opposed American independence. In an effort to reconcile the colonies and Great Britain, he devised a plan of union under which the legislative authority over the colonies would be held jointly by Parliament and a colonial legislature of elected delegates, each with veto power over the other's legislation. A Crown-appointed president general would serve as executive authority. The plan divided the Congress, and it was defeated by one vote. Galloway remained a Loyalist and refused to attend the Second Continental Congress. In 1777 he served as administrator of Philadelphia until its recapture by Continental troops in 1778. Fleeing to England, Galloway continued to criticize the war; his American properties were confiscated, and his request to return to the United States was denied.

Gallup, George (1901–84), surveyor of public opinion. In 1935 Gallup started the American Institute of Public Opinion, which became respected when it correctly predicted the outcome of the presidential election of 1936. Gallup continually refined his polling techniques, resulting in usually accurate predictions. His grass-roots polls on almost every conceivable issue expanded into over thirty countries.

Garbo, Greta (Greta Gustafsson; 1905–90), Swedish-born U.S. actress. The aloof and beautiful Garbo became one of the world's great actresses, starring in such silent films as *The Torrent* (1926), *Flesh and the Devil* (1927), and *Wild Orchids* (1929). Unlike some who started in silent films, Garbo, who had a mellow husky voice, made a successful transition to sound films. *Anna Christie* (1930), *Anna Karenina* (1935), and *Camille* (1937) are some of the best known. Her *Ninotchka,* made with Melvyn Douglas in 1939, ranks as a classic American film. In 1941 Garbo retired to an intensely private life.

Garfield, James A. (1831–81), twentieth president of the United States (1881). Born in Orange, Ohio, Garfield graduated from Williams College in Massachusetts and returned to Ohio to teach at Hiram College. He served as a general during the Civil War and as a member of the Ohio Senate for one year (1859) and the U.S. House of Representatives for seventeen years (1863–81). He won the Republican nomination for the ELECTION OF 1880 as a dark horse candidate because of a deadlock between supporters of Ulysses S. Grant and James G. Blaine. Garfield defeated the Democratic nominee, Gen. Winfield Scott Hancock, becoming the last president to be born in a log cabin. During his term of office he tried to reunite the STALWART and

HALF-BREED factions of the Republican party. After serving only four months, Garfield, on July 2, 1881, was shot by CHARLES GUITEAU, a deranged political office seeker, and died eighty days later.

Garland, Judy (Frances Gumm; 1922–69), singer and actress. The daughter of vaudeville performers, Garland costarred with Mickey Rooney in the Andy Hardy film series. She received a special Academy Award for her performance in *The Wizard of Oz* in 1939. Other films include *Meet Me in St. Louis* (1944), *Easter Parade* (1948), and *A Star Is Born* (1954). Garland, a skillful singer with a unique style, showcased her talent in films, television appearances, and concerts. During the 1950s and 1960s depression hampered her career, and in 1969 she died from an apparent overdose of sleeping pills. She was the mother of Liza Minelli, the actress and singer.

Garner, John Nance (1868–1967), Speaker of the House of Representatives (1931–33) and vice president of the United States (1933–41) under Franklin D. Roosevelt. Garner represented Texas as a Democrat in Congress from 1903 to 1933. He helped Roosevelt gain the Democratic nomination in 1932, thus earning the second spot on the ticket. Garner opposed Roosevelt's running for a third term, for he wanted the nomination for himself; the president dropped him as a running mate in favor of Henry A. Wallace in the 1940 election.

Garrison, William Lloyd (1805–79), ABOLITIONIST. Garrison founded the antislavery newspaper the *Liberator* in 1831 and published it until 1865, when slavery was abolished. He helped organize the American Anti-Slavery Society in 1833, serving as its president from 1843 to 1865. Once almost lynched by an angry Boston mob because of his extreme abolitionist views and such tactics as burning the Constitution and urging northern secession from the Union, Garrison railed against the federal government for years but eventually supported Abraham Lincoln after he issued the preliminary Emancipation Proclamation in 1862.

Garvey, Marcus (1887–1940), black nationalist leader. Garvey created a modern version of the "back to Africa" movement, believing that blacks would never achieve equality in countries where most of the people were white. He founded the Universal Negro Improvement Association in Jamaica in 1914 and acquired a huge following in the United States, the Caribbean, and Africa. He received substantial sums of money and started several black enterprises, including the Black Star Line, a steamship company. His projects faltered, however, and in 1923 he was convicted by the Justice Department for mail fraud. He was imprisoned in 1925, pardoned by Calvin Coolidge in 1927, and deported to Jamaica. Never able to regain his immense influence, he made London his permanent home.

Gaspee, Burning of the (June 9, 1772), an act of violence preceding the American Revolution. The *Gaspee,* a British custom ship patrolling the waters near Providence, Rhode Island, was set afire by American colonists to protest British antismuggling policy. This incident brought about stricter enforcement of the Navigation and Trade Acts.

Gates, Horatio (1728?–1806), American general during the AMERICAN REVOLUTION. A skilled political general, Gates was credited with the victory at the BATTLE OF SARATOGA in 1777; this suggested to some that he should replace Washington as commander in chief. In fact, Thomas Conway formed a secret group, the CONWAY CABAL, to plot such an action, but it quickly collapsed. When Gates later commanded Patriot forces in the South, he suffered a bad defeat at the Battle of Camden in South Carolina, which tarnished his reputation.

Gates, William (1955–), computer industry inventor and entrepreneur. Gates was born in Seattle, where he developed an interest in software and began programming computers at age thirteen. He left Harvard in his junior year to focus on Microsoft, a company he had begun in 1975 with childhood friend PAUL ALLEN. He began developing software for personal computers, and the Microsoft Corporation evolved into the world's leader in software, services, and Internet technologies. Although known for his brilliance, Gates established a reputation for questionable business practices resulting in a series of major antitrust actions brought both by the U.S. Department of Justice and individual companies against Microsoft in the late 1990s. Generally considered one of the richest men in the world, Gates, along with his wife, created the Bill and Melinda Gates Foundation, a charitable organization that provides funds for minority college scholarships, AIDS prevention, and other projects.

Gatling, Richard (1818–1903), inventor. Gatling, best known for his creation of a crank-operated, rapid-fire revolving machine gun called the Gatling gun, patented his invention in 1862. The army officially adopted it for use in 1866.

Gay Rights Movement, a movement to secure civil rights for homosexuals and lesbians. Partly due to the influence of religious beliefs, condemnation of and discrimination against homosexuals were common in the United States since colonial times, creating a climate in which, to a large extent, homosexual behavior was kept private. Changing social and economic conditions in the twentieth century led many

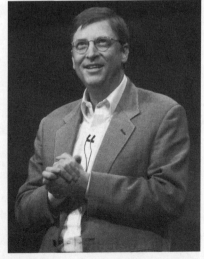

Bill Gates

homosexuals to acknowledge their sexuality openly and to form social and other organizations. This resulted in increasingly overt discrimination, particularly in the 1950s; for example, in 1953 President Eisenhower issued an executive order banning homosexuals from federal employment. The contemporary Gay Rights Movement took shape following the events of June 27, 1969, when a police raid on the Stonewall Inn, a gay bar in New York City's Greenwich Village, led to three nights of rioting and the spontaneous formation of a political and social grassroots activist movement. The emergence of the AIDS epidemic in the 1980s intensified the need for political mobilization among homosexuals and further solidified the movement.

By the early 2000s, several states had enacted laws protecting against discrimination in employment by private-sector employers based on sexual orientation. More companies began offering health care and other benefits to partners of gay and lesbian employees, and in 2003 the Episcopal Church elected the denomination's first openly gay bishop. Also in 2003, a Supreme Court decision in LAWRENCE V. TEXAS effectively struck down all state antisodomy laws, which is expected to fuel the debate for and against recognition of gay marriage.

In 2004 the high court of Massachusetts ruled that gay marriage was legal under its constitution, leading to the nation's first legal gay marriages in May 2004. In February 2004, the issue was pushed into the national spotlight when San Francisco mayor Gavin Newsom issued an unprecedented executive order allowing same-gender couples to be legally married in the city and county of San Francisco. This action ignited a trend and led to the issuing of same-sex licenses in several other communities in other states. Heated debates and legal challenges ensued, and the California Supreme Court ordered a halt to the practice while they determined whether the mayor had the power to authorize the unions.

Also in February 2004, President GEORGE W. BUSH endorsed a constitutional amendment banning same-sex marriages. It promised to be a divisive issue in the 2004 presidential election.

Gehrig, Lou (1903–41), baseball player. As first baseman for the New York Yankees, Gehrig, known as "the Iron Horse," played 2,130 consecutive games in sixteen seasons. He compiled a .340 lifetime batting average with 493 home runs and 1,990 runs batted in. Voted the American League most valuable player four times, Gehrig became a member of the Hall of Fame in 1939. His career was cut short when he became ill with a terminal form of sclerosis, now known as Lou Gehrig's disease.

Gemini Space Program (1965–66), series of ten two-man space flights, which comprised the second phase of the manned space program, following the MERCURY program and preceding the Apollo lunar landing. The goals of the Gemini program included testing whether astronauts could endure the lengthy weightlessness required of lunar journeys, developing rendezvous and docking techniques, and training new astronauts. The first manned Gemini mission, *Gemini 3*, was flown on March 23, 1965, by Virgil I. Grissom and John W. Young. *Gemini 12* ended the project.

General Court, the legislative assembly of the MASSACHUSETTS BAY COLONY. The court met four times a year and included the governor, his aides, and representatives of the colonists. It levied taxes and fines, passed regulations for the government of Massachusetts Bay, and deported undesirable settlers to England. The Massachusetts legislature is still called the General Court.

Genêt Affair (1793). France sent Citizen Edmond Genêt as minister to the United States to obtain American aid in the French war against Great Britain. President George Washington had proclaimed United States' neutrality in any European war, and when Genêt appealed directly to the American people for support, the president prepared to deport him. Genêt then asked for and received permission to remain in the United States as a private individual because he feared execution by the French government.

Geneva Conventions (1864), international agreements signed in Geneva, Switzerland, by almost every nation of the world establishing humane rules relating to war. Provisions include the care of the sick and wounded, identification of the dead, treatment of prisoners of war and hostages, and the neutrality of medical personnel in time of war. The rules, unfortunately, are too often ignored.

Gentlemen's Agreement (1907), an informal agreement between Japan and the United States in which Japan agreed to halt unrestricted emigration of its citizens to the United States. In return, the United States promised to stop discrimination against Japanese, thus ending its segregation of Asian children in San Francisco schools.

George, Henry (1839–97), California newspaperman and popular economist. George developed the single tax theory, whereby one tax would replace all other forms of taxation. Believing that land is a gift of nature to which all should have equal access, he advocated a tax on land equal to its rental price to fund government operations. He presented his theories in *Progress and Poverty* in 1879. George ran for mayor of New York in 1886 and finished second. He also was influential as an Irish nationalist.

Georgia (Empire State of the South), became the fourth state on January 2, 1788. (See maps, pages 540 and 541.) Founded by JAMES OGLETHORPE in 1732 as a colony for debtors, Georgia was named in honor of King George II of England. Savannah, the first city settled (1733), and Atlanta, its capital, have become important communication and transportation centers. As the largest state east of the Mississippi River, Georgia grows peanuts, tobacco, cotton, and peaches. Tourist attractions include the old cities of Savannah and Augusta; the Sea Islands along its coast; Stone Mountain, on which is carved a Confederate memorial, the world's largest sculpture; the

Okefenokee Swamp, the largest in the United States; and the Little White House in Warm Springs, Franklin D. Roosevelt's vacation home. Georgia was the last Confederate state to re-enter the Union after the Civil War. A strongly segregated state for years, it was the site of many voter registration and desegregation efforts during the civil rights movement in the 1950s and 1960s. Famous Georgians include JIMMY CARTER, ALEXANDER H. STEPHENS, MARTIN LUTHER KING, JR., JOEL CHANDLER HARRIS, and TED TURNER.

Germantown, Battle of (October 4, 1777), military engagement during the AMERICAN REVOLUTION. George Washington attempted a surprise attack on the British forces under Sir William Howe at Germantown, Pennsylvania. Despite inflicting heavy casualties, the American army suffered a defeat and was forced to retreat.

Geronimo (1829–1909), chief of the Apache nation. Geronimo led attacks during the Apache War (1871–76) against settlers in Arizona. Noted for his bravery and fierceness, he finally surrendered to Gen. Nelson Miles in 1886. He and his followers were exiled to Florida and later to Fort Sill in Indian Territory (now Oklahoma) where he became a successful farmer and a tourist attraction at fairs and exhibitions.

Gerry, Elbridge (1744–1814), leader for independence in Massachusetts, member of the Second Continental Congress, signer of the Declaration of Independence, and vice president of the United States under James Madison (1813–17). Gerry, a member of the CONSTITUTIONAL CONVENTION, opposed a strong central government and refused to sign the Constitution because it did not include a bill of rights. He served in Congress from 1789 to 1793 and was a member of the U.S. delegation to Paris whose visit resulted in the XYZ AFFAIR in 1797. As governor of Massachusetts for two terms, he was blamed for his party's gross rearrangement of election districts in 1812 to favor the Democratic-Republican party. The practice came to be called GERRYMANDERING after him — ironically, since he had nothing to do with it and privately opposed it.

Gerrymandering, a political device of drawing irregular district lines in order to favor one political power over another, usually the party in office, or to exclude a

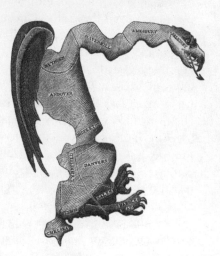

Gerrymandering
The original gerrymander as it appeared in a political cartoon in the periodical Broadsides, *January 1812.*

target group from full representation. The practice was named after ELBRIDGE GERRY. In 1812 a Massachusetts election district was redrawn so much out of shape that it resembled a salamander; Federalists combined that word with Gerry's name to coin the term *gerrymander*.

Gershwin, George (1898–1937), composer, and Ira Gershwin (1896–1983), lyricist. The Gershwins are responsible for some of the most popular music in America. George composed songs, musical comedies, film scores, and the classic black folk opera *Porgy and Bess* (1935). His first concert composition, *Rhapsody in Blue* (1924), combined classical piano and jazz elements. Ira wrote the lyrics of most of George's songs. Their musical *Of Thee I Sing* won the Pulitzer Prize in 1931. Their other musicals include *Funny Face* (1927), *Girl Crazy* (1930), and *An American in Paris* (1928).

Getty, Jean Paul (1892–1976), oil tycoon. Getty inherited his father's oil company and made his first million by age twenty-one, buying and selling oil leases. By the 1960s he was worth more than a billion dollars and considered to be the world's wealthiest man. Noted for frugality in his personal life, Getty was an art collector, founding the richly endowed J. Paul Getty Museum in Malibu, California.

Gettysburg Address (November 19, 1863), speech delivered by Abraham Lincoln at dedication ceremonies for a national cemetery at Gettysburg, Pennsylvania. The featured speaker, EDWARD EVERETT, gave a two-hour oration, but it was Lincoln's brief remarks that have come to be recognized as classic. The address, expressing grief for the dead and emphasizing the need to maintain the principles they had died to uphold, ended with the hope that "government of the people, by the people, and for the people shall not perish from the earth." Lincoln's ten sentences are the most famous speech in American history and, it has been argued, recast the principles of American government.

Gettysburg, Battle of (July 1–3, 1863), the turning-point battle of the CIVIL WAR. Gen. ROBERT E. LEE initiated a second invasion of the North (ANTIETAM was the first) when he crossed into southern Pennsylvania. His Army of Northern Virginia met the Union Army of the Potomac, led by Gen. GEORGE MEADE, at Gettysburg on July 1. The bloodiest battle of the war lasted three days. On July 3 at 3:00 P.M., Confederate general GEORGE PICKETT led his disastrous charge on Cemetery Ridge. The attack failed and Lee retreated into Virginia. General Meade, recognizing that his men were exhausted, refused to follow Lee's troops, and the Civil War continued for two more long and bloody years. Meade was criticized as overcautious for failing to pursue Lee, but military historians tend to exonerate him.

Ghent, Treaty of (December 24, 1814), agreement between the United States and Great Britain, signed in Ghent, Belgium, ending the WAR OF 1812. England agreed to surrender its forts in the Northwest Territory and to allow the United States fishing rights in Canadian waters. Neither side obtained any significant advantage as a result of the treaty. Because of slow communication, the United States won its most important victory, at the Battle of New Orleans, two weeks after the treaty was signed.

Giannini, Amadeo P. (1870–1949), banker. Though a school dropout in San Francisco, Giannini rose to found the Bank of America, which became the largest in the United States. He loaned money to help reconstruct San Francisco after the earthquake of 1906 and retired in 1936 after organizing his financial holdings into the Transamerica Corporation.

Gibbons v. Ogden (1824), a SUPREME COURT decision that interpreted the interstate commerce power of Congress. Written by Chief Justice John Marshall, it stated that national law was superior to state law when the two came into conflict.

G.I. Bill of Rights (1944), a series of programs designed to help veterans. This first G.I. bill, passed in 1944 during World War II and called the Servicemen's Readjustment Act, offered veterans funds for tuition and maintenance in educational institutions. The law also included hospitalization, pensions, and other benefits, as well as a provision for government-guaranteed loans for the purchase of homes, farms, and businesses. In 1952 similar benefits were granted to Korean War veterans in a second G.I. bill. Other bills have benefited people who served in the armed forces during the cold war.

Gibson, Althea (1927–2003), tennis player. After winning the first of ten consecutive national Negro women's singles titles in 1948, Gibson rose quickly in the tennis ranks. She became the first black athlete to play Forest Hills, Long Island, in 1950 and the first black American invited to Wimbledon in 1951, capturing both the British and the U.S. singles championships in 1957–58. As the first black tennis player to win all the world singles titles for women, she turned professional in 1959 to win the women's professional singles crown in 1960.

Gibson, Josh (1911–47), baseball player barred from the major leagues because he was black. As a star catcher for the Negro National League, Gibson led in home runs for ten consecutive years and was considered the greatest power hitter in baseball history. It is estimated that he hit over 950 home runs in his career and had a lifetime batting average of .347. He became a member of baseball's Hall of Fame in 1972.

Gideon v. Wainwright (1963), a U.S. Supreme Court decision ruling that states must provide qualified counsel for anyone accused of committing a felony who cannot afford a lawyer. The Court ruled that the Sixth Amendment guarantees this right to all Americans. Retried because Florida had not provided him with an attorney, Clarence Gideon was acquitted.

Gilded Age the period between 1865 and 1900. During this time of great, showy displays of wealth, large fortunes were made as a result of industrial expansion. The name, a derogatory one, was derived from the title of a novel by Mark Twain and Charles Dudley Warner in 1873.

Gillespie, Dizzy (John; 1917–93), black composer, trumpet player, and band-leader. Gillespie, with his original style and innovative technique, was one of the creators of modern jazz. With Charlie Parker, he pioneered bebop in the 1940s. Known for their harmonic, rhythmic, and tasteful sounds, many of his pieces, such as "A Night in Tunisia," have become jazz classics. Gillespie led his own groups, from small combos to full bands, throughout the world.

Gingrich, Newt (1943–), politician. A Republican from Georgia, Gingrich served in the House of Representatives (1978–98). He became a leader of the House conservatives, vocally opposing the majority Democrats and using ethics charges to force Speaker of the House Jim Wright to resign. He served as minority whip (1989–94), and in the 1994 election engineered the first Republican House majority in forty years, becoming Speaker in 1995. During his leadership, Congress attacked President BILL CLINTON's character, investigating various scandals and calling for impeachment. His CONTRACT WITH AMERICA attempted to unify the Republican party with promises that were only partially successful. Ultimately, Gingrich was saddled with ethics problems himself and was fined for violating House rules. Blamed for Republican losses in the 1996 and 1998 elections, he resigned both the speakership and his congressional seat in 1998.

Ginsburg, Ruth Bader (1933–), Supreme Court justice. Appointed by President BILL CLINTON in 1993, Ginsburg became the second female justice on the U.S. Supreme Court. A lawyer and former professor of law at Rutgers (1963–72) and Columbia (1972–80), she served as a fellow at the Center for Advanced Study in the Behavioral Sciences at Stanford (1977–78). She then became a judge on the U.S. Court of Appeals (1980–93). Generally considered a liberal, Ginsburg is known for her integrity and independent thinking.

Giuliani, Rudolph (1944–), politician. Born and raised in Brooklyn, Giuliani graduated from NYU Law School magna cum laude. He first gained prominence as a U.S. attorney for the southern district of New York for his aggressive prosecutions of white-collar criminals as well as organized crime. Elected mayor of New York in 1993, his two terms were considered successful. Although criticized by some for his temper and harsh manner, during his tenure the city's crime rate dropped, city services improved, and New York's reputation changed from dangerous and crime-ridden, to being one of the safest large cities in America. Giuliani dropped a bid for the U.S. Senate in 2000 against HILLARY RODHAM CLINTON as his marriage dissolved and he underwent prostate cancer treatment. His reputation was largely restored when Giuliani showed tremendous strength, courage, and sound leadership following the SEPTEMBER 11, 2001, TERRORIST ATTACKS, earning him praise and respect from around the world. For his work, he was selected *Time* magazine's Person of the Year in 2001 and was given an honorary knighthood by Queen Elizabeth II in 2002.

Glass, Carter (1858–1946), politician. A Democrat from Virginia, Glass served in the House of Representatives from 1902 to 1918, where he coauthored the Federal Reserve Act of 1913, which set up the FEDERAL RESERVE SYSTEM. Glass served as secretary of the treasury from 1918 to 1920 and in the Senate from 1920 to 1946, where he was president pro tempore from 1941 to 1945. He cosponsored the GLASS-STEAGALL ACT.

Glass-Steagall Act (June 16, 1933), law that established the FEDERAL DEPOSIT INSURANCE CORPORATION to insure bank deposits up to $5,000 (the amount was changed several times and is now $100,000). Also known as the Banking Act of 1933, the act prohibited the affiliation of banks with companies selling securities. (An earlier Glass-Steagall Act, February 27, 1932, addressed credit expansion in the United States.)

Gleason, Jackie (1916–87), comedian and actor. Called "the Great One," Gleason played in nightclubs, films, and television. Television successes include the "Cavalcade of Stars," the "Jackie Gleason Show," and the comedy classic "The Honeymooners," still shown in reruns. His film credits include *The Hustler* (1961) and *Requiem for a Heavyweight* (1962).

Glenn, John, Jr. (1921–), astronaut and U.S. senator. Glenn became a national hero in 1962 as the first American to orbit the earth in a space capsule (*Friendship 7*). Elected U.S. senator from Ohio in 1974 and reelected in 1980 and 1986, he made an unsuccessful bid for the Democratic party's nomination for president in 1984. In October, 1998, Glenn participated in a space shuttle mission to test effects of space travel on the elderly. At the age of seventy-seven, this made him the oldest person ever to go into space. Glenn retired from the Senate in 1999.

Glidden, Joseph (1813–1906), teacher, inventor, and farmer. Glidden perfected barbed or twisted wire, patenting it in 1874. The wire helped end the open range in the West. By keeping cattle contained, it made it possible for small farmers to operate. It was also used extensively in both world wars as a defense against attacks on men in trenches.

Goddard, Robert (1882–1945), rocket scientist, known as the father of American rocketry. As early as 1919 Goddard described the kind of rocket flight that would be necessary to reach the moon. Although his report, *A Method of Reaching Extreme Altitudes,* was received with skepticism, he continued his research and launched the world's first liquid-propelled rocket in 1926. The significance of Goddard's contribution was unappreciated until after his death and the advent of the space program.

Godkin, Edwin (1831–1902), editor and author. Godkin founded the *Nation,* a weekly periodical, and served as its editor from 1865 to 1901. An outspoken critic of the SPOILS SYSTEM, he worked vigorously for CIVIL SERVICE

REFORM. His campaign aroused public opinion in favor of the Pendleton Act (1883), establishing the civil service system.

Goethals, George Washington (1858–1928), army engineer. President Theodore Roosevelt appointed Goethals to direct the building of the PANAMA CANAL in 1907. After overcoming problems with organization, supplies, disease, climate, and labor, Goethals completed the canal ahead of schedule in 1914. He retired from the army and served as first governor of the Canal Zone from 1914 to 1916 and as the head of the Bureau of Purchase and Supplies during World War I.

Goldberg, Arthur (1908–90), jurist and public official. During the 1940s Goldberg served as general counsel for the United Mine Workers and the Congress of Industrial Organizations (CIO). Skilled as a mediator and negotiator, he was instrumental in the merger of the American Federation of Labor and the CIO in 1955. President John F. Kennedy appointed Goldberg, a Democrat, secretary of labor and later associate justice to the Supreme Court (1962–65). In an unusual decision to leave the Court in 1965, Goldberg accepted President Lyndon Johnson's appointment as ambassador to the United Nations and tried unsuccessfully to negotiate an end to the war in Vietnam.

Goldman, Emma (1869–1940), Russian-born U.S. political activist. Goldman immigrated to the United States in 1886 and copublished a monthly magazine, *Mother Earth* (1908), with fellow anarchist Alexander Berkman. Arrested several times for her activities supporting birth control and the rights of workers, she was sent to prison in World War I for opposing conscription. Upon her release in 1919, she was deported to Russia with other anarchists. She became disillusioned with the Soviet system and spent the rest of her life in Europe and Canada.

Gold Rushes, rapid mass movements of prospectors and adventurers to newly discovered goldfields. Upon discovery of a vein of gold, people would come from all parts of the world to seek their fortune. Towns and cities sprung up overnight, contributing to the development of the West. The most significant gold rush occurred in California in 1849 after gold was discovered in 1848 at John Sutter's mill in Coloma on the American River. The FORTY-NINERS came in such numbers that California became a state quickly. In 1859 others flocked to the Pike's Peak gold rush in Colorado, resulting in the development of the city of Denver. In 1896 the discovery of gold in the Klondike region of Canada near the Alaskan border caused a gold rush in 1897. Other gold rushes occurred in Arizona, Montana, Nevada, New Mexico, South Dakota, Utah, and Wyoming.

Gold Standard Act (March 14, 1900), an act establishing gold as the standard of value for money in the United States. It provided that all forms of currency in circulation should be redeemable in gold on demand.

Goldwater, Barry (1909–98), politician. A conservative Republican from Arizona, Goldwater served as U.S. senator from 1953 to 1965 and from 1969 to 1986. Opposed to "big government" and communism, he ran unsuccessfully for president against Lyndon B. Johnson in the ELECTION OF 1964. He retired from politics in 1987.

Goldwyn, Samuel (Samuel Goldfish; 1882–1974), film producer. Goldwyn produced his first film in 1913 and formed Goldwyn Pictures, which later merged with Metro Pictures to form Metro-Goldwyn-Mayer (MGM). As an independent producer he turned out such classics as *Wuthering Heights* (1939), *The Little Foxes* (1941), *The Best Years of Our Lives* (1946), and *Guys and Dolls* (1955).

Gompers, Samuel (1850–1924), labor leader. Gompers helped organize the AMERICAN FEDERATION OF LABOR in 1886 and served as its president, with the exception of one year, until his death. Gompers, a skilled debater and negotiator who favored collective bargaining, fought for higher wages, shorter work hours, and more freedom for workers. He advocated the organization of skilled workers on the basis of their trades and opposed industrial unions. He objected to unions being allied with any political party and also called for restrictions on immigration. Unions became more bureaucratic in the Gompers era.

Goodman, Benny (1909–86), clarinetist and bandleader. Known as "the King of Swing," Goodman performed for radio, film, and records. He helped develop a new style of music called swing, which swept the country as he introduced jazz to white audiences. He was the first important bandleader to integrate white and black musicians in his performing groups. Soloists featured with Goodman's small ensembles included Harry James, LIONEL HAMPTON, and GENE KRUPA.

Good Neighbor Policy (1933), President Franklin D. Roosevelt's approach to improved relations with Latin American countries. The earlier "Big Stick" approach of Theodore Roosevelt had been tempered by Calvin Coolidge and Herbert Hoover during the 1920s. Now FDR pledged to "dedicate this nation to the policy of the good neighbor." At the Seventh Pan-American Conference of 1933 (the Montevideo Conference), the countries of the Americas pledged that no nation would intervene in the affairs of another. The United States withdrew its Marines from Haiti, Cuba, and Nicaragua as part of this policy.

Goodyear, Charles (1800–60), inventor of the process of vulcanizing rubber, strengthening it and increasing its resistance to extreme temperatures. It made rubber useful for household articles and, later, automobile tires. Goodyear patented his process in 1844. Even though he sold the rights to many people, he spent his money on unsuccessful experiments and died in poverty.

GOP, initials for Grand Old Party, a term for the REPUBLICAN PARTY.

Gore, Al, Jr. (Albert; 1948–), vice president of the United States under BILL CLINTON. Gore is the son of Albert Gore, Sr. (1907–98), who served for over thirty years in the House and Senate as a liberal Democrat. Educated at Harvard and Vanderbilt Law School, Gore served during the Vietnam War as an army reporter and later wrote for the *Nashville Tennessean* (1971–76). He was elected to the House of Representatives (1977–85) as a Democrat from Tennessee and to the Senate (1985–93). In 1988 he made a creditable bid for the Democratic presidential nomination. Known first as a liberal, he moved to a moderate position. A strong spokesman for environmental issues, Gore was among the first U.S. politicians to draw attention to depletion of the ozone layer and pioneered efforts to clean up toxic waste dumps. His book, *Earth in the Balance: Ecology and the Human Spirit,* was published in 1992. He also specialized in arms control and foreign policy issues in the Senate. In the ELECTION OF 1992, he was selected as Bill Clinton's running mate. Gore (at age forty-four) and Clinton (at age forty-five) became the youngest team to run for the presidency in U.S. history. Gore's foreign policy experience was an asset to the ticket. The Clinton-Gore team won the election by a wide margin of the electoral vote. In the ELECTION OF 1996 Clinton and Gore won reelection. After two terms as vice president, Gore ran for president himself in the ELECTION OF 2000 and was narrowly defeated by GEORGE W. BUSH. He became the fourth presidential candidate in history to receive the largest share of the popular vote while losing the electoral votes. GROVER CLEVELAND in 1888, SAMUEL TILDEN in 1876, and ANDREW JACKSON in 1824 also lost the presidency with more popular votes than their opponents.

Gorgas, William (1854–1920), army officer and physician. In charge of the mosquito control and sanitation program in Panama from 1904 to 1914, Gorgas successfully suppressed yellow fever and malaria, making it possible to construct the Panama Canal. He served as surgeon general of the army from 1914 to 1918.

Gould, Jay (1836–92), financier and railroad owner. With JAMES FISK, Gould attempted to corner the gold market in 1869, causing the panic of BLACK FRIDAY on September 24 and making a fortune in the process. Gould was also involved with Fisk and Daniel Drew in a bitter struggle with CORNELIUS VANDERBILT to control the Erie Railroad in 1867. His tactics in these episodes and in his later activities in western railroad companies gave him a reputation as a major financial predator of his time.

Graham, Billy (1918–), fundamentalist Baptist minister and evangelist. Graham's sermons are distinguished by their persuasion and dramatic appeal, whether delivered in person or on the radio or television. He has served as a confidant to presidents and has traveled the globe spreading the gospel through his highly successful "Christian Crusades," emphasizing salvation through faith.

Graham, Katharine (1917–2001), newspaper and magazine publisher. The daughter of a publisher, Graham began work at the *Washington Post*, which her father had bought at a bankruptcy auction in 1933. In 1940 she married Philip Graham, who became publisher of the paper six years later. She and her husband bought the *Post* in 1948 from her father and enlarged the company in 1961 by buying *Newsweek* and several radio and TV stations. After her husband's suicide in 1963, Graham took control of the paper and transformed it into one of the most influential newspapers in the country. Her decision in 1971 to publish the PENTAGON PAPERS and to allow her journalists to pursue the WATERGATE break-in (1972) eventually forced the resignation of President RICHARD NIXON. Graham won a Pulitzer Prize in 1998 for her memoir, *Personal History*.

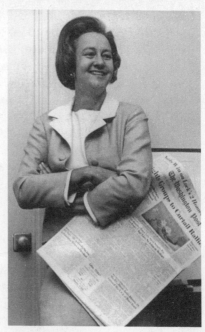

Katharine Graham

Graham, Martha (1894–1991), dancer, choreographer, and teacher. Graham rejected classical ballet and began her career in choreography in 1923, producing dances around social and literary themes. Her best-known works include "Primitive Mysteries" (1931), "Appalachian Spring" (1944), and "Clytemnestra" (1958). Influencing generations of modern dance teachers and performers with her unique free style, Graham was the first choreographer to employ a racially integrated troupe.

Graham, Otto (1921–2003), football player. After playing as an All-American quarterback at Northwestern University, Graham developed into one of the best T-formation quarterbacks in National Football League history. Selected the league's most valuable player in 1953 and 1955, Graham led the Cleveland Browns to three world championships. A great passer, he was elected to pro football's Hall of Fame in 1965.

Gramm-Rudman Act (1985), a law that revised budgeting procedures and required an end to the federal deficit by October 1, 1990. The act authorized the president to impose automatic spending reductions if Congress does not meet each year's deficit ceiling. Social Security and some programs for the poor are exempted from cuts. Representative Phil Gramm of Texas and Senator Warren Rudman of New Hampshire sponsored the bill.

Grand Army of the Republic (GAR) (1866), an organization of soldiers who served in the Union army during the Civil War. It lobbied for veterans' pensions and other benefits and exerted strong political influence, especially in the Republican party, during the 1870s and 1880s. The GAR started the observance of Memorial Day. Its last member died in 1956, ending the organization. Its only woman member was SARAH EDMONDS.

Grandfather Clauses, provisions added to southern state constitutions after the Civil War to keep blacks from voting, despite the passage of the Fifteenth Amendment. The clauses said in effect, "You can vote if your grandfather could vote," thus disfranchising the ex-slaves. The U.S. Supreme Court declared grandfather clauses unconstitutional in 1915.

Grange, Red (Harold; 1903–91), football player. Grange, three-time All-American halfback at the University of Illinois, earned the appellation "Galloping Ghost" because of his elusive maneuvers and exciting runs. In college he gained 3,637 yards and scored thirty-one touchdowns in twenty games. Grange scored 1,058 points during his professional career with the Chicago Bears. He was elected to the Hall of Fame in 1963.

Granger Laws, a series of western state laws passed after the Civil War to regulate grain elevator and railroad freight rates and rebates and to address long- and short-haul discrimination and other railroad abuses against farmers. When several Granger laws were declared unconstitutional by the Supreme Court, the federal INTERSTATE COMMERCE ACT of 1887 was passed to secure the same reforms. The Granger laws were so called because they were passed in response to the GRANGER MOVEMENT.

Granger Movement, organization of farmers formed to improve agricultural conditions. Officially called the National Grange of the Patrons of Husbandry, the movement began December 4, 1867, in Washington, D.C. The first branches, called Granges, were located in Minnesota, the home of founder Oliver Kelley. Members established cooperative banks and other cooperatives to buy seeds and supplies and sell their crops; they also pressed for the passage of GRANGER LAWS. The movement grew rapidly during the early 1870s, feeding on agrarian economic distress, and by 1875 its membership had reached 850,000. During the 1880s, because of improved agricultural conditions, membership dropped to 150,000, and the revolt moved to the South and West, where it became involved with the FARMERS' ALLIANCE movement.

Grant, Cary (Archibald Alexander Leach; 1904–86), actor. Born in England, Grant epitomized classic Hollywood glamour and sophistication for twenty-five years on the American film screen. Known for his poised and intelligent demeanor, as well as dashing good looks, Grant starred in a wide variety of screwball comedies, suspense dramas, and action adventures. In

Bringing Up Baby (1938) and *The Philadelphia Story* (1940), he appeared with KATHARINE HEPBURN. Later comic suspense films included *To Catch a Thief* (1955) and *Charade* (1963). Grant gave Oscar-nominated performances for *Penny Serenade* (1941) and *None but the Lonely Heart* (1944), and in 1969 he received an honorary Academy Award for his work. Often voted one of the most popular film stars of all time, Grant was honored with a U.S. Postage Service stamp in 2002. Writer Ian Fleming modeled the character of James Bond after Grant; he was originally offered the role in the first film, but turned it down.

Grant, Ulysses S. (1822–85), commander in chief of the Union army during the CIVIL WAR and eighteenth president of the United States (1869–77). Born in Point Pleasant, Ohio, Grant graduated from West Point and served in the Mexican War. He resigned from the army to become a farmer, but after years of hardship and financial failure, he reenlisted at the outbreak of the Civil War. Grant achieved Union victories at FORT HENRY, FORT DONELSON, SHILOH, the siege of VICKSBURG, CHATTANOOGA, LOOKOUT MOUNTAIN, and MISSIONARY RIDGE. In 1864 Abraham Lincoln appointed him commander of all Union forces. He led the Army of the Potomac in the WILDERNESS campaign, captured Richmond, and accepted the surrender of ROBERT E. LEE at APPOMATTOX COURT HOUSE, Virginia, on April 9, 1865. Nominated by the Republicans in the ELECTION OF 1868, Grant won over Democrat Horatio Seymour and was reelected over Horace Greeley in 1872. Major events during his administration included completion of the first transcontinental railroad (1869), the BLACK FRIDAY stock market crash (1869), ratification of the Fifteenth Amendment (1870), and the financial panic of 1873. Grant's administration was clouded by political scandals,

---

★ **Ulysses S. Grant**

An excerpt from Grant's *Personal Memoirs* (1885), describing his meeting with Robert E. Lee at Appomattox Court House, April 9, 1865, for the surrender of the Confederate army

What General Lee's feelings were I do not know. As he was a man of much dignity, with an impassable face, it was impossible to say whether he felt inwardly glad that the end had finally come, or felt sad over the result, and was too manly to show it. Whatever his feelings, they were entirely concealed from my observation; but my own feelings, which had been quite jubilant on the receipt of his letter, were sad and depressed. I felt like anything rather than rejoicing at the downfall of a foe who had fought so long and valiantly, and had suffered so much for a cause, though that cause was, I believe, one of the worst for which a people ever fought, and one for which there was the least excuse. I do not question, however, the sincerity of the great mass of those who were opposed to us.

including CRÉDIT MOBILIER, the WHISKEY RING, and the BELKNAP SCANDAL. After he retired, financial ventures plunged him into bankruptcy and his health collapsed. Dying from throat cancer, he wrote his memoirs to provide income for his family. *Personal Memoirs* (1886), published posthumously, is a classic of American literature, renowned for its clarity and narrative power.

Gray, Captain Robert (1755–1806), sea captain and explorer. Gray was the first American to sail around the world. In 1792 he discovered the Columbia River, which he named for his ship. This discovery became a basis of the U.S. claims to Oregon Territory.

Great Awakening, a series of religious revivals in the 1730s through the 1760s led by the ministers JONATHAN EDWARDS and George Whitefield, among others. The movement swept through all the colonies and was characterized by its emphasis on the sinfulness of humanity and the need for personal redemption through Jesus Christ. The revivals, which included Baptists, Congregationalists, and Presbyterians, extended the scope of religion to the poor, to blacks, and to women, many of whom had been excluded from mainstream established churches. It waned with the coming of the Revolution, but was followed in the 1820s and 1830s by a Second Great Awakening, this one associated with Charles Grandison Finney. He preached that people were "moral free agents" who could obtain salvation through their own efforts. The emphasis on personal improvement, the avoidance of sin, and hard work helped stimulate the many reform movements of the 1800s: temperance, abolition, moral reform, public education, and philanthropic endeavors, among others.

Great Compromise (Connecticut Compromise; July 16, 1787), a plan proposed by the Connecticut delegates to the CONSTITUTIONAL CONVENTION establishing a two-house legislature. The VIRGINIA PLAN, supported by the large states, called for a legislature in which representation was based on population. The NEW JERSEY PLAN, supported by the small states, favored a legislature in which each state would be represented equally. Under the Great Compromise the U.S. Senate became the body based on equal representation, with two senators from each state, and the House of Representatives the body based on population (although every state must have at least one member).

Great Depression (1929–40), a period of economic failure following the STOCK MARKET CRASH and panic of 1929. More than 15 million people were unemployed during the height of the depression, thousands of homes and farms were foreclosed for failure to pay mortgages, millions lost their savings, and huge losses were incurred by businesses. National income declined and thousands of banks went bankrupt. The depression hit its lowest point in 1933, just before Franklin D. Roosevelt declared a BANK HOLIDAY,

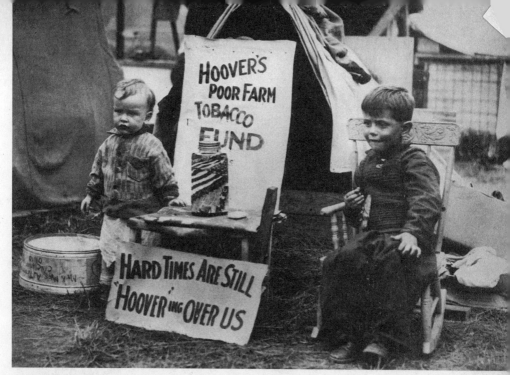

Great Depression
Children at a Hooverville camp.

ordering all banks in the country closed. Despite the efforts of the NEW DEAL, full recovery was not achieved until the onset of World War II.

Great Plains, a large area of land located in Middle America from Mexico to Canada (the Great Lakes) and from the Mississippi River to the Rocky Mountains. The plains cover a dry grassland area, important for its agricultural and mining industries. Farm products include wheat, rye, oats, barley, and alfalfa, and cattle, goats, and sheep are raised. The region is rich in coal, oil, and natural gas.

Great Society (1966), the term coined by President LYNDON B. JOHNSON to characterize his domestic program. Johnson believed government should be involved in improving the quality of life for Americans and promised a "war on poverty." The program included Volunteers in Service to America (VISTA), a domestic peace corps; a Job Corps for school dropouts; and the Head Start program for preschool education for underprivileged children. Johnson also declared a war on crime and disease, and increased financial support for public education, urban renewal, job training programs, housing subsidies, and environmental initiatives. Medicare and Medicaid were two of the most enduring legacies of the Great Society, as well as three landmark civil rights acts passed in 1964, 1965, and 1968.

Great White Fleet, sixteen American battleships sent on an around-the-world voyage between 1907 and 1909. The mission, initiated by President

THEODORE ROOSEVELT, was to promote goodwill and demonstrate the military might of the United States. The ships were painted white, giving the fleet its name.

Greeley, Horace (1811–72), newspaper publisher and politician. Greeley founded the *New York Tribune* in 1841 and served as its editor for thirty years. His editorials promoted his political views, which included advocating the organization of labor and a high protective tariff and opposition to the Mexican War, woman suffrage, and slavery. His advice, "Go West, young man, and grow up with the country," influenced thousands of settlers. He was sympathetic to utopian socialism and sponsored the founding of homesteading colonies in the West. Greeley, Colorado, is named for him. Greeley joined the Republican party in 1854 and supported the election of Abraham Lincoln. He advocated universal amnesty and suffrage following the Civil War and alienated some Northerners by signing the bail bond releasing Jefferson Davis from prison. The Liberal Republican party and the Democratic party nominated Greeley in the ELECTION OF 1872, but Ulysses S. Grant soundly defeated him.

Green, William (1872–1952), labor leader. With the support of JOHN L. LEWIS, Green succeeded SAMUEL GOMPERS as president of the AMERICAN FEDERATION OF LABOR in 1924 and held the position until his death. He opposed union militants and split with Lewis's Congress of Industrial Organizations in 1936, disagreeing over how labor should be organized — by a whole industry (Lewis) or by a particular trade or craft (Green).

Greenback Party, a political party that emerged around 1874. The party took its name from the paper money issued during the Civil War. Formed to address the problems of farmers and debtor groups, the party argued that increasing the number of greenbacks in circulation would cause farm prices to rise, thus giving farmers more money to pay off their debts. Perceived as the "party of the poor," it also appealed to some labor groups. The party nominated presidential candidates PETER COOPER in the ELECTION OF 1876, JAMES WEAVER in the ELECTION OF 1880, and BENJAMIN BUTLER in the ELECTION OF 1884. The party then faded and most of its members joined the POPULIST PARTY.

Greenberg, Hank (1911–86), baseball player. As one of baseball's great power hitters, Greenberg belted out 58 home runs in 1938. Playing first base for the Detroit Tigers, he was twice the American League's most valuable player, in 1935 and 1940. He hit 331 career home runs and led the league in runs batted in four times. He became a member of baseball's Hall of Fame in 1956.

Greene, Nathanael (1742–86), general during the AMERICAN REVOLUTION. Washington's second in command, Greene fought at BRANDYWINE TRENTON, and GERMANTOWN and later replaced Gen. Horatio Gates as commander of the Continental army in the South. He inflicted heavy losses on the British at the Battles of GUILFORD COURTHOUSE and COWPENS and is noted for the final defeat and harassment of the British forces in Georgia and the Carolinas.

Green Mountain Boys, armed groups formed in 1770 and led by ETHAN ALLEN to protect what is now Vermont from becoming part of New York State. During the AMERICAN REVOLUTION Allen and the Green Mountain Boys captured FORT TICONDEROGA in 1775 and helped win an important victory at BENNINGTON in 1777.

Greenspan, Alan (1926–), economist. Greenspan is chairman of the United States Federal Reserve Board. Appointed by President RONALD REAGAN in 1987, he was reappointed to an unprecedented five terms by GEORGE H. W. BUSH, BILL CLINTON, and GEORGE W. BUSH. He also serves as Chairman of the Federal Open Market Committee, the Federal Reserve System's principal monetary policy-making body. From 1974 to 1977, he was chairman of the President's Council of Economic Advisers under GERALD R. FORD. Generally considered a moderate conservative, Greenspan is credited for helping the economy grow while keeping inflation low. He is considered by many to be the leading authority and chief influence regarding U.S. domestic fiscal policy.

Greenville, Treaty of (August 3, 1795), an agreement ending a period of warfare with Indians, thus opening the Old Northwest Territory for whites to settle in apparent safety. It was signed following the defeat of the frontier Indians at the Battle of FALLEN TIMBERS by ("MAD") ANTHONY WAYNE.

Gregory, Dick (1932–), comedian and political activist. After an early career as a stand-up comic, Gregory became active in the anti-Vietnam War and civil rights movements. Prior to an unsuccessful presidential campaign in 1968 on the ticket of the radical Peace and Freedom party, Gregory wrote several books of humor commenting on racial matters. In the 1970s and 1980s, he became noted for his fasts to protest war and racial injustice.

Gretzky, Wayne (1961–), hockey player. The most dominant player in the history of hockey, "the Great One" holds or shares sixty-one National Hockey League (NHL) records, including most goals in one season (92 in 1981–82, when he became the first player to score over 200 points [212] in a season), most points (215, set in 1986), and most assists (163, set in 1986). He has led the national Hockey League (NHL) in scoring ten times (1981–87, 1990–91, 1994), and earned the Hart Trophy as NHL Most Valuable Player a record nine times (1980–87 and 1989). In 1995 he became the first NHL player to score 2,500 points. He also holds the career records for goals (894), assists (1,963), and points (2,857). Gretzky led the Edmonton Oilers to four Stanley Cups and was traded, at his own request, to the Los Angeles Kings in 1988, leading them to the Stanley Cup finals in 1992–93. He joined the New York Rangers in 1996, where he finished his twenty-year career in 1999. Gretzky became managing partner of the NHL's Phoenix Coyotes in 2001, and in 2002 he served as the executive director of Team Canada's gold-medal-winning Olympic Hockey Team.

Griffith, D. W. (David; 1875–1948), silent film director and producer. Griffith pioneered creative and skillful directing and editing techniques in film. *Birth of a Nation,* Griffith's 1915 historical spectacle about southern Reconstruction and the rise of the Ku Klux Klan, has been much criticized for its racist content and was banned in some cities when it was released. His other major films include *Broken Blossoms* (1919) and *Intolerance* (1916), in which he sought to make up for the harm done by *Birth of a Nation.*

Grimké Sisters, Sarah (1792–1873) and Angelina (1805–79), ABOLITIONISTS and women's rights activists. Members of a distinguished South Carolina slaveholding family, the Grimké sisters moved north because they disliked living in a slave society. Defying the prohibition against women speaking in public, they made lecture tours promoting abolitionism and women's rights. Angelina, in 1838, became the first American woman to address a legislative body: she presented to the Massachusetts legislature thousands of antislavery petitions the sisters had gathered on a lecture tour for the American Anti-Slavery Society. Both women also published important books and pamphlets laying the foundations for abolitionism and what later became feminist theory. Angelina married abolitionist THEODORE WELD in 1838.

Guadalcanal, Battle of (August 7, 1942–February 9, 1943), a combined U.S. sea and air attack on Guadalcanal in the Solomon Islands and a turning-point battle of WORLD WAR II. Guadalcanal, the first American offensive against the Japanese, followed American victories at MIDWAY and the CORAL SEA. The Marines landed and established control after months of fierce fighting, and Adm. William Halsey then soundly defeated the Japanese fleet. By February 1943 Japanese troops had been driven off the island.

Guadalupe Hidalgo, Treaty of (February 2, 1848), peace treaty ending the MEXICAN WAR. Under its terms the United States received the Mexican Cession, which included California and New Mexico and Utah Territories. In return the United States paid $15 million to Mexico and agreed to settle over $3 million in American claims against Mexico. Mexico also recognized the prior annexation of Texas into the Union in 1845 and agreed to the Rio Grande as the boundary between Texas and Mexico.

Guam, a territory of the United States, largest of the Mariana Islands in the Pacific Ocean. The United States acquired Guam from Spain as a result of the SPANISH-AMERICAN WAR in 1898. Captured in 1941 during WORLD WAR II by the Japanese and recaptured by the Americans in 1944, Guam has served as an important U.S. naval base in the Pacific. In 1950 Guam officially became a U.S. territory and its people U.S. citizens.

Guilford Courthouse, Battle of (March 15, 1781), a major military engagement in North Carolina near the end of the AMERICAN REVOLUTION between Americans led by Gen. NATHANAEL GREENE and British led by Gen. CHARLES CORNWALLIS. The colonists claimed victory when the battered British abandoned North Carolina and retreated to the coast.

Guiteau, Charles (1840?–82), assassin of President JAMES A. GARFIELD. Interested in politics, Guiteau offered to help with the Garfield campaign but was not welcomed. On July 2, 1881, after repeated rebuffs of his demand for an office, he shot Garfield in the back at Union Station in Washington, D.C. A STALWART REPUBLICAN, he claimed that he killed the president in order to put Chester A. Arthur into office. Refusing to plead not guilty by reason of insanity, Guiteau was tried for murder, found guilty, and hanged in Washington, D.C.

Gulf War *See* PERSIAN GULF WAR.

Guthrie, Woody (Woodrow Wilson Guthrie; 1912–67), guitarist, composer, and folksinger. Guthrie, a political radical, sang about America: the land, the ordinary people, the workers and victims of the Great Depression. He strongly influenced other folksingers and wrote over a thousand songs, including "This Land Is Your Land," "Hard Traveling," and "So Long — It's Been Good to Know You." His son, Arlo, followed in his footsteps as a folksinger and composer, writing the popular "Alice's Restaurant."

H **Habeas Corpus, Writ of,** a court order directing that anyone arrested be brought before the court to justify their being held for trial. Sufficient cause must be shown to continue holding the person. The writ prevents unjust imprisonment; it does not determine guilt or innocence. A keystone of English law, habeas corpus (meaning "you have the body") was brought to the colonies in the seventeenth century. Protected by the Constitution, the writ became an issue during the Civil War, when Abraham Lincoln suspended it. His opponents maintained that only Congress could suspend the writ; Congress quickly passed a law ratifying Lincoln's action.

Hagen, Walter (1892–1969), golfer. Hagen won the U.S. Open twice, the PGA five times, the British Open four times, and the Western Open five times. A popular showman, he helped make golf a national pastime.

Haig, Alexander (1924–), former general and secretary of state. A career army officer, Haig advanced through a number of military assignments, serving in Japan, Korea, Europe, Vietnam, and at the Pentagon. He served on the National Security Council as HENRY KISSINGER's military adviser in 1968. As President RICHARD NIXON's emissary, he assisted in the cease-fire negotiations with VIETNAM in 1972. Named White House chief of staff in 1973, he held this position until President GERALD R. FORD recalled him to active duty as supreme allied commander in Europe, responsible for the integrated military forces of NATO. After retiring from military service in 1979, Haig was appointed secretary of state by

President RONALD REAGAN in 1981, but he resigned in 1982 over policy differences. He ran unsuccessfully for the Republican presidential nomination in 1988. In 1992 Haig authored an autobiography, *How America Changed the World.*

Halas, George (1895–1983), football player, coach, and owner. "Papa Bear" cofounded the National Football League (NFL) in 1920 and founded, owned, and coached the Chicago Bears, leading them to seven NFL championships. His innovations helped revolutionize professional football, most noticeably his creation of the T-formation. He was inducted into pro football's Hall of Fame in 1963.

Haldeman, Bob (H. R.; 1926–93), chief of staff to Richard Nixon (1969–73). Haldeman resigned from his post on April 30, 1973, following disclosure of his role in the WATERGATE cover-up. Convicted of perjury, conspiracy, and obstruction of justice, he served a year and a half in federal prison. Haldeman had served as Nixon's campaign manager in 1968.

Hale, Nathan (1755–76), Patriot during the American Revolution. Hale, a schoolteacher, accepted a dangerous mission to obtain information about the movement of the British forces on Long Island, New York. Captured by the British as a spy, he was hanged without trial at age twenty-one. His final words were reported to be, "I only regret that I have but one life to lose for my country."

Haley, Alex (1921–92), author. Haley traced his family back through seven generations to an African village in Gambia for his Pulitzer Prize-winning book, *Roots: The Saga of an American Family* (1976). Made into a television miniseries in 1977, *Roots* was seen by over 130 million people. In the same year Haley received the NAACP's SPINGARN MEDAL for his work. He also helped write MALCOLM X's autobiography.

Haley, Bill (1927–81), musician. Haley, called the father of rock 'n' roll, was responsible for early hits of the rock era, including "Rock around the Clock" and "Shake, Rattle, and Roll." As leader of Bill Haley and the Comets, Haley, who was white, borrowed black musical styles for his new rock beat, which strongly influenced rock artists of the 1960s and 1970s, including the Beatles.

Half-Breeds, a name given to the reform wing of the Republican party after the election of 1876 to distinguish it from the STALWART, or conservative wing. Also called MUGWUMPS, the Half-Breeds advocated civil service reform, fought corruption in the Republican party, and favored a policy of forgiveness toward the South.

Hall, Joyce Clyde (1891–1982), businessman. Hall created Hallmark from a small engraving business in Kansas City, Missouri, developing it into the largest greeting card company in the world. He expanded the traditional Christmas and birthday card market to include cards for any occasion. Utilizing innovative merchandising, consumer research, and television advertising, he was the first to employ the works of such artists as Grandma Moses and Norman Rockwell on his Christmas cards.

Halsey, William, Jr. ("Bull"; 1882–1959), WORLD WAR II naval officer. As commander of the Allied naval forces in the South Pacific from 1942 to 1944, Halsey won great victories over the Japanese fleets at GUADALCANAL, the Solomon Islands, and LEYTE GULF in the Philippines. Promoted to the rank of five-star admiral in 1945, he retired in 1947.

Hamer, Fannie Lou (1917–77), civil rights activist. Hamer was cofounder of the Mississippi Freedom Democratic party, organized to challenge the mainstream white-supremacist Democratic party delegation to the 1964 national convention. The youngest of twenty children of Mississippi share-croppers, Hamer, at age forty-five, joined the STUDENT NONVIOLENT CO-ORDINATING COMMITTEE (SNCC) in 1962. She worked to register blacks to vote and to help agricultural workers organize.

Hamilton, Alexander (1755–1804), revolutionary, politician, and statesman. Born in the West Indies of Creole lineage, Hamilton served as aide-de-camp to George Washington during the AMERICAN REVOLUTION and was a hero at the Battle of Yorktown. He represented New York at the Constitutional Convention in 1787 and, with James Madison and John Jay, wrote the FEDERALIST PAPERS urging approval of the Constitution. Appointed the first secretary of the treasury in 1789 by President Washington, Hamilton was responsible for creating the First BANK OF THE UNITED STATES. He sought to encourage the growth of manufactures in the new nation and to put it on a sound monetary basis. In the 1790s disagreements between Hamilton and a group led by Thomas Jefferson and James Madison resulted in the founding of the FEDERALIST PARTY, led by Hamilton and John Adams, which advocated a strong federal government. Although never elected to public office, Hamilton remained influential in national politics. When the ELECTION OF 1800 ended in an electoral deadlock and was thrown into the House of Representatives, he supported his rival Jefferson in order to thwart AARON BURR's bid for the office. He also opposed Burr's campaign for governor of New York. In 1804 Burr fatally wounded Hamilton in a duel.

Hamlin, Hannibal (1809–91), vice president of the United States (1861–65) during Abraham Lincoln's first term. Hamlin, who served in Congress and as governor of Maine, was originally a Democrat, but helped form the REPUBLICAN PARTY and became a strong ABOLITIONIST. Lincoln chose not to select him as a running mate in the ELECTION OF 1864 because he wanted a Democrat to help unite the nation under the National Union party banner. Hamlin later returned to the Senate, where he supported strong Reconstruction policies to assist the freed slaves.

Hammerstein, Oscar, II *See* RICHARD RODGERS AND OSCAR HAMMERSTEIN II.

Hammett, Dashiell (1894–1961), writer. Hammett, once a Pinkerton detective, helped create the hard-boiled school of detective fiction. He featured his unsentimental hero Sam Spade in *The Maltese Falcon* (1930). Hammett also created the witty amateur detectives Nick and Nora Charles for *The Thin Man* (1932). Both books were made into classic American films, and Hammett became a scriptwriter. In the 1950s he refused to testify about his left-of-center political beliefs before the HOUSE UN-AMERICAN ACTIVITIES COMMITTEE and served a year in prison for contempt of Congress. His friend LILLIAN HELLMAN wrote about his principled stand in *Scoundrel Time* (1976).

Hampton, Lionel (1913–2002), jazz musician. Hampton rose to fame in the 1930s as part of the BENNY GOODMAN Quartet, in which he was featured as the first jazz soloist on the vibraphone. Hampton had his own band during the 1940s.

Hampton Roads Conference (February 3, 1865), an attempt to end the CIVIL WAR. Representatives of the Union and the Confederacy met on the steamer *River Queen* in Hampton Roads, Virginia. Representing the North, Abraham Lincoln and William H. Seward refused to change the terms of the Emancipation Proclamation (though Lincoln suggested possible compensation to slave owners) and demanded restoration of the Union and the surrender of the Confederacy. The Confederate delegates — Alexander H. Stephens, Robert M. T. Hunter, and John A. Campbell — would accept no terms except complete independence for the Confederate states. The conference ended in failure.

Hampton, Wade (1818–1902), Confederate general. Although initially opposed to secession, Hampton served in the Confederate army during the CIVIL WAR, first in the infantry and later gaining fame as a cavalry leader. He raised Hampton's Legion, which he led at the first Battle of BULL RUN (1861) and was promoted to brigadier general (1862). Active in most of J.E.B. STUART's operations, he succeeded to the command of the cavalry corps following Stuart's death. After the war, Hampton worked for peaceful reconstruction and was elected governor of South Carolina in 1876. He was reelected in 1878, and in 1879 became a U.S. senator. Hampton was the grandson of Gen. Wade Hampton, who fought in both the American Revolution and the WAR OF 1812.

Hancock, John (1737–93), colonial merchant and leader in the AMERICAN REVOLUTION. Hancock resisted British colonial rule by opposing the STAMP ACT (1765) and the TOWNSHEND ACTS (1768). As president (1775–77) of the Second CONTINENTAL CONGRESS, he was the first signer of the Declaration of Independence. Hancock became the first governor of Massachusetts in 1780 and served for nine terms. In 1788 he became an Antifederalist but, as president of the state convention held to consider adoption of the Constitution, helped work out compromises that secured its ratification by Massachusetts.

Hancock, Winfield Scott (1824–86), Union general in the CIVIL WAR. Hancock fought in the Battles of ANTIETAM, FREDERICKSBURG, and CHANCELLORSVILLE and commanded a corp on Cemetery Ridge in the Battle of GETTYSBURG. He ran as the Democratic party's nominee for president in 1880, but lost to Republican James Garfield.

Handy, W. C. (William Christopher; 1873–1958), black jazz musician and blues composer. Known as the father of the blues (which was the title of his 1941 autobiography), Handy composed such songs as "St. Louis Blues," "Beale Street Blues," and "Memphis Blues," and conducted a band for many years.

Hanks, Tom (1956–), actor, director, producer. An Academy Award–winning comic and dramatic actor, Hanks won consecutive Oscars for his performances in *Philadelphia* (1993) and *Forrest Gump* (1994). Known for playing conflicted, regular guys, he also starred in *Splash* (1984), *Big* (1988), *Sleepless in Seattle* (1993), and *You've Got Mail* (1998). His dramatic roles in STEVEN SPIELBERG's *Saving Private Ryan* (1988), *Apollo 13* (1995), *The Green Mile* (1999), and *Road to Perdition* (2002) earned critical acclaim. *That Thing You Do!* (1996) marked his directorial debut, a film which he also wrote and starred in. Hanks performed in drag on television's *Bosom Buddies* (1980–82) and made guest appearances on other popular 1980s sitcoms.

Hanna, Mark (Marcus Alonzo; 1837–1904), businessman and politician. Hanna managed the Republican presidential campaign of 1896 for his protégé, U.S. Congressman William McKinley of Ohio. He became the Republican national chairman, and his money, power, and success as a political boss led to his election to the U.S. Senate in 1897, where he became a champion of the interests of big business.

Hansberry, Lorraine (1930–65), black playwright and civil rights activist. Hansberry wrote *A Raisin in the Sun* (1959; film, 1961), the first play by a black woman to appear on Broadway. She was the youngest American to win the New York Drama Critics' Circle Award for her play, which presented the frustrations of a black family in the Chicago ghetto hoping to move into a white neighborhood. After her early death from cancer, excerpts from Hansberry's letters, journals, and speeches were published in *To Be Young, Gifted, and Black* (1969).

Hanson, John (1721–83), Revolutionary leader. Hanson was among those who opposed the STAMP ACT (1765) and the TOWNSHEND ACTS (1768); he helped arm Patriot troops during the AMERICAN REVOLUTION. He served as the first president (1781–82) of the Congress of the Confederation, which operated the first government of the United States following ratification of the Articles of Confederation.

Harding, Warren G. (1865–1923), twenty-ninth president of the United States (1921–23). Born near Corsica (now Blooming Grove), Ohio, Harding served as lieutenant governor of the state. Elected to the U.S. Senate in 1914, he became the compromise candidate of leaders of the Republican party for the presidential nomination in 1920. Campaigning on a slogan of "Back to Normalcy," he was elected in the largest landslide up to that time by a war-weary country.

Although Harding appointed a number of able men to high office, he sometimes chose badly. Corruption involving cabinet appointees ALBERT FALL and Harry Daugherty, as well as the TEAPOT DOME SCANDAL, plagued his administration. Harding, while returning from a speaking tour of Alaska to revive confidence in his administration, died of a stroke in San Francisco on August 2, 1923. During Harding's brief time in office, Congress placed quotas on immigration, and the Washington Naval Disarmament Conference met (1921).

Hardy, Oliver *See* STAN LAUREL AND OLIVER HARDY.

Harlan, John Marshall (1833–1911), jurist. Although a member of a Kentucky slaveholding family, Marshall fought for the Union during the Civil War. Appointed to the U.S. Supreme Court in 1877 by Rutherford B. Hayes, Harlan was often the lone dissenter in important cases. The only justice to oppose *PLESSY* v. *FERGUSON*, a decision upholding the "separate but equal" principle validating segregation, Harlan declared that the Constitution is "color-blind." His grandson, John Marshall Harlan (1899–1971), also served on the Court (1955–71).

Harlem Renaissance, black literary, artistic, and cultural movement centering in Harlem in New York City from the 1920s to the mid-1930s. With encouragement from the Urban League and the National Association for the Advancement of Colored People, Harlem witnessed a flowering of black music, theater, and literature. Many intellectuals explored black American culture and its African roots in detail. Major contributors to the Harlem Renaissance included W.E.B. DU BOIS, ZORA NEALE HURSTON, JAMES WELDON JOHNSON, and LANGSTON HUGHES. Although the movement faded during the 1930s with the onset of the Great Depression, it influenced many subsequent black writers and artists.

Harmon, Tom (1919–90), football player and sports announcer. As a two-time All-American running back for the University of Michigan and a Heisman Trophy winner in 1940, Harmon broke numerous records. During World War II he earned a Silver Star and a Purple Heart while serving in the Army Air Corps. He returned to play for the Los Angeles Rams in 1946 and 1947, and later became a radio and television sportscaster.

Harpers Ferry, town in West Virginia at the confluence of the Potomac and Shenandoah rivers. Harpers Ferry was the site of JOHN BROWN'S RAID in 1859. Its arsenal was at the forefront of American technology and weapons research prior to the CIVIL WAR. For that reason and because of its strategic location, the town was a major objective of both Union and Confederate raids. Confederate general Thomas ("Stonewall") Jackson won it from the Union in 1862, and it changed hands several times thereafter.

Harriman, Edward H. (1848–1909), railroad executive and financier. Harriman, at various times, controlled the Illinois Central, Union Pacific, and Southern Pacific Railroads. He lost a fight with JAMES HILL to gain control of the Northern Pacific Railroad in a struggle that contributed to the stock market panic of 1901. Hill, Harriman, and J. P. MORGAN combined forces to create a monopoly, the Northern Securities Company; in 1906, the Supreme Court ruled in favor of a government order to break up the firm. Although often berated for his ruthless operating methods, Harriman used much of his vast fortune for the public good.

Harriman, W. Averell (William; 1891–1986), businessman, politician, and diplomat; son of Edward H. Harriman. During World War II Harriman served as U.S. ambassador to the Soviet Union and in 1946 was appointed secretary of commerce by Harry S. Truman. An unsuccessful candidate for the 1956 Democratic presidential nomination, he was elected governor of New York in 1954. Later, as under secretary of state for political affairs, he helped negotiate the 1963 nuclear test ban treaty. In 1968 and 1969 he was a chief U.S. negotiator at the Paris peace talks on the Vietnam War.

Harrington, Michael (Edward; 1928–89), author and political activist. A democratic socialist, Harrington wrote *The Other America: Poverty in the United States* (1962), which focused national attention on America's poor. He pointed out that one-fourth of the American people were living below the poverty level. His work stimulated the antipoverty programs of the Kennedy and Johnson administrations.

Harris, Joel Chandler (1848–1908), white author and journalist. Harris entertained readers with his humorous tales of Uncle Remus, written in southern black dialect and featuring animals with human characteristics such as Brer Fox, Brer Bear, and Brer Rabbit. Although the narrator, Uncle Remus, reflects a stereotypical southern black found offensive by many, the stories he tells preserve West African animal tales as modified by the slaves. Harris heard them in conversations with southern blacks. Collections include *Uncle Remus, His Songs and His Sayings* (1880), *Nights with Uncle Remus* (1883), and *The Tar Baby* (1904).

Harris, Patricia Roberts (1924–85), lawyer and educator. Harris attended Howard University, graduating with highest honors. She received her law degree, also with honors, from George Washington University. Under President JOHN F. KENNEDY, she served as cochairman of the National Women's Committee on Civil Rights, where she gained the attention of LYNDON JOHNSON. In 1965 Harris became the first African-American woman to head a U.S. embassy when President Johnson appointed her ambassador to Luxembourg. From 1969 to 1972 she was the first female dean of the law school at Howard. In 1971, she became the first black woman to be a director of a major U.S. company (IBM), then she became the first black to chair a national political convention (Democrat). Harris was the first black woman to gain a cabinet position when President JIMMY CARTER named her secretary of housing and urban development in 1977. In 1979 Carter appointed her secretary of health, education, and welfare, which later became the Department of Health and Human Services, a post she held until 1982.

Harrison, Benjamin (1833–1901), twenty-third president of the United States (1889–93). Born in North Bend, Ohio, Harrison served as a brigadier general in the Civil War. Elected to the U.S. Senate from Indiana in 1881, Harrison was chosen by the Republicans to oppose incumbent Grover Cleveland in the ELECTION OF 1888. Although Cleveland won the most popular votes, Harrison received a majority of electoral votes, becoming the only grandson of a president (William Henry Harrison) to become president. Harrison in office supported the protective McKinley tariff and the SHERMAN ANTI-TRUST ACT. Again opposed by Cleveland in the ELECTION OF 1892, he lost his reelection bid. In 1899 he represented Venezuela in arbitration of the VENEZUELA BOUNDARY DISPUTE with Great Britain.

Harrison, William Henry (1773–1841), ninth president of the United States (March 4–April 4, 1841). Born into a wealthy slave-owning family in Charles City County, Virginia, Harrison served as governor of Indiana Territory (1800–12) and negotiated numerous treaties that opened up new lands to white settlers. He became an Indian fighter, defeating Shawnee chief TECUMSEH's forces at the Battle of TIPPECANOE (November 7, 1811). As a brigadier general in the WAR OF 1812, he defeated British and Indian forces in the Battle of the Thames (1813), during which Tecumseh was killed. Harrison served in the U.S. House of Representatives (1816–19) and the U.S. Senate (1825–28) from Ohio. Nominated by the Whig party for president in 1836, he lost to Democrat Martin Van Buren. In the ELECTION OF 1840, as the "log cabin and hard cider" candidate, Harrison became the first Whig president. Using torchlight parades, coonskin caps, and popular songs, the Whigs emphasized antics rather than issues. "Tippecanoe and Tyler Too" was the campaign slogan. Harrison, in a cold, pouring rain, gave the longest inauguration speech ever delivered, contracted pneumonia, and died a month later. He served the shortest time in office of any president and was the first to die in office.

Hart, Moss (1904–61), playwright and director, best known for the sophisticated comedies he wrote with George S. Kaufman. Hart's first hit was the Hollywood spoof *Once in a Lifetime* (1930). Other successes included the Pulitzer Prize–winning farce *You Can't Take It with You* (1936) and *The Man*

Who Came to Dinner (1939). Hart also wrote screenplays and directed the stage productions of *My Fair Lady* (1956) and *Camelot* (1960).

Harte, Bret (Francis; 1836–1902), author. Harte was one of the most powerful writers of fiction about the American West. Many of his vivid, local-color stories portray the gamblers, prospectors, and settlers of the California gold rush. He edited the *Overland Monthly,* where his best-known writings first appeared, including "The Luck of the Roaring Camp" (1868), "The Outcasts of Poker Flat" (1869), and "Plain Language from Truthful James" (1870).

Hartford Convention (December 15, 1814–January 5, 1815), a secret meeting of New England Federalists to protest inept Democratic-Republican management of the WAR OF 1812. Twenty-six delegates representing Connecticut, Massachusetts, New Hampshire, Rhode Island, and Vermont met in Hartford, Connecticut, and passed resolutions declaring the right of the states to nullify federal laws. A proposal of secession was discussed but rejected. The TREATY OF GHENT ending the war, signed while the convention was still in session, made its decisions moot. The actions of the convention appeared traitorous, resulting in the destruction of the FEDERALIST PARTY.

Harvard College (1636), first college established in the United States. Founded in Cambridge sixteen years after the arrival of the PILGRIMS at Plymouth, Harvard was named for its first benefactor, John Harvard, a Massachusetts minister who left his library and half of his estate to the institution upon his death in 1638. Beginning with nine students and one master, the college offered classic academic study based on the English university system, heavily influenced by the PURITAN philosophy of the early colonists. Many early graduates became clergymen, but the school was never associated with a specific religious denomination. Seven presidents of the United States were graduates of Harvard, more than any other college — John Adams, John Quincy Adams, Theodore Roosevelt, Franklin D. Roosevelt, Rutherford B. Hayes, John F. Kennedy, and George W. Bush. Today Harvard University has grown to an enrollment of more than 18,000 and a faculty of more than 2,000.

Hassam, Childe (1859–1935), Impressionist painter. Born in Boston, Hassam studied in Paris where he was influenced by French Impressionists. A master of watercolor, he developed a style characterized by brilliant light, vivid color, and descriptive realism. His subjects include the streets and parks of Boston, New York street scenes, New England landscapes, and his famed series of flag paintings created during World War I. In 1898 Hassam helped found the Ten American Painters, a group of Impressionist painters. He remained an influential and prolific artist throughout his career.

Hatch Act (August 2, 1939), law forbidding federal executive employees from participating in and contributing to any presidential or congressional election campaign. Designed to combat political corruption, the law imposed stiff penalties on any person who used political influence on federal officeholders. Amended in 1940, the act further included state and local employees whose salaries were paid for, even partially, by the federal government. It was also called the Federal Corruption Practices Act of 1939.

Hauptmann, Bruno *See* LINDBERGH KIDNAPPING.

Havlicek, John (1940–), basketball player. An All-American at Ohio State, Havlicek played forward and guard for the Boston Celtics from 1962 to 1978. Considered to be the best "sixth man" ever to play pro basketball, he led the Celtics to eight championship titles in the National Basketball Association and was named four times to the All-NBA first team.

Hawaii (Aloha State) became on August 21, 1959, the fiftieth state. (See maps, pages 540 and 541.) The only state that lies outside of North America, Hawaii is made up of over one hundred volcanic and coral islands. The eight largest are Hawaii, Maui, Oahu, Lanai, Molokai, Kauai, Niihau, and Kahoolawe. Polynesians first settled the islands about two thousand years ago. Capt. James Cook of England was the first European to discover the islands in 1778, naming them the Sandwich Islands. American whalers and traders arrived during the early 1800s. Later, missionaries dominated the economy and government. During the late 1800s sugar cane became a large industry, and the first pineapples, shipped from Jamaica, formed the basis of its world-leading pineapple industry.

Hawaii is the only state that was once an independent monarchy. Queen Liliuokalani, who opposed American political and business influence, was deposed in 1893 in a bloodless revolution led by Americans, thus forming the Republic of Hawaii with pineapple grower SANFORD DOLE as its president. Under pressure from American sugar planters in the islands, the United States annexed Hawaii as a possession in 1898, and it became a U.S. territory in 1900. The Japanese attack on PEARL HARBOR brought the United States into World War II.

Tourism is Hawaii's leading industry, with visitors enjoying the islands' beauty and pleasant climate. The island of Kauai is the site of the wettest place on earth — Mount Waialeale, with an average annual rainfall of 460 inches. Haleakala, on the island of Maui, is the largest volcanic crater in the world. Major cities are Honolulu, the capital, Pearl City, Kailua, and Hilo.

Hawley-Smoot Tariff *See* SMOOT-HAWLEY TARIFF.

Hawthorne, Nathaniel (1804–64), novelist and short story writer. Hawthorne set many of his works in the Puritan New England world of his ancestors, probing the dark side of human nature and the American character and exploring moral conflicts and contradictions. Examples are his masterpieces *The Scarlet Letter* (1850) and *The House of Seven Gables* (1851). From 1825 to 1850 Hawthorne wrote over a hundred short stories, many appearing in the collections *Twice-Told Tales* (1837, 1842) and *Mosses from an*

Old Manse (1846). During college Hawthorne became a friend of Franklin Pierce, who, as president, appointed him U.S. consul to Liverpool, England, a post he held for four years.

Hay, John (1838–1905), author, diplomat, and private secretary to Abraham Lincoln. As secretary of state under William McKinley and Theodore Roosevelt, Hay, a strong advocate of U.S. expansionism, was responsible for the OPEN DOOR POLICY toward China and treaties with Panama. The Hay-Pauncefote Treaties (1899, 1901) and the Hay-Bunau-Varilla Treaty (1903) helped pave the way for construction of the Panama Canal.

Hay-Bunau-Varilla Treaty *See* PANAMA CANAL.

Hayes, Helen (1900–93), stage and film actress, often called the First Lady of the American theater. Hayes began her career at age five in vaudeville and entertained radio, movie, and television audiences for over seventy-five years. She won Tony awards for her stage roles in *Happy Birthday* (1946) and *Time Remembered* (1957), and her role as Queen Victoria in *Victoria Regina* (1935) earned critical acclaim. Her first film, *The Sin of Madelon Claudet* (1932), earned her an Academy Award, as did her supporting role in *Airport* (1970). The Helen Hayes Theatre in New York was named in her honor at a celebration of her fiftieth year on the stage.

Hayes, Rutherford B. (1822–93), nineteenth president of the United States (1877–81). Born in Delaware, Ohio, Hayes graduated from Kenyon College and Harvard Law School and served in the Civil War as a general. He was governor of Ohio from 1868 to 1872 and the Republican candidate for president in the ELECTION OF 1876. His opponent, Democrat Samuel Tilden, won the most popular votes and led in the electoral college 184–165. But fraud and violence in three southern states and doubts about an Oregon elector's eligibility left 20 electoral votes in question. Congress created a special electoral commission to determine the winner, and Hayes won by 1 electoral vote. During the Hayes administration, all federal troops were removed from the South as part of the COMPROMISE OF 1877, thus ending military RECONSTRUCTION. Hayes was not renominated in 1880.

Hayes, Will (1879–1954), politician and motion picture executive. Hayes was an Indiana lawyer who became active in partisan politics and served as Republican national chairman (1918–21). He helped direct WARREN G. HARDING's successful presidential race, and served as postmaster general (1921–22) under Harding. As president of the Motion Picture Producers and Distributors of America (1922–45), Hayes administered the motion picture Production Code, which for almost forty years controlled the content of nearly all American films. Popularly called the Hayes Code, it was a response to a growing popular movement to regulate the movie industry, calming the public outcry for decency and morality in the movies and diverting possible censorship by the government.

Hay-Herran Treaty *See* PANAMA CANAL.

Haymarket Affair (May 4, 1886), violent incident in Chicago's Haymarket Square during the McCormick Harvester Machine Company Strike. Although the labor rally began peaceably, someone threw a bomb, killing seven policemen. Police responded by killing four demonstrators. Eight anarchists were found guilty of inciting a riot and murder. Four were hanged and one committed suicide. Seven years later, in an act that helped destroy his political career, Illinois governor JOHN PETER ALTGELD pardoned the remaining three, believing they had received an unfair trial.

Hay-Pauncefote Treaty *See* PANAMA CANAL.

Hays, Arthur Garfield (1881–1954), lawyer. Through his corporate practice in New York, Hays became a successful and wealthy lawyer representing the interests of power and fame. At the same time, he was drawn to society's underdogs, vigorously defending the individual liberty of victims of discriminatory laws. His famous cases include the SCOPES trial in 1925, in which he shared the defense of a Tennessee teacher who taught Darwin's theory of evolution; the SACCO-VANZETTI CASE (1927), defending two anarchists accused of a murder they denied committing; and the SCOTTSBORO CASE, defending nine black men accused of attacking two white women. Hays became general counsel of the AMERICAN CIVIL LIBERTIES UNION in 1920 and authored numerous books including *Let Freedom Ring* (1928), *Democracy Works* (1939), and *City Lawyer* (1942), his autobiography.

Head Right System, colonial system awarding a tract of land, usually fifty acres, to a person who paid for the passage of an immigrant to the colonies. Some wealthy people in Virginia and other southern colonies accumulated huge tracts of land through the system.

Health and Human Services, Department of (HHS), an executive department of the U.S. government that deals with social welfare, public health, and income security. Founded in 1953 as the Department of Health, Education, and Welfare, it was reorganized and renamed in 1979. It is supervised by a secretary who is part of the president's cabinet and is composed of five principal agencies: Public Health Service, Health Care Financing Administration, Office of Human Development Services, Social Security Administration, and Family Support Administration. It is the second largest federal department, after the Department of Defense.

Hearst, William Randolph (1863–1951), newspaper and magazine publisher. Hearst, who owned a chain of newspapers, including the *San Francisco Examiner,* the *New York Journal,* and the *Chicago American,* used sensationalism to appeal to his readers, a style called YELLOW JOURNALISM by his critics. Hearst's skill at manipulating public opinion fueled interest in the Spanish-American War in 1898. He was elected to the House of Representatives from New York in 1902 but lost a bid for the 1904 Republican presidential nomination. By 1920 he owned twenty large newspapers and six magazines, the world's greatest publishing empire. Hearst acquired numerous works of art, which form a priceless collection at his estate in San Simeon, California. The film classic *Citizen Kane* is said to be based on his life.

Held, John (1889–1958), illustrator and author. Held's covers for such magazines as *The New Yorker, Vanity Fair,* and *Harper's Bazaar* made him one of the most popular artists of the 1920s, influencing an entire era. His fanciful yet simple drawings were light, humorous, and sophisticated, showing flappers with bobbed hair and short skirts, and young men with raccoon coats and pennants. A full-time cartoonist at age sixteen, Held later created the newspaper comic strip "Merely Margie" and wrote several books.

Heller, Joseph (1923–99), novelist and playwright. Heller established his reputation with his satiric novel *Catch-22* (1961), which focuses on the grotesqueries of war as experienced by a bomber squadron during World War II. His other best-selling novels include *Something Happened* (1974) and *Good as Gold* (1979). His play *We Bombed in New Haven* (1967) addresses America's changing attitudes toward war.

Hellman, Lillian (1905–84), playwright and writer. Hellman wrote plays about destructiveness, selfishness, greed, and materialism. Her works, featuring tightly woven plots and reflecting her concern for social issues, include *The Children's Hour* (1934), *The Little Foxes* (1939), *Watch on the Rhine* (1941), *Another Part of the Forest* (1946), and *Toys in the Attic* (1960). The film industry blacklisted Hellman when she, like her friend DASHIELL HAMMETT, refused to cooperate with the HOUSE UN-AMERICAN ACTIVITIES COMMITTEE in 1952.

Helper, Hinton Rowan (1829–1909), author. A white southerner from North Carolina, Helper became unpopular in the South because of his opposition to slavery, especially in his book *The Impending Crisis* (1857). An examination of slavery's impact on Southern economy, the book condemned slavery not on humanitarian or moral grounds, but because it was an economic threat that victimized small-scale white farmers. In 1860 the Republican party showed support for the book, distributing more than 100,000 copies. It sold well in the North, but was outlawed in the South. Helper served as a diplomat to Argentina from 1861 to 1866. After claiming bankruptcy from a railroad venture, he committed suicide.

Hemingway, Ernest (1899–1961), writer. Hemingway won the 1953 Pulitzer Prize for his novella *The Old Man and the Sea* (1952) and received the Nobel Prize for literature in 1954. One of his favorite themes was war and its brutal effects on survivors; the typical Hemingway hero endures violence and defeat with courage. His influential writing style features plain, crisp, simple language and close descriptions of settings. Hemingway's experiences as an ambulance driver and soldier for the Italian army during World War I and his stint in the Spanish civil war provided inspiration for many of his short stories and novels. His most memorable works include *The Sun Also Rises* (1926), *A Farewell to Arms* (1929), and *For Whom the Bell Tolls* (1940). After a period of suffering in the 1950s, Hemingway committed suicide at his Idaho home.

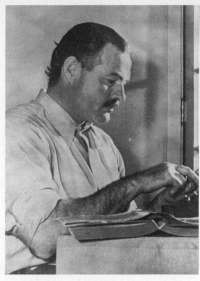
Ernest Hemingway

Hendrix, Jimi (James; 1942–70), rock performer. Hendrix's music featured a loud, powerful beat and long, emotional solo passages on an electric guitar. He worked with Little Richard and the Isley Brothers before putting together his own band, the Jimi Hendrix Experience, in 1966. A genius but self-destructive, he died of a drug overdose at the age of twenty-seven.

Henri, Robert (Robert Henry Cozad; 1865–1929), art teacher and painter. Henri founded the ASHCAN SCHOOL of realistic painting. As instructor at the Art Students League from 1915 to 1923, Henri fostered the development of modern painting in America and inspired a generation of young artists, including JOHN SLOAN, EDWARD HOPPER, and GEORGE BELLOWS. His influential book *The Art Spirit* (1923) expresses his philosophy on art.

Henry, O. (William Sydney Porter; 1862–1910), writer and journalist. O. Henry began writing while serving a three-year prison term for embezzlement. Known for his short, simple stories with ironic, surprise endings, he presents sentimental, sympathetic, usually lower-class characters in natural situations. O. Henry, under various pen names, wrote nearly three hundred works, achieving great success with such classic stories as "The Gift of the Magi" (1905) and "The Ransom of Red Chief." Collections of his works include *Cabbages and Kings* (1904) and *The Four Million* (1906).

Henry, Patrick (1736–99), colonial orator and statesman during the AMERICAN REVOLUTION. Henry served in the Virginia HOUSE OF BURGESSES, where he denounced the Stamp Act, and was a member of the CONTINENTAL CONGRESS, where he supported a boycott of English goods. He advocated war in his fiery speech to the Virginia Assembly in 1775 when he reportedly said, "I know not what course others may take; but as for me, give me liberty or give me death!" During and after the Revolution Henry served five times as governor of Virginia and was a member of the Virginia constitutional ratification convention. He strongly opposed ratification of the U.S. Constitution because he felt it gave too much power to the federal government. His objections, along with those of GEORGE MASON and others, led to the passage of the BILL OF RIGHTS.

Henson, Jim (1936–90), award-winning puppeteer. Henson created the Muppets, who first appeared on television in 1956 and were featured on the program "Sesame Street," beginning in 1969. The popular characters included Big Bird, Kermit the Frog, Bert and Ernie, Oscar, and the Cookie Monster.

Henson, Matthew (1867–1955), black explorer. Henson was the only American to accompany ROBERT PEARY 1909 on the first expedition to reach the North Pole. He traveled with Peary on expeditions for over twenty years, including seven trips to the Arctic. Henson published his autobiography, *Dark Companion*, in 1947.

Hepburn Act (June 29, 1906), law that strengthened the power of the Interstate Commerce Commission by increasing its membership from five to seven and allowing it to determine reasonable rates upon the complaint of a shipper. The act also prohibited free railroad passes and forbade railroads to haul commodities they had produced themselves.

Hepburn, Audrey (1929–93), actress and humanitarian. Born in Brussels, Belgium, Hepburn studied ballet and acting in London before moving to New York. Her poise, sense of style, and graceful demeanor gave her recognition in films such as *Roman Holiday* (1953), for which she won the Academy Award for best actress; *Breakfast at Tiffany's* (1961); *My Fair Lady* (1964); and the thriller *Wait until Dark* (1967). Over her career she was one of Hollywood's most popular box office attractions, and was nominated for best actress four more times. After 1988, Hepburn served as special ambassador to the United Nations Children's Fund. She received a posthumous Academy Award for her humanitarian efforts.

Hepburn, Katharine (1907–2003), actress. Noted for her dry, sophisticated style and crisp delivery of lines, Hepburn was nominated for an unprecedented twelve Academy Awards. She won four Oscars for her roles in *Morning Glory* (1932), *Guess Who's Coming to Dinner* (1967), *The Lion in Winter* (1968), and *On Golden Pond* (1981). She and her longtime friend Spencer Tracy costarred in many highly successful films.

Herblock (Herbert Lawrence Block; 1909–2001), editorial cartoonist.

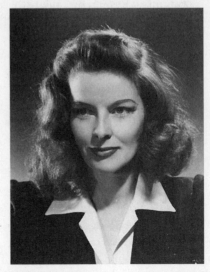

Katharine Hepburn

Block's cartoons, which appear in over two hundred newspapers, have defended civil liberties, attacked the misuse of political power, and opposed the arms race and the Vietnam War. He won three Pulitzer Prizes for cartooning.

Hersey, John (1914–93), author. Hersey's experiences as a World War II correspondent provided background for many of his books. The Pulitzer Prize-winning *A Bell for Adano* (1944) examines events in an American-occupied Italian village. *Hiroshima* (1946) is a moving nonfictional account of the atomic bombing of the Japanese city. Other novels include *The Wall* (1950) about the Warsaw ghetto, *The War Lover* (1959) about war's effect on people, and *The Child Buyer* (1960) on modern education. The son of American missionary parents, Hersey was born and raised in China.

Hessians, soldiers from the German state of Hesse. Because the rulers of Hesse owed the British Crown money, they sent about 30,000 Hessians to fight with the British against the colonists during the AMERICAN REVOLUTION. Well trained, they fought successfully in numerous battles but suffered defeat at Trenton, New Jersey, on Christmas Eve, 1776, in a surprise attack by George Washington's troops. Many Hessians deserted from British ranks and remained in the United States following the war.

Heston, Charlton (1924–), actor. Heston is known for his roles in epic films, including *The Ten Commandments* (1956), *Ben-Hur* (1959), and *El Cid* (1961), and various science fiction films. He won an Academy Award for his performance in the title role of *Ben-Hur*. He was president of the Screen Actor's Guild from 1966 to 1971 and worked closely with President RONALD REAGAN as the leader of the president's task force on arts and the humanities. Politically, Heston is a conservative Republican and has clashed at various times in his life with MARTIN LUTHER KING, JR., JOHN F. KENNEDY, and BILL CLINTON. A proud member of the NATIONAL RIFLE ASSOCIATION, a U.S. gun owner's rights lobbying group, he was its president and spokesman from 1998 to 2003. In 2002 Heston publicly announced he had Alzheimer's disease.

Hewlett, William (1913–2001), and **David Packard** (1912–96), computer industry pioneers. After meeting during their undergraduate days at Stanford, Hewlett and Packard put together $538 and formed an electronics business in Packard's garage in Palo Alto, California, in 1939. In 1989, that small garage was declared a historical landmark as the birthplace of "SILICON VALLEY," northern California's high-technology center. The first product developed was an audio oscillator designed by Hewlett, the first practical method of generating high-quality sound frequencies needed in communications, geophysics, medicine, and defense work. Their first commercial sale was to WALT DISNEY, who purchased eight oscillators to use in the award-winning soundtrack of the animated film *Fantasia*. The company, Hewlett-Packard, flourished and became one of the largest computer and printer manufacturing companies in the world. Hewlett was involved actively in management of the company until 1987, with time off as an army officer during World War II. Packard was active until his death in 1996, except for a stint as deputy secretary of defense in the first Nixon administration (1969–71). Both men created foundations to support their philanthropic interests.

Hickok, "Wild Bill" (James Butler; 1837–76), scout and frontier law officer. Hickok served as a scout and spy for the Union during the Civil War. Later he was a marshal in Fort Riley, Hays City, and Abilene, Kansas. On tour with BUFFALO BILL CODY's Wild West Show, Hickok displayed his legendary marksmanship and inspired many dime novels. He died after being shot in the back during a card game in Deadwood, South Dakota.

Hicks, Edward (1780–1849), folk painter. Painting in an untrained style, Hicks created over sixty interpretations of *The Peaceable Kingdom*. An itinerant Quaker preacher, he displayed his religious beliefs through his bold, strong paintings of ferocious animals lying at peace with the lamb. He also painted patriotic historical works and scenes of rural Pennsylvania.

Hill, Ambrose P. (1825–65), Confederate CIVIL WAR general. Hill served at the second Battle of BULL RUN and ANTIETAM and initiated the attack that began the Battle of GETTYSBURG. He died in the final days of the Civil War while defending Petersburg, Virginia.

Hill, James (1838–1916), financier and railroad magnate. Hill developed the Great Northern Railroad between the Great Lakes and the Pacific Northwest in 1893. Called "the Empire Builder," he opened a huge area of the United States through his transportation systems. He engaged in a stock market battle with J. P. MORGAN that caused the Wall Street panic of 1901. His estate was valued at over $100 million when he died.

***Hindenburg* Disaster** (May 6, 1937), a spectacular explosion of the German dirigible while it maneuvered to land at Lakehurst, New Jersey. The *Hindenburg*, the world's first transatlantic commercial airliner, was to provide luxurious air service between New Jersey and Germany. It was destroyed by fire when the airship's hydrogen ignited, claiming thirty-six lives. A radio broadcaster, there to describe the landing, gave a famous eyewitness account of the disaster as it occurred.

Hines, Earl ("Fatha") (1905–83), jazz pianist and bandleader. In the 1920s Hines became the first virtuoso piano soloist in jazz history. He developed the "trumpet style" of piano jazz, featuring single notes played by the right hand. Hines led his own bands during the bebop era and following World War II toured with all-star groups.

Hippies, young people during the 1960s and 1970s who rejected the values and ideas of mainstream society in regard to work, money, and material goods. They dressed distinctively, grew long hair, and ate vegetarian food; many experimented with drugs. They opposed the Vietnam War, arguing that love and peace could change the world. Many refused to work at traditional jobs; they often lived in communes or wandered from place to place. They were sometimes called "flower children."

Hiroshima *See* Atomic Bomb.

Hirshhorn, Joseph (1899–1981), financier and art collector. An immigrant from Latvia, Hirshhorn made a fortune through the sale of investments in the stock market just before the crash of 1929. He acquired one of the world's largest private modern art collections, which he later donated to the U.S. government. Congress established the Joseph H. Hirshhorn Museum and Sculpture Garden in Washington, D.C., in 1966 to house the collection of over six thousand pieces; the museum opened in 1974.

Hiss Case, celebrated case during the post–World War II red scare. In 1948 Whittaker Chambers (1901–61), an editor at *Time* and former Communist party member, appeared before the House Un-American Activities Committee (HUAC) and accused Alger Hiss (1901–96), a former State Department official, of passing him military secrets during the 1930s to be delivered to the Soviets. Chambers offered as evidence microfilms of what he claimed were secret documents, giving them to Representative Richard M. Nixon at Chambers's farm where he said they had been hidden in a hollowed-out pumpkin (hence, the "pumpkin papers"). Hiss denied the charges and was indicted for perjury. His first trial, at which Chambers was the chief prosecution witness, ended in a hung jury, but a second trial led to his conviction in 1950. After serving forty-four months in prison, Hiss was released in 1954, still protesting his innocence. The case made Nixon a national figure. In 1992, Dmitri Antonovich Volkogonov, Russian historian and chairman of a commission on the Soviet Union's KGB archives, publicly confirmed, after a thorough search of the files, that Hiss had never served as an intelligence agent for the Soviet Union.

Hitchcock, Sir Alfred (1899–1980), British-American film director and producer. Hitchcock was master of the suspense thriller, using innovative techniques to engage audiences. His film *Rebecca* won the 1940 Academy Award for best picture. Other masterpieces include *Rear Window* (1954), *North by Northwest* (1959), *The Birds* (1963), and *Psycho* (1960). Hitchcock produced and hosted a popular television series.

Hobart, Garret (1844–99), twenty-fourth vice president of the United States under William McKinley (1897–99). Hobart had never served in a major political office, but he was a powerful figure in New Jersey Republican politics. Hobart had served only half of his vice-presidential term when he died, opening the door of the vice presidency to Theodore Roosevelt, who stepped into the presidency when McKinley was assassinated in 1901.

Hobby, Oveta Culp (1905–95), public official and first woman to receive the Distinguished Service Medal. During World War II Hobby helped plan the Women's Auxiliary Army Corp (WAAC) and served as its director from

1942 to 1945. In 1953 Dwight Eisenhower appointed Hobby as the first secretary of the Department of Health, Education, and Welfare; she was the second woman to hold a cabinet position.

Hoffa, Jimmy (1913–75?), labor leader. As president of the International Brotherhood of Teamsters (1957–71), Hoffa helped secure the first national trucking company contract in the union's history. After successfully defending himself on numerous corruption charges, he was convicted of mail fraud and misuse of union funds in 1964 and sent to prison (1967–71). After his release, while trying to regain control of the union, he disappeared, presumably murdered. His body has never been found.

Hoffman, Dustin (1937–), actor. Known for his skillful representations of unusual characters, Hoffman achieved success with his role in *The Graduate* (1967). He won Academy Awards as best actor for his performances in *Kramer vs. Kramer* (1979) and *Rain Man* (1988). Hoffman has also received critical praise for his stage performances.

Hofstadter, Richard (1916–70), historian and author. During his twenty-four years on the faculty at Columbia University (1946–70), Hofstadter wrote fluently on the intellectual, social, and political history of the United States. Regarded as one of the most distinguished historians of his day, his influential works reflected a liberal philosophy and skeptical views of U.S. politics. His interest in contemporary affairs made his works relevant to the present day. Hofstadter's most influential works, which enjoyed popular as well as professional acclaim, include *The American Political Tradition* (1948) and his two Pulitzer Prize winners, *The Age of Reform* (1955) and *Anti-Intellectualism in American Life* (1963).

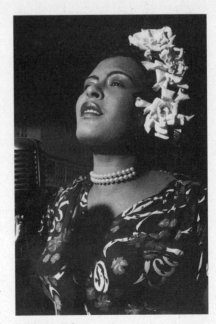

Billie Holiday

Hogan, Ben (William; 1912–97), golfer. One of golf's greatest players, Hogan dominated the sport in the 1940s and early 1950s, by winning over sixty tournaments, including the U.S. Open four times, the U.S. Masters twice, the PGA twice, and the British Open once. Though critically injured in an automobile accident at the peak of his career in 1949, he returned to the circuit to win numerous championships.

Holiday, Billie (Eleanora Fagan; 1915–59), black jazz singer. Holiday began singing in Harlem nightclubs in the 1930s and toured with major bands. She made her first recordings with Benny Goodman in 1933 and began a highly successful solo career, winning recognition for the expressive, bittersweet quality of her voice. Active in black protest movements, she grew increasingly bitter over racism, which led to an addiction to heroin and her death.

Holly, Buddy (Charles Hardin Holley; 1936–59), rock guitarist, composer, and singer. One of the first rock musicians, Holly became a celebrity after his band, the Crickets, recorded "That'll Be the Day" and "Peggy Sue" in 1957. Holly influenced other performers, including the Beatles (whose name derived from the Crickets). He died in a plane crash at the age of twenty-two.

Holmes, Oliver Wendell, Sr. (1809–94), physician and author. Known for his witty essays, poems, and novels, Holmes wrote the poem "Old Ironsides" (1830) in protest of the navy's plan to scrap the *Constitution*, which helped save the ship. In 1857 his column "The Autocrat of the Breakfast-Table," which appeared in the *Atlantic Monthly*, made him famous. As a physician and professor at Harvard Medical School from 1847 until 1883, he wrote influential articles on medical subjects. His most important article, "The Contagiousness of Puerperal Fever" (1842), urging cleanliness during childbirth, saved many lives.

Holmes, Oliver Wendell, Jr. (1841–1935), jurist. The son of Oliver Wendell Holmes, Sr., Holmes served as chief justice of the Massachusetts supreme court (1882–1902) and associate justice of the U.S. Supreme Court (1902–32). Called "the Great Dissenter," he was noted for his liberal dissenting opinions against majority decisions. Holmes strongly supported freedom of speech, stating it must be allowed except when it presents a "clear and present danger of imminent lawless action."

Homeland Security, Department of, one of the cabinet departments of the executive branch of the U.S. government. Created in the aftermath of the terrorist attacks against America on SEPTEMBER 11, 2001, the department's first priority is to protect the American homeland and the safety of American citizens. The new department officially began operation on January 24, 2003, under the direction of former Pennsylvania governor Tom Ridge. The plan is for several existing domestic agencies to merge into one department, the most significant change of the U.S. government in more than fifty years (since the U.S. Department of Defense was created by Harry S. Truman in 1947). Component agencies will analyze threats and intelligence, guard borders and airports, protect infrastructure, and coordinate the response of the nation for future emergencies.

Homer, Winslow (1836–1910), artist. Homer first gained attention as a contributor to *Harper's Weekly*, illustrating Civil War battle scenes. His oil landscapes and watercolor seascapes display intense feeling, vivid color, and realism. Homer's love for the life and drama of the sea are reflected in *Eight Bells* (1886) and *Gulf Stream* (1899).

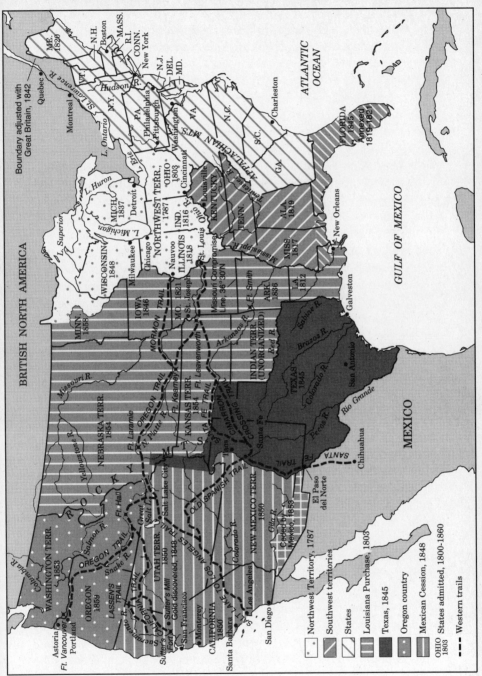

Westward Expansion, 1800–1860

BRITISH NORTH AMERICA

ATLANTIC OCEAN

GULF OF MEXICO

MEXICO

Boundary adjusted with Great Britain, 1842

ME.
1820

N.H.
Boston MASS.
R.I.
CONN.
New York
N.J.
PA.
DEL.
Philadelphia MD.
Pittsburgh
Washington

Quebec
Montreal
St. Lawrence R.
L. Ontario
L. Erie
Hudson R.

N.C.
S.C.
Charleston
GA.

VA.
APPALACHIAN MTS.

FLORIDA
1845
Annexed
1819–1821

L. Superior
L. Huron
L. Michigan
Detroit MICH.
1837
Milwaukee
Chicago
WISCONSIN
1848

NORTHWEST TERR.,
1787
OHIO
1803
Cincinnati
IND.
1816
ILLINOIS
1818
Nauvoo
St. Louis
KENTUCKY
TENN.
ALA.
1819
MISS.
1817
LA.
1812
New Orleans
Galveston

MINN.
1858
IOWA
1846
MO. 1821
St. Joseph
Ft. Leavenworth
Missouri Compromise
Line 36° 30'N
ARK.
1836
Ft. Smith
INDIAN TERR.
(UNORGANIZED)

MORMON TRAIL
Missouri R.
Yellowstone R.

NEBRASKA TERR.
1854

Ft. Laramie
Platte R.
OREGON TRAIL
Ft. Kearney
KANSAS TERR.
1854
SANTA FE TRAIL
Arkansas R.
Red R.

CIMARRON CROSSING
Santa Fe
Taos

R O C K Y M T S.

Columbia R.
WASHINGTON TERR.
1853
OREGON
1859
Portland
Ft. Vancouver
Astoria
Salmon R.
Snake R.
OREGON TRAIL

Ft. Hall
UTAH TERR.
1850
Great Salt Lake
Salt Lake City
Salt L.

CALIFORNIA TRAIL
LASSEN'S TRAIL
Sutter's Mill
Gold discovered, 1848
Sutter's Fort
Sacramento R.
San Francisco
Monterey
Santa Barbara
Los Angeles
San Diego
CALIFORNIA
1850

OLD SPANISH TRAIL
LOS ANGELES TRAIL

Colorado R.
Gila R.
NEW MEXICO TERR.
1850
Ceded by
Mexico, 1853
El Paso
del Norte
Chihuahua
SANTA FE TRAIL

TEXAS
1845
San Antonio
Rio Grande
Pecos R.
Colorado R.
Brazos R.
Sabine R.

Northwest Territory, 1787
Southwest territories
States
Louisiana Purchase, 1803
Texas, 1845
Oregon country
Mexican Cession, 1848
OHIO 1803 States admitted, 1800–1860
Western trails

Homestead Act (May 20, 1862), an act encouraging settlement in the West. Any adult citizen who headed a family and had not fought against the Union during the Civil War could receive 160 acres of unoccupied land by paying a small registration fee and promising to live on and cultivate the land for a period of five years. The Homestead Act ended in 1976 for all states except Alaska, where it expired in 1986. (For an overview of westward expansion, see map on page 245.)

Homestead Strike (1892), labor dispute between steel workers and the Carnegie Steel Company in Homestead, Pennsylvania, one of the most bitter strikes in American history. The striking trade union, the Amalgamated Association of Iron and Steel Workers, refused to accept a decrease in wages and stepped-up production demands by plant manager HENRY CLAY FRICK, who was determined to break the union. When he brought in three hundred Pinkerton guards to break the strike, they were met by ten thousand workers and violence erupted. Sixteen men were killed and many more injured. The governor then sent in eight thousand state militia who guarded non-union strike breakers running the plant. The strike ended after five months. The first major struggle between organized labor and big business resulted in failure for the most important craft union of the age and exhibited the power of American big business.

Hooker, Joseph (1814–79), Union general during the CIVIL WAR. Newspapers called Hooker "Fighting Joe" after the Battles of FREDERICKSBURG and ANTIETAM. Appointed commander of the Army of the Potomac by Abraham Lincoln, he suffered a serious defeat at the Battle of CHANCELLORSVILLE. He was relieved of command at his own request but later commanded a corps in the Chattanooga and Atlanta campaigns.

Hooker, Thomas (1586–1647), Puritan clergyman and founder of Connecticut. Dissatisfied with the conservative views of the leaders of the Massachusetts Bay Colony, Hooker left with a group of followers and established a settlement at Hartford, Connecticut, in 1636. He influenced the writing of the FUNDAMENTAL ORDERS OF CONNECTICUT in 1639, the first written constitution in America.

Hoover, Herbert (1874–1964), thirty-first president of the United States (1929–33). Born in West Branch, Iowa, Hoover graduated from Stanford University in engineering. He served as the U.S. food administrator during World War I. In 1921 Warren G. Harding appointed Hoover secretary of commerce, a post he held with distinction until 1928 when he received the Republican nomination for the presidency. Hoover defeated Democrat Alfred E. Smith in a landslide owing to the nation's apparent prosperity and nativist prejudice against the Catholic Smith. Seven months following his inauguration, the stock market crashed and the Great Depression began, seriously affecting his term of office. Hoover was criticized for his lack of action and his insistence that prosperity was "just around the corner," and suffered an overwhelming defeat in 1932 by Franklin D. Roosevelt. During his term the RECONSTRUCTION FINANCE CORPORATION was created, and Congress passed the Emergency Relief Act. In 1932 the BONUS ARMY, a group of unemployed World War I veterans, marched on Washington, D.C., and were forcibly ousted by federal troops at Hoover's request. After World War II Hoover again helped with relief efforts to foreign nations and headed the Hoover Commission, which recommended ways to improve the administration of the U.S. government.

Hoover, J. Edgar (John; 1895–1972), public official. Hoover directed the U.S. FEDERAL BUREAU OF INVESTIGATION (FBI) for forty-eight years (1924–72), serving under eight presidents and building it into an efficient law enforcement organization. Under Hoover's leadership, however, the FBI violated the civil liberties of many Americans. He became a controversial figure in the 1960s because of his illegal acts directed at Martin Luther King, Jr., and other civil rights workers, anti-Vietnam War activists, and hippies. He developed extensive secret files on individuals' private lives, which became accessible only after his death.

Hope, Bob (Leslie; 1903–2003), British-born comedian. After beginning his career in vaudeville, Hope achieved fame on radio and in movies. *The Big Broadcast of 1938* marked his film debut; he appeared in over fifty motion pictures, including many with Bing Crosby. The Motion Picture Academy honored Hope five times for his charitable activities.

Hopkins, Harry (1890–1946), public official and presidential adviser. A confidant of Franklin D. Roosevelt, Hopkins served as director of the Federal Emergency Relief Administration (1933) and the Works Projects Administration (1935–40). He helped establish the Social Security System, served as secretary of commerce, and headed the Lend-Lease Program. During World War II he attended all major wartime conferences with FDR and was the president's chief emissary to Great Britain and the Soviet Union.

Hopper, Edward (1882–1967), painter. Hopper studied with Robert Henri of the ASHCAN SCHOOL of realism. He has been called the "painter of loneliness," rendering starkly realistic scenes of contemporary life that convey somberness and isolation. Examples include *Early Sunday Morning, Nighthawks,* and *Second Story Sunlight.* His watercolors also reflect scenes of rural New England.

Horne, Lena (1917–), blues singer and actress. Horne began her career as a chorus girl in Harlem's Cotton Club and became the first black woman vocalist to be featured with a white band when she sang with Charlie Barnet's orchestra. She gained film stardom in *Stormy Weather* (1943). She celebrated fifty years in show business with her one-woman show, *The Lady and Her Music,* in the early 1980s and received the NAACP's SPINGARN MEDAL in 1983.

Hornsby, Rogers (1896–1963), baseball player and manager. After twenty-three seasons Hornsby compiled a lifetime batting average of .358, the highest in National League history. Playing second base for five major league teams, including the St. Louis Cardinals, he won seven NL batting titles, six in succession. His .424 average in 1924 was the highest in the twentieth century. Hornsby managed baseball teams following his retirement in 1937 and became a member of the Hall of Fame in 1942.

Horseshoe Bend, Battle of (March 27, 1814), clash during the WAR OF 1812 between American forces led by ANDREW JACKSON, and the Creek Indians at Horseshoe Bend on the Tallapoosa River in Alabama. The U.S. forces of about two thousand soldiers attacked about eight hundred Creeks, and several hours of hand-to-hand combat ensued, resulting in a victory for the Americans. All but fifty Indians were killed.

Houdini, Harry (Ehrich Weiss; 1874–1926), magician and escape artist. Particularly known for his ability to free himself from almost any restraint, Houdini gained international fame for his escape acts from straitjackets, ropes, chains, handcuffs, and locked chests and cabinets. He crusaded against mind readers and the like, exposing them as frauds. Houdini died from peritonitis following a stomach injury incurred during one of his stunts.

House of Burgesses, Virginia, the first representative legislative body in America. The sessions first met at Jamestown in 1619 and consisted of two elected citizens, called burgesses, from each of the eleven sections of Virginia. The House of Burgesses managed the affairs of the colony until its last session in 1774. It was a focus of colonial resistance to British policy in the 1760s and 1770s.

House of Representatives, one of the two chambers of the U.S. Congress, often referred to as the House. Larger than the U.S. Senate, it consists of 435 elected representatives apportioned according to the population of the states. Each state must have at least one representative. The Constitution requires a representative to be at least twenty-five years old, a U.S. citizen for at least seven years, and a legal resident of the state from which he or she is elected. Representatives are elected in even-numbered years, serve two-year terms, and may be reelected indefinitely. The Speaker of the House, selected from the majority party, presides over sessions.

House Un-American Activities Committee (HUAC) (1938), congressional committee set up to investigate subversive activities. In the 1940s HUAC investigated labor unions, liberal organizations, peace groups, and New Deal agencies, holding highly publicized public hearings and using guilt by association to "prove" disloyalty. In 1947 HUAC focused on communism in Hollywood. Although the committee uncovered no wrongdoing, film executives refused to hire anyone on its BLACKLIST, a practice that spread to stage, radio, and television. The committee's 1948 investigation of the HISS CASE brought Richard M. Nixon to national prominence. Re-named the Internal Security Committee in 1969, it was abolished in 1975.

Housing and Urban Development, Department of (HUD) (1965), executive department of the federal government that coordinates housing and community development programs. The secretary of housing and urban development, a member of the president's cabinet, heads the department. Formed in 1965 to solve problems of record growth during the 1950s and 1960s, HUD replaced the Housing and Home Finance Agency.

Houston, Sam (1793–1863), soldier and politician. Houston lived with the Cherokees as a boy and later served as a Democratic member of the House of Representatives and as governor of Tennessee (1827–29). After moving to Texas, Houston became commander in chief of the Texas forces in 1835. The defeat of Mexican General Santa Anna at the Battle of San Jacinto in 1836 secured Texas's independence, and Houston became its first president. Texas joined the Union in 1845 and elected Houston to the U.S. Senate. A strong Unionist, he supported the COMPROMISE OF 1850 and opposed the KANSAS-NEBRASKA ACT. He was elected governor of Texas in 1859, but could not prevent the people from voting to secede. He refused to support the Confederacy and was removed from office in 1861.

Howard, Oliver O. (1830–1909), Union general during the CIVIL WAR. Howard fought with the Northern army at BULL RUN, CHANCEL-LORSVILLE, GETTYSBURG, and the Georgia campaign. He served after the war as commissioner of the FREEDMEN'S BUREAU and commissioner to the Apaches. He also helped establish Howard University in Washington, D.C.

Howe, Elias (1819–67), inventor of the sewing machine. Howe patented his invention in 1846, making possible the inexpensive and rapid manufacturing of shoes, clothing, and other products previously made by hand.

Howe, Gordie (Gordon; 1928–), hockey player. Born in Canada, Howe played for the Detroit Red Wings for twenty-six years and helped lead them to four championships. He won the Hart Trophy as most valuable player six times and led the National Hockey League in scoring six times. He holds the career record for most games played (1,767), but his records for most goals scored (801) and most points (1,850) were broken by WAYNE GRETZKY. After retiring in 1971 Howe returned in 1973 to play for the Houston Aeros of the World Hockey Association. He finally retired in 1980 at age fifty-two and became a member of the hockey Hall of Fame in 1972.

Howe, Julia Ward (1819–1910), writer and social reformer. Howe is best known as the author of "The Battle Hymn of the Republic" (1862), which became the major war song of the Union forces during the Civil War. She assisted her husband, SAMUEL GRIDLEY HOWE, as coeditor of the abolitionist newspaper the *Commonwealth*. A leader in the New England woman suffrage movement, she also is known for her role in establishing Mother's

Day in the United States in 1872, although the day evolved into something different from what she had in mind. She proposed the day to honor women in their role as social activists and seekers of peace.

Howe, Louis (1871–1936), journalist and political adviser. Howe befriended New York state senator FRANKLIN D. ROOSEVELT in 1911 and became his political mentor, serving as personal secretary and strategist. He persuaded FDR to remain in politics after he was stricken with polio and managed his successful gubernatorial and presidential campaigns.

Howe, Samuel Gridley (1801–76), educator, physician, and social reformer. Howe in 1831 founded the first U.S. school for the blind, the New England Asylum for the Blind, later called the Perkins Institute, and served as director for forty-four years. He assisted HORACE MANN and DOROTHEA DIX in their campaigns for reforms in education, prisons, and treatment of the mentally ill. An ABOLITIONIST, Howe published the *Commonwealth,* an abolitionist newspaper, with his wife, JULIA WARD HOWE.

Howells, William Dean (1837–1920), novelist, critic, and editor. Howells's campaign biography *Life of Lincoln* (1860) earned him an appointment from Abraham Lincoln as U.S. consul in Venice, where he lived until 1865 and wrote the first of many travel books, *Venetian Life* (1866). In 1866 he became a member of the staff of the *Atlantic,* serving as editor in chief from 1871 until 1881. He exerted a strong influence on the development of realism in American literature, promoting such writers as HENRY JAMES and MARK TWAIN. After 1882 he devoted himself to writing fiction, publishing the realistic novels *A Modern Instance* (1882) and *The Rise of Silas Lapham* (1885), two of his major achievements. Howells's open denunciation in 1887 of the judicial murder of the Chicago anarchists in the HAYMARKET AFFAIR endangered his career. Asserting that their conviction was based on their political views rather than on evidence of murder, he wrote a famous letter to the *New York Tribune* just prior to their execution, urging clemency. A prolific writer, Howells published about a hundred books, including novels, plays, criticism, essays, and short stories.

Hubble, Edwin (1889–1953), astronomer. In 1919 Hubble joined the staff of Carnegie Institution's Mt. Wilson Observatory in California, later becoming its director. Using the 100-inch Hooker telescope, his observations established beyond doubt that nebulae seen earlier were not part of our Milky Way galaxy, but galaxies themselves. In what is now known as Hubble's law, he was the first to observe evidence to support the theory of the expanding universe. The orbiting Hubble Space Telescope is named in his honor.

Hudson, Henry (?–1611), English explorer. Hudson explored North America in an unsuccessful search for the Northwest Passage. During the third of his four voyages, he sailed up the Hudson River to the present-day site of Albany and as far south as North Carolina. Sailing under the Dutch flag, he claimed some of the land for the Netherlands. Later, representing England, he explored Hudson Bay. Set adrift by his mutinous crew, he was left to die and never seen again.

Hudson, Rock (born Roy Scherer; 1925–85), actor. Hudson, nominated for an Academy Award for his role in *Giant* in 1956, was paired with Doris Day in a series of romantic comedies. His admission just before he died that he had AIDS raised public awareness of the disease.

Hudson River School, group of nineteenth-century realistic landscape painters. Characterized by their close attention to details of nature, painters of this school created romantic impressions of the Catskill Mountains and the Hudson River valley. Later artists painted landscapes of various wilderness areas of North and South America. The school flourished from 1825, when THOMAS COLE's landscapes gained popularity, to 1880.

Hughes, Charles Evans (1862–1948), politician and chief justice of the United States (1930–41). Hughes served as Republican governor of New York from 1907 until 1910, when William Howard Taft appointed him associate justice of the U.S. Supreme Court. He resigned from the Court in 1916 to become the Republican party candidate for president but lost by a narrow margin to Woodrow Wilson. Hughes later served as secretary of state under Warren Harding and Calvin Coolidge, taking a leading role in the Washington Disarmament Conference. In 1930 Herbert Hoover appointed him chief justice on the Supreme Court, where he served during the New Deal. He played a pivotal role in turning back Franklin D. Roosevelt's 1937 COURT-PACKING PLAN.

Hughes, Howard (1905–76), financier and movie maker. At age seventeen, Hughes took over his father's Hughes Tool Company, which became the foundation of his fortune. As a Hollywood producer he made such films as *Hell's Angels* (1930), *Scarface* (1932), and *The Outlaw* (1941). He formed the Hughes Aircraft Company and set a world's speed record flying his own

---

★ **Some Painters of the Hudson River School**

Early Members
- THOMAS COLE (1801–48)
- ASHER B. DURAND (1796–1886)
- Thomas Doughty (1793–1856)

Late Members
- FREDERICK CHURCH (1826–1900)
- ALBERT BIERSTADT (1830–1902)
- GEORGE INNESS (1825–72)
- John F. Kensett (1816–72)
- Thomas Moran (1837–1926)

plane. After selling his controlling interest in Trans World Airlines, he invested heavily in Nevada real estate, acquiring much of Las Vegas's "Strip." During the 1960s Hughes became an increasingly eccentric recluse.

Hughes, Langston (James; 1902–67), African-American author, playwright, and poet. A major figure in the HARLEM RENAISSANCE of the 1920s, Hughes presented powerful depictions of the black experience in his writings. Although best known for his poetry, he also wrote memoirs and plays and worked with theater companies. His works include *The Weary Blues* (1926), *Not without Laughter* (1930), and *One-Way Ticket* (1949).

Huguenots, French Protestants who migrated to North America after 1685 because of religious persecution. Most settled in the Carolinas, contributing to the intellectual and economic growth of the colonies.

Hull, Bobby (1939–), hockey player. Hull played for the Chicago Blackhawks for fifteen years. Known as "the Golden Jet" because of his speed on skates, he led the National Hockey League in scoring three times and won the Lady Byng Trophy in 1965. As player-coach of the Winnipeg Jets of the World Hockey Association (WHA), he was chosen the MVP in 1973 and 1975 and led them to the WHA title in 1976. He became a member of the hockey Hall of Fame in 1983.

Hull, Cordell (1871–1955), statesman. Hull, who had represented Tennessee in Congress, served as secretary of state under Franklin D. Roosevelt from 1933 to 1944 and received the Nobel Peace Prize in 1945. He developed the GOOD NEIGHBOR POLICY toward Latin America and was responsible for the initial plans that resulted in the United Nations.

Hull House *See* JANE ADDAMS.

Hull, William (1753–1825), army officer and governor of Michigan Territory. Hull was a general during the WAR OF 1812. Because he surrendered Detroit to the British without a strong defense, he was court-martialed and convicted of cowardice and neglect of duty and sentenced to die. He escaped execution when President James Madison stayed his sentence because of his excellent military record during the Revolution.

Humphrey, Hubert H. (1911–78), vice president of the United States (1965–69) under Lyndon B. Johnson. Humphrey became mayor of Minneapolis in 1945 and entered the U.S. Senate from Minnesota in 1949. He lost his bid for the Democratic presidential nomination to John F. Kennedy in 1960. Although not always liberal in his positions, he supported civil rights, federal aid to education, and social welfare legislation. His support for the war in Vietnam as vice president cost him some of his liberal support and the election when he ran for president against Richard Nixon in 1968. Humphrey returned to the Senate in 1971, where he served until his death.

Huntington, Collis P. (1821–1900), railroad executive and financier. Huntington joined with Mark Hopkins to establish a prosperous mercantile company, capitalizing on the needs of the miners during the California Gold Rush. He and Hopkins joined with LELAND STANFORD and Charles Crocker to form the Central Pacific Railroad (CPR) in the 1860s. The CPR joined the Union Pacific at Promontory Point, Utah, in 1869, becoming the first TRANSCONTINENTAL RAILROAD. In 1884, the group expanded their railroad business to southern California by forming the Southern Pacific Railway, with Huntington succeeding Stanford as president in 1890. Huntington also invested in the Chesapeake and Ohio Railroad and a number of steamship companies.

Huntley, Chet (1911–74), and **David Brinkley** (1920–2003), newscast team. *The Huntley-Brinkley Report* was the prime nightly newscast from 1956 to 1970. The team won every major news-broadcasting award in television. Huntley's solemn, dry manner complemented Brinkley's wry and witty humor. After the pair broke up, Brinkley hosted *This Week with David Brinkley,* a Sunday morning news program. Brinkley retired from ABC News in 1997. The complete title of his 1995 memoir summed up his career: *David Brinkley: 11 Presidents, 4 Wars, 22 Political Conventions, 1 Moon Landing, 3 Assassinations, 2,000 Weeks of News and Other Stuff on Television and 18 Years of Growing Up in North Carolina.*

Hurston, Zora Neale (1891?–1960), black author and anthropologist. Known for her literary interpretations of African-American folklore of the southern United States and West Indies, Hurston used humor and lively, energetic metaphorical language in her works. She was the most prolific African-American woman writer of the 1930s and an important figure of the HARLEM RENAISSANCE. Hurston's novels include *Jonah's Gourd Vine* (1934) and *Their Eyes Were Watching God* (1937). *Mules and Men* (1935) and *Tell My Horse* (1938) are collections of folktales.

Huston, John (1906–87), motion picture director. Huston began his career directing *The Maltese Falcon* in 1941. He focused on stories involving adventure and honor with such classics as *The Asphalt Jungle* (1950), *The African Queen* (1951), and *Moby Dick* (1956). Huston directed his father, Walter, in *The Treasure of the Sierra Madre* (1948) and daughter, Anjelica, in *Prizzi's Honor* (1985); both won Academy Awards for their performances.

Hutchinson, Anne (1591–1643), New England Puritan religious leader. Hutchinson immigrated to Massachusetts in 1634 to follow the preachings of JOHN COTTON. In 1638 she was excommunicated from the church because of her religious beliefs, which asserted that salvation was God's gift and could not be earned, and because of her claim to immediate revelation from God. Her preachings divided the MASSACHUSETTS BAY COLONY, and she was banished in 1637. Hutchinson moved with her family to Rhode Island, where she founded Portsmouth. Following the death of her husband in 1642, she moved to New York, where she and all but one of her children were massacred in an Indian raid.

Hutchinson, Thomas (1711–80), colonial politician. In 1771 Hutchinson, a descendant of ANNE HUTCHINSON, was the last civilian royal governor of the Massachusetts colony. His refusal to order tea-laden ships to leave Boston Harbor resulted in the BOSTON TEA PARTY in 1773. Although he opposed the STAMP ACT, he enforced it, and a Boston mob destroyed his home. Colonial radicals published some of Hutchinson's private letters, ending his political effectiveness. Replaced by Thomas Gage in 1774, he went to England to serve as an adviser on American affairs.

Hutson, Don (1913–97), football player. An All-American end at the University of Alabama and superstar with the Green Bay Packers, Hutson led the National Football League in scoring from 1940 to 1944, pass receiving eight times, and touchdowns eight times. He became a member of the professional football Hall of Fame in 1963.

Iacocca, Lee (Lido Anthony; 1924–), automobile executive. Iacocca joined the Ford Motor Company in 1946 and gained a reputation as a marketing genius. He promoted such successful models as the Ford Mustang, Maverick, and Fiesta and became president of the company in 1970. Because of a dispute with Henry Ford II, Iacocca moved to the Chrysler Corporation in 1978. Through a series of maneuvers, including a $1.5 billion loan guarantee and tax concessions granted by Congress, he turned the financially ailing company around within five years.

Ickes, Harold (1874–1952), government official. A liberal Republican and important in reform politics, Ickes supported Theodore Roosevelt's Progressive party in 1912 and managed Hiram Johnson's unsuccessful campaign to win the presidential nomination in 1924. He later switched to the Democratic party. Appointed secretary of the interior by Franklin D. Roosevelt, he served from 1933 to 1946, the longest cabinet tenure in American history. He fought for the preservation of natural resources and also headed the Public Works Administration (PWA) from 1933 to 1939.

Idaho (Gem State) became the forty-third state on July 3, 1890. (See maps, pages 540 and 541.) A mountainous and wooded state with enormous natural resources and scenic beauty, Idaho lies in the Rocky Mountain region of the United States. The state produces more than a third of the silver mined in the nation. Its fertile soil produces many crops, most notably potatoes. Thick forests yield great quantities of pulp and paper products. Tourism is important, with visitors coming year-round to fish and boat in the summer and ski at Sun Valley in the winter. The state encloses eight national forests and parts of seven others. The deepest canyon in the United States, Hell's Canyon, divides Idaho and Oregon along the Snake River. Boise is the capital and largest city. Famous Idahoans include EZRA POUND and GUTZON BORGLUM.

Illinois (Land of Lincoln) became the twenty-first state on December 3, 1818. (See maps, pages 540 and 541.) Chicago, its largest city, is the industrial center of the Midwest, serving as a major iron and steel producer, grain exchange, and meat-packing center. O'Hare International Airport is the world's busiest. The country's tallest building, the Sears Tower, rises 1,454 feet. Other major cities are Springfield, the capital, Rockford, and Peoria. Rolling plains cover most of the state; its agricultural products include hogs, cattle, corn, and soybeans. Noted Illinoisans include RONALD REAGAN, JANE ADDAMS, and ERNEST HEMINGWAY.

Immigration Legislation, laws regulating who can immigrate into the United States. The first restriction on immigration was imposed by the ALIEN ENEMIES ACT in 1798. In 1875 Congress barred prostitutes and felons from entering the country, and in 1882 added the insane and any other persons who might need public care to the list. The same year, Congress passed the CHINESE EXCLUSION ACT, which suspended the immigration of Chinese laborers. This was followed in 1907 with the GENTLEMEN'S AGREEMENT with Japan, which prevented the immigration of Japanese laborers. Congress overrode a presidential veto in 1917 and required all adult immigrants to pass a literacy test. Quotas were introduced for the first time in 1921. Congress passed the National Origins Act in 1924, to take effect in 1929, which limited immigrants from outside the Western Hemisphere, and in 1952 the Immigration and Naturalization Act (McCarran-Walter Act) limited quotas for Asian countries. In 1965 quotas based on nationality were discontinued, and preference was extended to relatives of U.S. citizens, refugees, and persons with special skills. Immigration is now limited to 170,000 per year, with no more than 20,000 allowed from any one country.

Impeachment, a formal charge of wrongdoing brought against a public official. It is not removal from office; it is the first step in removing political and judicial officials from office before their terms expire, as provided for in Article I of the U.S. Constitution. Impeachable offenses include "Treason, Bribery, or other high Crimes and Misdemeanors." The House of Representatives has the sole power of impeachment; the Senate sits as the jury for the subsequent trial. Impeachment requires the passage of a resolution by a majority vote of the House. The vice president of the United States presides over the trial, unless that person or the president is the subject of the proceedings. In this case, the chief justice of the United States presides. A two-thirds vote is needed for conviction and removal from office. Since 1789 the House has impeached fifteen officials. Seven, all federal judges, have been convicted. Presidents ANDREW JOHNSON and BILL CLINTON were impeached but acquitted. President RICHARD NIXON resigned from office following recommendation of impeachment by the House Judiciary Committee.

Impeachment of Andrew Johnson (1868). Andrew Johnson, the seventeenth president of the United States, was the only president to have been impeached until the IMPEACHMENT OF BILL CLINTON in 1999. In this case the House of Representatives, by a vote of 126 to 47, charged Johnson with "high crimes and misdemeanors" for, among other things, violating the TENURE OF OFFICE ACT when he fired Secretary of War Edwin Stanton from the cabinet without the consent of the Senate. Chief Justice Salmon P. Chase presided over the trial, and the U.S. Senate sat as jury. The final vote of 35–19 was one short of the two-thirds necessary for conviction, so Johnson was acquitted. Senator EDMUND G. ROSS of Kansas cast the deciding vote of "not guilty," which ended his political career.

Impeachment of Bill Clinton (1998–99). Bill Clinton, the forty-second president of the United States, became the second president to be impeached. (ANDREW JOHNSON was the first.) On December 11–12, 1998, the House Judiciary Committee approved four articles of impeachment including two counts of perjury, obstruction of justice, and abuse of power. On December 12, the Republican-controlled House of Representatives, voting along party lines, charged Clinton with "high crimes and misdemeanors" on two counts, perjury and obstruction of justice. The Senate trial, with Chief Justice WILLIAM REHNQUIST presiding, was held from Jan. 7 to Feb. 12, 1999. With opinion polls showing that Clinton's job approval rating surpassed 70 percent despite his impeachment, and most Americans favoring a quick conclusion to the Senate trial, senators also realized there would not be enough votes to convict the president unless twelve Democratic senators voted to convict, an unlikely possibility. The Senate (which, like the House, was controlled by the Republican party) also voted along party lines and found Clinton not guilty with a vote of fifty-five to forty-five on the perjury charge. Regarding the obstruction of justice charge, the Senate split evenly, fifty-fifty. With the necessary two-thirds majority not achieved, Bill Clinton was acquitted on both charges and would serve out the remainder of his term of office through January 20, 2001.

Impeachment charges stemmed from investigations that began in 1994 when independent prosecutor Kenneth Starr began looking into some of the numerous scandals that overshadowed Clinton's presidency. Revelations from the WHITEWATER SCANDAL led to information on an alleged sexual encounter with a woman named Paula Jones (a case he later settled by paying $850,000) and his two-year relationship with White House intern Monica Lewinsky. The perjury charge was for lying under oath to a federal grand jury about his affair with Lewinsky. He was charged with obstruction of justice for encouraging Lewinsky to submit a false affidavit and give false testimony in court, plotting to hide his gifts to her, and attempting to find Lewinsky a job to prevent her truthful testimony.

Although this was the second impeachment trial in U.S. history, it marked the first time an elected president was faced with possible removal from office. (Andrew Johnson was not elected but assumed office following the assassination of President Abraham Lincoln.)

Imperialism, the foreign policy of controlling another country, usually by military means, or exploiting it economically. During the late 1800s, with the closing of the frontier, many Americans thought expansion elsewhere would be an efficient way to meet the continuing demands of the country's industry. New lands and colonies, it was thought, would strengthen its military power. By 1900 the United States had acquired Hawaii, Guam, the Philippines, and Puerto Rico in the name of imperialism.

Impressment, the forcible seizure of men from American ships to serve in the British navy during the early 1800s. Searching for deserters, the British had impressed over six thousand American sailors by the end of 1807, despite repeated American protests and interventions, including the EMBARGO ACT. Impressment was a major cause of the WAR OF 1812.

Inauguration, the formal ceremony in Washington, D.C., inducting the president into office. Originally, the inauguration took place on or about March 4. The Twentieth Amendment to the Constitution, ratified in 1933, changed the date to January 20 of the year following the election.

Income Tax, a tax on the earnings of people proportionate to their incomes and on corporations, estates, and trusts. Income tax, the major source of government revenue, is paid to the Internal Revenue Service (IRS), which distributes it for use by the government. The first income tax in the United States was levied following the Civil War so that the Union government could pay its bills. But in 1895 a later income tax was declared unconstitutional by the Supreme Court. The Sixteenth Amendment to the Constitution, authorizing the tax, was ratified February 25, 1913.

Indentured Servant, a person who worked without wages, usually for a period of five to seven years, in exchange for payment of the person's passage to the American colonies. The contract, called an "indenture," entitled the servant to food, clothing, shelter, and medical attention. Devised by the Virginia Company in the late 1610s, the system provided cheap labor. It is estimated that one-half to two-thirds of all European immigrants to the colonies participated in the system, some voluntarily, some as victims of penal servitude. The practice disappeared after 1800.

Independence Hall, a building in Philadelphia, Pennsylvania, that was the site of some of the most significant events in American history. Completed in 1741 as the State House, the building was the site of the colony's government. It housed the Liberty Bell from 1753 to 1976. The Second Continental Congress met there in 1775, and in 1776 adopted the Declaration of Independence there, leading to the popular designation Independence

Hall. In 1787 the Constitutional Convention met there to draft the U.S. Constitution.

Indiana (Hoosier State) entered the Union as the nineteenth state on December 11, 1816. (See maps, pages 540 and 541.) First explored by the Frenchman Robert LaSalle in 1679, Indiana became a British territory after the French and Indian War in 1763. It was the center of Indian uprisings until the victory at Tippecanoe in 1811 by William Henry Harrison. Large cities include the capital, Indianapolis, and Gary, Fort Wayne, Evansville, and Muncie. The Indianapolis 500 auto race, the biggest single spectator sport in America, takes place every Memorial Day. Indiana's leading industries include agriculture, manufacturing, coal mining, and limestone producing. Noted Indiana natives include BENJAMIN HARRISON, EUGENE DEBS, and COLE PORTER.

Indian Treaties, agreements between Native American nations or tribes and the U.S. government, providing for the voluntary or forcible removal of Indians from much of their lands to make room for white settlers. During President Andrew Jackson's administration alone, more than ninety treaties were signed. Because many were broken by whites, a special agency, the Bureau of Indian Affairs, was established in 1836 to deal with problems.

Industrial Revolution, the transformation, during the 1700s and early 1800s, from making goods in small shops or homes by hand to making them in factories with machines and, later, on assembly lines. The Industrial Revolution began in Great Britain, and its spread changed the Western world from a rural, agricultural society to an urban and industrial one. The rapid economic change following the Civil War has sometimes been called the New Industrial Revolution.

Industrial Workers of the World (IWW) (1905), labor organization formed to unionize unskilled workers in the mining, lumbering, and textile industries during the early 1900s. Members of the union, called Wobblies, used boycotts and strikes in their effort to improve working conditions and gain higher wages. Formed in opposition to the AMERICAN FEDERATION OF LABOR (AFL), which organized workers by trades, the IWW's goal was to form all workers into one union and eventually overthrow capitalism through a general strike. Strikes during World War I were broken by violence against the workers, and the union, labeled "unpatriotic," was suppressed. Numerous IWW leaders, including EUGENE DEBS, one of its founders, were imprisoned, and many states passed legislation outlawing what was called "criminal syndicalism."

Inness, George (1825–94), landscape painter. The early paintings of Inness reflect the careful detailed style of the HUDSON RIVER SCHOOL. He later developed his own style — a subtle rendering of glowing light and color that produced shimmering landscapes. Inness, a believer in mysticism, attempted to give his works a spiritual quality by, among other things, blurring and smudging edges. Examples of his landscapes include *Peace and Plenty* (1865) and *The Coming Storm* (1878).

Inouye, Daniel K. (1924–), politician. A U.S. senator from Hawaii since 1963, Inouye was the first person of Japanese ancestry to be elected to Congress. Inouye, confined to a JAPANESE-AMERICAN INTERNMENT camp early in World War II, later lost his left arm while fighting with the 442ND IN-FANTRY in Europe. He came to national prominence through the 1973 WATERGATE investigation, when he sat on the Select Committee on Presidential Campaign Activities. He also chaired the joint congressional committee to investigate the IRAN-CONTRA AFFAIR in 1986. Inouye was a key architect of the federal government's 1988 apology and payment of reparations to Japanese-Americans who had been interned.

Interior, Department of (1849), executive department of the federal government responsible for the conservation and development of natural resources, including land, minerals, water, and wildlife. The secretary of the interior, a member of the president's cabinet, heads the department and its five divisions — Fish and Wildlife and Parks, which manages the National Park Service and the U.S. Fish and Wildlife Service; Water and Science, which manages the U.S. Geological Survey, the Bureau of Mines, and the Bureau of Reclamation; Land and Minerals Management, which oversees the Bureau of Land Management, Minerals Management Service, and Office of Surface Mining, Reclamation, and Enforcement; Indian Affairs, which operates the Bureau of Indian Affairs; and Territorial and International Affairs, which coordinates the affairs in U.S.-administered territories. Congress created the department in 1849 to administer the country's huge landholdings (especially the Louisiana Purchase and Oregon Territory) and its relations with Indians.

International Space Station (ISS), unfinished space module orbiting 250 miles above the earth. The *ISS* continues the work done by *SKYLAB* and Russia's *Mir*, representing a human presence in space. It is the largest and most complex international scientific project in history. Led by the United States and Russia, it draws upon the scientific resources and expertise of fifteen other nations: Canada, Japan, Russia, eleven nations of the European Space Agency, and Brazil. Its mission is to enable long-term exploration of space and provide benefits to people on earth. The first piece of the station, Russian control module *Zarya*, was launched into orbit in 1998. It was followed two weeks later by the U.S. module *Unity*, and the two were connected. The first crew entered the station November 2, 2000, and stayed 136 days, until March 18, 2001. More than one hundred components are scheduled to be connected before the completion of the station. Completion, however, is uncertain due to costs, delays, and skepticism. Critics of the project view it as a waste of time and money, and after the Columbia Disaster on February 1, 2003, and the resulting freeze on the Space Shuttle program, the future of the *ISS* is in question.

Interstate Commerce Act (February 4, 1887), law passed by Congress stating that all railroad charges should be fair and reasonable, and that forbade interstate railroad abuses. It established a five-member Interstate Commerce Commission to administer the provisions of the law.

Intolerable Acts (1774), also called the Coercive Acts, five laws passed by the British Parliament in response to the colonial defiance of the tea tax and the Boston Tea Party. The first act, the Boston Port Bill, closed the port of Boston. The second, the Administration of Justice Act, provided that British soldiers arrested for serious crimes against colonists would be returned to England for trial. The Massachusetts Government Act reduced the power of the colony's local government and forbade town meetings. The Quartering Act required the colonists to provide food and housing for British troops. The Quebec Act added western territory north of the Ohio River to the province of Quebec, eliminating the claims of some of the colonies to the region. The colonists strongly objected to the acts, calling them "intolerable," and their issuance prompted the calling, in September 1774, of the First Continental Congress.

Iowa (Hawkeye State) joined the Union as the twenty-ninth state on December 28, 1846. (See maps, pages 540 and 541.) Major cities include the capital, Des Moines, Cedar Rapids, Davenport, and Sioux City. The name *Iowa* comes from an Indian word meaning "the beautiful land." Its black soil is among the richest in the nation. Iowa is one of the foremost agricultural states, producing one-tenth of the country's food supply and more corn than any other state. Manufacturing, mining, and livestock are major industries. Noted Iowans include Herbert Hoover, John L. Lewis, Glenn Miller, and Grant Wood.

Iran-Contra Affair (1986), secret effort by officials of the Reagan administration to obtain release of U.S. hostages in Lebanon by selling U.S. weapons to Iran. Profits of the sales were secretly funneled to the Contras in Nicaragua (American-backed rebels who were trying to overthrow their government) at a time when Congress had prohibited such aid. A joint congressional committee held televised hearings in the spring of 1987 to investigate the covert operation. Implicated were National Security Council members Adm. John Poindexter and Lt. Col. Oliver North. Both men were convicted on criminal charges by federal juries in 1988 and 1989, but their convictions were set aside and finally dropped in 1991. Still at issue was whether President Ronald Reagan knew anything about the diversion of money to the Contras.

Iraq War (March 19–May 1, 2003), U.S. and British invasion of Iraq, leading to the collapse of the Iraqi government. Ground forces from Australia and

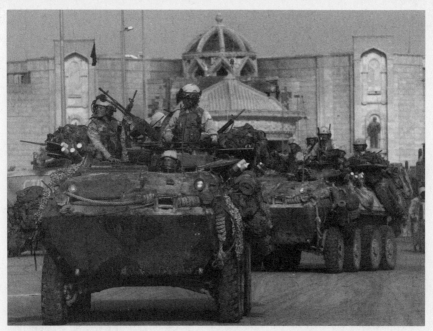

Iraq War
U.S. Marines occupy Saddam Hussein's palace in Tikrit.

Poland, and naval forces from Denmark and Spain also took part, as well as Iraqi Kurdish militia troops supported by the coalition forces. The war, dubbed Operation Iraqi Freedom, divided the international community and led to global protests and peace demonstrations.

Throughout 2002, the Bush administration focused on Iraq as part of its WAR ON TERRORISM, claiming that Iraq was part of an "axis of evil," supporting terrorist organizations and producing weapons of mass destruction. The UN launched weapons inspections in the country, but by early 2003 the United States and Britain, claiming that Iraq was not cooperating with the inspectors, sought UN authorization of force against Iraq. Many countries, including France, Germany, and Russia, opposed military action, arguing that more time was needed. Lacking the support needed for UN approval, the United States pursued military action with a coalition of willing countries.

U.S.-led forces, under the command of Gen. TOMMY FRANKS, invaded Iraq in late March with the goals of removing Iraqi leader Saddam Hussein from power and destroying the country's banned weapons. In less than a month, they took control of all major cities and oil fields, including the capital city of Baghdad, and overthrew the government of Hussein, whose whereabouts were unknown. The United States and its allies then began the process of rebuilding Iraq and establishing an interim government, with plans to remain until a transition to stable civilian rule could be made.

Just forty-three days after announcing the start of the war, President GEORGE W. BUSH officially declared that it had been won and announced the end of combat on May 1, 2003. However, casualties continued as conflicts erupted between Iraqi resistance and occupying troops. The capture of Saddam Hussein in December 2003 did not quell the violence in Iraq. The failure to uncover chemical, biological, or nuclear weapons led to controversy over the U.S. rationale for going to war, suggesting that the administration may have exaggerated the threat posed by Iraq. The United States sustained a total of one hundred thirty-eight casualties between March 20 and May 1, 2003. By March 19, 2004, the one-year anniversary of the war, there had been five hundred seventy-two American deaths. The rising death toll prompted a reversal in the Bush administration's Iraq policy. In a deal with the Iraqi Governing Council, the United States agreed to transfer power to an interim government in July 2004.

In April 2004 the revelation of abuse of Iraqi detainees at a U.S.-run prison near Baghdad further damaged the U.S. effort and stirred international outrage. Army investigations led to court martial, prison terms, and dishonorable dismissal of several military personnel.

Irving, John (1942–), author. Irving's novels present a sentimental view of humanity through the lively and sometimes absurd adventures of eccentric characters. *The World According to Garp* (1978) earned him a huge following and a National Book Award nomination. Other best sellers include *The Hotel New Hampshire* (1981); *The Cider House Rules* (1985) (Irving won an Oscar for best screenplay of the movie version); *A Prayer for Owen Meany* (1989); *A Widow for One Year* (1998); and *The Fourth Hand* (2001).

Irving, Washington (1783–1859), writer. Irving's extensive European travel inspired a varied collection of works, from humorous stories to satirical essays to history and biography. A respected writer during his own time, he exerted significant influence on other writers and helped establish the popularity of the short story. Best known for his collection *The Sketch Book of Geoffrey Crayon, Gent.* (1820), which includes "Rip Van Winkle" and "The Legend of Sleepy Hollow," Irving also wrote a five-volume biography, *The Life of George Washington* (1855–59).

Isolationism, a national policy of avoiding political or economic entanglements with other nations. Isolationism in the United States had its roots in the colonial period, when settlers hoped to find social, religious, and political structures distinct from and superior to those which they had left behind in Europe. Advocated by influential early leaders such as Washington and Jefferson, isolationism remained the dominant U.S. policy into the twentieth century. Even during the nineteenth century, however, isolationism was undermined by increasing social and economic ties with

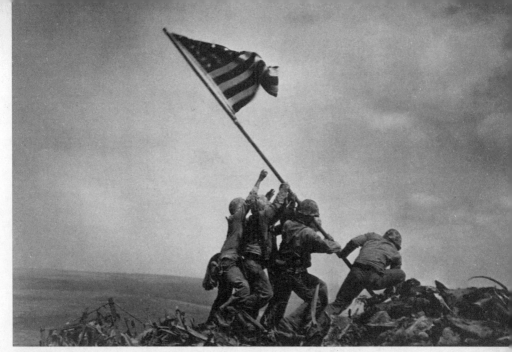

Iwo Jima
Marines raising the American flag on Iwo Jima.

Europe, urbanization, the growth of international finance, and improved international transportation and communications. The two World Wars — and especially the Japanese attack on PEARL HARBOR — effectively discredited the position of self-protective neutrality and forced the United States to assume a leadership role in the defense and spread of democracy.

Iwo Jima, Battle of (February 19–March 17, 1945), battle in the Pacific campaign during WORLD WAR II, when the U.S. Marines invaded the strongly fortified island. Although the capture of the island boosted morale of American forces in the last stages of the war, it came at the cost of heavy casualties. An estimated 4,600 Americans and 20,000 Japanese lost their lives. Following the victory the United States used the island as a base from which to bomb Japanese cities. A Pulitzer Prize-winning photo of the flag raising atop Iwo Jima's Mount Suribachi became one of the most famous pictures of World War II.

J **Jackson, Andrew** (1767–1845), seventh president of the United States (1829–37). Born in Waxhaw, South Carolina, Jackson served as a lad in the colonial army during the American Revolution and was later elected to the House of Representatives (1796–97) and the U.S. Senate from Tennessee (1797–98). He gained a reputation as an Indian fighter when he defeated the Creeks in the Battle of HORSESHOE BEND and became the hero of the WAR OF 1812 with his decisive 1815 victory over the British at New Orleans. Jackson then led successful campaigns against the Seminoles and became the first governor of the Florida Territory in 1821.

Jackson ran for president in the ELECTION OF 1824, one of four candidates. Although he received a plurality of the popular votes, he did not receive a majority of the electoral votes, so the decision went to the House of Representatives. There the Speaker of the House HENRY CLAY threw his support to JOHN QUINCY ADAMS, thereby electing Adams. Jackson claimed a "corrupt bargain" had taken place when Adams appointed Clay secretary of state. As leader of the DEMOCRATIC PARTY, Jackson easily won the presidency in 1828, becoming the first man from west of the Appalachians to be elected president. He was called the "common man's president," for he had grown up poor and was sympathetic to the non-elite.

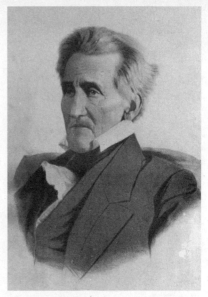

Andrew Jackson

The EATON AFFAIR in 1829 tarnished the beginning of his term of office and resulted in a reorganization of his cabinet in 1831. Jackson used the SPOILS SYSTEM to reward his backers during his presidency and vetoed the rechartering of the Second Bank of the United States. A hard-money advocate, he thought the Bank would give too much power over people's money to a few private individuals — the bankers. He threatened to use force to collect the tariff in South Carolina and was a key player in the relocation of American Indians from the Southeast to Indian Territory known as the TRAIL OF TEARS. As president he affirmed the supremacy of the federal government over the states. The reforms and reform movements stimulated by Jackson resulted in what is called JACKSONIAN DEMOCRACY. His reelection in 1832 marked the first time national political conventions chose candidates for president.

Jackson, Helen Hunt (1830–85), author. As a result of her book *A Century of Dishonor* (1881), which documented U.S. government injustices against American Indians, Jackson led a special commission to investigate living conditions of Native Americans in the California missions. A determined crusader for Indian rights, Jackson later wrote the classic novel *Ramona* (1884), a story about Native American mistreatment that was the basis for three motion pictures.

Jackson, Jesse (1941–), clergyman, civil rights leader, and politician. In the ELECTIONS OF 1984 and 1988, Jackson became the first black to be a serious contender for the U.S. presidency. Although he failed to secure the Democratic nomination, he gained recognition as an effective orator and advocate of minorities. An ordained Baptist minister, Jackson became the youngest worker with MARTIN LUTHER KING, JR., in 1965. After King's death in 1968, Jackson directed Operation Breadbasket and founded People United to Serve Humanity (PUSH) to promote economic opportunity for blacks. He also headed the Rainbow Coalition, an independent political organization aimed at uniting racial minorities. Jackson won the 1989 NAACP SPINGARN MEDAL and continues to be an important leader and spokesman on national and international issues.

Jackson, Mahalia (1911–72), black gospel singer. Jackson helped popularize gospel music with her renditions of such songs as "He's Got the Whole World in His Hands" and "When I Wake Up in Glory." Known for her rich, powerful voice, she toured internationally and sang on radio and television; because of her religious convictions, she refused to appear in nightclubs. Jackson worked closely with the civil rights movement of the 1960s.

Jackson, Maynard (1938–2003), politician. In 1965 Jackson became a lawyer with the first and largest black law firm in Atlanta, Georgia. In 1974 he was elected mayor of Atlanta, the first black mayor of a major southern city, and served until 1982. He was reelected in 1989.

Jackson, Michael (1958–), rock singer and songwriter. The integration of his singular voice and intricate dancing with music that combines soul, rhythm and blues, and rock has made him an international solo star. *Thriller* (1982) became the largest-selling album ever when it sold 40 million copies. He also helped pioneer the music video as art form and advertising. In 2004 Jackson was indicted for and pleaded not guilty to child molestation charges.

Jackson, Robert H. (1892–1954), lawyer and judge. Franklin D. Roosevelt appointed Jackson attorney general in 1940 and associate justice of the U.S. Supreme Court in 1941. He went on leave from the Court in 1945 to serve as chief U.S. prosecutor at the Nuremberg war crimes trials. A devoted civil libertarian and the master of a terse but elegant literary style, Jackson wrote several books including *The Case against the Nazi War Criminals* (1946) and *The Supreme Court in the American System of Government* (1955).

Jackson, Shirley (1919–65), writer. Known for her stories mixing the conventions of the Gothic tale with psychological horror, Jackson could detect the evil in everyday life. Her best-known short story, "The Lottery" (1947), and her novel, *The Haunting of Hill House* (1959), depict tragedy and sacrifice. Jackson also wrote humorous stories about her family in *Life among the Savages* (1953) and *Raising Demons* (1957).

Jackson, "Shoeless" Joe (1887–1951), baseball player. One of the finest natural hitters in baseball history, Jackson played for the Philadelphia Athletics, Cleveland Indians, and Chicago White Sox, achieving a .356 career batting average. In the 1919 "Black Sox" scandal, he was tried with seven other White Sox players for taking bribes to throw World Series games and was barred from major league baseball for life. He maintained his innocence, but the scandal cost him membership in baseball's Hall of Fame. Jackson played a game in the minor leagues without shoes owing to an injury, thus acquiring the appellation "Shoeless."

Jackson, "Stonewall" (Thomas J.; 1824–63), Confederate general during the CIVIL WAR. Jackson won the name "Stonewall" for his determined stand against the Union forces at the first Battle of BULL RUN in 1861. During the Shenandoah Valley campaign of 1862, he displayed his outstanding talent for strategy and military leadership. He led troops in the first and second Battles of Bull Run, FREDERICKSBURG, SEVEN DAYS' BATTLES, and CHANCELLORSVILLE, all Southern victories. Jackson, like his Union counterpart WILLIAM TECUMSEH SHERMAN, pioneered the use of destructive war against the enemy's economic and agricultural resources and civilian population. He was accidentally shot by one of his own troops after the Battle of Chancellorsville and died a week later.

Jacksonian Democracy, a concept that flourished during the presidency of ANDREW JACKSON and the generation that followed. The national nominating convention replaced the party caucus. With religious and property qualifications for voting abolished, the ordinary man (though only the *white man*) could vote and hold public office. The insane, the blind, the deaf, and prisoners began to receive better treatment. Movements formed that advocated free public education and women's rights. But there was a dark side to the Jacksonian era, too: a resurgence of nativism, hostility to immigrants and those espousing minority religious and political views, the condoning of the evils of slavery, and aggressive racist measures against Native Americans. The tenor of the time was much influenced by Jackson's own sympathies, as well as his prejudices.

James, Henry (1843–1916), novelist and critic. James published short stories, novels, plays, reviews, and essays on literary criticism. Many of his works emphasize psychological subtlety, the clash of values within a character's mind and heart, and the contrast between the manners and morals of complex, sophisticated Europeans and fresh, innocent Americans. Some of his many novels include *The Portrait of a Lady* (1881), *Washington Square* (1881), *The Wings of the Dove* (1902), and *The Turn of the Screw* (1898). The brother of philosopher WILLIAM JAMES he made his home in England, moving there permanently in 1875 and becoming a citizen in 1915.

James, Jesse (1847–82), outlaw. James began his life of crime in Missouri at age fifteen as a member of a Confederate guerrilla band led by WILLIAM

QUANTRILL. He became infamous following the Civil War as the leader of the James gang, a band of raiders that included his brother, Frank. They robbed banks, trains, and coaches, killing many of their victims and eluding Pinkerton detectives. James was murdered by gang member Bob Ford, who hoped to collect a large reward offered by the Missouri governor.

James, William (1842–1910), psychologist and philosopher. As a major philosopher of the 1900s, James codeveloped the philosophy of pragmatism with Charles Peirce and JOHN DEWEY. He helped popularize the movement through his writings, which stressed the importance of evaluating ideas by their consequences and outcomes rather than their origins. His major works include *The Principles of Psychology* (1890), *The Varieties of Religious Experience* (1902), *Pragmatism* (1907), and *The Meaning of Truth* (1909). He was the brother of novelist HENRY JAMES.

Jamestown, the first permanent English settlement in North America. Founded in 1607 on the James River in present-day Virginia, it was named for King James I of England. Originally settled by about a hundred people, the colony suffered from disease and starvation, which killed about two-thirds of the settlers. Capt. JOHN SMITH's discipline helped save the colony until new settlers and supplies arrived from England. JOHN ROLFE turned the cultivation of tobacco into a major cash crop to be traded with England.

Japanese-American Internment, a WORLD WAR II action decided on by the president and his advisers in February 1942, following Japan's attack on PEARL HARBOR, and carried out under Executive Order 9066. Federal officials, fearing groundlessly that Americans of Japanese ancestry might cooperate with a West Coast invasion by Japan, forcibly relocated over 100,000 Japanese-Americans, including U.S. citizens, to internment camps inland and seized their property. In 1944 the order was rescinded and by 1945 the camps were closed. The CIVIL LIBERTIES ACT of 1988 provided compensation of $20,000 each to the 60,000 surviving internees.

Jaworski, Leon (1905–82), special prosecutor in the WATERGATE scandal. His investigations led to President RICHARD M. NIXON's resignation in 1974.

Jay, John (1745–1829), diplomat and first chief justice of the United States. Jay began his political career as member and later president of the CONTINENTAL CONGRESS and as minister to Spain. As a member of the American peace commission at the end of the American Revolution, Jay helped negotiate the TREATY OF PARIS in 1783 with England. He strongly urged ratification of the Constitution in his essays for the FEDERALIST PAPERS. Appointed by George Washington as first chief justice of the United States in 1789, Jay resigned in 1795 to become governor of New York. He negotiated the JAY TREATY with England in 1794.

Jay Treaty (1794–95), agreement between the United States and Great Britain to resolve violations of the TREATY OF PARIS following the American

Revolution. Negotiated by Chief Justice JOHN JAY, this became the United States' first treaty. The English agreed to withdraw from their fur-trading posts in the Northwest Territory, settle boundary disputes, and pay American shipowners for ships they had seized. The treaty failed to solve the problem of British impressment of American sailors, contributing to its unpopularity, especially among the Democratic-Republicans.

Jazz Age *See* ROARING TWENTIES.

Jeffers, Robinson (1887–1962), poet. Isolated from civilization in his home near Carmel on the California coast, Jeffers was inspired by nature and came to view human beings as insignificant in contrast. His works include *Tamar and Other Poems* (1924) and an adaptation of Euripides' *Medea* (1946).

Jefferson, Joseph (1829–1905), actor. Jefferson began his career at age three. He grew up acting with traveling troupes, performing in over a hundred plays by the time he was thirty. Jefferson coauthored the dramatization of WASHINGTON IRVING's short story *Rip Van Winkle* (1865). With Jefferson playing the title role for thirty-eight years, it was one of the most popular comedies on the American stage from 1866 to 1905.

Jefferson, Thomas (1743–1826), third president of the United States (1801–09). Born in Goochland, Virginia, Jefferson studied at the College of William and Mary in Williamsburg before entering politics. He became a member of the Virginia House of Burgesses (1769–75), where his advocacy of American rights earned him a place in the Second Continental Congress. There he wrote the Declaration of Independence in 1776. Jefferson resigned from Congress and returned to Virginia, where he promoted reforms; he wrote Virginia's statute establishing freedom of religion and became governor (1779–81).

Jefferson succeeded Benjamin Franklin as minister to France and served as the first secretary of state under George Washington. Sharp differences between Jefferson and Secretary of the Treasury ALEXANDER HAMILTON resulted in the formation of the first political parties. The Federalists adopted Hamilton's philosophies; Jefferson helped bring together the DEMOCRATIC-REPUBLICAN PARTY. His vice presidency (1797–1801) under John Adams (a Federalist) strengthened the Democratic-Republicans, who secured his election as president in the ELECTION OF 1800 and reelection in 1804. During his presidency Jefferson in 1803 acquired the Louisiana Territory from France (doubling the size of the country) and authorized its exploration by the LEWIS AND CLARK EXPEDITION. The LIBRARY OF CONGRESS and the U.S. Military Academy were established. Jefferson sent a naval force against the BARBARY PIRATES and imposed the EMBARGO ACT in 1807, which was repealed before he left office.

Honored as a statesman and intellectual, Jefferson is also recognized as an agriculturist, musician, inventor, and one of America's foremost architects. His architectural designs include his home in MONTICELLO, the

University of Virginia, which he founded in 1819, and the Virginia Capitol. Both he and John Adams died on July 4, 1826, the fiftieth anniversary of the Declaration of Independence. He directed that his epitaph read: "Author of the Declaration of Independence, the Statute of Virginia for Religious Freedom, and father of the University of Virginia."

Jeffersonian Democracy, a political concept fostered by THOMAS JEFFERSON and the generation that followed him. Jefferson advocated a simple, frugal government geared to the average citizen rather than the rich and well-born. He began his administration by walking to his inauguration rather than riding in a carriage. He ended the glittering presidential receptions of his predecessors and sent written messages to Congress rather than delivering a formal address in person. He tried to eliminate the national debt, reduce the size of the army and navy, cut spending, and lower taxes. Jefferson's ideal was an agrarian republic in which states' rights and the individual's civil liberties were foremost.

Jennings, Peter (1938–), network news anchor. Born in Toronto and raised in Ottawa, Jennings had his own children's radio show on the Canadian Broadcasting Company (CBC) called *Peter's People* when he was nine years old. He worked with CBC radio and television, then joined ABC News in 1964, becoming America's youngest national network anchor ever as host of the *ABC Evening News* (1965–68). Following three years of poor ratings, Jennings became a foreign correspondent, establishing the first American television news bureau in the Middle East. He became anchor and senior editor of *World News Tonight* (1983–), which has often been the top-rated news show. Jennings became a U.S. citizen in 2003, legally acquiring dual citizenship with the United States and Canada.

Jim Crow Laws, laws that segregated races in the South beginning in the 1880s following Reconstruction. Jim Crow laws discriminated against blacks in public schools, railroads, buses, restaurants, theaters, hotels, and other public facilities. The Supreme Court decision PLESSY v. FERGUSON (1896) declared segregation constitutional. But decisions in the 1950s and 1960s, such as BROWN V. BOARD OF EDUCATION OF TOPEKA and the civil rights movement of the same period overturned these laws. "Jim Crow" was a character in a popular song of the 1830s, and the name was commonly used to refer to blacks.

Jobs, Steve (1955–), computer designer and executive. Along with Steve Wozniak, Jobs founded Apple Computer, Inc., in a garage in 1976. With Jobs as its chairman, Apple Computer quickly became a major competitor in the high-tech world. He helped make California's SILICON VALLEY a world-renowned center of high technology. After leaving Apple in 1986, Jobs founded NeXT Software, Inc., and Pixar, an Academy-Award-winning animation studio. He returned to Apple in 1997 as CEO and initiated a number of successful new hardware and software products.

John Birch Society, ultraconservative political organization. Founded in 1958 by retired business executive Robert Welch, the goal of this membership-based organization was originally to fight what was perceived to be the infiltration of communism within the United States. It was named after a Baptist missionary and intelligence agent killed by Communists in China in 1945. Other objectives include cutting federal taxes, repealing the Social Security Act, the impeachment of various high government officials, U.S. withdrawal from the United Nations, reclaiming the Panama Canal, and ending busing for the purpose of school integration.

John Brown's Raid (October 16–18, 1859), seizure of the U.S. arsenal at Harpers Ferry, Virginia. JOHN BROWN, an ardent ABOLITIONIST who had been part of the strife in BLEEDING KANSAS, planned to distribute rifles to slaves and start a massive rebellion against southern slave owners. The venture failed when, in the course of the raid, Brown and his followers were captured by a force commanded by Col. Robert E. Lee and Lt. J.E.B. Stuart. Brown was tried for treason, convicted, and hanged along with six of his men on December 2, 1859. The raid created political turmoil and inflamed the South, creating an even sharper division between pro- and antislavery forces prior to the CIVIL WAR.

Johns, Jasper (1930–), painter and sculptor. Johns began his career in POP ART, but later worked in a more abstract style. He became famous for paintings of everyday objects such as flags, targets, and numbers, as well as sculptures of beer cans, light bulbs, and flashlights. Johns sometimes combined mediums, including paint, sculpture, and collage.

Johnson, Andrew (1808–75), seventeenth president of the United States (1865–69) and the first president ever to be impeached, though he was acquitted. Born in Raleigh, North Carolina, Johnson moved to Greeneville, Tennessee, where he worked as a tailor. His interest in politics and the plight of the working man led to his election to several local offices and service in the Tennessee state legislature. A Jackson Democrat, Johnson served five terms in the House of Representatives (1843–53), two terms as governor of Tennessee (1853–57), and in the U.S. Senate (1857–62). In the Senate he pushed for the HOMESTEAD ACT and took a middle course on the slavery issue, favoring both the Union and slavery. In 1862 President Abraham Lincoln appointed him military governor of Tennessee after the state seceded. Johnson remained loyal to the Union, the only U.S. senator from seceding states to do so.

Although a Democrat, he became Lincoln's vice-presidential running mate in 1864 to help unite the Union, and succeeded to the presidency on April 15, 1865, when Lincoln was assassinated. He became embroiled in disputes with Congress over how to treat the South following the war. Johnson's vetoes of the Freedmen's Bureau and civil rights bill were overridden by the RADICAL REPUBLICANS. The president's removal of Secretary of War EDWIN STANTON in defiance of the TENURE OF OFFICE ACT prompted the House of Representatives to pass resolutions of IMPEACHMENT. Johnson was not removed from office because the U.S. Senate failed by one vote to secure the two-thirds majority needed for conviction. He completed his term and became the only president to return to the Senate, though he served only briefly before his death. During Johnson's administration, the Thirteenth and Fourteenth Amendments were ratified.

Johnson, Eastman (Jonathan Eastman; 1824–1906), artist. Johnson's studies in Holland influenced his skillful genre paintings of country life and portraits of many of his famous contemporaries. Known as "the American Rembrandt," he imitated the naturalistic style of the Dutch masters in his works, which include *The Fugitive Slaves* and *Cranberry Pickers.*

Johnson, Hiram (1866–1945), politician. Johnson's success as a prosecuting attorney in San Francisco led to his election as a liberal Republican governor of California in 1910. He broke the political domination of the Southern Pacific Railroad in California and promoted political and social reforms. A founder of the PROGRESSIVE PARTY, he was THEODORE ROOSEVELT's running mate in the ELECTION OF 1912, losing to the Democrats and WOODROW WILSON. Johnson was reelected governor, but resigned in 1917 to enter the U.S. Senate (1917–45). An initial supporter of the Hoover administration, Johnson later became its bitter opponent, in 1932 giving his support to FRANKLIN D. ROOSEVELT and the NEW DEAL. A strong isolationist, Johnson opposed the LEAGUE OF NATIONS and America's entry into both WORLD WARS I and II.

Johnson, Hugh (1882–1942), U.S. Army general, business executive. After graduation from the U.S. Military Academy in 1903, Johnson joined the army and became a brigadier general. He designed and directed the draft during World War I and served on the War Industries Board. In 1933 FRANKLIN D. ROOSEVELT appointed Johnson to head the newly created National Recovery Administration. He adopted the famous blue eagle emblem with the slogan "We Do Our Part" to be displayed by businesses and industries committed to ensuring shorter work hours, better wages, and fairer labor standards. He broke with F.D.R. over the SUPREME COURT PACKING PLAN and later opposed both the president and his programs. From 1935 until his death, Johnson wrote a syndicated column for the Scripps-Howard newspapers.

Johnson, Jack (1878–1946), boxer. Johnson became the first black to win the world's heavyweight championship, defeating Tommy Burns in Sydney, Australia, in 1908. Resentment among whites induced Jeffries J. James to come out of retirement in 1910 to unsuccessfully challenge Johnson for the title. This loss caused racial unrest and violence in many cities across the country. For seven years Johnson defeated all challengers until he was knocked out by Jess Willard in Havana, Cuba, in 1915. Later Johnson wrote that he had thrown the fight and let Willard win.

Johnson, James Weldon (1871–1938), black writer, lawyer, and diplomat. A leader in the HARLEM RENAISSANCE of the 1920s, Johnson wrote and compiled anthologies of black American poetry and songs, including "Lift Every Voice and Sing," as well as novels such as *The Autobiography of an Ex-Coloured Man* (1912). The first black to be admitted to the Florida bar in 1897, Johnson was a founder and secretary (1916–30) of the NATIONAL ASSOCIATION FOR THE ADVANCEMENT OF COLORED PEOPLE (NAACP). He served under Presidents Theodore Roosevelt and William Howard Taft as a consul in Venezuela and Nicaragua.

Johnson, John Harold (1918–), black publisher and banker. Johnson founded the Johnson Publishing Company in Chicago in 1942. He became the most successful black publisher in America, founding *Negro Digest* (1942) and *Ebony* (1945). Johnson also published *Jet,* a weekly news magazine. His magazines were the first black publications with substantial national advertising. He received the NAACP's SPINGARN MEDAL in 1966.

Johnson, Lyndon Baines (1908–73), thirty-sixth president of the United States (1963–69). Born in Stonewall, Texas, Johnson began his career as a speech and debate teacher. In 1937 he was elected to the U.S. House of Representatives as a New Deal Democrat. He joined the U.S. Senate in 1948 and served as majority leader from 1955 to 1961.

After losing the 1960 presidential nomination to John F. Kennedy, Johnson agreed to run as vice president, and the Kennedy-Johnson ticket narrowly won the ELECTION OF 1960. Johnson succeeded to the presidency following Kennedy's assassination on November 22, 1963. He obtained support for civil rights legislation in 1964, and after his landslide victory in the presidential ELECTION OF 1964, he convinced Congress to pass his domestic programs for a GREAT SOCIETY. But his popularity waned because of his escalation of the VIETNAM WAR. Johnson astounded the nation when he decided not to run for reelection in 1968 and retired to his ranch at Johnson City, Texas.

Johnson, "Magic" (Earvin; 1959–), basketball player. A guard for the Los Angeles Lakers, Johnson has been described by his peers as the greatest star (along with MICHAEL JORDAN) in the history of the sport. As an All-American at Michigan State, he led his team to the National Collegiate Athletic Association championship in 1979. With him, the Lakers won five National Basketball Association championships. Johnson was named most valuable player three times and led the NBA in assists four times; in 1991 he became the all-time NBA assist leader. Johnson retired from play in 1991 after testing positive for the HIV virus and became involved in efforts to promote public awareness and prevention of AIDS. In 1992, Johnson played on the gold-medal U.S. Olympic team in Barcelona, Spain. He briefly attempted a return to the NBA before retiring with the NBA record for career assists (9,921).

Johnson, Rafer (1935–), track athlete. While a student at UCLA, Johnson made his mark in the decathlon. He won the Pan-American decathlon championship in 1955. As the world record holder at the time, he took the silver medal at the 1956 Melbourne Olympics and the gold in 1960 in Rome. After retiring from track and field competition following the 1960 games, Johnson became a sportscaster, film actor, and successful business man. Widely regarded as one of the greatest all-around athletes of all time, he was honored as torch lighter for the opening ceremonies of the Los Angeles Olympic Games in 1984.

Johnson, Richard (1780–1850), vice president of the United States (1837–41) under Martin Van Buren. Johnson served in the U.S. House of Representatives and the Senate from Kentucky and fought in the War of 1812. It was he who killed the Indian leader Tecumseh. Johnson was the only vice president ever elected by the Senate, because he did not receive a majority of the electoral votes in the ELECTION OF 1836.

Johnson, Robert L. (1946–), founder and CEO of Black Entertainment Television (BET). Born the ninth of ten children to a poor family in Hickory, Mississippi, Johnson was an accomplished student, becoming the first person in his family to attend college. He earned a scholarship to the University of Illinois and got his master's degree in international affairs from Princeton. In 1980 Johnson launched BET, a cable network geared to black audiences, whose reach grew to seventy-four million homes in 2003. In 2001 he became the first African-American billionaire when he sold his company to Viacom for $3 billion. In 2003 he became the first African-American to be a majority owner of a pro sports team, purchasing the NBA expansion franchise in Charlotte, North Carolina, as well as the Charlotte Sting of the Women's National Basketball Association. To be called the Charlotte Bobcats, the team will play their inaugural season in 2004–05. Johnson is also the first black person to hold a controlling interest in a team in any of the four major pro sports leagues: the NBA, NFL, NHL, and MLB.

Johnson, Walter (1887–1946), baseball pitcher. Called "the Big Train" and noted for his fastball, Johnson won 416 games for the Washington Senators in the American League during his twenty-one-year career. He won twenty or more games for ten straight years with a season high of thirty-six in 1913. Johnson holds the major league record of 110 shutouts and pitched 801 games for the Senators, a record for the most with one baseball team. He became a member of the baseball Hall of Fame in 1936.

Johnston, Albert Sidney (1803–62), Confederate general during the CIVIL WAR. Johnston served in the Texas army and later as secretary of war for the Texas Republic. He resigned from office and entered the U.S. Army, conducting a successful, bloodless campaign against the Mormons in 1857. With the outbreak of the Civil War, Johnston joined the Confederacy. His attack on Ulysses S. Grant's forces at SHILOH almost won the battle, but he was killed in action the day before the Southern troops retreated.

Johnston, Joseph E. (1807–91), Confederate general during the CIVIL WAR. In command of the Army of Northern Virginia, Johnston helped rout the Union at the first Battle of BULL RUN. He watched as Vicksburg surrendered to Ulysses S. Grant and later became commander of the Army of Tennessee. President Jefferson Davis relieved Johnston of command in 1864, but he returned in 1865 only to surrender to Union Gen. William Tecumseh Sherman at Durham Station, North Carolina. Johnston later served in the U.S. House of Representatives (1879–81) from Virginia.

Jolson, Al (Asa Yoelson; 1886–1950), Russian-born singer and actor of the 1920s and 1930s. Best known for his blackface singing routines, Jolson became one of Broadway's top stars, singing such classics as "Swanee," "Mammy," "Sonny-Boy," and "April Showers." Jolson made film history when he starred in the first full-length sound feature, *The Jazz Singer,* in 1927.

Jones, Bobby (Robert Tyre, Jr.; 1902–71), golfer. Jones dominated golf by winning thirteen major championships in an amateur career that lasted only eight years. These included the U.S. Open four times, the British Open three times, and the U.S. Amateur five times. His record sweep in 1930 of the U.S. Open, British Open, U.S. Amateur, and British Amateur (collectively known as the Grand Slam of golf) has never been equaled. Jones established the Masters' Tournament in Augusta, Georgia, in 1934.

Jones, James (1921–77), novelist. Service in the army during World War II, during which he won a Purple Heart, gave Jones firsthand experience for his classic war novel *From Here to Eternity* (1951) about army life in Hawaii prior to the attack on Pearl Harbor. Other naturalistic novels include *Some Came Running* (1958), *The Pistol* (1959), and *The Thin Red Line* (1963).

Jones, James Earl (1931–), actor. Jones achieved stardom playing Jack Jefferson, the black prizefighter, in *The Great White Hope* (1968). A veteran Shakespearean actor, Jones starred in *Othello* and *King Lear.* He used his well-known deep, rich, melodic voice in the role of Darth Vader in the classic *Star Wars* trilogy. Jones is also a civil rights activist.

Jones, John Paul (1747–92), Scottish-born naval hero of the AMERICAN REVOLUTION. Jones commanded several ships for the Continental navy, including *Bonhomme Richard,* which he named as a tribute to Benjamin Franklin. In 1779 he defeated the more heavily armed British ship *Serapis* in the North Sea. When asked to surrender, Jones replied, "I have not yet begun to fight," words that have become part of the U.S. naval battle cry. After the war, Jones served as an admiral in the Russian navy.

Jones, Mary Harris ("Mother" Jones; 1830–1930), labor leader. Horrified by the conditions in which miners, railroad workers, women, and children were forced to work, Mother Jones devoted her life to labor causes. She led strikes and organized and supported unions across the nation. Jones continued to work among striking coal miners from Colorado to West Virginia into her nineties.

Joplin, Janis (1943–70), rock singer. Joplin's performance at the 1967 Monterey International Pop Festival launched her career. In a style until then uncharacteristic of white performers or of women, Joplin screamed and wailed in a harsh, rasping voice. She received a frenzied reception usually reserved for male performers at the time. Joplin died at age twenty-seven from an overdose of heroin.

Joplin, Scott (1868–1917), black pianist and composer. Joplin composed and played lively, rhythmic ragtime music. Best known for the "Maple Leaf Rag" (1897), he wrote over two hundred works, including a ballet and two operas. The public's declining interest in rag affected Joplin's life, and he spent his last years in a New York mental hospital. A revival of ragtime in the 1970s featured Joplin's music in the film *The Sting*. He received a special Pulitzer citation in 1976 for his contribution to American music.

Jordan, Barbara (1936–96), educator and politician. Jordan was educated at Texas Southern and Boston Universities, becoming the first black student to graduate from B. U. Law School. A Democrat, she was the first black woman elected to the Texas State Senate (1966–72). When she was elected to the U.S. House of Representatives (1972–78), she became the first back woman to represent a previously Confederate state in Congress. Jordan championed the causes of poor, black, and disadvantaged people. As a member of the House Judiciary Committee, she gained national prominence during the 1974 impeachment hearing of President RICHARD NIXON. Recognized for her dignified oratory, Jordan was chosen as a keynote speaker for the Democratic National Conventions in 1976 and 1992, the first black woman to be selected. Jordan retired from politics due to illness and became a professor at the University of Texas at Austin. In 1994 she was awarded the Presidential Medal of Freedom.

Jordan, Michael (Jeffrey; 1963–), basketball player, businessman. One of the most exciting players in National Basketball Association (NBA) history, Jordan played both guard and forward for the Chicago Bulls. Known for his spectacular shooting and dunk shots and his vertical "air time," Jordan won the most valuable player award five times. Chosen rookie of the year in the 1984–85 season, he led the league in scoring six times, and in 1997 became the third-highest scorer in NBA history. Jordan retired from basketball after the 1993 season to play professional baseball, but returned to the Bulls late in the 1994–95 season. He led the Bulls to six NBA titles between 1991 and

1998 before retiring again in 1999. In 2001 he announced his second return to the NBA to play for the Washington Wizards, retiring from play for a third time at the end of the 2002–03 season.

As a first-team All-American at the University of North Carolina, Jordan helped lead the team to a national championship in 1982 and led the 1984 and 1992 U.S. Olympic basketball teams to gold medals.

Joseph, Chief (1840?–1904), chief of Nez Percé tribe. When gold was discovered in Oregon in the 1870s, the U.S. government appropriated a large part of the Nez Percé reservation in the area without the consent of the Indians whose land it was. When strife ensued over settlers intruding on the land, the tribe decided to flee to Canada. Eluding the pursuing U.S. Army with whom

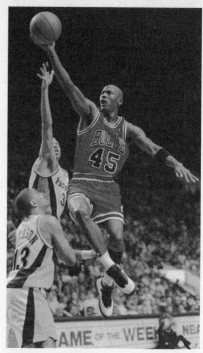

Michael Jordan

they engaged in skirmishes during the summer of 1877, they reached Bear Paw, Montana, forty miles south of the Canadian border, on September 23 and stopped to rest. But Gen. Nelson Miles and the U.S. Cavalry overtook them and forced their surrender on October 5. It was then that Joseph made his famous speech of surrender (for an excerpt, see page 277). He and his tribe were exiled to Indian Territory (present-day Oklahoma) and later were sent to Colville Reservation in Washington, where Joseph died and was buried.

Judah, Theodore D. (1826–63), engineer and railroad builder. By the time he was twenty-eight, Judah had engineered the Niagara Gorge railroad and had completed several eastern railway constructions. Arriving in California in 1854, he became an ardent advocate of a transcontinental railroad, and by 1860 he had drawn a passage through the Sierra Nevada Mountains. Judah interested a number of men in the plan, including COLLIS HUNTINGTON, Mark Hopkins, LELAND STANFORD, and Charles Crocker. The Central Pacific Railroad was formed with Judah as chief engineer. Bitter arguments ensued with his associates, and Judah was on his way to the east to obtain capital and support when he died of yellow fever, never to see the completion of his dream.

★ **Chief Joseph**

An excerpt from Chief Joseph's speech of surrender, delivered October 5, 1877

I am tired of fighting. Our chiefs are killed. . . . The old men are all killed. . . . It is cold and we have no blankets. The little children are freezing to death. My people, some of them, have run away to the hills and have no blankets, no food; no one knows where they are, perhaps freezing to death. I want time to look for my children and see how many of them I can find. Maybe I shall find them among the dead. Hear me, my chiefs, I am tired; my heart is sick and sad. From where the sun now stands, I will fight no more forever.

Judicial Review, the term applied to the power of the U.S. SUPREME COURT to determine the constitutionality of the laws and acts of all branches of government. Although not specifically granted to the Court by the Constitution, the power of judicial review was assumed by the Court in the case of *MARBURY V. MADISON,* in which Chief Justice John Marshall asserted that judicial review was a necessary function of the courts (1803). Since this case, it has been generally accepted as a basic principle of the American government that the power of declaring state and federal laws constitutional or not belongs solely to the U.S. Supreme Court.

Judiciary Act (September 24, 1789), one of the first laws passed by the U.S. Congress under the new Constitution. The Judiciary Act created the office of attorney general, organized the U.S. Supreme Court, and established a system of lower federal courts across the nation.

Judiciary Act (February 13, 1801), law passed by the FEDERALIST-controlled Congress creating sixteen new federal judgeships. Outgoing president JOHN ADAMS filled the posts with Federalists, including John Marshall as chief justice of the Supreme Court, following the DEMOCRATIC-REPUBLICAN victory in the ELECTION OF 1800 but before the inauguration of Thomas Jefferson. The Democratic-Republicans called the appointments the "MIDNIGHT JUDGES," and Congress repealed the act in 1802, restoring the Judiciary Act of 1789.

Justice, Department of, executive department of the U.S. government that has charge of the nation's legal affairs. Created by Congress in 1870, the department enforces federal laws and provides legal advice to the president and other members of government. Its head, the attorney general, appointed by the president with Senate approval, prosecutes those who break federal laws and conducts cases before the Supreme Court. Department of Justice agencies include the Bureau of Prisons, Drug Enforcement Administration, FEDERAL BUREAU OF INVESTIGATION (FBI), and the Immigration and Naturalization Service.

K Kaiser, Henry (1882–1967), industrialist. Kaiser's construction companies were responsible for the building of Hoover, Bonneville, and Grand Coulee Dams, and the San Francisco-Oakland Bay Bridge. His West Coast shipyards during World War II perfected assembly line production of almost 1,500 cargo ships. Kaiser pioneered a nonprofit medical care program, the Kaiser Foundation Medical Care Plan, as a model for health care systems throughout the nation.

Kalamazoo Case (1874), decision by the Michigan Supreme Court that stated tax money could be used to support public high schools and colleges. The decision promoted growth of the U.S. public high school system because it led to the establishment of tax-supported public schools.

Kalb, Johann (1721–80), Germany-born military officer in the Continental army during the AMERICAN REVOLUTION. Kalb came to America with the MARQUIS DE LAFAYETTE in 1777 to fight the British. Known for his bravery, Kalb was mortally wounded at the Battle of Camden in South Carolina.

Kanagawa Treaty (March 31, 1854), agreement between the United States and Japan providing for the opening of two Japanese ports to American merchant ships. The treaty also established an American consulate in Japan and promised the protection of American sailors shipwrecked in Japanese waters. It was the culmination of MATTHEW PERRY's efforts to open up Japan to western powers.

Kansas (Sunflower State) joined the Union as the thirty-fourth state on January 29, 1861. (See maps, pages 540 and 541.) The name is derived from a Sioux word meaning "people of the south wind." Between 1854 and 1861 a civil war existed between proslavery and antislavery settlers in Kansas Territory, giving rise to the label BLEEDING KANSAS. The present-day state leads all others in wheat production, and the nation's largest grain elevator is located near Hutchinson. Major cities include Wichita, one of the country's chief civilian aircraft manufacturing centers, Kansas City, and Topeka, the capital. Noted Kansans include CHARLES CURTIS, AMELIA EARHART, JAMES NAISMITH, and ROBERT DOLE.

Kansas-Nebraska Act (January 4, 1854), bill creating the Kansas and Nebraska Territories on the principle of popular sovereignty: the settlers would decide if their state would be free or slave. Introduced by Senator STEPHEN A. DOUGLAS of Illinois, the Kansas-Nebraska Act repealed the MISSOURI COMPROMISE of 1820. Hostility between free and slave interests escalated, leading to a civil war within Kansas Territory, which became known as BLEEDING KANSAS.

Kaye, Danny (David Daniel Kominski; 1913–87), actor and comedian. Known for his lively pantomimes and creative songs, Kaye starred in films and television, and toured the world entertaining children on behalf of the United Nations Children's Emergency Fund (UNICEF). His films include

The Secret Life of Walter Mitty (1947), *The Inspector General* (1949), *Hans Christian Andersen* (1952), and *White Christmas* (1954).

Kazan, Elia (1909–2003), film and stage director, producer, and writer. Kazan directed numerous critically acclaimed films, winning Academy Awards as best director for *Gentleman's Agreement* (1947) and *On the Waterfront.* (1954). He gained fame for his powerful and realistic direction of the stage productions of *A Streetcar Named Desire* (1947) and *Death of a Salesman* (1948), which became two of the most influential dramas in Broadway history. Other stage successes were *The Skin of Our Teeth* (1942), *All My Sons* (1947), and *Tea and Sympathy* (1953). In 1947 he helped found the Actor's Studio, where, with Lee Strasberg, he pioneered Method Acting, a style based upon inner emotional experience. Many of Kazan's achievements were overshadowed in 1952 when he was called before the HOUSE UN-AMERICAN ACTIVITIES COMMITTEE (HUAC). He confessed his own past Communist party membership and named eight people who had been fellow members in the 1930s; all of them were blacklisted. His decision was seen as a betrayal to the acting community and lost him friends but allowed him to continue to work in Hollywood. Kazan also wrote several novels including *America, America* (1962), *The Arrangement* (1967), and *A Life* (a 1988 autobiography in which he attempted to defend his decision to give names of his former friends to the HUAC). In 1999 the Motion Picture Academy gave him a third Academy Award, for lifetime achievement.

Kearney, Denis (1847–1907), Irish-born political and labor leader. After immigrating to San Francisco about 1868, Kearney organized the Workingman's party of California, leading workers in protests over unfair employment practices and unjust taxes. He bitterly opposed the hiring of Chinese laborers and, later, Japanese immigrants. "Kearneyism" became a synonym for "racism" throughout the American West.

Kearny, Stephen (1794–1848), military leader. Kearny commanded the western armies of the United States during the MEXICAN WAR, conquering New Mexico and California. He joined with Commodore Robert Stockton in 1847 to take control of California and, in a conflict of authority with Stockton, arrested JOHN FRÉMONT for insubordination, resulting in Frémont's court-martial. Ordered to Mexico, Kearny served as military governor of Vera Cruz until his death.

Keating-Owen Child Labor Law (1916), act passed by Congress prohibiting interstate shipment of goods made by children under age fourteen or by children ages fourteen through sixteen who worked more than eight hours per day. In 1918 the U.S. Supreme Court ruled that such an attempt to regulate child labor was unconstitutional, stating that it infringed upon freedom of contract and interfered with the states' right to regulate local manufacturing conditions.

Keaton, Buster (Joseph; 1895–1966), silent film comedian. Sometimes called "the Great Stone Face," Keaton played an unsmiling character who wins out through cleverness and determination. Noted silent films include *Sherlock, Jr.* (1924), *The Navigator* (1924), and *The General* (1927). At the peak of his career he rivaled Charlie Chaplin in popularity, but like Chaplin's later career, Keaton's declined with the arrival of sound films.

Keene, Laura (Mary Moss; 1820?–73), English-born American actress and theatrical manager. Keene, upon arrival in America, performed on tour with Edwin Booth and became the first woman in the United States to work as a major theatrical producer, opening the Laura Keene Theatre in New York in 1866. Her production of *Our American Cousin* achieved critical acclaim, and it was during her performance at Ford's Theatre in Washington, D.C., that Abraham Lincoln was assassinated.

Kefauver, Estes (Carey; 1903–63), politician. Kefauver served as a member of the House of Representatives from Tennessee (1939–49) and then in the U.S. Senate, where he became a national figure in 1950 as head of a committee for investigating organized crime. He unsuccessfully sought the Democratic presidential nomination in 1952 and 1956. He was the vice-presidential candidate on the ticket with Adlai E. Stevenson in the ELECTION OF 1956, losing to Dwight D. Eisenhower and Richard M. Nixon.

Keller, Helen (1880–1968), educator and author. Keller lost her sight and hearing as a result of scarlet fever at age nineteen months. With the help of her teacher, Anne Sullivan, she overcame these disabilities to graduate cum laude from Radcliffe College in 1904. She became a champion of the handicapped upon publication of *The Story of My Life* (1903). Keller wrote books and lectured widely to inspire the blind and deaf and educate the public about the plight of the handicapped. She was also very active in the early twentieth-century peace and civil-liberties movements. Her early experiences with Sullivan were immortalized in William Gibson's play and movie, *The Miracle Worker* (1959).

Kelley, Florence (1859–1932), social reformer. A graduate of Cornell, Northwestern University Law School, and the University of Zurich, Kelley developed socialist views while in Europe. In 1891 she became a resident at JANE ADDAMS's Hull House in Chicago, promoting industrial reform and pro-labor legislation, particularly for women and children. She served as director of the National Consumers' League, helped establish the NATIONAL ASSOCIATION FOR THE ADVANCEMENT OF COLORED PEOPLE (NAACP), and for many years was vice president of the NATIONAL AMERICAN WOMAN SUFFRAGE ORGANIZATION (NAWSO). Also vice president of the Woman's International League for Peace and Freedom, Kelley was a committed pacifist, opposing United States involvement in WORLD WAR I. Kelley crusaded for minimum wage, workmen's compensation, and other social legislation throughout her life.

Kellogg, Frank (1856–1937), political leader. In his role as secretary of state (1925–29), Kellogg negotiated the KELLOGG-BRIAND PACT in 1928 with the aid of French foreign minister Aristide Briand. Kellogg received the Nobel Peace Prize in 1929 and served as a justice on the Permanent Court of International Justice (the World Court) from 1930 to 1935.

Kellogg-Briand Pact (August 27, 1928), an agreement in which more than sixty nations agreed to "outlaw war as an instrument of national policy." Also called the Pact of Paris, and organized by Secretary of State Frank Kellogg and French foreign minister Aristide Briand, the pact was broken when the Japanese invaded Manchuria, China, in 1931. It provided no method to enforce its provisions.

Kelly, Colin (1915–41), military aviator. Kelly was awarded the Distinguished Service Cross posthumously for his heroic bombing attack on a Japanese naval task force in the Philippines. On December 10, 1941, following the Japanese attack on Pearl Harbor, Kelly destroyed the battleship *Haruna*. His plane was hit and Kelly ordered his crew to bail out; he died in the crash.

Kelly, Emmett (1898–1979), clown and circus performer. Kelly created his sad sack "Weary Willie" clown character, a melancholy tramp dressed in a ragged suit. He appeared often with Ringling Brothers and Barnum & Bailey Circus and also entertained before games of the Brooklyn Dodgers and St. Louis Hawks.

Kelly, Gene (1912–96), actor, dancer, director, and choreographer. Gaining attention for his performance in the Broadway production of *Pal Joey* (1940), Kelly made his musical film debut in *For Me and My Gal* (1942). His imaginative, energetic dancing routines have been featured in numerous Hollywood musicals such as *An American in Paris* (1951) and *Singin' in the Rain* (1952). Kelly sang in many of his movies and directed the film *Hello Dolly!* in 1969.

Kelly, Grace (1928–82), film actress and princess of Monaco. Kelly rose to fame as a movie actress, winning an Academy Award for her role in *The Country Girl* in 1954. Other films include *High Society* (1956) and the Hitchcock classics *Rear Window* (1954) and *Dial M for Murder* (1954). Kelly retired from films upon her 1956 marriage to Prince Rainier III of Monaco. She died in an automobile accident near Monaco.

Kelly, Walt (1913–73), cartoonist. His comic strip "Pogo," which first appeared in 1948, peopled the Okefenokee Swamp with 150 animals and satirized politicians and contemporary events. Pogo gained national stature by earning numerous votes in a 1952 presidential write-in campaign. In his most famous strip, Kelly had Pogo declare, "We have met the enemy and he is us," which became a slogan for the environmental movement. Pogo appeared in the comics for twenty-five years and was carried by over 450 newspapers. In 1990 Kelly's children revived the comic strip.

Kemp, Jack (1935–), politician. Kemp was a football quarterback for thirteen years, playing primarily for the San Diego Chargers and the Buffalo Bills. His career in public office began in 1970 when he was elected to the U.S. House of Representatives from New York (1971–89). A conservative Republican, Kemp supported tax cuts and deregulation. He served as secretary of housing and urban development (1989–93) under President GEORGE H. W. BUSH and was the Republican vice presidential candidate in the ELECTION OF 1996.

Kennan, George (1904–96), diplomat and historian. Kennan helped formulate the policy of containment of Soviet Union expansion after World War II. He served as ambassador to Moscow in 1952 and later to Yugoslavia from 1961 to 1963. A key figure in the emergence of the cold war, he wrote an article under the pseudonym "X" expressing Washington's vigorous anti-Soviet policy. Kennan had played an important role in the creation of the MARSHALL PLAN and later became an outspoken critic of American foreign policy. He wrote *Russia Leaves the War* (1956) and *Memoirs, 1925–50* (1967); both books received the Pulitzer Prize and the National Book Award.

Kennedy, Edward M. (Ted; 1932–), politician. The youngest of the nine children of JOSEPH P. KENNEDY, Ted Kennedy was elected to the U.S. Senate from Massachusetts as a Democrat in 1962. Following the deaths of his brothers, JOHN and ROBERT, he became a leader of the liberal congressional forces, advocating social welfare legislation and national health insurance. His political ambitions were crippled in 1969 when he drove his car off a bridge, in Chappaquiddick, Massachusetts, resulting in the drowning death of his companion, Mary Jane Kopechne. Kennedy unsuccessfully challenged Jimmy Carter for the presidential nomination in 1980.

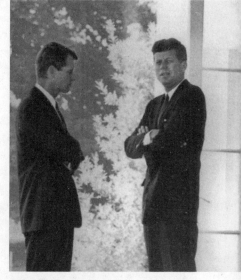

John F. Kennedy and Robert Kennedy
President Kennedy (right) and Robert F. Kennedy conferring at the White House in 1962.

Kennedy, John F. (1917–63), the thirty-fifth president of the United States (1961–63). Born in Brookline, Massachusetts, Kennedy graduated from Harvard and commanded a PT boat during World War II. He became a hero when his boat was sunk and he helped his crew survive. Groomed by his father, JOSEPH

KENNEDY, for high political office, he served in both the House of Representatives (1947–53) and the Senate (1953–60). Chosen as the Democratic candidate for president in the ELECTION OF 1960, Kennedy narrowly defeated Republican Richard M. Nixon. He became the youngest man and first Roman Catholic to be elected president.

Kennedy's charisma, enthusiasm, and intelligence inspired many. Calling his program the NEW FRONTIER, he pushed for federal aid for education, medical care for the aged, and civil rights legislation, but most of his proposals were blocked by Congress. The BAY OF PIGS invasion of Cuba in 1961 marked the low point of his administration, but his handling of the CUBAN MISSILE CRISIS in October 1962, when he forced the Soviet Union to remove its missiles from Cuba, was a highlight of his presidency. Kennedy signed the nuclear test ban treaty in 1963, established the PEACE CORPS, and committed increased numbers of U.S. military "advisers" to South Vietnam. On November 22, 1963, he was assassinated in Dallas, Texas, allegedly by LEE HARVEY OSWALD. He wrote *While England Slept* (1940) and *Profiles in Courage* (1956), which won the Pulitzer Prize in 1957.

Kennedy, Joseph P. (1888–1969), businessman and diplomat. Kennedy served as the first chairman of the Securities and Exchange Commission (1934–35) and as the U.S. ambassador to Great Britain (1937–40). After World War II he bought Chicago's Merchandise Mart, the world's largest commercial building. The father of U.S. senators EDWARD M. KENNEDY and ROBERT F. KENNEDY, and of President JOHN F. KENNEDY, he amassed a huge fortune in oil, real estate, stock speculation, motion pictures, and the importation of Scotch whisky (even during Prohibition).

Kennedy, Robert F. (1925–68), politician. After running his brother JOHN F. KENNEDY's successful senatorial and presidential campaigns, Bobby became U.S. attorney general (1961–64) and JFK's closest adviser. After his brother's death, he resigned to run for the Senate from New York in 1964. As a senator he became a leader of the liberal Democrats, speaking out against poverty and injustice. In 1968 he announced his candidacy for the Democratic nomination for president, running on an anti–Vietnam War platform. On the evening he won the California primary, June 6, 1968, he was assassinated by Sirhan Sirhan following his victory speech.

Kent, James (1763–1847), jurist. Kent strongly influenced the formulation of judicial procedure and legal principles as a member of the New York State Supreme Court from 1798 to 1823. His major work was the four-volume *Commentaries on American Law* (1826–30). Kent helped integrate British common law and American law as modified by the U.S. Constitution.

Kent State Incident (May 4, 1970), episode involving student protesters and National Guardsmen at Kent State University, Ohio. Following RICHARD M. NIXON's announcement on April 30 of the invasion of Cambodia and the need to draft 150,000 more soldiers for the VIETNAM WAR effort, protesters staged antiwar rallies at Kent State. Governor James Rhodes ordered National Guardsmen to the university, where they used tear gas to disperse the dissenters. A shot was heard, and the Guard opened fire on the unarmed students, killing four and wounding nine. The incident evoked massive protests across the country. It was followed ten days later by a similar incident at Jackson State University, an all-black school in Mississippi. Although two students were killed and nine wounded, it went mostly unnoticed, angering many blacks.

Kenton, Stan (1912–79), jazz musician and bandleader. Kenton was known for his innovative and unusual arrangements combining modern jazz and classical music, as well as Latin rhythms. He acquired a national reputation after recording his theme, "Artistry in Rhythm," and led a succession of original bands from the 1950s to the mid 1970s. He helped start the careers of many jazz greats including Maynard Ferguson and Shelly Manne.

Kentucky (Bluegrass State) became the fifteenth state and the first state west of the Appalachian Mountains on June 1, 1792. (See maps, pages 540 and 541.) Its name comes from an Indian word meaning "land of tomorrow." DANIEL BOONE helped blaze the Wilderness Trail through Cumberland Gap and founded Boonesboro. The state's northern border is formed by the Ohio River, making it a border state during the CIVIL WAR, during which it remained in the Union. The capital is Frankfort, and other large cities include Lexington, the horse center of America, and Louisville, famed for the Kentucky Derby held the first Saturday of every May at Churchill Downs. Kentucky is a major producer of horses, tobacco, and whiskey, and it leads the nation in coal production. The country's gold depository is located at Fort Knox. Noted Kentuckians include ABRAHAM LINCOLN, JEFFERSON DAVIS, ALBEN BARKLEY, and ROBERT PENN WARREN.

Kerouac, Jack (1922–69), writer. A leader of the "beatnik" generation, Kerouac chronicled his spontaneous, free-spirited travels around the United States in his best-seller, *On the Road* (1957), making him a cult hero in the beat movement of the 1950s and 1960s. His honest, relaxed, readable style deteriorated in later years, owing to his alcoholism, from which he died.

Kerry, John Forbes (1943–), politician. The son of a career foreign service officer for the U.S. State Department, Kerry spent much of his early life abroad, attending boarding schools in Switzerland and New Hampshire. Following graduation from Yale in 1966, he joined the Navy to serve in the VIETNAM WAR, and was awarded a Silver Star, a Bronze Star, and three Purple Hearts for being wounded in battle three times. Kerry's Vietnam experience disillusioned him about the war, and he became a leading activist against U.S. involvement. He helped found Vietnam Veterans of America and served as the spokesperson for Vietnam Veterans Against the War. Kerry earned a law degree from Boston College in 1976 and won a U.S. Senate seat from Massachusetts in 1984, where he has served for two decades.

A liberal Democrat, Kerry supports gun control, abortion rights, gay rights (but not gay marriage), and has a strong vote on environmental issues. Critical of the foreign policy of GEORGE W. BUSH and his handling of the Iraq War, Kerry was the Democratic candidate for president in the election of 2004.

Key, Francis Scott (1779–1843), lawyer, poet, and writer of "The Star-Spangled Banner" (1814). Sent to secure the release of a friend who had been captured by the British after the burning of Washington, D.C., during the WAR OF 1812, Key was held in temporary custody aboard a prisoner-exchange ship. Throughout the night, he witnessed the British attack on Fort McHenry in Baltimore Harbor. The next morning, the sight of the American flag still flying over the fort inspired him to write on the back of an envelope the poem that later became "The Star-Spangled Banner." The words were set to the music of "To Anacreon in Heaven," an English drinking song. Congress proclaimed it the national anthem in 1931.

King, B. B. (Riley; 1925–), blues singer and guitarist. King's music and innovative manner of playing influenced the development of rock music in the late 1960s, as many white guitarists copied his style. Known as the "Blues Boy from Beale Street" (later shortened to "B. B."), King toured the country's nightclubs for two decades and became the first blues performer to tour the Soviet Union in 1979.

King, Billie Jean (1943–), tennis player. King significantly influenced the growth and popularity of women's sports. She won four U.S. Open and six Wimbledon titles. Playing in various combinations of singles, women's doubles, and mixed doubles, King won a record total of twenty Wimbledon championships. She became *Sports Illustrated*'s first Sportswoman of the Year in 1972 and attracted national attention for women's equality when she defeated former tennis champion Bobby Riggs in the televised "winner-take-all" $100,000 "battle of the sexes" in 1973.

King, Ernest J. (1878–1956), U.S. admiral and commander of the U.S. fleet, and naval operations chief during WORLD WAR II. King was the first man to occupy both posts. In this dual capacity he was responsible for the conduct of all naval warfare in both the Pacific and the Atlantic.

King, Martin Luther, Jr. (1929–68), Baptist minister and black civil rights leader. King, who received a Ph.D. in divinity from Boston University, returned south and led a successful bus boycott protesting segregation in Montgomery, Alabama, in 1955. He founded the Southern Christian Leadership Conference in 1957 to combat segregation and racism, following Mahatma Gandhi's philosophy of nonviolent civil disobedience. An eloquent and charismatic orator, he addressed over a quarter of a million supporters at the Lincoln Memorial with his "I Have a Dream" speech during the March on Washington, D.C., in August 1963. King won the Nobel Peace Prize in 1964. Frequently arrested and the target of violence, he became the subject of FBI investigations and harassment because of J. Edgar Hoover's conviction that he was a Communist and because of his stance against the Vietnam War. He called increasingly for help for the nation's poor and blacks, before assassin James Earl Ray shot and killed him April 4, 1968, in Memphis, Tennessee. In 1986 Congress established King's birthday, January 15, as a federal holiday, to be celebrated on the third Monday in January.

King, Rufus (1755–1827), politician and diplomat. A delegate to the Continental Congress and the Constitutional Convention, King played a key role in the framing of the Constitution. He ran unsuccessfully as the Federalist candidate for vice president in 1804 and 1808 and for the presidency in the ELECTION OF 1816.

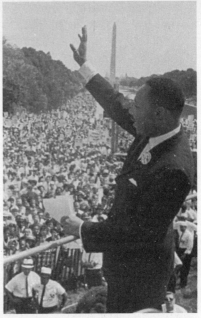

Martin Luther King, Jr.
King addressing demonstrators outside the Lincoln Memorial during the 1963 march on Washington.

King, William Rufus (1786–1853), vice president of the United States (1853). King was elected to the House of Representatives from North Carolina in 1810, serving until he resigned in 1816. In 1818 he settled in Alabama and became one of that state's first U.S. senators, elected first as a Democratic-Republican and later as a Jacksonian (1819–44). He served as president pro tempore for five years. In 1844 President JOHN TYLER appointed King minister to France, where his mission was to convince France not to join Britain in opposing the annexation of Texas. Appointed and later elected as a Democrat to the Senate (1848–52), he later resigned due to poor health. King was elected vice president of the United States with FRANKLIN PIERCE in the ELECTION OF 1852. Because he was suffering from the final stages of tuberculosis, Congress passed a special act enabling him to take the oath of office in Havana, Cuba, where he was seeking a cure, and thus he became the only vice president to take the oath on foreign soil. King died before he could ever serve. In honor of his inauguration, the newly formed Washington Territory created a county, which includes Seattle, that still bears his name.

King Cotton, phrase used by southerners before the Civil War to convey the importance of the production of cotton to the South and the nation.

Southern plantations provided more than three-fourths of the world's supply of raw cotton before 1861. Southern leaders hoped that Great Britain's need for cotton for its textile industry would result in Britain's recognizing the Confederacy as an independent nation, an expectation that failed.

King Philip's War (1675–76), an attempt to oust white settlers from New England. Metacomet (known to the whites as King Philip), son of MASSASOIT, led the uprising, which included forces from the Wampanoag, Narragansett, Nipmuck, and Pocumtuck tribes. Determined to drive all white settlers from New England, the bands destroyed twelve of ninety Puritan towns and attacked forty others. About a thousand Indians were killed, in turn, in the Great Swamp Massacre. The war ended shortly after Metacomet's capture and murder in August 1676. Many of his supporters escaped to Canada while others were sold into slavery in the West Indies.

Kinsey, Alfred (1894–1956), biologist. One of the first scientists to study human sexual behavior, Kinsey founded the Kinsey Institute and conducted research that contributed to the understanding of human relationships. His controversial studies, *Sexual Behavior in the Human Male* (1948) and *Sexual Behavior in the Human Female* (1953), became known as the *Kinsey Report.*

Kissinger, Henry (1923–), German-born foreign policy specialist. Kissinger taught at Harvard University during the 1950s and 1960s. He served as national security adviser from 1969 to 1975, strongly influencing foreign policy. He held the post of secretary of state under Richard M. Nixon and Gerald R. Ford from 1973 to 1977. Kissinger negotiated the cease-fire agreements ending U.S. involvement in the VIETNAM WAR in 1973, for which he won the Nobel Peace Prize. He also opened relations with the People's Republic of China in preparation for Nixon's 1972 visit. Kissinger helped establish the policy of détente with the Soviet Union and was instrumental in the overthrow of the Allende government in Chile in 1975. In 2002, President GEORGE W. BUSH appointed Kissinger to lead a probe into the events of the SEPTEMBER 11, 2001, ATTACKS on New York and Washington, D.C. His appointment led to widespread criticism, and he resigned over possible conflicts of interest.

Kitchen Cabinet, a term applied to political friends of President ANDREW JACKSON, who met with him unofficially in the kitchen of the White House to discuss political affairs. Members of the group included Secretary of State Martin Van Buren; Secretary of War John Eaton; Amos Kendall, fourth auditor of the Treasury; Maj. William Lewis, second auditor of the Treasury; Senator Isaac Hill; and Francis Blair, of the *Washington Globe.* Jackson frequently followed the advice of his friends rather than that of his official cabinet, which was reorganized following the EATON AFFAIR in 1831.

Knights of Labor, the major U.S. workers' organization from 1880 to 1890. First organized in 1871 by URIAH STEVENS (1821–82) as a secret society to protect workers against abuse from employers, the Knights of Labor became one of the first large labor unions in the United States. Its membership consisted of skilled and unskilled workers, farmers, and small businessmen. Its objectives included better working conditions, an eight-hour day, equal pay for men and women, prohibition of child labor, and arbitration of labor disputes. Stephens led the union until 1879, when TERENCE V. POWDERLY took over. Under Powderly, membership reached over 700,000 in 1885. It declined sharply after 1886 because of the HAYMARKET AFFAIR and competition from the craft union-oriented AMERICAN FEDERATION OF LABOR. The Knights formally dissolved in 1917.

Know-Nothing Party, also called the American party, formed in the 1850s to oppose immigration and the election of Roman Catholics to political office. Because its members originally met in secret and were unwilling to divulge what they stood for, their name came from their response to questions: "I know nothing." They nominated ex-president Millard Fillmore in 1856 and won the electoral votes of Maryland. The party failed because of its unwillingness to take a stand on the issue of slavery.

Knox, Henry (1750–1806), general of the AMERICAN REVOLUTION. A friend and adviser to George Washington, Knox took part in all major engagements of the war. He commanded at West Point and served in President Washington's first cabinet as secretary of war (1789–94).

Korean War (1950–53), conflict pitting South Korea and U.N. forces against North Korea and later the People's Republic of China. The war began when the North Korean Communist army crossed the thirty-eighth parallel on June 25, 1950, invading the Republic of South Korea. The UNITED NATIONS Security Council, declaring North Korea an aggressor, sent troops to counter the invasion. Gen. DOUGLAS MACARTHUR led the forces until 1951 when President HARRY S. TRUMAN removed him from command for repeated insubordination and replaced him with Gen. Matthew Ridgway. Sixteen nations sent troops and forty-one countries sent food and supplies, but the United States was the largest contributor of arms, troops, and equipment. After pushing the North Korean troops back above the thirty-eighth parallel, MacArthur pursued them into the North, which resulted in the intervention of Chinese troops. The war reached a stalemate in June 1951, and after two years of negotiations an armistice was signed July 27, 1953, with the thirty-eighth parallel designated as the border between North and South Korea.

Korematsu v. United States (1944), a U.S. Supreme Court decision upholding President Franklin D. Roosevelt's Executive Order 9066, ordering the JAPANESE-AMERICAN INTERNMENT of World War II. The Court upheld the ruling on the ground of military necessity.

Kosciusko, Thaddeus (1746–1817), Polish-born military leader in the AMERICAN REVOLUTION. Appointed colonel of engineers, Kosciusko was instrumental in the colonial victory at Saratoga, for which he was given honorary U.S. citizenship. Upon returning to Europe following the war, Kosciusko led an unsuccessful rebellion for Polish independence.

Koufax, Sandy (1935–), baseball player. A hard-throwing left-handed pitcher during the 1960s for the Brooklyn/Los Angeles Dodgers, Koufax led the Dodgers to four National League pennants and three World Series championships. He became the first in the major leagues to pitch four no-hit games and received three Cy Young awards. Koufax retired in 1966 because of an arthritic elbow condition. In 1972, at age thirty-six, he became the youngest man ever elected to the baseball Hall of Fame.

Kovacs, Ernie (1919–62), comedian. Kovacs, one of the most original and innovative television comedians of the 1950s, made creative use of new technology and video effects more than a decade before they became standard fare in the 1960s. Brandishing his trademark cigar and wearing horn-rimmed glasses, Kovacs gained admiration for his wide repertoire of zany characterizations and offbeat visual humor. He hosted "The Ernie Kovacs Show" (1955–56), "The Tonight Show" (1956–57), and various quiz and panel shows in the 1960s before his death in an automobile accident.

Krock, Arthur (1886–1974), journalist. Krock was the only person to win four Pulitzer Prizes (1935, 1938, 1950, and 1955). He worked sixty years as a political reporter and editor, serving as chief correspondent and bureau chief of the *New York Times* Washington office from 1932 to 1953. Krock covered every president from William Howard Taft to Richard M. Nixon and was the only reporter granted exclusive interviews with Franklin D. Roosevelt and Harry S. Truman. His editorial column, "In the Nation," became a mainstay of conservative opinion from 1933 to 1966.

Krupa, Gene (1909–73), jazz musician. Krupa, the first jazz drum soloist, was an original member of the BENNY GOODMAN trio (with Goodman and Teddy Wilson). He was a dominant personality of the swing era, noted for his energetic and enthusiastic performances. He later formed his own band and made many recordings and film appearances.

Krutch, Joseph Wood (1893–1970), author, critic, and naturalist. A literary critic and editor of the *Nation,* Krutch wrote biographies of Samuel Johnson and Henry David Thoreau. He left his professorship at Columbia University in 1952 to move to the Arizona desert, where he gained fame as a naturalist. *The Measure of Man* won the 1954 National Book Award.

Kubrick, Stanley (1928–99), film director, screenwriter, producer. Kubrick began directing independent films while working as a photographer for *Look* magazine. He is noted for his technical perfection and intellectual symbolism, but some critics have accused him of a cold and distant style. His numerous films include *Spartacus* (1960), *Lolita* (1962), *Dr. Strangelove*

(1963), *A Clockwork Orange* (1971), and *2001: A Space Odyssey* (1968). *Eyes Wide Shut* (1999) was completed only days before his death.

Ku Klux Klan (KKK), secret organization founded in the southern states by ex-Confederates, during RECONSTRUCTION following the Civil War, to terrorize and intimidate ex-slaves and keep them from voting or holding public office. In order to reestablish white supremacy, the KKK assaulted freed people and resorted to arson and lynching. Its members disguised themselves in white robes and hoods and held secret meetings. The Klan was officially disbanded in 1869, but a second Klan emerged in 1915 as an antiblack, anti-Catholic, and anti-Semitic organization. It eventually numbered over 3 million members, but disbanded in 1944. A third Klan emerged in 1946, focusing on communism and the civil rights movement.

L

Labor, Department of (1913), executive department of the U.S. government promoting the welfare of American workers by monitoring laws that relate to child and agricultural labor, the minimum wage, and other areas of worker concerns. The secretary of labor, a member of the president's cabinet, heads the department and serves as the chief adviser to the president on labor matters. The secretary of labor was the first cabinet post held by a woman, FRANCES PERKINS, appointed by Franklin D. Roosevelt in 1933.

Labor Unions, groups of men and women who unite to promote the welfare of wage earners. The first labor unions in the United States were local and began around 1794 when shoemakers in Philadelphia organized. By 1837 labor unions numbered over two hundred. After the Civil War, with the tremendous expansion of industry, frequent depressions, the gradual closing of free land in the West, and the overwhelming power of large corporations, workers organized national labor unions. The first during this period was the KNIGHTS OF LABOR in 1871. The unionization of skilled workers such as printers led to the formation of the AMERICAN FEDERATION OF LABOR (AFL) in 1886. The twentieth century opened with the formation of the INDUSTRIAL WORKERS OF THE WORLD (IWW) in 1905, followed in 1939 by the CONGRESS OF INDUSTRIAL ORGANIZATIONS (CIO) during the Depression. The AFL and CIO merged in 1955, becoming the AFL-CIO. Labor unions today face declines in membership and in the nation's industrial base, as well as increasing automation. Less than 15 percent of American workers now belong to unions.

Lafayette, Marquis de (1757–1834), soldier of the AMERICAN REVOLUTION. Lafayette, a French soldier and statesman, became so moved by America's fight for independence that he sailed to America at his own expense and received the rank of major general at the age of nineteen. Wounded at the Battle of BRANDYWINE, he spent the winter at Valley Forge with Gen. George Washington, establishing a lifelong friendship. Lafayette cooperated closely with Benjamin Franklin in efforts to obtain financial support from France for the American cause. In 1781 he played a major role in the victory at the Battle of YORKTOWN. The names of Lafayette's children, George Washington Lafayette and Virginie Lafayette, exemplified his love for America. When Lafayette returned to France after his final visit to the United States, he took with him several tons of American soil, in which he ultimately was buried.

Laffite, Jean (1780?–1825?), pirate and patriot. As leader of a band of pirates, Laffite commanded a fleet of ships that raided Spanish vessels in the Gulf of Mexico. Spurning an offer from the British to help seize New Orleans in 1814, he joined forces with Andrew Jackson to defend the city and defeat the invading British. President James Madison granted Laffite and his men pardons for their invaluable help in the victory. He returned to piracy, however, and when he destroyed an American ship, the navy set out after him. He escaped capture and was never seen again.

La Follette, Robert (1855–1925), politician. In 1957 a U.S. Senate committee named La Follette one of the five most outstanding senators of all time. He spent most of his life in public service, serving in the U.S. House of Representatives (1855–91), as governor of Wisconsin (1901–05), and as a U.S. senator (1906–25). As a pacifist and isolationist, La Follette became a controversial figure when he voted against the U.S. entry into World War I and opposed ratification of the Treaty of Versailles and joining the League of Nations. He helped found the Progressive movement and was the Progressive party candidate for president in the ELECTION OF 1924, receiving nearly 6 million votes. La Follette earned the nickname "Fighting Bob" because of his deep commitment to his beliefs.

La Guardia, Fiorello (1882–1947), politician. La Guardia served for three terms as mayor of New York City (1933–45), initiating major reforms against political corruption, substandard housing, and gambling. He developed streets, bridges, parks, sewer systems, schools, and airports. La Guardia also served in the U.S. House of Representatives, where he cosponsored the Norris-La Guardia Anti-Injunction Act of 1932, which protected the rights of striking workers. La Guardia Airport in New York City is named for him.

Lajoie, Napoleon ("Nap") (1874–1959), baseball player. Lajoie earned the distinction of having the highest batting average for a season in baseball's American League (AL). In 1901, during the first season of the AL, Lajoie compiled a .422 batting average while playing for the Philadelphia Athletics; this still stands as a league record. He moved to Cleveland to serve as player-manager for the Indians (1905–09), which was nicknamed the Naps under his leadership. He later returned to the Athletics, retiring in 1916. Lajoie was elected to the Hall of Fame in 1937.

Lake Erie, Battle of (September 10, 1813), major naval engagement during the WAR OF 1812. The American fleet of ten ships under Commodore

OLIVER HAZARD PERRY forced the British to surrender six ships under Capt. Robert Barclay. Perry sent his famous report to Gen. William Henry Harrison: "We have met the enemy, and they are ours." The American victory assured control of Lake Erie and free entry into Canada.

Lame Duck Amendment (1933), the Twentieth Amendment to the U.S. Constitution, which abolished lame duck sessions of Congress. Prior to its enactment, national elections were held in November, but the president and the new Congress did not take office until March 4 of the next year. As a result, defeated officials, called "lame ducks," remained in office for four months but with diminished power since they were soon to leave. The amendment provides for the president to be inaugurated on January 20 and for the new Congress to convene on January 3.

L'Amour, Louis (1908–88), novelist. L'Amour achieved recognition for his novels about frontier life. He wrote more than one hundred books, thirty of which were turned into movies. Most of them are westerns, portraying fictional families in historically accurate situations. His own family heritage and stories told by his grandfather about the CIVIL WAR provided much of the background for L'Amour's stories. His books have sold hundreds of millions of copies and include *The Westward Tide* (1950), *Hondo* (1953), and *The Daybreakers* (1960). In 1983 L'Amour became the first novelist to be awarded the Congressional Gold Medal in honor of his life's work.

Land, Edwin (1909–91), inventor and scientist. Land's name became a household word with his introduction of the Polaroid Land Camera in 1947. This camera produces a finished print in sixty seconds. Land served as president of the Polaroid Corporation (1937), continually improving his company's photographic products.

Landis, Kenesaw Mountain (1866–1944), jurist and first commissioner of major league baseball. Appointed a U.S. federal judge by THEODORE ROOSEVELT, Landis earned a reputation for fairness and integrity when he fined John D. Rockefeller and Standard Oil nearly $30 million for accepting freight rebates in 1907. Landis was selected commissioner of major league baseball (1920–44) in response to a scandal among players of the Chicago White Sox, who fixed the 1919 WORLD SERIES. He supervised the sport firmly, bringing an attitude of respectability, discipline, and honesty. However, Landis was a firm segregationist, opposed to allowing black players to play major league baseball, and his detractors note that he prolonged the segregation of organized baseball.

Landon, Alf (1887–1987), businessman and politician. Landon served two terms as governor of Kansas and ran as the Republican candidate for president in the ELECTION OF 1936, losing to Franklin D. Roosevelt in a landslide; he won only the electoral votes of Maine and Vermont. Following his defeat he pursued business interests as a petroleum producer.

Land Ordinance of 1785 (May 20), establishment of a system for surveying and subdividing public land outside the states. Passed by the Congress of the Articles of Confederation, the statute provided for the surveying of blocks of land thirty-six square miles each, to be known as townships. Each township was to set aside one section for public education and schools, with each block or section containing 640 acres. Congress established the prices at which the land was to be sold to the public.

Landrum-Griffin Act (September 14, 1959), law passed by Congress to eliminate corruption and suppress the influence of organized crime in labor unions. Also called the Labor Management Reporting and Disclosure Act, it requires that unions file annual financial reports showing how the dues of union members are spent.

Langley, Samuel (1834–1906), astronomer, physicist, and airplane pioneer. Langley made valuable studies of the dynamics of air in his attempts to prove the possibility of mechanical flight. Although his machines did not fly as he hoped, Langley developed the principles upon which other inventors were able to construct successful airplanes. He invented the bolometer (1881), which measures the sun's radiation.

Lansing, Robert (1864–1928), U.S. secretary of state under President WOODROW WILSON (1915–20). Lansing helped purchase the Virgin Islands in 1917 and negotiated the Lansing-Ishi agreement with Japan, which validated the OPEN DOOR POLICY with China. He attended the Versailles Peace Conference in 1919, but broke with President Wilson over the LEAGUE OF NATIONS. When Wilson learned that Lansing called several cabinet meetings during the president's illness, he asked him to resign. Lansing, a conservative on foreign affairs, also supported nonrecognition of the Bolshevik government with Russia. He wrote *The Peace Negotiations* (1921) and founded the *American Journal of International Law* (1907), remaining its editor until his death.

Lardner, Ring, Sr. (Ringgold W.; 1885–1933), journalist and author. Beginning his career as a baseball writer, Lardner gained a reputation for his literary skill, humor, and use of satire. *You Know Me, Al* (1915) drew on his sports experiences; his masterly story collections include *How to Write Short Stories* (1924) and *Round Up* (1929). Lardner collaborated in the theater with George M. Cohan and George S. Kaufman. His son, also a writer, was one of the BLACKLISTED Hollywood Ten.

Larson, Gary (1950–), cartoonist. Appearing in over 1,900 newspapers, Larson's one-panel comic strip, "The Far Side," became a pop-culture phenomenon of the 1980s, thriving for fourteen years until Larson's retirement in 1995. In his cartoons Larson contrasts intelligent and cunning animals with human beings who are often depicted as stupid and pathetic. Larson has also completed two animated films, *Gary Larson's Tales from the Far*

Side I (1994) and *Gary Larson's Tales from the Far Side II* (1997), both featured at international film festivals.

LaSalle, Robert (1643–87), French explorer. LaSalle led an expedition from Canada down the Mississippi River to the Gulf of Mexico in 1682, claiming the territory for France and naming it Louisiana in honor of King Louis XIV. He returned to France to organize an expedition to colonize the area. While searching for the original site, he was murdered by his men.

Latrobe, Benjamin Henry (1764–1820), architect. Called the father of American architecture, Latrobe is best known for his work on the White House and the United States Capitol. Born in England, Latrobe immigrated to America, where he quickly achieved attention in Philadelphia for his work in the Greek Revival style. In 1803 President THOMAS JEFFERSON appointed him surveyor of public buildings and summoned him to Washington to complete the Capitol. He constructed the building's south wing and rebuilt the interior of the north wing. After the British burned the Capitol in 1814, Latrobe oversaw restoration. He resigned in 1817 over an authority dispute and was succeeded by CHARLES BULFINCH. Latrobe also built Baltimore Cathedral, the first vaulted church and the first Roman Catholic cathedral in America.

Laurel, Stan (Arthur Stanley Jefferson; 1890–1965), and Oliver Hardy (1892–1957), comedy motion picture team of the 1920s and 1930s. The skinny Laurel portrayed an innocent, timid man who frustrated his partner, the fat Hardy, a pompous know-it-all, resulting in many slapstick routines. The team starred in over two hundred silent and sound films, winning an Academy Award in 1932 for *The Music Box.*

Laurens, Henry (1724–92), statesman of the Revolutionary period. A merchant and planter in Charleston, South Carolina, Laurens served as president of the CONTINENTAL CONGRESS. Captured by the British while en route to negotiate a treaty with the Dutch, Laurens was imprisoned in the Tower of London, but later exchanged for Gen. Charles Cornwallis.

Laurens, John (1754–82), general of the AMERICAN REVOLUTION. Laurens served on George Washington's staff and saw action at BRANDYWINE. The son of HENRY LAURENS, he served as an envoy to France and helped negotiate the British surrender at YORKTOWN. He was killed in action while fighting with Gen. Nathanael Greene in South Carolina.

Lawrence, Jacob (1917–2000), painter and educator. Lawrence trained in fine arts at the Harlem Art Workshop and the American Art School in New York. Influenced by social realism, he painted scenes from African-American life, historical figures, social issues, and African history. His paintings, influenced by cubism and expressionism, are characterized by bold, angular, richly colored decorative effects. Many of them are created as a series on a single historic figure or topic. His *Migration* series (1941–42), describing the great migration of blacks from the rural south to northern urban areas during the depression, made him nationally famous. Lawrence taught painting at New York's Pratt Institute (1958–65) and the University of Washington (1970–83). He wrote and illustrated *Harriet and the Promised Land* (1993), a children's book of verse about HARRIET TUBMAN.

Lawrence, James (1781–1813), naval officer during the WAR OF 1812. Lawrence, in command of *Chesapeake,* lost his life when the British frigate *Shannon* captured his ship near Boston. Lawrence's dying words, "Don't give up the ship!" have lived on.

Lazarus, Emma (1849–87), poet. As a result of a wave of Jewish immigration, Lazarus, a Jew, wrote the sonnet "The New Colossus" in 1883, which is inscribed on a plaque at the base of the STATUE OF LIBERTY. Much of her writing protested Jewish persecution in Russia during the late 1800s.

Leadbelly (Huddie Ledbetter; 1888–1949), folk singer and composer. Born in Louisiana of Cherokee and black descent, Leadbelly sang and played a twelve-string guitar and led a drifter's life. He gathered songs from prisons and toured the country singing folksongs. Eventually "discovered" by early folk music recorders, he made a series of important and popular records, including the songs "Irene, Good Night" and "Rock Island Blues."

League of Nations (1920–46), the first major international association of countries dedicated to the prevention of war. Proposed by President Woodrow Wilson as part of his FOURTEEN POINT program at the end of World War I, organization of the League was included in the TREATY OF VERSAILLES. Members of the League included France, Great Britain, Italy, and Japan, but Wilson could not persuade the U.S. Senate to ratify the League Covenant. The League proved ineffective in preventing aggression, and it dissolved in April 1946, to be replaced by the UNITED NATIONS.

League of Women Voters (1920), nonpartisan organization that encourages public participation in government. Founded in Chicago by CARRIE CHAPMAN CATT and members of the National American Woman Suffrage Association, the League of Women Voters has branches in the United States, Puerto Rico, and the Virgin Islands. The league, which welcomed men in 1974, promotes political education and voter registration. It has sponsored presidential campaign debates since 1976.

Lecompton Constitution *See* BLEEDING KANSAS.

Lee, Henry (1756–1818), military leader and statesman. Known as "Lighthorse Harry," Lee served as a cavalry commander during the AMERICAN REVOLUTION. He was a member of the Continental Congress, governor of Virginia, and a congressman in the U.S. House of Representatives. He also commanded the U.S. soldiers who suppressed the WHISKEY REBELLION. It was Lee who said, when George Washington died, that he was "first in war, first in peace, and first in the hearts of his countrymen."

Lee, Richard Henry (1732–94), statesman of the Revolutionary period. A member of Virginia's House of Burgesses, Lee opposed British taxation.

As a delegate from Virginia to the Continental Congress, he introduced a resolution on June 7, 1776, to declare independence. Lee served as president of the Congress in 1784 and opposed the ratification of the Constitution because of its limitation of states' rights. As a U.S. senator from Virginia (1789–92), he was part of the movement to add a bill of rights.

Lee, Robert E. (1807–70), Confederate CIVIL WAR general. Lee commanded the U.S. troops who cut short JOHN BROWN'S RAID at Harpers Ferry, Virginia, in 1859. Offered the command of the Union army at the outbreak of the Civil War, Lee refused and instead joined the Confederate army as military adviser to Confederate president JEFFERSON DAVIS when his home state of Virginia seceded. He assumed command of the Army of Northern Virginia in 1862 and immediately achieved his first success near Richmond in the SEVEN DAYS' BATTLES (June 26–July 2). Following his victory at the second Battle of BULL RUN (August 29–30), Lee suffered defeat at ANTIETAM (September 17), prompting him to reorganize his army. Lee's troops then defeated Union forces at FREDERICKSBURG (December 13) and CHANCELLORSVILLE (May 2–4, 1863). Defeat at GETTYSBURG (July 1–3) was followed by fierce battles of the WILDERNESS campaign (May 5–6, 1864) and further defeat at Petersburg (June 15–18). Lee became commander in chief of all Confederate armies just prior to the fall of Richmond in April 1865. He surrendered to ULYSSES S. GRANT at APPOMATTOX COURT HOUSE on April 9, 1865, thus ending the Civil War. Lee spent his final years as president of Washington College (now Washington and Lee University) in Lexington, Virginia.

Lee, Spike (1957–), African-American writer, filmmaker, and actor. Lee is noted for his bold and sometimes controversial political films, which confront racism and African-American issues. He studied filmmaking at Morehouse College and committed himself to making films that would capture the black experience. *She's Gotta Have It* (1986) earned him recognition not only as a director but as a comic actor. Other films include *Do the Right Thing* (1989), *Jungle Fever* (1991), *Malcolm X* (1992), *4 Little Girls* (1997), *Summer of Sam* (1999), *The Original Kings of Comedy* (2000), and *Rent* (2004). Lee's activism and success in Hollywood have influenced the careers of many black actors and filmmakers by creating opportunities in the movie industry. Lee also produces and directs music videos, commercials,

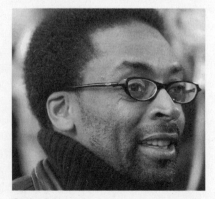

Spike Lee

and has authored several books on the making of his films including *Five for Five* (1992).

Lehman, Herbert H. (1878–1963), banker and politician. A partner in the successful banking firm of Lehman and Brothers in New York City, Lehman, a liberal Democrat, served as both lieutenant governor (1928–32) and governor of New York (1932–42), and in the U.S. Senate (1949–57). He supported the New Deal and became the first director general of the United Nations Relief and Rehabilitation Administration.

Lemieux, Mario (1965–), hockey player. Lemieux was the first player picked by the Pittsburgh Penguins in the 1984 draft and in 1985 won the Calder Memorial trophy for the National Hockey League (NHL) Rookie of the Year. Playing center, he led the Penguins to both of their Stanley Cup titles in 1991 and 1992. He led the NHL in scoring six times and won the Hart Memorial trophy as the league's most valuable player. Ranked with the greatest hockey players in the NFL, Lemieux suffered some serious injuries and battled Hodgkins's disease. He retired in 1997, but returned as a player and owner of the Penguins in 2000.

Lend-Lease Act (March 11, 1941), act passed by Congress during WORLD WAR II authorizing the president to lend or lease war matériel to any nation whose defense was considered necessary for U.S. national security. Initiated by President FRANKLIN D. ROOSEVELT, the program provided aid to Great Britain, the Soviet Union, China, Brazil, and other countries.

L'Enfant, Pierre Charles (1754–1825), soldier and architect. L'Enfant came to America in 1776 from France to volunteer for army service in the AMERICAN REVOLUTION. He formed a friendship with GEORGE WASHINGTON, and later, when Congress decided to build a capital federal city on the Potomac (1791), L'Enfant prepared a design and Washington hired him. Washington dismissed L'Enfant the following year because of L'Enfant's insistence on complete control of the project. L'Enfant died penniless and alone and was buried in Maryland. In 1908, by a special act of Congress, his remains were disinterred and moved to ARLINGTON NATIONAL CEMETERY, where his monument stands.

Leonard, Sugar Ray (Ray Charles; 1956–), boxer. Named after former boxing champion Sugar Ray Robinson, Leonard became the first boxer to win titles in five different weight classes, including the light welterweight gold medal at the 1976 Summer Olympics. Surgery for a detached retina in 1982 interrupted his career, but he made a comeback to win two more titles. After winning thirty-five of thirty-six bouts over twelve years, he retired in 1991.

Leopold, Nathan, Jr. (1904–71) and **Richard Loeb** (1905–31), murderers. Both wealthy University of Chicago students, Leopold and Loeb in a sensational case admitted to kidnapping and murdering fourteen-year-old

Bobby Franks for the thrill of it in 1924. Defended by CLARENCE DARROW, they pleaded guilty, and Darrow organized his case as a plea against capital punishment. The court sentenced them both to prison for life plus ninety-nine years. Loeb was murdered in prison, and Leopold was paroled toward the end of his life.

Leutze, Emmanuel (1816–68), German-born historical painter. Chiefly known for his painting of *Washington Crossing the Delaware* (1851), one of his several works depicting scenes from American history, Leutze settled in the United States in 1859 after being commissioned by Congress to paint a mural for the U.S. Capitol. Called *Westward Ho the Course of Empire Takes Its Way*, the allegorical mural represents the settlement of the frontier.

Levitt, William (1907–), builder of mass-produced, low-cost, quality housing. With his brother and father, Levitt established the building firm of Levitt and Sons in 1929 and served as its president. Combining lessons he learned from building homes for defense workers during World War II with production-line techniques he observed at Detroit auto plants, Levitt revolutionized the U.S. housing industry. His firm built mass-produced tract housing, first for the U.S. Navy, then for servicemen following the war. The communities, called Levittowns, featured affordable, single-family homes with a uniform look in a suburban community. Levittowns were built on Long Island, New York, and in Pennsylvania, New Jersey, and Florida, and eventually totaled about 125,000 homes. Levitt sold the company to International Telephone and Telegraph Corporation in 1968.

Lewis, Carl (1961–), track and field athlete. A champion sprinter and long jumper, Lewis won the Sullivan Award in 1981, given annually to the top U.S. amateur athlete. In 1983 he won three world championship medals, and in 1984 he equaled JESSE OWENS's record by winning four Olympic gold medals. He won two more gold medals in the 1988 Olympics and again in 1992.

Lewis, John L. (1880–1969), labor leader. Lewis, head of the United Mine Workers of America from 1920 to 1960, founded and was first president of the CONGRESS OF INDUSTRIAL ORGANIZATIONS from 1936 to 1940. Strikes by the miners after World War II gained benefits for the workers but alienated the public. Helpful in getting safety legislation passed for miners, Lewis was once quite powerful, but his influence waned in his later years, owing partly to his arbitrary personality.

Lewis, Meriwether (1774–1809), explorer and public official. Private secretary to (and kinsman of) President Thomas Jefferson, Lewis commanded the expedition to explore the LOUISIANA PURCHASE territory in 1804 with WILLIAM CLARK. Lewis served as governor of the Louisiana Territory from 1806 until 1809 when he died, either by suicide or murder, while en route to Washington, D.C.

Lewis, Sinclair (1885–1951), novelist. Lewis received critical acclaim and international recognition for his works, which criticized aspects of American life in the Midwest. *Main Street* (1920) was his first success, and *Arrowsmith* earned him the 1926 Pulitzer Prize, which he declined. Other notable works include *Babbit* (1922), *Elmer Gantry* (1927), and *Dodsworth* (1929). In 1930 Lewis became the first American writer to win the Nobel Prize for literature.

Lewis and Clark Expedition (1804–06), a venture commissioned by President Thomas Jefferson to explore the wilderness area in the territory acquired by the LOUISIANA PURCHASE. In the spring of 1804 the party, led by MERIWETHER LEWIS and WILLIAM CLARK, left St. Louis, Missouri. They traveled up the Missouri River, crossed the Rocky Mountains, and followed the Snake and Columbia rivers to the Pacific Ocean. They were guided by SACAJAWEA, a Shoshone woman, for part of their journey. When they returned to St. Louis in 1806, they had accumulated a vast store of information about topical features, natural resources, plant and animal life, and the Indians of the territory.

Lexington, Battle of (April 19, 1775), first battle of the AMERICAN REVOLUTION. Because of unrest following the passage of the INTOLERABLE ACTS, British troops were sent to capture SAMUEL ADAMS and JOHN HANCOCK, and to destroy military supplies at Concord, Massachusetts. En route to Concord, the Redcoats were met at the village green in Lexington, Massachusetts, by Minutemen who had been alerted the previous night by PAUL REVERE and SAMUEL PRESCOTT. No one knows who fired the first shot, but both sides suffered casualties and the colonials withdrew. The British continued on and engaged next in the BATTLE OF CONCORD.

Leyte Gulf, Battle of (October 23–25, 1944), naval battle during WORLD WAR II. The U.S. and Japanese fleets met in Leyte Gulf, off the coast of the Philippines, near the end of the war. During the engagements the larger U.S. naval and air forces destroyed Japan's naval and air power. The landing of U.S. Marines followed the victory and started the American reconquest of the islands.

Liberalism, a political concept that has changed meaning over the years. In the late eighteenth and early nineteenth centuries, liberalism emphasized the desirability of allowing individuals to follow their own wishes and pursue their own goals rather than thinking first of the common good. It was the political theory that led to the AMERICAN REVOLUTION and is evidenced in the writings of THOMAS JEFFERSON and the DECLARATION OF INDEPENDENCE. By the late nineteenth century political and economic liberalism had come to reflect the belief that a society functions best with little government regulation. Liberals favored free trade and an unregulated economy. The conditions deriving from that philosophy led to twentieth-century liberalism, which supports an activist government intervening to regulate the economy and remedy social problems. Today liberals support government programs to ensure freedom of opportunity for individuals suffering discrimination, to provide help for those in economic need, and to set standards and regulations in such matters as the environment, safety in the workplace, and business practices. Contrasted with conservatism, liberalism tends to be associated with the DEMOCRATIC PARTY.

Liberty Party, political party organized by ABOLITIONISTS in New York in 1840. The party advocated the abolition of slavery and nominated its leader, James Birney, for president in 1840 and 1844. The party merged with other antislavery groups in 1848 to form the FREE-SOIL PARTY.

Library of Congress, the world's largest library. Located in Washington, D.C., just east of the Capitol, the Library of Congress provides reference materials to the U.S. Congress. Established in 1800 as a legislative library at the urging of THOMAS JEFFERSON, it was burned by the British in 1814. To begin a new library, Jefferson sold his personal library of about six thousand volumes to Congress. In 1865 Congress declared that two copies of all books and materials that claim a copyright must be submitted to the library. By 2004, the collection totaled more than 126 million items on approximately 530 miles of bookshelves.

Lieberman, Joseph (1942–), politician. With a reputation for strong moral convictions and character, Lieberman was elected to the U.S. Senate from Connecticut in 1988 and reelected in 1994 and 2000. AL GORE JR., who was seeking to distance himself from the scandals of the BILL CLINTON presidency, selected Lieberman as his Democratic vice presidential running mate in the ELECTION OF 2000, thus making Lieberman the first Jewish American to run on a major party ticket. Lieberman is known as a moderately conservative Democrat, crossing party lines on issues such as capital gains taxes, military spending, and school vouchers. He is ranking member and former chairman of the Senate Governmental Affairs Committee and led the push to establish a DEPARTMENT OF HOMELAND SECURITY. Lieberman has authored six books, including *An Amazing Adventure* (2003), detailing his experiences on the vice presidential campaign trail in 2000.

Lin, Maya (1959–), artist and architect. Lin gained national attention when, as a senior at Yale, she created the winning design for the Vietnam Veterans Memorial in Washington, D.C. Her commission initially sparked controversy due to the unusual design, as well as the age, gender, and ethnic identity of Lin herself, but she personally oversaw the construction process, and it was dedicated in 1982. It has become one of the most visited and appreciated memorials in the United States. Among her other projects, Maya also designed the Civil Rights Memorial in Montgomery, Alabama, honoring the people who shaped the struggle for civil rights, and the Langston Hughes Library in Tennessee.

Lincoln, Abraham (1809–65), sixteenth president of the United States (1861–65) who led the nation through its greatest crisis, the CIVIL WAR. Born in a log cabin near Hodgenville, Kentucky, Lincoln had less than one year of formal schooling. He moved to Indiana in 1816 and then to Illinois, where he became a storekeeper and rail-splitter, studying law in his free time. He served in the Illinois legislature from 1834 to 1841 and then moved to Springfield, where he practiced law. He was elected to the U.S. House of Representatives as a Whig for one term (1847–49). After joining the REPUBLICAN PARTY in 1856, he opposed

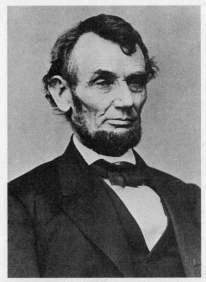

Abraham Lincoln
A portrait of Abraham Lincoln attributed to photographer Mathew Brady; this image appears on the five-dollar bill.

Stephen A. Douglas for a seat in the U.S. Senate from Illinois in 1858. During the Campaign, the two men conducted the famous LINCOLN-DOUGLAS DEBATES over the extension of slavery, which Lincoln opposed. He lost the election, but the campaign had made him a national figure.

In 1860 Lincoln received the Republican nomination for president and won the election, partly because of a split in the Democratic party. Seven southern states seceded from the Union to form the CONFEDERATE STATES OF AMERICA before his inauguration, and four more did so when he made clear his determination to preserve the Union by calling for volunteers after the South fired on Fort Sumter. Although Lincoln's foremost goal in the

---

★ **Abraham Lincoln**
The concluding lines of Lincoln's Second Inaugural Address, delivered March 4, 1865

With malice toward none; with charity for all; with firmness in the right, as God gives us to see the right, let us strive on to finish the work we are in; to bind up the nation's wounds; to care for him who shall have borne the battle, and for his widow, and his orphan — to do all which may achieve and cherish a just and lasting peace, among ourselves, and with all nations.

beginning was the preservation of the Union, by 1863 he had become convinced that it could be preserved only by the destruction of slavery, which he abhorred on moral grounds. Despite personal tragedies and bitter criticism from all sides, Lincoln was one of the most effective war leaders in the nation's history. A first-rate administrator and an able commander in chief, he also did a masterful job of articulating the moral goals of the war and the American experiment in government. His eloquent speeches have become a textbook on liberty and democratic government.

On April 14, 1865, five days after Robert E. Lee surrendered to Ulysses S. Grant at Appomattox, the president and his wife attended a performance at Ford's Theatre, where JOHN WILKES BOOTH shot him in the back of the head. He never regained consciousness and died the next day. Lincoln has since been recognized as one of the greatest presidents of the United States, as well as a towering figure in Western civilization.

Lincoln-Douglas Debates (1858), a series of seven debates between Democrat STEPHEN A. DOUGLAS and Republican ABRAHAM LINCOLN during a campaign for the U.S. Senate seat from Illinois. The major issue was the question of the legal status of slavery in the territories. Douglas supported the concept of POPULAR SOVEREIGNTY to decide whether a given territory would be free or slave, and Lincoln opposed the expansion of slavery. Douglas won the senatorial election, because U.S. senators at that time were chosen by state legislatures, and the Democrats carried the Illinois legislature that year. Lincoln, however, became a national political figure and two years later defeated Douglas for the presidency.

Lindbergh, Charles (1902–74), and **Anne Morrow Lindbergh** (1906–2001). Charles, an aviator, made the first solo nonstop flight across the Atlantic Ocean in the *Spirit of St. Louis* on May 20–21, 1927, flying from New York to Paris in 33½ hours. Called the "Lone Eagle" and "Lucky Lindy," he received a hero's welcome on his return and was awarded the Congressional Medal of Honor. In the 1930s, Lindbergh became an outspoken isolationist and a member of the America First Committee prior to World War II. When war came, however, he flew combat missions in the Pacific and

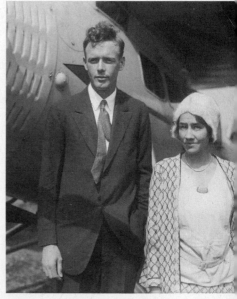

Charles Lindbergh and Anne Morrow Lindbergh

served as a technical expert on aeronautical matters. In 1954 he won the Pulitzer Prize for his autobiography, *The Spirit of St. Louis* (1953). His wife, Anne Morrow Lindbergh, was a poet and essayist known for the sensitive nature of her works. Especially well known are her *Gift from the Sea* (1955), a book of essays, and *The Unicorn and Other Poems* (1956). She made many flights with her husband, which provided inspiration for several other books. The couple's early life was marred by the tragedy of their infant son's kidnapping and murder in 1932. The resulting sensational coverage of the trial forced the couple to seek refuge and privacy in Europe. They eventually settled in Hawaii.

Lindbergh Kidnapping (1932), the kidnapping and murder of the twenty-month-old son of CHARLES LINDBERGH and ANNE MORROW LINDBERGH. Bruno Hauptmann, German-born carpenter and escaped criminal, was convicted of the crime in a trial marked by sensational coverage in the press and highly controversial evidence. Hauptmann maintained his innocence until his execution in 1936, and his widow pursued the matter for many years. The event moved Congress to pass a federal law on kidnapping known as the "Lindbergh Law."

Lindsay, Ted (Robert; 1925–), hockey player. A left-winger for the Detroit Red Wings of the National Hockey League, Lindsay played on the NHL all-star team nine times, led Detroit to win the Stanley Cup four times, and led the league in scoring in 1950. He also played for the Chicago Black Hawks. He held the NHL record for penalty minutes and earned the appellation of "Terrible Ted" because he was such a fierce competitor.

Lippmann, Walter (1889–1974), journalist and author. Noted for his commentaries on political and economic affairs, Lippmann founded and edited the *New Republic* (1914) and edited the *New York World* (1921–31). He wrote a column for the *New York Tribune*, "Today and Tomorrow," from 1931 to 1967, which eventually appeared in over two hundred newspapers. Lippmann received Pulitzer honors in 1958 and 1962 for his reporting and commentaries. He advised President Woodrow Wilson on his FOURTEEN POINTS proposal and attended the Paris Peace Conference. His books include *Public Opinion* (1922) and *A Preface to Morals* (1929).

Literacy Test Act (1917), law passed by Congress requiring immigrants to be able to read English before being admitted to the United States. Congress passed the act over President Woodrow Wilson's veto.

Livingston, Robert R. (1746–1813), lawyer and statesman. Livingston was a New York delegate to the CONTINENTAL CONGRESS and joined the five-member committee that formulated the DECLARATION OF INDEPENDENCE. As chancellor of New York, the state's highest ranking equity judge (1777–1801), Livingston administered the oath of office to President George Washington in 1789. President Thomas Jefferson appointed him minister to France, where he negotiated the treaty for the Louisiana Purchase. He aided

Robert Fulton in the creation of the first successful steamboat, *Clermont,* which was named after Livingston's New York estate.

Lloyd, Harold (1893–1971), actor and comedian. Lloyd won fame making more than two hundred comic silent and sound films during a thirty-four-year career, becoming one of Hollywood's first movie stars. At the height of his career, he was one of the most popular and highest-paid stars of his time. Wearing his trademark straw hat, wrinkled suit, and round horn-rim glasses, he created his signature character, an ordinary, timid weakling who wins battles against overwhelming odds. Called the "king of daredevil comedy," Lloyd performed precarious physical stunts and chase sequences. Some of his highly acclaimed films include *Grandma's Boy* (1922), *Safety Last* (1923), *Girl Shy* (1923), and *Speedy* (1928).

Lobbyist, an individual or organization, paid or unpaid, who seeks to influence legislators to vote for or against proposed legislation that affects their special interest. The word refers to the lobby of the legislature, where much discussion takes place. The Federal Regulation of Lobbying Act of 1946 attempts to control corruption and bribery in the practice of lobbying.

Lockwood, Belva Ann (1830–1917), lawyer and social reformer. Nominated by the National Equal Rights party to run for president in the ELECTIONS OF 1884 and ELECTIONS OF 1888, Lockwood was one of the few women who have run for president. She was responsible for a law requiring equal pay for equal work by women in government jobs. After helping to pass a law permitting women to practice before the U.S. Supreme Court, Lockwood became the first woman to do so.

Lodge, Henry Cabot (1850–1924), political leader and author. Elected to represent Massachusetts in the U.S. House of Representatives in 1886 and the U.S. Senate in 1893, Lodge espoused conservative Republican beliefs. As an outspoken critic of President Woodrow Wilson, chairman of the Senate Foreign Relations Committee, and a fervent isolationist, he led the opposition in the Senate against ratifying the TREATY OF VERSAILLES and joining the LEAGUE OF NATIONS. Born into an aristocratic Boston family, Lodge began his career as an editor and noted historian, writing several biographies of famous Americans.

Lodge, Henry Cabot, II (1902–85), political leader and diplomat. Elected to the U.S. Senate as a Republican from Massachusetts in 1936, Lodge lost his seat to John F. Kennedy in 1952. He was Richard M. Nixon's running mate in the ELECTION OF 1960, losing to the Kennedy-Johnson ticket. As a diplomat under four presidents, Lodge served as U.S. ambassador to the United Nations, ambassador to South Vietnam, and ambassador to West Germany. He unsuccessfully sought the Republican presidential nomination in 1964, and in 1969 became Nixon's chief negotiator at the Paris peace talks on Vietnam. He was the grandson of Henry Cabot Lodge.

Loeb, Richard *See* NATHAN LEOPOLD, JR. AND RICHARD LOEB.

Lombardi, Vince (1913–70), football coach. Lombardi gained national stature by turning the losing Green Bay Packers into a disciplined, aggressive team that won five league championships and two Super Bowls, in 1967 and 1968. With the attitude that "winning isn't everything; it is the only thing," Lombardi insisted on hard work, dedication, and pride. He was inducted into the pro football Hall of Fame in 1971. President Richard M. Nixon cited Lombardi often as one of his heroes; some saw a resemblance between Nixon's drive to win and Lombardi's.

London, Jack (1876–1916), sailor, adventurer, and novelist of adventure tales. The time London spent in the Yukon Territory of Canada provided inspiration for some of his best works including *The Call of the Wild* (1903), *The Sea Wolf* (1904), and *White Fang* (1906). His writings deal with the struggle for existence; many of them, such as his autobiographical *Martin Eden* (1909), have an anticapitalist theme. He promoted socialist reform in his novel *The Iron Heel* (1908) and once ran for mayor of Oakland, California, on the Socialist ticket. London became wealthy and spent money lavishly before his death of acute uremia.

London Naval Conferences. In 1930 the United States, Great Britain, Japan, France, and Italy attempted to limit the size and number of warships not already restricted by the Washington Naval Conference of 1921–22. France and Italy withdrew because of disagreements, but the remaining three powers agreed to terms. In 1936 another conference was held to try to establish limits. Japan withdrew, but the United States, Great Britain, and France signed an agreement reaffirming the treaty of 1930.

Lone Star Republic, nickname taken by Texas after it won its independence from Mexico in 1836. The Texas Republic existed for nearly ten years until annexed by the United States in 1845. The name derives from the single star on its flag.

Longfellow, Henry Wadsworth (1807–82), one of America's best-known poets. Highly respected as a writer in his lifetime, Longfellow wrote many poems on historical topics. Some of his best-known works include *Evangeline* (1847), *The Song of Hiawatha* (1855), *The Courtship of Miles Standish* (1858), and "Paul Revere's Ride" (1861). He became the first American to be recognized in the Poet's Corner of London's Westminster Abbey.

Long, Huey (1893–1935), politician. A demagogue and virtual dictator of the state of Louisiana, Long became governor in 1928 on a populist platform of "every man a king." Elected to the U.S. Senate in 1930, Long, called the "Kingfish," at first supported President Franklin D. Roosevelt's New Deal. As the 1936 election approached, he spoke of mounting a challenge to Roosevelt for the presidency using the slogan of "Share Our Wealth." Long was assassinated in the marble corridors of the state capitol in Baton Rouge by the son of a political opponent; the assassin was slain by Long's bodyguards.

Long Island, Battle of (August 27, 1776), a military engagement of the AMERICAN REVOLUTION. Gen. William Howe led the British troops from Staten Island to Brooklyn Heights on Long Island, dislodging and badly beating George Washington and the outnumbered colonial forces. Under the cover of night they retreated across the East River to Manhattan and temporary safety, leaving Long Island to the British.

Longstreet, James (1821–1904), Confederate general during the CIVIL WAR. Known by his troops as "Old Peter," Longstreet won a major victory at BULL RUN and led the right wing of Robert E. Lee's army at ANTIETAM. His service at GETTYSBURG caused controversy because his delay in carrying out Lee's orders to attack possibly caused the Confederate defeat. Longstreet also served at LOOKOUT MOUNTAIN and the last defense of Richmond, Virginia. President Ulysses S. Grant appointed Longstreet U.S. minister to Turkey in 1880.

Lookout Mountain, Battle of (November 23–25, 1863), CIVIL WAR battle that marked the beginning of the North's victory in the Chattanooga campaign. JOSEPH HOOKER led the Union troops in the plan to capture the Confederate transportation center of Chattanooga, Tennessee. He and his forces cleared Lookout Mountain of troops led by Confederate general JAMES LONGSTREET. The Southern troops retreated across Chattanooga Creek to join other forces at MISSIONARY RIDGE.

Los Angeles Riots (April 29–May 3, 1992), the nation's worst civil disorder of the twentieth century, with a toll of 60 people killed, more than 4,000 injured, and an estimated $850 million in property damage. Rioting broke out in the South Central section of the city following the acquittal of four white police officers accused of beating black motorist Rodney G. King. The beating had attracted international attention because an amateur photographer's videotape recording of the incident showed the officers repeatedly kicking King and striking him with their batons as he lay on the ground. Anger at the apparent condoning of police brutality and frustration with a lack of economic opportunity and with the perceived unfairness of the justice system exploded in five days of rioting in Los Angeles and in scattered violence in Atlanta, Las Vegas, Seattle, and other U.S. cities.

Lost Colony of Roanoke, English settlement on Roanoke Island, off the coast of present-day North Carolina. Arriving in 1587, the settlers, led by John White, realized they had insufficient food to last the winter and would need more supplies from home. White sailed to England but was not able to make the return voyage for three years because of war between England and Spain. Upon his return to Roanoke, he found that the entire colony had disappeared. No trace remained of the settlers but the letters *Cro* and *Croatoan* carved on two trees. To this day, no one knows what really became of John White's lost colony.

Louis, Joe (Joseph Louis Barrow; 1914–81), boxer. Called the "Brown Bomber," Louis put his title on the line twenty-five times and held it longer than any other heavyweight champion. He won the championship in 1937, defeating James Braddock, and retired in 1947 at age thirty-four. His efforts at a comeback in 1950 were thwarted by defeats at the hands of Ezzard Charles and Rocky Marciano.

Louisiana (Pelican State) joined the Union as the eighteenth state on April 30, 1812. (See maps, pages 540 and 541.) It seceded in 1861 and was readmitted in 1865. New Orleans, its most famous city and major tourist attraction, boasts the Mardi Gras and the famous restaurants of the French Quarter. Site of the birth of jazz, this multicultural city houses the Superdome, the world's largest enclosed stadium. It was also the site of the greatest American victory over the British in the War of 1812. Other important cities include Shreveport and Baton Rouge, the capital. Home to the greatest number of game birds in the United States, Louisiana leads the country in oil products, cotton, rice, soybeans, and sugar. Famous Louisianans include ZACHARY TAYLOR, HUEY LONG, and LOUIS ARMSTRONG.

Louisiana Purchase (1803), the acquisition from France of the area between the Mississippi River and the Rocky Mountains on the east and west and between Canada and the Gulf of Mexico on the north and south. A major achievement of President Thomas Jefferson, the $15 million purchase of the Louisiana Territory doubled the size of the United States and opened the West to American settlement.

Lovejoy, Elijah (1802–37), editor and ABOLITIONIST. Lovejoy attacked slavery as editor of the *St. Louis Observer,* a religious newspaper. Ignoring threats to his life, he later published an abolitionist newspaper in Alton, Illinois. Lovejoy's antislavery position provoked hostility, resulting in his murder by an angry mob. Many northerners joined the abolitionist cause in outraged sympathy.

Low, Juliette (1860–1927), founder of the Girl Scouts of America. Inspired by scouting organizations in England, Low organized the first troop in 1912 in her hometown of Savannah, Georgia. In 1915 the Girl Scouts of America was formed, and Low served as its president until 1920.

Lowell, James Russell (1819–91), author and diplomat. Under Lowell's editorial leadership, the *Atlantic Monthly* and the *North American Review* achieved major literary importance. Three of his best-known works, *A Fable for Critics, The Biglow Papers,* and *The Vision of Sir Launfal,* were published in 1848. Lowell succeeded Henry Wadsworth Longfellow as professor of modern language at Harvard and later served as U.S. ambassador to both Spain and England (1877–85).

Loyalists, also called Tories, were American colonists who remained loyal to England during the AMERICAN REVOLUTION. Loyalists made up about one-third of the colonial population. Many fled to England and

Canada after the war; those who remained were treated harshly by the
PATRIOTS.

Lucas, George (1944–), motion picture producer, writer, and director.
His first film success came with the direction of *American Graffiti* (1973).
Becoming known for action-packed films with spectacular special effects,
Lucas wrote and directed *Star Wars* (1977), one of the most popular films
in movie history; its successors, *The Empire Strikes Back* (1980) and *The
Return of the Jedi* (1983); and the Indiana Jones Trilogy, which included
Raiders of the Lost Ark (1981), *The Temple of Doom* (1984), and *The Last
Crusade* (1989). The prequels to *Star Wars* were released in 1999 and 2000.

Luce, Clare Boothe (1903–87), playwright, politician, and diplomat. Luce
edited *Vogue* and *Vanity Fair* magazines during the 1930s and became a
noted playwright with such plays as *The Women* (1936) and *Kiss the Boys
Good-Bye* (1938). From 1943 to 1947 she represented Connecticut in the U.S.
House of Representatives as a conservative and from 1953 to 1956 served as
U.S. ambassador to Italy. In 1959 Luce was appointed ambassador to Brazil
but resigned after winning a bitter Senate confirmation fight. She was married to HENRY LUCE.

Luce, Henry (1898–1967), editor and publisher. Credited with creating the
modern news magazine, Luce achieved immediate success with his publication of *Time* in 1923, followed by *Fortune* (1930), *Life* (1936), and *Sports Illustrated* (1954). His radio program and movie newsreels, "March of Time,"
ran from 1928 to 1943. Born in China to American missionaries, he urged a
vigorous pro-China and anti-Communist foreign policy. Luce also produced television programs and operated radio and television stations. He
was married to CLARE BOOTHE LUCE.

Luciano, Lucky (Charles Salvadore Lucania; 1897–1962), Italian-born racke-
teer. Luciano, one of the most powerful figures in organized crime, was arrested twenty-five times between 1919 and 1936, but was convicted only
once. During World War II he helped U.S. military intelligence through his
Mafia connections and was given a suspended sentence on condition that
he leave the country. Luciano returned to Naples, Italy, where he lived out
his life in luxury.

Luisetti, Angelo ("Hank") (1916–2002), basketball player. Luisetti was a
three-time All-American forward at Stanford (1935–38) and revolutionized
the game of basketball with his running, one-handed shot. This ended the
era of the traditional two-handed set shot and evolved into today's jump
shot. Known for quick, controlled dribbling, he introduced the behind-the-
back dribble and the no-look pass. In 1938 Luisetti became the first college
player to score fifty points in a game. He played for various teams at the
AAU level, but his career ended at age twenty-eight when he contracted
spinal meningitis.

Lundy, Benjamin (1789–1839), ABOLITIONIST. Lundy organized the Union Humane Society of Ohio in 1815, one of the first antislavery organizations. As a publisher he founded and edited the antislavery newspapers *Genius of Universal Emancipation* and the *National Enquirer.* Lundy traveled widely, writing and speaking against slavery. He influenced JOHN QUINCY ADAMS to oppose the extension of slavery when Adams was a congressman.

Lusitania, British passenger liner sunk without warning by a German submarine, May 7, 1915, during WORLD WAR I. The world's largest passenger liner, the *Lusitania* was torpedoed off the coast of Ireland, resulting in 1,198 deaths, 128 of them U.S. citizens. Although the United States was neutral at the time, this act of piracy increased anti-German sentiment and support for the Allies. Later disclosures showed that the ship did carry a cargo of British munitions, despite Allied claims that it was only a passenger ship.

Lyon, Mary (1797–1849), pioneer in women's education. Lyon founded Mount Holyoke Female Seminary of Massachusetts (now Mount Holyoke College) in 1837, contributing significantly to the quality of women's education. She served as its president from 1837 to 1849.

M

MacArthur, Douglas (1880–1964), general during WORLD WAR II and the KOREAN WAR. MacArthur was chief of staff of the armed forces from 1930 to 1935; in 1932 he directed the suppression of the BONUS ARMY. During World War II he led the American campaign in the Pacific. His defense of the Philippines at BATAAN and CORREGIDOR earned him the Medal of Honor, but his impending defeat prompted President Franklin D. Roosevelt to send him to Australia in 1942. When he left, he declared, "I shall return." MacArthur recaptured the Philippines in 1944 at LEYTE GULF and accepted the Japanese surrender in Tokyo Bay aboard the USS *Missouri* in 1945.

After the war MacArthur took over as supreme commander of the Allied occupation forces in Japan and directed the establishment of a constitutional monarchy there. In 1950 he commanded U.N. forces in Korea, but differed with President Harry S. Truman over military strategy by wanting to extend the war into North Korea. MacArthur's public criticism of the government led Truman to remove him from command for insubordination in 1951. He received a hero's welcome on his return to America, and some conservative Republicans unsuccessfully tried to nominate him for the presidency in 1952 (as they had in 1948). He retired then from public life.

MacDonough, Thomas (1783–1825), naval commander. MacDonough received many honors for defeating an invading British fleet during the WAR OF 1812. As head of the U.S. naval force on Lake Champlain, MacDonough faced the more powerful British naval squadron in 1814 and averted an invasion of New York State by forcing their retreat into Canada.

Mack, Connie (Cornelius McGillicuddy; 1862–1956), baseball manager. Mack helped organize the American League and was owner and manager of the Philadelphia Athletics from 1901 to 1950. He led the Athletics to nine AL pennants and five World Series championships. His fifty-year career in baseball included 3,755 wins and 3,967 losses, both all-time records that earned him a place in the baseball Hall of Fame in 1937.

McAdoo, William Gibbs (1863–1941), lawyer and statesman. McAdoo practiced law in New York City, and as president of the Hudson and Manhattan Railroad Company, he developed and built the system of rapid-transit tunnels under the Hudson River between New York and New Jersey. The son-in-law of President WOODROW WILSON, McAdoo acted as treasury secretary from 1913 to 1918 during WORLD WAR I. He also served as director-general of the railways and first chairman of the Federal Reserve Board, the Federal Farm Loan Board, and the War Finance Corporation. In 1932, as a supporter of the NEW DEAL, he was elected to the U.S. Senate from California, serving until 1938. McAdoo's attempts to secure the Democratic presidential nominations in 1920 and 1924 failed: in 1924 the nomination was tied up between McAdoo and New York governor ALFRED E. SMITH for 102 ballots, then on the 103d ballot, the delegates turned to compromise candidate JOHN W. DAVIS. His autobiography, *Crowded Years*, was published in 1931.

McCarran-Walter Immigration Act (June 30, 1952), law, also known as the Immigration and Nationality Act, tightening controls over aliens and immigrants. The act replaced the National Origins Act of 1924 and modified the 1929 quota formula by allowing a limited number of Asians to enter the United States. The law removed racial barriers and made citizenship available to people of all origins for the first time, but required screening of aliens to eliminate security risks.

McCarthy, Eugene (1916–), politician. McCarthy won election to the House of Representatives in 1948 and the U.S. Senate in 1958 as a liberal Democrat from Minnesota. A contender for the Democratic presidential nomination in the ELECTION OF 1968, McCarthy campaigned on a platform of opposition to the war in Vietnam, attracting widespread grass-roots and student support in important primaries. President Lyndon B. Johnson defeated him in the opening New Hampshire primary, but the narrowness of the victory margin was a factor in Johnson's deciding not to run for reelection. Robert F. Kennedy then joined the race for the Democratic nomination and defeated McCarthy in several primaries. With Kennedy's murder after he won the California primary, the nomination went to Vice President Hubert H. Humphrey. In 1976 McCarthy ran for president as an independent but fared poorly.

McCarthy, Joseph R. (1909–57), politician. McCarthy went to the U.S. Senate as a Republican from Wisconsin in 1946 and in 1950 gained national prominence when he made unsubstantiated charges that Communists had infiltrated the State Department and the U.S. Army. McCarthy's accusations fed an already-brewing anti-Communist hysteria in the country. His reckless and vicious attacks cost hundreds of people their jobs and careers. The televising in 1954 of the Army-McCarthy hearings made clear to a national audience his methods and bullying manner and led to his loss of public support and to his censure by the U.S. Senate on December 2, 1954.

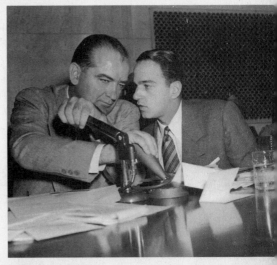

Joseph McCarthy

Senator McCarthy and his chief counsel, Roy Cohn, at the Army-McCarthy hearings in 1954.

McCarthy, Mary (1912–89), writer. In the course of a long and productive career, McCarthy published novels, short stories, criticism, essays, and travel books. One of her best-known novels, *The Group* (1963), follows the lives of several Vassar graduates in the 1930s. Noted for her satiric wit and perceptiveness, McCarthy won both the Edward MacDowell Medal and the National Medal for Literature in 1984.

McClellan, George B. (1826–85), Union general during the CIVIL WAR and politician. At the outbreak of the Civil War McClellan commanded volunteers from Ohio and in 1861 became commander of the Army of the Potomac. His youth, reputation for brilliance, and arrogance led to his nickname "the Young Napoleon." Popular with his men, he scorned his civilian superiors, especially President Abraham Lincoln. Because of his overcautiousness in confronting the Confederate forces, Lincoln removed him from command in 1862 but reinstated him after the Confederate victory at the second Battle of BULL RUN. He led Union forces at the Battle of ANTIETAM, winning a narrow victory. But when he failed to pursue the retreating Confederates, Lincoln again removed him from command. As the Democratic presidential candidate in 1864, McClellan lost the election to Lincoln. He became governor of New Jersey in 1878.

McClintock, Barbara (1902–92), pioneering geneticist. McClintock began her groundbreaking work in the genetics of corn in 1942 at a time when genes were not well understood. She discovered that genes can move on and between chromosomes. The phenomenon, called jumping genes, was questioned at the time, but superior molecular study techniques of the 1970s and 1980s allowed other scientists to confirm her discovery. McClintock was awarded the Nobel Prize in Physiology or Medicine in 1983.

McCormick, Cyrus Hall (1809–84), inventor and industrialist. McCormick revolutionized farming in 1832 with his invention of the mechanical reaper, a device to gather and cut grain. Horsedrawn, it enabled farmers to reduce the number of laborers while increasing the speed of harvesting. His invention eventually cut costs for both farmers and consumers.

McCulloch v. *Maryland* (1819), landmark decision by the U.S. Supreme Court ruling that Congress has not only the powers specifically granted by the CONSTITUTION but also those implied powers necessary or helpful in carrying out its authority. The Court ruled that when federal and state powers conflict, federal powers prevail. James W. McCulloch, a teller at a Baltimore branch of the Bank of the United States, had refused to pay a Maryland state tax on the bank. The state court ruled against him, but the Supreme Court reversed the decision, declaring the U.S. Banking Act of 1816 constitutional.

McGillivray, Alexander (1759?–93), Creek chief. The son of a Scottish father and a French-Creek mother, McGillivray was educated in South Carolina before becoming chief of the Creek Federation. A Loyalist during the American Revolution, he sought to protect Creek lands from American settlers by helping with British raids. After the war he joined with the Spanish in attacks against U.S. frontier settlements in Georgia and Tennessee. In 1790 George Washington persuaded McGillivray to sign a peace treaty guaranteeing Creek sovereignty over certain lands.

McGovern, George (1922–), politician. McGovern won a seat in the House of Representatives as a liberal Democrat from South Dakota in 1956 and a U.S. Senate seat in 1962. As the Democratic presidential nominee in 1972, McGovern pledged broad reforms and removal of U.S. troops from Vietnam, but lost to the incumbent Richard Nixon in a landslide. He was defeated for a fourth term in the Senate in 1980 and withdrew from the 1984 presidential race after failing to win early primaries.

McGuffey, William Holmes (1800–73), educator and clergyman. McGuffey's series of illustrated reading books for elementary schools, begun in 1836, became an immediate success and eventually sold over 120 million copies. Titled *Eclectic Readers,* the books became popularly known as *McGuffey's Readers* and were the basic primer for American schoolchildren, particularly in the Midwest, for about a hundred years. The content included proverbs, grammar, and selections from Shakespeare. The tone was moralistic, extolling patriotism, religion, good behavior, and games and sports.

McKinley, William (1843–1901), twenty-fifth president of the United States (1897–1901). Born in Niles, Ohio, McKinley fought for the Union during the

Civil War. He served in the House of Representatives as a Republican (1876–90); as chairman of the Ways and Means Committee he sponsored the MCKINLEY TARIFF, the unpopularity of which contributed to his reelection defeat in 1890. McKinley won the governorship of Ohio in 1891 and 1893 and made widespread improvements of the state's transportation systems.

With the support of Cleveland millionaire MARK HANNA, McKinley won the Republican presidential nomination in 1896 and defeated Democrat William Jennings Bryan. During McKinley's administration, Americans won the SPANISH-AMERICAN WAR. As a result, GUAM, the PHILIPPINES, PUERTO RICO, HAWAII, and AMERICAN SAMOA became U.S. possessions in 1899. McKinley won reelection to the presidency in 1900, but six months into his second term, on September 6, 1901, he was shot by anarchist LEON CZOLGOSZ at the Pan-American Exposition in Buffalo, New York. He died on September 14 of an infection in his wound, becoming the third president to be assassinated and the fifth to die in office.

McKinley Tariff (1890), law establishing record-high tariffs on many imported items. Sponsored by Representative William McKinley, chair of the House Ways and Means Committee, the act was designed to protect American industries from foreign competition. Its unpopularity led to its replacement by the Wilson Act in 1894.

McNamara, Robert Strange (1916–), business executive and public official. McNamara taught business administration at Harvard Business School (1940–43). He later joined the Ford Motor Company (1946), becoming president (1960), the first from outside the Ford family. As secretary of defense (1961–68), McNamara was a member of President JOHN F. KENNEDY's inner circle of advisers. He continued his cabinet position under President LYNDON B. JOHNSON and was a leading proponent of the escalation of the VIETNAM WAR. He resigned from his office in 1968 after becoming disillusioned with the war and became president of the World Bank (1968–81). McNamara wrote a memoir, *The Tragedy and Lessons of Vietnam* (1995), calling it a "terrible, terrible mistake" and becoming the most prominent national official to apologize for the U.S. involvement in the war.

Macon's Bill No. 2 (May 1, 1810), law enacted by Congress during the Napoleonic Wars to motivate Great Britain and France, then at war, to cease illegal seizures of American commercial vessels. Macon's Bill affirmed American trade with all countries but would ban trade with either France or Great Britain unless seizure of neutral ships stopped. This bill replaced the Non-Intercourse Act but failed to stop the seizure of ships.

Madison, Dolley (1768–1849), wife of President James Madison. Born in Philadelphia, Dolley Payne Todd was a young widow when Madison married her in 1795. Considered the ultimate Washington hostess, she presided over the White House with elegant style when her husband became president. She had already served eight years as White House hostess for widowed President Thomas Jefferson while Madison was Jefferson's secretary of state. When, during the War of 1812, the British burned the White House, Dolley Madison earned the nation's enduring gratitude by rescuing the original Declaration of Independence and a Gilbert Stuart portrait of George Washington and carried these historical treasures to safety.

Madison, James (1751–1836), fourth president of the United States (1809–17). Born in Port Conway, Virginia, Madison graduated from Princeton and began his forty-year political career by becoming involved in Virginia's politics. In 1776, as a member of the Virginia convention that wrote the state's pioneering constitution and declaration of rights, he took a strong stand for religious liberty. In the 1780s Madison was a key member of the Virginia legislature, where he won enactment of many of the statutes drafted in 1779 by his friend and mentor Thomas Jefferson, including the Virginia Statute for Religious Freedom. He was also a leading advocate of reform of the ARTICLES OF CONFEDERATION, a key delegate to the ANNAPOLIS CONVENTION of 1786, and one of the foremost members of the CONSTITUTIONAL CONVENTION of 1787.

Because of his pathbreaking VIRGINIA PLAN (the basis of the convention's work in framing the Constitution), his brilliant analyses of American politics and governance, and his extensive notes on debates in the convention, he has been dubbed the father of the Constitution (a title he himself always rejected). Madison campaigned for ratification of the document in the FEDERALIST PAPERS, a collection of essays he wrote with John Jay and Alexander Hamilton. As a representative in Congress (1789–97), Madison was a leader in the drive to add the BILL OF RIGHTS to the Constitution.

After serving for eight years as secretary of state in Jefferson's administration, Madison became the Democratic-Republican party's choice for president, winning in 1808 and again in 1812. His presidency was tainted by the unpopular WAR OF 1812, derided as "Mr. Madison's War." With its end, however, the country regained its optimism, opening the ERA OF GOOD FEELINGS and restoring Madison's popularity.

Mahan, Alfred Thayer (1840–1914), naval strategist and historian. Mahan graduated from the U.S. Naval Academy in 1859 and served in the Civil War. A prominent American historian who emphasized the importance of sea power in war and peace, he influenced the growth of the U.S. Navy and promoted U.S. imperialism. Mahan wrote *The Influence of Sea Power upon History, 1660–1783* (1890), which had a strong impact on U.S. and world naval strategy and foreign policy preceding World War I.

Mailer, Norman (1923–), novelist and journalist. Mailer first gained prominence with his novel of World War II, *The Naked and the Dead* (1948). He used fictional, autobiographical, and journalistic styles to present his sharp views on the violence and corruption of social values in American society.

Mailer won two Pulitzer Prizes, one in 1968 for *The Armies of the Night*, a journalistic account of the 1967 anti-Vietnam War demonstration at the Pentagon, and the other for *The Executioner's Song* (1979), about the life and death of murderer Gary Gilmore. In 1969 Mailer ran unsuccessfully for mayor of New York City on a platform calling for the city to become the fifty-first state in the Union.

Maine (Pine Tree State) became the twenty-third state when it joined the Union on March 15, 1820. (See maps, pages 540 and 541.) The most eastern of the states, it occupies a region explored by Samuel de Champlain in 1604. Maine was part of Massachusetts until it was admitted as a free state under the Missouri Compromise. Tourism is a major industry. The state is more than 90 percent forested, so people come to hunt for deer and bear, and to fish and boat in its thousands of lakes and rivers. Maine, known for its lobster caught off the rocky coastline, leads the nation in production of wood products, potatoes, sardines, and blueberries. Important, too, is the manufacture of textiles and shoes. Maine's largest cities are Portland, Bangor, Lewiston, and Augusta (the capital). Noted personalities born in Maine include HANNIBAL HAMLIN, NELSON A. ROCKEFELLER, MARGARET CHASE SMITH, and EDNA ST. VINCENT MILLAY.

Malcolm X (Malcolm Little; 1925–65), black militant leader. The son of a Baptist minister who followed the teachings of Marcus Garvey, he converted to Islam in 1952 while imprisoned for burglary and adopted the name Malcolm X, the X being symbolic of the slaves' stolen identity. He became a Muslim minister and spent a decade as a charismatic speaker on behalf of black separatism and black nationalism and pride. In 1963 Malcolm broke with the more militant wing of the movement and softened his black separatist views, forming a rival group, the Organization of Afro-American Unity (OAAU). In 1965 while giving a speech at Harlem's Audubon Ballroom, he was assassinated, allegedly by Black Muslims. His book *The Autobiography of Malcolm X* (1965), written in collaboration with ALEX HALEY, became a classic.

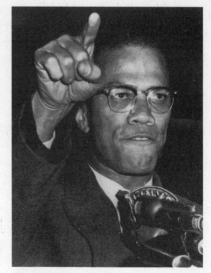

Malcolm X

Manhattan Project *See* ATOMIC BOMB.

Manifest Destiny, the belief of many political leaders in the nineteenth century that the United States was destined by Divine Providence to stretch from the Atlantic to the Pacific Ocean. Many Americans justified western territorial acquisitions on the basis of manifest destiny, as well as the lands gained as a result of the Mexican and Spanish-American wars.

Manila Bay, Battle of (May 1, 1898), the first important battle of the SPANISH-AMERICAN WAR. With the outbreak of war, Commodore GEORGE DEWEY led the American fleet's attack on the Spanish fleet at Manila Bay in the Philippines. Within seven hours the ten-vessel Spanish fleet had been destroyed; American damages and casualties were slight. Dewey blockaded Manila Harbor, and the city surrendered three and a half months later.

Mankiller, Wilma (1945–), author, activist, and former chief of the Cherokee Nation. Mankiller became the first woman chief of the Cherokee Nation of Oklahoma in 1985 and the first female in modern history to lead a major Native American tribe. Born in Oklahoma to a Cherokee father and a Dutch-Irish mother, she moved with her family to San Francisco as part of the Bureau of Indian Affairs relocation program in the 1950s. In 1969 she was inspired by the American Indian Movement protest on Alcatraz Island, leading to her involvement in the struggle for Native American rights. In 1976 Mankiller returned to Oklahoma to promote women's and children's issues, winning many grants to finance Cherokee self-sufficiency programs. She resigned as chief in 1995 but continued her influence as an author and political speaker.

Mann, Horace (1796–1859), educator and reformer. Called the father of the American common school, Mann played a leading role in shaping the American elementary school system, as his movement to improve free public schools in Massachusetts spread nationwide. As secretary of the Massachusetts State Board of Education (1837–48), Mann fought for reforms that resulted in a doubling of the amount of money allocated to schools, increased teacher salaries, and an extended school year. He founded the first state normal school for teacher training in 1839. Mann took a seat in the U.S. House of Representatives in 1848 as an antislavery Whig but lost his quest to become governor as a Free-Soil candidate in 1850.

Mantle, Mickey (1931–1995), baseball player. Mantle played center field for the New York Yankees from 1951 to 1968 and ranks among the leading home run hitters in the history of baseball, with 536 in regular season play. He also hit a record eighteen home runs in World Series play. Mantle won the most valuable player award in the American League three times and won the triple crown in 1956 (batting average, runs batted in, home runs). Mantle helped lead the Yankees to twelve World Series and seven championships and became a member of the baseball Hall of Fame in 1974.

Marbury v. Madison (1803), landmark decision marking the first time the Supreme Court declared a law passed by Congress unconstitutional. William Marbury, a member of the Federalist party, was named by outgoing Federalist president John Adams as a justice of the peace in the capital district during the final hours of Adams's administration. Incoming president Thomas Jefferson, a member of the rival Democratic-Republican party, ordered Secretary of State James Madison to withhold Marbury's commission. As one of the MIDNIGHT JUDGES appointed under the Judiciary Act of 1801, Marbury sued in accordance with Section 13 of the JUDICIARY ACT OF 1789, asking the Court to force Madison to grant the appointment. In his decision Chief Justice JOHN MARSHALL established the principle of JUDICIAL REVIEW. In denying Marbury's request, Marshall ruled that because Section 13 gave the Supreme Court powers not provided by the Constitution, it was unconstitutional and invalid, so the Court lacked jurisdiction. The decision established supremacy of the Constitution over laws passed by Congress and the power of the Court to decide on the constitutionality of legislation.

March, Fredric (Frederick Bickel; 1897–1975), actor. March, during a long career, made a graceful transition from playing debonair leading men to character roles. He won Academy Awards for his acting in *Dr. Jekyll and Mr. Hyde* (1932) and *The Best Years of Our Lives* (1946). Broadway hits included *A Bell for Adano* (1944) and *Long Day's Journey into Night* (1956), for which he won a Tony Award. March was noted in private life for his antifascist activities.

Marciano, Rocky (Rocco Marchegiano; 1923–69), boxer. Marciano won the world heavyweight championship with a knockout in 1952 and successfully defended his title until he retired in 1956. His career record of forty-nine victories (forty-three by knockouts) and no defeats earned him the appellation "the Brockton Blockbuster," a reference to his hometown in Massachusetts.

Marcy, William (1786–1857), politician. Marcy coined the phrase "spoils system." While serving in the U.S. Senate as a Democrat from New York, he delivered a speech in 1832 in defense of an important appointment by President Andrew Jackson in which he stated, "To the victor belongs the spoils." He was a member of a dominant New York political group called the Albany Regency and later became governor. Marcy was secretary of war under James K. Polk and secretary of state under Franklin Pierce.

Marion, Francis (1732–95), leader of South Carolina troops during the AMERICAN REVOLUTION. Marion, a former Continental officer, earned the appellation "Swamp Fox" when he led his men in and out of the marshes for quick raids and surprise attacks against British and Loyalist troops. He and his men, ranging in number from twenty to two hundred, fought without compensation, using their firsthand knowledge of the geography of the land to cripple British advances.

Maris, Roger (Roger Maras; 1934–85), baseball player. Maris made sports history in 1961 when he broke Babe Ruth's single-season home run record of sixty by hitting sixty-one homers. Both totals are considered records because Maris hit his in a 162-game schedule and Ruth had a 154-game schedule. Maris, an outfielder, won the most valuable player award in the American League in 1960 and 1961 and hit a total of 275 career home runs.

Marne, Battles of the, two WORLD WAR I battles fought in France near the Marne River. In the first battle (September 5, 1914), the Allies halted the German invasion of France and transformed the war into four years of trench warfare. The fierce French offensive drove the Germans back to the Aisne River, where they became entrenched. In the second Battle of the Marne (July 18, 1918), the Allied forces led a victorious counteroffensive against the Germans, forcing them to retreat from the Marne. This offensive counterattack included American forces and was the start of the Allies' offenses that ended the war.

Marshall, George C. (1880–1959), military leader and statesman. A career military officer and chief of staff of the army during WORLD WAR II, Marshall served as adviser to Franklin D. Roosevelt. He was responsible for the military planning that led to American victory in the war. Appointed secretary of state by Harry S. Truman, he helped launch the MARSHALL PLAN in 1947 to assist European recovery after the war, receiving the Nobel Peace Prize in 1953 for his efforts. Marshall was instrumental in the formation of the NORTH ATLANTIC TREATY ORGANIZATION (NATO) and served as secretary of defense during the KOREAN WAR.

Marshall, John (1755–1835), fourth chief justice of the U.S. Supreme Court (1801–35). Marshall fought in the Continental Army during the American Revolution and served as a member of Virginia's House of Burgesses. A Federalist, he served in the House of Representatives and held the post of secretary of state. In 1797 he was one of the U.S. commissioners sent to France to resolve the XYZ AFFAIR. President John Adams appointed Marshall chief justice in 1801, just prior to the end of his presidential term. Marshall's thirty-four-year tenure on the Court had an immense impact on the judicial system. He advocated a strong central government and gave the Court power to overrule states when conflicts arise. He established judicial review and exercised it in the landmark case *Marbury* v. *Madison* (1803). In 1807 Marshall presided over the controversial treason trial of AARON BURR.

Marshall, Thomas R. (1854–1925), twenty-eighth vice president of the United States, under President Woodrow Wilson (1913–21). Marshall was the first vice president in nearly a hundred years to work with the same president for two terms, and he was the first to preside over a cabinet meeting. He supported Wilson's League of Nations and opposed woman suffrage and Prohibition. Marshall had served as governor of Indiana from 1909 to 1913. When he sought the Democratic nomination for president in 1912 as a favorite son candidate, he won the vice presidency instead. He is known for his statement, "What this country needs is a good five-cent cigar." When President Wilson was incapacitated by a stroke, Marshall was urged to take over. But he refused, afraid he would be accused of seizing power unconstitutionally.

Marshall, Thurgood (1908–93), jurist and civil rights advocate. Marshall gained national recognition between 1934 and 1961 as legal counsel for the National Association for the Advancement of Colored People (NAACP). Called "Mr. Civil Rights" for his support of racial justice, he argued thirty-two cases before the Supreme Court, including *Brown* v. *Board of Education of Topeka* (1954),

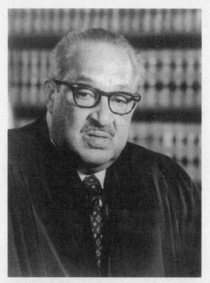

Thurgood Marshall

which brought about integration in public schools. Appointed by President Lyndon B. Johnson in 1967, Marshall became the first black member of the U.S. Supreme Court. He took outspoken liberal positions on capital punishment, free speech, school integration, and affirmative action. Marshall retired from the Court in 1991.

Marshall Plan (1947) (also called the European Recovery Program), a five-year program to help war-torn Europe recover economically after World War II. Proposed by Secretary of State George C. Marshall, the plan provided $13 billion in loans between 1948 and 1951 to European countries who pledged to control inflation and lower tariffs to receive the aid. Sixteen countries, including Germany and Italy, were recipients.

Marx Brothers, comedy team. The group consisted of Groucho (Julius; 1890–1977), Chico (Leonard; 1886?–1961), Harpo (born Adolph, later Arthur; 1893–1964), Gummo (Milton; 1894?–1977), and Zeppo (Herbert; 1901–79). Zeppo left the team in 1934 and Gummo left after their stage days. The Marx brothers became famous for their zany antics in vaudeville, Broadway, and motion pictures. They starred in *The Cocoanuts* (1925; film 1929) and *Animal Crackers* (1928; film 1930), and *A Night at the Opera* (1935) is considered a classic by film historians. Other memorable films include *Monkey Business* (1931) and *Duck Soup* (1933). Later Groucho established a solo career as host of the successful radio and television quiz show "You Bet Your Life," where he specialized in quick wit and insults.

Maryland (Old Line State) became on April 28, 1788, the seventh state to enter the Union. (See maps, pages 540 and 541.) After the area was explored by Capt. JOHN SMITH in 1608, King Charles I of England granted a royal charter to George Calvert (Lord Baltimore) to establish a colony there in 1632. Because the Chesapeake Bay nearly splits the state in two, Maryland has a long coastline. It is a leader in shipping and fishing, and the bay yields excellent seafood, especially crabs, oysters, and clams. Tobacco, vegetable canning, and manufacturing are also important industries. The largest cities include Baltimore, Silver Spring, and Bethesda. Annapolis is the capital and the home of the U.S. Naval Academy. Noted Marylanders include FRANCIS KEY, FREDERICK DOUGLASS, HARRIET TUBMAN, EDWIN BOOTH, JOHN WILKES BOOTH, BABE RUTH, and H. L. MENCKEN.

Mason, George (1925–92), political leader. An important Virginia Patriot, Mason served as a member of the Constitutional Convention of 1787 and helped draft the CONSTITUTION, which he refused to sign because it lacked a declaration of rights. It was Mason's Declaration of Rights, which he had prepared for the Virginia legislature in 1776, that eventually became the basis for the BILL OF RIGHTS.

Mason-Dixon Line, the east-west boundary line between Pennsylvania and Maryland and the north-south boundary between Delaware and Maryland. It became famous as the border between the North and the South during the Civil War. The line is named for two English surveyors, Charles Mason and Jeremiah Dixon, who were employed by William Penn and Lord Baltimore in 1763–67 to settle a boundary dispute.

Massachusetts (Bay State) became on February 6, 1788, the sixth state to join the Union. (See maps, pages 540 and 541.) The PILGRIMS settled PLYMOUTH COLONY in 1620 and the PURITANS settled the MASSACHU- SETTS BAY COLONY in 1628. Massachusetts, a leader in the events that led to the American Revolution, was the site of the first skirmishes of the war at LEXINGTON and CONCORD. Boston, the state's largest city and capital, has been called the "Cradle of Liberty" because of the important revolutionary events that occurred there, including the BOSTON MASSACRE and the BOSTON TEA PARTY. The sea for years was a mainstay of the economy, with New Bedford (once the whaling capital of the world), Boston, and Glouces- ter serving as important fishing ports. Cape Cod, the popular vacation is- lands of Martha's Vineyard and Nantucket, and western Massachusetts (the site of Tanglewood) contribute to the tourism industry. Still the leader in the manufacturing of shoes and textiles (though the industries have de- clined in recent years), Massachusetts leads also in communications equip- ment and electronics. The state is the largest producer of cranberries in the United States. The first college in North America, Harvard, was founded in Cambridge in 1636. The state has produced an impressive collection of pub- lic figures and writers including JOHN ADAMS, JOHN QUINCY ADAMS, JOHN F. KENNEDY, GEORGE H. W. BUSH, SAMUEL ADAMS, JOHN HAN- COCK, NATHANIEL HAWTHORNE, LOUISA MAY ALCOTT, HENRY THOREAU, EMILY DICKINSON, and RALPH WALDO EMERSON.

Massachusetts Bay Colony (1628), one of the first settlements in New England. Established by the PURITANS in Salem, Massachusetts, the Massachusetts Bay Company comprised settlers who wanted to "purify" the Anglican Church of England. It elected JOHN WINTHROP its first governor in 1630. In 1691 Plymouth Colony joined it to become one of the largest and most important colonies in North America.

Massasoit (1580?–1661), Wampanoag chief. Massasoit made a peace treaty with Governor JOHN CARVER of the Plymouth Colony shortly after the arrival of the Pilgrims in 1621. He remained friendly with white settlers throughout his life, teaching them survival skills. Massasoit and many of his men were invited to a feast to celebrate the first THANKSGIVING in Plymouth Colony in 1621.

Masters, Edgar Lee (1869–1950), author. As a writer of novels, poetry, plays, and historical biographies, Masters is best known for his volume of poems *Spoon River Anthology* (1915). Reflecting on the meaning of life, the collection is made up of over two hundred poetic monologues spoken by residents of Spoon River Cemetery. Masters also practiced law in the firm of defense attorney Clarence Darrow from 1903 to 1911.

Mather, a family of PURITAN clergymen. Richard Mather (1596–1669) came to the Massachusetts Bay Colony in 1635 to pursue religious freedom and became the pastor of Dorchester Church. A founder of the Congregational church, he married the widow of John Cotton after the death of his first wife. Increase Mather (1639–1723), son of Richard, served as the influential pastor of Old North Church, Boston. He married the daughter of John Cotton in 1662 and served as president of Harvard from 1685 to 1701. He aided in the renegotiation of the Massachusetts Bay's original charter at the courts of James II and William III. His *Cases of Conscience concerning Evil Spirits* (1693) reflected on the events of the Salem witchcraft crisis and helped end the executions. Cotton Mather (1663–1728), son of Increase, succeeded his father as pastor of Old North Church, Boston. Through his prolific writings and his support of witchcraft persecution, he contributed to the hysteria during the trials. The most important of his more than five hundred published works was *Magnalia Christi Americana* (1702) about early New England. Mather was the first American elected to the Royal Society of London in recognition of his scientific writings.

Mathewson, Christy (1880–1925), baseball player. A star right-handed pitcher for seventeen years with the New York Giants and the Cincinnati Reds, Mathewson won 373 games, a record for the National League shared with Grover Alexander. Called "Big Six," Mathewson became the first player in the twentieth century to win twenty-two or more games a season twelve years in a row. Known for developing the screwball pitch, he pitched three shutouts in the 1905 World Series. In 1936 Mathewson became one of the first players elected to baseball's Hall of Fame.

Mauldin, Bill (1921–2003), editorial cartoonist. Mauldin during World War II depicted army life in *Stars and Stripes,* an armed forces newspaper. His cartoons often featured Willie and Joe, two GIs displaying their long-suffering resentment of officers. Mauldin won the Pulitzer Prize for cartooning in 1945 and 1959.

Maximilian Affair (1864–67), diplomatic crisis in 1864 between the United States and France when Napoleon III appointed Archduke Maximilian of Austria as emperor of Mexico in an effort to establish a French empire there. The act was a violation of the MONROE DOCTRINE. Refusing to recognize the new government, the United States demanded removal of the French armies. After the Civil War, the United States posted a military force along the Rio Grande, and Napoleon removed his troops in 1866. The Mexicans overthrew the government and executed Maximilian.

Mayer, Louis B. (1885–1957), Russian-born motion picture producer. Mayer formed Metro Pictures Corporation and Louis B. Mayer Productions, which merged in 1924 to form Metro-Goldwyn-Mayer (MGM). He served as general manager of MGM for twenty-seven years. In partnership with Irving Thalberg, Mayer created a huge studio system and became the highest paid executive in the country for several years. He cornered the market on Hollywood stars and showcased them in classics such as *Ben Hur* (1926) and *The Good Earth* (1937). Mayer discovered such talents as the European star GRETA GARBO, CLARK GABLE, JOAN CRAWFORD, and SPENCER TRACY, as well as numerous writers and directors. He left MGM in 1951 and served briefly as chairman of Cinerama Productions before he died of leukemia.

Mayflower Compact (November 21, 1620), the first written agreement of self-government in America. When colonists on the *Mayflower* discovered they had landed several hundred miles north of their Virginia destination owing to storms at sea, they realized they were outside the area of English jurisdiction. The male heads of families drew up a compact aboard ship and required all to sign it before going ashore to settle in Plymouth. They pledged to obey just and equal laws passed by the majority. The Mayflower Compact remained in effect until the late 1600s. (See box, page 323, for the complete text.)

Mayo Brothers Charles (1865–1939), and William (1861–1939), surgeons. Natives of Minnesota, the Mayo brothers were sons of a frontier physician. They began their careers with their father in Rochester, Minnesota, at St. Mary's Hospital. In 1905 they began to broaden their staff to include highly skilled specialists in various medical fields. Seeking out the latest medical advances, the Mayos were instrumental in establishing sterile conditions in the operating room and in using X rays as a diagnostic tool. They began the Mayo Clinic in 1889, the first private cooperative medical organization in the United States. The Mayo Clinic grew to be one of the world's

★ The Mayflower Compact

In the Name of God, Amen. We, whose names are underwritten, the Loyal Subjects of our dread sovereign Lord King James, by the Grace of God, of Great Britain, France, and Ireland, King, Defender of the Faith, &c.

Having undertaken for the Glory of God, and Advancement of the Christian Faith, and the Honour of our King and Country, a Voyage to plant the first colony in the northern Parts of Virginia; Do by these Presents, solemnly and mutually in the Presence of God and one another, covenant and combine ourselves together into a civil Body Politick, for our better Ordering and Preservation, and Furtherance of the Ends aforesaid; and by Virtue hereof do enact, constitute, and frame, such just and equal Laws, Ordinances, Acts, Constitutions, and Offices, from time to time, as shall be thought most meet and convenient for the general Good of the Colony; unto which we promise all due Submission and Obedience.

In witness whereof we have hereunto subscribed our names at Cape Cod the eleventh of November, in the Reign of our Sovereign Lord King James of England, France, and Ireland, the eighteenth and of Scotland, the fifty-fourth. Anno Domini, 1620.

largest medical centers. The brothers established the Mayo Foundation for Medical Education and Research in 1915 as part of the University of Minnesota.

Mays, Willie (1931–), baseball player. An outstanding hitter, Mays played center field for the New York (later San Francisco) Giants from 1951 to 1972, thrilling crowds with his skill and enthusiasm for the game. He won the National League's most valuable player award twice (1954 and 1965) and in 1954 and 1962 helped lead the San Francisco team to a World Series (winning in 1954). Mays's total of 660 career home runs is fourth only to Hank Aaron, Barry Bonds, and Babe Ruth. He entered baseball's Hall of Fame in 1979.

Mead, Margaret (1901–78), anthropologist. Known for her pioneering studies on culture and human behavior, Mead spent many years living among the island tribes of the South Pacific. She observed the development of social behavior, particularly among children, and contrasted values between cultures. She examined the importance of time and environment on human values and the influence of traditional male-female roles on personality. Mead's studies of primitive cultures led her to delve into American cultural standards, publishing one of her most important books, *Male and Female: A Study of the Sexes in a Changing World*, in 1949. She lectured widely and wrote on family life and child rearing.

Meade, George G. (1815–72), Union general during the CIVIL WAR. After commanding the Pennsylvania volunteers and fighting in most of the important battles of the Civil War, including ANTIETAM, FREDERICKSBURG, and CHANCELLORSVILLE, Meade was appointed commander of the Army of the Potomac in 1863. He led the Union victory at GETTYSBURG. Although criticized (unfairly, some historians say) for allowing the Confederate troops to retreat into Virginia, Meade kept his position when Gen. Ulysses S. Grant became supreme Union commander in 1864.

Meany, George (1894–1980), labor leader. Meany served as president of the New York State Federation of Labor during the Great Depression. In 1952 he became president of the AMERICAN FEDERATION OF LABOR and negotiated its merger with the CONGRESS OF INDUSTRIAL ORGANIZATIONS in 1955, remaining as head of the AFL-CIO until 1979. He was instrumental in the expulsion of the Teamsters from the union in 1957 because of corruption, and tried to strengthen anticommunist forces in labor. In 1953 he received the Presidential Medal of Freedom.

Medicare/Medicaid (July 30, 1965), two publicly funded health insurance programs established with the passage of amendments to the SOCIAL SECURITY ACT. Medicare provides most citizens or permanent residents of the United States over age sixty-five with basic health insurance, covering hospital and physician services. A younger person with a disability or with chronic kidney disease may also qualify. Medicare is funded by a tax on the earnings of employees that is matched by the employer. In November 2003 a new prescription drug benefit was added to the program, becoming the largest expansion in its history. Medicaid provides federal matching-fund grants to the states to provide health insurance for the poor. The Medicare and Medicaid programs are facing challenges caused by a growing population of senior citizens; by 2030 it is expected to double to 76 million Americans. As a result, there is growing concern about the cost of financing care for future generations. Both Medicare and Medicaid are administered by the Centers for Medicare and Medicaid Services (CMS).

Mellon, Andrew W. (1855–1937), financier and industrialist. Mellon took over his father's banking firm in 1886 and built a fortune in steel and public utilities industries. Appointed secretary of the treasury by Warren G. Harding, he served from 1921 until 1932 under Presidents Harding, Calvin Coolidge, and Herbert Hoover. As a conservative Republican, he drastically lowered taxes on the rich and reduced the World War I debt by $9 billion. He later served as ambassador to Great Britain. Mellon gave his $25 million art collection to the U.S. government with enough money to build the National Gallery of Art in Washington, D.C.

Melville, Herman (1819–91), author. Melville, who came from an impoverished home, first went to sea as a cabin boy in 1839. A subsequent trip on a whaler in 1841–42 took him to the South Seas, where he jumped ship and lived for a time in the Marquesas Islands. At one point, he was held captive by savages before escaping to Tahiti, where he worked as a laborer, observing the people. These and subsequent experiences as a seaman provided the material for a series of highly popular sea novels, including *Typee* (1846), *Omoo* (1847), *Mardi* (1849), and *Redburn* (1849). These were followed by his masterpiece, *Moby-Dick* (1851). Through its story of a whaling voyage and Captain Ahab's obsessive search for the "great white whale" that for him embodies evil, Melville explored symbolically the conflict between human beings and their fate. This and later books were not well received at the time by critics or his audience, who failed to understand his departure from pure adventure tales, and his popularity waned. He spent the last nineteen years of his life in obscurity, writing and working as a customs inspector. It was not until some thirty years after his death that his mastery of style, his narrative power, and his keen insights into the human condition came to be recognized by critics and readers.

Mencken, H. L. (Henry Louis; 1880–1956), writer, editor, and critic. One of the most influential journalists of the twentieth century, Mencken started his writing career with the *Baltimore Morning Herald* in 1899 and later moved to the *Baltimore Sun,* where he remained for over forty years. In 1923 he cofounded and edited the *American Mercury,* a magazine of humor and social criticism. Mencken became a severe critic of American society and literature, attacking with biting wit and satire what he saw as the superficiality of the middle class. He wrote *The American Language* (1919), an authoritative study of American English, as well as a three-volume autobiography, *Happy Days* (1940), *Newspaper Days* (1941), and *Heathen Days* (1943).

Menéndez de Avilés, Pedro (1519–74), Spanish explorer. Menéndez firmly established Spanish power in Florida when he was sent by King Philip II of Spain to drive the French away. He founded St. Augustine in 1565, which became the first permanent European settlement in the New World. As governor of St. Augustine, Menéndez led an attack on the French Huguenots' Fort Caroline on the St. Johns River. The Spanish massacred the French, ending any further French attempts to settle in Florida.

Menninger, family of psychiatrists who pioneered mental health treatment in a clinic setting. Charles Menninger (1862–1953) and his son Karl (1893–1990) founded the Menninger Clinic in the 1920s, which became an important center of psychiatric therapy and research. Joined in 1926 by another son, William (1899–1966), the family established the Menninger Foundation in 1941 to help Americans understand the issues about mental health. Located in Topeka, Kansas, the Menninger Foundation is one of the most prominent psychiatric centers in the world. Karl served as chairman of the board of trustees. His numerous books on psychiatry and mental illness include *The Human Mind* (1930), *Man against Himself* (1938), and *The Crime of Punishment* (1968). William became general secretary of the foundation and won the Distinguished Service Medal for his service as psychiatry consultant during World War II. His writings include *Psychiatry in a Troubled World* (1948) and *Psychiatry: Its Evolution and Present Status* (1948).

Mercantilism, economic system in which countries gained wealth by acquiring colonies to provide raw materials usually not available at home. During the 1700s the British government employed the system, requiring the colonists to send raw materials to Great Britain, to be manufactured into goods purchased in the colonies. The mercantile system thus implied that the colonies existed to benefit the mother country.

Mercury Project (1961–63), America's first manned space program, designed to put a man in space and to gather information about the capabilities of humans in space. The first manned suborbital flight (Mercury 3) was undertaken on May 5, 1961, by astronaut ALAN SHEPARD in *Freedom 7*. Lt. Col. JOHN GLENN became the first American to orbit the earth when he circled the globe three times aboard the Mercury capsule *Friendship 7*. The final flight of the project (Mercury 9) occurred May 15–16, 1963, when Maj. Gordon Cooper, Jr., made the longest flight, completing twenty-two earth orbits aboard Mercury capsule *Faith 7*. Project Mercury was succeeded by the GEMINI program.

Meuse-Argonne, Battle of (September 26–November 11, 1918), one of the last major engagements of WORLD WAR I. The Allied offensive, led by U.S. general JOHN PERSHING, attacked and destroyed the German defenses in the heavily fortified Argonne Forest along the Meuse River in France. The offensive involved over a million American troops and culminated with the negotiation of the armistice on November 11, 1918.

Mexican Cession (1848), territory acquired from Mexico by the terms of the TREATY OF GUADALUPE HIDALGO, which ended the MEXICAN WAR. America's southern border became the Rio Grande, and the United States acquired what are now California, Utah, Nevada, and parts of New Mexico, Arizona, and Wyoming. This acquisition of over 500,000 square miles cost the United States $15 million. (See map on page 245.)

Mexican War (1846–48), conflict between the United States and Mexico. The revolt and declaration of independence of Texas from Mexico in 1836 eventually resulted in the annexation of Texas to the Union in 1845. Mexico refused to recognize the annexation and disputed the boundary of the Rio Grande. After a still-controversial incident along the border, President JAMES K. POLK, a proponent of EXPANSIONISM and MANIFEST DESTINY, asked Congress for a declaration of war. He sent Gen. ZACHARY TAYLOR to invade northern Mexico. Col. STEPHEN KEARNY led U.S. troops to take New Mexico and California, and Gen. WINFIELD SCOTT led his forces to capture Vera Cruz and Mexico City. All three campaigns were successful.

The TREATY OF GUADALUPE HIDALGO ended the war on February 2, 1848. Mexico ceded all claims to Texas, and the United States acquired the lands known as the MEXICAN CESSION; it also agreed to assume outstanding claims of American citizens against Mexico. The acquisition of new lands intensified the slavery controversy in the United States, raising the question of whether the territories should be slave or free. The debate raged for twelve years, culminating in the Civil War. Participants in the later conflict who received firsthand experience in the Mexican War included ULYSSES S. GRANT, WILLIAM TECUMSEH SHERMAN, GEORGE B. MCCLELLAN, ROBERT E. LEE, STONEWALL JACKSON, and JEFFERSON DAVIS.

Michener, James (1907–1997), author. Michener served as a naval historian in the South Pacific at the end of World War II and received the 1948 Pulitzer Prize for *Tales of the South Pacific* (1947), a collection of stories of his experiences. These stories provided the inspiration for the musical *South Pacific* (1949), which won the 1950 Pulitzer Prize for drama. Some of Michener's other works include *The Bridges at Toko-Ri* (1953), *Sayonara* (1954), and such epic novels as *Hawaii* (1959) and *Centennial* (1974).

Michigan (Wolverine State) became on January 26, 1837, the twenty-sixth state to enter the Union. (See maps, pages 540 and 541.) Michigan is surrounded by four of the Great Lakes and is the only state divided into two separate land areas, the Upper Peninsula and the Lower Peninsula. The first permanent settlement was Sault Sainte Marie, established by Father Marquette. Detroit, the largest city, is a center of the automobile industry in the United States. Other major cities include Grand Rapids, Warren, Flint, and Lansing, the capital. Battle Creek is known as the "Cereal Bowl of America" because it produces more breakfast cereal than any city in the world. Michigan is also a leader in the manufacture of airplane parts and machine tools. Its farm products include cherries, navy beans, and Christmas trees. Tourism is an important industry, with visitors coming to fish, hunt, and explore the scenic beauty. Noted personalities born in Michigan include HENRY FORD, SUGAR RAY ROBINSON, RING LARDNER, EDNA FERBER, and CHARLES A. LINDBERGH.

Midnight Judges, judicial appointments made by JOHN ADAMS just before the end of his presidential term in 1801. The Federalist-controlled Congress passed the JUDICIARY ACT OF 1801, which created sixteen federal judgeships. Adams appointed Federalists who opposed the Democratic-Republican principles of his successor, THOMAS JEFFERSON. Many of the papers were signed just before midnight as a gesture of antagonism toward Jefferson, who called the men "midnight judges." Jefferson did not want to recognize the appointments, eventually leading to the repeal of the Judiciary Act of 1801 and the landmark *Marbury* v. *Madison* case.

Midway, Battle of (June 3–6, 1942), the first decisive U.S. naval victory over the Japanese in WORLD WAR II. In the three-day battle, U.S. carrier-based planes countered the Japanese naval and air assault of Midway Island in the Pacific. All four of Japan's aircraft carriers were sunk, devastating its naval air power, halting momentum, and relieving the threat to Hawaii. The Battle of Midway was a turning point in the Pacific war.

Mies van der Rohe, Ludwig (1886–1969), German-born architect. Mies became known during the 1930s for his introduction of glass skyscrapers. He designed clear, elegant constructions of brick, steel, and glass, including the campus of the Illinois Institute of Technology, where, as director of the School of Architecture, Mies taught "less is more." He codesigned, with Philip Johnson, the acclaimed Seagram Building in New York in 1958.

Mikan, George (1924–), basketball player. Mikan became the first big man to dominate the game by using his height (6'10") and hook shot. Chosen by the Associated Press as the greatest basketball player in the first half of the twentieth century, Mikan played in the National Basketball Association for the Minneapolis Lakers and helped his team win five championships and led the league in scoring three times. When the American Basketball Association was formed in 1967, Mikan became its first commissioner. He entered the basketball Hall of Fame in 1959.

Miles, Nelson (1839–1925), soldier and commander of the U.S. army. After service in major Civil War battles, Miles continued his military career in many of the western Indian campaigns. He forced the surrender of CHIEF JOSEPH in 1877 and GERONIMO in 1886. At Wounded Knee his troops massacred the Sioux, ending the Indian wars. In 1894 Miles commanded troops at the PULLMAN STRIKE in Chicago and became commander of the U.S. Army in 1895. During the SPANISH-AMERICAN WAR Miles led the forces that invaded and took control of Puerto Rico.

Millay, Edna St. Vincent (1892–1950), poet. Millay wrote sentimental but witty poetry about love, death, and rebelliousness, earning the 1923 Pulitzer Prize for *The Harp Weaver and Other Poems*. She also experimented with drama; a commission by the Metropolitan Opera Company resulted in the libretto for the opera *The King's Henchman* (1927). A master of the sonnet, Millay often portrayed her political and social ideas in her poetry. She donated money to defend SACCO AND VANZETTI and personally appealed to the governor for their lives.

Miller, Arthur (1915–), playwright. Miller's works explore the conflicts between individual and social morality. He won two Pulitzer Prizes, one for his masterpiece *Death of a Salesman* (1949) and the other for *A View from the Bridge* (1955). Other works include *The Crucible* (1953), in which the Salem witchcraft trials serve as a parable for McCarthyism, and *After the Fall* (1964), a semiautobiographical account of his marriage to Marilyn Monroe. Miller wrote the screenplay for *The Misfits* (1961), the last film made by both Monroe and Clark Gable.

Miller, Glenn (1904–44), trombonist and bandleader of the 1930s and 1940s. The Glenn Miller Orchestra, highly popular during the big-band swing era, played such hits as "Moonlight Serenade," "Tuxedo Junction," and "Chattanooga Choo-Choo." Miller dissolved his band in 1942 to lead the U.S.

Army Air Force Band in Europe. He disappeared on a flight from England to Paris in 1944; his plane's wreckage has never been found.

Mineta, Norman Y. (1931–), politician. Elected mayor of San Jose, California, in 1971, Mineta became the first Japanese-American mayor of a major U.S. city. A Democratic member of the U.S. House of Representatives since 1974, he was chosen by his colleagues in 1992 to chair the House Public Works and Transportation committee, the first Asian-American to head a major congressional committee. Mineta served as secretary of commerce during the Clinton administration and was selected by President GEORGE W. BUSH as the nation's first Asian-American to serve as secretary of transportation (2001–). The only Democrat appointed to Bush's cabinet, Mineta is the first Department of Transportation (DOT) secretary to have served in a previous cabinet position and the first to have served presidents of different parties consecutively. His position became very visible following the events of September 11, 2001, when Mineta took action to shut down the nation's air system and coordinate interim security measures to ensure safety. As a child, Mineta was one of 120,000 Americans of Japanese ancestry who were evacuated from the West Coast and placed in internment camps during World War II. He was a driving force behind the passage of the Civil Liberties Act of 1988, which provided reparations for former internees. In 1995 George Washington University awarded the Martin Luther King, Jr. Commemorative Medal to Mineta for his contributions to the field of civil rights and in 2001 the San Jose Airport was renamed the Norman Y. Mineta San Jose International Airport.

Minnesota (Gopher State) became on May 11, 1858, the thirty-second state to join the Union. (See maps, pages 540 and 541.) Minneapolis is the largest city, separated from its "twin," St. Paul, the capital, by the Mississippi River. Other large cities include Duluth, Bloomington, and Rochester, location of the world-famous Mayo Clinic. Minnesota leads the United States in iron ore production and has become an important trading center. Major agricultural products include grain, sugar beets, rice, and cheese and butter. Its scenic beauty, lakes, and forests make it an attractive vacation destination. The Mississippi River and its branches, which begin as a small stream flowing out of Lake Itasca, eventually drain over 50 percent of the state. Notable natives of Minnesota include WARREN E. BURGER, WILLIAM O. DOUGLAS, WALTER F. MONDALE, EUGENE McCARTHY, SINCLAIR LEWIS, and CHARLES SCHULZ.

Minority Presidents, those elected by a plurality of less than 50 percent of the popular vote. Fourteen men (three of them twice) became president of the United States without winning a majority of the popular votes. (SEE TABLE.) On the other hand, four candidates lost the presidency even though they had a plurality of the popular vote, because they did not have

Minority Presidents

Year	President	Percentage of Popular Vote
1824	John Quincy Adams	30.92
1844	James K. Polk	49.54
1848	Zachary Taylor	47.28
1856	James Buchanan	45.24
1860	Abraham Lincoln	39.82
1876	Rutherford B. Hayes	47.95
1880	James Garfield	48.27
1884	Grover Cleveland	48.50
1888	Benjamin Harrison	47.82
1892	Grover Cleveland	46.05
1912	Woodrow Wilson	41.84
1916	Woodrow Wilson	49.24
1948	Harry S. Truman	49.51
1960	John F. Kennedy	49.72
1968	Richard M. Nixon	43.42
1992	Bill Clinton	42.97
1996	Bill Clinton	49.2
2000	George W. Bush	47.87

a majority of the electoral votes. These were Andrew Jackson in the election of 1824 (41.34 percent), Samuel Tilden in the election of 1876 (50.97 percent), Grover Cleveland in the election of 1888 (48.62 percent), and Al Gore, Jr. in the election of 2000 (48.38 percent).

Mint, U.S., a division of the Department of the Treasury responsible for manufacturing coins and official medals. Congress created the first U.S. Mint in 1792 in Philadelphia. Its director, appointed by the president, supervises the mints at Philadelphia and Denver, as well as the assay office and the Mint Museum at San Francisco. The U.S. Mint also administers the government's silver holdings at West Point, New York, and its gold holdings at Fort Knox, Kentucky.

Minuit, Peter (1580–1638), Dutch colonial leader. Appointed governor of New Netherlands by the Dutch West India Company in 1625, Minuit purchased Manhattan Island in 1626 from the Indians for about $24 worth of trinkets. He built Fort Amsterdam on the site, which later became New York City. Representing Sweden, Minuit established New Sweden in Delaware and built Fort Christina in 1638 at what is now Wilmington.

Minutemen, members of New England's volunteer militia in the AMERICAN REVOLUTION. Minutemen were so called because they were expected to fight "at a minute's notice." Massachusetts Minutemen fought the British at LEXINGTON and CONCORD.

Miranda v. *Arizona* (1966), U.S. Supreme Court decision stating that police must inform suspects of their constitutional rights at the time of their arrest. The Court ruled 5–4 that prior to being questioned, suspects must be informed of their rights to remain silent, that anything they say can be used against them in court, that they have the right to the presence of an attorney, and that if they cannot afford one the court will appoint one. These rights, guaranteed to all citizens, are rooted in the Bill of Rights, particularly the Fifth and Sixth Amendments, and the due process clause of the Fourteenth Amendment. An extensive review of police practices and training manuals preceded the decision, and the majority of the justices decided that only a formal statement could ensure that those arrested would have their rights respected.

Missionary Ridge, Battle of (November 25, 1863), Union victory during the CIVIL WAR on a hill near Chattanooga, Tennessee. Gen. WILLIAM TECUMSEH SHERMAN and his army attacked the Confederate forces under Gen. BRAXTON BRAGG at Missionary Ridge, forcing their retreat. This victory helped restore Tennessee to the Union.

Mississippi (Magnolia State) became on December 10, 1817, the twentieth state admitted to the Union. (See maps, pages 540 and 541.) Its name comes from an Indian word meaning "father of waters." It seceded from the Union on January 9, 1861, and was readmitted on February 23, 1870. Jackson is the capital and largest city. Other large cities include Biloxi, Hattiesburg, Greenville, and Gulfport. Mainly an agricultural state, Mississippi produces cotton, rice, soybeans, pecans, sorghum, and sugar cane. Manufacturing has increased in recent years, especially forestry and oil products. Vicksburg is an important port on the Mississippi River. Once tightly segregated, Mississippi was the site of many struggles during the civil rights movement of the 1950s and 1960s. Prominent Mississippians include MEDGAR EVERS, WILLIAM FAULKNER, ELVIS PRESLEY, TENNESSEE WILLIAMS, and JOHN GRISHAM.

Missouri (Show Me State) became on August 10, 1821, the twenty-fourth state to join the Union. (See maps, pages 540 and 541.) It was admitted as part of the MISSOURI COMPROMISE of 1820. It is often called the "Gateway to the West" because of its historical location on the edge of the frontier: the Santa Fe and Oregon trails and the PONY EXPRESS all began in St. Joseph. The Harry S. Truman Library, the first presidential library, is located in Independence. The tallest monument in the country is the Gateway Arch, located in St. Louis, the state's largest city and an important transportation center. Other important cities include Kansas City, Springfield, and the capital, Jefferson City. Missouri is noted for its production of transportation equipment; leading products include beer, tobacco, and horses. Noted personalities born in Missouri include HARRY S. TRUMAN, WALTER

CRONKITE, MARK TWAIN, LANGSTON HUGHES, and THOMAS HART BENTON.

Missouri Compromise (March 3, 1820), legislation dealing with the extension of slavery to new areas of the country. When Missouri applied for admission to the Union, the balance of slave and free states was eleven each, which meant that slave and free states had equal representation in the Senate. Admitting Missouri as a slave state would upset that balance of power. The opportunity for a compromise came when Maine requested admission as a free state, allowing the Senate to admit Missouri as a slave state and maintain the balance. In addition, the agreement prohibited slavery in the territory of the Louisiana Purchase north of 36°30' latitude. The KANSAS-NEBRASKA ACT of 1854 repealed the Missouri Compromise.

Mitchell, Billy (William; 1879–1936), army officer and aviator. Mitchell commanded U.S. air units during World War I and became an early enthusiastic supporter of air power. He believed the airplane had made the battleship obsolete and warned against the Japanese military threat. Mitchell charged the Departments of War and Navy with incompetence and neglect, resulting in his court-martial in 1925 for insubordination. Rather than accept a five-year suspension, Mitchell resigned. Events during World War II confirmed many of his predictions, and in 1946 Congress awarded him the Medal of Honor posthumously.

Mitchell, John (1870–1919), labor leader. Mitchell served as president of the United Mine Workers from 1898 to 1908 and organized and directed the successful anthracite coal strike in 1902. He served as vice president of the AMERICAN FEDERATION OF LABOR from 1899 to 1914 and chaired the New York State Industrial Commission from 1915 to 1919.

Mitchell, John N. (1913–88), lawyer and politician. Mitchell served as attorney general of the United States from 1969 to 1972. A former law partner of Richard M. Nixon and his campaign manager during the ELECTION OF 1968, Mitchell closely advised him on domestic and international issues. He resigned in 1972 to direct the Committee to Re-Elect the President (CREEP) and became a central figure in the WATERGATE political scandal. In 1975 Mitchell became the only attorney general ever convicted of a felony. He served nineteen months of his prison sentence before receiving a parole in 1979.

Mitchell, Margaret (1900–49), novelist. *Gone with the Wind* (1936), Mitchell's Pulitzer Prize–winning novel, sold a record one million copies in its first six months of publication and has remained one of the most popular novels in the world. Its success was enhanced by the equally popular 1939 film based on the novel and starring Vivien Leigh and Clark Gable. Mitchell, a writer for the *Atlanta Journal,* spent ten years writing the story of the Civil War and Reconstruction from a white southerner's point of view.

Molasses Act (1733), act passed by Parliament placing a heavy duty on all sugar, molasses, and rum imported into the American colonies from non-British islands in the Caribbean. Parliament passed the act at the request of planters of the British West Indies, who feared that American trade with other islands would destroy the British sugar industry. The Molasses Act proved ineffective owing to colonial smuggling and Parliament's failure to enforce it. It was repealed by the SUGAR ACT.

Molly Maguires, secret and criminal society of Irish-American coal miners in western Pennsylvania. From 1865 to the 1870s the Molly Maguires settled labor disputes by the same methods employed by mine owners to break strikes — intimidation, destruction of property, and murder. The group was finally infiltrated by a Pinkerton detective, James McParlan, whose testimony in a series of murder trials from 1875 to 1877 resulted in conviction and hanging of several of the members and in the destruction of the society. The group's name came from a widow named Molly Maguire, who had led antilandlord agitators in the 1840s.

Mondale, Walter F. (1928–), vice president of the United States (1977–81) under Jimmy Carter. A former attorney general for the state of Minnesota, Mondale replaced Senator Hubert Humphrey in the Senate when Humphrey became vice president in 1964. As a liberal Democrat, Mondale supported civil rights, federal aid to education, child-care legislation, and arms limitations. Carter and Mondale ran for reelection in the ELECTION OF 1980 but were defeated by Republican opponents Ronald Reagan and George Bush. Mondale became the Democratic presidential nominee in the ELECTION OF 1984, selecting as his running mate the first woman to be nominated by a major political party, Congresswoman GERALDINE FERRARO. The Mondale-Ferraro ticket lost to Reagan and Bush. Mondale served as U.S. ambassador to Japan (1993–96) and was President Clinton's representative in Indonesia in 1998. In 2002, as a last-minute replacement on the Minnesota ballot to replace recently deceased Senator Paul Wellstone, Mondale narrowly lost the election.

***Monitor* v. *Merrimack*,** the first battle in history between ironclad warships, occurring during the CIVIL WAR at Hampton Roads, Virginia, on March 9, 1862. The Confederates fitted the captured Union frigate *Merrimack* with iron sides and renamed it *Virginia*. After sinking several wooden ships, it engaged in battle with the Northern ironclad *Monitor,* designed by JOHN ERICCSON. Neither vessel could sink the other, and both withdrew after several hours of battle. The confrontation signaled the end of an era of wooden fighting ships.

Monmouth, Battle of (June 28, 1778), the heaviest one-day battle of the AMERICAN REVOLUTION. Following their evacuation of Philadelphia, the British headed for New York. Gen. GEORGE WASHINGTON, seeking to inflict a crippling defeat, sent Gen. Charles Lee to lead an attack. Lee fumbled the mission and led his troops in retreat. Washington himself re-formed the troops to attack in heavy combat. Ten thousand men fought on each side, leading to a British withdrawal under the darkness of night. Lee was court-martialed and convicted for disobeying orders.

Monopoly, an economic arrangement in which a single company controls the production and sale of a product. Efforts to create monopolies were frequent in the late nineteenth and early twentieth centuries. Examples are the U.S. Steel Corporation and the Standard Oil Company. The abuse of monopolies led to the enactment of such federal laws as the SHERMAN ANTI-TRUST ACT, the CLAYTON ANTI-TRUST ACT, and the Federal Trade Commission Act. Today the U.S. Postal Service and many public utilities are monopolies, but state and federal governments have laws to control them, often enforced by the FEDERAL TRADE COMMISSION.

Monroe, James (1758–1831), fifth president of the United States (1817–25). Born in Westmoreland County, Virginia, Monroe was an aide to George Washington during the Revolution. He served as a member of the Continental Congress, as a U.S. senator from Virginia, as U.S. minister to France, Spain, and England, and as governor of Virginia (1799–1802). Appointed secretary of state by James Madison, Monroe also held the post of secretary of war during the War of 1812. Because the Federalist party had dissolved and most people belonged to the Democratic-Republican party during his administration, his two terms became known as the ERA OF GOOD FEELINGS. The country prospered with the growth of industry and settlement of the West. During Monroe's years in office, Florida was purchased from Spain and became part of the United States, the MISSOURI COMPROMISE took place, and the MONROE DOCTRINE became part of the foreign policy of the United States.

Monroe, Marilyn (Norma Jean Baker; 1926–62), actress. Ambitious to become a serious actress, Monroe achieved stardom as a comedienne in *Gentlemen Prefer Blondes* (1953). Her numerous box-office successes included *The Seven Year Itch* (1955) and *Some Like It Hot* (1959). Monroe, married successively to baseball player JOE DiMAGGIO and playwright ARTHUR MILLER, was known for her great beauty and was idolized by both the public and the press. Her fine performances in *Bus Stop* (1956) and *The Misfits* (1961), her last film, held great promise for her acting career. But her tragic personal life led to her premature death from an overdose of sleeping pills.

Monroe Doctrine (December 2, 1823), statement of policy issued by President James Monroe in his annual message to Congress. Influenced and developed by Secretary of State John Quincy Adams, the Monroe Doctrine declared a hands-off policy in the Western Hemisphere. It asserted that the United States would not interfere with European colonies already established in North and South America but that it would not tolerate further colonization. The United States in turn would not interfere in the affairs of

Europe. Any attempt by any European nation to interfere in the Western Hemisphere would be looked upon as a threat to American safety and could be reason for war. In 1904 President Theodore Roosevelt extended the Monroe doctrine with his ROOSEVELT COROLLARY.

Montana (Treasure State) became on November 8, 1889, the forty-first state in the Union. (See maps, pages 540 and 541.) The Battle of Little Bighorn, known as "Custer's Last Stand," took place in Montana in 1876, and it was at Bear Paw, Montana, that CHIEF JOSEPH surrendered to the U.S. Cavalry in 1877, effectively ending the resistance of Plains Indians to U.S. expansion in the West. Popular tourist attractions in Montana include old gold camps, dude ranches, hunting, and the scenic beauty of Glacier National Park. Helena is the capital; other major cities include Billings, Great Falls, and Butte. Coal, petroleum, gold, silver, copper, and lead are major products of the state, as well as wheat, barley, sheep, and cattle. Noted Montanans include CHET HUNTLEY, GARY COOPER, and JEANNETTE RANKIN.

Montana, Joe (1956–), football player. As the star quarterback for the San Francisco 49ers, Montana led the team to four Super Bowl championships, won the most valuable player award in 1989 and 1990, and was named the Super Bowl most valuable player three times. He established a National Football League career record for passing efficiency of 94 percent and the most consecutive 300-yard games (five) in 1982.

Monticello, the home of Thomas Jefferson, near Charlottesville, Virginia. The house stands on a hill justifying its name, which means "little mountain." Designed by Jefferson and built over his lifetime, it combines elements of Italian, Greek, Roman, and colonial architecture. Acclaimed by architects as one of America's most beautiful buildings, Monticello was Jefferson's home for fifty-six years; he is buried on the grounds.

Moon Landing *See* APOLLO SPACE PROGRAM.

Moore, Marianne (1887–1972), poet. Moore's works were praised for their wit, crisp form, and intellectual grounding. Her collections include *Selected Poems* (1935), *Collected Poems* (1951, Pulitzer Prize), and *Predilections* (1955). A graduate of Bryn Mawr (1909), Moore taught in a U.S. Indian school. She edited *Dial* magazine (1925–29) and encouraged other writers by publishing their work.

Moral Majority, an organization of fundamentalist Christians formed by Baptist televangelist Jerry Falwell. The group backed conservative political candidates and supported school prayer. It opposed abortion, gay rights, and school busing. The Moral Majority influenced the election of Ronald Reagan in 1980 but was dissolved by Falwell later in the decade.

Morgan, Daniel (1736–1802), general during the AMERICAN REVOLUTION. Morgan led the American force that achieved an important victory at the Battle of COWPENS near the North Carolina-South Carolina border. Morgan later became commander of the Virginia militia sent to end the

WHISKEY REBELLION in Pennsylvania. Morgan, a Federalist, represented Virginia in the U.S. House of Representatives (1797–99).

Morgan, John Pierpont (1837–1913), financier. Morgan joined his father's banking firm in 1856 and established J. P. Morgan and Co. in 1895, which became a leader in financing American business and marketing U.S. government bonds. Morgan helped organize the U.S. Steel Corporation in 1901 and the International Harvest Corporation in 1902. He controlled many railroads and formed the Northern Securities Corporation, which was dissolved by the Supreme Court in 1904 because it violated the SHERMAN ANTI-TRUST ACT. Congress, suspicious of his great wealth, conducted an investigation of Morgan in 1912 but uncovered no illegal activities. A collector of art, Morgan donated his huge collection to the Metropolitan Museum of Art in New York City.

Morison, Samuel Eliot (1887–1976), historian and author. Morison, whose writing is much admired for its literary style, was especially interested in U.S. maritime history, winning Pulitzer Prizes for his biographies of Columbus, *Admiral of the Ocean Sea* (1942), and *John Paul Jones* (1959). Other works include *The European Discovery of America* (1971) and a widely used textbook written with Henry Steele Commager, *The Growth of the American Republic* (1930). Morison taught at Harvard from 1915 to 1955 and was the U.S. Navy's official historian, writing the fifteen-volume *History of U.S. Naval Operations in World War II* (1947–62).

Mormons, members of the Church of Jesus Christ of Latter-day Saints, a religious sect founded by JOSEPH SMITH in western New York in 1830. He published the six-hundred-page *Book of Mormon* the same year. Their beliefs made Mormons unpopular with their neighbors in the early years. Following the murder of Smith in Illinois by a mob, leadership shifted to BRIGHAM YOUNG who led the Mormons' western migration to Great Salt Lake in 1847. Here the Mormons prospered, building Salt Lake City and becoming desert farming experts. An effort to create their own state, DESERET, failed, but Congress created Utah Territory and appointed Young governor in 1850. Hostility toward the sect because of its control of political life, its economic practices, and its acceptance of polygamy persisted into the 1880s. The church agreed to abolish these practices in 1890, and Utah became a state in 1896. The Mormon church operates several educational institutions, including Brigham Young University in Provo, Utah, as well as a daily newspaper and a media network, and is influential in Utah's politics.

Morrill Act (July 2, 1862), bill granting the states more than 17 million acres of land to raise revenue for the establishment of colleges. The act, named for its sponsor, Representative Justin Morrill of Vermont, gave tracts of land to each state that remained in the Union during the Civil War, the number of acres determined by the number of its congressional delegates multiplied by 30,000. The land was to be sold and the profits used to create colleges for agriculture and the mechanical arts. These schools provided instruction in business and agriculture, opening up higher education to a larger part of the population. Also called the Land-Grant Act of 1862, the Morrill Act established over seventy colleges and universities, many of which were the first in their state. Land-grant schools include the University of California and Michigan State University. In 1890 a second Morrill Act awarded similar land grants to southern states.

Morrill Tariff (March 2, 1861), law passed to increase tariff rates in an effort to help business because of poor economic conditions during the Civil War. The rates were gradually increased during and after the conflict, bringing in revenue to help pay for the war.

Morris, Gouverneur (1752–1816), statesman. Becoming a lawyer at age nineteen, Morris (who lost a leg as a young man) supported the colonial cause during the American Revolution, even though many members of his well-to-do family were Loyalists. Morris, under the ARTICLES OF CONFEDERATION, served as assistant superintendent of finance under ROBERT MORRIS and made recommendations for the first national currency, based on the decimal system. As a Pennsylvania delegate to the CONSTITUTIONAL CONVENTION, he was an eloquent and persuasive speaker, supporting a strong central government controlled by the wealthy; he headed the committee that prepared the final draft of the Constitution. Morris served in the U.S. Senate as a member of the Federalist party. Morris supported the idea of New England's secession during the War of 1812 and became a key promoter of the Erie Canal.

Morris, Robert (1734–1806), English-born financier and political leader. As superintendent of finance under the ARTICLES OF CONFEDERATION, Morris helped raise money for the Americans during the American Revolution, signed the Declaration of Independence, and served as a delegate to the CONSTITUTIONAL CONVENTION, favoring a strong central government. He founded and organized the Bank of North America in 1782 and served in the U.S. Senate from Pennsylvania until 1795. Unwise investments in land speculations resulted in his financial ruin, and he was incarcerated in debtors' prison from 1798 to 1801. He spent the rest of his life in near poverty, supported by his former assistant, GOUVERNEUR MORRIS.

Morrison, Toni (Chloe Anthony Wofford; 1931–), African-American author and educator. Considered by many as America's greatest living writer, Morrison uses brutal truth and historical fact to delineate the individual pain and triumph of black women and men in America. Her books are infused with changing perspective, a lyrical style, and richly detailed prose. She won the National Book Critics Award for the family chronicle *Song of Solomon* (1977), and the 1998 Pulitzer Prize for *Beloved* (1987), a tale of slavery and infanticide. In 1993 she became the first black woman to receive the Nobel Prize in Literature. Morrison graduated from Howard and Cornell, and has taught at various universities including Yale, Rutgers, Howard, and the State University of New York. She worked in publishing for almost twenty years while establishing herself as a writer. Other novels include *Jazz* (1992) and *Paradise* (1998).

Morse, Samuel F. B. (1791–1872), inventor and painter. Principally known for his invention of the telegraph (first inaugurated in 1844) and his development of the Morse code for telegraphic messages, Morse revolutionized communications. His work on the telegraph, however, occurred relatively late in his life, only after he was unable to make a living at his first passion, art. After studying painting in London

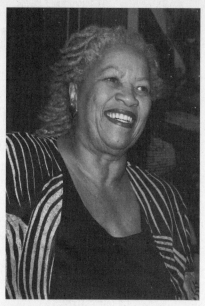

Toni Morrison

with Benjamin West and Washington Allston, Morse returned to America in 1815, where he painted portraits of many well-known figures. He founded the National Academy of Design, serving as its president from 1826 to 1842. Morse also exerted an influence on nineteenth-century politics. An avid anti-Catholic, he wrote a series of newspaper articles (collected in a best-selling book in 1835) that denounced the Roman Catholic church and opposed immigration of Catholics into the United States. This stirred nativist feelings that persisted for many years.

Morse, Wayne (1900–74), politician. A liberal from Oregon, Morse served in the U.S. Senate as a Republican from 1945 to 1951 and as a Democrat from 1957 to 1967. An outspoken opponent of the war in Vietnam, Morse was one of two senators who voted against the TONKIN GULF RESOLUTION in 1964. He lost bids for reelection in 1968 and 1972. Morse once filibustered against offshore oil drilling for 22½ hours.

Morton, Jelly Roll (Ferdinand; 1885–1941), jazz musician and composer. A pioneer of ragtime piano, Morton rose to national fame with his group, the Red Hot Peppers. He made a series of popular recordings during the 1920s, the best known being "King Porter Stomp" and "Jelly Roll Blues."

Morton, Levi P. (1824–1920), twenty-second vice president of the United States, under President Benjamin Harrison (1889–93). Morton, a Republican, had served in the House of Representatives from New York from 1879 to 1881 and as minister to France from 1881 to 1885. He was not renominated for vice president in 1892 because he made enemies within his party while presiding over the Senate, by not favoring the party's positions. He served as governor of New York from 1895 until 1897.

Mosby, John Singleton (1833–1916), Confederate ranger during the CIVIL WAR. The commander of a Confederate cavalry unit, Mosby made sudden rapid attacks on isolated Union outposts. Known as Mosby's Rangers, his men avoided capture by dispersing immediately after their raids and regrouping later at a designated location. In 1863 Mosby led a daring attack behind Federal lines and captured Gen. Edwin Stoughton and about a hundred Union soldiers. After the war he returned to Virginia to practice law, became a Republican, and supported Ulysses S. Grant for president.

Moses, Grandma (Anna Mary Robertson; 1860–1961), painter. Known for her folk-art paintings of typical American life, Grandma Moses began painting in her late seventies. She originally copied paintings from Currier and Ives and then painted from memories of her early farm life. Although Moses never had an art lesson, her works received popular and critical acclaim and were exhibited throughout the world. She created over a thousand works, twenty-five of them after her one hundredth birthday.

Moses, Robert (1888–1981), urban planner. Moses achieved unequaled success in the planning and development of hundreds of parks, recreation areas, bridges, public works, and highways for New York City and New York State between 1924 and 1968. Sometimes called the master builder, he accomplished a great deal in a short amount of time. Among his most notable work was the Verrazano Narrows Bridge, for many years the world's longest suspension bridge. Moses served as president of the Long Island Park Commission, actually drafting the legislation creating his post, assuring himself of absolute power. As commissioner of the New York Council of Parks (1934–60), Moses pushed projects while often displacing minorities, the elderly, and the poor who could not afford to move back to the new housing that was created on their former homesites. During the 1960s the city began prioritizing preservation and restoration over Moses's plans to run a highway through Washington Square Park and build a parking lot in Central Park. Eventual disapproval of his use of power and ruthless tactics caused Mayor Robert Wagner to appoint him in 1960 to run the 1964 World's Fair, for which he had to give up his city projects. Governor NELSON ROCKEFELLER took away his state jobs as well, forcing him into retirement following the fair.

Mott, Lucretia (1793–1880), Quaker reformer and abolitionist. One of the original members of the American Anti-Slavery Society, Mott served as a delegate to the World Anti-Slavery Convention in London in 1840 but was denied a seat on account of her sex. This led to her work for women's rights. She and ELIZABETH CADY STANTON organized the 1848 women's rights convention in Seneca Falls, New York, an early event of the women's rights movement. Mott traveled and lectured widely against slavery and refused to use products produced by slave labor. After the Civil War, she continued to agitate for black suffrage as well as woman suffrage, the latter through her work with SUSAN B. ANTHONY as head of the NATIONAL WOMAN SUFFRAGE ASSOCIATION.

Mount Rushmore National Memorial, massive sculpture on Mount Rushmore in South Dakota's Black Hills. The heads of four presidents — George Washington, Thomas Jefferson, Theodore Roosevelt, and Abraham Lincoln — were carved into the granite under the supervision of GUTZON BORGLUM. Beginning in 1927 workers used drills and dynamite to shape the granite into sixty-foot-tall sculptures, the largest in the world. The memorial was completed in 1941, shortly after Borglum's death.

Mount Vernon, George Washington's estate along the Potomac River in Virginia. Washington owned the home for forty-five years. He left in 1775 to command the Continental Army during the American Revolution and again in 1789 to assume the duties of president, but always returned. In 1799 he died there and is buried on the grounds with his wife, Martha.

Moynihan, Daniel Patrick (1927–2003), politician and diplomat. An Irish-American who grew up in the slums of New York City and worked as a dock worker and bartender, Moynihan became a Fulbright scholar and earned advanced degrees, eventually teaching at Syracuse, Harvard, and M.I.T. He joined the DEPARTMENT OF LABOR in 1961 and helped draft antipoverty legislation. Although a Democrat, he served as ambassador to India (1973–75) and to the United Nations (1975–76) during the Nixon and Ford administrations. Moynihan was elected to the U.S. Senate from New York four times (1977–2001). He promoted antipoverty legislation and opposed President Ronald Reagan's cuts in social programs, his nuclear weapons buildup, and his policies in Central America. Known for his scholarship and intelligence, Moynihan was one of the earliest proponents of welfare reform, an expert on foreign affairs, and a champion of urban development.

Muckrakers, name applied in 1906 by President Theodore Roosevelt to a group of journalists who exposed the abuses of power and corruption in American political and business life. Writers UPTON SINCLAIR, LINCOLN STEFFENS, JACOB RIIS, and IDA TARBELL among others, exposed filth in food processing, fraudulent advertising, political corruption, and other abuses through sensationalized accounts in such publications as *McClure's*, *Everybody's*, and *Collier's*. Muckrakers were largely responsible for mobilizing public opinion in favor of the progressive reform of the period.

Mugwumps, a group of independent Republicans who refused to support James G. Blaine, the party's candidate in the ELECTION OF 1884. Instead, they supported Grover Cleveland, the Democratic candidate, and their votes were a strong factor in Cleveland's victory. Derived from an Indian word meaning "big chief," *mugwump* came to be applied to any independent voter.

Muhammad, Elijah (1897–1975), former leader of the Nation of Islam. Born Elijah Robert Poole, Muhammad was the son of former slaves. In 1923 he moved to Detroit and became assistant to Fard Muhammad, also known as W. D. Fard, who had founded the Nation of Islam, a black nationalist and religious organization. Poole became a leader of this movement, which denounced Christianity as a tool of white supremacy. In 1934 he adopted the surname Muhammad and later organized his own movement, which became known as the BLACK MUSLIMS.

Muhlenberg, Frederick Augustus (1750–1801), politician and first Speaker of the House of Representatives (1789). Muhlenberg studied theology in Germany with his brother, JOHN PETER MUHLENBERG, and was ordained as a Lutheran pastor in Pennsylvania in 1770. A staunch supporter of the American Revolution, he became a member of the CONTINENTAL CONGRESS (1779–80) and presided over the Pennsylvania convention in its ratification of the federal Constitution in 1787. A Federalist and later a Republican, Muhlenberg was elected to the House of Representatives (1789–97), serving as Speaker during the First and Third Congresses. He was the first signer of the Bill of Rights before it was sent to the states for ratification. Muhlenberg cast the deciding vote in favor of the controversial JAY TREATY, which was viewed as anti-German. This decision ended his political career and nearly cost him his life when he was stabbed in a knife attack shortly thereafter.

Muhlenberg, John Peter Gabriel (1746–1807), politician, soldier, patriot. Muhlenberg studied for the ministry in Germany, later serving congregations in Philadelphia and Virginia. After a Sunday service in 1775, he removed his robe to reveal a military uniform and enrolled men in his parish into a German regiment, becoming its leader and later a general in the CONTINENTAL ARMY. Muhlenberg was a member of the HOUSE OF BURGESSES when PATRICK HENRY delivered his famous speech in 1775. A close friend of GEORGE WASHINGTON, he commanded troops at Brandywine, Germantown, and Yorktown, where he witnessed the surrender of Cornwallis's army. He served three terms in the U.S. House of Representatives (1789–91, 1793–95, 1799–1801), and in 1801 he was elected to the U.S. Senate. He resigned shortly thereafter when President THOMAS JEFFERSON appointed him supervisor of internal revenue of Pennsylvania, serving in this post until his death. Muhlenberg's statue represents Pennsylvania in the Capitol's Statuary Hall.

Muir, John (1838–1914), Scottish-born explorer, naturalist, and writer. Muir played a leading role in the conservation movement. He roamed on foot through many regions of the United States, discovering and writing about natural wonders and urging federal action to protect them from development. He was responsible for the establishment of Yosemite and Sequoia National Parks and the formation of the Sierra Club, an organization devoted to conservation. Muir was a major influence on President Theodore Roosevelt's decision to increase significantly the amount of protected public land.

Murfreesboro, Battle of (December 31, 1862–January 2, 1863), battle in Tennessee during the CIVIL WAR. Confederate forces under Gen. BRAXTON BRAGG were forced to retreat toward Chattanooga after suffering heavy losses at the hands of the Union army under command of Gen. WILLIAM ROSECRANS.

Murrow, Edward R. (1908–65), radio and television broadcaster and journalist. Murrow gained recognition as a war correspondent during World War II for his vivid radio descriptions of German bomb attacks on London. His on-the-scene reporting style was featured on radio's "Hear It Now" (1950–51), followed by "See It Now," a popular television program he narrated from 1951 to 1958. In 1954 Murrow's strong attack on Senator Joseph McCarthy received particular attention. On his most popular program, "Person to Person" (1953–61), he interviewed subjects in their homes. President John F. Kennedy selected Murrow to head the U.S. Information Agency in 1961, a post he held until 1964.

Musial, Stan (1920–), baseball player. Musial won seven batting titles and was chosen the National League's most valuable player three times. An outfielder and first baseman for the St. Louis Cardinals, "Stan the Man" appeared in a record twenty-four all-star games. He helped lead the Cards to four World Series and three championships. Musial joined baseball's Hall of Fame in 1969.

Muskie, Edmund (1914–96), politician. Muskie's political career began in 1946 when he won a seat as a Democrat to Maine's House of Representatives. In 1955 he became governor of Maine. The first Democrat to be elected to the U.S. Senate from Maine, he served from 1958 to 1980. He ran unsuccessfully for vice president with Hubert Humphrey in 1968 and lost a bid for the Democratic presidential nomination in 1972. Muskie served as secretary of state under President Jimmy Carter in 1980 and 1981.

My Lai Massacre (March 16, 1968), incident during the VIETNAM WAR during which American soldiers invaded a hamlet in Vietnam and opened fire on about 350 unarmed Vietnamese civilians, mostly women, children, and old men. They then burned and destroyed the village, killing anyone they found still alive. When journalists learned of the massacre over a year later, Americans became more divided over the war. The leader of the unit, Lt. William Calley, Jr., who maintained he was "only following orders," was tried and found guilty on twenty-two counts of murder. His sentence of life imprisonment caused more public controversy, with some insisting his actions were justified and some seeing him as a scapegoat for others equally or more guilty. His sentence was eventually reduced to ten years, of which he served three years under house arrest in his apartment. He was paroled on September 10, 1975.

N **Nader, Ralph** (1934–), consumer advocate and lawyer. Nader gained national attention with his exposé of safety standards in the automobile industry in his best-selling book, *Unsafe at Any Speed* (1965). Both the book and revelations of a secret campaign by General Motors to discredit Nader and his findings of design defects in the Chevrolet Corvair led to the passage of the National Traffic and Motor Vehicle Safety Act in 1966. As one of the most prominent consumer advocates in the United States, Nader enlisted the aid of volunteers, called Nader's Raiders, to investigate threats to the environment, the record of government regulatory agencies, industrial hazards, and issues of tax reform. Their published reports made the public more aware of problems involving radiation dangers, pesticides, harmful food additives, and coal mine safety hazards, and contributed to the enactment of numerous consumer reforms. During the 1990s, Nader launched two unsuccessful bids for the presidency: in 1992 as an independent write-in candidate and in 1996 as the candidate for the Green party. Running again as a Green party candidate in 2000, Nader fell short of his goal of winning 5 percent of the vote, which would have been enough to qualify for federal election funds in 2004. However, he ran for president in 2004 as an independent candidate.

Naismith, James (1861–1939), Canadian-born physical educator. Naismith invented the game of BASKETBALL in 1891. As a physical education teacher at the YMCA Training College in Springfield, Massachusetts, Naismith created the game so that students would have a sport to play indoors in winter. He nailed two peach baskets at either end of the gymnasium and made up a simple set of rules for the game, played with a soccer ball.

Namath, Joe (1943–), football player. After leading his University of Alabama team to three bowl games and a national championship, Namath became the first of the highly paid athletes in 1965 when he signed a record-setting financial contract with the New York Jets of the American Football League. He achieved sports stardom when he accurately predicted and led a Jets upset over the Baltimore Colts in 1969's Super Bowl III. He was known for accurate passing and his skill as a quarterback. Repeated knee injuries shortened his career, and he played his last year with the Los Angeles Rams. Namath was called "Broadway Joe" for his glamorous life-style. He was inducted into the football Hall of Fame in 1985.

Nash, Ogden (Frederic; 1902–71), poet and humorist. Nash published many volumes of light-hearted humorous and satirical verse. Skillful creative use of puns, asides, and invented words contributed to the humor that Nash saw as an important ingredient for survival in the world.

Nashville, Battle of (December 15–16, 1864), one of the last major military engagements of the CIVIL WAR. Gens. George Thomas and John Schofield, leading the Union forces, inflicted heavy casualties on the Confederate troops under Gen. John Bell Hood. The North's victory eventually led to the restoration of Tennessee to the Union.

Nast, Thomas (1840–1902), German-born editorial and political cartoonist. Nast's influential cartoons appeared in the popular magazine *Harper's Weekly* during the 1860s and 1870s. Nast created or popularized such political symbols as the Democrats' donkey, the Republicans' elephant, and the Tammany tiger. His cartoons about the corruption of the TWEED RING and Tammany Hall in New York City (1869–72) helped mold public opinion and bring about the downfall of William "Boss" Tweed and his supporters.

Nation, Carry A. (1846–1911), temperance agitator and reformer. The widow of an alcoholic, Nation became a dedicated temperance leader. She began her violent antisaloon campaign in the prohibition state of Kansas in the 1890s with prayer and a hatchet, smashing bottles, furnishings, and fixtures. She crusaded throughout the state, lecturing and selling souvenir hatchets. Arrested, imprisoned, and fined several times for disturbing the peace, Nation's actions helped bring about PROHIBITION with the Eighteenth Amendment in 1919.

National Aeronautics and Space Administration (NASA) (1958), a federal agency established by Congress to supervise U.S. space flights and activities within and beyond the earth's atmosphere. The agency is involved in the research, building, and testing of spacecraft for peaceful purposes. Its accomplishments include the launching of hundreds of satellites and space probes, and missions to all the planets in the solar system except Pluto. But the most well-known of its efforts are the human spaceflight initiatives. These began with Projects Mercury and Gemini in the 1960s and hit a

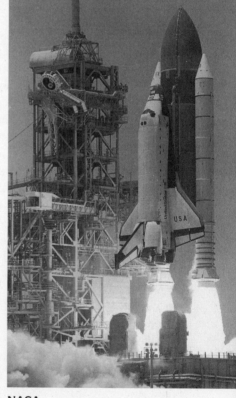

NASA
The Space Shuttle Columbia *launches July 1, 1997, at the Kennedy Space Center in Florida.*

peak with the six successful moon landings of the APOLLO SPACE PRO-GRAM. They continued in the 1970s with the orbiting *SKYLAB*, and then carried on to the manned SPACE SHUTTLE program beginning in the 1980s and the *INTERNATIONAL SPACE STATION* in the late 1990s. The 1986 *CHALLENGER* DISASTER set the program back, and investigations uncovered inadequate safety standards. Reforms were enacted that attempted to preclude another occurrence of such an accident, and launches resumed in 1988. The shuttle program continued without serious incident until the *COLUMBIA* DISASTER on February 1, 2003, which again halted the program.

National American Woman Suffrage Association (NAWSA) (1890), group formed by the joining of the NATIONAL WOMAN SUFFRAGE ASSOCIATION and the AMERICAN WOMAN SUFFRAGE ASSOCIATION. Under the leadership of CARRIE CHAPMAN CATT, the NAWSA was instrumental in securing passage and ratification of the Nineteenth Amendment in 1920. The group dissolved in the same year, but many of its leaders remained politically active and founded the LEAGUE OF WOMEN VOTERS.

National Association for the Advancement of Colored People (NAACP) (1909–10), organization established to oppose racial inequality, segregation, and discrimination against blacks and other minority groups. Originating in New York City with the purpose of gaining political, economic, social, and civil equality for all Americans, the NAACP broadened its focus to the entire world during the 1970s. Under the leadership of JAMES WELDON JOHNSON, the NAACP became a significant force in the civil rights movement. The NAACP Legal Defense Fund, led by Charles Hamilton Houston and THURGOOD MARSHALL, won many legal victories in the courts, including the 1954 Supreme Court decision *Brown* v. *Board of Education of Topeka*, which ordered the desegregation of public schools.

National Geographic Society (1888), nonprofit scientific and educational organization established to promote knowledge of geography. Located in Washington, D.C., the society has sponsored research projects and exploratory expeditions all over the world, including ROBERT PEARY's trip to the North Pole in 1909 and RICHARD BYRD's polar expedition. It publishes the popular monthly *National Geographic* magazine.

National Industrial Recovery Act (June 16, 1933), NEW DEAL legislation creating the Federal Emergency Relief Administration (FERA) and the National Recovery Administration (NRA). FERA, later renamed the Public Works Administration (PWA), helped create jobs in public works. The NRA required business and labor to accept fair competition codes that regulated wages, hours, working conditions, and collective bargaining. In *Schechter Poultry Corp.* v. *U.S.* (1935), the U.S. Supreme Court declared the act unconstitutional because its assignment of lawmaking power to the NRA violated the Constitution's allotment of such powers to Congress.

National Labor Relations Act (1935), NEW DEAL legislation prohibiting unfair labor practices against unions and granting organized labor the right of collective bargaining. It also outlawed discrimination against union members and forbade the use of blacklists. The act created the National Labor Relations Board (NLRB) to help settle union-management disputes over unfair labor practices. Often called the Wagner Act because it was written by Senator Robert Wagner of New York, the act was amended in 1947 by the TAFT-HARTLEY ACT.

National Organization for Women (NOW) (1966), an organization formed to seek equality for women. Cofounded by BETTY FRIEDAN and other feminist leaders, NOW consists of men and women who press for better education, employment, and political opportunities for women. The organization campaigned vigorously for the EQUAL RIGHTS AMENDMENT (ERA) and works to end discrimination at both state and federal levels.

National Rifle Association (NRA) (1871), organization that encourages the civilian use of firearms for hunting and sharpshooting. The NRA sponsors competitions and strongly lobbies against gun control legislation.

National Security Council (NSC) (1947), board of government officials that administers and coordinates activities concerned with the national security and defense of the United States. The NSC consists of four principal members — the president, vice president, secretary of state, and secretary of defense. Advisers include the chair of the Joint Chiefs of Staff and the director of the CENTRAL INTELLIGENCE AGENCY. As part of the Executive Office of the President, the council advises the president on military and intelligence matters and foreign policy. It also supervises the Central Intelligence Agency. Originally intended to have only policymaking and coordinating functions, the NSC expanded its powers in the 1970s and 1980s to carry out intelligence and covert operations. Its involvement in the IRAN-CONTRA AFFAIR led to demands that it return to its original purposes.

National Union Party *See* UNION PARTY.

National Woman Suffrage Association (NWSA) (1869), organization formed by SUSAN B. ANTHONY and ELIZABETH CADY STANTON to promote women's rights. In contrast to the AMERICAN WOMAN SUFFRAGE ASSOCIATION (AWSA), the NWSA went beyond suffrage issues and supported the active participation of women in politics, including VICTORIA WOODHULL, the first woman to run for president of the United States (1872). The NWSA merged with the AWSA in 1890 to become the NATIONAL AMERICAN WOMAN SUFFRAGE ASSOCIATION (NAWSA).

Nat Turner's Rebellion (August 13–23, 1831), slave rebellion at Southampton County, Virginia. Literate slave preacher Nat Turner and a band of about sixty followers killed about sixty white men, women, and children. Turner was captured and tried, and hanged on November 11, 1831, along with many of his followers. Southerners blamed radical northern abolitionists for inciting the rebellion and passed harsh laws forbidding teaching slaves to read and write and eliminating whatever freedoms they had.

Navigation Acts, a series of acts passed by the English Parliament during the seventeenth century to protect England's trade and to prevent the American colonies from directly trading with foreign countries or other colonies. The act of 1651 provided that all goods imported to England must be carried on English ships. The Navigation Act of 1660 stated that all colonial produce and tobacco must be exported on English vessels or colonial-owned ships with English captains. The act of 1663, generally ignored, specified that all foreign imports to the colonies pass through England first. The Navigation Act of 1673 required English officials to collect duties on any goods not sent to England. The acts helped make England "Queen of the Seas," but Americans greatly resented them. After eighty years of lax British enforcement and extensive American smuggling, the British began to crack down after 1763, helping to bring about the AMERICAN

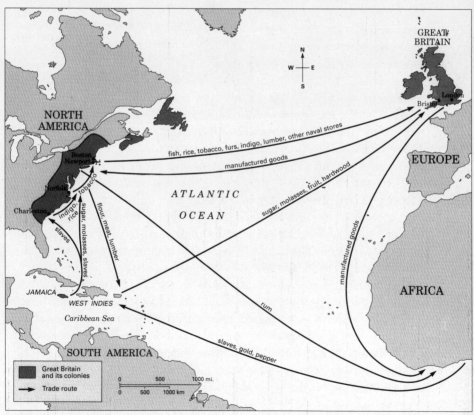

The Atlantic Trade Cycle

REVOLUTION. Parliament repealed all Navigation Acts in 1849 and 1854. See map on page 347.

Navratilova, Martina (1956–), Czechoslovakian-born tennis player. Navratilova became a U.S. citizen in 1981 and earned the title of number one player in the world seven times (1978–79 and 1982–86). A left-hander known for her powerful style of play, Navratilova captured 167 singles tournaments, including nine Wimbledon titles, the U.S. Open four times, the French Open twice, and the Australian Open three times. She officially retired from professional tennis in 1994, but came out of retirement in 1995 to continue competitive play. With partner Leander Paes, her 2003 mixed doubles win at the Australian Open made her the oldest player to win a Grand Slam title. Also in 2003, she equaled BILLIE JEAN KING's record of twenty Wimbledon titles in various combinations of singles, mixed doubles, and women's doubles. In 1999 she was named by ESPN as one of the century's twenty greatest American athletes, joining BABE DIDRIKSON ZAHARIAS as the only two women to make the list. She is involved with various charities that benefit animal rights, underprivileged children, and gay rights.

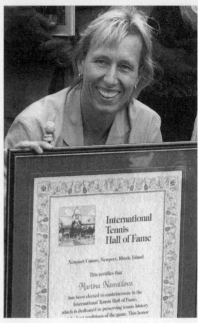

Martina Navratilova
Inducted into the International Tennis Hall of Fame in July 2000.

Nebraska (Corn Husker State) joined the Union on March 1, 1867, as the thirty-seventh state. (See maps, pages 540 and 541.) It had become a territory in 1854. The first homestead claim under the HOMESTEAD ACT was made in Nebraska. Nebraska's largest cities include Lincoln, its capital, Omaha, Grand Island, and North Platte. In 1937 Nebraska's legislature became the only unicameral state legislature in the country, with one house called the senate. A leading farming state, Nebraska produces rye, corn, and wheat. Cattle and hogs are raised, and Omaha is the largest meatpacking center in the United States. Tourist sites include Ogallala, Broken Bow, and Chimney Rock. Noted Nebraskans include GERALD FORD, FRED ASTAIRE, HENRY FONDA, and JOHNNY CARSON.

Nelson, Byron (John, Jr.; 1912–), golfer. Nelson won every major U.S. championship including the U.S. Open in 1939, the Masters twice, and the

Professional Golfers' Association tournament twice. In 1944 he won eleven consecutive open titles, a record that has never been approached.

Nelson, Willie (1933–), country and western singer. During the 1970s Nelson recorded many best-selling albums, earning him the title "King of Country Music." He won the Country Music Association's Entertainer of the Year Award in 1979 and in the 1980s drifted into popular music with hit albums such as *Always on My Mind*. Nelson organized charity concerts including Farm Aid concerts to raise money to benefit U.S. farmers.

Neutrality, Proclamation of (April 22, 1793), declaration by George Washington of neutrality toward all warring nations. Issued during the European wars between England and France, the proclamation forbade American ships from carrying war supplies to the fighting countries. Congress passed the Neutrality Act of June 5, 1794, to reinforce the proclamation.

Neutrality Acts (1935, 1936, 1937, 1938, 1939), series of laws passed prior to the outbreak of WORLD WAR II for the purpose of keeping the United States neutral in foreign affairs and out of wars. The first four acts banned arms sales and loans to any country engaged in war, but in 1939 the law allowed munitions sales to the Allies on a "cash and carry" basis. The acts were replaced by the LEND-LEASE ACT in 1941, which did not require immediate payment.

Nevada (Silver State) joined the Union on October 31, 1864, as the thirty-sixth state. (See maps, pages 540 and 541.) Thousands of fortune seekers moved to Nevada in 1859 in search of gold and silver with the discovery of the COMSTOCK LODE. Nevada's largest cities include Carson City, its capital, and Las Vegas, Reno, Sparks, and Henderson. Las Vegas is called the entertainment and gambling capital of the world; gambling taxes account for 45 percent of the state's tax revenues. Easy divorce laws have made that another important industry. Nevada has many tourist attractions, including Lake Tahoe, Reno, Lake Mead, and Pyramid Lake. It is the driest state in the Union, with an average annual rainfall of only 3.73 inches.

Nevins, Allan (1890–1971), historian. Nevins received two Pulitzer Prizes for his extensive works in American history: *Grover Cleveland: A Study in Courage* (1932) and *Hamilton Fish: The Inner History of the Grant Administration* (1936). His critically acclaimed *Ordeal of the Union* (1947–71) was a series of histories of the Civil War. Nevins held editorial posts at the *New York Sun* and *New York World* and taught American history at Columbia University.

New Deal (1933–39), umbrella label for a wide range of programs adopted by President FRANKLIN D. ROOSEVELT to offer relief and stimulate economic recovery from the GREAT DEPRESSION of the 1930s. In his speech accepting the presidential nomination at the 1932 Democratic National

Convention, Roosevelt declared, "I pledge . . . myself to a new deal for the American people." In a session of Congress called the Hundred Days, numerous laws were passed creating programs and policies to promote economic activity and reduce unemployment. The National Recovery Administration (NRA) and Agricultural Adjustment Administration (AAA) were intended to assist businesses and farmers, but were later declared unconstitutional by the Supreme Court. The Securities and Exchange Commission (SEC) supervised stock market reform, and the FEDERAL DEPOSIT INSURANCE CORPORATION (FDIC) addressed problems in the banking system. To provide jobs, the CIVILIAN CONSERVATION CORPS (CCC), the Civil Works Administration (CWA), and the Federal Emergency Relief Administration (FERA) were established. Although they did not end the depression, these measures and others relieved hardship for many and established a commitment on the part of the federal government to deal with American economic problems. The New Deal promoted competition in politics and economics and increased the popularity of the Democratic party. Prosperity was not achieved, however, until World War II, when military and private spending increased, creating a demand for workers and goods.

New Freedom (1912), Democrat WOODROW WILSON's political and economic reform program proposed during the presidential ELECTION OF 1912. To reduce corporate power and return government to the people, Wilson proposed to lower tariffs, revise the monetary system, break up monopolies, and reinvigorate the free enterprise system.

New Frontier (1960), domestic program of JOHN F. KENNEDY proposed during the presidential ELECTION OF 1960. Kennedy called for federal aid to education, Medicare, equal opportunity in employment, advances in space exploration, and vigorous leadership. Most of his program stalled in Congress, but after his assassination, some of his ideas were carried out by his successor, LYNDON B. JOHNSON, in his War on Poverty.

New Hampshire (Granite State) joined the Union on June 21, 1788, as the ninth state. (See maps, pages 540 and 541.) In 1830 John Mason named the colony after the English county of Hampshire. After thirty-eight years as part of Massachusetts, it became a separate colony in 1679. New Hampshire was the first colony to vote for the Declaration of Independence and the ninth state to accept the Constitution, which put it into effect. The largest cities in New Hampshire are Concord, the capital, Manchester, and Nashua. With mountains and forests covering much of its land, tourism is an important industry. Other important industries include manufacturing of textiles, leather goods, machinery, and wood and metal products. Noted New Hampshirites include DANIEL WEBSTER, FRANKLIN PIERCE, HENRY WILSON, SALMON P. CHASE, HARLAN FISKE STONE, and MARY BAKER EDDY.

New Jersey (Garden State) on December 18, 1787, became the third state to join the Union. (See maps, pages 540 and 541.) Almost one hundred battles of the American Revolution took place on New Jersey soil. Although small in size, it has more people per square mile than any other state. Its largest cities include Trenton, the capital, Camden, Newark, Jersey City, Elizabeth, and Patterson. New Jersey's vacation areas and resort cities along the Atlantic coast attract many visitors. Atlantic City is famous for its boardwalk, beach, hotels, and gambling. The chief industries are chemicals and pharmaceuticals. Agriculture is also important, with tomatoes, soybeans, vegetables, and chickens being major products. The first professional baseball game was played in Hoboken in 1846. THOMAS EDISON invented the electric light bulb and phonograph and SAMUEL F. B. MORSE developed the telegraph in New Jersey. Famous people born in the state include GROVER CLEVELAND, AARON BURR, MOLLY PITCHER, and STEPHEN CRANE.

New Jersey Plan (June 15, 1787), plan introduced at the CONSTITUTIONAL CONVENTION favoring small states. Presented by delegate William Paterson of New Jersey, the plan called for a single federal legislative body in which all states, regardless of size, would have one vote. The New Jersey Plan was an alternative to the VIRGINIA PLAN, which favored the large states. Parts of each plan were incorporated into the GREAT COMPROMISE, or Connecticut Compromise, providing for a two-house legislature, with the U.S. Senate representing the states on an equal basis and the House of Representatives representing the people on the basis of population.

Newman, Paul (1925–), actor. A major box-office attraction, Newman won the 1986 Academy Award as best actor for his performance in *The Color of Money.* Known for his good looks and blue eyes, he often plays outsiders or independent characters. Newman achieved stardom in *The Long, Hot Summer* (1958). Other films include *The Hustler* (1961), *Butch Cassidy and the Sundance Kid* (1969), and *Mr. and Mrs. Bridge* (1990). Newman directed his wife, Joanne Woodward, in *Rachel, Rachel* (1968) and *The Effect of Gamma Rays on Man-in-the-Moon Marigolds* (1972). He has been involved in liberal political activities and has marketed a line of food products, the profits from which he donates to charity.

New Mexico (Land of Enchantment) became on January 12, 1912, the forty-seventh state to join the Union. (See maps, pages 540 and 541.) The original inhabitants of the region, the Pueblo Indians, built cliff dwellings, many of which are still occupied. The territory became linked to the rest of the United States with the completion of the southern transcontinental railroad in 1881. The largest cities today include Santa Fe, the capital, Albuquerque, Las Cruces, and Roswell. Hunting, fishing, skiing, and sightseeing, as well as the Carlsbad Caverns and the Palace of Governors, the oldest public building in the United States, attract many visitors each year, making tourism a major industry. The first atomic bomb blast took place in 1945 at Los Alamos. New Mexico is a leader in energy research, and uranium, potassium, and oil products. Spanish and English are the official state languages. Prominent people who have made New Mexico their home include ROBERT H. GODDARD and GEORGIA O'KEEFFE. BILL MAULDIN and political leader Dennis Chavez were born there.

New Nationalism, the Progressive political platform of Theodore Roosevelt during the ELECTION OF 1912. New Nationalism emphasized political, social, and economic reforms to be coordinated by the federal government. The philosophy stressed an increase in safety and welfare laws, as well as taxation of business. Roosevelt opposed Woodrow Wilson's NEW FREEDOM program, arguing that monopolies and big business should not be destroyed but be controlled by regulatory commissions.

New Orleans, Battle of (January 8, 1815), final military engagement between British and American troops during the WAR OF 1812. Unknown to either side, the TREATY OF GHENT had been signed ending the war two weeks before the battle was fought. The British fleet, hoping to gain control of the Mississippi River, faced an army of frontier militiamen headed by Gen. ANDREW JACKSON near New Orleans, Louisiana. Aided by French pirate JEAN LAFFITE, the American victory resulted in the loss of over a thousand British soldiers and fewer than twenty American casualties in a battle that lasted about an hour. This victory made Jackson a national hero and enhanced his political future.

New York (Empire State) on July 26, 1788, became the eleventh state to join the Union. (See maps, pages 540 and 541.) The Dutch originally settled New York with the first permanent settlement at Fort Orange (now Albany). It became an English colony in 1664 and was named for the duke of York. New York City became the first capital of the United States under the Constitution (1789–90), and George Washington took the presidential oath there in 1789. As the largest city in the United States, it is a leading center of banking, finance, foreign trade, manufacturing, fashion, publishing, broadcasting, culture, and tourism. The Port of New York is the busiest port in the country. The state's capital is Albany and other large cities include Buffalo, Yonkers, Rochester, and Syracuse. Attractions such as Niagara Falls, the Erie Canal, the Finger Lakes, and New York City itself make tourism a major industry. New York was the birthplace of four presidents (MARTIN VAN BUREN, MILLARD FILLMORE, THEODORE ROOSEVELT, FRANKLIN D. ROOSEVELT) and eight vice presidents. Other noted New Yorkers include JOHN JAY, CHARLES EVAN HUGHES, EUGENE O'NEILL, LOU GEHRIG, ALEX HALEY, J. P. MORGAN, and ARTHUR MILLER.

Nicholson, Jack (1937–), film actor. With his Cheshire-cat grin and arching eyebrows, Nicholson has shown versatility as an actor in his portrayal of cynical, neurotic, nonconformist, emotional, and comic characters. His breakthrough came with *Easy Rider* (1969) for which he earned his first Oscar nomination. He received Oscars for his performances in *One Flew Over the Cuckoo's Nest* (1975) *Terms of Endearment* (1984), and *As Good as It Gets* (1997). His twelfth Academy Award nomination, for *About Schmidt* (2002), made him the recipient of more Oscar nominations than any other male performer. Other highly acclaimed films include *The Shining* (1979), *Prizzi's Honor* (1985), *Batman* (1989), *A Few Good Men* (1992), and *Something's Gotta Give* (2003).

Nicklaus, Jack (1940–), golfer. While playing golf on the professional tour, Nicklaus posted more major tournament victories than any player in the history of the game. Called "the Golden Bear" because of his blond hair and heftiness, Nicklaus became the first golfer to win all four professional tournaments more than once. His pro wins include six Masters, five PGAs, four U.S. Opens, and three British Opens.

Niebuhr, Reinhold (1892–1971), theologian and educator. Niebuhr was best known for his efforts to relate Christian faith to the reality of modern politics and diplomacy. Educated at Yale Divinity School, he became an evangelical minister in working-class Detroit, where he was troubled by the demoralizing effects of industrialism on workers. He became an outspoken critic of HENRY FORD and what he considered to be inhumane conditions of assembly lines, and often allowed his pulpit to be used by union organizers to preach about workers' rights. Niebuhr attacked liberal Protestantism for its failure to deal with everyday moral dilemmas and promoted his ideas in his numerous books including *Moral Man and Immoral Society* (1932), *The Irony of American History* (1952), *The Democratic Experience* (1969), and *The Nature and Destiny of Man* (1941).

Nimitz, Chester W. (1885–1966), admiral who commanded the Pacific fleet during WORLD WAR II. Assuming command three months after the Japanese bombing of Pearl Harbor, Nimitz supervised the expansion of the naval force in the Pacific and directed U.S. victories at the battles of MIDWAY (1942), the Philippine Sea (1944), and the LEYTE GULF (1944). He became a five-star admiral in 1944 and signed the document securing the Japanese surrender in 1945 aboard his flagship, USS *Missouri.*

Nisei, native-born American citizens who are the children of Japanese immigrants. Their name meaning "second generation," the Nisei along the Pacific Coast were harshly treated during World War II when thousands were evacuated from their homes in the JAPANESE-AMERICAN INTERNMENT following the bombing of Pearl Harbor.

Nixon, Richard M. (1913–94), thirty-seventh president of the United States (1969–74). A lifelong Republican, Nixon became a member of the U.S. House of Representatives in 1947, where he gained national attention with his involvement in the HISS CASE. He was elected to the U.S. Senate in 1951. Still remembered for his emotional "Checkers" speech during the presidential ELECTION OF 1952, Nixon served as vice president in the administration of Dwight D. Eisenhower. He narrowly lost the presidency to John F. Kennedy in the ELECTION OF 1960 and was soundly defeated by Pat Brown in his bid for the governorship of California in 1962, resulting in a bitter announcement that he would never again seek public office. After practicing law in New York for several years, however, Nixon actively campaigned for and narrowly won the presidency in the ELECTION OF 1968 in a race with Hubert H. Humphrey; he won reelection by a landslide over George McGovern in the ELECTION OF 1972. As president, Nixon opened relations with the People's Republic of China and ended U.S. involvement in Vietnam. A break-in at the Democratic party headquarters in the WATERGATE complex, Washington, D.C., during the 1972 campaign, led to an investigation of Nixon's campaign committee's involvement. The administration's cover-up and obstruction of justice in the case led to a congressional committee's recommendation that Nixon be impeached. To avoid impeachment proceedings he resigned, the only president to do so. After his resignation, President Gerald Ford pardoned him for any federal crimes he may have committed while in office, leading to a national outcry. Nixon subsequently wrote memoirs and other books and served as a consultant to Republican presidents.

Noguchi, Isamu (1904–88), Asian-American sculptor. After spending part of his childhood in Japan, Noguchi studied sculpture with GUTZON BORGLUM in the United States and Constantin Brancusi in France, as well as calligraphic drawing in Peking. Successfully blending traditional Oriental principles and modern Western design, Noguchi created works that won him international recognition. After six months of voluntary internment in a California detention camp during World War II, Noguchi designed sets for MARTHA GRAHAM's dance company. His outdoor projects include two bridges for the Peace Park at Hiroshima and the Garden of Peace at the UNESCO Building in Paris. The Isamu Noguchi Museum in New York houses some five hundred of his sculptures.

Non-Intercourse Act (March 1, 1809), American effort to induce Britain and France to change their policy toward neutral shipping and impressment during Europe's Napoleonic Wars. The act allowed U.S. ships to trade with any country except Great Britain and France and opened American ports to all but British and French ships. It failed to convince England and France that they should change their policies, however. Following its expiration in 1810, the act was replaced by MACON'S BILL NUMBER 2.

Normandy Invasion *See* D-DAY.

Norris, George W. (1861–1944), politician. A liberal Republican from Nebraska, Norris acted independently as a member of Congress for forty years. He served five terms in the House of Representatives (1903–13) and five terms in the Senate (1913–43). In 1910 Norris led the successful fight to strip the dictatorial powers of Speaker Joe Cannon. He opposed U.S. entry into World War I and the League of Nations, sponsored the Twentieth Amendment to the Constitution, helped establish the TENNESSEE VALLEY AUTHORITY, cosponsored the NORRIS-LA GUARDIA ACT, and supported aid to Great Britain during the early years of World War II.

Norris-La Guardia Act (March 23, 1932), law limiting the use of injunctions in labor disputes, including nonviolent strikes. The act encouraged labor union activity and prohibited employers from discriminating against workers who broke "yellow-dog contracts" (promises by employees not to join or support a union). Because such contracts became unenforceable, employers stopped using them. The Norris-La Guardia Act was sponsored by Republican Senator GEORGE W. NORRIS of Nebraska and Republican Representative FIORELLO LA GUARDIA of New York.

North American Free Trade Agreement (NAFTA). Signed in 1992, NAFTA is an accord to establish a free trade zone between Canada, Mexico, and the United States. NAFTA took effect on January 1, 1994, immediately lifting restrictions on the flow of goods, services, and investment in North America. NAFTA's purpose was to improve the economies of all three nations by increasing the purchasing power of Mexico and Canada and improving production, sales, and employment in the United States over a fifteen-year period. Major industries affected are agriculture, automobile and textile manufacture, energy, financial services, telecommunications, and financial services. Detractors of the pact claim it has led to numerous American job losses because manufacturers have moved plants to Mexico to avoid paying higher wages. Proponents argue that U.S. jobs have increased due to a rise in imports by Mexico and Canada.

North Atlantic Treaty Organization (NATO) (1949), a Western military alliance of twelve nations formed in response to the COLD WAR. Providing for joint action in an attack on any member nation, NATO was intended to defend against Soviet aggression. It also promoted joint military aid and economic cooperation during peacetime. Original members of NATO included Belgium, Canada, Denmark, France, Iceland, Italy, Luxembourg, the Netherlands, Norway, Portugal, the United Kingdom, and the United States. Greece and Turkey joined in 1952, West Germany (now Germany) in 1955, and Spain in 1982. The end of the cold war in 1989, the collapse of East Germany in 1990 and its incorporation into the Federal Republic of Germany, the end of the Warsaw Pact, and the collapse of the Soviet Union in 1991 reduced military tensions and led to the expansion of NATO as former Warsaw Pact members applied for admission. The Czech Republic, Hungary, and Poland joined the Alliance in March 1999, and by 2003 plans had been made to admit Bulgaria, Estonia, Latvia, Lithuania, Romania, Slovakia, and Slovenia by 2004. As NATO's role in world affairs began to change, it saw its first military engagements during the YUGOSLAV CRISES of the 1990s, and the core provision of the treaty was used for the first time in the treaty's history in response to the SEPTEMBER 11, 2001, TERRORIST ATTACKS.

North Carolina (Tarheel State) on November 21, 1789, joined the Union as the twelfth state. (See maps, pages 540 and 541.) In 1585 SIR WALTER RALEIGH established the first English colony in the New World at Roanoke Island. A second group of settlers who arrived in 1587 became the LOST COLONY OF ROANOKE when they disappeared around 1590. The largest cities in North Carolina include Raleigh, the capital, Charlotte, Greensboro, Winston-Salem, and Durham. A long thin strip of sandbars extending along the Atlantic coastline forms a protective barrier for the coast. The site of many shipwrecks, the area is called Cape Fear, Cape Lookout, and Cape Hatteras, which has the tallest lighthouse in the United States. The WRIGHT BROTHERS flew their first airplane for twelve seconds at Kitty Hawk. North Carolina is the nation's largest tobacco and textile producer and is a leader in the production of furniture, bricks, corn, cotton, peanuts, and vegetables. Three presidents were born in North Carolina: ANDREW JACKSON, JAMES K. POLK, and ANDREW JOHNSON. Other famous North Carolinians include JESSE JACKSON and RICHARD GATLING.

North Dakota (Sioux State) became on November 2, 1889, the thirty-ninth state to join the Union. (See maps, pages 540 and 541.) The geographic center of North America is in North Dakota near the town of Rugby. The largest cities include Bismarck, the capital, Fargo, Grand Forks, and Minot. The Badlands, a valley of sandstone, shale, and clay displaying unusual formations, is the major tourist attraction of the state. North Dakota, 90 percent farmland, is the most rural of the fifty states. Agriculture and mining dominate the economy, with farm products including wheat, rye, flaxseed, barley, and hay, and mining products including petroleum, natural gas, and coal. THEODORE ROOSEVELT lived in the Badlands in 1884 before he became president. Noted North Dakotans include Lawrence Welk and ROGER MARIS.

North, Oliver (1943–), former military officer. A Vietnam veteran, North was assigned to the National Security Council staff by President RONALD REAGAN and became deeply involved in the IRAN-CONTRA AFFAIR. When his role became public in 1986, he resigned. Televised congressional hearings in 1987 led to the prosecution of North and National Security adviser John M. Poindexter. Both were convicted on criminal charges, and North was given a three-year suspended sentence. In 1991 all charges against North were dropped because it could not be proved that the conviction was not influenced by his 1987 televised testimony while under immunity from prosecution. North lost a bid for the U.S. Senate in 1994 and later became a political pundit, radio personality, and television war reporter.

Northwest Ordinance (July 13, 1787), legislation passed under the Articles of Confederation creating the NORTHWEST TERRITORY, the area north of the Ohio River, east of the Mississippi, and west of Pennsylvania. The ordinance specified how territories could become states, and eventually five were formed from the area — Ohio, Indiana, Illinois, Michigan, and Wisconsin. Dividing the region into several territories, the law stated that each should have a Congress-appointed governor, a secretary, and three judges. When the adult male population reached five thousand, the territory could send a nonvoting representative to Congress, and when the total population reached sixty thousand, it was eligible for statehood. The ordinance also forbade slavery, guaranteed trial by jury and freedom of religion, and encouraged support for education, all of which attracted thousands of settlers to the region.

Northwest Passage, the sea route thought to exist through northern Canada and Alaska linking the Atlantic and Pacific oceans. French navigator Jacques Cartier explored the St. Lawrence River in search of the Northwest Passage as early as 1534. Martin Frobisher discovered Frobisher Bay on Baffin Island in 1576 and Henry Hudson discovered Hudson Bay in 1610 in their searches for the passage. Numerous other explorers followed, but it was not until Robert McClure's expedition in 1854 that the existence of such a route was proven. The first successful all-water crossing was achieved by Roald Amundsen, who sailed from Oslo, Norway, to Nome, Alaska, between 1903 and 1906. The first commercial vessel made the journey in 1969, but the route has not been used commercially since because of the numerous icebergs.

Northwest Territory (1787), area west of Pennsylvania between the Ohio and Mississippi rivers. Established by the Continental Congress on July 13, 1787, by the NORTHWEST ORDINANCE, the territory consisted of what would become the states of Ohio, Indiana, Illinois, Michigan, Wisconsin, and part of Minnesota.

Noyce, Robert (1927–90), scientist and entrepreneur. Noyce invented the integrated circuit in 1959, a tiny computer chip that revolutionized the electronics industry and became the basis of the personal computer.

Nuclear Regulatory Commission (NRC) (1974), government agency responsible for licensing and regulating civilian uses of nuclear energy, including setting safety standards. Established by President Gerald Ford as successor to the Atomic Energy Commission, the NRC was strongly criticized for its handling of the nuclear disaster at Three Mile Island in 1979.

Nullification Proclamation (1832), presidential proclamation by President Andrew Jackson to the people of South Carolina in response to the state's Ordinance of Nullification, in which it declared the TARIFF OF ABOMINATIONS null and void and threatened to secede. Jackson defended the principle of federal supremacy and the unity of the Union. He declared the

Ordinance of Nullification treasonable and threatened to hang anyone who opposed government authority. The crisis was averted when both sides accepted HENRY CLAY's Compromise Tariff in 1833.

Nuremberg Trials (November 20, 1945, to October 1, 1946), trials of twenty-four Nazi leaders for war crimes committed during WORLD WAR II. An international military tribunal established by the United States, Great Britain, the Soviet Union, and France met in Nuremberg, Germany, where after lengthy trials, it handed down twelve death sentences, nine prison sentences, and three acquittals. Associate Justice ROBERT JACKSON took leave of his post on the U.S. Supreme Court to act as chief U.S. prosecutor.

O

Oakland–San Francisco Earthquake *See* SAN JOSE–OAKLAND–SAN FRANCISCO EARTHQUAKE.

Oakley, Annie (Phoebe Anne Oakley Mozee; 1860–1926), rodeo performer. A sharpshooter with Buffalo Bill's Wild West Show, Oakley gained fame for her amazing accuracy with pistol, rifle, or shotgun. She could shoot a dime in midair and a cigarette from the lips of her husband, marksman Frank Butler, from ninety feet away. The popular Irving Berlin musical *Annie Get Your Gun* (1946) was based on her life.

Occupational Safety and Health Administration (OSHA), a federal agency of the Department of Labor established by Congress in 1970 to maintain safe conditions in the workplace. It carries out on-site inspections and educates the public about industrial hazards related to fire, asbestos, lead, and other dangers.

O'Connor, Sandra Day (1930–), jurist. Appointed by President Ronald Reagan in 1981, O'Connor was the first female justice on the U.S. Supreme Court. A lawyer and former Arizona State Senate majority leader, she served on the Arizona Superior Court before her appointment to the Supreme Court. O'Connor usually allies herself with the conservative members of the Court, but at times votes independently, depending on the issues. During the early 1990s she became part of a centrist bloc on the Court, helping to moderate the Court's positions on abortion and civil rights.

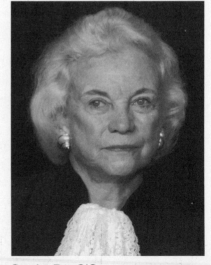

Sandra Day O'Connor

Oglethorpe, James (1696–1785), English colonial founder. A member of the British House of Commons for thirty years, Oglethorpe and his associates received a charter to establish the colony of Georgia in 1732. He led debtors and other poverty-stricken emigrants to Savannah in 1733 and was the colony's first governor until 1743, when he returned to England.

O'Hara, John (1905–70), writer. Admired for his crisp dialogue and realism, O'Hara wrote about the American middle class. His works include *Appointment in Samarra* (1934), *Butterfield 8* (1935), and *From the Terrace* (1958). His short stories are collected in *The Doctor's Son* (1935), *Cape Cod Lighter* (1962), and others.

Ohio (Buckeye State) joined the Union on March 1, 1803, as the seventeenth state and the first one formed from the NORTHWEST TERRITORY. (See maps, pages 540 and 541.) Ohio's name comes from an Iroquois word meaning "beautiful." Its largest cities include Columbus, the capital, and Cleveland, Cincinnati, Dayton, and Toledo. Ohio is one of the nation's industrial and manufacturing leaders. Major products are iron, steel, rubber, auto parts, glass, and machinery. It also produces clay, salt, sandstone, and gravel. Important agricultural products include dairy products, hogs, sheep, popcorn, and vegetables. Ohio was the birthplace of seven U.S. presidents (ULYSSES S. GRANT, RUTHERFORD B. HAYES, JAMES A. GARFIELD, BENJAMIN HARRISON, WILLIAM MCKINLEY, WILLIAM HOWARD TAFT, and WARREN G. HARDING). Other native Ohioans include THOMAS EDISON, ANNIE OAKLEY, JOHN GLENN, NEIL ARMSTRONG, CY YOUNG, ORVILLE WRIGHT, and JACK NICKLAUS.

Oil Embargo (1973), restrictions imposed on the United States and other industrialized nations by the Arab-controlled Organization of Petroleum Exporting Countries (OPEC) in retaliation for their support of Israel during that year's Yom Kippur War. The oil shortage caused gas rationing, long lines at gas stations and increased consumer prices. A national speed limit of 55 mph helped reduce gasoline consumption. In 1974 President Richard Nixon sent HENRY KISSINGER to negotiate an Egypt-Israel cease-fire and the resumption of the shipment of oil to the United States.

O'Keeffe, Georgia (1887–1986), painter. Known for portraying such natural subjects as flowers, rolling hills, rocks, and bleached bones, O'Keeffe painted in a clear, precise, dramatic style. The New Mexico desert provided inspiration for many of her works, which are often presented from an oversized and close-up perspective. *Cow's Skull, Red, White and Blue* (1931) and *Black Iris* (1926) are two of her noted works.

Okies, migrant farm laborers displaced by the DUST BOWL of the 1930s. In the midst of the Great Depression, when the land of Oklahoma, Texas, and Arkansas became exhausted by erosion and pest destruction, more than 150,000 families followed the crops west. Called Okies because many came from Oklahoma, they sought work on West Coast farms and lumber camps. JOHN STEINBECK wrote of their poverty and desperation in his Pulitzer Prize–winning novel *The Grapes of Wrath* (1939).

Okinawa, Battle of (1945), three-month air, sea, and land battle between American and Japanese forces in the Pacific near the end of WORLD WAR II. U.S. troops invaded the island of Okinawa on April 1, 1945, and finally achieved victory on June 21, with heavy casualties on both sides. Okinawa remained under U.S. control until 1972, when it was returned to Japan.

Oklahoma (Sooner State) joined the Union on November 16, 1907, as the forty-sixth state. (See maps, pages 540 and 541.) Its name comes from the Choctaw word meaning "red people." Between 1830 and 1842 the area was the final destination of the TRAIL OF TEARS, when the U.S. government forced Indians out of southeastern United States. In 1889 what was then called Indian Territory was opened to settlers, and thousands of people lined up along the border to claim land. Others sneaked in early and became known as *Sooners* because they were there "sooner" than the legal settlers. Oklahoma now ranks as a leader in production of natural gas and petroleum. It is the only state with oil wells on the grounds of the state capitol. Its largest cities include Oklahoma City, the capital, Tulsa, Lawton, and Norman. Noted Oklahomans include WILL ROGERS, WOODY GUTHRIE, JIM THORPE, and MICKEY MANTLE.

Oklahoma City Bombing (April 19, 1995), domestic terrorist attack on a federal office building in Oklahoma City. A rented truck loaded with explosives was detonated outside the Murrah Federal Building, collapsing the walls and floors of much of the nine-story structure. Killing 168 and injuring more than 1,000, it was the worst terrorist attack on U.S. soil until the SEPTEMBER 11, 2001, ATTACK on the WORLD TRADE CENTER. Timothy McVeigh and former army buddy Terry Nichols were tried and convicted of the antigovernment attack, which they committed in retaliation against the Branch Davidian WACO SIEGE exactly two years earlier. McVeigh was sentenced to death and executed for conspiracy and murder; Nichols received life imprisonment for conspiracy and involuntary manslaughter. A memorial honoring those who died now stands at the site.

Olds, Ransom Eli (1864–1950), automobile engineer and manufacturer. As builder of the first automobile factory, Olds pioneered mass production, setting the stage for the assembly line later perfected by HENRY FORD. Olds built the Oldsmobile and the Reo (his initials).

Olive Branch Petition (July 5, 1775), an appeal to King George III requesting an end to all military action against the colonists and seeking a peaceful solution to the differences between the colonies and England. Written by John Dickinson of Pennsylvania and adopted by the Second Continental Congress, it was ignored by the British government.

Olmsted, Frederick Law (1822–1903), landscape architect. Olmsted was a leader of American landscape architecture, famous for designing many sites and planned communities. He designed New York's Central Park and served as administrative head of the U.S. Sanitary Commission (forerunner of the American Red Cross) before forming his own firm in 1883. Between 1872 and his retirement in 1895, Olmsted designed 550 projects including the grounds of the U.S. Capitol, the Biltmore Estate in North Carolina, the Stanford University campus in California, and Boston's "Emerald Necklace" of parks. He served as the first head of the commission to preserve Yosemite Valley and was a leader in establishing the Niagara Falls Reservation.

Olney, Richard (1835–1917), politician. As U.S. attorney general (1893–95) under Grover Cleveland, Olney obtained the injunction against the American Railway Union that broke the PULLMAN STRIKE in 1894. As Cleveland's secretary of state (1895–97) he helped settle the VENEZUELA BOUNDARY DISPUTE with Great Britain in 1897. His position that the United States had the right to intervene in international disputes in the Western Hemisphere became known as the Olney Corollary to the MONROE DOCTRINE.

Omnibus Bill *See* COMPROMISE OF 1850.

Onassis, Jacqueline Bouvier Kennedy (1929–94), first lady of the United States (1961–63). As the wife of President John F. Kennedy, Jacqueline Kennedy set international fashion trends, restored and redecorated the White House, and had it declared a national museum. In 1968 she married Greek shipping magnate Aristotle Onassis and, following his death in 1975, became an editor with a publishing firm in New York City.

O'Neill, Eugene (1888–1953), playwright. Winner of four Pulitzer Prizes, O'Neill became the only American playwright to win the Nobel Prize for literature (1936). Plagued by a tragic family life, he drifted as a seaman, actor, reporter, and derelict during his early years. While recovering from tuberculosis, O'Neill became inspired by the works of Swedish playwright August Strindberg and embarked upon his writing career. Most of his over forty plays are tragedies, drawing upon his experiences and presenting realistic characters in search of life's meaning and encountering love, disappointment, and disillusion. *Beyond the Horizon* (1920; Pulitzer), the first of his full-length plays to be performed, is considered America's first native stage tragedy. Other works include *Anna Christie* (1921; Pulitzer), *Strange Interlude* (1928; Pulitzer), the eleven-act *Mourning Becomes Electra* (1931), and his autobiographical masterpiece *Long Day's Journey into Night* (produced posthumously in 1956; 1957 Pulitzer). O'Neill's only comedy was *Ah, Wilderness!* (1933).

O'Neill, Thomas Philip, Jr. (Tip; 1912–94), politician. A liberal Democrat from Massachusetts, Tip O'Neill was elected to the U.S. House of Representatives in 1952, where he served for thirty-four years. He was majority whip from 1971 to 1973, majority leader from 1973 to 1977, and Speaker from 1977 to 1987. O'Neill opposed U.S. involvement in the Vietnam War and many of President Ronald Reagan's policies.

Open Door Policy (1899), principle stating that all nations have equal trading rights and commercial opportunities in China. In the nineteenth century Japan and other nations had divided China into separate spheres of influence, with each power maintaining economic dominance in its area. The Open Door policy was proposed by U.S. Secretary of State JOHN HAY in 1899 and again following China's Boxer Rebellion in 1900. In it, American policymakers reluctantly accepted the spheres of influence already established but sought equal privileges for the United States. Because most nations, especially Japan, disregarded the provisions, the Nine-Power Treaty, signed at the 1922 Conference on the Limitation of Armament in Washington, D.C., reaffirmed the Open Door policy. It ended with the recognition of China's sovereignty after World War II.

Oppenheimer, J. Robert (1904–67), physicist. Oppenheimer supervised the development of the ATOMIC BOMB as director of the Manhattan Project in Los Alamos, New Mexico, from 1942 to 1945. He chaired the General Advisory Committee to the Atomic Energy Commission (AEC) from 1947 until 1952 and directed the Institute for Advanced Study at Princeton from 1947 to 1966. In 1954, at the height of the RED SCARE, because of his opposition to the escalation of the nuclear arms race and the development of the hydrogen bomb, as well as his alleged former left-wing associations, Oppenheimer was declared a security risk and barred from participation in government programs. In 1963, however, the AEC presented him with the prestigious Fermi Award for his contributions to theoretical physics.

Oregon (Beaver State), joined the Union on February 14, 1859, as the thirty-third state. (See maps, pages 540 and 541.) Oregon became part of the United States in 1846 when a treaty was signed with England dividing the OREGON TERRITORY along the forty-ninth parallel. Tourism is an important industry, with such attractions as Crater Lake (the deepest lake in the United States), ocean beaches, Bonneville Dam, and the Columbia Gorge. The largest cities include Salem, the capital, Portland, Eugene, and Springfield. Oregon is a leader in the wood-processing industry and salmon fishing and in the production of lumber, peppermint oil, pears, plums, and grass seed. The city of Portland is known as the City of Roses because of its beautiful gardens. Noted personalities born in Oregon include LINUS PAULING and CHIEF JOSEPH.

Oregon Territory, area south of the forty-ninth parallel (excluding Vancouver Island), north of California, and west of the Rocky Mountains. Early in the nineteenth century the Oregon Territory had been jointly occupied by the United States and Great Britain under the terms of the Treaty of 1818. American claims were based on Capt. ROBERT GRAY's discoveries, explorations by the LEWIS AND CLARK EXPEDITION, and the establishment of Astoria by JOHN JACOB ASTOR. Great Britain's claims were based on discoveries by Sir Francis Drake, Capt. James Cooke, and Capt. George Vancouver. During the ELECTION OF 1844, U.S. expansionists cried, "Occupy Oregon" and "Fifty-four forty or fight," calling for annexation of the entire Oregon Territory up to 54°40' north latitude. In 1846 the United States and Great Britain signed a treaty dividing the territory and making the forty-ninth parallel the boundary between the United States and Canada.

Oregon Trail, chief overland route from Missouri to the Pacific Northwest followed by fur traders and pioneers during the 1840s and 1850s. The two-thousand-mile journey took about six months for the average wagon train. Beginning in Independence, Missouri, settlers traveled northwest along the Platte and North Platte rivers to South Pass, where the journey through the Rocky Mountains led them to the Snake River. They left the Snake to cross the Blue Mountains and join the Columbia River to the Willamette Valley or Fort Vancouver. Use of the Oregon Trail declined with the completion of the TRANSCONTINENTAL RAILROAD in 1869.

Organization of American States (OAS) (1948), a regional political body of thirty-two countries in the Western Hemisphere organized to foster better relations among the American nations. Concerned with political matters, particularly the maintenance of peace and human rights, the OAS succeeded the Pan-American Union.

Oriskany, Battle of (August 6, 1777), bloody confrontation during the AMERICAN REVOLUTION between American and British forces. Colonists under Gen. Nicholas Herkimer and British under Gen. Barry St. Leger met near Lake Oswego in central New York. The American victory forced a British retreat into Canada, destroying their campaign plan and leading to the surrender of British general JOHN BURGOYNE at SARATOGA.

Orr, Bobby (1948–), Canadian-born U.S. hockey player. Orr led the Boston Bruins to two Stanley Cup championships and as a defense man broke every record in the National Hockey League. Orr won the Hart Most Valuable Player award three times, the Norris Trophy for best defense man nine straight times, and the Ross Trophy as leading scorer twice. He also won the Calder Trophy in 1966–67 as rookie of the year and the Smythe Trophy as playoff MVP twice. In 1979 at age thirty-one Orr became the youngest man ever inducted into the hockey Hall of Fame.

Ostend Manifesto (October 18, 1854), secret document stating the American demand that Spain sell Cuba to the United States and asserting that if Spain refused to sell, the United States would be justified in seizing it. Meeting in Ostend, Belgium, Minister to France John Mason, Minister to Great Britain JAMES BUCHANAN, and Minister to Spain Pierre Soulé were authorized by Secretary of State WILLIAM MARCY to negotiate the purchase, which failed.

Southern expansionists had hoped that by this agreement the island of Cuba would become a southern slave state. When news of the manifesto's contents reached the press, however, northern protests caused Marcy to disclaim it as official U.S. policy.

Oswald, Lee Harvey (1939–63), alleged assassin of President John F. Kennedy. On November 22, 1963, Oswald was arrested and charged with killing President Kennedy in Dallas, Texas. Two days later, while being transferred to another jail, he himself was assassinated by Dallas nightclub owner Jack Ruby. The Warren Commission Report concluded that Oswald acted alone, but speculation continues that he may have been set up or that he was part of a conspiracy.

Otis, James (1725–83), Revolutionary lawyer and Patriot. Otis strongly opposed the WRITS OF ASSISTANCE, objecting to unlawful search and seizure without proper cause. A member of the Massachusetts Committee of Correspondence, he is given credit for writing "Taxation without representation [in Parliament] is tyranny."

Owen, Ruth Bryan (1885–1954), diplomat. The first woman to represent the United States in a foreign country, Owen served as minister to Denmark from 1933 to 1936. She represented Florida in the House of Representatives

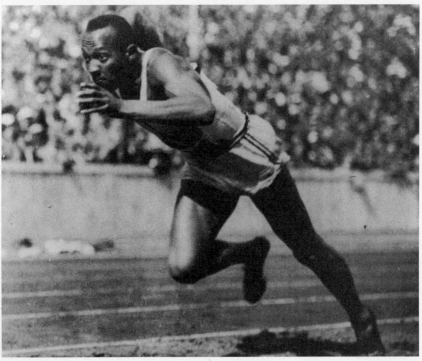

Jesse Owens
Running in a 200-meter preliminary heat at the 1936 summer Olympic Games in Germany.

from 1929 to 1933 and was an alternate U.S. representative to the United Nations in 1949. She was the daughter of WILLIAM JENNINGS BRYAN.

Owens, Jesse (1913–80), African-American track and field athlete. During the 1936 Olympic Games in Berlin, Germany, Owens won four gold medals for the United States, tying the 100-meter dash record and breaking Olympic records in the 200-meter dash, long jump, and 4 × 100-meter relay. This sensational feat by a black athlete so upset Adolf Hitler and his theory of a white master race that the German dictator left the stadium rather than congratulate Owens. Owens finally received the Presidential Medal of Freedom for his legendary accomplishment in 1976.

P

Paige, Satchel (LeRoy; 1906–82), African-American baseball player. Paige pitched in the Negro Leagues from 1924 to 1947, before the major leagues admitted black players. He was a legend, reportedly pitching dozens of career no-hitters and winning 103 of 105 games in 1934. In 1948, at age forty-two, Paige became the first black pitcher in the American League when he joined the Cleveland Indians and later the St. Louis Browns. He pitched in the majors for six years, for a 28–31 record, and tossed in over 2,500 games during his career. Paige joined baseball's Hall of Fame in 1971.

Paine, Thomas (1737–1809), English-born Revolutionary, political philosopher, and writer. Paine's influential pamphlet *Common Sense* (1776) was the first to advocate independence for the American colonies. During the AMERICAN REVOLUTION he wrote a series of sixteen pamphlets called *The Crisis* (1776–83), which helped inspire the Revolutionaries. After the Revolution Paine returned to England, where he defended the French Revolution in his *Rights of Man* (1791–92). Charged with libel, Paine fled to France, where he was elected to the National Convention but was later imprisoned. While in prison, he wrote *Age of Reason* (1794), which upset many with its deist religious views. James Monroe obtained Paine's release, and he returned to the United States in 1802, where he died in poverty.

Palmer, Arnold (1929–), golfer. Palmer's popularity brought golf to new heights as a spectator sport with the help of television and his loyal supporters, known as "Arnie's Army." He won more than eighty events including the Masters four times, the British Open twice, and the U.S. Open once.

Palo Alto, Battle of (May 8, 1846), one of the earliest battles of the Mexican War. U.S. general ZACHARY TAYLOR's troops defeated Mexican forces led by Gen. Mariano Arista at Palo Alto, Mexico, near Brownsville, Texas. The Mexicans, who numbered six thousand, lost over three hundred men, while the Americans lost nine. This battle enabled President James K. Polk to induce Congress to declare war on Mexico on May 13.

Panama Canal waterway built across the Isthmus of Panama by U.S. military engineers to connect the Atlantic and Pacific oceans. Forty miles in length, the canal eliminates the need to travel around South America, saving a distance of over seven thousand miles. It takes a ship seven to eight hours to travel through two lakes and the six locks of the canal. Planning began in 1850, when the Clayton-Bulwer Treaty between the United States and Great Britain ensured that neither country would seek individual rights over such a canal. This agreement was superseded by the Hay-Pauncefote Treaty of 1901, when the British relinquished any claims and gave the United States sole rights to construct and control the canal. In 1903 Congress ratified the Hay-Herran Treaty, granting the United States a ten-mile strip of land across the isthmus, but the Colombian government refused to approve the treaty. A Panamanian uprising supported by the United States led to Panama's independence and the Hay-Bunau-Varilla Treaty in 1903, allowing the United States to build the canal. Construction, begun in 1906, spanned eight years. DR. WILLIAM C. GORGAS successfully eliminated the threat of malaria and yellow fever, and chief engineer GEORGE WASHINGTON GOETHALS is generally credited with the success of the project. In 1977 the United States ratified the Panama Canal Neutrality Treaty, which guaranteed neutrality after the year 2000, and the Panama Canal Treaty, which allowed U.S. supervision until December 31, 1999, when Panama took over control of the canal's operations.

Papp, Joseph (Yosl Papirofsky; 1921–91), director and producer. Papp opened the world of theater to huge audiences by persuading New York City authorities to let him stage plays in Central Park. His program, the New York Shakespeare Festival, became so popular that the city built an amphitheater seating over two thousand to house it. Papp acquired and transformed the Astor Library into the five-auditorium Public Theatre.

Paris, Treaty of (February 10, 1763), agreement signed by Great Britain, France, and Spain ending the Seven Years' War — in America the FRENCH AND INDIAN War. France lost its major North American possessions to England, except Louisiana, which it had ceded to Spain. Spain recovered Cuba and the Philippines, but ceded Florida to England.

Paris, Treaty of (September 3, 1783), agreement between the United States and Great Britain ending the AMERICAN REVOLUTION and recognizing American independence. Negotiated by JOHN ADAMS, BENJAMIN FRANKLIN, and JOHN JAY, the treaty doubled the size of the new country by extending its western boundary to the Mississippi River; agreed upon were a northern boundary with Canada and a southern boundary with Florida, which was ceded to Spain. It also allowed free navigation of the Mississippi River to all nations and gave the United States fishing rights off the banks of Newfoundland.

Paris, Treaty of (December 10, 1898), agreement ending the SPANISH-AMERICAN WAR. Spain ceded Puerto Rico, the Philippines and Guam to the United States and granted independence to Cuba.

Parker, Alton B. (1852–1926), jurist. As chief justice of the New York Court of Appeals (1897–1904), Parker held one of the highest judicial positions in the United States. He was known for his liberal decisions in labor cases, and had refused to run for governor and U.S. senator from New York, believing the bench should not serve as a stepping stone to executive positions. However, he resigned as chief judge after he received the Democratic nomination for the presidency. Hoping for an upset over popular Republican president THEODORE ROOSEVELT, Parker suffered an overwhelming defeat. Unable to return to the bench due to his resignation, he had to give up his dream of one day serving on the U.S. Supreme Court, and returned to his law practice.

Parker, Charlie ("Bird"; 1920–55), jazz saxophonist. Closely associated with DIZZY GILLESPIE, Parker helped develop the bebop style of jazz in the 1940s and creatively improvised on all themes from ballads to the blues. Noted works include "Now's the Time" and "Parker's Mood."

Parker, Dorothy (1893–1967), author. Noted for her satirical short stories and poetry, Parker published her first collection of light verse, *Enough Rope,* in 1926. Originally a drama critic for *Vanity Fair* and a book reviewer for the *New Yorker,* Parker became famous for her acerbic wit. Parker published several collections of short stories and also wrote for motion pictures and the stage.

Parker, Theodore (1810–60), clergyman and social reformer. A strong abolitionist, Parker served as the minister of the Congregational Society of Boston and was a leader of the Unitarian movement. He advocated a variety of social reforms, including abolition, temperance, and women's education, and was one of the secret planners of JOHN BROWN'S RAID in 1859 at Harpers Ferry, Virginia.

Parkman, Francis (1823–93), historian and author. Although in poor health much of his life, Parkman in 1846 took a seven-month journey westward on the OREGON TRAIL and lived among the Sioux Indians to gather material for his classic, *The Oregon Trail* (1849). Parkman wrote about the Indian revolt following the British conquest of Canada in *History of the Conspiracy of Pontiac* (1851), the first volume of *France and England in North America* (1851–92), a ten-volume account of the struggle for control of North America. Although he was a great literary stylist, recent historians have charged him with bias against Native Americans.

Parks, Rosa (1913–), African-American civil rights activist. In December 1955 Parks refused to give up her seat on a bus in Montgomery, Alabama, to a white passenger as the law required. Her arrest led to the loss of her job and a year-long citywide boycott, which brought national prominence to Dr. MARTIN LUTHER KING, JR., who led the resistance. The incident resulted in a U.S. Supreme Court decision outlawing segregation on city buses. Parks was awarded the SPINGARN MEDAL in 1979.

Paterson, William (1745–1806), jurist and political leader. As a delegate to the Constitutional Convention from New Jersey, Paterson helped write the New Jersey Plan, which favored the small states by giving each state an equal number of representatives in the federal legislature. Paterson served in the U.S. Senate and was appointed an associate justice of the U.S. Supreme Court by President George Washington in 1793.

Patriots, appellation for American colonists who fought for independence against the English during the American Revolution.

Patrons of Husbandry *See* Granger Movement.

Patton, George S. (1885–1945), general during World War II. Known as "Old Blood and Guts" for his toughness, Patton played a major role as commander of a tank corps in the invasion of North Africa in 1942 and was instrumental in the capture of Sicily in 1943. After the D-Day invasion of Normandy, his Third Army led in the liberation of France as it swept across Europe into Germany. Patton also helped halt the German counterattack in the Battle of the Bulge.

Paul, Alice (1885–1977), social reformer and feminist. Paul was an early leader in the movement that eventually gave women the right to vote in 1920. At odds with the National American Woman Suffrage Association (NAWSA) because she advocated more militant tactics, Paul left the group in 1914 to cofound the Congressional Union for Woman Suffrage, which became the National Woman's party in 1916. She submitted the first version of the Equal Rights Amendment to Congress in 1923.

Pauling, Linus (1901–94), chemist. One of the few people to have received two Nobel Prizes, Pauling won the 1954 chemistry prize for his work on molecular structure and the 1962 peace prize for his efforts to ban nuclear weapons. His later contributions to medicine include advocacy of large doses of vitamin C to fight colds. His notable works include *The Nature of the Chemical Bond* (1939) and *No More War!* (1958).

Payne, John Howard (1791–1852), actor and playwright. Credited with writing, adapting, or translating over sixty plays, Payne was the first American playwright to achieve international recognition. His first play was produced when he was fourteen. He began acting at seventeen and while in Europe collaborated with Washington Irving on several plays, including *Charles the Second* (1824) and *Richelieu* (1826). Payne is best known for having written the words to the song "Home, Sweet Home" for his opera *Clari, or The Maid of Milan* (1823). Payne aggressively campaigned for Native American rights, particularly on behalf of the Cherokees, and served as U.S. consul in Tunisia from 1842 to 1845 and 1851 to 1852.

Payne-Aldrich Tariff (1909), controversial legislation signed by President William Howard Taft lowering some tariffs and raising others. Honoring Taft's 1908 campaign pledges to lower tariffs, the House of Representatives passed a bill introduced by Representative Sereno E. Payne of New

York that lowered tariff rates. Senator Nelson W. Aldrich of Rhode Island and other protectionists in the Senate added numerous amendments to the bill, and as finally passed, the Payne-Aldrich Tariff preserved a high protective tariff. Taft's failure to veto the bill caused controversy.

Payton, Walter (1954–99), professional football player. At Jackson State University, Payton broke the NCAA record for most career points with 464. As a running back for the Chicago Bears of the National Football League (NFL) from 1974 to 1987, Payton broke JIM BROWN's career records for rushing and total yardage. His record held until 2002 when it was broken by EMMITT SMITH. Known for his strength and balance, he scored 125 career touchdowns and led the Bears to a Super Bowl championship in 1986. He died of cancer at age forty-five.

Peace Corps (1961), overseas volunteer program started as part of President JOHN F. KENNEDY's NEW FRONTIER. Volunteers at the request of developing countries, usually for two years, in fields such as education, health care, and agriculture. Its goals are to help obtain everyday necessities, promote world peace, and improve relations between Americans and the people of other countries. In 1971 the Peace Corps became part of ACTION, a government agency that coordinates several volunteer programs, and in 1981 it became an independent agency.

Peace Democrats *See* COPPERHEADS.

Peale, distinguished family of early American painters, headed by Charles Willson Peale (1741–1827). Twenty members of the family, spanning three generations, were artists. A founder of the Philadelphia Academy of the Fine Arts in 1805, Charles studied with John Singleton Copley and Benjamin West. He is noted for his portraits of noted Americans including Benjamin Franklin, Thomas Jefferson, and about sixty of George Washington alone. Peale's scientific pursuits included taxidermy (he opened a natural history museum of stuffed animals and artifacts, the first of its kind, at Independence Hall in Philadelphia), dentistry (he invented false teeth), and with Thomas Jefferson, the invention of the polygraph, a device for writing two copies of a document at the same time. His brother James Peale (1749–1831) was known for his still lifes and miniatures. Charles taught several of his seventeen children, many of whom were named for noted European artists. They included Titian Peale (1799–1885), animal painter and naturalist; Rubens Peale (1784–1865), painter of still life nature subjects; Raphaelle Peale (1774–1825), painter of still lifes and portraits; and Rembrandt Peale (1778–1860), portrait painter, student of Benjamin West, and founder of the Peale Museum in Baltimore, Maryland.

Peale, Norman Vincent (1898–1993), Protestant clergyman. Peale influenced millions through his weekly radio and television programs. *The Art of Living* continued for a record fifty-four years as the longest-running religious radio program. A dynamic motivational speaker, Peale conveyed simple, optimistic messages, offering courage, compassion, and a positive outlook on living. Ordained in the Methodist Episcopal Church in 1922, he preached at several churches in New York and Rhode Island. Changing his affiliation to the Dutch Reformed Church, he served as pastor of the Marble Collegiate Church in Manhattan for more than fifty years (1932–84). Peale cofounded the Blanton-Peale Institute of Religion and Health, the first school for pastoral psychology. The best-known of his more than forty books, *The Power of Positive Thinking* (1952) sold nearly twenty million

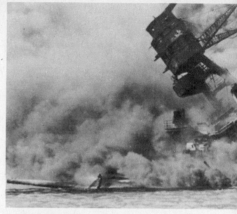

Pearl Harbor
The sinking of the U.S.S. Arizona *at Pearl Harbor, December 7, 1941; a memorial has been built over the sunken ship.*

copies. Other books include his autobiography *The True Joy of Positive Living* (1984) and *This Incredible Century* (1991).

Pearl Harbor, natural harbor on the Hawaiian island of Oahu, best known as the site of an important U.S. naval base. On December 7, 1941, Pearl Harbor was the target of a surprise air attack by the Japanese. The U.S. casualties were heavy, with eighteen ships sunk or badly damaged, about two hundred planes destroyed, and 2,323 U.S. servicemen killed. Although a military success for Japan, it was a political blunder, for it mobilized U.S. public opinion against the Japanese and the Axis powers. The attack spurred Congress to declare war on Japan, bringing the United States into WORLD WAR II on December 8, 1941. Pearl Harbor is now a National Historic Site.

Peary, Robert (1856–1920), Arctic explorer. Accompanied by his black aide MATTHEW HENSON, Peary led numerous expeditions in an attempt to reach the North Pole, finally becoming the first person to reach it on April 6, 1909. Peary wrote several books including *Northward over the Great Ice* (1898) and *The North Pole* (1910). He retired from the navy as a rear admiral in 1911.

Peck, Gregory (1916–2003), actor. Known for his characterizations of strong, reserved heroes, Peck achieved stardom with his second film, *The Keys of the Kingdom* (1944), and earned an Academy Award for his performance in *To Kill a Mockingbird* (1962).

Pei, I. M. (1917–), Chinese-American architect. Working in an elegant style depicting broad, irregular geometric shapes, Pei gained respect for his unique designs for shopping centers, skyscrapers, museums, and government buildings. His first recognition was for Denver's Mile-High Center. Award-winning buildings include Kips Bay Plaza (New York City, 1962),

John Hancock Tower (Boston, 1973), and the East Wing of the National Gallery of Art (Washington, D.C., 1978). Pei won numerous honors for his work, notably the Gold Medal of the American Institute of Architects (1979) and the Pritzker Architecture Prize (1983).

Pelosi, Nancy (1940–), politician. Pelosi was elected Democratic (minority) leader of the U.S. House of Representatives in 2002, becoming the highest-ranking woman in the history of the U.S. Congress. Pelosi won the position after fifteen years in the House, representing a San Francisco area district. Before becoming leader, she served as House Democratic whip for one year, as ranking Democrat on the House Permanent Select Committee on Intelligence, and as a senior member of the powerful House Appropriations Committee. Known for her liberal views, she is an active supporter of gun control, legal abortion, and gay rights, and has opposed trade with China, citing human rights violations by the Chinese government.

Pendleton Act (January 16, 1883), act passed by Congress during the administration of CHESTER A. ARTHUR establishing a Civil Service Commission, which required competitive examinations for some federal jobs. It was the first comprehensive national merit system. The Pendleton Act helped dismantle part of the SPOILS SYSTEM.

Peninsular Campaign (April 4–July 1, 1892), series of battles during the CIVIL WAR, which ended an unsuccessful Union military advance toward the Confederate capital of Richmond, Virginia. Gen. GEORGE B. McCLELLAN landed his forces on the peninsula between the York and James rivers. The Union won the siege of Yorktown, forcing Confederate general JOSEPH E. JOHNSTON to move his troops back. The Union forces pushed the Southern units back at Fair Oaks. In the SEVEN DAYS' BATTLES, the Confederates under Gen. ROBERT E. LEE forced McClellan and the Union men to retreat to Harrison's Landing, and the campaign ended in failure.

Penn, William (1644–1718), reformer and colonizer. An English Quaker and believer in religious toleration, Penn founded the American colony of Pennsylvania, obtaining the land grant from King Charles II to establish a haven of religious freedom and democracy.

Pennsylvania (Keystone State) became on December 12, 1787, the second state to join the Union. (See maps, pages 540 and 541.) In 1681 King Charles II of England gave a grant of land in North America to William Penn; this became the colony of Pennsylvania, meaning "Penn's Woods." Its largest cities include Philadelphia, Pittsburgh, Erie, Scranton, and Allentown. The capital is at Harrisburg. Philadelphia is called the "birthplace of the nation" because the Continental Congress met there, the Declaration of Independence was signed there, and the writing and adoption of the U.S. Constitution took place there. Philadelphia also served as the capital of the country from 1790 to 1800. Titusville was the site of the first oil well in the world. The U.S. Steel Corporation located in the state emerged as one of the largest companies in the world. Gettysburg was the site of the most important battle of the Civil War and of Abraham Lincoln's Gettysburg Address. Pennsylvania leads in the production of steel, coal, cement, glass, and wood products. The world's largest chocolate factory is located in Hershey. Famous Pennsylvanians include JAMES BUCHANAN, BETSY ROSS, DANIEL BOONE, STEPHEN FOSTER, BENJAMIN WEST, THOMAS EAKINS, MARY CASSATT, ANDY WARHOL, ALEXANDER CALDER, and W. C. FIELDS.

Pentagon, headquarters for the Department of Defense, and of the army, the navy, and the air force. Located in Arlington, Virginia, across the Potomac River from Washington, D.C., the Pentagon is a five-story, five-sided building. Covering an area of thirty-four acres and 3.7 million square feet of office space, it is one of the largest office buildings in the world. Completed in 1943, it is thought to be one of the most efficient office buildings in the world. Despite 17.5 miles of corridors, it takes only seven minutes to walk between any two points in the building. One side of the Pentagon was damaged by the SEPTEMBER 11, 2001, TERRORIST ATTACK when a hijacked airplane was intentionally crashed into the building. The crash and subsequent fire killed 184 people, including the passengers and crew of the jetliner. The attack was coordinated with a similar one on the twin towers of the WORLD TRADE CENTER. Congress has authorized the development of a Pentagon Memorial honoring those who perished in the attack on the Pentagon, to be built entirely from gifts and contributions.

Pentagon Papers, popular name given to secret documents of a military history conducted by the U.S. Department of Defense regarding the U.S. involvement in Vietnam. In 1971 Daniel Ellsberg, a former government researcher who helped research and write the secret history, leaked the papers to the *New York Times,* which began publishing them as a series. They showed how presidents and high-ranking civilian and military leaders had misled the American people about the role of the United States in Southeast Asia. The Justice Department ordered the *Times* to stop publishing, but the Supreme Court ruled in favor of the newspaper on the basis of the First Amendment, allowing the continuation of the articles, which earned the *Times* a Pulitzer Prize in 1972. Ellsberg was indicted for theft, espionage, and conspiracy in 1971, but charges were dismissed in 1973 after revelations of government misconduct.

Pepper, Claude (1900–89), politician. Elected to the U.S. Senate from Florida in 1936, Pepper, a Democrat, served until 1951, losing his renomination bid in 1950 because of his supposedly pro-Soviet positions. As a senator Pepper was a strong supporter of the New Deal and civil liberties. He backed the nation's first minimum-wage law and urged aid for the Allies that later became the Lend-Lease program. He helped create the World Health Organization and the National Institutes of Health. Pepper's second political career began in 1962, when he was elected to the House of

Representatives from a district that included such minority groups as Hispanics, blacks, and senior citizens. As the oldest member of Congress, he became the nation's most powerful advocate of legislation and programs to benefit the elderly. In 1977 Pepper became chairman of the House Select Committee on Aging, where he sponsored an important bill to modify or eliminate age as a factor for mandatory retirement.

Perkins, Frances (1880–1965), social reformer and the first female cabinet member. Appointed by Franklin D. Roosevelt as secretary of labor, Perkins served in the cabinet from 1933 to 1945. She had served as New York State's industrial commissioner before joining FDR's administration. A social reformer, she supported Social Security, federal public works legislation, minimum wages, and the abolishment of child labor.

Perot, Henry Ross (1930–), business executive and political figure. The son of a Texas cotton trader, Perot founded Electronic Data Systems in 1962 with $1,000 borrowed from his wife. The company made him a billionaire by the time he sold it to General Motors in 1984, and he later founded Perot Systems (1988), a computer services company. Perot used his wealth to back causes ranging from inner-city schools to airports to helping Americans in crisis. In 1969 he crusaded for the release of American POWs in Vietnam, and in 1978 he financed and arranged a commando raid to free two captives held in Iran. Although he never held public office, he created a political phenomenon in 1992 when he announced on cable talk show *Larry King Live* that he would run as an independent candidate for the presidency if supporters would petition to ensure him a ballot spot in all fifty states. Criticizing the budget, the national debt, education, corporate America, taxes, and the energy policy, Perot spent more than $65 million of his own money and earned 19 percent of the popular vote in the ELECTION OF 1992. In 1995 he founded the United States Reform party and mounted a second unsuccessful presidential bid in 1996.

Perry, Matthew (1794–1858), naval officer. In 1853 Perry (the younger brother of OLIVER H. PERRY) led a naval mission to Japan that opened the nation's ports to world trade. He entered Tokyo Bay with four vessels and presented President MILLARD FILLMORE's proposal for an agreement to protect shipwrecked American seamen and to expand commerce and trade with the United States. Negotiations resulted in the KANAGAWA TREATY in 1854, giving the United States trading rights with Japan.

Perry, Oliver H. (1785–1819), naval officer. The commander of U.S. naval forces on Lake Erie during the WAR OF 1812, Perry and his fleet of ten ships defeated the British fleet at the BATTLE OF LAKE ERIE in September 1813. This significant victory gave the United States control of the lake and the Ohio Valley. He sent a famous message to Gen. WILLIAM HENRY HARRISON stating, "We have met the enemy and they are ours." (He was the older brother of MATTHEW PERRY.)

Pershing, John J. (1860–1948), military leader. In 1916 Pershing led a difficult punitive expedition of eleven thousand men against Pancho Villa in Mexico. As commander of the American Expeditionary Forces in France during WORLD WAR I, he organized and trained the American forces, which eventually numbered 2 million, and led them in action at CHATEAU-THIERRY, BELLEAU WOOD, ST. MIHIEL, and MEUSE-ARGONNE. Pershing returned from the war a hero, and Congress created a new rank for him, general of the armies. He served as army chief of staff from 1921 to 1924. His book, *My Experiences in the World War* (1931), won a Pulitzer Prize for history in 1932.

Persian Gulf War (August 2, 1990–April 6, 1991), conflict between an international coalition of forces led by the United States and the Iraqi army under Saddam Hussein. Iraq's August 1990 invasion and annexation of Kuwait led to speculation that Iraq intended to invade Saudi Arabia and take control of the region's oil supplies. The U.N. Security Council outlawed trade with Iraq and authorized the use of force if it did not withdraw from Kuwait by January 15, 1991. President GEORGE H. W. BUSH ordered U.S. troops to protect Saudi Arabia, and the protective Operation Desert Shield began. The January deadline ignored, Bush secured authorization from Congress to take military action against Iraq.

In Operation Desert Storm, Allied planes began an air assault on Iraq and Kuwait to oust Hussein's army from the country. A ground war began on February 24, and in only four days of combat the United States and coalition forces defeated Hussein's troops. Bush declared the war ended on February 27, and on April 6 a cease-fire was signed.

The U.N. Security Council demanded Hussein's agreement to tough financial and military conditions, requiring a renouncement of terrorism, payment of billions of dollars in damages to Kuwait, the acceptance of borders negotiated with Kuwait in 1963, and Iraq's destruction of its chemical and biological weapons. In June the Pentagon estimated 100,000 Iraqi soldiers had died in combat. Allies killed totaled less than 200.

Personal Liberty Laws (1780–1861), statutes passed by northern states to protect runaway slaves. By 1843 personal liberty laws prohibited state officials to aid in the arrest or use the jails to hold runaway slaves. Earlier personal liberty laws stated that fugitives would receive a fair trial.

Pet Banks, name applied to state banks selected by the Department of the Treasury to receive government deposits in 1833 when President Andrew Jackson removed government funds from the Bank of the United States. By 1836 pet banks, chosen not because of monetary fitness but on the basis of the SPOILS SYSTEM, numbered eighty-nine.

Peter, Paul, and Mary (Peter Yarrow, 1938– ; Mary Travers, 1937– ; Noel Paul Stookey, 1937–), folk singers. Peter, Paul, and Mary (PP&M) was one of the most successful folk singing groups of the 1960s, with popular recordings of such songs as "Puff the Magic Dragon," "If I Had a Hammer," "Blowin' in the Wind," and "Leaving on a Jet Plane." PP&M was at the forefront of the civil rights movement and has promoted the causes of farm workers, hunger, homelessness, antiapartheid, and numerous other contemporary causes. Having earned many Grammy Awards, they continued to perform into the new century.

Petersburg, Battle of (June 15, 1864–April 2, 1865), siege during the CIVIL WAR. In hopes of seizing the railroads of Petersburg, Virginia, an important railroad center for the Confederate states, Gen. ULYSSES S. GRANT began a battle of trench warfare and bombardment of the town that lasted nine months. Grant finally broke through Gen. ROBERT E. LEE's lines on April 2, 1865, and nearby Richmond fell the next day. A week later Lee surrendered to Grant at APPOMATTOX COURT HOUSE.

Philip (King Philip) (1639?–76), Wampanoag chief. Metacomet (his Indian name) was the son of MASSASOIT. Angry that Indian land was being taken over by white settlers in New England, Philip set out to massacre the colonists. During KING PHILIP'S WAR he wiped out many settlements before being hunted down and killed in a swamp near Bristol, Rhode Island. His head was displayed at Plymouth for twenty-five years.

Philippine Islands, island country in the southwest Pacific Ocean. An Asian land, the country came under Spanish influence in 1521 when Ferdinand Magellan arrived and it became the only Christian nation in Asia. The Spaniards ruled the Philippines until fleet commander George Dewey's defeat of Spanish ships at Manila Bay during the Spanish-American War. The United States gained possession of the country under terms of the TREATY OF PARIS (1898). America ruled the islands until they became a commonwealth in 1935, but U.S. authority continued in the areas of foreign affairs and national defense. During WORLD WAR II, Japan conquered the islands in 1941, despite heroic U.S.-Philippine efforts at BATAAN and CORREGIDOR. The United States recaptured the islands in 1945 and granted the Philippines independence on July 4, 1946.

Phillips, Wendell (1811–84), abolitionist, labor reformer, and orator. A friend of abolitionist WILLIAM LLOYD GARRISON, Phillips gave up a successful law practice to join Garrison's antislavery campaign. He became one of the country's most popular, influential, and powerful orators. Denouncing the Constitution because it supported slavery, he served as president of the American Anti-Slavery Society from 1865 until 1870 and the adoption of the Fifteenth Amendment. Following the Civil War, Phillips crusaded on behalf of woman suffrage, labor reform, and temperance.

Pickering, Timothy (1745–1829), military and political leader. During the American Revolution Pickering served as quartermaster general (1780–85) of the Continental army. President George Washington appointed him postmaster general, and he also held the cabinet positions of secretary of war and then secretary of state. While secretary of war Pickering founded the U.S. Military Academy at West Point. President John Adams fired Pickering in 1800 for insubordination when he discovered that Pickering was working with Alexander Hamilton, then a private citizen, to make foreign and military policy. Representing Massachusetts, Pickering served as leader of the Federalists in the U.S. Senate from 1803 to 1811 and in the House of Representatives from 1813 until 1817.

Pickett, George (1825–75), Confederate general during the CIVIL WAR. Commander of a Virginia division at the Battle of GETTYSBURG, Pickett led the famous and ill-fated Pickett's Charge on Cemetery Ridge on July 3, 1863. Although the Confederates broke momentarily through the Union lines in hand-to-hand combat, the Union forces reunited and the attack was repulsed. The Confederates were forced to retreat and the manpower of the Army of Northern Virginia was greatly weakened. More than 60 percent of Pickett's men were killed or wounded.

Pickford, Mary (Gladys Mary Smith; 1893–1979), Canadian-born silent film actress. Promoted by director D. W. GRIFFITH, Pickford became known as "America's Sweetheart" and won an Academy Award in 1929 for *Coquette*. Together with CHARLIE CHAPLIN, her husband Douglas Fairbanks, and Griffith, Pickford founded United Artists in 1919. She received a special Academy Award in 1976 honoring her lifetime contribution to film. Notable films included *Rebecca of Sunnybrook Farm* (1917), *The Poor Little Rich Girl* (1917), and *Pollyanna* (1920).

Pierce, Franklin (1804–69), fourteenth president of the United States (1853–57). Born in Hillsborough, New Hampshire, Pierce studied law at Bowdoin College. He served in the U.S. House of Representatives (1833–37) and the U.S. Senate (1837–42). He fought in the Mexican War, becoming a brigadier general in 1847, Known for his proslavery views and his support of the COMPROMISE OF 1850, Pierce in 1852 seemed to be acceptable to the southern delegates and won the Democratic presidential nomination on the forty-ninth ballot. He went on to defeat the Whig candidate, Gen. Winfield Scott, for the presidency. During his administration, the Senate ratified the GADSDEN PURCHASE, the KANSAS-NEBRASKA ACT passed, the OSTEND MANIFESTO failed, and a trade treaty with Japan went into effect.

Pike, Zebulon (1779–1813), soldier and explorer. Pike is best known for his 1806 discovery of Pike's Peak, a 14,110-foot peak in the Rocky Mountains near Colorado Springs. He explored the American Southwest to learn about the land and its resources. Pike was suspected of conspiring with Gen. James Wilkinson and AARON BURR in a scheme to create an empire in the Southwest, but the accusation proved false. During the War of 1812 Pike led an attack on York, Toronto, Canada, in which he lost his life.

Pilgrims, a group of English Separatists who founded PLYMOUTH COLONY in New England in 1620. In an effort to separate from the Anglican Church of England, the Pilgrims first fled to Holland and then to North America. Along with other, non-Separatist passengers, they sailed on the *Mayflower* under the leadership of WILLIAM BRADFORD and William Brewster. Before landing in what became Plymouth, Massachusetts, they drew up the MAYFLOWER COMPACT to govern themselves.

Pinchot, Gifford (1865–1946), politician and conservationist. Pinchot served as chief of the Development of Agriculture's Division of Forestry during the presidency of Theodore Roosevelt, significantly influencing Roosevelt's conservation policies. During President William Howard Taft's administration, he became embroiled in the BALLINGER-PINCHOT CONTROVERSY over national land use. Pinchot founded the National Conservation Association and developed a systematic forestry program. He later served two terms as governor of Pennsylvania (1923–27, 1931–35).

Pinckney, notable South Carolina family who played leading roles in the American Revolution. Elizabeth Lucas Pinckney (1722–93), a colonial planter, grew indigo and shared her growing methods, helping it become a leading export for the colony. Two of her children, Charles Cotesworth Pinckney (1746–1825) and Thomas Pinckney (1750–1828), became important statesmen. Charles gained prominence as a member of the CONSTITUTIONAL CONVENTION, helping to draft and signing the document. President John Adams sent him, with Elbridge Gerry and John Marshall, to Paris to resolve conflicts with France, an unsuccessful mission that became known as the XYZ AFFAIR. Pinckney was an unsuccessful Federalist vice-presidential candidate in the ELECTION OF 1800, as well as an unsuccessful candidate for president in the ELECTIONS OF 1804 and 1808. His brother Thomas, a soldier and diplomat, served in the American Revolution and as governor of South Carolina and minister to Great Britain. His negotiation of PINCKNEY'S TREATY with Spain (1795) secured the free navigation of the Mississippi. Defeated as a Federalist candidate for vice president in the ELECTION OF 1796, Pinckney later served in the U.S. House of Representatives and as a major general in the War of 1812. Charles's and Thomas's cousin Charles Pinckney (1757–1824) also served in the Revolution, as a delegate to the Continental Congress, and as a member of the Constitutional Convention. Advocating a strong central government, he submitted to the convention the "Pinckney Plan" or "Pinckney Draught," more than thirty provisions of which were included in the finished document, which he signed. He served as governor of South Carolina and as minister to Spain, helping to win Spain's acceptance of the LOUISIANA PURCHASE.

Pinckney's Treaty (October 27, 1795), agreement establishing U.S. commercial relations with Spain and fixing the southern boundary of the United States at the thirty-first parallel. The treaty, negotiated by Thomas Pinckney, also allowed Americans to land goods at New Orleans tax-free and granted free navigation of the Mississippi River.

Pinkerton, Allan (1819–84), Scottish-born detective. Pinkerton organized the Pinkerton National Detective Agency in Chicago in 1850, one of the first such agencies in the United States. In 1861 he guarded Abraham Lincoln on his journey to inauguration ceremonies in Washington, D.C. During the Civil War he directed a network of spies behind Confederate lines at the request of Gen. George B. McClellan to learn Southern military secrets. After the war his agency specialized in railroad robberies and labor union disputes, gaining attention for infiltrating and breaking up the MOLLY MAGUIRES, an organization of coal miners allegedly engaged in terrorism. Pinkertons were also called in to help break up the HOMESTEAD STRIKE against Carnegie Steel Company in 1892.

Pitcher, Molly (Mary Ludwig Hays; 1754–1832), heroine of the AMERICAN REVOLUTION. Pitcher earned her appellation by carrying water for her husband, John, and other soldiers in the Battle of Monmouth in 1778. A legend that she commanded her husband's cannon following his death may be doubtful, arising from confusion with MARGARET CORBIN, who lived about the same time.

Plath, Sylvia (1932–63), poet and author. Plath showed her talents at a young age when she published her first poem at age eight. Her grief over the death of her father at about the same time provided much of the inspiration for her poetic themes of trouble and loss. Her later poems were noted for their personal imagery and intensely honest focus. By the time she graduated from Smith College she was an acclaimed author, having already published numerous prize-winning poems and short stories. Plath's first collection of poetry was *Colossus* (1960); her autobiographical novel, *The Bell Jar* (1963), was written under the pseudonym Victoria Lucas. Plagued by mental illness, Plath committed suicide at age thirty-one. Collections of her poetry published posthumously include the celebrated *Ariel* (1965) and *The Collected Poems* (1981), which was awarded the Pulitzer Prize in poetry in 1982.

Platt Amendment (1901), agreement between the United States and Cuba giving the United States the rights to intervene in Cuban affairs and to lease naval bases on the island. In effect it made Cuba a U.S. dependency. The United States invoked the amendment several times before its 1934 repeal.

Plessy* v. *Ferguson (1896), decision of the U.S. Supreme Court concerning racial segregation. The Court upheld Louisiana's power to segregate railroad cars, holding that the Fourteenth Amendment of the U.S. Constitution guaranteed political but not social equality. The decision and its recognition of "separate but equal" facilities as constitutional led to widespread segregation laws in the South, which persisted for over fifty years until overturned by the *Brown* v. *Board of Education of Topeka* decision in 1954.

Plymouth Colony (1620), first English settlement in New England and the second permanent English settlement in America, founded by about one hundred PILGRIMS in Massachusetts on the western shore of Cape Cod

Bay. Because they had landed farther north than their planned destination in Virginia, owing to storms at sea, they lacked the governance of their original charter. Thus, while aboard the *Mayflower,* the Pilgrim leaders established a governing order through the MAYFLOWER COMPACT, binding themselves to obey certain laws. During the first winter, despite the help of friendly Indians, they endured great suffering and more than half of the colony died. JOHN CARVER was chosen as the first governor of the colony, followed by WILLIAM BRADFORD. The Plymouth Colony remained independent for nearly seventy years before it became part of the short-lived Dominion of New England in 1686 and then the MASSACHUSETTS BAY COLONY in 1691.

Pocahontas (c. 1596–1617), Indian princess and daughter of Chief Powhatan of the Algonquin Indians of Virginia. Pocahontas contributed to the survival of the Jamestown Colony by providing food and serving as an informer of Indian plans to the colonists. JOHN SMITH claimed that she saved his life when her father was about to execute him by placing her head upon his, though this story may be inaccurate. Later the English held Pocahontas captive near Jamestown, where she converted to Christianity and was baptized Rebecca. She married JOHN ROLFE, a tobacco planter, and accompanied him to England. There she was presented at the court of King James as "Lady Rebecca" and an example that Indians could adopt English ways. Pocahontas died of illness while preparing to return to America.

Poe, Edgar Allan (1809–49), poet, short-story writer, and literary critic. Poe became noted for his tales of terror and his creation of the modern detective story. Orphaned at age three and raised by John Allan, a Virginia tobacco exporter, Poe attended private schools near London. He excelled in studies at the University of Virginia, but as a student at West Point he was dismissed for disobedience of orders. Poe achieved success as an editor, critic, and short-story writer for newspapers in Richmond, Philadelphia, and New York City. Many of his works, which possess a haunting quality, feature bizarre, yet beautiful settings. His short stories include "The Gold Bug" (1843), considered the first detective story, "The Tell-Tale Heart" (1843), "The Fall of the House of Usher" (1839), and "The Murders in the Rue Morgue" (1841). "The Raven" (1845) brought him fame as a poet.

Point Four Program, a foreign aid program proposed by President Harry S. Truman as the fourth point of his 1949 inaugural address. Administered by the Department of State from 1950 to 1953, it was later integrated into other foreign policy programs. Intended as a defense against communism, the Point Four Program promoted improved agricultural production and technological skills in underdeveloped and developing nations.

Poitier, Sidney (1924–), black actor and director. Beginning his career with the American Negro Theatre in New York, Poitier appeared on Broadway in *Anna Lucasta* (1948) and *A Raisin in the Sun* (1959). He won an Academy

Award in 1963 for his performance as a handyman in *Lilies of the Field* and became the first black superstar in the motion picture industry. He directed and starred in *A Patch of Blue* (1965) and *Uptown Saturday Night* (1974).

Polk, James K. (1795–1849), eleventh president of the United States (1845–49). Born in Mecklenburg County, North Carolina, and educated at the University of North Carolina, Polk served in the U.S. House of Representatives from Tennessee (1825–39), acting as Speaker from 1835 to 1839. He then became governor of Tennessee from 1839 to 1841. He gained the Democratic nomination for president in 1844 as a dark horse and compromise choice because neither Martin Van Buren nor John C. Calhoun could win the nomination outright. Polk campaigned on a program of MANIFEST DESTINY with slogans of "Annex Texas" and "Occupy Oregon," defeating his Whig opponent Henry Clay. More territory was added to the United States during Polk's administration than any other except that of Thomas Jefferson. Texas became part of the Union just before Polk took office. During his administration the Oregon Treaty with Great Britain divided the OREGON TERRITORY, the independent Treasury System was reestablished, and the Walker Tariff lowered duties. Polk called for and directed the MEXICAN WAR, after which the United States acquired the MEXICAN CESSION. Polk did not pursue renomination for a second term.

Pollard, Fritz (Frederick; 1894–1986), black football player. Pollard became the first black All-American football player in 1916 when he played halfback at Brown University. He became the first black inducted into the college football Hall of Fame in 1954. Pollard also played in the National Football League and in 1920 became the league's first black coach at Akron.

Pollock, Jackson (1912–56), painter. As originator of a painting technique called "drip" or "action" painting, Pollock attained worldwide influence as a leader of the abstract expressionist movement in the United States during the 1940s and 1950s. Believing that an artist must be a part of his paintings and that the act of painting was as important as the work itself, Pollock walked over his huge canvasses, pouring, dripping, and swirling paint into free, loose patterns. His early teacher and lifelong friend was realistic painter THOMAS HART BENTON.

Poll Tax, also called a "head" tax, is a tax collected equally from everyone. Southern states used poll taxes as a discriminatory device to keep poor people and blacks from voting. In 1964 the use of poll taxes in federal elections became unconstitutional with the ratification of the Twenty-fourth Amendment, and in 1966 the Supreme Court outlawed them at the state level.

Ponce de León, Juan (1460–1521), Spanish explorer. Ponce de León reached America in 1513, searching for the legendary "fountain of youth." He gave the name "Florida" to his landing place and gave Spain a claim to the southeast peninsula of what is now the United States.

Pontiac (c. 1720–69), Ottawa Indian chief. Pontiac's efforts to unite tribes in the Great Lakes area in order to maintain Indian control of the region during the FRENCH AND INDIAN WAR resulted in what is known as Pontiac's Rebellion. In 1763 Pontiac attacked all British forts on the Great Lakes. Although he captured eight of the twelve posts, the rebellion was unsuccessful because the French failed to send reinforcements. Pontiac's Rebellion prompted King George III to issue the PROCLAMATION OF 1763, forbidding white settlers to move west of the Appalachian Mountains. In 1769 Pontiac visited Cahokia, Illinois, where a young Peoria warrior killed him after being bribed by a British trader.

Pony Express (1860–62), a horseback mail delivery service between St. Joseph, Missouri, and San Francisco, California. Relays of about seventy-five ponies or horses covered about two hundred miles a day for ten days. Notable among the riders, many of whom were teenagers, were BUFFALO BILL CODY and WILD BILL HICKOK. Pony Express service ended after not quite two years, upon completion of the Western Union Telegraph Company's transcontinental telegraph and the transcontinental railroad.

Pop Art, modern art movement of the 1950s and 1960s. Objects from popular culture such as road signs, Coca-Cola bottles, comic strips, and soup cans provided the subjects of many pop art works. The movement encouraged various styles in painting and sculpture, but emphasized almost photographic precision in such commercial techniques as silkscreens and stenciling. Pop art was a reaction against abstract expressionism, which developed following World War II. Leading pop artists include JASPER JOHNS, Robert Rauschenberg, Roy Lichtenstein, and ANDY WARHOL.

Pope, John (1822–92), military leader. Pope was the Union general during the CIVIL WAR in charge of the Army of the Potomac when it met the Confederate forces led by Gens. STONEWALL JACKSON and JAMES LONGSTREET at the second Battle of BULL RUN on August 30, 1862. Pope had a good offensive plan to smash the Confederates' right flank, but for some reason the

★ **Pony Express**
An early advertisement for Pony Express riders

Wanted: Young, skinny, wiry fellows not over eighteen. Must be expert riders, willing to risk death daily. Orphans preferred.

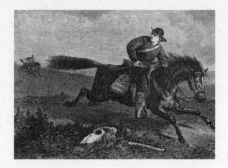

Pony Express
A woodcut from 1861 showing a Pony Express rider on the westward journey from Missouri to San Francisco.

Union soldiers halted, allowing the Confederates to repel assaults to the center of their line. The battle involved fierce hand-to-hand combat, and under tremendous pressure from the Confederates, Pope pulled his troops back and retreated to Washington, D.C. He blamed his defeat on disobedient subordinates and Gen. GEORGE B. MCCLELLAN for holding back troops and supplies. Historians are divided on whether his charges were correct. On September 5, Pope was relieved of his command and for the rest of the war served in departments in the West.

Popular Sovereignty, the doctrine that people of a territory could decide for themselves whether they wanted slavery. First suggested in 1847 by Michigan Senator Lewis Cass, popular sovereignty was proposed as a compromise between the antislavery North and the proslavery South on how to deal with the land acquired from Mexico after the Mexican War. It was incorporated into the 1854 KANSAS-NEBRASKA ACT. STEPHEN A. DOUGLAS, its most popular advocate, called it "popular sovereignty"; antislavery advocates called it "squatters' sovereignty."

Populist Party, political party formed in Omaha, Nebraska, in 1892. Also called the People's party, it consisted of farmer groups, Grangers, and remnants of the GREENBACK PARTY who supported an increase in the money supply, free silver, greater government regulation of business, and increased political power of ordinary voters. In 1892 the Populist party nominated JAMES WEAVER for president and James Field for vice president, winning more than a million popular votes and twenty-two electoral votes. In 1896 the Populists supported Democratic presidential candidate WILLIAM JENNINGS BRYAN, who endorsed many Populist ideas including free coinage of silver, but nominated their own vice president, Thomas Watson of Georgia. The Republicans won the election, and remnants of the Populist party merged with the Democrats.

Porter, family name of two naval officers, father and son. David Porter (1780–1843) served in the war against Tripoli (1801–05) and the WAR OF 1812. As commander of the *Essex,* he was the first American to operate a naval vessel in the Pacific. Porter's adopted son was DAVID FARRAGUT, Civil War naval commander. His son David Dixon Porter (1813–91) served under Farragut in an attack on New Orleans during the Civil War. Acting as head of the Union's Mississippi Squadron, he was active in the takeover of Fort Pickens, Vicksburg, and Wilmington, North Carolina. At the end of the war he became superintendent of the U.S. Naval Academy. In 1870 he was promoted to admiral, only the second person to hold that rank, succeeding his adopted brother, Farragut.

Porter, Cole (1891–1964), songwriter. Porter, known for his witty, poetic, sophisticated lyrics and imaginative melodies, composed for such Broadway musicals as *Anything Goes* (1934), *Kiss Me Kate* (1948) (based on Shakespeare's *Taming of the Shrew*), and *Silk Stockings* (1955), and for such films as

Born to Dance (1936) and *High Society* (1956). Popular songs include "Night and Day" (1932), "Begin the Beguine" (1935), and "I've Got You under My Skin" (1936).

Porter, Katherine Anne (1890–1980), writer. Known for the accomplished style of her short stories, Porter won the 1966 Pulitzer Prize for fiction and the National Book Award for *Collected Short Stories* (1965). She also achieved popular success with her only novel, *Ship of Fools* (1962), a moral allegory focusing on the passengers of a ship bound for Germany in 1931 during the rise of Nazism.

Post, Wiley (1899–1935), aviator. In 1933 Post pioneered the use of an automatic pilot system and became the first person to make a solo flight around the world, covering the distance in seven days, eighteen hours, forty-nine minutes. Two years earlier, with navigator Harold Gatty, he had earned fame when they flew the same course and described the journey in a book, *Around the World in Eight Days.* Post died with his friend, humorist WILL ROGERS, in a plane crash near Point Barrow, Alaska.

Potsdam Conference (July 17–August 2, 1945), the final BIG THREE summit of WORLD WAR II to deal with issues arising from the recent defeat of Germany and the war against Japan. Held in Potsdam, Germany, near Berlin, representatives included President HARRY S. TRUMAN of the United States, Prime Minister Winston Churchill (later replaced by his successor Clement Attlee) of Great Britain, and Premier Joseph Stalin of the Soviet Union. They discussed peace terms for the defeated nations and demanded Japan's unconditional surrender. They also approved earlier agreements to divide Germany into four occupation zones (American, British, Russian, and French) and to try Nazi leaders as war criminals. Numerous disagreements between the Soviet Union and other members caused breaches in the alliance and resulted in the COLD WAR.

Pottawatomie Massacre (May 24–25, 1856), the murder of five proslavery settlers at Pottawatomie Creek in Franklin County, Kansas. John Brown, his sons, and antislavery followers were accused of the massacre. Warrants for their arrest were issued, but the case never came to trial. The murders were part of the state's civil war over slavery, which led to its being called "BLEEDING KANSAS."

Pound, Ezra (1885–1972), poet, critic, and editor. An influential and controversial literary figure, Pound left the United States in 1908 to live in Venice and London. In 1912 he founded imagism, advocating a tight, clear, unsentimental style of poetry. With painter and writer Wyndham Lewis, Pound founded vorticism, which was concerned with the form rather than the content of art. Pound exerted significant influence on the careers of T. S. ELIOT, ERNEST HEMINGWAY, and James Joyce, helping them edit and promote their works. His lifelong effort, the epic *Cantos* (1917–61), deals with corruption in American life. Other works include *Homage to Sextus*

Propertius (1918) and *Hugh Selwyn Mauberley* (1920). As an admirer of Mussolini, Pound broadcast fascist and anti-Semitic propaganda during World War II. Arrested by the United States in 1945 for treason, he was judged insane and unfit to stand trial, and spent thirteen years in a mental hospital. He returned to Italy following his release in 1958.

Powderly, Terence V. (1849–1924), labor leader. Powderly joined the KNIGHTS OF LABOR in 1874, and the union reached its height under his leadership as president beginning in 1879. By 1886 its membership had reached over 700,000, challenging many powerful monopolies. Powderly's greater achievement was his educating the public about the needs and goals of working people. Powderly was dismissed from the presidency in 1893 partly because he opposed use of the strike as a union weapon. Powderly also served as mayor of Scranton, Pennsylvania (1878–84), U.S. commissioner of immigration (1897–1902), and chief of the Division of Information, Bureau of Immigration (1907–21).

Powell, Adam Clayton, Jr. (1908–72), clergyman and political leader. Powell succeeded his father as pastor of Abyssinian Baptist Church in Harlem, America's oldest and largest African-American Protestant congregation. Through his crusades for jobs and housing for the poor, he earned recognition as a compassionate, charismatic, self-assured, and effective leader with loyal support. In 1944 he was elected to the House of Representatives as a Democrat from Harlem (1945–70), the first African-American representative from a northeastern state. There he became a strong and controversial force, chairing the House Committee on Education and Labor (1960–67), vocally and vigilantly promoting reforms for social equality and civil rights, and becoming the most powerful black political leader in the country. Powell's outspokenness and flamboyant lifestyle earned him enemies, however, and his personal excesses and financial indiscretions led to his fall. Members of the House accused him of misuse of House funds, and he was deprived of his seat for a time; later he suffered defeat in the primary election of 1970.

Powell, Colin (1937–), U.S. secretary of state under President George W. Bush (2001–), former U.S. Army general, and chairman of the Joint Chiefs of Staff. A four-star general, Powell served two tours of duty in the VIETNAM WAR and later commanded ground forces in South Korea, West Germany, and the United States. President Ronald Reagan named him deputy national security adviser in 1986, and he became the national security adviser the next year. Appointed chairman of the Joint Chiefs of Staff by George H. W. Bush in 1989, Powell was the youngest man and the first African-American to hold the post. He served from 1989 to 1993 under both President George H. W. Bush and President Bill Clinton. With Secretary of Defense RICHARD CHENEY, he codirected the Allied efforts in the 1991 PERSIAN GULF WAR. After retiring from the army in 1993, Powell wrote his autobiography, *My American Journey* (1995). In 1997 he established America's Promise — The Alliance for Youth, an organization to help needy and at-risk children. After being unanimously confirmed by the Senate, he was sworn in as the sixty-fifth secretary of state on January 20, 2001, the first African American to hold that position. Powell was a voice of moderation in the early months of the Bush administration. In the months leading up to America's 2003 war in Iraq, Powell urged the U.N. Security Council to approve a resolution calling for unconditional access for weapons inspectors and the right to use force if Saddam Hussein failed to comply. As the postwar violence and the projected cost of the occupation of Iraq increased, Powell tried — with limited success by the end of 2003 — to win support at the U.N. for broader international aid in Iraq.

Powell, John Wesley (1834–1902), geologist and explorer. Powell made the first of many exploratory trips into the Rocky Mountain region in 1867. In 1869 he led an expedition financed by the SMITHSONIAN INSTITUTION and Congress down the Colorado River and through the Grand Canyon. Powell studied the Indians of the West closely. In 1879 he became the first director of the Smithsonian's Bureau of American Ethnology and two years later the second director of the U.S. Geological Survey.

Prescott, Samuel (1751?–77), Revolutionary Patriot. A physician in Concord, Prescott completed PAUL REVERE's famous ride of warning on the night of April 18, 1775, following Revere's capture by the British. Returning home from Lexington, Prescott met Revere and William Dawes, who were spreading news of the British march on Concord. When stopped by British officers, Dawes and Revere were seized, but Prescott escaped and continued to Concord. Prescott served at FORT TICONDEROGA, where he was captured by the British. He died in prison.

Prescott, William (1726–95), soldier of the AMERICAN REVOLUTION. Ordered by Gen. Artemas Ward to fortify BUNKER HILL in Boston, Prescott and his men fortified nearby Breed's Hill instead because it commanded a better view of Boston Harbor. On June 17, 1775, Prescott and his troops successfully defended the hill against three British attacks, but were forced to retreat when they ran out of ammunition. Prescott saw further action at Saratoga and in the New York campaign.

Prescott, William Hickling (1796–1859), historian. Best known for his classics, *History of the Conquest of Mexico* (1843) and *The Conquest of Peru* (1847), Prescott specialized in the Spanish conquest of the New World. Prescott wrote prolifically despite near blindness. His works, noted for their accuracy, reflected careful research and use of original sources, making him one of the first historians to use a more scientific approach.

Presidency, the office held by the elected head of the executive branch of the U.S. government, who also serves as commander in chief of the armed forces. Often called the chief executive, the president is elected for a four-year term by the people of the fifty states through the ELECTORAL COL-LEGE system. The Twenty-second Amendment provides that no one may be elected president more than twice. Established under Article II, Section 1, of the Constitution, the office was principally delineated by JAMES WILSON of Pennsylvania at the CONSTITUTIONAL CONVENTION. The Constitution stipulates that the president must be at least thirty-five years old, have lived in the United States fourteen years, and be a natural-born citizen.

Although the powers and authorities of the president are set by the Constitution, the position itself has evolved with the personalities of the men who have held the office and the particular requirements of the times. GEORGE WASHINGTON basically shaped the duties of the office for future presidents. Others, such as THOMAS JEFFERSON, ANDREW JACKSON, and ABRAHAM LINCOLN, defined and strengthened the chief executive's role through their bold interpretations of the Constitution. The office was weakened following the Civil War, as Congress increased its influence beginning with its impeachment of ANDREW JOHNSON. Following the Spanish-American War, however, THEODORE ROOSEVELT brought increased power and prestige to the presidency through his reforms. WOODROW WILSON, FRANKLIN D. ROOSEVELT, HARRY S. TRUMAN, and JOHN F. KENNEDY further enlarged the scope and influence of the office through aggressive measures, beginning in WORLD WAR I and extending through the CUBAN MISSILE CRISIS. Although presidential decisions during the VIETNAM WAR and the WATERGATE scandal raised questions about the uses of presidential power, the position remains one of the most powerful in the world.

Presidential Succession, provision in Article II, Section 1, of the Constitution, stating that the vice president becomes president upon the death, resignation, or removal from office of the president. The Presidential Succession Act of 1886, amended in 1947, defines the succession further, stating that the SPEAKER OF THE HOUSE of Representatives and then the PRESIDENT PRO TEMPORE of the Senate are next in succession. The fourteen cabinet members follow, starting with the secretary of state and continuing through the departments in the order in which they were established. The Twentieth Amendment (1933) and the Twenty-fifth Amendment (1967) clarify the succession under a variety of circumstances — for example, if a president or vice president has not been selected by January 20, if a president-elect dies before assuming office, if a president becomes disabled while in office, or if a vacancy occurs in the office of vice president.

President Pro Tempore, the presiding officer of the U.S. Senate, elected by the members to officiate at sessions when the president of the Senate (the vice president of the United States) is not available. The position of president pro tempore is usually filled by the member of the majority party with the most seniority, but it does not include much political power.

Presley, Elvis (1935–77), rock singer. Presley, influenced by blues and country western music, popularized rock and roll in the 1950s. He became a musical and cultural phenomenon, known for his African-American-influenced vocal mannerisms, his manner of hair and dress, and a sexually provocative (for the time) performance style. His rise to stardom in 1956 with "Heartbreak Hotel" was solidified with other hits including "Don't Be Cruel," "Love Me Tender," and "All Shook Up." Presley's fame spread worldwide with concerts, television appearances, and over thirty movies. He died from an accidental drug overdose. Graceland, his Memphis, Tennessee, home, has become a major tourist attraction and national shrine for his many fans. In 1993 Presley became the first rock star to be honored with a U.S. postage stamp.

Price, Leontyne (1927–), African-American opera singer. After graduating from Juilliard School of Music, Price debuted on Broadway in 1952. A lyric soprano, she achieved fame in her performance of Bess in *Porgy and Bess* (1952–54), touring nationally and internationally. Despite racial protests, she achieved critical acclaim when she sang the title role in a television production of *Tosca* (1955), becoming the first black singer in a television opera production. In 1960 she became the first black singer to sing a leading role at La Scala in Milan, Italy, as the lead in *Aida*, which became her signature role. Price spent most of her career at the Metropolitan Opera House in New York, where she performed until her retirement in 1985. Price has won eighteen Grammy Awards.

Privateers, privately owned armed ships commissioned by the government to prey upon enemy naval or merchant ships in time of war. They were first authorized by the Continental Congress in 1776, and the U.S. government commissioned many during the American Revolution and the War of 1812. The United States refused to sign the Declaration of Paris (1856), which outlawed privateering and continued the practice through the Civil War.

Proclamation of Neutrality (1914), executive notice issued by President WOODROW WILSON at the outbreak of WORLD WAR I in Europe. He urged Americans to be neutral in thought as well as in action.

Proclamation of 1763, order issued by King George III of England at the end of the FRENCH AND INDIAN WAR establishing the lands west of the Appalachians as an Indian reserve. In response to PONTIAC's Rebellion, during which hundreds of white settlers had been killed along the western frontier, the proclamation prohibited settlers from moving west of the Appalachians and ordered those already there to return to the East. The American colonists strongly opposed and largely ignored the order.

Progressive Movement (1889–1920), a broad-based campaign for economic, political, and social reforms. The movement addressed the power of big business and advocated aid for farmers and protection for consumers. The reforms included passage of the Sixteenth and Seventeenth

Amendments, the Pure Food and Drug Act, the Meat Inspection Act, and the Sherman and Clayton Anti-Trust Acts. Progressives supported initiative, recall, referendum, and direct primary laws. Also during this time, attacks were made on child labor, sweatshops, slum conditions, and women working excessive hours. Leading figures in the Progressive Era included the MUCKRAKERS, THEODORE ROOSEVELT, WOODROW WILSON, ROBERT LA FOLLETTE, EUGENE V. DEBS, JOHN PETER ALTGELD, Hiram Johnson, WILLIAM JAMES, JOHN DEWEY, and GEORGE NORRIS.

Progressive Parties (1912, 1924, and 1948), three political parties.

The Progressive party of 1912: Splitting from the Republican party, this group nominated THEODORE ROOSEVELT for president and Senator Hiram Johnson for vice president. It was also called the Bull Moose party. Its platform included woman suffrage, conservation, minimum wage laws, abolition of child labor, direct election of U.S. senators, and advocacy of the initiative, recall, and referendum. The party outpolled the Republicans, thereby defeating incumbent President William Howard Taft; it won over 25 percent of the popular vote but only eighty-eight electoral votes and lost the election to the Democrat WOODROW WILSON.

The Progressive party of 1924: This group also split from the Republicans and nominated U.S. Senator ROBERT LA FOLLETTE of Wisconsin as its presidential candidate. Its platform favored intensive monopoly control, abolition of the Supreme Court's power of JUDICIAL REVIEW, extended farm relief, and the initiative, recall, and referendum. It received the support of the AMERICAN FEDERATION OF LABOR and the U.S. Socialist party. The party received one-sixth of the popular votes but took only the electoral votes of Wisconsin, losing to Republican incumbent CALVIN COOLIDGE.

The Progressive party of 1948: Splitting from the Democrats, this Progressive party nominated former vice president HENRY A. WALLACE as its presidential candidate. Its platform called for the repeal of the TAFT-HARTLEY ACT, demanded strong civil rights legislation, urged reconciliation of United States-Soviet Union conflicts, and opposed the MARSHALL PLAN and the TRUMAN DOCTRINE. The party polled only 2 percent of the popular votes and received no electoral votes, losing to Democratic incumbent HARRY S. TRUMAN.

Prohibition, the forbidding of the manufacture, transportation, and sale of intoxicating liquors in the United States, usually associated with the period 1920–33. Following decades of temperance activities, Congress in 1919 approved the Eighteenth Amendment to the Constitution banning alcohol and adopted the VOLSTEAD ACT to provide for its enforcement. Although consumption sharply declined at first, enforcement efforts were unable to stem the increased smuggling, racketeering, bootlegging, and violence that Prohibition brought in its train. Although Herbert Hoover called

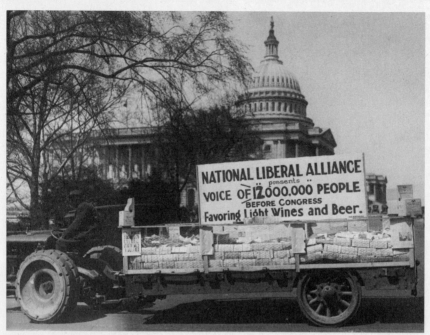

Prohibition
Beer truck used as a polling place.

Prohibition a "noble . . . experiment," toward the end of the 1920s a repeal movement gathered force. The Democrats, in the presidential campaign of 1932, endorsed its repeal, and with Franklin D. Roosevelt's decisive victory, Congress approved the Twenty-first Amendment, repealing the Eighteenth. Although Prohibition ended on December 5, 1933, a few states retained the policy until the 1960s.

Prosser, Gabriel (1775?–1800), black slave. Prosser planned a revolt to end slavery in Virginia and create an independent state for blacks. He organized about a thousand slaves for an attack on Richmond, intending to kill most whites and free the slaves. The attack, planned for August 30, 1800, was postponed when bridges and roads were washed out by a storm. Two slaves betrayed the plans, resulting in the capture and hanging of Prosser and thirty-four others.

Puerto Rico, formerly Porto Rico Island, now a self-governing commonwealth and territory of the United States in the Caribbean Sea. Reached in 1493 by Christopher Columbus, who claimed it for Spain, Puerto Rico was colonized by JUAN PONCE DE LEÓN in 1508. In 1898 the island became an American colony when it was ceded to the United States as part of the TREATY OF PARIS ending the SPANISH-AMERICAN WAR. President McKinley appointed the first U.S. governor under the terms of the

Foraker Act in 1900, and in 1917 the Jones Act granted U.S. citizenship to island residents, and they participated in World War I, World War II, and the Korean War. As U.S. citizens, Puerto Ricans may travel freely in the United States but may not vote in presidential elections while living on the island. During the 1940s the United States contributed to Operation Bootstrap, a program aimed at improving living conditions and educational programs. Proclaimed the Commonwealth of Puerto Rico in 1952, the island continues to receive U.S. assistance but governs itself under its own Constitution. Questions concerning its statehood or complete independence persist.

Pulaski, Casimir (1748–79), Polish-born military leader during the American Revolution. After offering his services to American representatives Benjamin Franklin and Silas Deane in France, Pulaski sailed to America to organize the first American cavalry unit, the Pulaski Legion. He died from wounds sustained during a cavalry charge against the British near Savannah, Georgia.

Pulitzer, Joseph (1847–1911), Hungarian-born editor and publisher. Pulitzer earned a fortune as a result of his merging of two St. Louis newspapers, the *Dispatch* and the *Evening Post*. The success of the *Post-Dispatch* led to his purchase in 1883 of the troubled *New York World*. Under Pulitzer's leadership its circulation grew to be the largest in the nation, and it became America's most influential newspaper, with the addition of such features as sports, comics, and women's fashions. Competition with William Randolph Hearst's *New York Journal* led to its sensationalistic coverage of domestic and foreign problems that came to be called "yellow journalism." Pulitzer's and Hearst's newspapers helped provoke the Spanish-American War. Pulitzer left funds to establish a school of journalism at Columbia University and to endow the Pulitzer Prizes, which are awarded for distinguished work in journalism, literature, and music.

Pulitzer Prizes, awards given annually for distinguished work in journalism, literature, and music. Funded through an endowment left by newspaper magnate Joseph Pulitzer, prizes of $1,000 each have been bestowed since 1917 on the recommendation of a Columbia University advisory board. A gold medal is awarded for public service.

Pullman, George (1831–97), inventor and industrialist. Pullman developed the first modern railroad sleeping car. His Pioneer, the first of the cars called Pullmans, was built in 1865 with the assistance of a friend, Ben Field. It had a folding upper berth with seat cushions that could be made into a lower berth. In 1867 Pullman founded the Pullman Palace Car Company, which built and operated sleeping cars for all major railways. He also designed a dining car in 1868 and a vestibule car in 1887. Pullman pioneered the development of company towns when he founded Pullman, Illinois, to house his workers.

Pullman Strike (May 11–July 20, 1894), violent strike between the American Railway Union (ARU) and the Pullman Palace Car Company of Illinois. About 2,500 employees went on strike against the company to protest wage cuts and high rents in the company's town of Pullman, south of Chicago. EUGENE V. DEBS led the ARU in a nationwide boycott of Pullman cars. When the railroads fired union members, the strike became national. United States Attorney General RICHARD OLNEY obtained a federal court injunction barring the union from interfering with the running of the trains after he had deputized about 3,600 men to keep the trains moving. A rioting mob wrecked a mail train on July 1, causing President Grover Cleveland to call in federal troops to Chicago; on July 4 rioting broke out again and several strikers were killed. By July 10 troops had broken the strike and labor leaders were jailed for disobeying the injunction. The U.S. Supreme Court upheld the use of the injunction by the government in 1895.

Pure Food and Drug Acts, legislation to protect consumers from adulterated food, drugs, and cosmetics. After the publication of UPTON SINCLAIR's *The Jungle* (1906) exposing atrocities of the meatpacking industry in Chicago, as well as other sensational articles by MUCKRAKING journalists, President THEODORE ROOSEVELT urged legislation to prohibit the movement of adulterated foods and drugs in interstate commerce and to require honest labeling on packaging. The result was the Pure Food and Drug Act and the Meat Inspection Act (both passed June 30, 1906). On June 24, 1938, Congress enacted the Food, Drug, and Cosmetic Act, which greatly extended the number of commodities under federal control. The Food and Drug Administration became responsible for enforcing the acts.

Puritans, early New England Protestants who settled in Boston after leaving England in the early seventeenth century. With a strong emphasis on family, devotion, education, and the Bible, the Puritans influenced the development of the American colonies. JOHN COTTON and the MATHERS — Richard, Increase, and Cotton — provided clerical leadership in the MASSACHUSETTS BAY COLONY. JOHN WINTHROP, who became the colony's first governor, believed that the colonists were to act as an advance guard in setting up the kingdom of God to await the return of Jesus Christ.

Pyle, Ernie (Ernest; 1900–45), illustrator and journalist. In 1940 Pyle reported on the German air bombardment of London. He covered the U.S. invasion of North Africa in 1943 and the Normandy invasion in 1944, presenting intimate accounts from the front. In 1944 he received the Pulitzer Prize for his distinguished war correspondence. While observing the advance of U.S. troops near Okinawa in the Pacific, he was killed by Japanese machine-gun fire. Pyle wrote several popular books, including *Here Is Your War* (1943), in which he brought home to his readers the realities of war.

Quakers, popular name for the Society of Friends, a religious sect that developed in England in the 1600s. Religious persecution in England led Quakers, one of the Separatist groups, to immigrate to America, where WILLIAM PENN established the colony of PENNSYLVANIA in 1681. Known for their simplicity, humanitarianism, and pacifism, Quakers have advocated abolitionism, prison reform, education, women's rights, temperance, and humane treatment of mental patients. Quakers rely on inner spiritual experiences, believing everyone can communicate directly with God. They therefore do not consider churches and the Bible to be necessary mediators between God and human beings. They stress religious tolerance, receiving their guidance from what they perceive as an "inner light," sharing their inspiration with their brethren.

Quantrill, William (1837–65), leader of Confederate guerrilla band during the CIVIL WAR. Although Quantrill and his band joined the Confederate forces in 1862, they operated independently, destroying and looting towns and farms indiscriminately. On August 21, 1863, he and his men burned much of the town of Lawrence, Kansas, killing about 150 civilians. Quantrill incurred mortal wounds at the hands of Union troops during a raid in Kentucky in 1865.

Quartering Act *See* INTOLERABLE ACTS.

Quayle, Dan (James Danforth; 1947–), Republican vice president of the United States under GEORGE H. W. BUSH. Before becoming vice president in 1989, Quayle, a strong conservative, served two terms in the House of Representatives (1977–81) and as a senator from Indiana (1981–89). In 1982 he cosponsored the Job Training Partnership Act with Senator Edward M. Kennedy of Massachusetts, providing training for disadvantaged workers. Bush and Quayle lost their 1992 reelection bid. Quayle bid unsuccessfully for the 2000 Republican presidential nomination.

Quebec, the first permanent French settlement in North America. Founded by Samuel de Champlain in 1608 on the cliffs overlooking the St. Lawrence River, Quebec was the site of the Battle of Quebec (1759) during the FRENCH AND INDIAN WAR. The English decisively defeated the French, leading France to give up its American empire in the TREATY OF PARIS (1763). Quebec is now a province of Canada.

Quebec Act (1774), punitive legislation issued by Parliament, one of the INTOLERABLE ACTS that helped bring about the AMERICAN REVOLUTION. The act protected Indians from white settlement by extending the boundaries of Quebec to the Ohio and Mississippi rivers. Angered Americans, who had already been banned from the territory by the PROCLAMATION OF 1763, resisted this threat to self-government. The law also granted religious freedom to Catholics in Quebec, alarming Protestants who held no tolerance for Roman Catholicism.

Quincy, Josiah (1772–1864), educator and politician. A member of the U.S. House of Representatives from Massachusetts (1805–13), Quincy was a Federalist who opposed the policies of Presidents Thomas Jefferson and James Madison. He refused to support the War of 1812 and argued for states' rights. Quincy served as mayor of Boston (1823–29), and as president of Harvard (1829–45) he instituted many reforms. He wrote the two-volume *History of Harvard University* (1840).

Quinn, Anthony (1916–2001), Mexican-born stage and film actor. Quinn, known for the strength and vitality of his acting, won two best supporting actor Academy Awards for *Viva Zapata!* (1952) and *Lust for Life* (1956). He also starred in *The Guns of Navarone* (1961), *Requiem for a Heavyweight* (1962), and *Zorba the Greek* (1964).

Radical Republicans, Republican members of Congress dissatisfied with the policies of Presidents ABRAHAM LINCOLN and ANDREW JOHNSON during and after the CIVIL WAR. Usually strong abolitionists, they took a punitive stance toward the South after the war, advocating strong measures called Radical Reconstruction. THADDEUS STEVENS was their leader in the House, as were CHARLES SUMNER and BENJAMIN WADE in the Senate. Passage of the TENURE OF OFFICE ACT in 1868 led to Johnson's impeachment, but the Senate failed to remove him from office by one vote. Radical Republicans were noted for waving the BLOODY SHIRT to win elections.

Rainey, Joseph (1832–87), legislator. Rainey, son of a free black man, was the first black elected to the House of Representatives, serving from 1869 to 1879 as a Republican from South Carolina. After receiving death threats from the KU KLUX KLAN in 1871, he urged President Ulysses S. Grant to propose a tough law against the Klan, which ultimately passed Congress. Rainey supported the Fourteenth and Fifteenth Amendments to the Constitution, as well as legislation to improve conditions on Indian reservations. He had previously served in South Carolina's state senate.

Rainey, Ma (Gertrude Pridgett; 1886–1939), black singer. An influential pioneer of blues music, Rainey's notable records include *See See Rider, Trust No Man,* and *Slave to the Blues.*

Raleigh, Sir Walter (1552?–1618), English explorer. A favorite of Queen Elizabeth I, Raleigh organized the first English attempt at colonization in North America, which ended with the ill-fated LOST COLONY OF ROANOKE in 1587. He named the unknown land Virginia in honor of Elizabeth who, being unmarried, was called "The Virgin Queen." Raleigh is credited with introducing the potato plant and tobacco into England.

Randolph, family name of four generations of Virginians. William Randolph (1651?–1711), an English-born settler, became a leading planter of Virginia. He served as attorney general for the Crown in Virginia and was a cofounder of the College of William and Mary. His grandson Peyton Randolph (1721?–75) served as president of both the First and Second Continental Congresses in 1774 and 1775. A member of the Virginia House of Burgesses for many years, he served as speaker from 1766 to 1775. He opposed the Stamp Act and served as chairman of the first three Virginia conventions. William Randolph's great-grandson and Peyton Randolph's nephew Edmund Randolph (1753–1813) was one of America's Founding Fathers. He served as the first attorney general of the United States and later became the second secretary of state, succeeding Thomas Jefferson. He served as Gen. George Washington's aide-de-camp during the American Revolution and played an important role at the Constitutional Convention. Randolph introduced the Virginia Plan at the convention and helped draft the U.S. Constitution to include a strong central government. He also had been a member of the Continental Congress and governor of Virginia. Randolph later served as senior counsel for Aaron Burr during Burr's treason trial. His cousin John Randolph (1773–1833) was also a great-grandson of William Randolph and a descendant of Pocahontas and John Rolfe. Known as John Randolph of Roanoke, he served in both the House of Representatives and the Senate as a Democratic-Republican from Virginia. Originally a strong supporter of Thomas Jefferson, he broke with Jefferson over the proposed acquisition of Florida and became a leader of states' rights. Randolph founded a political faction known as the Quids and opposed the national bank, protective tariffs, western expansion, and the War of 1812. He also opposed the Missouri Compromise and Henry Clay, with whom he had a bloodless duel in 1826.

Randolph, A. Philip (1889–1979), black labor and civil rights leader. Randolph played a leading role in the struggle for black civil rights from the 1920s through the 1960s. He directed the marches on Washington, D.C., in 1941 and 1963 and served as vice president of the AFL-CIO in 1957. Randolph organized the Brotherhood of Sleeping Car Porters in 1925 and during the 1930s served as president of the National Negro Congress. Randolph fought for fair employment practices to protect blacks in industry and government and to abolish segregation in the armed forces. He won the Spingarn Medal in 1942.

Rankin, Jeannette (1880–1973), pacifist, feminist, social reformer, and legislator. Rankin became the first woman elected to Congress when in 1916 she won Montana's at-large seat in the House of Representatives for one term. She voted against U.S. entry into World War I, and when she returned to the House in 1941 she cast the only vote against the U.S. entry into World War II. Rankin worked diligently for women's rights and world peace, and in 1968 led the five-thousand-strong Jeannette Rankin Brigade to Washington, D.C., to oppose the Vietnam War.

Rather, Dan (1931–), journalist and television newscaster. Joining CBS in 1962, Rather earned a reputation for careful, thoughtful, and direct reporting. On November 22, 1963, in Dallas, he broke the news of the death of President JOHN F. KENNEDY. He served as war correspondent during the VIETNAM WAR and as White House correspondent during the Nixon administration. Rather succeeded WALTER CRONKITE in 1981 as anchor and managing editor for the *CBS Evening News*. Rather has interviewed every U.S. president since Eisenhower, and in 1990 he was the first American journalist to interview Saddam Hussein after Iraq's invasion of Kuwait. Just prior to the IRAQ WAR in 2003, Rather sparked controversy when he conducted a second interview, the first interview between the Iraqi leader and an American journalist in a decade. Rather appears on *48 Hours* and *60 Minutes II* and has hosted a radio show since 1977.

Rayburn, Sam (1882–1961), politician. As a Democrat Rayburn served in the Texas legislature from 1907 to 1913 and won election to the U.S. House of Representatives in 1912, where he served continuously for forty-eight years, a congressional record. Elected Speaker in 1940, Rayburn held that post for nearly seventeen years (1940–46, 1949–53, 1955–61) until his death, longer than anyone in U.S. history. Rayburn strongly supported Franklin D. Roosevelt and helped establish New Deal programs.

Reagan, Ronald (1911–2004), fortieth president of the United States (1981–89). Born in Tampico, Illinois, Reagan graduated from Eureka College in Illinois. At age sixty-nine, he became the oldest man to be inaugurated president and the first actor to hold the office. Reagan as an actor appeared in over fifty films. He served as president of the Screen Actors Guild from 1947 to 1952 and from 1959 to 1960.

Originally a Democrat active in liberal causes, Reagan developed strong anticommunist feelings and joined the Republicans in 1962. He won the governorship of California in 1966 and 1970 as a conservative. He tried unsuccessfully for the Republican nomination for president in 1968 and 1976. Winning the nomination in 1980, he was elected over Jimmy Carter and Walter Mondale, and in 1984 he and George Bush were reelected over Walter Mondale and Geraldine Ferraro in a landslide.

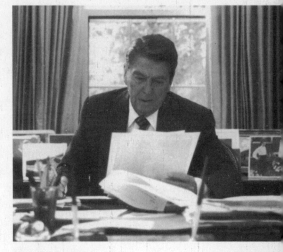

Ronald Reagan

Reagan campaigned on a platform of balancing the budget, reducing federal spending and taxes, and increasing the U.S. military strength. He achieved the latter goal but failed to balance the budget and the national debt soared. On his inauguration day in 1981, fifty-two American hostages were released from Iran, and just over two months later Reagan survived an assassination attempt that hospitalized him for several weeks. During his administration in 1987, a historic arms-control agreement with the Soviet Union took place. Increased involvement in Central America resulted in the controversial IRAN-CONTRA AFFAIR. He appointed Sandra Day O'Connor as the first woman to serve on the U.S. Supreme Court.

In 1994 Reagan, in a farewell letter to the American public, disclosed that he suffered from Alzheimer's disease, an act that heightened recognition and concern about the degenerative illness that affects millions of elderly Americans. On February 6, 1998, President Bill Clinton signed into law a bill renaming Washington National Airport as Ronald Reagan Washington National Airport.

Reconstruction (1865–77), period following the Civil War dominated by controversies over restoring the Union, aiding the former slaves, and rebuilding the devastated South. The Civil War left the South in physical, social, and economic ruin. In 1863 President Abraham Lincoln offered the Ten Percent Plan for readmitting the Confederate states into the Union once the war was over, but Congress denounced it as too lenient. Lincoln's successor, Andrew Johnson, and Congress were at odds as to how to readmit the eleven Confederate states and carry out the rebuilding process. Congress, including the RADICAL REPUBLICANS led by BENJAMIN WADE, CHARLES SUMNER, and THADDEUS STEVENS, rejected Johnson's plans. In addition to proposing the Thirteenth, Fourteenth, and Fifteenth Amendments to the Constitution, they created the FREEDMEN'S BUREAU, wrote a civil rights act, and passed the RECONSTRUCTION ACTS, all over Johnson's vetoes. President Johnson was impeached by the House of Representatives in 1868 for violating the TENURE OF OFFICE ACT, but the Senate, by a single vote, failed to convict him.

During Reconstruction southern state governments were run by CARPETBAGGERS, SCALAWAGS, and former slaves because the Fourteenth Amendment prevented former Confederate soldiers and officeholders from voting or holding office. Some southern whites responded by organizing the KU KLUX KLAN to terrorize black people and their supporters.

Reconstruction ended with the COMPROMISE OF 1877 and the election of Rutherford B. Hayes to the presidency. Hayes removed the last of the federal troops from the South, eliminating protection for blacks and the Reconstruction governments. The hope of the black people for equality collapsed as southern whites regained control of their state governments and took away many of the rights that had been assured during Reconstruction.

Reconstruction Acts (1867), laws passed by Congress abolishing the southern state governments formed under President Andrew Johnson's plan for Reconstruction. They divided the ten Confederate states not yet readmitted to the Union (only Tennessee was) into five military districts each governed by an army commander and patrolled by federal troops to help enforce the acts. The laws also outlined the process by which a state would be readmitted into the Union: each state was to hold a convention, write a new constitution, allow black men to vote, elect a governor and a state legislature, and ratify the Fourteenth Amendment. Johnson vetoed the Reconstruction Acts, but Congress, controlled by the RADICAL REPUBLICANS, overrode his vetoes.

Reconstruction Finance Corporation (RFC), a federal agency created by Congress on February 2, 1932, during the Great Depression to make loans to help stimulate commerce, industry, and agriculture. Backed by President Herbert Hoover, the RFC made loans to banks, insurance companies, industrial corporations, and railroads. During World War II the RFC played an important role in financing war industries. The agency was abolished by Congress in 1956 after lending over $13 billion.

Red Cloud (Mahpiua Luta; 1822–1909), chief of Oglala Sioux tribe. During the 1860s Red Cloud attacked white settlers using the Bozeman Trail to travel to the Montana gold fields because they were crossing a favorite hunting ground east of the Bighorn Mountains. The U.S. Army built three forts to protect the trail, but Red Cloud kept them under attack for two years. In 1868, after the slaughter of over eighty troops at Fort Kearney, the government signed a treaty and abandoned the forts. Red Cloud has been called the only Indian ever to win a war against the U.S. government.

Red Scare (1919–20), a fear of communism that swept the United States following World War I. After the 1917 Bolshevik Revolution in Russia, American leaders, fearing a similar revolution might break out in the United States, set into motion a federal crackdown on suspected radicals. Attorney General A. Mitchell Palmer initiated the Palmer Raids (1920) against "suspicious" foreigners across the country. These raids violated many suspects' and detainees' civil liberties and led to the formation of the AMERICAN CIVIL LIBERTIES UNION to protect the rights of the many innocent people jailed. A wave of strikes and a few terrorist bombings heightened the tensions. The red scare sparked a fear and intolerance of foreigners that led to deportation of many radicals, a revival of the KU KLUX KLAN, the enactment of stiff immigration quota laws and laws against "criminal syndicalism" (labor unions), and long sentences for the Industrial Workers of the World leaders tried and convicted for their strike activities.

Redford, Robert (1937–), actor, director, and producer. Known for his rugged good looks, Redford was among the biggest movie stars of the 1970s. After stints as an oil worker and a painter, Redford turned to stage acting in the 1960s, earning critical acclaim in the Broadway production of *Barefoot* *in the Park.* This led to film roles with PAUL NEWMAN in *Butch Cassidy and the Sundance Kid* (1969) and *The Sting* (1973), which have become classics. Redford won an Academy Award for his direction of *Ordinary People* (1980). He has remained in the forefront of the motion picture industry as a film director and founder of the Sundance Institute, an influential organization that promotes independent filmmaking. He devotes private efforts toward political causes and environmentalism.

Reed, John (1887–1920), journalist and political radical. Reed is best known for his eyewitness account of the 1917 Bolshevik Revolution in Russia, *Ten Days That Shook the World* (1919). Reed had established his reputation with his coverage of the revolt of Pancho Villa in Mexico and his World War I reports from Europe. After his return to the United States in 1919 he was expelled from the Socialist party and then helped form the Communist Labor party. Indicted for treason, he fled to the Soviet Union. He died in Moscow and was buried within the walls of the Kremlin.

Reed, Stanley F. (1884–1980), jurist. Appointed by Franklin D. Roosevelt, Reed served as associate justice on the U.S. Supreme Court from 1938 to 1957. Before joining the Court, he served as counsel to both the Federal Farm Board and the RECONSTRUCTION FINANCE CORPORATION. He also served as U.S. solicitor general and defended the constitutionality of some of the major programs of the New Deal.

Reed, Thomas (1839–1902), politician. A Republican, Reed served in the House of Representatives from Maine from 1877 to 1899, including two terms as Speaker of the House. Called "Czar" Reed because of his arbitrary use of power, his "Reed Rules," adopted by the House in 1890, increased the Speaker's power. Reed lost his bid for the Republican nomination for president to William McKinley in 1896.

Reed, Walter (1851–1902), military surgeon. In 1900 Reed headed a commission of physicians sent to Cuba to investigate a yellow fever epidemic among American troops. He proved through experiments that yellow fever was caused by a virus transmitted by the *aedes aegypti* mosquito, and elimination of breeding sites in Cuba and Panama halted the epidemic. Reed also had helped control the spread of typhoid fever by flies during the Spanish-American War in 1898. Walter Reed Medical Center, founded in 1909 outside Washington, D.C., is named for him.

Rehnquist, William H. (1924–), sixteenth chief justice of the U.S. Supreme Court, appointed by President Ronald Reagan in 1986. Despite liberal opposition Rehnquist won confirmation after being appointed associate justice by President Richard Nixon in 1971. A conservative, Rehnquist supports "law and order" and opposes labor measures. He has been criticized for insensitivity to civil rights and liberties and women's rights. Rehnquist served as assistant attorney general during Nixon's administration, heading the Department of Justice's Office of Legal Counsel from 1969 to 1971. In 1999 he presided over the Senate trial in the IMPEACHMENT OF BILL CLINTON, only the second chief justice to preside over a presidential trial.

Remington, Frederic (1861–1909), painter, sculptor, and author. Remington first made his reputation as a realistic painter of the cowboys, Indians, horses, and soldiers of the American West. He illustrated articles written by Theodore Roosevelt for *Century* magazine and Henry Wadsworth Longfellow's poem "Song of Hiawatha." Remington also illustrated his own books, including *Pony Tracks* (1895) and *The Way of an Indian* (1906). As a sculptor Remington is best known for *Bronco Buster*.

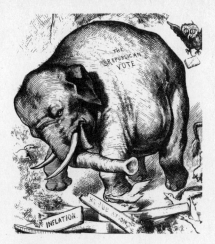

Republican Party
The first representation — in a cartoon by Thomas Nast — of the Republican party emblem.

Reno, Janet (1938–), first woman attorney general of the United States (1993–2001). A graduate of Harvard Law School, Reno was Florida's first female state attorney (1978–93). As attorney general during the Clinton administration she made many controversial decisions, including ordering the raid that resulted in the WACO SIEGE. Her candor and acceptance of full responsibility of the incident earned respect, however. Reno was the longest-serving attorney general in the twentieth century (eight years), and her tenure saw a decline in national crime rates, the conviction of those responsible for the OKLAHOMA CITY BOMBING, and the independent prosecutor's investigation of President BILL CLINTON. In 2002 she lost a bid to run for governor of Florida.

Republican Party, the younger and more conservative of the two major political parties in the United States. Also known as the GOP (for Grand Old Party), an appellation that dates back to the 1880s, the Republican party was organized in 1854 to oppose the extension of slavery. John C. Frémont was the party's first but unsuccessful presidential candidate in 1856, and in 1860 Abraham Lincoln became the first Republican candidate elected to the presidency. By 2004 the Republicans had been in the White House a total of eighty-eight years.

Republican Party (1792–1824). *See* DEMOCRATIC-REPUBLICAN PARTY.

Reuther, Walter (1907–70), labor leader. Reuther served as president of the United Auto Workers (UAW) from 1946 until his death. As president of the CONGRESS OF INDUSTRIAL ORGANIZATIONS (1952–55) and vice president of the AMERICAN FEDERATION OF LABOR–CONGRESS OF INDUSTRIAL

ORGANIZATIONS (1955–58), Reuther helped plan the merger of the two unions and served as president of one of its departments from 1955 to 1968. He was the first union leader to gain a contract with a major industry tying wages to the cost of living.

Revels, Hiram (1822–1901), clergyman, educator, and politician. Revels was the first black to serve in the U.S. Senate, winning election as a Republican in Mississippi in 1870 to fill the seat once held by Jefferson Davis. Revels supported civil rights for blacks and full restoration of civil and political rights for all ex-Confederates. After his term he became president of Alcorn Agricultural and Mechanical College in Mississippi. An ordained minister of the African Methodist Church, he founded a school for freedmen in St. Louis, Missouri, in 1863 and during the Civil War helped recruit black soldiers for the Union, himself enlisting as a chaplain.

Revere, Paul (1735–1818), patriot and silversmith. An official courier for the Massachusetts Committee of Correspondence, Revere became a hero for his legendary ride across the Massachusetts countryside on the night of April 18, 1775, riding from Charlestown to Lexington to warn SAMUEL ADAMS and JOHN HANCOCK of approaching British troops. Joined in Lexington by SAMUEL PRESCOTT and William Dawes, Revere went on to warn the MINUTEMEN at Concord, but British troops allowed only Prescott to get through. HENRY WADSWORTH LONGFELLOW immortalized Revere's adventure in the famous but inaccurate poem "Paul Revere's Ride" (1863). A leader of the SONS OF LIBERTY, Revere participated in the BOSTON TEA PARTY and engraved a number of political cartoons and propaganda for the colonial cause. Revere manufactured gunpowder and cast musket balls and cannons during the American Revolution and designed and printed the first Continental currency. He was a leading silversmith and founded the country's first sheet-copper mill.

Rhode Island (Ocean State) joined the Union on May 29, 1790, as the thirteenth state. (See maps, pages 540 and 541.) ROGER WILLIAMS started the colony of Providence in 1636 after being banished from Massachusetts because of his religious beliefs. In 1776 Rhode Island was the first of the colonies to declare its independence from Great Britain, but it was the last to sign the Constitution, waiting for the addition of a bill of rights. Although Rhode Island is the smallest state in the Union, it became a center of the textile industry in the 1800s and is now a leading producer of wool, silver, and jewelry. Fishing, chickens, and agriculture are also important. The largest cities include Providence, the capital, Warwick, Cranston, and Pawtucket. The state is not actually an island, but is made up of thirty-six islands and a mainland separated by Narragansett Bay, all of which help make the state a leading vacation land for boating, fishing, and other water sports. Noted Rhode Islanders include NATHANAEL GREENE, GILBERT STUART, and Thomas Wilson Dorr, leader of the DORR REBELLION.

Rice, Condoleezza (1954–), national security adviser to President GEORGE W. BUSH (2001–). Born in Birmingham, Alabama, Rice entered the University of Denver at age fifteen, graduating cum laude and Phi Beta Kappa. She earned a master's degree at the University of Notre Dame and a doctorate from the University of Denver's Graduate School of International Studies. An expert on Russia and Eastern Europe who is fluent in Russian, Dr. Rice taught political science at Stanford University and served as provost (1981–99). From 1989 to 1991 she served in the first Bush administration as director of Soviet and East European Affairs in the National Security Council, and as special assistant to the President for National Security Affairs. She became the second African-American and first woman to hold the office of assistant to the president for National Security Affairs in 2001, and supported the U.S. strike against Iraq in 2003, advocating against giving weapons inspectors additional time. She has written and coauthored numerous articles and several books on international relations and foreign policy, including *Germany Unified and Europe Transformed: A Study in Statecraft* (1995).

Rice, Grantland (1880–1954), sportswriter. Rice, the first American journalist to gain prominence writing about sports, wrote a syndicated column, "The Sportlight." Credited with naming the Notre Dame backfield "the Four Horsemen," Red Grange "the Galloping Ghost," and Jack Dempsey "the Manassa Mauler," Rice also coined the phrase "It's not whether you won or lost but how you played the game." His autobiography was titled *The Tumult and the Shouting: My Life in Sport* (1954).

Rice, Jerry (1962–), football player. Rice was drafted in the first round by the San Francisco 49ers in 1985, won rookie of the year, and has dominated his position as wide receiver more than any player in National Football League (NFL) history. He was SUPER BOWL XXIII most valuable player in 1989 and also helped lead the 49ers to three Super Bowl championships in 1989, 1990, and 1995 before signing to play with the Oakland Raiders. Rice holds every NFL wide receiver record including career receptions, receiving yardage, most receiving touchdowns, and most career touchdowns. He was selected to twelve Pro Bowls and twice named NFL Player of the Year.

Richard, Maurice (1921–2000), Canadian-born hockey player. Richard was the first hockey player to score fifty goals in a fifty-game season (1944–45). In nineteen seasons with the Montreal Canadiens, he led his team to eight league titles and eight Stanley Cups. Richard was called "Rocket" because of his speed and power. He played on thirteen all-star teams and scored 544 goals during his career and 82 in playoff games.

Richardson, Elliot L. (1920–99), political leader. Under President Richard M. Nixon, Richardson held three cabinet positions: secretary of health, education, and welfare, secretary of defense, and attorney general. He resigned from the last position to protest the firing of Special Watergate

Prosecutor ARCHIBALD COX in 1973. He also served as secretary of commerce in 1976–77, thus holding more cabinet positions than anyone in U.S. history. Early in his career Richardson served as lieutenant governor and attorney general in the state of Massachusetts. After Watergate he became the U.S. ambassador to Great Britain.

Rickenbacker, Eddie (1890–1973), aviator and airline executive. Rickenbacker was the most decorated American combat pilot during WORLD WAR I. Credited with shooting down twenty-two enemy planes and four balloons, he received the Congressional Medal of Honor. As president and chairman of the board of Eastern Airlines from 1938 to 1963, Rickenbacker turned the company into one of the nation's major airlines. During a World War II government inspection trip, he and seven others were forced down in the Pacific, where they drifted on rafts until rescued twenty-four days later, an experience he described in *Seven Came Through* (1943).

Rickey, Branch (1881–1965), baseball executive. In 1947 Rickey made one of the most important moves in sports history when he broke the color barrier and signed JACKIE ROBINSON as the first black man to play in major league baseball. Serving as manager for the St. Louis Browns, St. Louis Cardinals, Brooklyn Dodgers, and Pittsburgh Pirates, Rickey developed the farm system of training minor league players. He became a member of the Hall of Fame in 1967.

Rickover, Hyman (1900–86), Polish-born naval officer. Rickover pioneered the development of the USS *Nautilus* (1954), the first nuclear-powered submarine. In 1947 he took charge of the navy's nuclear-power program and became head of the Atomic Energy Commission's Naval Reactor Branch. He received the 1964 Enrico Fermi Medal, the highest atomic science award, for his contributions to the development of nuclear energy, won a congressional gold medal in 1959, and was awarded the Presidential Medal of Freedom in 1980. An outspoken critic of the U.S. educational system, Rickover wrote *Education and Freedom* in 1959 and *American Education: A National Failure* in 1963.

Ride, Sally (1951–), astronaut. In June 1983 Ride became the first American woman to travel in space when she made a six-day flight on the space shuttle *Challenger*. Her second flight took place in October 1984. In 1986 Ride served on the presidential commission to investigate the CHALLENGER DISASTER. She resigned from NASA in 1987 to work at Stanford and in 1989 became a professor of physics at U.C. San Diego, and director of the California Space Institute. In 2001 she founded Imaginary Lines, a company to promote the scientific interests of girls.

Ridgway, Matthew (1895–1993), WORLD WAR II and KOREAN WAR military leader. Ridgway succeeded Gen. Douglas MacArthur as supreme commander of the U.N. forces in Korea in 1951 and succeeded Gen. Dwight Eisenhower as supreme NATO Allied commander in Europe the following year. In 1963 Ridgway became chief of staff of the U.S. Army. He commanded the 82d Airborne Division during World War II and in 1943 led the first important airborne attack in U.S. military history in the assault on Sicily. He led his troops in the Normandy invasion in France on June 6, 1944, D-DAY.

Riis, Jacob (1849–1914), Danish-born photographer, author, and social reformer. A MUCKRAKER, Riis published *How the Other Half Lives* (1890), which exposed the poverty and squalor of living conditions in New York City slums and led to corrective legislation. As a reporter for the *New York Tribune* and the *New York Evening Sun,* Riis documented slum conditions with his camera, campaigning for improvements in education, child labor laws, housing codes, and playground construction. Riis wrote twelve books, including his autobiography, *The Making of an American* (1901).

Ringling Brothers, family of circus owners and performers. Five brothers (Albert, 1852–1916; Otto, 1858–1911; Alfred, 1861–1919; Charles, 1863–1926; John, 1886–1936), founded the world-famous Ringling Brothers Barnum & Bailey Circus. Beginning in 1884 with a modest traveling wagon show, the brothers developed their business through shrewd management and by buying up their competition. They purchased the Barnum & Bailey circus, largest of the time, in 1907, merging it with theirs in 1919, making it the world's largest by 1930. The family sold the circus in 1967, but the new owners kept the original name.

Ripken, Cal, Jr. (1960–), baseball player. Born in Maryland to the Baltimore Oriole's coach and manager, Ripken signed with Baltimore right out of high school. He was chosen rookie of the year in 1982 and became one of baseball's best all-time shortstops. Ripken was chosen the American League (AL) most valuable player in 1983 and 1991, and set the record for most home runs by a shortstop at 345. Noted for breaking LOU GEHRIG's fifty-six-year-old major league record of 2,130 consecutive games played, Ripken ended his streak in 1995 at 2,632 consecutive games. He was an outstanding fielder as well as hitter.

Roanoke Company *See* LOST COLONY OF ROANOKE.

Roaring Twenties, also called the jazz age, the period after World War I from 1921 to 1929. It was a time of ISOLATIONISM, escapism, and some social reform. PROHIBITION prompted a wave of lawbreaking when many Americans made liquor at home, gangsters bootlegged liquor, and organized crime escalated. The 1920s was an era of apparent business prosperity under Presidents Warren G. Harding, Calvin Coolidge, and Herbert Hoover, although political corruption caused embarrassment during the Harding administration. Many Americans enjoyed what seemed to be a rising standard of living, evidenced by enormous overspeculation in the stock market and excessive amounts of easy credit. The 1920s were the time of the flapper and of a flourishing entertainment industry, with crowds flocking to theaters and sports stadiums. Critical agricultural, industrial, and financial problems, however, led to the STOCK MARKET CRASH OF 1929 and the GREAT DEPRESSION, thus ending the prosperity and recklessness of the Roaring Twenties.

Robber Barons, derogatory term used to describe big businessmen in the late nineteenth century who used ruthless, unscrupulous, and sometimes illegal means to build monopolies and develop great economic power. Ten percent of American businessmen controlled over 90 percent of U.S. wealth. Industrial leaders ANDREW CARNEGIE, JOHN D. ROCKEFELLER, CORNELIUS VANDERBILT, and William Vanderbilt were called robber barons, as well as bankers JAY GOULD and J. PIERPONT MORGAN.

Robbins, Jerome (1918–98), dancer and choreographer. Robbins achieved fame for his work in ballet and as director and choreographer of Broadway musicals. *The King and I* (1951), *Peter Pan* (1954), *West Side Story* (1957), and *Fiddler on the Roof* (1964) featured his blend of all aspects of theatrical production — acting, singing, and dancing. Robbins won two Academy Awards for the film version of *West Side Story.* From 1959 he was associated with the New York City Ballet, and from 1983 until his retirement in 1990 he served as codirector, succeeding GEORGE BALANCHINE.

Robertson, Oscar (1938–), basketball player. Robertson made the National Basketball Association (NBA) all-star team nine times and led the Milwaukee Bucks to a championship in 1970–71. The "Big O" is one of the all-time leaders in NBA assists and the second player (after Wilt Chamberlain) to score over 25,000 points. He had been a three-time consensus All-American at the University of Cincinnati. Robertson became a member of basketball's Hall of Fame in 1979.

Robeson, Paul (1898–1976), black actor, singer, and political activist. Robeson displayed versatility and talent in many fields, achieving respect and recognition worldwide. After becoming a two-time collegiate football All-American at Rutgers and graduating valedictorian of his class and earning Phi Beta Kappa honors, he received a law degree from Columbia University before turning to the stage. He performed throughout the world on radio, stage, and film, earning praise for his interpretations of the folk music of many countries. Robeson's career as an actor was marked by spectacular success in roles previously not awarded to black actors. He starred in *Emperor Jones* (1924; film 1933) and *Othello* (1943) on Broadway, receiving the Donaldson Award as best actor.

In spite of his success, Robeson suffered the realities of prejudice and racism. After several trips to the Soviet Union, where he experienced little racism, he became friendly with American communists and became an activist for blacks' rights. These associations, plus his acceptance of the Stalin Peace Prize in 1952, alienated some Americans during the McCarthy era and led to his effective banishment from the stage. The State

Department denied him a passport, labeling him "dangerous." Regaining his passport in 1958, Robeson resided in Great Britain until 1963, when he returned to the United States in poor health and lived out his life in obscurity.

Robinson, Bill "Bojangles" (1878–1949), black tap dancer. Affectionately known as Mr. Bojangles, Robinson's tap dance routine up and down staircases became a classic. Featured in vaudeville, nightclubs, and on Broadway, Robinson won fame for appearances with Shirley Temple in films including *The Little Colonel* (1935) and *Rebecca of Sunnybrook Farm* (1938).

Robinson, Edward G. (1893–1973), film actor. A noted character actor with a cigar and a sneer, Robinson portrayed memorable gangsters (*The Racket,* 1927) tough guys (*Little Caesar,* 1931), and criminals (*Key Largo,* 1948). He also played more sympathetic parts in films like *Double Indemnity* (1944) and *Woman in the Window* (1944). Born Emmanuel Goldenberg in Bucharest, Romania, Robinson immigrated to New York City as a child. He attended the American Academy of Dramatic Arts and made his Broadway debut in 1915, then spent fifteen years on the stage. His film career spanned fifty years and included more than eighty movies. Robinson was given an honorary Academy Award posthumously, and his autobiography, *All My Yesterdays,* was published following his death in 1973.

Robinson, Edwin Arlington (1869–1935), poet. Robinson's works bear the stamp of his Puritan New England ancestry. A master of verse forms and possessing a moving poetic vision, he is best known for his poems "Richard Cory" and "Miniver Cheevy." Robinson's disillusioned and unhappy characters were modeled after his own dysfunctional family and local townspeople. Robinson won Pulitzer Prizes for *Collected Poems* (1921), *The Man Who Died Twice* (1924), and *Tristram* (1927).

Robinson, Frank (1935–), baseball player and manager. Robinson is the only man in baseball history to win the most valuable player award in both the National League (1961 with the Cincinnati Reds) and the American League (1966 with the Baltimore Orioles). He became the first black manager of a major league baseball team in 1975 with the Cleveland Indians. Under his management, the Baltimore Orioles won two World Series titles. He served as Major League Baseball's vice president of on-field operations (2000–01) before becoming manager of the Montreal Expos in 2002. He joined the baseball Hall of Fame in 1982.

Robinson, Jackie (1919–72), baseball player. Robinson became the first black player in major league baseball when he joined the Brooklyn Dodgers in 1947 after a year with the Montreal Royals, the top Dodger farm club. Robinson played all ten years of his major league career with the Dodgers, leading the team to six World Series appearances. Accepting BRANCH RICKEY's challenge not to respond to abuse, he withstood jeers, insults, bean balls, hate mail, and death threats to break the color line in professional sports. An exceptional hitter and base-stealer, he won the rookie of the year award in 1947 and the most valuable player award in 1949. Breaking his silence in 1949, Robinson became an outspoken opponent of racial discrimination. He received the SPINGARN MEDAL in 1956 and retired from baseball in 1957 to engage in business, political, and civil rights activities. In 1962 he became the first black to enter baseball's Hall of Fame.

Robinson, Sugar Ray (Walker Smith; 1921–89), boxer. Robinson became welterweight champion in 1946 and won the middleweight title in 1951, setting a record by winning the middleweight crown five times. He is considered by many boxing experts as the greatest fighter in the history of boxing. During retirement, he spent most of his time helping children in the Sugar Ray Youth Foundation in Los Angeles, California.

Rockefeller, John D. (1839–1937), businessman and philanthropist. Rockefeller founded the Standard Oil Company in 1870, which led in 1882 to the Standard Oil Trust, controlling almost all of the U.S. oil industry. As a near-monopoly, the Standard Oil Trust was dissolved in 1892 by the Ohio Supreme Court but was replaced by Standard Oil Company of New Jersey. This trust was dissolved by the U.S. Supreme Court in 1911. Rockefeller retired from active business in 1897 but retained the title of president of the Standard Oil Company until it was dissolved. He devoted the rest of his life to philanthropy, establishing the Rockefeller Institute for Medical Research, the General Education Board, and the Rockefeller Foundation, giving away about $550 million during his lifetime.

Rockefeller, Nelson A. (1908–79), politician. Rockefeller, a grandson of John D. Rockefeller, served four terms as governor of New York from 1959 to 1973. He greatly expanded state services in transportation, welfare, housing, education, and environmental protection. Although his administration raised taxes substantially, it also established the State University of New York system and the New York State Thruway. Rockefeller served as vice president under President Gerald Ford from 1974 to 1977; he was appointed by Ford under the provisions of the Twenty-fifth Amendment after Richard M. Nixon resigned, making Ford president. Rockefeller in this post headed a commission to investigate the Central Intelligence Agency. He unsuccessfully sought the Republican nomination for the presidency in 1960, 1964, and 1968.

Rockne, Knute (1888–1931), Norwegian-born college football player and coach. Playing receiver at Notre Dame, Rockne and quarterback Gus Dorais made the forward pass a primary offensive weapon in 1913, marking a turning point in the evolution of the game. As coach, Rockne led Notre Dame to five undefeated seasons, compiling a record of 105 victories, 12 defeats, and 5 ties, and a winning percentage of .881, the best record of any coach in college football history. His inspirational half-time talks to his team became legendary, and his success as a master strategist helped popularize the sport.

Among the notable players he developed were George Gipp and the "Four Horsemen" backfield, whose exploits were immortalized by the sports press. Gipp's dying words to Rockne, "Win one for the Gipper," became a national catchphrase. Rockne's death at age forty-three in a plane crash was mourned throughout the country. He became a member of the college football Hall of Fame in 1951.

Rockwell, Norman (1894–1978), illustrator and painter. Rockwell became very popular through his more than three hundred *Saturday Evening Post* magazine covers. His meticulously detailed paintings present sentimental, usually humorous scenes of rural and small-town life in America. For his *Four Freedoms* series, made into posters and used by the Office of War Information during World War II, Rockwell received the Presidential Medal of Freedom from President Gerald Ford in 1977.

Rodgers, Richard (1902–79), and **Oscar Hammerstein II** (1895–1960), musical-drama team. During a seventeen-year partnership Rodgers and Hammerstein produced the Pulitzer Prize-winning *Oklahoma!* (1943) and *South Pacific* (1949), as well as such notable musicals as *Carousel* (1945), *The King and I* (1951), and *The Sound of Music* (1959).

Roebling, family name of two engineers who pioneered the development and building of suspension bridges and wire cable. John Roebling (1806–69), born in Germany, produced the first wire cable in the United States in 1841 and from 1845 until his death designed five major suspension bridges, including a double railroad-vehicle bridge over Niagara Falls (1855). The only two to survive today are the Cincinnati-Covington Bridge (1867) and the Brooklyn Bridge (1883). His spectacular plans for the Brooklyn Bridge were approved in 1869, but he was killed while siting the position of the Brooklyn tower before construction was even under way. The task of bringing his ambitious designs to reality passed to his son, Washington A. Roebling (1837–1926), who became chief engineer of the Brooklyn Bridge until its completion in 1883. Three years after he took his father's place, he in turn was injured and left an invalid for the rest of his life. He continued to direct the work from his home in Brooklyn, watching by telescope as his wife, Emily Roebling (1844–1903), supervised the construction and conveyed her husband's instructions.

Roe v. Wade (1973), decision by the U.S. Supreme Court concerning a woman's right to an abortion. The Court legalized abortion by ruling that state laws could not restrict it during the first three months of pregnancy. During the second trimester a state may regulate abortions only to protect a woman's health. States may prohibit abortions during the final trimester unless the pregnancy endangers the woman's health. The decision has been much challenged and modified, but remains in place.

Rogers, Ginger (1911–95), actress and dancer. Rogers made more than twenty films on her own before teaming with FRED ASTAIRE in 1933. They soon became the most successful dance team in motion pictures, making eleven musicals together including *The Gay Divorcee* (1934) and *Top Hat* (1935). Although known for romantic comedies, Rogers won an Academy Award for her dramatic role in *Kitty Foyle* (1940). She later played on Broadway in the title roles of *Hello Dolly* and *Mame* and toured through Europe and Canada. Her autobiography, *Ginger, My Story,* was published in 1991.

Rogers, Will (1879–1935), humorist and actor. Known for his clever, home-spun commentaries on current events, Rogers popularized easygoing satire on business, government, the economy, and politics. He was an author, lecturer, and vaudeville, radio, and film star. Often opening with the phrase "All I know is what I read in the papers," Rogers wrote a syndicated column that appeared in over 350 daily newspapers. He died in a plane crash near Point Barrow, Alaska, with aviator WILEY POST.

Rolfe, John (1585–1622), English colonist. After settling at JAMESTOWN Colony in 1610, Rolfe married POCAHONTAS, an Indian princess, in 1614 bringing peace to the colony. He is credited with developing a method of curing tobacco, making it the staple crop of Virginia.

Rooney, Mickey (Joe Yule, Jr.; 1920–), actor. Rooney became part of his family's vaudeville act when he was a baby and made his film debut at age six in the silent short *Not to Be Trusted* (1926) playing a cigar-smoking midget. From 1927 to 1933 he starred in the two-reel comedy series, *Mickey McGuire*. He took the name Mickey Rooney in 1932 and became a national star as the title character in the lighthearted *Andy Hardy* series (1937–47). After memorable performances in *Boys' Town* (1938), and several musicals with JUDY GARLAND, Rooney became America's biggest box-office attraction. His best-known films include *Babes in Arms* (1939), *National Velvet* (1947), and *The Bridges at Toko-Ri* (1954). Rooney received two honorary Oscars for his achievement in motion pictures.

Roosevelt Corollary (1904), foreign policy statement attached to the MONROE DOCTRINE by President Theodore Roosevelt, declaring that the United States would exercise police power to maintain stability in the Western Hemisphere. Directed at Europe, the Roosevelt Corollary stated that the United States would consider any interference in the affairs of small, poor Latin American nations a violation of the Monroe Doctrine. The first application of the Corollary occurred in 1905, when Roosevelt sent Marines to the Dominican Republic to manage the country's European debts.

Roosevelt, Eleanor (1884–1962), humanitarian, diplomat, and first lady (1933–45). The wife of President Franklin D. Roosevelt and niece of Theodore Roosevelt, Eleanor Roosevelt expanded the role of first lady to one of influence and power. The mother of six children (one of whom died in infancy), she was a tireless worker for social causes. Roosevelt held press conferences, had her own radio show, and wrote a daily newspaper column. She traveled widely, supporting the underprivileged and minority groups, and visiting military posts and hospitals during World War II to boost morale. She resigned from the DAUGHTERS OF THE AMERICAN REVOLUTION when it refused to allow black singer MARIAN ANDERSON to sing in Constitution Hall, and arranged for her to sing on the steps of the Lincoln Memorial. After the death of her husband and her departure from the White House, she served as a U.N. delegate from 1945 to 1952 and influenced the organization's adoption of the Declaration of Human Rights in 1948. In 1961 she headed the U.N. Commission on Human Rights.

Roosevelt, Franklin D. (1882–1945), thirty-second president of the United States (1933–45). Roosevelt was the only president to be elected to more than two terms. Born in Hyde Park, New York, the only child of an old patrician family, Roosevelt was educated at Harvard and entered politics early. He served as assistant secretary of the navy in World War I and in 1920 ran unsuccessfully for vice president with Democratic presidential candidate James Cox. In 1921 he was partially paralyzed from an attack of poliomyelitis. Encouraged to reenter politics by his wife, Eleanor, Roosevelt won the governorship of New York by a narrow margin in 1928 and became

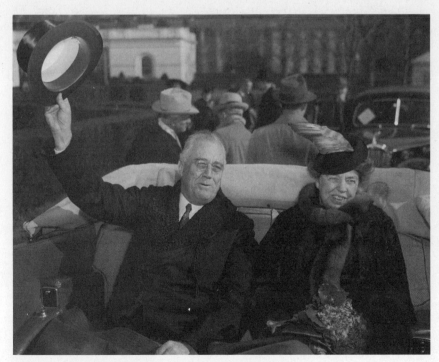

Franklin Delano Roosevelt and Eleanor Roosevelt
President and Mrs. Roosevelt riding in a car on the president's third inauguration day.

the Democratic candidate for president in 1932 in the midst of the Great Depression. Forging a new Democratic coalition among urban voters, immigrants, young first-time voters, blacks, women, the working class, and the southern states, FDR defeated Herbert Hoover in a landslide.

Roosevelt promised the American people in his inaugural address a NEW DEAL. His buoyant personality helped restore the country's morale, and he and the many fresh faces he brought to Washington tackled problems of the economy with groundbreaking programs of public works, relief, and reform. Programs and agencies set up under the New Deal included the SECURITIES AND EXCHANGE COMMISSION, to oversee the stock market; the TENNESSEE VALLEY AUTHORITY, to bring electricity and conservation programs to rural areas in the South; the FEDERAL DEPOSIT INSURANCE CORPORATION, to insure people's bank deposits; the SOCIAL SECURITY SYSTEM, to provide old-age pensions and unemployment insurance; and the FAIR LABOR STANDARDS ACT, to set a national minimum wage and limit hours of work. Other, more temporary programs — like the Works Progress Administration and the CIVILIAN CONSERVATION CORPS — relieved unemployment on a short-term basis. Roosevelt's administration did not end the depression (it took World War II to do that), but it did

---

★ Franklin Delano Roosevelt

The Four Freedoms

An excerpt from Roosevelt's inaugural address of January 6, 1941; the Second World War had begun in Europe and the Pacific, but the United States did not enter it until December, following the Japanese attack on Pearl Harbor.

In the future days which we seek to make secure, we look forward to a world founded upon four essential human freedoms.

The first is freedom of speech and expression — everywhere in the world.

The second is freedom of every person to worship God in his own way — everywhere in the world.

The third is freedom from want — which, translated into world terms, means economic understandings which will secure to every nation a healthy peacetime life for its inhabitants — everywhere in the world.

The fourth is freedom from fear, which, translated into world terms, means a world-wide reduction of armaments to such a point and in such a thorough manner that no nation will be in a position to commit an act of physical aggression against any neighbor — anywhere in the world. . . .

Freedom means the supremacy of human rights everywhere. Our support goes to those who struggle to gain those rights and keep them. Our strength is in our unity of purpose.

To that high concept there can be no end save victory.

greatly expand the role and power of the federal government and of the presidency itself. He won reelection in a landslide in 1936 and an unprecedented third term in 1940.

Always both a balance-of-power realist and an idealist in foreign policy, Roosevelt grew increasingly alarmed by the rise of fascism and Nazism abroad in the 1930s and tried to steer the nation away from ISOLATIONISM. After Japan attacked Pearl Harbor in 1941 and the United States entered WORLD WAR II, he became a highly effective commander in chief, leading the country in the immense mobilization of manpower and resources required to fight the war. His articulation of Allied war aims in the ATLANTIC CHARTER and the FOUR FREEDOMS speech and his proposal for a UNITED NATIONS after the war reflected his belief in democracy and America's role of leadership in the postwar world.

Roosevelt was reelected for a fourth term in 1944, but the next year, he died suddenly of a cerebral hemorrhage on April 12 in Warm Springs, Georgia. Many historians rank him among America's strongest presidents.

Roosevelt, Theodore (1858–1919), twenty-sixth president of the United States (1901–09). Roosevelt became a national hero when he led his ROUGH RIDERS up Kettle Hill in Cuba during the SPANISH-AMERICAN WAR in 1898. He then served as Republican governor of New York before being elected vice president in 1900.

Roosevelt became president in 1901 after the assassination of William McKinley. He is known for his trust busting, programs for conservation of natural resources, and creation of national parks. His ROOSEVELT COROLLARY to the MONROE DOCTRINE claimed the United States could intervene militarily in the Latin American states. He won the Nobel Peace Prize in 1906 for helping negotiate an end to the Russo-Japanese War. He also initiated the building of the PANAMA CANAL.

Roosevelt supported Republican WILLIAM HOWARD TAFT for president in 1908 but tried for the Republican nomination in 1912. When he lost it to Taft, he split with the Republicans and started the PROGRESSIVE, or Bull Moose party, with himself running for president. The split Republicans lost the election to the Democrats and Woodrow Wilson. Roosevelt hoped to gain the Republican nomination in

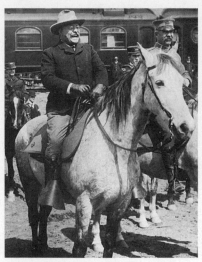

Theodore Roosevelt
President Roosevelt in Yellowstone Park.

1916, but the delegates chose Charles Evans Hughes as their standard-bearer.

Root, Elihu (1845–1937), politician. Root won the Nobel Peace Prize in 1912 for his efforts to ensure international peace. As secretary of war under William McKinley and Theodore Roosevelt, he reorganized the army and established the Army War College. As Roosevelt's secretary of state, he negotiated the 1908 GENTLEMEN'S AGREEMENT with Japan. Root served in the U.S. Senate as a Republican from New York from 1909 to 1915.

Rose, Pete (1942–), baseball player and manager. Known as "Charlie Hustle," Rose hit safely in forty-four consecutive baseball games, tying the National League record. He made 4,256 career hits, breaking TY COBB's record of 4,191. He is also baseball's career leader in singles (3,215), at-bats (14,053), and games played (3,562). After playing for the Cincinnati Reds, Philadelphia Phillies, and Montreal Expos, Rose became player-manager of the Reds in 1985. In 1989 Baseball Commissioner A. Bartlett Giamatti banned Rose from baseball for life for betting on baseball games. In 1990 he was convicted of tax evasion and served a five-month prison sentence.

Rosecrans, William (1819–98), Union general during the CIVIL WAR. Rosecrans led his troops to victory at Iuka and Corinth, Mississippi, in 1862 and maneuvered the Confederate troops out of Chattanooga. But he suffered a disastrous defeat at Chickamauga, and Ulysses S. Grant relieved him of his command. Rosecrans served as minister to Mexico in 1868 and represented California in the House of Representatives from 1881 to 1885.

Rosenberg Case, case resulting in the execution of Julius (1918–53) and Ethel (1915–53) Rosenberg for espionage. The Rosenbergs were convicted on charges of giving the Soviet Union information about U.S. nuclear weapons during the cold war. They became the first U.S. citizens ever put to death for wartime spying. The major witness testifying against the Rosenbergs was Ethel's brother, David Greenglass, who claimed that Julius had recruited him for information about the Los Alamos atomic bomb project, on which he had worked. In 1951 a jury found the Rosenbergs guilty of conspiracy to commit espionage. Worldwide protests took place, and the case was appealed to the U.S. Supreme Court but the Court denied all appeals. President Dwight D. Eisenhower twice rejected pleas for clemency, and the Rosenbergs were executed on June 19, 1953, at Sing Sing Prison in New York. Greenglass served ten years of a fifteen-year prison sentence.

Ross, Betsy (1752–1836), Patriot and seamstress. Ross, according to legend, made the first American flag at George Washington's request in June 1776. The story has never been proven because it first surfaced in 1870 when her grandson wrote about the stories his grandmother used to tell him. Records do show that she made flags for the Pennsylvania navy in 1777.

Ross, Edmund G. (1826–1907), politician. Ross, a Republican senator from Kansas, opposed President ANDREW JOHNSON but joined with six other

Republicans and the Democrats to vote against Johnson's removal from office during the impeachment trial of 1868. By supposedly withholding the last unknown swing vote until voting took place at the trial, Ross wrecked his political career.

Rough Riders, the First U.S. Volunteer Cavalry Regiment, which fought during the SPANISH-AMERICAN WAR. Col. Leonard Wood originally headed the group of one thousand cowboys, miners, football players, and others, and later THEODORE ROOSEVELT commanded the unit. Roosevelt led the "Rough Riders" in a successful charge up Kettle Hill near San Juan Hill in Cuba (July 1, 1898). Having been forced to leave their horses in Florida, most of the Rough Riders, however, fought on foot.

Rozelle, Pete (Alvin Ray; 1926–96), football executive and commissioner. Named commissioner of the National Football League in 1960, Rozelle expanded the league from twelve to fourteen teams and negotiated the first single-network television agreement, making professional football a lucrative sport. Attendance rose from 3.1 million in 1960 to 10.7 million in 1973. Rozelle, *Sports Illustrated's* sportsman of the year in 1963, helped negotiate the 1965 merger of the American Football League and the NFL, which took effect in 1970. Rozelle was elected to the Hall of Fame in 1985.

Rudolph, Wilma (1940–94), sprinter. Rudolph was born the twentieth of twenty-two children. Crippled by polio, she was told she would never walk. After years of therapy, braces, and corrective shoes, she was able to walk normally at age twelve, and decided to become an athlete. She became a star basketball player in high school, leading her school to a state championship. Turning to track, she won an Olympic bronze medal in 1956 at the age of sixteen. In 1960 in Rome, she set two world records and became the first American woman to earn three gold medals at the Olympics when she won the 100-meter dash, the 200-meter dash, and ran anchor on the 400-meter relay. Retiring from competition in 1964, Rudolph became a teacher and coach. She wrote her autobiography, *Wilma* (1977), and died from brain cancer at the age of fifty-four.

Rumsfeld, Donald H. (1932–), business executive and twice U.S. secretary of defense. Born in Chicago, Rumsfeld served as an aviator and flight instructor in the U.S. Navy (1954–57) before he turned to investment banking. He was elected to the U.S. House of Representatives from Illinois (1962–69), resigning during his fourth term to join President Nixon's cabinet. He served as director of the Office of Economic Opportunity and assistant to the president (1969–70), and from 1971 to 1972 he was counselor to the president and director of the Economic Stabilization Program. He served as ambassador to NATO in Brussels (1973–74). Rumsfeld continued under the Ford administration in various positions including White House chief of staff (1974–75) and became the thirteenth U.S. secretary of defense, the youngest in the country's history (1975–77). After many successful years in private business, Rumsfeld was again appointed secretary of defense in 2001, this time in the administration of GEORGE W. BUSH. A blunt and outspoken hawk, Rumsfeld argued aggressively for a strike against Iraq and favors a national missile defense system.

Runyon, Damon (1884–1946), journalist and short story writer. Writing in the colorful slang of the underworld, Runyon created humorous stories about gangsters, gamblers, and chorus girls of New York City's Broadway district. His best-known work, *Guys and Dolls* (1931), became a Broadway musical comedy hit in 1950. His other collections of stories include *Blue Plate Special* (1934) and *Money from Home* (1935).

Rush, Benjamin (1745–1813), physician and reformer. A leading physician, Rush established the first free dispensary in the United States in 1786. He pioneered the humane and scientific treatment of the mentally ill and wrote the first American text on the subject in 1812. Rush helped found the first American antislavery society, and as a member of the Continental Congress he signed the Declaration of Independence. During the American Revolution, Rush served as surgeon general of the Continental army but resigned when Congress ignored his accusations, later proved true, of malpractice. After the war he campaigned for ratification of the U.S. Constitution without a bill of rights. In 1812 he performed a great service when he persuaded Thomas Jefferson and John Adams to patch up their differences and resume their friendship.

Rush, Richard (1780–1859), politician. Rush served as attorney general in 1814 under President James Monroe and as interim secretary of state while John Quincy Adams was in Europe. During this time he negotiated the Rush-Bagot Agreement providing for mutual American and British disarmament of ships on the Great Lakes. As minister to Great Britain he negotiated the TREATY OF 1818, which extended the United States-Canadian border westward from the Lake of the Woods along the forty-ninth parallel and provided for joint U.S.-British occupation of Oregon. In 1828 Rush was chosen to be John Quincy Adams's vice-presidential running mate, but they were soundly defeated by the Democrats. He went to England to pursue litigation by James Smithson and brought back the money that established the SMITHSONIAN INSTITUTION. Rush served as minister to France from 1847 to 1849.

Rusk, Dean (1909–94), politician, U.S. secretary of state (1961–69). Following service in WORLD WAR II (1940–46), Rusk joined the Department of State in 1946, and was appointed director of its office of United Nations Affairs. As assistant secretary of state for Far Eastern affairs (1950–52), Rusk played a major role in the U.S. decision to take military action in Korea. Rusk headed the Rockefeller Foundation (1952–61), where he expanded its international operations. As secretary of state for Presidents Kennedy and Johnson, Rusk dealt with the CUBAN MISSILE CRISIS and supported the country's growing involvement in the VIETNAM WAR. Following his retirement, Rusk authored several books including *Waging Peace and War: Dean Rusk in the Truman, Kennedy, and Johnson Years* (1988) and *As I Saw It: A Secretary of State's Memoirs* (1990).

Russell, Bill (1934–), basketball player and coach. Russell led the Boston Celtics to eleven National Basketball Association championships in his thirteen-year career. He earned selection to the all-NBA team eleven times, pulled down 21,620 rebounds, and earned the most valuable player award a record five times. He became the first black head coach in major league professional sports when he served as player-coach for the Celtics from 1966 to 1969. Russell was named to the Hall of Fame in 1974.

Russell, Charles Marion (1864–1926), painter and sculptor. Russell was famous for his portrayal of life in the American west. His love of animals, cowboys, and Indians took him from St. Louis to the Montana Territory where his experiences as a herder, trapper, hunter, and cowboy provided authentic material for his paintings and sculptures. Working in pen and ink, oils, watercolors, and clay, Russell created works depicting vivid, detailed action of the Montana countryside that were shown and sold worldwide. His small wax figures were cast in bronze and sold at Tiffany and Co. in New York, and by 1920 one of his paintings sold for $10,000. Russell created more than two thousand paintings during his lifetime. His statue represents Montana in Statuary Hall in the U.S. Capitol.

Rustin, Bayard (1910–87), civil rights leader. A Quaker and pacifist, Rustin believed in pursuing black civil rights by nonviolent means. He helped plan the organization of the SOUTHERN CHRISTIAN LEADERSHIP CONFERENCE led by MARTIN LUTHER KING, JR., and was chief organizer of the 1963 march on Washington. In 1965 Rustin founded the A. Philip Randolph Institute, an educational, civil rights, and labor organization, which he directed until his death.

Ruth, Babe (George Herman; 1895–1948), baseball player. Ruth hit sixty home runs in the 1927 season, a record that stood until ROGER MARIS hit sixty-one in 1961. Called the "Sultan of Swat" and the "Bambino," fans filled the ballparks to watch Ruth play. He helped lead the New York Yankees to four world championships and led or tied the American League in home runs

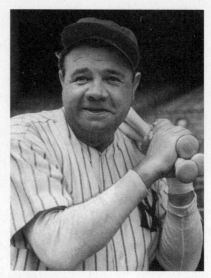

Babe Ruth

twelve times. Originally a pitcher for the Boston Red Sox, Ruth won twenty-three games in 1916 and helped them win the AL pennant, but he was sold to the Yankees in 1920, where he was switched to the outfield. He had 714 career homers and compiled a .342 lifetime batting average. Ruth was elected to the baseball Hall of Fame in 1936.

Rutledge, John (1739–1800), political leader. Rutledge signed the Declaration of Independence and served as governor of South Carolina during the American Revolution. He also served as a member of the First and Second Continental Congresses and as a delegate to the Constitutional Convention. Called "Dictator John," Rutledge was appointed to the U.S. Supreme Court in 1789 by President George Washington but resigned to become chief justice of the South Carolina State Supreme Court. Nominated by Washington in 1795 as U.S. Supreme Court chief justice, Rutledge served only one month because the U.S. Senate refused to confirm him owing to his bitter attacks on the Jay Treaty and rumors about his mental instability.

Ryan, Nolan (1947–), baseball player. On August 22, 1989, Ryan became the first major league pitcher to strike out five thousand batters. He pitched seven career no-hit games, the only pitcher to do so. Known for his blazing fastball, he also holds the record for most strikeouts (383) in a season. He has played for the New York Mets, the California Angels, the Houston Astros, and the Texas Rangers. At the time of his retirement in 1993, Ryan had the most career strikeouts (5,714). Averaging 9.55 strikeouts per nine innings over his career, he joined SANDY KOUFAX as the only pitcher in history to average one strikeout per inning. He surpassed GEORGE BLANDA's season record, playing the longest of anyone in baseball history (twenty-seven seasons). In professional team sports history, only GORDIE HOWE has played more seasons than Ryan.

Sabin, Albert (1906–93), virologist. Sabin developed the live-virus oral polio vaccine during the 1950s; its widespread use during the 1960s brought about a significant decline in polio throughout the world. Sabin's oral vaccine proved to be longer lasting and much easier to take than the vaccine developed earlier by JONAS SALK, which required injection.

Sacajawea (1784?–1812), Shoshone Indian woman who served as a guide and interpreter during part of the LEWIS AND CLARK EXPEDITION. Also spelled *Sacagawea*, her name means "bird woman." The only woman on the journey westward to the Pacific, she helped communicate with the Indians when they reached Shoshone territory in the Rocky Mountains, enabling them to secure horses for their journey. In 2000 the U.S. Mint issued a new "golden dollar" coin with her image.

Sacco-Vanzetti Case, controversial prosecution of Nicola Sacco (1891–1927), a shoemaker, and Bartolomeo Vanzetti (1888–1927), a fish peddler, for

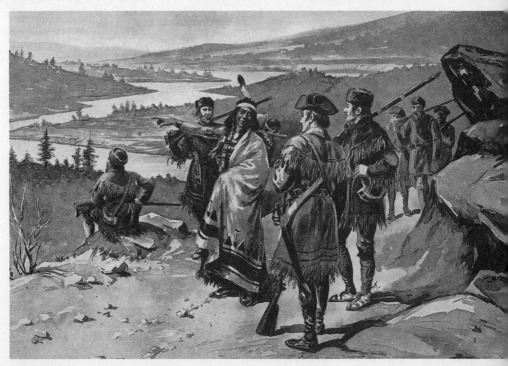

Sacajawea
Sacajawea guiding the Lewis and Clark expedition.

the holdup and murder of a shoe factory paymaster in South Braintree, Massachusetts, on April 15, 1920. The trial of the defendants, both Italian immigrants and acknowledged anarchists, took place against a backdrop of national hysteria over radicals and communists. The two were convicted and sentenced to death. Worldwide protesters questioned the evidence, citing abuses by the prosecution and alleging that the real reasons for conviction were the men's unpopular beliefs. After six years of appeals, Sacco and Vanzetti, maintaining their innocence to the end, were electrocuted August 23, 1927. In 1977, on the fiftieth anniversary of the executions, Governor Michael Dukakis of Massachusetts after a review of the case vindicated the pair in a proclamation that recognized the faults of the trial and declared that "any stigma and disgrace should be forever removed from their names."

Sagan, Carl (1934–96), astronomer and author. Sagan's books, articles, educational films, and television appearances have contributed to the popular understanding of science. A professor of astronomy and space science at Cornell University since 1968, Sagan created, wrote, and hosted "Cosmos," a public television series (1980). He wrote numerous books, including *The Dragons of Eden* (1977), a Pulitzer Prize–winning account of the evolution of the human brain. He also made major contributions to planetary astronomy and the U.S. program to explore the solar system.

St. Augustine, Florida, the oldest city in the United States. St. Augustine was founded in 1565 by Spanish explorer Pedro Menéndez de Avilés, who became the settlement's first governor. It remained a Spanish colony until 1819, when the United States purchased it from Spain under terms of the ADAMS-ONÍS TREATY.

St. Mihiel, Battle of (September 12–16, 1918), major Allied military engagement of WORLD WAR I. Under Gen. JOHN J. PERSHING, the American forces attacked the outnumbered German troops from St. Mihiel and forced them to retreat.

Sainte-Marie, Buffy (1941–), Native American singer, songwriter, and activist. Born on a Cree reservation in Canada, Sainte-Marie was adopted and raised in Maine and Massachusetts. Known for her protest and love songs of the 1960s, she recorded "Universal Soldier," which became prominent during the peace movement. She toured extensively, using her art and music as teaching tools to promote awareness of Native American cultural perspectives. Buffy and her son Dakota Starblanket Wolfchild spent five years on *Sesame Street* (1976–81), entertaining and educating children. In 1982 she won an Academy Award for her song "Up Where We Belong" from the film *An Officer and a Gentleman.* A Ph.D. in fine arts from the University of Massachusetts, she is also an art teacher and internationally exhibited artist.

Salem Witchcraft Trials (May–October 1692), trials that resulted from witchcraft hysteria in Salem Village, MASSACHUSETTS BAY COLONY. When a group of teenaged girls began to behave oddly, officials concluded that they were bewitched. Under pressure, they identified local residents as witches and wizards, resulting in dozens of arrests. Of the twenty-seven people who went to trial, nineteen were hanged and one man was pressed to death. The community was torn apart by accusations and fear. Boston clergyman Cotton Mather supported the persecutions, but his brother Increase Mather argued against the convictions and attempted to play a moderating role during the crisis. Governor William Phips forbade further trials, and a new court acquitted or discharged the remaining prisoners.

Salinger, J. D. (Jerome David; 1919–), author. Salinger's only novel, *The Catcher in the Rye* (1951), established his reputation. Holden Caulfield, the main character, set a style for the youth of the 1950s, who responded to the adolescent's language and disgust with "phoniness." The book became a modern classic, studied in many U.S. schools. Salinger's short story collections include *Nine Stories* (1953) and *Franny and Zooey* (1961). Noted for his insistence on privacy, he refuses to grant interviews or make public appearances. Salinger has also stopped publishing his writing.

Salk, Jonas (1914–95), virologist. Working in the field of preventive medicine, Salk developed the first vaccine against polio, which in 1955 was declared safe and effective. This vaccine helped reduce the incidence of the disease until ALBERT SABIN introduced an oral vaccine that was easier to administer. Earlier, Salk developed a vaccine against influenza; in 1960 he became director of the Salk Institute for Biomedical Studies. In 1977 Jimmy Carter awarded him the Presidential Medal of Freedom.

Salomon, Haym (1740–85), Polish-born patriot and banker. A Jewish immigrant, Salomon became a successful banker, making numerous loans to the government to finance the American Revolution. Arrested twice for spying on the British, Salomon escaped the second time and continued to support the American cause. Working under U.S. Superintendent of Finance Robert Morris, Salomon helped establish the Bank of North America.

Samoa, American, a group of five volcanic islands and two atolls in the South Pacific acquired by the United States in 1899. (Western Samoa is a separate independent country.) The capital of American Samoa is Pago Pago, located on the island of Tutuila and the site of a U.S. naval base until 1951. In 1899 the United States, Great Britain, and Germany signed a treaty that gave the United States possession of eastern Samoa. The islands were variously ceded by their chiefs during the early 1900s, and in 1929 Congress formally accepted control of the islands. The Department of the Navy administered them from 1900 to 1951, when the Department of the Interior took over. Samoan citizens, called U.S. nationals, elect a governor and legislature and send a nonvoting representative to Congress.

Sandburg, Carl (1878–1967), poet and historian. A two-time recipient of the Pulitzer Prize, Sandburg helped change the style of American poetry with his free verse form and simple, colloquial style. Collections include *Chicago Poems* (1916), *Cornhuskers* (1918), *The People, Yes* (1936), *Complete Poems* (1950; 1951 Pulitzer), and *Harvest Poems, 1910–60* (1960). Sandburg wrote of the spirit of the common man, often of the Midwest. As a historian and admirer of Abraham Lincoln, Sandburg wrote the two-volume *The Prairie Years* (1926) and won the 1940 Pulitzer Prize for the four-volume *Abraham Lincoln: The War Years* (1939). Sandburg also wrote children's stories, two collections of folk songs, memoirs, and other books.

San Francisco Earthquake (April 18, 1906), major earthquake and resulting three-day fire, which left most of the city in ruins. Measuring 8.3 on the Richter Scale, the quake destroyed about 28,000 buildings and left over 3,000 people dead. Rupture of the city's water mains prevented firefighters from dousing the fires, resulting in property damage in excess of $500 million.

San Francisco Earthquake (October 17, 1989). *See* SAN JOSE–OAKLAND–SAN FRANCISCO EARTHQUAKE.

Sanger, Margaret (1883?–1966), social reformer. A leader of the birth control movement during the early 1900s, Sanger founded the American Birth Control League in 1921 and became the first president of the International Planned Parenthood Federation in 1953. Appalled by her observations while working as a nurse with the poor, Sanger opened the first birth control clinic in the United States in Brooklyn, New York, in 1916, for which she was arrested and sent to prison. She organized the first World Population Conference in Geneva (1927) and helped obtain passage of laws allowing doctors to give birth control advice.

San Jacinto, Battle of (April 21, 1836), the last important military engagement between the Texans and the Mexicans in the war for Texas independence. Gen. SAM HOUSTON led a surprise attack on the Mexicans camped at San Jacinto and destroyed their forces quickly, an important victory for the Texans. Although significantly outnumbered, the Texans suffered minor casualties, about thirty killed or wounded, while Mexican casualties numbered over eight hundred killed or wounded and over seven hundred taken prisoner. Among the prisoners was Mexican president Gen. Antonio López de Santa Anna, who agreed to give Texas its independence in return for his release.

San Jose–Oakland–San Francisco Earthquake (October 17, 1989), major quake centered in the Loma Prieta area of the Santa Cruz Mountains, sixty miles south of San Francisco. Measuring 7.1 on the Richter Scale, the quake caused sixty-seven deaths and about $6 billion in property damage. Twelve of the deaths resulted from the collapse of an elevated section of the Nimitz Freeway in Oakland. The heaviest property damage occurred in San Francisco, Santa Cruz, Los Gatos, and Watsonville.

Saratoga, Battles of (September 19–October 17, 1777), turning-point battles of the American Revolution, which ended the hopes of Great Britain to divide the colonies. Fought in upper New York State just north of Albany, the battles ended with the surrender of British general JOHN BURGOYNE to U.S. general HORATIO GATES. The first assault by the British at Freeman's Farm took place on September 19, 1777, and resulted in heavy losses of British troops. The second assault, at Bemis Heights on October 7, again resulted in heavy losses by the British, who were repulsed by forces led by Gates, BENEDICT ARNOLD, and DANIEL MORGAN. Outnumbered and surrounded, Burgoyne surrendered on October 17. The colonists' victory persuaded France to form an alliance with the Americans against the British.

Sarazen, Gene (Eugene Saraceni; 1902–99), golfer. In 1922 at age twenty, Sarazen won two of golf's most prestigious tournaments, the U.S. Open and the Professional Golfers' Association Championship. Sarazen also won the British Open in 1932 and the Masters in 1935, thereby becoming the first of only six golfers to win the four titles that constitute the Grand Slam of golf. He won the PGA three times and represented the United States six times in Ryder Cup matches against Great Britain.

Sargent, John Singer (1856–1925), Italian-born painter. Born to American expatriates, Sargent achieved worldwide fame for his portraits of eminent and fashionable people of his time. Among his well-known subjects were Henry James, Robert Louis Stevenson, Theodore Roosevelt, Woodrow Wilson, and Edwin Booth. Sargent also painted murals for public buildings and impressionistic watercolor landscapes.

Sarnoff, David (1891–1971), radio executive. A Russian immigrant, Sarnoff worked for the Marconi Wireless Company and won recognition for his narration of the news of the *Titanic* disaster in 1912. As president and chairman of the board of the Radio Corporation of America (RCA) from 1930 until 1970, Sarnoff pioneered the development of radio and television. At his urging, RCA formed the National Broadcasting Company (NBC) in 1926, the first radio network in America. He served as a communications consultant to DWIGHT D. EISENHOWER in WORLD WAR II.

Saroyan, William (1908–81), writer. Best known for stories and plays that combine optimism in the midst of adversity, sentimentality, and pride of country, Saroyan first gained recognition with his collection of stories *The Daring Young Man on the Flying Trapeze* (1934). A major work is his novel *The Human Comedy* (1943). In 1940, citing his disapproval of literary prizes, Saroyan refused the Pulitzer Prize for his play *The Time of Your Life* (1939) about a group of eccentrics in a San Francisco waterfront bar.

Saturday Night Massacre *See* ARCHIBALD C. COX.

Sayers, Gale (1943–), football player. A two-time All-American running back from the University of Kansas, Sayers was drafted by the Chicago Bears in 1965. He received the National Football League (NFL) rookie of the year award after scoring twenty-two touchdowns, an NFL record at the time. Known for his agility and speed, he scored a record six touchdowns in one game (1965), and after only three years in the NFL, the organization named him the best halfback in the first fifty years of professional football in 1969. Sayers won rushing titles in 1966 and 1969, but his career was cut short by two severe knee injuries that ended his play in 1971. In 1977 at age thirty-four, he was the youngest player ever to be inducted into the Professional Football Hall of Fame. Sayers wrote an acclaimed book, *I Am Third*, which was made into the movie, *Brian's Song*, depicting the relationship with his friend and teammate Brian Piccolo, who died of cancer.

Scalawags, derogatory term used by southern Democrats to describe southern white Republicans who worked with blacks and northern Republicans during RECONSTRUCTION. Some sought political profit and were guilty of corruption, but others were farmers and planters who stressed economic development and a gradual, moderate reform. Scalawags helped to bring about educational and social reforms and to pass laws leading to black suffrage. They had gradually disappeared by 1876, when southern Democrats gained control of state and local governments.

Schechter v. United States (1935), unanimous decision of the U.S. Supreme Court ruling unconstitutional the NATIONAL INDUSTRIAL RECOVERY ACT (NIRA) (1933). The Court in *Schechter Poultry Corporation* v. *United States* invalidated NIRA on three grounds: that the act delegated legislative power to the executive; that there was a lack of constitutional authority for such legislation; and that it sought to regulate businesses that were wholly intrastate in character.

Schenck v. United States (1919), unanimous decision by the U.S. Supreme Court that upheld the Espionage Act of 1917, which stated that people who interfered with the war effort were subject to imprisonment. Justice Oliver Wendell Holmes, Jr., wrote that freedom of speech may be limited when there is a "clear and present danger" situation.

Schlesinger, Arthur, Jr. (1917–), historian. A two-time Pulitzer Prize recipient, Schlesinger won the 1946 history award for *The Age of Jackson* (1945) and the 1966 biography award for *A Thousand Days: John F. Kennedy in the White House* (1965). His three-volume biography of Franklin D. Roosevelt, *The Age of Roosevelt* (1957–60), analyzed the New Deal period. The award-winning *Robert Kennedy and His Times* was published in 1978 and *The Disuniting of America* in 1991. As a liberal Democrat, Schlesinger served as special assistant for Latin American affairs under Presidents Kennedy and Lyndon B. Johnson from 1961 to 1964.

Schulz, Charles (1922–2000), cartoonist. After selling his first cartoons to the *Saturday Evening Post* in 1948, Schulz rose to fame with the creation of the "Peanuts" comic strip in 1950; it became one of the most widely syndicated features of all time. Featuring child characters with adult problems and attitudes, the strip presented the emotional world of Charlie Brown, Lucy, Linus, their friends, and Charlie's philosophical, fantasizing dog Snoopy. "Peanuts" inspired numerous television specials and the musical *You're a Good Man, Charlie Brown*. The final Sunday strip appeared in February 2000 the day after Schulz died.

Schurz, Carl (1829–1906), German-born Union general and political leader. In his various roles as a diplomat, soldier, author, and politician, Schurz campaigned for black and Indian rights, civil service reform, and conservation. He served as U.S. minister to Spain (1861–62); as a Republican in the Senate from Missouri (1869–75), helping form the Liberal Republican party in 1872; and as secretary of the interior (1877–81). A leader of the MUGWUMPS, he edited the *New York Evening Post* (1881–83) and was an editorial writer for *Harper's Weekly* (1892–98). During the CIVIL WAR, Schurz fought as a Union general at the second Battle of Bull Run, Chancellorsville, and Gettysburg.

Schwarzenegger, Arnold (1947–), former bodybuilder, actor, business-man, and politician. Born in Austria, Schwarzenegger turned to bodybuild-ing, eventually winning the Mr. Olympia title seven times (1970–75, 1980). After graduating from the University of Wisconsin with a degree in busi-ness and economics he tried films, eventually gaining recognition as an ac-tion star in 1982's *Conan the Barbarian* and its 1984 sequel, *Conan the De-stroyer*. In 1984 he starred in *The Terminator* playing an unstoppable killer android from the future, reprising his role in several sequels. Alternating violent action films with lighter comedic fare, Schwarzenegger's other films include *Twins* (1988), *Kindergarten Cop* (1990), and *Junior* (1994). Despite never before holding public office, Schwarzenegger announced his candi-dacy for the governorship of California on *The Tonight Show with Jay Leno* on August 6, 2003. In October, running as a Republican, he led a successful campaign to appeal to people on a bipartisan basis, defeating 134 other can-didates and ousting recalled Governor GRAY DAVIS. Despite reports that he allegedly sexually harassed at least fifteen women in the past, about 47 per-cent of female voters backed him. His wife, television journalist Maria Shriver, and her mother, Eunice Kennedy Shriver, sister of the late President JOHN F. KENNEDY, offered public support.

Schwarzkopf, H. Norman (1934–), commander in chief of Operation Desert Storm in charge of Allied forces during the PERSIAN GULF WAR of 1991. Schwarzkopf planned operations and directed the more than 540,000 U.S. men and women and a total of 750,000 coalition troops under his com-mand. He had served as deputy chief for operation and plans from 1987 to 1988 and deputy commander, Joint Task Force, in Granada in 1983, as well as two tours in the Vietnam War.

Scopes Trial (July 10–21, 1925), trial of Tennessee pubic school biology teacher John Scopes for illegally teaching Darwin's theory of evolution. Tennessee state law prohibited the teaching of any theory that denied the biblical story of the divine creation of man. In the trial, often called the "Monkey Trial," WILLIAM JENNINGS BRYAN represented the state of Tennessee, and the AMERICAN CIVIL LIBERTIES UNION hired the famous lawyer CLARENCE DARROW to defend Scopes. After a dramatic court battle that received extensive nationwide publicity, Scopes was found guilty. The Tennessee Supreme Court acquitted him on a technicality, but upheld the constitutionality of the law itself.

Scott, Winfield (1786–1866), military and political leader. In his fifty-year career with the U.S. Army, Scott served in the War of 1812, the Mexican War, and the beginning of the Civil War. He became a hero when he captured Vera Cruz and Mexico City, bringing an end to the Mexican War. The pres-idential nominee for the Whig party in 1852, Scott lost to the Democratic candidate, Franklin Pierce. Known by his troops as "Old Fuss and Feathers" because of his clean appearance, elaborate uniforms, and obsession with details, Scott wrote *Infantry Tactics* (1835), the first complete manual of military procedures for the U.S. Army. He served as commanding general of the army from 1841 to 1861. Although born in Virginia, Scott remained loyal to the Union when the Civil War broke out.

Scottsboro Case (1931–37), important civil rights case. The name refers to several court cases that lasted almost seven years during the 1930s. Nine black youths were indicted on charges of raping two white women in Scottsboro, Alabama. In a series of trials the boys were found guilty and sentenced to prison terms of seventy-five to ninety-nine years or to death. The U.S. Supreme Court twice reversed the verdicts, ruling that the defendants had not been fairly represented, and blacks had not been allowed to serve on juries in Alabama. Even though one of the alleged victims retracted her story, Alabama officials refused to drop the charges and initiated new trials, which resulted in conviction and long prison sentences for five of the defendants (charges against the other four were dropped). The case focused national attention on the racial injustice in the South.

Secession *See* CIVIL WAR.

Secret Service, a division of the U.S. Department of the Treasury whose functions are to protect the president and to investigate crimes against the Treasury Department. Established in 1865 by President Abraham Lincoln, its function then was to detect counterfeiters, smugglers, and illegal liquor manufacturers. After the assassination of President William McKinley in 1901, it was assigned its task of protecting the president. Later its role was expanded to include protection of the president's family, other high government officials, presidential candidates, and ex-presidents.

Securities and Exchange Act (1934), measure creating the Securities and Exchange Commission to supervise licensing of stock exchanges. The act provided a program of regulatory control over the purchase and sale of stocks and bonds to prevent a recurrence of the STOCK MARKET CRASH of 1929. Regulations established standards for the conduct of stock brokers, the control of unrestricted speculation, and the illegality of false advertising.

Sedition Act (May 16, 1918), law passed by Congress during WORLD WAR I providing for punishment of persons who interfered with the war effort, spoke disloyally of the U.S. Constitution or federal government, or hindered the production of war materials. EUGENE V. DEBS, leader of the U.S. Socialist party, was imprisoned under this act. Congress repealed the law in 1921.

Seeger, Pete (1919–), folksinger, composer, and conservationist. In 1948 Seeger founded the group the Weavers, whose hits included "Irene, Good Night" and "On Top of Old Smoky." Later, as a solo performer, he influenced other folksingers with such compositions as "Where Have All the Flowers Gone?" and "If I Had a Hammer." Playing the five-string banjo,

Seeger toured with his own groups and with WOODY GUTHRIE, performing labor and antifascist songs. In 1955 he appeared before the HOUSE UN-AMERICAN ACTIVITIES COMMITTEE; his subsequent indictment for contempt was dismissed, but he was BLACKLISTED for many years.

Selective Service Acts *See* DRAFT.

Seminole Wars, series of conflicts between the United States and the Seminole Indians of Florida. The first (1817–18), set off by Gen. Andrew Jackson's excursions to capture runaway slaves, involved possession of Spanish Florida and was a factor in Spain's cession of Florida to the United States in 1819. The second struggle (1835–42) resulted from the Indian Removal Act of 1830 and efforts to move the Seminoles to Indian Territory. Lasting seven years, it resulted in the loss of thousands of lives. Gradually most of the Seminoles were sent west. A small group, however, remained in the Everglades. The third war (1855–58) erupted after efforts were renewed to track down the Seminole remnant still in Florida. In 1859 all but about a hundred Seminoles agreed to leave the state.

Senate, United States, one of the two branches of Congress and called the upper house. To ensure a balance of power between large and small states, the Framers of the Constitution provided that the Senate consist of two senators from every state, each elected to serve a six-year term. Currently the Senate has one hundred members. The Constitution requires that senators must be at least thirty years of age, citizens of the United States for at least nine years, and residents of the state they represent. The Senate has sole authority to ratify treaties (requires a two-thirds majority) and to confirm presidential appointments to federal judgeships, ambassadorships, and cabinet positions (requires a simple majority). The Senate sits as jury at impeachment trials, conducted by the chief justice of the Supreme Court, with a two-thirds majority necessary for conviction and removal. The vice president of the United States serves as president of the Senate but has no vote except in the case of a tie. The president pro tempore (usually the senator from the majority party ranking in seniority) presides in the absence of the vice president.

Sendak, Maurice (1928–), author and illustrator. In 1970 Sendak became the first American to receive the International Hans Christian Andersen Medal, the highest honor in children's book publishing. Sendak's stories focus on the imaginations, feelings, and fears of children. *Where the Wild Things Are* (1963), his best-known book, won the 1964 Caldecott Medal for its illustrations. Sendak designs sets and costumes for operas as well as for stage productions of his own works.

Seneca Falls Convention (July 19–20, 1848), meeting marking the formal beginning of the women's rights movement. Called by LUCRETIA MOTT and ELIZABETH CADY STANTON who, because of their sex, had been denied admission to an international antislavery convention in London, the assembly, at Seneca Falls, New York, was attended by some two hundred women and men (including abolitionist FREDERICK DOUGLASS). They endorsed the Seneca Falls Declaration of Sentiments (modeled on the Declaration of Independence), which included a demand for the right of women to vote. The convention was the first of many and gave impetus to the women's rights movement.

Sennett, Mack (Michael Sinnott; 1880–1960), Canadian-born silent film producer and director. Noted for his slapstick comedies, Sennett produced or directed over one thousand short films featuring the top silent stars of the day, such as CHARLIE CHAPLIN and BUSTER KEATON, and bathing beauties, pie-throwing, frantic chases, and the Keystone Kops. Unable to meet the demands of sound films, Sennett lost his fortune and closed his studio in 1933. His films included America's first feature-length comedy, *Tillie's Punctured Romance* (1914).

September 11, 2001, Terrorist Attacks, terrorist attacks of four fully fueled passenger jets headed for California from Boston, Massachusetts, Washington, D.C., and Newark, New Jersey. The planes were almost simultaneously commandeered in midair by Arab terrorists who deliberately crashed two jets into the twin towers of the WORLD TRADE CENTER; one more jet was crashed into the PENTAGON; a fourth, thought to be headed for the U.S. Capitol or the White House, crashed into a field in rural Pennsylvania after passengers and crew struggled to take control. The government shut down all air traffic in the United States for two days as fighter jets patrolled the skies. The total dead and missing numbered 2,752, including the nineteen hijackers and hundreds of emergency workers. President GEORGE W. BUSH immediately announced a war on terrorism and initiated security measures including the formation of a DEPARTMENT OF HOMELAND SECURITY. New legislation was enacted, including the U.S.A. PATRIOT ACT. Although the twin towers of the WORLD TRADE CENTER survived the impacts of the two Boeing jets, the intense heat from burning jet fuel weakened the steel framework of both buildings, resulting in their collapse. In addition to the towers, five other buildings were destroyed and scores were damaged. The fires continued to burn for three months while rescue workers removed debris, and at the end of May 2002, ceremonies to mark the end of over eight months of removal took place. No group claimed official responsibility for the attack, but the Islamic al-Qaeda organization and Osama bin Laden, a wealthy Saudi terrorist with close ties to the Afghan Taliban fundamentalist government, were identified by U.S. authorities as being responsible.

Sequoyah (1770?–1843), Cherokee silversmith who developed a written alphabet for his people. Sequoyah's system, completed in 1821 and consisting of over eighty symbols, enabled thousands of Cherokees to read and write in their own language. The giant sequoia tree and Sequoia National Park are named for him.

Serra, Junípero (Miguel José; 1713–84), Spanish Franciscan missionary. Father Serra founded nine of the twenty-one missions in California. Sent to Baja California in 1767, he cooperated with Spanish plans to establish missions in upper California and founded the first in San Diego in 1769, the first European settlement in California. Father Serra continued as a leader in white occupation, building eight more missions extending northward as far as San Rafael, including those at Carmel, San Luis Obispo, San Juan Capistrano, Santa Clara, and San Francisco. Noted for his religious dedication and self-discipline, Father Serra constantly traveled on foot between missions, even though he suffered from an ulcerated leg. Serra has become a controversial figure. In the 1980s, high-ranking members of the Roman Catholic church proposed that he be canonized, and in 1988, he was beatified, the last step before sainthood. Native American leaders opposed the action, claiming that as director of the mission churches, Serra led a system that enslaved Indians. His defenders conceded that harsh treatment occurred under the mission system, but they argued that Serra himself was innocent of wrongdoing and always acted as a strenuous advocate of Indian rights. The matter is still under consideration.

Seton, Elizabeth Bayley (1774–1821), religious leader. Mother Seton founded the Sisters of Charity in 1813, the first Roman Catholic religious community in America, and was a pioneer in the parochial school movement. She established a successful Roman Catholic school in Emmitsburg, Maryland, for well-to-do families and a day school for orphan and poor children. In 1907 Mother Seton was proposed for sainthood, and in 1975 she became the first person born in the United States to be recognized as a saint by the Roman Catholic church.

Seuss, Dr. (Theodor Seuss Geisel; 1904–91), writer and illustrator of children's books. Dr. Seuss's works create a whole new world, combining wildly imaginative tales with humorous illustrations, often conveying a moral message. Written in simple verse, his stories teach children that reading is a joy, not a chore; they include *Horton Hears a Who* (1954), *How the Grinch Stole Christmas* (1957), *The Cat in the Hat* (1957), and *Green Eggs and Ham* (1960). *Oh, the Places You'll Go!* (1990), a metaphorical account of the journey through life, is a story for all ages. Readers enjoy his clever rhymes and drawings and invented words. Seuss received a special citation from the Pulitzer Prize board in 1984 "for his contribution over nearly half a century to the education and enjoyment of America's children and their parents."

Seven Days' Battles (June 25–July 1, 1862), a series of battles during the CIVIL WAR, which were part of the peninsular campaign of the Union to capture the Confederate capital of Richmond, Virginia. Union troops led by

Gen. GEORGE B. MCCLELLAN were opposed by Confederate forces under Gen. ROBERT E. LEE. When McClellan tried to move south, the Confederates launched a counteroffensive but were repeatedly repulsed by Union forces. Despite heavy Confederate losses, the Union army retreated to the James River, thus allowing Lee to save Richmond.

Seward, William H. (1801–72), politician. The first Whig governor of New York (1839–43) and a member of the U.S. Senate (1849–61), Seward opposed slavery and helped form the Republican party. Although he was the party's most prominent member, he lost the 1860 presidential nomination to Abraham Lincoln on the third ballot. To preserve party unity and acknowledge Seward's influence, Lincoln appointed him his secretary of state, in which capacity he negotiated the TRENT AFFAIR and the ALABAMA CLAIMS, and took a strong stand in inducing the French to leave Mexico in the MAXIMILIAN AFFAIR. One of the targets in JOHN WILKES BOOTH's plot against Lincoln and his administration, Seward survived numerous stab wounds. An expansionist, he negotiated the ALASKA PURCHASE from Russia in 1867, an act derided as "Seward's Folly."

Seymour, Horatio (1810–86), politician. Seymour was the unsuccessful Democratic candidate for president in 1868, losing to Ulysses S. Grant. A two-term governor of New York, Seymour was instrumental in obtaining legislative agreement for the construction of the ERIE CANAL. He also helped Governor SAMUEL TILDEN drive BOSS TWEED from power. During the Civil War he denounced the Emancipation Proclamation as unconstitutional and opposed the draft.

Sharecropping, a system of farming in which the tenant farmer provides the labor for a share of the income, usually about half, and the owner of the land supplies the land, housing, and expenses for food, clothing, and supplies. The system, which flourished in the southern states after the Civil War and the destruction of slaved-based plantation agriculture, was often abused by landowners, leading to both black and white tenants being reduced to near-peonage status.

Shawn, Ted (Edwin Meyers; 1891–1972), choreographer and dancer. Shawn formed a troupe of male dancers that performed from 1933 to 1940. His work helped bring respect and prestige to male performers. Shawn also established an important summer dance school and theater, Jacob's Pillow, at Lenox, Massachusetts, in 1933.

Shays's Rebellion (August 1786–February 1787), an umbrella term for a series of revolts by farmers from Vermont to South Carolina, though concentrated in New England. The farmers rebelled against state courts' foreclosing on their farms for failure to pay debts or state taxes. The most serious rebellion, which broke out in western Massachusetts, was led by Daniel Shays (c. 1747–1825). The farmers attempted to seize a federal arsenal in Springfield and prevented state courts there from holding sessions. The state militia ended the rebellion quickly in early 1787. Shays fled to Rhode Island and Vermont. Most of the rebels were pardoned in 1787, and Shays, in 1788. The rebellion became a rallying point for advocates of a strong central government, and Federalists often cited it as a justification for the adoption of the U.S. Constitution.

Sheen, Fulton J. (1895–1979), Roman Catholic archbishop. A persuasive spokesman for the Roman Catholic church, Bishop Sheen became an influential radio personality on his weekly "The Catholic Hour" during the 1930s and presented a popular series of television lectures called "Life Is Worth Living" during the 1950s. He wrote about fifty books, including *Life Is Worth Living* (1953), *Walk with God* (1965), and *The Moral Universe* (1967).

Shepard, Alan (1923–98), astronaut. Selected in 1959 as one of the original seven astronauts, Shepard, on May 5, 1961, became the first American launched into space. His flight aboard *Freedom 7* lasted fifteen minutes. An ear disorder grounded him from 1963 to 1969, but he recovered to command *Apollo 14*, the third manned mission to the moon. The fifth man to walk on the moon, he spent 4 ½ hours exploring the lunar surface.

Sheridan, Philip (1831–88), Union general during the CIVIL WAR. Best known for victories as a cavalry leader in the Shenandoah Valley in Virginia, Sheridan helped force ROBERT E. LEE's surrender at APPOMATTOX. In 1862 Sheridan commanded Union troops in victories at Perryville, Kentucky, and MURFREESBORO, Tennessee. He also led battles at CHICKAMAUGA, Georgia, and MISSIONARY RIDGE and CHATTANOOGA in Tennessee. Sheridan's cavalry raid on Richmond, Virginia, resulted in the death of Confederate cavalry leader Gen. J.E.B. STUART. Following the war Sheridan served along the Rio Grande and became involved in the MAXIMILIAN AFFAIR. He acted as military governor of Louisiana and Texas until President Andrew Johnson relieved him of command for his harsh Reconstruction policies. Sheridan was transferred to the West, where he continued the army's campaign against the Plains Indians.

Sherman, James (1855–1912), twenty-seventh vice president of the United States under William Howard Taft (1902–12). Sherman, former mayor of Utica, New York, and U.S. congressman, was the only vice-presidential candidate in U.S. history to receive 3 million votes after he was dead. After serving one term, he was renominated at the 1912 Republican convention, but died six days before the election. The Democrats won, and Sherman's electoral college votes went to Nicholas Murray Butler, president of Columbia University.

Sherman, John (1823–1900), statesman. Noted for the silver purchase and antitrust acts that bear his name, Sherman, a Republican, held numerous political offices during his forty-three-year career, but never gained the presidential nomination he sought three times in the 1880s. He served in the House of Representatives (1855–61), in the Senate (1861–77, 1881–97), as secretary of the treasury (1877–81), and as secretary of state (1897–98). A conservative financial expert, Sherman sponsored the SHERMAN ANTI-TRUST ACT and the SHERMAN SILVER PURCHASE ACT in 1890. He was the younger brother of Gen. WILLIAM TECUMSEH SHERMAN.

Sherman, Roger (1721–93), statesman. Sherman signed the Articles of Association (1774), the Declaration of Independence (1776), the Articles of Confederation (1777), and the U.S. Constitution (1787), the only person to sign all four documents. He represented Connecticut at the First and Second Continental Congresses and was a member of the committee assigned to write the Declaration of Independence. At the Constitutional Convention, he and OLIVER ELLSWORTH introduced the GREAT COMPROMISE (Connecticut Compromise) resolving differences between small and large states on representation in Congress. Sherman served in Congress in both the House of Representatives (1789–91) and the Senate (1791–93).

Sherman, William Tecumseh (1820–91), Union general during the CIVIL WAR, second in importance only to Ulysses S. Grant. Sherman's expertise in planning and executing long marches earned him fame with his March to the Sea across Georgia in 1864 and his devastating march through the Carolinas in 1865. His troops destroyed much of the military and economic resources of the South, and he received the surrender of Gen. JOSEPH E. JOHNSTON on April 26, 1865. Sherman served as colonel at the first Battle of BULL RUN. Promoted, he fought with Grant at the Battles of Shiloh, Vicksburg, and Chattanooga before beginning his march to Savannah. Sherman was among the first military leaders to conceive and put into practice the methods of modern warfare. He succeeded Grant in the post of commanding general of the U.S. Army from 1869 to 1884. He was the older brother of political leader JOHN SHERMAN.

Sherman Anti-Trust Act (July 2, 1890), legislation passed by Congress to break up monopolies. The first of several antitrust acts designed to curb the power and growth of monopolies, the law forbade companies to join in a trust in order to control interstate trade. The law was also used to break up unions. Penalties for violation included a $5,000 fine, a year's imprisonment, or both. Because its wording was unclear and it was difficult to enforce, the Sherman Anti-Trust Act was supplemented by the CLAYTON ANTI-TRUST ACT in 1914.

Sherman Silver Purchase Act (July 14, 1890), coinage law increasing the amount of silver coined to 4.5 million ounces a month, which came to about the total being mined at the time. Superseding the Bland-Allison Act (1878), the Sherman Silver Purchase Act also permitted the U.S. government to print paper currency backed by silver. The law was passed because of pressure from silver miners, farmers, and debtors. The act failed to expand the money supply, and Congress repealed it after the financial panic of 1893 because it had caused the gold reserve to dwindle to a dangerous point.

Shiloh, Battle of (April 6–7, 1862), one of the bloodiest battles of the CIVIL WAR, also known as the Battle of Pittsburgh Landing, Tennessee. Although Confederate troops caught Union forces by surprise, the Union army led by Gen. ULYSSES S. GRANT defeated the Confederates led by Gen. ALBERT SIDNEY JOHNSTON after a brutal battle with high casualties on both sides. The Union's force of 63,000 suffered more than 12,000 dead or wounded; the 40,000 Confederates incurred more than 10,000 casualties. During the fighting, Johnston was killed and command passed to Gen. P.G.T. BEAUREGARD. With the arrival of Gen. DON CARLOS BUELL's fresh troops, the Union took the offensive and won the final victory.

Shirer, William L. (1904–93), newsman and author. Shirer's best-selling book *The Rise and Fall of the Third Reich* (1960), traces the history of Nazi Germany from its beginning after World War I to its destruction in World War II. The work won the National Book Award in 1961. Shirer served as European correspondent for the *Chicago Tribune* and for Universal News Service and as a commentator for CBS and the Mutual Broadcasting System. His first book, *Berlin Diary: The Journal of a Foreign Correspondent, 1934–1941* (1941) also became a best-seller.

Shoemaker, Bill (Willie) (1931–2003), jockey. "The Shoe" rode in more horse races than any jockey in history (40,350), earning purses of more than $120 million. Retiring from riding in 1990, he was the most successful jockey in history until his lifetime victory record of 8,883 wins was broken in 1999 by Lafit Pincay. Winning with nearly 22 percent of his mounts, Shoemaker won four Kentucky Derbys, two Preaknesses, and five Belmont Stakes. In 1991 he was paralyzed in an automobile accident that injured his neck and spinal cord, causing him to work from a wheelchair, but he enjoyed modest success as a trainer until 1997.

Shubert, family of theatrical managers and producers. Three brothers, Lee (1872–1953), Sam S. (1875–1905), and Jacob J. (1880–1963), dominated management of American theater during the first half of the twentieth century. After becoming managers of the Herald Square Theatre in New York City in 1900, they formed the Shubert Theatrical Company, eventually building and controlling a national chain of over sixty theaters. In 1950 the federal government instituted antitrust action against the Shuberts for having a monopoly over the American stage.

Sickles, Dan (1825–1914), military leader during the CIVIL WAR and politician. Sickles represented New York as a Democrat in the House of Representatives from 1857 to 1861. On February 27, 1859, he shot and killed Philip Barton Key, son of Francis Scott Key, because of Key's attentions to Mrs. Sickles. Sickles pleaded temporary insanity and was acquitted of murder, the first time this defense was used in a U.S. court. At the outbreak of the Civil War, Sickles led a New York brigade in the Union army, fighting in the peninsular campaign at CHANCELLORSVILLE and at GETTYSBURG, where he lost his right leg. After the war he was appointed military governor of the Carolinas, but President Andrew Johnson relieved him of his position because of his harsh measures. Sickles served as minister to Spain from 1869 to 1873 and again in the House from 1893 to 1895.

Silicon Valley, a narrow valley in northern California, about twenty-five miles long, stretching from Palo Alto to San Jose. The area became a center for computer and electronics companies in the 1970s. It is so named because silicon is the major component of the tiny chips that compose the basic part of computers.

Silver Purchase Act (June 19, 1934), act that established the nationalization of domestic silver holdings until the price reached a predetermined level. The Department of the Treasury was to issue silver certificates against all silver purchases. The purpose was to increase the price of silver following the depression by inflating the currency, but the act failed to do so.

Simpson, O. J. (Orenthal James; 1947–), football player and broadcaster. Called "the Juice," Simpson gained over two hundred yards in a game six times, a National Football League record. He won All-American honors twice at the University of Southern California, leading the team to a national championship in 1967 and winning the Heisman Trophy in 1968. Simpson played pro ball for the Buffalo Bills and the San Francisco 49ers. He won the NFL's most valuable player award in 1973 when he broke the record for most yards (2,003) gained in a season (broken in 1984 by Eric Dickerson with 2,105). He was elected to pro football's Hall of Fame in 1985 and went on to a career in sports broadcasting.

Simpson's sports fame was overshadowed, however, in 1994 when he was arrested for the double murder of his ex-wife Nicole Brown Simpson and her friend Ronald Goldman. After a sixteen-month investigation and trial, he was acquitted in 1995 by a Los Angeles jury that deliberated for fewer than four hours. In 1996, though, he lost a civil trial, a wrongful death suit brought by the victims' families, and was ordered to make financial reparations.

Sinatra, Frank (Francis; 1915–98), singer and actor. Achieving stardom with Tommy Dorsey's orchestra, Sinatra gained the mass adulation of teenagers during the 1940s. His fans, called bobby-soxers, created a pop-star hysteria unequaled until the Beatles in the 1960s. During the McCarthy era, allegations of communist sympathies damaged his career, but his role in *From Here to Eternity* (1953), for which he won an Academy Award, opened a new career. He later became a strong conservative, closely associated with President Ronald Reagan. Sinatra starred in over fifty films, ranging from comedy to musicals to drama, including *Guys and Dolls* (1955), *Pal Joey* (1957), *The Man with the Golden Arm* (1955), and *The Manchurian Candidate* (1962).

Sinclair, Upton (1878–1968), novelist and social reformer. Sinclair is best known for his muckraking novel *The Jungle* (1906), which exposed conditions in the meatpacking industry in Chicago. Outrage fueled by the book led to reform legislation such as the PURE FOOD AND DRUG ACTS. In 1934 he was narrowly defeated in his bid for governor of California as a Democrat with the slogan "EPIC — End Poverty in California." Sinclair helped establish the American Civil Liberties Union in the state. In 1940 he launched a series of eleven novels about Lanny Budd. The third, *Dragon's Teeth*, about Hitler's rise to power, won the 1943 Pulitzer Prize for fiction.

Sioux Wars (1854–90), series of skirmishes and battles between Sioux Indians and white settlers and soldiers. The Sioux, a confederation of nine tribes, lived throughout the northern plains. Known for their bravery and fighting ability, they had fought on the side of the British in the American Revolution and the War of 1812. As white settlers and gold seekers encroached on Sioux hunting grounds during the last half of the 1800s, hostilities increased. Strong leaders such as RED CLOUD, SITTING BULL, and CRAZY HORSE led the Sioux in their resistance to having their land taken from them and being forced onto reservations. In 1862 in Minnesota, Chief Little Crow launched an unsuccessful uprising against the white settlers. From 1865 to 1867 Red Cloud rebelled against the use of Sioux territory as a route to the mines of western Montana. Lt. Col. GEORGE ARMSTRONG CUSTER attacked the Sioux at the Little Bighorn River in 1876, resulting in his troops being wiped out in what came to be known as "Custer's Last Stand." In 1890 Gen. NELSON A. MILES ordered the arrest of Sitting Bull, who was killed when he resisted. The army then conducted the massacre of 146 Sioux men, women, and children at WOUNDED KNEE, SOUTH DAKOTA, on December 29, 1890. This was the last violent encounter between American Indians and the U.S. military.

Sirica, John J. (1904–92), judge. Sirica served as chief judge on the U.S. District Court for the District of Columbia at the 1973 trial of the seven original WATERGATE defendants. He ruled that executive privilege did not allow President RICHARD M. NIXON to refuse to turn over confidential White House tapes. Sirica sentenced some of the president's top aides to prison for obstruction of justice. His account of the Watergate affair is *To Set the Record Straight* (1979).

Sitting Bull (Tatanka Iyotake; c. 1831–90), Sioux leader of the Hunkpapa Teton tribe. Leader in many of the SIOUX WARS, Sitting Bull was present, although not a leader, at the Battle of Little Bighorn in 1876, when Lt. Col. GEORGE ARMSTRONG CUSTER and his troops were massacred. Because he had predicted the deaths of many soldiers, Sitting Bull's followers believed his powers had brought victory to the Sioux. He fled to Canada but returned in 1881 to surrender. After being held for two years at Fort Randall,

South Dakota, he lived on Standing Rock Reservation, where he continued to urge the Sioux to resist giving up their lands. In 1885 he traveled with BUFFALO BILL CODY's Wild West Show. On December 15, 1890, he was shot and killed by Indian police allegedly for resisting arrest.

Skelton, Red (Bernard Richard Skelton; 1913–97), comedian and actor. After appearing in vaudeville and on Broadway as a teenager, Skelton embarked on his show business career in the 1930s with his successful radio program, *Red Skelton's Scrapbook of Satire.* He made numerous films during the 1940s including *I Dood It* (1943) and *Bathing Beauty* (1944). His popularity peaked in the early days of television with *The Red Skelton Show,* which ran from 1951 through 1971. A master of mime and comedy, Skelton created and portrayed a variety of comic characters, including his best-known clown, Freddie the Freeloader, as well as Willie Lump-Lump, and the goofy Clem Kadiddlehopper.

Skinner, B. F. (Burrhus Frederic; 1904–90), psychologist. As a behaviorist, Skinner studied animal and human behavior and influenced the fields of psychology and education during his tenure as head of the psychology department at Harvard University. Skinner supported "programmed instruction" and developed a teaching machine that used the reward principle. Skinner wrote several books, including *Walden Two* (1948) and *Beyond Freedom and Dignity* (1971), both of which deal with ideal planned societies.

Skylab (1973–74), earth-orbiting space station, meant to demonstrate human ability to work and live in space for extended periods. Originally the third stage of a Saturn V rocket, *Skylab* orbited about three hundred miles above the earth. Astronauts entered from an Apollo spacecraft that had docked with it. The three-man crews visited the station for twenty-eight, fifty-nine, and eighty-four days and conducted scientific and medical experiments. Because of solar storms, *Skylab* fell from its orbit in 1979, most of it disintegrating as it reentered earth's atmosphere. Remaining pieces crashed in Australia and the Indian Ocean.

Slater, Samuel (1768–1835), British-born inventor and businessman. Slater, called the father of the American factory system, began the U.S. textile industry. After emigrating in 1789 from England to New York, he built a number of textile machines like those he had seen in England and set up the first American textile factory in Pawtucket, Rhode Island, in 1793.

Slaughterhouse Cases (1873), landmark Supreme Court decision that had profound effects on the interpretation of the Fourteenth Amendment. In 1869 the Louisiana legislature granted a monopoly to a slaughterhouse company in New Orleans with the intention of protecting people's health. A group of independent white butchers sued, claiming that their property rights had been denied in violation of the Fourteenth Amendment. The Court, in a 5–4 decision, upheld the grant of the butcher's monopoly because it did not violate the privileges and immunities of competitors, nor deny them equal protection of the laws, nor deprive them of property without due process. This decision generally upheld business regulations by the states until 1886 in *Santa Clara County* v. *Southern Pacific Railroad Co.*

Slavery, system of forced labor in which one person owns another as property. The first slaves were brought to Central and South America from Africa by the Spaniards before the founding of Jamestown. Dutch traders then followed, selling slaves to the Jamestown colonists as early as 1619 and eventually establishing a lucrative SLAVE TRADE between the colonies and Africa. Slavery existed in all thirteen colonies by 1690, filling the need for cheap, abundant labor. Between 1744 and 1804 the northern states abolished slavery, but the "peculiar institution" flourished in the South. Although Congress abolished the importation of slaves from other countries in 1808, the institution continued, eventually leading to the CIVIL WAR in 1861. Abraham Lincoln's EMANCIPATION PROCLAMATION took effect January 1, 1863, and adoption of the Thirteenth Amendment to the Constitution completed the abolition of slavery in 1865.

Slave Trade, the exchange of African people for money or for such items as guns, cloth, molasses, or rum. Before 1808 the trade flourished both between other countries and America and within the colonies or states. In 1808 the importation of slaves into the United States from other countries was abolished, but the trade continued within the states. The first African slaves were introduced into Jamestown, Virginia, in 1619 by Dutch traders to provide colonists with workers for their fields. A flourishing trade developed. Most slaves were either prisoners taken in wars in Africa or villagers captured by slave hunters who then sold them to traders. For their voyage across the Atlantic (called the Middle Passage), they were chained and crammed into the ships' holds. Once in America, they were sold as laborers or, in the case of women, as laborers and bearers of future slaves. The extremely profitable TRIANGULAR TRADE brought thousands of slaves to America before Congress prohibited the trade with other countries. Domestic trade continued until the Civil War, except in Washington, D.C., where it ended with the passage of the COMPROMISE OF 1850.

Slidell, John (1793–1871), politician and diplomat. Slidell, as a member of the Texas-Mexico Border Commission, unsuccessfully attempted to purchase California and New Mexico from Mexico in 1845. Mexico's refusal to recognize him as a representative of President JAMES K. POLK was a factor in the outbreak of the MEXICAN WAR. A Louisiana Democrat, Slidell served in the U.S. House of Representatives (1843–45) and the Senate (1853–61). When the Civil War broke out, he joined the Confederacy. Slidell, as the Confederate envoy to France, and James Mason, assigned to London, became involved in the *TRENT* AFFAIR, which delayed their arrival in Europe. Once there, Slidell failed in his attempt to persuade France to recognize the Confederate States of America as an independent country.

Sloan, John (1871–1951), etcher, painter, and illustrator. Sloan was a teacher and leader in the ASHCAN SCHOOL of American art. He realistically portrayed scenes from everyday life including city streets, bars, and cafés. Beginning in 1917 Sloan, a Socialist, headed the Independent Artists and taught at the Art Students League. He was well known for such city scenes as *McSorley's Bar* (1912).

Smith, Alfred E. (1873–1944), politician. Al Smith, a leading Tammany Hall Democrat, served four terms as reform governor of New York. He lost his bid for the 1924 Democratic presidential nomination but received it in 1928 with the help of his friend Franklin D. Roosevelt, who called him "the Happy Warrior." In a campaign dominated by Prohibition (which he opposed), prosperity (which the Republicans claimed as their doing), and religion (Smith was the first Roman Catholic to be a major party's candidate), Smith lost the election to Republican Herbert Hoover. He received a majority of the urban immigrant vote, however, which presaged the later Democratic coalition. Smith finally broke with FDR, who defeated him for the nomination in 1932, and did not support the New Deal.

Smith, Bessie (1895?–1937), African-American blues singer. Known for her imposing physical size (six feet tall and some two hundred pounds) and full-bodied delivery, Smith sang and recorded with many of the great jazz musicians of the 1920s, becoming the most successful black performing artist of her time. Her rendition of "St. Louis Blues" with LOUIS ARMSTRONG is considered by many to be one of the finest recordings of the 1920s. During the 1930s her career suffered due to alcoholism, as well as the decline of the recording industry during the Depression. Smith died from injuries sustained in an automobile accident. Reports that she bled to death because she had been turned away from a white hospital proved not to be true, but EDWARD ALBEE's 1960 play, *The Death of Bessie Smith,* helped perpetuate the myth.

Smith, David (1906–65), artist and sculptor. Smith revolutionized modern sculpture by adapting for artistic purposes scrap metal, machine parts, used tools, and junk steel, which he welded into abstract and geometric sculptures.

Smith, Emmitt (1969–), football player. Smith was selected by the Dallas Cowboys as their first pick in the 1990 draft. Although he stands only five feet nine inches tall, Smith won the NFL rushing title four times (1991, '92, '93, and '95). In 2002 Smith broke WALTER PAYTON's rushing record and is the current leading rusher, with more than 17,000 yards. In 2003 he was released by the Cowboys and signed with the Arizona Cardinals.

Smith, John (1580–1631), English soldier, colonist, and writer. Smith helped establish JAMESTOWN, Virginia, as the first permanent English colony in North America. As president of the colony, he organized and enforced discipline among the settlers. Smith treated the Indians harshly and they feared him. During his absence while on a trip to England in 1609, Indian attacks almost wiped out the colony. According to one of Smith's later accounts, he had been captured by unfriendly Indians in 1607 and the chief, Powhatan, intended to kill him, but POCAHONTAS, the chief's daughter, stopped the execution. The accuracy of this report has been questioned, but it has become a popular legend.

Smith, Joseph (1805–44), religious leader. As founder of the Mormon faith, the Church of Jesus Christ of Latter-day Saints, Smith became its first president in 1830. Claiming an angel named Moroni guided him to a set of inscribed golden plates, he published his translation of the inscriptions, *The Book of Mormon,* in 1830. Smith, calling himself "Prophet," organized churches in Ohio and Missouri. In 1839 he established the city of Nauvoo, Illinois, where he built a temple and served as mayor. In 1843 Smith secretly instituted the practice of polygamy among a select group of Mormons. Rumors of this, coupled with jealousy of Nauvoo's prosperity, led to persecution of the Mormons. Smith and his brother Hyrum were jailed in Carthage, Illinois, on charges of rioting and treason. An angry mob attacked the jail and killed the brothers. After Smith's death, BRIGHAM YOUNG led the main body of Mormons to Great Salt Lake Valley, Utah.

Smith, Margaret Chase (1897–1995), politician. Smith, the first woman to serve in both houses of Congress, succeeded her husband, a Republican congressman from Maine who died in 1940. Smith served four terms in the House of Representatives (1940–49) and four in the Senate (1949–73), longer than any other woman. Smith's 1950 address to the Senate, "Declaration of Conscience," distinguished her as the first Republican senator to oppose the tactics of Senator JOSEPH MCCARTHY. In 1964 Smith became the first woman of a major political party to campaign for the presidency.

Smith Act (June 28, 1940), law passed by Congress making it a crime to advocate or teach the forceful overthrow of a government in the United States or to belong to a group that does so. Also called the Alien Registration Act, it requires registration and fingerprinting of all aliens living in the United States. Representative Howard W. Smith of Virginia sponsored the act, which was passed when fears of communism and fascism were growing just before the U.S. entry into World War II.

Smithsonian Institution, a scientific and cultural museum comprising several branches and located in Washington, D.C. Congress established the Smithsonian Institution in 1846. English scientist James Smithson bequeathed $500,000 to the United States (which he never visited) to establish an institution for the "increase and diffusion of knowledge among men." Among its branches are the National Museum of Natural History, the National Gallery of Art, the National Museum of American Art, the National Zoological Park, the National Air and Space Museum, and the National Museum of History and Technology. The Smithsonian promotes research, publishes books, maintains a library, and sponsors expeditions throughout the world. It is governed by a board of regents, which consists of the vice president, the chief justice, three senators, three representatives, and six private citizens appointed by Congress.

Smoot-Hawley Tariff (June 17, 1930), one of the highest tariffs in American history. Passed during the administration of President Herbert Hoover, the act contributed to a decline in world trade and aroused deep resentment among foreign countries. Meant to protect American commodities, it resulted only in a slump in foreign trade. It was sponsored by Representative Willis C. Hawley (Oregon) and Senator Reed Smoot (Utah).

Snead, Sam (1912–2002), golfer. As the most successful golfer ever, winning over 150 tournaments, Snead was called "Slammin' Sammy" because of his almost perfect golf swing. Snead won the U.S. Masters three times, the Professional Golfers Association title three times, and the British Open once. His long, colorful career helped popularize the sport. He became a member of golf's Hall of Fame in 1953.

Socialist Party, a party founded by labor organizer EUGENE V. DEBS in 1898, which merged with a faction of the Socialist Labor party in 1901. Between 1900 and 1920 Debs was the Socialist candidate for president five times, polling nearly a million votes in the ELECTION OF 1920 while serving a term in prison. Socialists elected more than a thousand local officials across the country. In the ELECTION OF 1924 the Socialists endorsed ROBERT M. LA FOLLETTE, the Progressive party candidate. Norman Thomas headed the party through the 1930s and 1940s, becoming its candidate in every election from 1928 to 1948. The party supported Social Security, increased suffrage, improved labor conditions, welfare legislation, and more educational opportunities. Its popularity declined after 1932, although Socialists continued to win some local elections, such as Bernie Sanders, who became mayor of Burlington, Vermont, in 1981 and is now a member of the U.S. House of Representatives.

Social Security Act (August 14, 1935), law providing for a system of old-age insurance for workers at age sixty-five and survivor benefits for children or spouses of insured workers who die before age sixty-five. The act was a central element in the NEW DEAL program of President Franklin D. Roosevelt. The Social Security Administration, part of the Department of Health and Human Services, administers the system. Money for the pensions is collected from a Social Security tax taken out of workers' and employers' earnings. The act also provided that money be returned to the states so they could set up systems of unemployment insurance.

Somalia Conflict (1992–95), U.S./U.N. military intervention. Years of civil war and a devastating famine in Somalia led the United Nations (U.N.) to officially begin to provide humanitarian relief for the nation in 1992. When the U.N. asked its members for assistance, President George H. W. Bush, in one of his last acts as president, sent more than 25,000 U.S. troops in a deployment called Operation Restore Hope. Objectives to restore trade routes and provide security for the safe passage of relief supplies were somewhat successful, but incidents of violence continued among warring clans and against U.S. and U.N. peacekeepers. Although newly elected President BILL CLINTON supported the action in Somalia, he ordered the number of U.S. troops reduced in preparation for a transition to a U.N. peacekeeping force in May 1993. U.N. efforts to reestablish a central government were unsuccessful, due largely to forcible resistance by Somali clan leader Mohammad Farah Aidid. Months of attacks and efforts to capture Aidid climaxed in October 1993 in the capital city of Mogadishu when eighteen U.S. soldiers were killed and eighty-four were wounded by Somali militiamen. International news reports showed bodies of the dead Americans dragged through the streets, and President Clinton responded by withdrawing U.S. troops from Somalia. Clan-based fighting increased in 1994 as the United States and other nations withdrew their forces; the last U.N. peacekeepers left the following year.

Sons of Liberty (1765), a secret radical patriotic organization formed before the American Revolution to oppose the STAMP ACT. Sons of Liberty groups sprang up in all the colonies, with Massachusetts and New York the most active. The organization disbanded in 1766 after repeal of the Stamp Act, but the Sons of Liberty label became associated with those persons or groups who supported the independence movement.

Sousa, John Philip (1854–1932), composer and bandmaster. Called "the March King" for the more than 130 marches he wrote, Sousa also composed operettas and popular songs. Some of his best-known marches include "The Stars and Stripes Forever" (1896), "The Washington Post March" (1889), and "Semper Fidelis" (1888). Sousa led the U.S. Marine Band from 1880 until 1892, when he left to form his own successful band. He served as bandmaster for the U.S. Navy from 1917 to 1919.

South Carolina (Palmetto State) became the eighth state in the Union on May 23, 1788. (See maps, pages 540 and 541.) More battles were fought in South Carolina than in any other state during the American Revolution. In December 1860, South Carolina was the first state to secede from the Union. The Civil War started in Charleston on April 12, 1861, when Confederate units fired upon Fort Sumter in the city's harbor. The state's largest cities include Columbia (the capital), Charleston, and Greenville. Charleston has many beautiful gardens, and the first public museum was opened there. South Carolina is noted for its agriculture, especially peaches, cotton, tobacco, and soybeans. It is also a leader in the production of textiles, wood, glass, and asbestos. Noted South Carolinians include ANDREW JACKSON, JOHN C. CALHOUN, CHARLES COTESWORTH PINCKNEY, FRANCIS MARION, WILLIAM WESTMORELAND, and MARY MCLEOD BETHUNE.

South Dakota (Coyote State) became the fortieth state in the Union on November 2, 1889. (See maps, pages 540 and 541.) When gold was discovered in the Black Hills in 1874, boomtowns sprung up, including Deadwood with such colorful characters as WILD BILL HICKOK and CALAMITY JANE. The state's largest cities include Sioux Falls and Rapid City; the capital is Pierre. Tourism is important to South Dakota, with attractions like MOUNT RUSHMORE in the Black Hills, the Badlands, the carving of Chief Crazy Horse near Custer, and Dinosaur Park. Agriculture is the state's most important industry, and it leads in livestock, grains, and processed foods. Prominent politicians born in South Dakota include HUBERT H. HUMPHREY and GEORGE McGOVERN.

Southeast Asia Treaty Organization (SEATO) (1955–77), a military alliance of eight nations formed to check communist territorial expansion in the Pacific and Southeast Asia. Organized under the Manila Pact of 1954, the members included Great Britain, France, the Philippine Republic, Thailand, Pakistan, Australia, New Zealand, and the United States. The treaty was initiated by the United States after communist troops defeated France in Indochina. Members agreed to act together if anyone was attacked militarily. Pakistan left in 1968, France withdrew financial support in 1975, and SEATO dissolved in 1977.

Southern Christian Leadership Conference (SCLC), a civil rights organization founded by Dr. MARTIN LUTHER KING, JR., in 1957 in Atlanta, Georgia. Its intent is to gain equal rights for blacks and other minorities through assertive but nonviolent means. In 1963 the SCLC organized the August 28 March on Washington, when over 250,000 Americans gathered at the Lincoln Memorial in support of civil rights legislation. The SCLC worked to integrate public facilities and conducted voter registration drives in the South. After King's assassination in 1968, the organization lost some of its power and influence in the civil rights movement.

Space Shuttle, reusable spacecraft designed to be launched into orbit by rockets and to return to earth by gliding and landing on a runway. Until 1981 the NATIONAL AERONAUTICS AND SPACE ADMINISTRATION (NASA) used for its manned programs — Mercury, Gemini, Apollo, and Skylab — single-use launch vehicles and spacecraft. The shuttle replaced booster rockets for launching satellites and was designed to deliver payloads to earth orbit repeatedly. The orbiter, the main part of the shuttle system, can be reused more than a hundred times. Six orbiters have been built through 2003: *Enterprise* (a test vehicle), *Columbia* (twenty-eight launches), *Challenger* (ten launches), *Discovery* (thirty launches), *Atlantis* (twenty-six launches), and *Endeavour* (seventeen launches). The first shuttle flight, by *Columbia,* lifted off on April 12, 1981, at Kennedy Space Center in Cape Canaveral, Florida. The twenty-fifth ended in the tragedy known as the *CHALLENGER* DISASTER (1986), which forced a long delay in the program while NASA designed improvements to prevent future malfunctions. In early 2003 the COLUMBIA DISASTER caused further delays when it broke apart during a reentry mishap, causing a suspension of the space shuttle program until at least March 2005. By 2003, the number of missions flown stood at 111, including several that serviced and provided crews for the INTERNATIONAL SPACE STATION, but in the wake of the COLUMBIA DISASTER a shift toward using safer, cheaper unmanned rockets to launch payloads was being considered.

Spahn, Warren (1921–2003), baseball player. Spahn held the distinction of being the winningest left-handed pitcher of all time, with 363 wins. He won twenty games for thirteen seasons, a major league record for left-handers. Spahn led the National League in strikeouts for four consecutive years (1949–52) and won the Cy Young Award in 1957. He led the Boston Braves to a NL pennant in 1948, the Milwaukee Braves to a pennant in 1957 that ended with a World Series championship, and a NL pennant in 1958. He was inducted into the Hall of Fame in 1973.

Spanish-American War (April 25–August 12, 1898), conflict between the United States and Spain. Begun over the cause of Cuban independence, the war marked the emergence of the United States as a world power and the beginning of American overseas imperialism. Most of the fighting occurred in the Spanish possessions of Cuba and the PHILIPPINES on opposite sides of the world. The expansionists in the United States wanted to acquire Cuba, and in 1895 Cuban nationalists began an insurrection against the Spanish government. After Gen. Valeriano Weyler herded Cuban farmers into concentration camps and took other measures to put down the insurrection, WILLIAM RANDOLPH HEARST and JOSEPH PULITZER started their YELLOW JOURNALISM newspaper war, molding public opinion in favor of U.S. intervention against Spain and the annexation of Cuba. With the blowing up of the battleship USS *Maine* in Havana Harbor and the loss of 266 lives, President WILLIAM MCKINLEY was pressured by Congress into asking for a declaration of war.

Starting on April 25, 1898, the bloody combat lasted only a few months, so that Secretary of State JOHN HAY called it "the splendid little war." In the Pacific, Commodore GEORGE DEWEY's squadron slipped into Manila Bay on May 1 in the Philippines and destroyed the obsolete Spanish fleet lying at anchor. Aided by army reinforcements, Dewey captured the city of Manila on August 13. The U.S. Navy then seized Spanish GUAM and unclaimed Wake Island, and Congress, by a joint resolution, annexed the Hawaiian Islands. In May 1898 the Spanish fleet at Santiago, Cuba, was blockaded. American troops under Gen. William Shafter landed in Cuba and the ROUGH RIDERS, led by LEONARD WOOD and THEODORE ROOSEVELT, were victorious at the Battles of El Caney and San Juan (Kettle's) Hill. The Spanish fleet made a dash for the open seas but was destroyed by the U.S.

fleet led by Rear Adm. William Sampson in less than four hours. On July 17, twenty-four thousand Spanish troops surrendered.

In the TREATY OF PARIS (1898) Cuba became independent, and the United States claimed PUERTO RICO, Guam, and the Philippine Islands. The treaty barely passed the Senate, with only two votes over the two-thirds needed for ratification.

Speaker, Tris (Tristan; 1888–1958), baseball player. Known as "the Gray Eagle," Speaker holds the American League record for most putouts by an outfielder (6,794) and compiled a lifetime batting average of .344. Known for his defense and speed, he set a major league record for doubles (793). Speaker played for the Boston Red Sox and Cleveland Indians, serving as player-manager for the Indians from 1919 to 1926. He led the Indians to the World Series championship in 1920. Speaker became a member of the baseball Hall of Fame in 1937.

Speaker of the House, the presiding officer of the U.S. House of Representatives, as provided in Article I, Section 2, of the U.S. Constitution. The Speaker, always a member of the majority party, is elected every two years by the entire House at its first session. The Speaker presides over the sessions, recognizes speakers, refers bills to committees, and decides points of order. Influential Speakers have included HENRY CLAY, JAMES K. POLK, THOMAS REED, JOSEPH CANNON, SAM RAYBURN, and THOMAS "TIP" O'NEILL. The Speaker follows the vice president in presidential succession.

Specie Circular (July 11, 1836), order of President Andrew Jackson and his Treasury secretary, Levi Woodbury, directing that all future purchases of public lands be made in gold and silver. Jackson hoped thereby to end the widespread speculation in public lands that had resulted from his actions against the second BANK OF THE UNITED STATES, when he had withdrawn government deposits and placed them in state PET BANKS. The Specie Circular's failure contributed to the panic of 1837.

Spielberg, Steven (1947–), film director, writer, and producer. Spielberg's films capitalize on imaginative technical effects and feature adventure, fantasy, and humor. The creator of many box-office hits, Spielberg's films include *Jaws* (1975), *Raiders of the Lost Ark* (1981), *Close Encounters of the Third Kind* (1977), and *ET: The Extra-Terrestrial* (1982). Spielberg's later films are noted for their more serious subject matter and powerful impact. He earned Best Director Oscars for *Schindler's List* (1993) and *Saving Private Ryan* (1998), and became known for his willingness to take on controversial issues. Spielberg's multimedia entertainment company, DreamWorks SKG, produces film, television, music, computer software, and Internet technology.

Spillane, Mickey (Frank Morrison Spillane; 1918–), author of crime novels. Spillane became a best-selling author with his creation of tough, hard-boiled, hard-fighting private eye, Mike Hammer. Spillane's novels, which rely on violence, sex, and stereotypes, have been questioned by critics, but have sold 200 million copies worldwide according to the author, and several have been made into motion pictures. Novels include *I, the Jury* (1947), *One Lonely Night* (1951), and *Black Alley* (1996).

Spingarn Medal, award given each year to an outstanding black American. It was instituted in 1914 by Joel Elias Spingarn (1875–1939), a white literary critic and chairman of the board of the NATIONAL ASSOCIATION FOR THE ADVANCEMENT OF COLORED PEOPLE (NAACP). The gold medals are awarded by a committee appointed by the NAACP board.

Spitz, Mark (1950–), Olympic swimmer. Spitz is the only athlete to win seven gold medals in a single Olympic Games. In 1972 at Munich, Spitz won the 100- and 200-meter freestyle and butterfly events, and was a member of the winning 4 × 100 and 4 × 200 freestyle relay teams and the 4 × 100 meter medley relay team. He broke world records in every event. Spitz also won four medals (two gold, a silver, and a bronze) in the 1968 Games for a total of eleven overall. He shares the record for the most Olympic gold medals overall (nine). His comeback try for the 1992 Olympic team was unsuccessful.

Spock, Benjamin (1903–98), pediatrician, author, and political activist. Dr. Spock is best known for his *Common Sense Book of Baby and Child Care* (1946), which has sold more than 30 million copies and greatly influenced child-rearing practices. His other books include *A Baby's First Year* (1955) and *Dr. Spock Talks with Mothers* (1961). A political activist, Spock was the presidential candidate of the People's party in 1972. He criticized U.S. involvement in Vietnam, advocated nuclear disarmament, and was arrested several times for civil disobedience. In 1968 a federal district court found Spock guilty of violating the Selective Service Act by encouraging draft resistance, but the U.S. First Circuit Court of Appeals reversed the decision in 1969.

Spoils System, a policy of giving government jobs to political party workers who have supported a particular victorious candidate. The practice began during the presidency of Thomas Jefferson when he, a Democratic-Republican, followed a policy of not selecting Federalists for appointments. During the administration of President Andrew Jackson, government employees of the rival party were dismissed from their positions and replaced by members of the Democratic party. The term *spoils system* was used as early as 1812, but came into general use when Jackson's friend Senator William Marcy declared in 1832, "To the victor belong the spoils of the enemy." The system gradually became associated with corruption, and it was modified when Congress passed the PENDLETON ACT in 1883 establishing the Civil Service Commission. Although education, experience, and examinations have become important as a basis for appointment to public office, the practice of patronage continues.

Spotsylvania Courthouse, Battle of (May 8–19, 1864), CIVIL WAR conflict between Union troops led by ULYSSES S. GRANT and Confederate forces under ROBERT E. LEE at Spotsylvania Courthouse, Virginia. Despite heavy losses suffered during the Battle of the Wilderness, Grant pushed his troops on toward Richmond, where they clashed with Lee's army, with both sides suffering heavy losses. Although Grant lost more men and he gradually withdrew, the battle resulted in no real victory for either side.

Springsteen, Bruce (1949–), singer and songwriter. Springsteen, called "The Boss" (for his exacting musical standards), is known for his personal rock ballads that reflect sympathy for blue-collar life. In the early 1970s he formed the Bruce Springsteen Band, later renamed the E Street Band following the release of their second album, *The Wild, the Innocent & the E Street Shuffle* (1973). *Born to Run* (1975) was their first big success, followed by several others including *Born in the U.S.A.* (1984), which followed up with a successful tour and video. Springsteen won an Academy Award and four Grammy Awards for the song "Streets of Philadelphia" for the 1994 film *Philadelphia*. In 2001 he reunited with the E Street Band to record *The Rising* (2002), inspired by the terrorist attacks of September 11. The album earned three Grammys, including Best Rock Album.

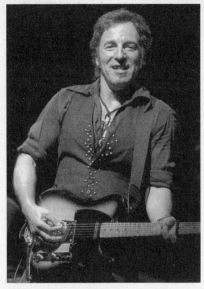

Bruce Springsteen

Spruance, Raymond (1886–1969), naval officer. Admiral Spruance was an outstanding commander of aircraft carrier task forces in the Pacific during WORLD WAR II. When Pearl Harbor was attacked by the Japanese on December 7, 1941, Spruance became commander of the cruiser division in the Pacific, serving under Adm. Chester Nimitz. He won the Battle of Midway (1942) and directed successful attacks on the Gilbert Islands (1943), the Marshall Islands, and Saipan (1944), when he was promoted to admiral, and the Battle of the Philippine Sea (1944). Spruance led naval forces in the invasions of Iwo Jima (February 1945) and Okinawa (April 1945). In November 1945 he succeeded Nimitz as commander in chief of the Pacific Fleet. After the war, Spruance served as president of the Naval War College (1946–48) and as ambassador to the Philippines (1952–55).

Squanto (Tisquantum; 1585?–1622), Pawtuxet Indian leader. Squanto befriended the PILGRIMS of PLYMOUTH COLONY and helped them survive by teaching them how to plant corn and advising them on where to hunt and fish. Acting as interpreter between Wampanoag chief MASSASOIT and the settlers, Squanto helped arrange a peace treaty.

Stalwarts, the name given to the conservative right wing of the Republican party after 1876, to distinguish it from the Half-Breed liberal left reform wing of the party. Led by ROSCOE CONKLING of New York, SIMON CAMERON of Pennsylvania, and John Logan of Illinois, the Stalwarts supported the policies of ULYSSES S. GRANT and wanted Grant to be nominated for a third term. They also opposed the reform programs of President RUTHERFORD B. HAYES, including civil service reform, and advocated high tariffs and a strong Reconstruction policy.

Stamp Act (1765), measure passed by the British Parliament requiring tax stamps on all legal documents, newspapers, almanacs, and pamphlets issued in the colonies. Intended to help pay for the maintenance of British troops in the colonies, the act aroused so much opposition that the Stamp Act Congress (October 1765) took place in New York City to protest it. The congress issued a statement that only the colonial government, not the British Parliament, could levy taxes on the colonists. The colonists boycotted the Stamp Act, and it was repealed by Parliament in 1766. The congress was the first united colonial action against Great Britain.

Standish, Miles (1584?–1656), English colonist and soldier. Hired by the PILGRIMS to accompany them on the *Mayflower* to the New World, Standish was the military leader of the new colony of PLYMOUTH, Massachusetts, in 1621, where he explored the territory, tended the sick, trained a militia, and fought Indians. He later served as assistant to the governor and as treasurer of Plymouth Colony. He helped establish the town of Duxbury in 1631. There is no factual basis for Henry Wadsworth Longfellow's account of Standish's wooing of Priscilla Mullens in his poem "The Courtship of Miles Standish" (1858).

Stanford, Leland (1824–93), businessman, politician, and philanthropist. Stanford served as Republican governor of California from 1861 to 1863. A strong supporter of Abraham Lincoln and the Union during the CIVIL WAR, he was instrumental in preventing California from seceding from the Union. He founded and presided over the Central Pacific Railroad Company and served as president of the Southern Pacific Railroad. Stanford represented California in the U.S. Senate from 1885 to 1893 and established Stanford University in memory of his son who died young.

Stanley Cup, trophy awarded annually to the winner of the National Hockey League (NHL) championship series. The Stanley Cup is the oldest award given to a professional team in North America. First presented in 1893 by Lord Stanley of Preston, governor general of Canada, it is now controlled by the NHL. Considered by many to be the most difficult trophy to win because of the two months of exhaustive playoffs required to earn it, it is the only trophy in professional sports to have the name of every member of the winning team engraved upon it. The most-winning American team is the Detroit Red Wings, with ten Stanley Cup championships.

Stanton, Edwin (1814–69), politician. A "War Democrat" who opposed slavery and secession, Stanton served President James Buchanan as attorney general and President Abraham Lincoln as secretary of war; he later played a part in the impeachment of President Andrew Johnson. As secretary of war Stanton played a vital role in the CIVIL WAR through his control of the Union military. He participated in the investigation and trial of the conspirators following Lincoln's assassination. Stanton continued in his post under Johnson but soon clashed with him over RECONSTRUCTION policy, and Johnson tried to remove him from office. This led to Johnson's impeachment on the ground that he violated the TENURE OF OFFICE ACT. Stanton resigned in 1868 following Johnson's acquittal. He died four days after his appointment to the Supreme Court by Ulysses S. Grant.

Stanton, Elizabeth Cady (1815–1902), reformer and a leader in the fight for women's rights. She and LUCRETIA MOTT organized the SENECA FALLS CONVENTION in 1848, the first women's rights conference in the United States. With Susan B. Anthony she cofounded the NATIONAL WOMAN SUFFRAGE ASSOCIATION and coedited a women's rights journal, *Revolution* (1868–69). In 1878, at Stanton's urging, a woman suffrage amendment was proposed for the U.S. Constitution. Reintroduced annually, it was finally approved by Congress in 1919 and became the Twentieth Amendment. A prolific writer, Stanton helped compile the first volumes of the six-volume *The History of Woman Suffrage* (1881–86) and wrote *Eighty Years and More* (1898), an autobiography, and *The Woman's Bible* (2 vols., 1895, 1898), in which she interprets women in the Bible.

Starr, Belle (Myra; 1848–89), female outlaw. Under the name "the bandit queen," Starr stole horses and cattle in the Southwest. She became the common-law wife of a Cherokee named Sam Starr in 1880. Their cabin in Indian Territory provided a hideout for outlaws including Jesse James. She was shot by an unknown assailant.

State, Department of, the executive department of the U.S. government that advises the president on foreign policy. The oldest federal department, it was created by Congress in 1789. The department negotiates treaties, maintains embassies, and processes information from throughout the world. Its head, the secretary of state, is appointed by the president and approved by the Senate. Fourth in order of succession to the presidency, the secretary serves as the senior member of the president's cabinet.

States' Rights Doctrine, a doctrine seeking to protect the rights and powers of the states in relation to those of the federal government. The states' rights doctrine, a theory held by many southerners before the Civil War, asserted that the U.S. Constitution was a compact among the states, that the states could block (called interposition) or overrule (called nullification) actions of the Union that affected their interests, and that states had the right to secede from the Union. The doctrine or variants of it appeared in the VIRGINIA AND KENTUCKY RESOLUTIONS (1798), the HARTFORD CONVENTION (1814), the WEBSTER-HAYNE DEBATE (1830), and the Ordinance of Nullification (1832). JOHN C. CALHOUN, "the Voice of the South," was the leading spokesman for the doctrine.

Statue of Liberty, huge copper statue located on Liberty Island at the entrance to New York Harbor near Ellis Island. The figure represents freedom as a woman who has escaped the chains of tyranny, which lie at her feet. Designed by Frédéric Auguste Bartholdi and completed in Paris in 1884, the Statue of Liberty was unveiled as a gift from the French people in 1886, honoring the first centennial of American independence. It stands as a symbol of welcome to immigrants entering the United States.

Steffens, Lincoln (1866–1936), journalist, author, and reformer. As a leading MUCKRAKER and managing editor of *McClure's* magazine, Steffens exposed corruption in government, business, and labor during the early twentieth century. His articles appeared in book form as *The Shame of the Cities* (1906) and *The Struggle for Self-Government* (1906).

Steichen, Edward J. (1879–1973), photographer and artist. Steichen was one of the most prominent and influential photographers of the twentieth century. In both black and white and color, his subjects included portraits, landscapes, fashion, advertising, and dance. He mastered a command of aerial photography as commander of the photographic division of the Army Expeditionary Forces in World War I and during World War II became director of the U.S. Naval Photographic Institute, in charge of all combat photography. Together with ALFRED STIEGLITZ, he founded the Little Galleries of the Photo Secession (later the 291 Gallery) in New York. As director of photography at the Museum of Modern Art in New York City (1947–62), Steichen presented the popular exhibition *The Family of Man,* which toured the world and also became a best-selling book. His career helped establish photography as a modern art medium.

★ **Statue of Liberty**

An excerpt from "The New Colossus," a sonnet composed by Emma Lazarus in honor of the Statue of Liberty and carved into its base

"Give me your tired, your poor, Your huddled masses yearning to breathe free, The wretched refuse of your teeming shore. Send these, the homeless, tempest-tost to me.

I lift my lamp beside the golden door!"

Stein, Gertrude (1874–1946), author. Stein introduced a unique style of writing based on extreme simplification and repetition, illustrated by her famous statement "Rose is a rose is a rose is a rose." She used little punctuation, believing it distracts the reader, and emphasized sounds of words rather than sense. She was also a pioneer in the "stream of consciousness" technique. After she moved to Paris in 1903, her home became a gathering place for writers such as ERNEST HEMINGWAY, F. SCOTT FITZGERALD, and SHERWOOD ANDERSON and painters such as Cézanne, Picasso, and Matisse. Stein was a vital part of the artistic ferment of the time. A prolific author, she wrote novels, short stories, critical essays, "cubist" poetry, drama, and opera. Her autobiographical work, *The Autobiography of Alice B. Toklas* (1933), presents a view of Stein from the perspective of her lifelong companion and secretary.

Steinbeck, John (1902–68), author. Steinbeck won the 1940 Pulitzer Prize for his classic novel, *The Grapes of Wrath* (1939), and the 1962 Nobel Prize for literature. Steinbeck's childhood in the California farming community of Salinas and his early work as a laborer inspired many of his books, which often deal with the struggle of poor farmers and laborers to survive in modern society. Noted works include *Tortilla Flat* (1935), *Of Mice and Men* (1937), *Cannery Row* (1945), *The Pearl* (1947), *East of Eden* (1952), and *Travels with Charley* (1962).

Steinem, Gloria (1934–), feminist writer and political activist. Cofounder and editor of *Ms.* magazine (1972–87), Steinem campaigned for women's rights in employment, politics, and social life. In 1971 she helped organize both the National Women's Political Caucus and the Woman's Action Alliance, which fights discrimination against women. She has been active in the civil rights and peace movements, supporting the efforts of the United Farm Workers and opposing the Vietnam War. She published *Outrageous Acts and Everyday Rebellions* (1983), a collection of articles she wrote during her journalistic career, and *Revolution from Within: A Book of Self-Esteem* (1992), a memoir.

Steinmetz, Charles (Karl; 1865–1923), German-born mathematician and engineer. Steinmetz made important contributions to the understanding of electricity, particularly alternating-current systems. While consulting for General Electric Company, he patented over two hundred inventions. His experiments led to techniques for protecting power lines from lightning.

Stengel, Casey (Charles; 1890–1975), baseball player and manager. Stengel gained celebrity status during his twenty-two years as manager of the Brooklyn Dodgers, Boston Braves, New York Yankees, and New York Mets, known for his colorful antics, outgoing personality, and tangled sentences. Under him, the New York Yankees won ten pennants and seven World Series championships. Prior to managing, Stengel played for the National

League from 1912 to 1925 with several teams. He was elected to the baseball Hall of Fame in 1966.

Stephens, Alexander H. (1812–83), vice president of the CONFEDERATE STATES OF AMERICA (1861–65). Stephens represented Georgia as a Whig and later Democratic member of the U.S. House of Representatives from 1843 to 1859. Though disapproving of secession, he supported Georgia when it voted to leave the Union in 1861. Stephens headed the unsuccessful Confederate commission that met with Abraham Lincoln at the HAMPTON ROADS CONFERENCE in 1865, and after the war was imprisoned at Fort Warren in Boston. He was elected to the U.S. Senate but was denied a seat, being from a "rebel" state. Later, however, he served as a member of the House from 1873 to 1882. He was elected governor of Georgia in 1882 but died a few months after taking office.

Stephens, Uriah (1821–82), labor leader. Stephens, a tailor, helped organize the Garment Cutter's Association of Philadelphia. In 1869 he cofounded the Noble Order of the Knights of Labor, the first national labor union in the United States, and became its first leader, or grand master. Stephens opposed strikes and promoted secrecy and ritual at his meetings. These issues sparked controversy and conflict, and Stephens resigned in 1879 when TERENCE POWDERLY took over.

Steuben, Baron Friedrich Wilhelm von (1730–94), German-born general during the AMERICAN REVOLUTION. Steuben's service to the Continental army proved invaluable, as he brought discipline to the troops. After serving with the Prussian army through the Seven Years' War, he drilled and trained the colonial army at Valley Forge at the request of George Washington. Steuben wrote *Regulations for the Order and Discipline of the Troops of the United States* (1779), the army's standard drill manual until the War of 1812. He commanded troops at the Battle of MONMOUTH, served under the MARQUIS DE LAFAYETTE in Virginia when Gen. Charles Cornwallis invaded the state, and commanded a division of Washington's army at the siege of YORKTOWN, where the British met final defeat.

Stevens, Thaddeus (1792–1868), lawyer and politician. As a Pennsylvania congressman (1849–53, 1859–68), Stevens vigorously opposed slavery and led RADICAL REPUBLICANS in forming a RECONSTRUCTION plan for stern treatment of the South. He insisted on strict requirements for readmission of southern states into the Union and was instrumental in denying them seats in Congress. Stevens helped secure passage of the Fourteenth Amendment guaranteeing civil rights and chaired the committee that recommended the impeachment of President Andrew Johnson.

Stevens, Wallace (1878–1955), poet. A successful lawyer and Connecticut insurance company executive for most of his life, Stevens achieved acclaim for his influential poetry. Noted for his philosophical verse and use of alliteration, Wallace explored the importance of imagination in giving meaning to life. His *Collected Poems* (1954) won the Pulitzer Prize. His strong belief in order was also reflected in his poetry and essays. He presented his theories in a book of essays, *The Necessary Angel* (1951).

Stevenson, family of Democratic politicians from Illinois. Adlai Ewing Stevenson I (1835–1914) served as vice president of the United States (1893–97) under Grover Cleveland. As the first assistant postmaster general in Cleveland's first administration, Stevenson angered Republicans when he replaced some forty thousand Republican postmasters with Democrats. Following his vice presidency, he was sent to Europe by William McKinley to serve as chairman of a commission to promote international bimetallism. His grandson and namesake, Adlai Ewing Stevenson II (1900–65), became governor of Illinois and, as assistant to the secretary of state, helped found the UNITED NATIONS. He became noted for the eloquence and wit of his speeches. Twice, in 1952 and 1956, he was the Democratic candidate for president, defeated both times by Dwight D. Eisenhower. After losing the Democratic nomination to John F. Kennedy in 1960, Stevenson was appointed in 1961 by Kennedy as chief representative to the United Nations, a post he held until his death. His son Adlai Ewing Stevenson III (1930–), represented Illinois in the U.S. Senate from 1970 to 1981 and lost bids for the governorship in 1982 and 1986.

Stewart, Jimmy (James Maitland Stewart; 1908–97), actor. Stewart earned a degree in civil engineering and architecture from Princeton (1932) before making his acting debut on Broadway. Known for his roles as clean-cut good guys and his all-American image, Stewart starred in many highly acclaimed films including *You Can't Take It with You* (1938), *Mr. Smith Goes to Washington* (1939), *It's a Wonderful Life* (1946), *Harvey* (1950), and *The Glenn Miller Story* (1953). He won a Best Actor Oscar for his performance in *The Philadelphia Story* (1940). In 1980 he was awarded an American Film Institute Lifetime Achievement Award, and in 1985 he was awarded a special career Oscar. Stewart was a decorated bomber pilot in WORLD WAR II and remained in the reserves, retiring as brigadier general in 1968.

Stewart, Martha (1941–), lifestyle entrepreneur and businesswoman. Stewart started a catering business in 1979 that eventually led to a billion-dollar media and merchandising empire devoted to home, food, and entertainment. Through books, instructional videos, a daily nationally syndicated television show, and her *Martha Stewart Living* magazine, Stewart inspires millions with her meticulous, hands-on instruction. She became one of America's wealthiest women by taking her company, Martha Stewart Omnimedia, public in 1999. Stewart was indicted in 2003 on charges of obstruction of justice, conspiracy, and lying to federal investigators, stemming from the 2001 sale of biotech stock. She pleaded innocent to all charges and resigned as CEO of Omnimedia after the indictment. In 2004 she was found guilty of all charges. She vowed to appeal her conviction.

Stieglitz, Alfred (1864–1946), photographer. While documenting the transformation of American society during the first half of the twentieth century through photography, Stieglitz led a movement called Pictorialism that promoted the photograph as art, to take its place beside painting. He was honored in 1924 by having his work requested by the Metropolitan Museum of Modern Art in New York, the first time a major American art museum considered photographs for display. At first subscribing to a theory that the subject of a photo should be in sharp focus while the secondary elements should be left out of focus, Stieglitz later pioneered a more precise and descriptive style. Through his several galleries, Stieglitz showcased the work of many modern artists including Picasso, Rodin, and Matisse. Some of his most famous pictures include *The Terminal, The Steerage,* and the portrait collection of his future wife, GEORGIA O'KEEFFE.

Stilwell, Joseph T. (1883–1946), army general during WORLD WAR II. Stilwell commanded all U.S. forces in the China-Burma-India theater and also served as chief of staff to Chiang Kai-shek, becoming the first American general to command a Chinese army. In 1942, when the Allied forces were defeated in Burma by the Japanese, Stilwell led the retreat through the jungles to India. He opened a route from India to China in 1944 and took command of the U.S. Tenth Army in Okinawa in 1945. He was called "Vinegar Joe" for his strongly stated opinions and sharp comments, including his denunciations of the corruption in Chiang's government and the reflexive anticommunism of America's China policy.

Stimson, Henry L. (1867–1950), lawyer and statesman. Stimson served as secretary of state under Herbert Hoover and was appointed secretary of war by both William Howard Taft and Franklin D. Roosevelt. In 1932 his Stimson Doctrine was criticized as an unduly mild response to the 1931 Japanese invasion of Manchuria. The doctrine (January 7, 1932) simply stated that the United States would not recognize territorial changes brought about by force or in violation of treaties. As secretary of war Stimson guided the mobilization, training, and operation of U.S. troops throughout WORLD WAR II. He served as a chief adviser to Presidents Roosevelt and Harry S. Truman on atomic policy and in 1945 headed the committee that recommended the use of the atomic bomb against Japan.

Stock Market Crash (October 29, 1929), also known as Black Tuesday, the day on which thousands of investors tried to sell their stocks, ending the prosperity of the ROARING TWENTIES. The crash was caused by the overspeculation of the 1920s; investors, taking risks in hopes of profits, bought their stock on margin with money they did not have. On that day, over 16 million shares of stock were traded. With an overabundance of sellers and few buyers, the prices of stocks dropped far below the prices paid for them, and investors lost billions of dollars in paper profits within a matter of hours. Banks and businesses had also invested in the stock market, and with the falling prices, the values of their investments plunged, causing them to fold. Although the crash did not "cause" the GREAT DEPRESSION, it was the opening event of the era.

Stone, Harlan Fiske (1872–1946), chief justice of the United States (1941–46). Stone, serving as attorney general under Calvin Coolidge, reorganized the FEDERAL BUREAU OF INVESTIGATION and named J. EDGAR HOOVER as its head. He resigned in 1925 to become associate justice of the Supreme Court. Later, as chief justice appointed by Franklin D. Roosevelt, Stone upheld many of Roosevelt's New Deal measures.

Stone, Lucy (1818–93), reformer and feminist. Stone was prominent in efforts to emancipate slaves and gain rights for women. In 1869 she cofounded, with JULIA WARD HOWE, the AMERICAN WOMAN SUFFRAGE ASSOCIATION and toured the country advocating equality for women. Stone married Dr. Henry Blackwell, also a crusader for woman suffrage, and, unusual for the time, retained her maiden name. Together they founded and edited the *Woman's Journal*, which was published for nearly fifty years. Their daughter, Alice Stone Blackwell (1857–1950), was a writer, editor, and advocate of woman suffrage.

Stone, Oliver (1946–), film director and screenwriter. The critical and popular success of *Platoon* (1986) brought Stone recognition as an independent filmmaker. Based on his wartime experiences in Vietnam, the film was nominated for eight and won four Academy Awards, including best director and best picture. Other films include *Salvador* (1986), *Born on the Fourth of July* (1989), *The Doors* (1991), *JFK* (1991), a highly controversial film about the Kennedy assassination, *Nixon* (1995), and *Any Given Sunday* (1999).

Story, Joseph (1779–1845), jurist. A Massachusetts native and Harvard graduate, Story practiced law and served in the U.S. House of Representatives (1808–09) before being appointed by President JAMES MADISON to the Supreme Court in 1811. Appointed at age thirty-two, he remains the youngest person to be selected for the Court. Known for his scholarship and great legal mind, Story helped shape American concepts of the common law; principles that had influenced the development of the Constitution and the Bill of Rights. He usually voted with Chief Justice JOHN MARSHALL's opinions, giving the federal government supremacy over the states. He held that a state court decision could be reviewed by the Court. Story later became a popular professor of law at Harvard (1829–45) and wrote a number of influential legal works, including a commentary on the U.S. Constitution.

Stowe, Harriet Beecher (1811–96), author. An abolitionist and sister of Henry Ward Beecher, Stowe wrote the influential antislavery novel *Uncle Tom's Cabin* (1852). Her book attracted international attention for its attack on the system of slavery, selling 300,000 copies in the first year. It intensified the unrest between the North and South prior to the Civil War. Stowe wrote other essays, poetry, and novels, including *Sam Lawson's Oldtown Fireside Stories* (1872), *The Minister's Wooing* (1859), *The Pearl of Orr's Island* (1862), and *Oldtown Folks* (1869).

Strategic Arms Limitation Talks (SALT), negotiations between the Soviet Union and the United States, begun in 1969 at the request of President Lyndon B. Johnson, in an attempt to limit the production and distribution of nuclear weapons and slow down the nuclear arms race. The first series of meetings occurred between 1969 and 1972 in Helsinki, Vienna, and Geneva. The second round lasted from 1972 to 1979 in Geneva. Agreements were reached in 1972 (SALT I) during the Nixon administration to put limitations on antiballistic missile systems and in 1979 (SALT II) during the Carter administration. But SALT II was not approved by the Senate partly as a protest against the 1979 Soviet invasion of Afghanistan. In 1982 the Reagan administration abandoned SALT and began a new series of negotiations called START (Strategic Arms Reduction Talks), which led to agreements in arms reductions.

Stratemeyer, Edward (1862–1930), author. Stratemeyer created some of the most popular children's book characters. A prolific writer, Stratemeyer turned out several series of books before he founded the Stratemeyer Syndicate, in which he used a staff of writers and built the largest publishing company of juvenile fiction in the country. He wrote over 160 books using many pseudonyms, and provided the plots, outlines, and characters for about eight hundred more. His best-known series include the Hardy Boys, Tom Swift, the Bobbsey Twins, and Nancy Drew, which his daughter Harriet continued under the name of Carolyn Keene after his death.

Strauss, Levi (1829?–1902), German-born clothing manufacturer. Strauss founded Levi Strauss and Co., the world's first and largest manufacturer of denim jeans. Settling in California in 1850 during the gold rush, Strauss opened a wholesale business in San Francisco and sold pants made of tent canvas to gold miners. Later, at the suggestion of Nevada tailor Jacob Davis, rivets were added to reinforce the seams, and the company expanded to produce other clothing.

Stravinsky, Igor (1882–1971), Russian-born composer. One of the most important composers of the 1900s, Stravinsky helped to revolutionize modern music with his freshness, meticulous craftsmanship, and experimentalism. Known first for his ballets, it was in his landmark *The Rite of Spring* (1913), that he departed from tradition by using primitive beats, harsh rhythms, and dissonance. Living at times in Switzerland and France, Stravinsky experimented with an austere, neoclassical style in *Octet for Wind Instruments* (1923) and *Dumbarton Oaks Concerto* (1938). He became an American citizen in 1945, turning to the controversial serial composition, in which all notes have equal importance, giving no sense of key. His serial works include *Threni* (1958) and *Elegy for J.F.K.* (1964).

Streisand, Barbra (1942–), singer and actress. Streisand achieved stardom on both stage and screen with her portrayal of comedienne FANNY BRICE in *Funny Girl* (1964; film, 1968). She won an Academy Award as best actress for her performance in the film. Respected for her dramatic interpretations of popular songs, Streisand starred in several musicals including *Hello, Dolly!* (1969), *A Star Is Born* (1976), and *Yentl* (1983), which she also directed. Nonmusical films include *The Way We Were* (1973) and *Prince of Tides* (1991), which she also directed. Streisand is active in liberal and peace causes.

Stuart, Gilbert (1755–1828), portrait painter. Of his nearly one thousand portraits, Stuart's lifelike portraits of George Washington gained the most fame. They proved so popular that he painted over one hundred replicas. One, the "Athenaeum" version, appears on the U.S. one-dollar bill. Trained in London under American artist Benjamin West, Stuart opened studios in New York, Philadelphia, Washington, D.C., and Boston. He painted many of the most prominent Americans of his day.

Stuart, J.E.B. (James Ewell Brown; 1833–64), Confederate cavalry general during the CIVIL WAR. Stuart commanded forces at BULL RUN in 1861 and later at the second Battle of BULL RUN, ANTIETAM, and FREDERICKSBURG. He served with Stonewall Jackson at CHANCELLORSVILLE and gained respect for a dash he made around Gen. George B. McClellan's army, gathering information that led to the Union defeat in the SEVEN DAYS' BATTLES. Stuart's reports of enemy troop movements were invaluable for the South. Late reaching GETTYSBURG because he was on a raid, he handicapped Robert E. Lee's efforts. Stuart was killed in a cavalry maneuver against Gen. Philip Sheridan at Yellow Tavern, Virginia.

Student Nonviolent Coordinating Committee (SNCC), civil rights organization of the 1960s (also called snick). The SNCC was founded in 1960 in North Carolina to coordinate nonviolent protests against segregation. Black and white college students organized peaceful demonstrations and helped thousands of blacks to register to vote. In 1966 STOKELY CARMICHAEL assumed leadership of SNCC. His frustration with the organization's slow progress led to the "black power" movement and rejection of white support. The organization disbanded in 1969.

Stuyvesant, Peter (1610?–1672), Dutch soldier and colonial official. Stuyvesant was the last Dutch governor of New Netherland (later New York). Prior to his appointment in 1647 to head the colony, he served in the

Dutch West India Company and as governor of Curaçao and other nearby Dutch possessions. He lost his right leg in battle against the Portuguese, replacing it with a silver-ornamented wooden peg. As administrator of New Netherland, Stuyvesant brought about major political and economic reforms, but his dictatorial style and religious intolerance angered settlers. In 1664 an English fleet, sent by Charles II of England, ordered the surrender of New Amsterdam. The citizens refused to support him or defend the city and surrendered to the enemy.

Suffrage, the right or privilege of voting. Suffrage in the United States has progressed from the colonial period, when only wealthy white males of sufficient property and acceptable religious beliefs had the *privilege* of voting, to today, when all male and female citizens over the age of eighteen, regardless of wealth, race, or religion, have the *right* to vote. Milestones in this halting progress toward universal enfranchisement include the Fifteenth Amendment (1870) to the Constitution, which prohibited discrimination against voters based on race or previous condition of servitude; the Nineteenth Amendment (1920), which granted women the right to vote; the VOTING RIGHTS ACT (1965), which helped to eradicate the remnants of discriminatory poll taxes, literacy tests, and other measures aimed at preventing southern blacks from registering to vote; and the Twenty-sixth Amendment (1971), which lowered the voting age from twenty-one to eighteen. (*See also* WOMAN SUFFRAGE and the text of the Constitution, including all amendments, in the APPENDIX.)

Sugar Act (1764), measure passed by Parliament placing heavy duties on sugar, textiles, coffee, indigo, and wine imported to the American colonies from foreign countries to help pay the costs of keeping British troops in America. It lowered the duty on molasses to discourage the smuggling that had followed the MOLASSES ACT of 1733, but raised the duty on refined sugar and other foreign goods. Unlike the Molasses Act, the Sugar Act was strictly enforced. Colonists saw it as taxation without representation, and it was one of the causes of the American Revolution.

Sullivan, Anne (1866–1936), educator. A pupil of SAMUEL GRIDLEY HOWE at the Perkins Institution for the Blind in Boston, Sullivan taught HELEN KELLER how to read and write. Nearly blind herself, Sullivan became Keller's lifelong companion. William Gibson's play *The Miracle Worker* (1959; film, 1962) dramatizes how she made contact with Keller by teaching the connection between words and objects through the sense of touch.

Sullivan, Ed (1902–74), television personality. Beginning his career as a columnist and radio emcee, Sullivan hosted television's popular variety show, *The Ed Sullivan Show* (originally *Toast of the Town*) from 1948 to 1971. Noted for his deadpan expressions and flat, monotone voice, he was often caricatured by comedians, but Sullivan's talent at discovering and publicizing newsworthy entertainers kept him at the top of television ratings for twenty-three years. The 1956 appearance of ELVIS PRESLEY was viewed by sixty million people (more than 80 percent of the television audience), the largest single audience in television history up to that time.

Sullivan, John L. (1858–1918), boxer. Called "the Great John L." and "the Boston Strong Boy," Sullivan was the last boxer to fight with bare knuckles. He won the heavyweight championship in 1882 and held the crown for ten years. An Irishman, he had a large following among Irish immigrants. He won his last bare-knuckle championship when he knocked out Jake Kilrain in 1889 after seventy-five rounds. Sullivan was inducted into the boxing Hall of Fame in 1954.

Sullivan, Louis (Henri; 1856–1924), architect. Sullivan designed the first steel-skeleton skyscraper and pioneered modern design. He established a partnership with Dankmar Adler, a well-known Chicago acoustical and structural engineer, in 1881, and together they promoted the philosophy that a building's form should express its function. Sullivan greatly influenced FRANK LLOYD WRIGHT, who studied with him. He was one of the founders of the Chicago School of Architecture and is recognized for his work on skyscrapers including the Auditorium Building (1886–89) in Chicago, the Wainwright Building (1890–91) in St. Louis, the Stock Exchange Building (1893–94), and the Guaranty (now Prudential) Building (1894–95) in Buffalo. Sullivan ended his partnership with Adler in 1895 and became an articulate spokesman for organic architecture. He died in poverty and obscurity in Chicago.

Sumner, Charles (1811–74), politician and antislavery leader. As a member of the U.S. Senate from Massachusetts from 1851 to 1874, Sumner was the Senate's chief advocate of antislavery sentiment and an eloquent orator. Following a powerful speech, which included accusations against Senator Andrew P. Butler of South Carolina, Representative Preston Brooks, Butler's nephew, attacked Sumner in the Senate with a heavy cane on May 22, 1856, inflicting injuries that prevented Sumner from returning to the Senate for three years. The event made Sumner a martyr throughout the North and intensified antislavery attitudes outside the slave states. Sumner had helped organize the FREE-SOIL PARTY in 1848 and the REPUBLICAN PARTY in 1854–55. A leading RADICAL REPUBLICAN after the Civil War, he favored harsh treatment of the South and took a prominent part in the impeachment proceedings against President Andrew Johnson.

Sunday, Billy (William; 1862–1935), evangelist and baseball player. Sunday played baseball for Chicago, Pittsburgh, and Philadelphia before undergoing a conversion experience that led him to work with the YMCA. As a Presbyterian minister, he conducted revivals all over the country, particularly during World War I. His mass meetings converted over a million people through his use of a flamboyant style involving acrobatics, his baseball background, and sophisticated high-pressure promotional techniques.

Super Bowl (since 1967), the championship game of the National Football League (NFL). Played between the winning teams of the NFL's American Football Conference (AFC) and the National Football Conference (NFC), the Super Bowl occurs in January, and the winner is recognized as the world champion. The Super Bowl has become an American cultural phenomenon, attracting over 100 million television viewers. Nielsen ratings report that ten of the top twenty television programs ever were Super Bowl Games. The broadcast has also become the premier spot for extravagant and entertaining commercials. The Dallas Cowboys hold the record for the most Super Bowl Games played, at eight; the record for most games won is five, held by both the San Francisco 49ers and the Cowboys.

Supreme Court, the highest court in the nation. The Supreme Court heads the judicial branch of the federal government. The only court specified in the Constitution (Article III), its function is threefold: to oversee the federal judicial system, to provide authoritative interpretations of federal law, and to decide major constitutional questions. Supreme Court decisions interpreting the Constitution are final, except when they are overturned by constitutional amendment. They bind all other courts in the United States in cases interpreting the Constitution. Under the JUDICIARY ACT OF 1789, which established the times of sessions and rules of procedure, the Court originally consisted of a CHIEF JUSTICE and five associate justices. Congress

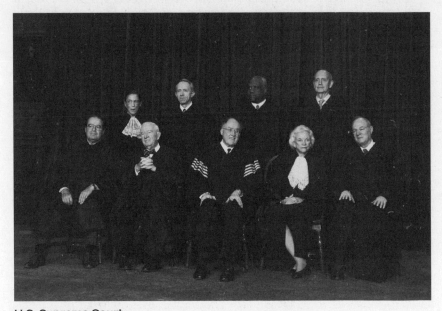

U.S. Supreme Court
The nine-member court. Seated from left: Antonin Scalia, John Paul Stevens, William H. Rehnquist, Sandra Day O'Connor, and Anthony M. Kennedy. Standing from left: Ruth Bader Ginsburg, David Hackett Souter, Clarence Thomas, and Stephen G. Breyer.

has varied the size of the Court, but since 1869 it has had a chief justice and eight associate justices, each appointed by the president with the advice and consent of the Senate. Justices serve for life or until they resign; they can be removed only through impeachment. The first chief justice, JOHN JAY, began sessions in 1789. JOHN MARSHALL, chief justice from 1801 to 1835, first made the Court a power in the government because of his exposition of the doctrine of JUDICIAL REVIEW. His decisions greatly strengthened the federal government.

Supreme Court–Packing Plan (1937), proposal by President FRANKLIN D. ROOSEVELT to reform the federal judiciary. During the 1930s, when several conservative justices were inclined to declare parts of Roosevelt's NEW DEAL program unconstitutional, Roosevelt sought to shift the power of the judicial branch by asking Congress for the power to appoint one additional judge for every justice who had reached the age of seventy but declined to retire. Opposition to the proposal was strong. Congress would not allow the number of justices to be increased, and Roosevelt was criticized for trying to undermine the independence of the Court.

Sutter, John (1803–80), German-born pioneer and settler in California. After immigrating to the United States from Switzerland in 1834, Sutter founded the colony of Nueva Helvetia (New Switzerland) on the site of present-day Sacramento. He built Sutter's Fort, a frontier trading post, and enjoyed a lucrative business. But the discovery of gold in the area brought on disaster, as squatters and fortune hunters took over his land, destroying livestock and property. Sutter died bankrupt after U.S. courts denied his claims for losses.

T

Taft, Robert A. (1889–1953), politician. As a Republican from Ohio, Taft served in the U.S. Senate from 1939 to 1953, where he was known as "Mr. Republican." An isolationist before World War II, Taft became an active backer of the United Nations after the war. As a conservative, he cosponsored the TAFT-HARTLEY ACT. The son of President William Howard Taft, he unsuccessfully sought the Republican presidential nomination in 1940, 1948, and 1952.

Taft, William Howard (1857–1930), twenty-seventh president of the United States (1909–13) and tenth chief justice of the United States (1921–30). Born in Cincinnati, Ohio, Taft graduated from Yale University. A Republican, he served as the first governor-general of the Philippines and as secretary of war under Theodore Roosevelt. Roosevelt chose Taft as the candidate to succeed him, and he defeated the Democratic candidate William Jennings Bryan in the ELECTION OF 1908. During Taft's administration, the Sixteenth Amendment was passed, allowing Congress to levy a federal income tax. Although Taft was not considered a trust-buster, he instituted twice as many antitrust proceedings as his predecessor. Taft also instituted DOLLAR DIPLOMACY, an unproductive program that promoted the use of trade and commerce to increase the nation's diplomatic influence, especially in the Caribbean and Asia. Although Taft survived a challenge for the Republican nomination in 1912, Roosevelt's formation of the PROGRESSIVE PARTY split the party, and Democratic candidate Woodrow Wilson won the election. President Warren G. Harding named Taft chief justice on the Supreme Court in 1921, the job he had always wanted. He was the only man to serve as both president and chief justice.

Taft-Hartley Act (1947), measure outlawing the closed shop, the practice of hiring only union members. The act also ordered unions to register and file their financial status with the Department of Labor, limited union political activity, and provided that strikes that would affect a national emergency be delayed for eighty days as a cooling-off period. Passed over the veto of President Harry S. Truman, the act was opposed by unions, which tried to repeal or amend it. Also called the Labor-Management Relations Act, it was cosponsored by Republican Senator ROBERT A. TAFT of Ohio and Republican Representative Fred A. Hartley, Jr., of New Jersey.

Tallchief, Maria (1925–), ballet dancer. Born to an Osage Indian father and a mother of Irish and Scottish descent, Tallchief became the first American-trained ballerina to achieve international acclaim. Dancing for the New York City Ballet from 1947 to 1965, her performance in the title role of *The Firebird* established her reputation. She received the highest salary ever paid any dancer as guest artist with the Ballet Russe de Monte Carlo in 1955 and 1956. Tallchief founded the Chicago City Ballet in 1980, serving as artistic director until 1987.

Tammany Hall, powerful political force in New York City originally formed to preserve the nation's independence. Organized in 1789 as the Society of St. Tammany, it was named after a legendary Delaware Indian chief. Eventually developing a close association with the Democratic party, Tammany Hall became a political machine dominating New York City and state politics during the nineteenth and twentieth centuries. Many scandals were connected with the organization, including the infamous 1871 affair involving WILLIAM "BOSS" TWEED and his gang, who were convicted of defrauding New York City of millions of dollars. Tammany regained power until the 1930s, revived in the 1950s, and subsequently disappeared as a political power after the 1970s.

Tampico Incident (1914), confrontation between the United States and Mexico at Tampico Bay, Mexico. An American fleet sailed to Tampico to protect American lives and property. When some American sailors were arrested by the Mexican government on April 9, 1914, the United States demanded their release and an apology. The Mexican government agreed, but when a German warship arrived with guns and supplies for the Mexicans, war threatened. President Woodrow Wilson ordered the American naval forces to occupy Tampico, and the navy bombarded Veracruz. The issue was settled through the ABC Conference held in Niagara Falls, Canada, and the United States withdrew its naval force from Mexico.

Taney, Roger B. (1777–1864), chief justice of the United States (1836–64). Taney, as attorney general and secretary of the treasury under President ANDREW JACKSON, supported Jackson's struggle against the BANK OF THE UNITED STATES by removing federal funds from the Bank. Jackson then appointed him chief justice. Taney became reviled among ABOLITIONISTS in the North because of his decisions enforcing the FUGITIVE SLAVE LAWS. He is best known for his decision in the *DRED SCOTT CASE*, ruling that a black could not be a citizen and therefore could not sue in court. He compounded his unpopularity during the Civil War by opposing Abraham Lincoln's suspension of the writ of HABEAS CORPUS.

Tanner, Henry (1859–1937), black painter. At the encouragement of his teacher, THOMAS EAKINS, Tanner began a career as a professional painter. He first gained recognition for his depiction of southern black life. Among his best-known pieces is *Banjo Lesson,* showing an old black man teaching a boy to play. Tanner moved to Paris in 1891 to escape the racial prejudice he experienced in the United States. His later paintings on religious themes show the influence of Rembrandt in their warm colors and dramatic contrasts of light and shadow.

Tarawa, Battle of (November 21–24, 1943), one of the bloodiest battles of WORLD WAR II between American and Japanese forces. Tarawa, one of the Gilbert Islands in the South Pacific, was occupied by the Japanese in 1942. As part of the Allied island-hopping campaign toward the Philippines, U.S. Marines bombarded the island, meeting heavy Japanese resistance but forcing an evacuation. In four days of fighting, 4,500 Japanese soldiers died, leaving fewer than 20 alive; 3,000 Marines were killed or wounded.

Tarbell, Ida (1857–1944), historian, journalist, and reformer. Tarbell became famous as a leading MUCKRAKER through her series of articles in *McClure's* magazine on political and corporate corruption. Her *History of the Standard Oil Company* (1904) led to the outlawing of monopolies in the United States. She also wrote biographies of Napoleon I and Abraham Lincoln, and an autobiography, *All in the Day's Work* (1929).

Tariff of Abominations (1828), a federal statute placing high tariffs on imports. The highest tariff imposed in America up to that time, it was labeled the "Tariff of Abominations" by southern leaders, who bitterly opposed the bill and spoke of secession. HENRY CLAY worked out the COMPROMISE TARIFF OF 1833, which reduced tariffs gradually until 1842.

Taylor, Elizabeth (1932–), English-born actress. Beginning her career as a child actress in *Lassie Come Home* (1943) and *National Velvet* (1944), Taylor became a Hollywood star. She won an Academy Award for her roles in *Butterfield 8* (1960) and *Who's Afraid of Virginia Woolf?* (1966). Other films include *Cleopatra* (1963) and *The Taming of the Shrew* (1967). Taylor is a leader in efforts to promote research on AIDS.

Taylor, Frederick W. (1856–1915), mechanical engineer and business efficiency expert. Taylor originated scientific management in business by developing detailed systems intended to gain maximum efficiency from both workers and machines in factories. These systems relied on time and motion studies, which helped determine the best methods for performing a task in the least amount of time. He is best known for his introduction of technological and organizational changes at the Midvale Steel Company in Philadelphia and the Bethlehem Steel Company. Taylor's writings on efficient and scientific management were widely read and translated into several languages, giving his ideas influence around the world. He wrote *The Principles of Scientific Management* (1915).

Taylor, Maxwell D. (1901–87), army general. During World War II Taylor commanded airborne divisions in Europe and then led U.S. forces in Korea and the Far East in 1953 and 1954 before serving as army chief of staff from 1955 to 1959. He resigned from his position because of a disagreement with President Dwight D. Eisenhower over the need for an expanded flexible army. Appointed by President John F. Kennedy, he served as chairman of the Joint Chiefs of Staff from 1962 to 1964. President Lyndon B. Johnson appointed him to serve as ambassador to South Vietnam where he urged U.S. support for the Vietnam War.

Taylor, Zachary (1784–1850), twelfth president of the United States (1849–50). Born in Montebello, Virginia, Taylor had little formal education. Because of his family's position, he gained entrance to West Point and became a career military officer. Fondly called "Old Rough and Ready" by his troops, he never lost a battle. Taylor served in the BLACK HAWK WAR and received BLACK HAWK's surrender in 1832. He participated in the SEMINOLE WARS in Florida in 1837 and in 1846 became a hero of the MEXICAN WAR, defeating Mexican forces at the Battles of PALO ALTO and Resaca de la Palma, Monterrey, and BUENA VISTA. After a forty-year military career Taylor won the presidential nomination of the Whig party in 1848 and defeated Democratic candidate Lewis Cass and Free-Soil candidate Martin Van Buren. During his brief sixteen-month administration the Clayton-Bulwer Treaty was ratified. Although a slave owner, Taylor opposed secession and did not oppose admitting California and New Mexico into the Union as free states during his administration. Taylor died of cholera while in office.

Tea Act (1773), act passed by the British Parliament removing export duties on tea to help the financially troubled British East India Company. The act allowed the company to sell tea directly to the colonies without the tea first going to Britain. Because colonial merchants were being undersold, it caused great resentment in the colonies, and protests eventually led to the BOSTON TEA PARTY.

Teagarden, Jack (1905–64), jazz musician. Teagarden became one of the few white jazz masters, arriving on the jazz scene in the 1920s with blues-inspired sound. A self-taught trombonist, he had great range and brilliant technique, which he featured with his own band (1939–46) as well as the LOUIS ARMSTRONG All-Stars. In 1951 Teagarden formed his own Dixieland sextet, which he led through the remainder of his career. Also one of the best white vocalists of the era, his relaxed, comfortable drawl is associated with "Basin Street Blues," "Stars Fell on Alabama," and "Pennies from Heaven."

Teapot Dome Scandal (1921–24), incident during the administration of President Warren G. Harding involving fraudulent leases of naval oil reserves at Teapot Dome, Wyoming, and Elk Hills, California. Secretary of the Interior Albert Fall leased the reserves to oil men Harry Sinclair and Edward Doheny in return for $300,000 in cash. In 1929 Fall was convicted of accepting bribes and was fined $100,000 and sentenced to one year in prison. He became the first cabinet member to go to jail for crimes committed while in office.

Tecumseh (1768?–1813), Shawnee chief and political leader. With the help of his brother TENSKWATAWA ("the Prophet"), Tecumseh, hoping to stop the advance of white settlers in the Old Northwest, tried to unite many of the eastern Indian tribes in a confederation. After the Indians were defeated by the Americans at the Battle of TIPPECANOE in 1811, Tecumseh joined the British forces during the WAR OF 1812. He was killed in the Battle of the Thames at Chatham, Ontario, in 1813 while leading his warriors against the invading Americans.

Teheran Conference (November 28–December 1, 1943), the first meeting of Allied leaders during WORLD WAR II. Meeting in Iran were Premier Joseph Stalin of the Soviet Union, Prime Minister Winston Churchill of Great Britain, and President Franklin D. Roosevelt of the United States. The leaders agreed to open a western front in occupied France in 1944 and settled on the Soviet Union's entering the war against Japan after Germany's defeat. They also discussed the establishment of the UNITED NATIONS at the end of the war. The success of the conference created optimism for future cooperative efforts between the war leaders, such as the YALTA CONFERENCE in 1945.

Teller, Edward (1908–2003), Hungarian-born physicist and atomic scientist. After joining the Manhattan Project in Los Alamos, New Mexico, Teller worked with ENRICO FERMI on nuclear fission. His research in nuclear physics led in 1952 to the development and production of the hydrogen bomb. From 1952 to 1960 Teller, a hard-liner in the cold war, designed nuclear weapons at the Lawrence Livermore Laboratory in Livermore, California. He received the Atomic Energy Commission's Fermi Award in 1962 for his scientific contributions.

Telstar, a series of communications satellites that used electronic equipment to amplify signals. Manufactured by Bell Telephone Laboratories for the American Telephone and Telegraph Company, which paid the National Aeronautics and Space Administration to launch them, *Telstar 1* and *Telstar 2* became the first commercial experiments of satellites in low orbits and opened an era of transatlantic television transmission. *Telstar 1* was launched by Delta Rocket from Cape Canaveral on July 10, 1962, and transmitted the first direct television pictures from the United States to Europe, becoming the first satellite to relay signals from the earth to a satellite and back. It ceased operations in 1963 after being damaged by radiation and was replaced by *Telstar 2*, launched May 7, 1963, which transmitted the first transatlantic color television program. Telstar operations ended in May 1965.

Temple Black, Shirley (1928–), film star and stateswoman. A child star of enormous popularity, Temple made her film debut at age three and sang, tap-danced, and charmed her way to stardom in twenty-five films during the 1930s, including *Little Miss Marker* (1934), *The Little Colonel* (1935), *Wee Willie Winkie* (1937), and *Rebecca of Sunnybrook Farm* (1938). Temple retired from films in 1949 and later married Charles Black. A conservative Republican, she served as U.S. representative to the United Nations (1969), ambassador to Ghana (1975), the first woman chief of protocol in the State Department (1976), and ambassador to Czechoslovakia (1989–92).

Tennessee (Volunteer State) became the sixteenth state in the Union on June 1, 1796. (See maps, pages 540 and 541.) It received its appellation because over thirty thousand men volunteered to fight in the Mexican War in 1846. During the Civil War its divided loyalties were apparent: Tennessee was the last state to secede from the Union and the first to return. The largest cities include the capital, Nashville, Memphis, Knoxville, and Chattanooga. Nashville is a mecca for fans of country western music, with the Grand Ole Opry and the Country Music Hall of Fame. Graceland, Elvis Presley's home in Memphis, has become a national shrine. The TENNESSEE VALLEY AUTHORITY, created in 1933, provides irrigation, electric power, and flood control on the Tennessee River. Leading products are tobacco, wood, textiles, chemicals, and clothing. Noted Americans born in Tennessee include DAVY CROCKETT, CORDELL HULL, and W. C. HANDY.

Tennessee Valley Authority (TVA) (1933), government agency established by NEW DEAL legislation as part of a long-range planning project to bring electricity to rural areas of the Tennessee River valley in seven states and to conserve the region's resources. The TVA was authorized to build dams to control flooding of the Tennessee River and power plants for the production and sale of electric power. Republican Senator GEORGE NORRIS of Nebraska supported the plan, which helped prevent flooding and rebuilt eroded farmland in Tennessee, Alabama, Mississippi, Kentucky, Virginia, North Carolina, and Georgia.

Tenskwatawa (1775?–1834), Shawnee Indian religious leader. An alcoholic as a young man, this younger brother of TECUMSEH experienced visions that made him stop drinking and begin to preach. Changing his name to Tenskwatawa ("open door"), he urged Indians to give up alcohol and return to their traditional ways. He joined with his brother to resist white settlers' encroaching on Indian lands. Called "the Shawnee Prophet" by whites because he predicted an eclipse of the sun, he lost prestige after the Indians' defeat at the Battle of TIPPECANOE in 1811 and lived many years thereafter on a British pension.

Tenure of Office Act (March 2, 1867), controversial law passed by Congress over President ANDREW JOHNSON's veto stating that a president could not remove without the Senate's approval an officeholder appointed with the consent of the Senate. In 1868 Johnson, believing the law to be unconstitutional, fired Secretary of War EDWIN STANTON. The House of Representatives impeached Johnson three days later for high crimes and misdemeanors. Johnson was acquitted by the Senate by one vote less than the two-thirds needed for removal. The Tenure of Office Act was repealed in 1887; in 1926 it was declared to have been unconstitutional by the U.S. Supreme Court.

Terman, Lewis (1877–1956), psychologist. Terman pioneered intelligence tests in the United States. Working at Stanford University, he conducted studies of the brightest children in California. He adapted the Binet intelligence test, creating the individually administered Stanford-Binet test, which became the most widely used of all mental tests for children. Terman introduced the term *intelligence quotient* (IQ). The reliability of his test has been questioned in recent years.

Terrell, Mary Church (1863–1954), educator and civil rights activist. Born in Memphis, Tennessee, to former slaves in the year of the EMANCIPATION PROCLAMATION, Terrell graduated from Oberlin College in Ohio (1884). An active feminist, she founded the Colored Women's League (1892), which later merged with the National Federation of Afro-American Women to become the National Federation of Colored Women; Terrell was elected its first president. A popular speaker and lecturer, she wrote many articles denouncing segregation, and her appointment to the Washington, D.C., Board of Education in 1895 became a first for an African-American woman. Terrell was a charter member of the National Association of Colored

Women (NACW) and served as its first president. She wrote an autobiography, *A Colored Woman in a White World* (1940).

Tet Offensive (January 30, 1968), massive offensive attack on South Vietnam by the North Vietnamese and the Vietcong during the VIETNAM WAR. Tet, the traditional Vietnamese lunar new year, had previously been observed with a truce. The Communists chose this day to launch their offensive, though a holiday cease-fire had been agreed upon by both sides. The attack on over one hundred cities and towns, including Saigon and Hue, was launched in hopes of sparking a rebellion against the American-backed government, but this did not happen. American military intelligence had thought the cease-fire might not be observed, but the size and scope of the attack surprised them. Many South Vietnamese civilians were tortured and murdered. By April the Tet offensive had failed militarily, and Americans had retaken the cities and towns, killing in turn thousands of Vietcong and civilians caught in the middle. The American bombings turned many of the South Vietnamese against the United States and the Saigon government. The Tet offensive also contributed to the growth of the antiwar movement among the American people.

Texas (Lone Star State) became the twenty-eighth state in the Union on December 29, 1845. (See maps, pages 540 and 541.) It won its independence from Mexico in 1836 after SAM HOUSTON and his Texas troops defeated General Santa Anna and the Mexican forces at the Battle of SAN JACINTO. It was during this war that the siege at the ALAMO took place. Sam Houston became the first president of the LONE STAR REPUBLIC, which existed as a country from 1836 to 1845, when it became part of the United States. Texas is the second largest state in size and has the third largest population. Austin is its capital, and other major cities include Houston, Dallas, San Antonio, El Paso, and Fort Worth. It leads the nation in oil, cotton, sheep, cattle, and mineral production. It also produces peanuts, poultry, and rice. Noted people born in Texas include DWIGHT D. EISENHOWER, LYNDON B. JOHNSON, JOHN NANCE GARNER, OVETA CULP HOBBY, SAM RAYBURN, and BABE DIDRIKSON ZAHARIAS.

Texas War for Independence (1835–36), a revolution by American colonists in a section of Mexico called Texas in which they secured independence and established the LONE STAR REPUBLIC. Many Americans settled in Texas during the 1820s, and by the 1830s they outnumbered the Mexicans living there. Mexico's dictator, General Santa Anna, placed heavy restrictions upon Texans, including a ban on slavery and the imposition of extra taxes. The American settlers rebelled. They won a victory at Gonzales, but were slaughtered at the ALAMO. The Texans declared independence on March 2, 1836. At SAN JACINTO, in a surprise attack on April 21, SAM HOUSTON and his forces routed the Mexican troops and captured Santa Anna.

Mexican troops withdrew from Texas, Santa Anna was released, and the independent Texas Republic was founded. It remained independent until 1845, when it consented to annexation by the United States.

Thanksgiving, an annual holiday celebrated in the United States on the fourth Thursday in November for giving thanks to God for the blessings received during the year. The first Thanksgiving was celebrated by the PILGRIMS in PLYMOUTH COLONY in 1621 in gratitude for their first harvest, which assured survival through the upcoming winter. Other Thanksgivings occurred on an irregular basis, usually determined by individual states. President George Washington proclaimed a Thanksgiving Day on November 26, 1789, to honor the adoption of the Constitution. President James Madison declared a Thanksgiving Day in 1815 to celebrate the end of the War of 1812. President Abraham Lincoln made Thanksgiving an official national holiday in 1863.

Thirteen Colonies, early settlements that eventually became the United States. The original thirteen colonies fell into three sectional groups: the New England colonies consisted of Massachusetts, Rhode Island, Connecticut, and New Hampshire; the middle colonies, New York, New Jersey, Pennsylvania, and Delaware; and the southern colonies, Maryland, Virginia, North Carolina, South Carolina, and Georgia. The population of the colonies had reached nearly 2 million by 1770.

Thomas, George (1816–70), Union general during the Civil War. As Union commander of the Army of the Cumberland, Thomas helped win the Battle of CHATTANOOGA, a major Confederate transportation center, and the Battle of Nashville. He was called "the Rock of Chickamauga" for his strong defense at the Battle of CHICKAMAUGA, which permitted an orderly Union withdrawal. Thomas commanded military governments in Kentucky and Tennessee and died while commanding the military division of the Pacific.

Thomas, Norman (1884–1968), political leader. As leader of the Socialist party from 1926 to 1955, Thomas ran unsuccessfully for the presidency six times, beginning in 1928. A Presbyterian minister, he became a pacifist and opposed U.S. entry into both world wars and the Vietnam War. An opponent of communism, Thomas campaigned for social welfare measures, civil liberties, and world peace. He helped found the AMERICAN CIVIL LIBERTIES UNION.

Thoreau, Henry David (1817–62), writer, naturalist, and abolitionist. Chiefly known for *Walden* (1854), an artistic account of his life in the woods at Walden Pond near Concord, Massachusetts (1845–47), Thoreau published only one other book, *A Week on the Concord and Merrimack Rivers* (1849). He demonstrated his opposition to slavery in 1846 when he spent time in jail for refusing to pay poll taxes. "Civil Disobedience," Thoreau's influential essay promoting passive resistance, inspired such world leaders as Leo Tolstoy, Mahatma Gandhi, and MARTIN LUTHER KING, JR. Guided by his mentor RALPH WALDO EMERSON, who encouraged and criticized his writing, Thoreau was a key figure in the philosophical movement known as transcendentalism and helped edit the *Dial,* where some of his poems and essays were published.

Thornton, William (1759–1828), physician and self-taught architect, recognized as the first architect of the U.S. Capitol. In 1792, Thornton's design for the Capitol won a national competition. Following the dismissal of PIERRE L'ENFANT in 1792, President GEORGE WASHINGTON appointed Thornton and two others commissioners of the federal district to lay out the federal city and oversee construction of the first government buildings, including the Capitol. Although praised for its beauty and simplicity, execution was difficult. BENJAMIN HENRY LATROBE succeeded Thornton in 1803 when Thornton became the first superintendent of the U.S. Patent Office, a position he held until his death.

Thorpe, Jim (1888–1953), Olympic and professional athlete of Sauk and Fox descent. In 1950 the Associated Press selected Thorpe as the greatest male athlete in the first half of the twentieth century. In the 1912 Olympic Games he became the first athlete to win gold medals and set records in both the decathlon and pentathlon. Although he was stripped of the medals because he had played semiprofessional baseball, they were returned to his family by the International Olympic Committee in 1983 after years of appeals. An all-American football player at Carlisle Indian School in Pennsylvania, Thorpe played professional football with several teams and became a charter member of the professional football Hall of Fame in 1963. At the same time Thorpe played major league baseball with three National League teams. He served as the first president of the American Professional Football Association, now known as the National Football League.

Three-fifths Compromise, a compromise at the CONSTITUTIONAL CONVENTION between northern and southern states on how slaves were to be counted for direct taxation and representation in the House of Representatives. The South believed that slaves should be considered as persons in determining population but as property in determining taxes; the North held the opposite view. The compromise provided that "three-fifths" of all slaves would be added to the number of free persons in determining the population of a state for purposes of representation and taxation.

Three Mile Island Nuclear Disaster (March 28, 1979), accident in a nuclear reactor located near Harrisburg, Pennsylvania, which lasted twelve days. A combination of improper design, equipment failure, and operator error led to a partial core meltdown in the reactor, resulting in the release of radioactive gases into the atmosphere. The core came within thirty minutes of large-scale melting, reaching a temperature of almost 5,000 degrees. About 100,000 residents of the area had to be evacuated. A federal investigation recommended revisions in the structure and function of the

Nuclear Regulatory Commission, and the construction of nuclear power plants in the United States all but ceased. Ten years later, the reactor itself was still unusable and hardly even approachable.

Thurber, James (1894–1961), humorist, cartoonist, and writer. Many of Thurber's works centered on the theme of a timid middle-aged man with rebellious children and married to a strong woman. He wrote stories and essays, and drew cartoons for the *New Yorker* magazine, including his short story "The Secret Life of Walter Mitty" (1939). Thurber's works include *Is Sex Necessary?* with E. B. White (1929), *My Life and Hard Times* (1933), and *The Middle-Aged Man on the Flying Trapeze* (1935). He coauthored a play, *The Male Animal* (1940), with Elliott Nugent.

Thurmond, J. Strom (1902–2003), politician. Thurmond was governor of South Carolina from 1947 to 1951. He served in the U.S. Senate from South Carolina from 1954, when he was elected as a write-in candidate, until 2003. A strong supporter of states' rights and racial segregation, he was originally elected as a Democrat but left the party in 1964 to join the Republicans. Thurmond ran for the presidency in the ELECTION OF 1948 as the candidate of the DIXIECRAT PARTY, opposing the Democrats' civil rights policies. He carried four states and won thirty-nine electoral votes. He served as chairman of the Senate Judiciary Committee from 1981 to 1987. He and Jesse Helms formed far-right political action committees in the 1970s. In 2002 Thurmond, age 100, became the oldest person and first centenarian to serve in the U.S. Senate. Shortly after his death in 2003 it was revealed that as a young man he fathered a child with an African-American maid who worked in his household.

Tilden, Bill (1893–1953), tennis player. The top-ranked player during the 1920s and 1930s, Tilden became a sports idol. He won seven U.S. Open championships, three Wimbledons, two professional singles championships, and seven Davis Cups during his career. His flamboyant style of play influenced the growth of tennis into a major spectator sport.

Tilden, Samuel (1814–86), political leader. Tilden was the Democratic candidate for president in the ELECTION OF 1876 after serving as reform governor of New York. He lost the election to Republican Rutherford B. Hayes by one electoral vote, even though he won the popular vote by over 250,000. Tilden had gained national prominence as the New York City district attorney who led the attack on the TWEED RING, helping convict WILLIAM "Boss" TWEED and his Tammany Hall associates.

Tippecanoe, Battle of (November 7, 1811), battle between troops led by Indiana Territory governor WILLIAM HENRY HARRISON and the Shawnee Indians led by TENSKWATAWA on the Tippecanoe River. Harrison burned the Indian village there and then withdrew. Because casualties on each side were nearly equal, the victory was indecisive, but helped make Harrison a national hero.

Tomb of the Unknowns (1921), formerly called the Tomb of the Unknown Soldier. Originally created to commemorate a serviceman killed in WORLD WAR I, the Tomb of the Unknowns is located in the ARLINGTON NATIONAL CEMETERY in Virginia. Serving as a monument to honor all war dead, it contained the remains of four unknown Americans from WORLD WAR I, WORLD WAR II, the KOREAN WAR, and (until 1998) the VIETNAM WAR. In 1998 the body of the Vietnam unknown was disinterred, identified through DNA testing, and returned to his family for burial. In 1998 the Department of Defense announced that the Vietnam crypt would remain empty, citing technological and scientific advances that made the chances of having an unknown from Vietnam very small. In a ceremony on September 17, 1999, the following inscription was dedicated on the empty crypt: "Honoring and Keeping Faith with America's Missing Servicemen."

Tompkins, Daniel D. (1774–1825), sixth vice president of the United States under James Monroe (1817–25). Tompkins served on the New York State Supreme Court and was elected governor of the state three times. He was plagued by rumors that he had cheated the state out of money, but in 1824 Congress established his innocence.

Tonkin Gulf Resolution (August 7, 1964), resolution passed by Congress concerning the VIETNAM WAR. The resolution gave President LYNDON B. JOHNSON authority to "take all necessary measures to repel any armed attack against forces of the United States and to prevent further aggression." When two North Vietnamese torpedo boats allegedly attacked U.S. ships *Maddox* and *Turner Joy* in the Gulf of Tonkin, President Johnson requested broad emergency powers and was overwhelmingly backed by Congress. The House of Representatives voted unanimously for the resolution and the Senate vote was 88 to 2, with Senators WAYNE MORSE of Oregon and Ernest Gruening of Alaska dissenting. The resolution, though short of a formal declaration of war, increased U.S. involvement in Vietnam. Many congressmen later protested that they had been deceived about the extent of the peril to U.S. forces.

Tories, colonists during the AMERICAN REVOLUTION who remained loyal to King George III. Also called Loyalists, the Tories opposed the Declaration of Independence and regarded the PATRIOTS as traitors.

Toscanini, Arturo (1867–1957), cellist and musical conductor. Toscanini, born in Italy, is recognized as one of the world's great conductors. Known for his energy, power of command, and perfectionism, he suffered from vision problems that caused him to commit scores to memory. First chief conductor and artistic director at La Scala in Milan (1898–1907, 1921–31), Toscanini's American career began as conductor of the Metropolitan Opera in New York (1908–14). After returning to Italy during World War I, he moved to the United States to conduct the New York Philharmonic Orchestra (1926–36) and the NBC Symphony Orchestra (1937–54), which was formed especially for him. His family donated his private archives to the New York Public Library in 1987.

Townsend, Francis (1867–1960), physician and advocate of social change. Townsend, who practiced medicine in southern California during the GREAT DEPRESSION, became convinced of the need for a national old-age pension. He launched the Townsend Plan in 1933, calling for pensions of $200 monthly to be financed by a 2 percent sales tax. Citizens over sixty would be eligible only if they spent the money within a month and promised not to look for work, thus, Townsend reasoned, stimulating the economy and freeing jobs for younger workers. The movement gathered an enormous following in the form of Townsend Clubs, but with the passage of the SOCIAL SECURITY ACT in 1935 and the gradual improvement of the economy, the movement dissolved.

Townshend Acts (June 15–July 2, 1767), measures passed by Parliament to raise revenue from the colonies after the repeal of the Stamp Act. Initiated by Chancellor of the Exchequer Charles Townshend, one of the acts placed duties on glass, paper, paint, lead, and tea imported into the American colonies. Another created a Board of Customs Commissioners to collect and enforce the duties. The Townshend Acts threatened colonial liberty; at the urging of the SONS OF LIBERTY, the colonists launched a boycott of British goods. In 1770 Parliament withdrew all the duties except the tax on tea, which led to the BOSTON MASSACRE, the BURNING OF THE GASPÉE (1772), and the BOSTON TEA PARTY (1773).

Tracy, Spencer (1900–67), actor. Tracy delivered two Academy Award-winning performances, in *Captains Courageous* (1937) and *Boys Town* (1938). Playing a number of versatile roles, whether rough, tough, shrewd, or sympathetic, Tracy appeared in over seventy films. He costarred with KATHARINE HEPBURN in nine films including *Pat and Mike* (1952) and *Guess Who's Coming to Dinner* (1967). He played convincing political personalities in three of his later films, *The Last Hurrah* (1958), *Inherit the Wind* (1960), and *Judgment at Nuremberg* (1963).

Trail of Tears, the name given to the forced journey of the Cherokees from Georgia to Indian Territory (modern-day Oklahoma) during the 1830s. Although Chief Justice John Marshall ruled that Indians had a right to stay in Georgia, President Andrew Jackson ordered their removal under the terms of the Indian Removal Act of 1830, intended to provide more land for white settlement. Under the supervision of Gen. WINFIELD SCOTT, the U.S. Army uprooted thousands of Indians from their homes, stripped them of their possessions, and herded them west on foot. About four thousand died on the long journey through summer heat and winter snow. The Trail of Tears became a national monument in 1987.

Transcontinental Railroad (1869), railway lines connecting the Atlantic to the Pacific. The Pacific Railway Act (1862) authorized the Union Pacific

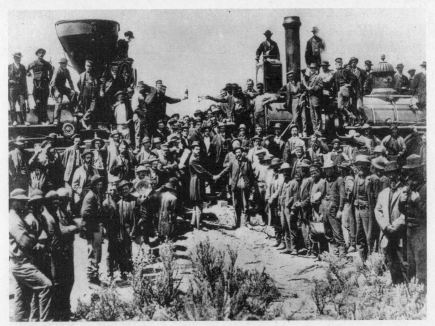

Transcontinental Railroad
Joining the tracks for the first transcontinental railway, Promontory, Utah Territory, 1869.

Railroad Company to build a line westward from Omaha, Nebraska, and the Central Pacific Railway of California to build a connecting line eastward from Sacramento. The companies recruited armies of workers in what became a competition to put down the most track. The Central Pacific hired seven thousand Chinese immigrants at one dollar a day, and the Union Pacific hired Irish immigrants. Construction began in 1865, and after years of grueling labor and hardship, the two lines met on May 10, 1869, at Promontory Point, Utah. The Central Pacific had built 689 miles of track, much of it through the Sierra Nevadas, and the Union Pacific 1,086 miles. California governor Leland Stanford, who was also president of the Central Pacific, drove in the final "golden spike" connecting the two lines.

Transportation, Department of (1966), executive department of the federal government, responsible for the development and promotion of national transportation policies and programs. Headed by the secretary of transportation, a member of the president's cabinet, the department promotes safety, conducts research, and supervises federal divisions responsible for aviation, highways, railroads, mass transit, and maritime services, as well as the St. Lawrence Seaway Development Corporation, and the National Transportation and Safety Board. The Homeland Security Act of 2002 established the DEPARTMENT OF HOMELAND SECURITY, which, in 2003, assumed management of the U.S. Coast Guard and the

Transportation Security Administration, formerly Department of Transportation agencies.

Treasury, Department of the (1789), executive department of the federal government responsible for collecting federal taxes and customs. Headed by the secretary of the treasury, a member of the president's cabinet, the department manufactures currency and coins, prepares federal securities, and prints postage stamps. It manages all money borrowed and paid out by the U.S. government and supervises national banks. Its bureaus include the U.S. Secret Service, the Internal Revenue Service, and the Bureaus of Narcotics, Engraving and Printing, Public Debt, Law Enforcement Training, Customs, the Mint, and Alcohol, Tobacco, and Firearms.

Treaty of 1818, agreement that settled a boundary dispute between the United States and Great Britain over the northern border of the Louisiana Territory. The treaty fixed the boundary at the forty-ninth parallel. It also gave the United States fishing rights off Labrador and Newfoundland and provided for joint occupation of the Oregon Territory by the United States and Great Britain for a ten-year renewable period.

***Trent* Affair** (November–December 1861), naval incident between Great Britain and the United States during the CIVIL WAR. Two Confederate diplomats, James Mason and JOHN SLIDELL, were sent to Europe to enlist the aid of neutral France and England for the Southern cause. Sailing on the British ship *Trent,* they were taken prisoner by Union captain Charles Wilkes and sent to Boston. The British government demanded an apology for this violation of international law and almost joined the war on behalf of the South. The envoys were released on order of President Abraham Lincoln and went on to Europe, but their mission was unsuccessful.

Trenton, Battle of (December 26, 1776), engagement between George Washington's forces and HESSIANS during the AMERICAN REVOLUTION. During the night of December 25 Washington made his famous crossing of the Delaware River from Pennsylvania and the next morning surprised the sleeping Hessians, who were supposed to guard the town of Trenton, New Jersey. The British commander suffered fatal wounds, and the Americans captured about a thousand prisoners. This victory, coupled with a victory at Princeton, helped raise American morale and encouraged enlistment in the Continental army.

Trevino, Lee (1939–), golfer. Trevino's winning streak of the Canadian, U.S., and British Opens earned him numerous awards including the Professional Golf Association (PGA) player of the year and *Sports Illustrated* sportsman of the year. In 1975 he was struck by lightning at the Western Open, leading to back problems. Trevino, a popular favorite for his constant chatter, quick wit, and jokes, has a following of fans called "Lee's Fleas." Trevino retired from the PGA tour in 1985 with thirty-four victories.

Triangle Shirtwaist Fire (March 25, 1911), tragedy at the Triangle Shirtwaist Company, which led to improvements in job safety. A fire swept through the eighth floor of a factory in the Greenwich Village section of New York City, lasting thirty minutes. Because there were no fire escapes and exit doors were locked by management to keep the workers from stepping outside for a break, 146 workers, mostly young women, died. Max Blanck and Isaac Harris, co-owners of the company, were indicted for first and second degree manslaughter. When they were acquitted, public outrage over the tragedy intensified and provoked demands for reform. The incident led to numerous new factory inspection laws and improved sanitary and safety conditions in industry. It also boosted the International Ladies Garment Workers Union, which had been formed in 1900.

Triangular Trade, profitable trade routes connecting the northern colonies, the West Indies, and England or Africa. The most infamous of the triangular trade routes involved the shipping of molasses and sugar from the West Indies to New England, where it was made into rum; then the New England rum went to West Africa, where it was traded for slaves who were shipped from West Africa to the West Indies. There the slaves were "seasoned" and auctioned off to plantation owners in the southern colonies.

Trudeau, Garry (1948–), cartoonist and cultural critic. In 1975 Trudeau became the first comic strip artist to receive the Pulitzer Prize for editorial cartooning. His "Doonesbury" satirizes public figures and politics.

Truman, Harry S. (1884–1972), thirty-third president of the United States (1945–53). Born in Lamar, Missouri, Truman served in World War I. After serving as vice president for only eighty-two days, Truman became president during one of the most critical moments in American history, when Franklin D. Roosevelt died on April 12, 1945. Involved deeply in World War II, the United States, during the first weeks of Truman's administration, was victorious in Europe. Truman then made the decision to use the ATOMIC BOMB against Japan to put an end to the war. The first bomb was dropped on Hiroshima on August 6, 1945, and the second on Nagasaki on August 9, 1945, forcing a Japanese surrender. Truman conferred with Joseph Stalin, Winston Churchill, and later Clement Attlee at POTSDAM in 1945 to secure peace for the postwar world. In 1947 he proposed the TRUMAN DOCTRINE as a keystone of American foreign policy, followed by the MARSHALL PLAN and the development of the policy of containing Soviet Union expansion. In the ELECTION OF 1948, Truman won over Republican Thomas Dewey in a great political upset. He set forth his administration's domestic program, calling it the FAIR DEAL, and promoted the NORTH ATLANTIC TREATY ORGANIZATION in 1949. Truman became a vigorous supporter of South Korea when the KOREAN WAR broke out in 1950. He sparked controversy in 1951 when he relieved Gen. DOUGLAS MACARTHUR from command in

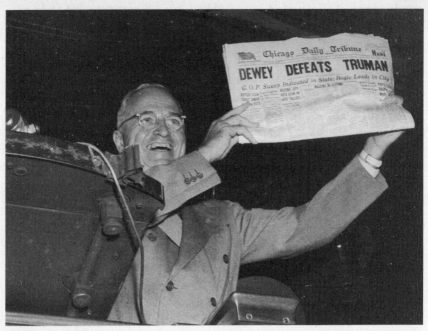

Harry S. Truman
The famous photograph of Truman after his surprise victory in the 1948 election, holding up the headline falsely announcing his defeat.

Korea for insubordination. Truman decided against running for reelection in 1952 and retired to his home in Independence, Missouri.

Truman Doctrine (March 12, 1947), plan of international resistance to communist expansion. In an address to Congress, President HARRY S. TRUMAN declared it to be the foreign policy of the United States to grant moral and economic assistance to any country whose stability was threatened by communism or the Soviet Union. Congress then voted for financial and military aid to Greece and Turkey, totaling $400 million. The Truman Doctrine led to the MARSHALL PLAN later the same year.

Trumbull, John (1756–1843), painter. Trumbull, an aide to George Washington during the AMERICAN REVOLUTION, studied painting with BENJAMIN WEST in London. Known for his portraits of George Washington, Alexander Hamilton, and other leaders, Trumbull also painted American historical events; works include *The Battle of Bunker Hill*, *The Declaration of Independence*, and *The Surrender of Lord Cornwallis at Yorktown*.

Trumbull, Lyman (1813–96), jurist and politician. Trumbull served as a Republican senator from Illinois from 1855 and 1873 and helped draft the Thirteenth Amendment to the Constitution, making slavery unconstitutional, and the Fourteenth Amendment, giving ex-slaves the rights of citizenship. He supported Abraham Lincoln and was one of the few Republicans who

★ Sojourner Truth

An excerpt from a speech proclaiming women's equal right to vote

Look at my arm! I have ploughed and planted and gathered into barns . . . and ain't I a woman? I could work as much and eat as much as a man — when I could get it — and bear the lash as well . . . I have borne thirteen children and seen most of 'em sold into slavery, and when I cried out with my mother's grief, none but Jesus helped me — and ain't I a woman?

supported Andrew Johnson during his impeachment trial. Trumbull also urged civil service reform legislation and served as counsel to presidential hopeful SAMUEL TILDEN before the electoral commission in 1876.

Truth, Sojourner (1797?–1883), evangelist, abolitionist, and feminist. Born into slavery as Isabella Baumfree, Truth escaped in 1827 to a Quaker family named Van Wagener (whose name she took) shortly before mandatory emancipation in New York State. In 1843, after changing her name again to Sojourner Truth, she became the first black woman orator to speak out against slavery and became well known for her quick wit, inspiring faith, and powerful oratory. She traveled widely throughout New England and the Midwest and in 1850 joined the struggle for equal rights for women. Truth visited Abraham Lincoln in the White House in 1864, pledging her support, and stayed in Washington, D.C., to try to improve the living conditions of blacks.

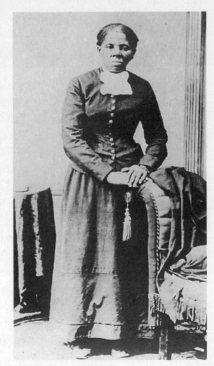

Harriet Tubman

Tubman, Harriet (1821?–1913), abolitionist, spy, and scout on the UNDERGROUND RAILROAD during the 1850s. Tubman, who was called "the Moses of her people," traveled to the South at least nineteen times to lead more than three hundred slaves to freedom in the northern states and Canada via the Underground Railroad. An escaped slave herself, Tubman had fled to Philadelphia from Maryland in 1849 and received financial help from the ABOLITIONISTS in New York and Boston for her rescue work. At one time the reward for her capture reached $40,000, but she successfully eluded bounty hunters. During the CIVIL WAR Tubman served as a nurse, scout, and spy for the Union in Florida and the Carolinas. After the war she turned her residence into the Home for Indigent and Aged Negroes.

Tunney, Gene (James Joseph; 1898–1978), boxer. Tunney stunned the boxing world by defeating JACK DEMPSEY in ten rounds for the world heavyweight championship in 1926. He defended his title against Dempsey in 1927, winning a decision in the famous "long count" match, and retired the following year.

Turner, Frederick Jackson (1861–1932), historian. Turner's influential paper "The Significance of the Frontier in American History" (1893) presented the theory that an abundance of free land strengthened democratic beliefs and national development in the United States. Turner viewed the frontier as a process in constant change, formed by the area's natural resources and the heritage and beliefs of the people who moved into it. He won the Pulitzer Prize for history in 1933 for *Significance of Sections in American History* (1932).

Turner, Nat. *See* NAT TURNER'S REBELLION.

Turner, Ted (Robert Edward, III; 1938–), business executive and sportsman. Turner took the advertising business he inherited from his father and expanded into television in 1970. In 1975 he transformed WTBS into the first "superstation" by transmitting programs by satellite to cable networks throughout the United States. In 1980 Turner established the Cable News Network (CNN), the first twenty-four-hour newscast station. An avid sportsman, Turner purchased the Atlanta Braves baseball team and the Atlanta Hawks basketball team and won the America's Cup yachting race against an Australian team in 1977. His Turner Broadcasting System, Inc. merged with Time Warner Inc. in 1995 with Turner as vice chairman, head of Time Warner's cable network division. In 2000 Time Warner merged with AOL to become AOL Time Warner, and Turner resigned in 2003.

Turner's contributions to charities have been considerable. In 1994 he personally gave $200 million to charity and his 1998 gift of $1 billion to the United Nations may be the largest single donation by a private individual in history.

Twain, Mark *See* SAMUEL CLEMENS.

Tweed, William Marcy "Boss" (1823–78), political boss and criminal. Known as Boss Tweed, he served as New York City commissioner of public works in 1870. Tweed helped set in motion a series of frauds and corrupt deals that drained millions of dollars from the New York City treasury. Through his control of TAMMANY HALL, Tweed and his associates, known as the TWEED RING, dominated the New York City government. Arrested for fraud, Tweed escaped from jail to Spain in 1875. In 1876 he was identified by a Spanish police officer from one of THOMAS NAST's cartoons and was arrested and returned to the United States for trial. He died in prison before his trial began.

Tweed Ring, a group of corrupt New York City politicians led by "Boss" William Marcy Tweed, the leader of TAMMANY HALL. After the Civil War the Tweed Ring stole millions of dollars from New York City through bribery, padded contracts, and other dishonest practices. The efforts of district attorney SAMUEL TILDEN, editorial cartoonist THOMAS NAST, and other reformers aroused public opinion against the Tweed Ring's corruption. Many members of the ring, including Tweed himself, were tried, convicted, and sent to jail.

Tyler, John (1790–1862), tenth president of the United States (1841–45). Tyler served in the U.S. House of Representatives as a Democrat, as governor of Virginia, and as a U.S. senator from Virginia. In 1840 he became the WHIG PARTY'S vice-presidential candidate with presidential nominee William Henry Harrison. When Harrison died April 4, 1841, after serving only one month, Tyler became the first vice president to succeed to the presidency because of the death of a president. During his administration the WEBSTER-ASHBURTON TREATY (1842) was negotiated between the United States and Canada, and TEXAS was annexed in 1845. Tyler used the president's veto power to block many of the Whigs' domestic programs, and because of his opposition to Whig policies, he was not renominated for president in 1844.

Tyler, Royall (1757–1826), author and lawyer. Tyler was a successful lawyer and judge, but it is for his writing that he is remembered. In 1787 he wrote a play entitled *The Contrast,* the first comedy written by an American to be professionally produced. It contrasted American honesty with British snobbishness and introduced the character of Jonathan, the first of many stage Yankees. The play was very popular and served as a model of American comedy for over fifty years.

U **U-2 Incident** (May 1, 1960), in which an American U-2 spy plane was shot down over the USSR in 1960. While photographing troop movements and missile sites, pilot Francis Gary Powers (1929–77) was shot down and captured by the Soviets. Although the United States had routinely flown such missions for four years, President Dwight Eisenhower at first denied Powers had been spying, but had to admit it when the Soviets produced Powers and the plane. The incident led Soviet premier Nikita Khrushchev to cancel a planned summit meeting with Eisenhower, heightening tensions during the COLD WAR. Powers, imprisoned in the Soviet Union, was released in exchange for Soviet spy Rudolf Abel in 1962.

Uncle Sam, symbol of the United States, which first came into use during the War of 1812 as a derogatory name for troops. It may have come from the letters "US" on government uniforms and property. In 1961 Congress asserted that Samuel "Uncle Sam" Wilson, a supplier of provisions to the army, was the inspiration for the symbol. Cartoonist THOMAS NAST created the popular image of today: a tall, slender gentleman with long white hair and beard, dressed in a coat decorated with stars, a pair of striped trousers, and a top hat.

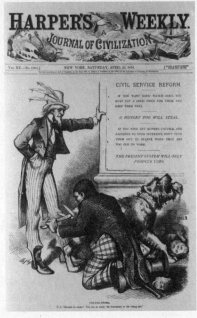

Uncle Sam
A Thomas Nast depiction of Uncle Sam.

Uncle Tom's Cabin, antislavery novel written by HARRIET BEECHER STOWE in 1852. To expose the evils of slavery, Stowe wrote a melodrama about the compliant slave, Uncle Tom, who lives under three slaveholders and dies from a beating. Simon Legree, who whips his slaves and cares only for money, became a classic villain of American literature. Stowe portrayed slaves as feeling human beings, something new to American fiction at the time. The book, an immediate best-seller, sold 300,000 copies within one year and ultimately about 7 million worldwide. It was made into a successful play, playing to packed houses throughout the North, and changed the attitudes of many northerners toward slavery.

Underground Railroad, secret route of safe houses used by runaway slaves to escape to the northern states and Canada. Although neither a railroad nor underground, it was so named to assure secrecy. "Stations" were barns, stables, or houses with hiding places. "Conductors" were escaped slaves such as HARRIET TUBMAN.

Underwood Tariff Act (October 3, 1913), act passed by Congress during the administration of Woodrow Wilson that lowered tariffs on hundreds of items that could be produced more cheaply in the United States than abroad. Sponsored by Representative Oscar W. Underwood of Alabama (1862–1929), the tariff reduced the rates of the Payne-Aldrich Tariff (1909) by about 10 percent. As the first bill since the Civil War to lower tariff rates, the Underwood Tariff included an income tax to make up for the loss in revenues caused by the lower tariffs.

Union, northern states during the CIVIL WAR. They included Oregon, California, Kansas, Minnesota, Iowa, Wisconsin, Illinois, Michigan, Indiana, Ohio, Pennsylvania, New York, Vermont, New Hampshire, Maine,

Massachusetts, Rhode Island, Connecticut, and New Jersey, and the border states of Delaware, Maryland, Missouri, and Kentucky. West Virginia separated from Virginia in 1861 and joined the Union in 1863. More broadly, the Union refers to the United States of America.

Union Party (also called National Union party), the name used by the RE-PUBLICAN PARTY during the ELECTION OF 1864. To unite Republicans, who advocated abolition of slavery, and northern Democrats who supported Abraham Lincoln (War Democrats) and to emphasize preservation of the Union by merging all antislavery forces in the North regardless of partisanship, Lincoln called the alliance the National Union, or Union party. Andrew Johnson, a War Democrat, was nominated for vice president and the party won the election.

Unitas, John (1933–2002), football player. Unitas won the National Football League most valuable player award three times and the Jim Thorpe Trophy twice. A star quarterback for the Baltimore Colts for seventeen seasons, he led the Colts to two NFL titles in 1958 and 1959 and to a Super Bowl championship in 1971. Unitas was named Associated Press man of the decade for the 1960s and the NFL man of the year in 1970. After playing for the San Diego Chargers in 1973–74, he became a sports analyst and joined the professional football Hall of Fame in 1979.

United Mine Workers of America (UMW), an industrial labor union representing workers in most of the coal mines and coal-processing industries of the United States. Formed in Columbus, Ohio, in 1890, the UMW gained recognition under the leadership of John Mitchell during the early 1900s. The UMW belonged to the AMERICAN FEDERATION OF LABOR (AFL) until 1936, helped form the CONGRESS OF INDUSTRIAL ORGANIZATIONS (CIO) in 1935, but withdrew in 1942. Except for a brief period when it rejoined the AFL in 1946–47, it has remained independent. JOHN L. LEWIS served as president from 1920 to 1960, leading the union to progressive reforms and increased membership. Its numbers, however, then declined — from 500,000 in 1946 to fewer than 65,000 in 1990.

United Nations (October 24, 1945), international organization formed after World War II that works for world peace and security, and seeks cooperation in solving cultural, economic, humanitarian, and social problems. At the United Nations Conference on International Organization in San Francisco in 1945, delegates from fifty nations developed a peace plan and outline for international cooperation called the Charter of the United Nations. The Charter was signed by all fifty nations, and since then over one hundred other nations have joined. Each member nation sends representatives to U.N. headquarters in New York City. The United Nations seeks the causes of incipient wars and tries to eliminate them before fighting occurs. If war breaks out, the United Nations may try to stop it, and once fighting stops, it will try to keep it from starting again. The six major organs, provided for in the Charter, are the General Assembly, the Security Council, the Secretariat, the Economic and Social Council, the International Court of Justice, and the Trusteeship Council. The Secretariat, headed by a secretary general, handles administrative functions. Other specialized agencies deal with such problems as agriculture, health, communications, and living and working conditions around the world.

United States v. *Nixon* (1974), unanimous ruling by the U.S. Supreme Court stating that President Richard M. Nixon's secret taped conversations with White House aides were to be released to the federal grand jury investigating the WATERGATE scandal. The justices held that the president could in theory withhold information under the doctrine of executive privilege but that federal judges had the final say in balancing the need for secrecy against the need for disclosure. Nixon's claim of executive privilege was rejected because national security issues were not at stake.

Updike, John (1932–), writer and critic. Updike's works deal with the tensions and anxieties of American middle-class life. His series of novels about an everyday American named Harry "Rabbit" Angstrom received both critical and popular praise. *Rabbit Is Rich* (1981) won a Pulitzer Prize and an American Book Award. Other works include *Couples* (1968), *Bech: A Book* (1970), and *The Witches of Eastwick* (1984). Updike has also written literary criticism, poetry, plays, short stories, and stories for children.

U.S.A. Patriot Act (October 26, 2001), legislation of the GEORGE W. BUSH administration in the aftermath of the SEPTEMBER 11, 2001, ATTACKS on the WORLD TRADE CENTER and PENTAGON. Introduced on October 23, it was passed that same day by the House 356 to 66. The Senate passed the bill 98 to 1, and the president signed it into law on October 26, approximately seventy-two hours after it was first introduced. The act gives federal investigators sweeping new powers to probe terrorism. Among its provisions, it allows the government much greater freedom to share information, seize property, expand wiretaps, track electronic and Internet communications, and conduct searches. It triples the number of personnel along U.S. borders and expands the powers of the attorney general to detain any foreigner believed to be involved in terrorist activity. Many oppose the law, saying it threatens civil liberties and violates the Constitution by giving law enforcement too much power.

Utah (Beehive State) became the forty-fifth state in the Union on January 4, 1896. (See maps, pages 540 and 541.) In 1847 BRIGHAM YOUNG initiated white settlement of Utah by leading the MORMONS to their new home near the Great Salt Lake. A year later swarms of crickets started to eat all of the crops, but seagulls flew in from the lake and ate the crickets, saving the Mormons from disaster. The seagull, therefore, became the state bird. In 1869 the TRANSCONTINENTAL RAILROAD met at Promontory Point, connecting the east and west by rail. The Great Salt Lake is four times saltier than the ocean, and the Bonneville Salt Flats, where auto racing takes place, is part of the Great Salt Lake Desert. Utah's largest cities include Salt Lake City (the capital), Provo, and Ogden. Tourism, manufacturing, and mining are the major industries. Notable people born in Utah include William Dudley ("Big Bill") Haywood, organizer of the INDUSTRIAL WORKERS OF THE WORLD, and Maude Adams, actress.

Valentino, Rudolph (Rodolfo d'Antonguolla; 1895–1926), Italian-born silent film star. Known for his dark, brooding good looks, Valentino became the leading romantic screen idol of the Roaring Twenties after achieving stardom in *The Four Horsemen of the Apocalypse* (1921). In his brief five-year career he aroused female adulation in such films as *The Sheik* (1921), *Blood and Sand* (1922), *Monsieur Beaucaire* (1924), and *The Eagle* (1925). His sudden death from peritonitis caused mass hysteria among his fans.

Vallandigham, Clement (1820–71), politician. Vallandigham, a Democrat, represented Ohio in the U.S. House of Representatives from 1857 to 1863. An opponent of federal policy during the CIVIL WAR, he became a leader of the Peace Democrats, or COPPERHEADS, in the North. Vallandigham opposed Abraham Lincoln's Civil War policies and advocated compromise with the South, leading to his imprisonment in 1863. Lincoln ordered his release and banishment to the Confederacy. Escaping to Canada and eventually to Ohio, Vallandigham never regained political stature.

Valley Forge, the site in Pennsylvania where, from December 19, 1777, to June 19, 1778, the American forces, led by Gen. GEORGE WASHINGTON, camped. Coming on the heels of defeats at Brandywine and Germantown during the AMERICAN REVOLUTION, the winter at Valley Forge was the darkest hour of the Revolution for the colonists. Neglected by the Continental Congress, the men lacked food, clothing, shoes, and supplies. Of an estimated 10,000 troops, about 2,500 died. By spring, however, under the tutelage of BARON VON STEUBEN, the Continental army had become disciplined and well trained. The area now is a national historic park.

Van Buren, Martin (1782–1862), eighth president of the United States (1837–41) and vice president under ANDREW JACKSON (1833–37). Born in the Dutch community of Kinderhook, New York (the first president to be born after the Revolution), Van Buren became a leader of the DEMOCRATIC PARTY in the state of New York. Before joining the U.S. Senate in 1821 he established the "Albany Regency," a political organization to run the state in his absence. In the Senate Van Buren successfully led the fight to abolish debtors' prison and tried to stop the extension of the slave trade.

As a supporter of Andrew Jackson for president in the ELECTION OF 1828, Van Buren ran for and won the post of governor of New York to ensure that Jackson would receive the state's electoral votes. Jackson rewarded him by appointing him secretary of state in 1829. Van Buren supported Jackson's unpopular policies toward the BANK OF THE UNITED STATES and stood by him when Jackson reorganized his cabinet during the EATON AFFAIR. In 1831 Van Buren was, by one vote, denied confirmation as minister to Great Britain by anti-Jackson forces in Congress. Van Buren, for his loyalty, became Jackson's chosen successor, first as Jackson's running mate in the ELECTION OF 1832, when they won handily, and then as presidential nominee in the ELECTION OF 1836 when Jackson stepped down. Van Buren defeated the Whig WILLIAM HENRY HARRISON.

Van Buren's term as president was a rocky one. The panic of 1837 ushered in a depression, causing hundreds of banks to fail. Van Buren's laissez-faire measures to alleviate the economic distress in the country were seen as inadequate, and this, along with an aggressive campaign by Harrison and the Whigs, cost him the ELECTION OF 1840. He tried again for the nomination in 1844, but was defeated by expansionists and southerners because of his opposition to the annexation of Texas and to the extension of slavery to the territories. The FREE-SOIL PARTY nominated him in 1848 to run for president, but he suffered defeat again.

Vandenberg, Arthur (1884–1951), politician. Vandenberg was active in formulating U.S. foreign policy following World War II. Representing Michigan, he became a Republican leader during his terms in the Senate from 1928 and 1951. He was a delegate to the UNITED NATIONS conference in San Francisco in 1945 and to the U.N. General Assembly in 1946. As chairman of the Senate Foreign Relations Committee, he led Senate approval of the Marshall Plan and encouraged the formation of the North Atlantic Treaty Organization (NATO).

Vanderbilt, Cornelius (1794–1877), financier and businessman. Vanderbilt, called "Commodore" because of his shipping interests, amassed a steamship and railroad empire and pioneered the nation's transportation system. Beginning by forming ferry and schooner service in New York and along the East Coast, Vanderbilt eventually established a shipping line from the East Coast to California via Nicaragua during the gold rush. When river traffic fell during the Civil War, Vanderbilt gained control of the New York and Harlem Railroad in 1863 and the Hudson River Railroad in 1865. He merged these lines in 1869 with the New York Central Railroad, and by 1873 his lines stretched from New York City to Chicago. Vanderbilt's questionable business tactics contributed to instability in the stock market, and Congress and other authorities investigated his operations. He left a fortune of over $100 million to his family and endowed Vanderbilt University in Tennessee.

Vaudeville, popular type of stage entertainment consisting of a variety of acts including plays, songs, dances, monologues, juggling, gymnastics, and comedy routines. Flourishing in the United States between 1880 and 1930, vaudeville suffered a setback with the development of radio and sound motion pictures but served as a starting place for many stars. Well-known vaudeville performers were actress Lillian Russell, magician HARRY HOUDINI, songwriter GEORGE M. COHAN, and comedians WILL ROGERS, W. C. FIELDS, GEORGE BURNS, and JACK BENNY.

Vaughan, Sarah (1924–90), jazz singer and pianist. Born in Newark, New Jersey, Vaughan began singing gospel music as a child. She won a talent competition at the Apollo Theater in Harlem, catching the attention of singer Billy Eckstine and bandleader EARL HINES, who signed her to sing and play piano. Vaughn was best known for her multi-octave range, with its sweeping highs and deep lows. Nicknamed Sassy, she launched her solo career in 1946, becoming an international star and one of the top female singers of her time. She expanded her audiences during the 1950s as she added pop to her repertoire, singing to sellout crowds well into her sixties.

Veblen, Thorstein (1857–1929), economist, social critic, and author. Veblen taught at many leading universities including Stanford, the University of Chicago, and the New School for Social Research during the 1890s and the first quarter of the twentieth century. A noted social critic, he wrote the influential *Theory of the Leisure Class* (1899), in which he protested false values and waste in American society.

V-E Day (May 8, 1945), Victory in Europe Day. In WORLD WAR II, V-E Day was the day following Germany's unconditional surrender to the Allies.

Venezuela Boundary Dispute (1895), conflict between Great Britain and Venezuela over the boundary between British Guiana and Venezuela; the controversy arose when gold was discovered in the disputed area. In 1895 Secretary of State Richard Olney declared that Great Britain's claim to this territory violated the MONROE DOCTRINE and demanded a settlement. The threat of war was averted when Great Britain agreed to arbitration in 1897. A Paris tribunal in 1899 awarded the land taken for gold back to Venezuela; the rest of the land in dispute reverted to Great Britain.

Vermont (Green Mountain State) became the fourteenth state in the Union on March 4, 1791. (See maps, pages 540 and 541.) Its name comes from the French words for "green mountains." Originally the colonies of New York and New Hampshire disputed possession of the region between the Connecticut and Hudson rivers for nearly a century. In 1761 Great Britain awarded the territory to New York, but settlers in the region thought of themselves as independent from that colony. Led by ETHAN ALLEN, the settlers supported independence in 1776, and it was Allen's GREEN MOUNTAIN BOYS who captured Fort Ticonderoga. In 1777 delegates from the region at a meeting declared it a republic independent not only from Great Britain but from New York and New Hampshire as well. Vermont continued as an independent republic until 1791, when it became the first new state to join the Union.

Major cities include Montpelier, its capital, Burlington, and Rutland. Vermont leads the United States in maple syrup production. Other important products include cattle, asbestos, granite, marble, and slate. Tourism is an important industry, with skiing a top attraction. Noted Americans born in Vermont include CHESTER A. ARTHUR, CALVIN COOLIDGE, JOHN DEERE, JOHN DEWEY, GEORGE DEWEY, STEPHEN A. DOUGLAS, and JAMES FISK.

Versailles, Treaty of (June 28, 1919), peace agreement ending WORLD WAR I. Drawn up at the Paris Peace Conference, the treaty was signed by the United States, Great Britain, France, Italy, Japan, and the other Allied powers, and Germany. It put the blame on Germany for starting the war, calling for the payment of heavy reparations to the Allies and for Germany's immediate disarmament. Because the treaty included the Covenant of the LEAGUE OF NATIONS, the United States was the only Allied country not to ratify it; opposition to the League of Nations in the Senate led that body to reject it. A separate peace treaty between the United States and Germany was concluded in 1921 (the Treaty of Berlin). The severe terms of the Treaty of Versailles led to German resentment, which contributed to the rise of Adolf Hitler and Nazism, and ultimately World War II.

Vesey, Denmark (1767?–1822), free black insurrectionist. Vesey purchased his freedom from slavery in 1800. In 1822 he secretly planned an uprising of some nine thousand slaves in and around Charleston, South Carolina. When the plot was discovered, Vesey and the participants were seized. They were put on trial and thirty-five, including Vesey, were found guilty and hanged, while four white men involved were fined and imprisoned. News of the conspiracy created fear among whites, who adopted harsher laws affecting blacks and more vigorously enforced existing laws.

Veterans Affairs, Department of (VA), cabinet-level department of the federal government that administers laws and authorizes benefits for veterans of U.S. military service, their dependents, and the dependents of deceased veterans. Benefits include medical care and treatment, disability payments, pensions, education assistance, rehabilitation, home loans, death compensation and burial assistance, and life insurance. The Department of Veterans Affairs was created on March 15, 1989, from the Veterans Administration, an independent government agency established in 1930.

Vice Presidency, the second highest executive office in the U.S. government. The vice president is first in line to succeed to the presidency in the event of the president's death, resignation, or removal from office. Official duties are few. The vice president presides over the U.S. Senate but can vote only in case of a tie. The vice president presides over impeachment trials, but not if the case involves the president or vice president. Nine vice presidents have succeeded to the presidency, four of them because of assassination of the president. (SEE TABLE.) The Twenty-fifth Amendment to the

Vice-Presidential Succession to the Presidency

Vice Presidents	Year	Reason
John Tyler	1841	William Henry Harrison's death
Millard Fillmore	1850	Zachary Taylor's death
Andrew Johnson	1865	Abraham Lincoln's assassination
Chester A. Arthur	1881	James Garfield's assassination
Theodore Roosevelt	1901	William McKinley's assassination
Calvin Coolidge	1923	Warren G. Harding's death
Harry S. Truman	1945	Franklin D. Roosevelt's death
Lyndon B. Johnson	1963	John F. Kennedy's assassination
Gerald Ford	1974	Richard M. Nixon's resignation

Constitution, passed in 1967, provides that when a vacancy occurs, a new vice president is appointed by the president and confirmed by a vote of both houses of Congress. The first appointed vice president was Gerald Ford, appointed by President Richard M. Nixon when Vice President Spiro Agnew resigned in 1973. When Nixon in turn resigned, President Ford appointed Nelson Rockefeller in 1974.

Vicksburg, Battle of (May 19–July 4, 1863), major military engagement of the CIVIL WAR. Guarding the Mississippi River between Memphis and New Orleans, the heavily armed Confederate city of Vicksburg, Mississippi, proved a challenge to Union general ULYSSES S. GRANT, who sought to split the Confederacy in two. After his attacks had been repeatedly repulsed by the Confederates, Grant laid siege to the city, approaching from the south and east. For six weeks the bombardment continued. Finally outmanned and out of food and supplies, Confederate general John Pemberton surrendered to Grant on July 4, 1863 (one day following the Southern defeat at Gettysburg), thus giving control of the Mississippi River to the North and dividing the Confederacy.

Vidal, Gore (Eugene Vidal, Jr.; 1925–), writer and critic. Best known for his novels, Vidal has written of political power and corruption in American politics in *Washington, D.C.* (1967), *Burr* (1974), and *Lincoln* (1984). He has also written essays, short stories, and plays, including a fantasy, *Visit to a Small Planet* (1957), and a political drama, *The Best Man* (1960). Vidal's satires of modern life include *Myra Breckenridge* (1968), *Myron* (1974), and *Kalki* (1978). He served as a television political commentator and made several unsuccessful bids for political office as a liberal Democrat.

Vietnam War (1955–75), military conflict in Vietnam between the U.S.-backed South Vietnamese government and the Communist-led guerrilla forces backed by North Vietnam. The war, the nation's longest, resulted in the loss of 58,000 American lives and was the first in which the United States failed to achieve its goals. The tonnage of bombs dropped on North

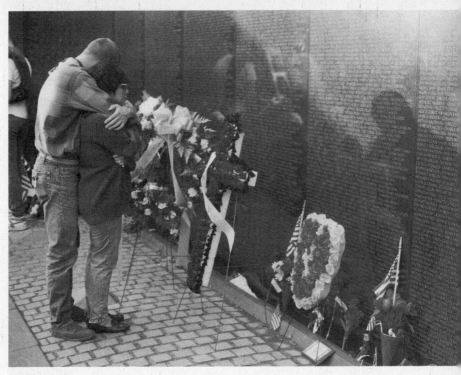

Vietnam War
The Vietnam Veterans Memorial, Washington, D.C., honoring the men and women who served in Vietnam; the monument lists the names of every American killed or missing in the war.

Vietnam by the United States was greater than the total of that dropped on Germany, Italy, and Japan during World War II. The war left up to 10 million refugees and caused sharp divisions among the American people.

The Vietnam War followed the Indochina War (1946–54) in which the Vietnamese overthrew French rule when France tried to reestablish its colonial control of Southeast Asia after World War II. The Geneva Accords, which ended the struggle in 1954, created two nations: Communist-ruled North Vietnam and noncommunist South Vietnam. The accords required the holding of elections to determine what government a reunified Vietnam would have, but South Vietnam refused to comply. When North Vietnam, allied with the insurgent Vietcong, sought to overthrow the government of South Vietnam, the United States tried to stop it. American involvement has its roots in Harry S. Truman's decision to contain the spread of communism anywhere. Presidents Dwight D. Eisenhower, John F. Kennedy, and Lyndon B. Johnson carried on this policy, each one escalating U.S. involvement and the number of advisers and (after 1965) combat troops in Vietnam. The number of American troops exceeded 500,000 in 1968.

Congress passed the TONKIN GULF RESOLUTION in 1964, authorizing the president to use military force without a formal declaration of war, and Johnson accordingly ordered bombing raids on North Vietnam. The TET OFFENSIVE of 1968 made it clear that the war would not end easily, and American opposition to the conflict increased at home. Although Richard M. Nixon ran for president with a promise to end the war, he actually expanded it by authorizing secret raids into Laos and an incursion into Cambodia. With each escalation, popular demonstrations (including one at KENT STATE) and political pressure to end the war mounted.

Finally in 1973 a cease-fire was negotiated and U.S. troops were withdrawn. During 1973–74 the North Vietnamese continued to attack South Vietnam. In January 1975 a major attack was launched by the Vietcong, and the South Vietnamese government collapsed. The Communists then gained control of Vietnam and Cambodia and Laos, as well.

Vinson, Fred M. (Frederick Moore; 1890–1953), chief justice of the U.S. Supreme Court (1946–53). Vinson served as a Democratic representative for Kentucky, supporting the New Deal, and served as director of the Office of Economic Stabilization and of War Mobilization and Reconversion during World War II. In 1945 Harry S. Truman appointed him secretary of the treasury and the following year chief justice of the United States.

Virginia (Old Dominion) became the tenth state in the Union on June 25, 1788. (See maps, pages 540 and 541.) JAMESTOWN, founded in 1607, was the first permanent English settlement in North America. Williamsburg served as Virginia's capital from 1699 to 1780, and part of the city has been restored as a popular tourist attraction. Virginia seceded from the Union on April 17, 1861, and Richmond became the second capital of the Confederate States of America the same year. Many battles of the Civil War were fought in the state. Part of Virginia broke away during the war and became the state of West Virginia. Gen. Robert E. Lee of the South surrendered to Gen. Ulysses S. Grant of the North at APPOMATTOX COURT HOUSE, ending the Civil War in 1865. Virginia was readmitted to the Union in 1870. Richmond is the state's capital; other large cities include Virginia Beach, Norfolk, and Newport News. Virginia's major products include hams, seafood, tobacco, peanuts, and turkeys. Mining and the dairy industry are also important to the economy. Tourist attractions include Williamsburg, Mount Vernon, Monticello, Arlington National Cemetery, and numerous Civil War battlefields. Virginia is known as "the Mother of Presidents," with eight having been born there. Other noted Americans born in Virginia include JOHN MARSHALL, SAM HOUSTON, BOOKER T. WASHINGTON, GEORGE MASON, and PATRICK HENRY.

Virginia and Kentucky Resolutions (1798–99), series of statements in support of state sovereignty approved by the legislatures of Kentucky and Virginia in response to the unpopular Federalist ALIEN AND SEDITION ACTS, which the resolution sought to have repealed. The resolutions passed in Virginia were written by JAMES MADISON. They argued the doctrine of *interposition,* under which a state can interpose its authority between an arguably unconstitutional federal law and its citizens, forcing a constitutional test of the federal law in question. The resolutions passed in Kentucky were written by THOMAS JEFFERSON. They stood for the doctrine of *nullification,* under which a state has the authority to nullify or cancel the operation of an arguably unconstitutional federal law within its borders.

Virginia Plan (1787), proposal for a form of government for the new United States presented by Governor Edmund Randolph and the Virginia delegation at the CONSTITUTIONAL CONVENTION. The plan recommended a national government with three branches — legislative, judicial, and executive. The legislative branch would have two houses with representation based on population. One house would be directly elected by the people; that house would then elect the second house. This plan was favored by large states because representation in both houses would be based on population. Delegates from small states resisted the Virginia Plan and proposed the NEW JERSEY PLAN, which called for a one-house legislature and one vote per state. The basics of the Virginia Plan, plus elements of the New Jersey Plan, resulted in the GREAT COMPROMISE at the convention.

Virgin Islands, self-governing American territory that lies east of Puerto Rico in the Caribbean Sea. Consisting of about sixty-eight rugged and hilly islands, only St. Croix, St. Thomas, and St. John are inhabited. Bought by the United States from Denmark in 1917, the United States built a naval base there to protect the Panama Canal and prevent Germany's seizure of the islands during World War I. As citizens of the United States, Virgin Islanders rely on it for most products. An elected governor and unicameral legislature govern the islands, and a nonvoting delegate is elected to the U.S. House of Representatives. The scenic beauty and mild climate of the Virgin Islands attract many tourists.

***Virginius* Affair** (1873), incident during the Cuban rebellion against Spain, which almost involved the United States in a war with Spain. Spanish authorities captured *Virginius,* a Cuban merchant ship commanded by an American, which was illegally flying the American flag. Fifty-three passengers and crew members, including some Americans, were shot as pirates on the assumption that they were aiding Cuban rebels. Spain agreed that the action was inappropriate and paid reparations to the families of the American victims.

V-J Day (August 15, 1945), Victory over Japan Day. V-J Day marked Japan's surrender to the Allied forces, bringing an end to the fighting in the Pacific during WORLD WAR II. The formal surrender took place aboard USS *Missouri* in Tokyo Bay on September 2, 1945.

Voice of America (VOA), a radio broadcasting network operated by the U.S. Information Agency. Formed in 1942 as part of the Office of War Information, VOA transmitted information about the United States and its policies during World War II. It now broadcasts news, music, and other programs in over forty languages throughout the world, excluding North America, to promote support and understanding for the United States.

Volstead Act (October 28, 1919), law providing for the enforcement of PROHIBITION. Introduced by Representative Andrew Volstead of Minnesota and passed over President Woodrow Wilson's veto, the Volstead Act backed up the Eighteenth Amendment to the Constitution, which prohibited the sale, manufacture, or transportation of alcoholic beverages within the United States. But routine violation of Prohibition laws by many and the difficulty of enforcement prompted calls to repeal the amendment. Also called the National Prohibition Enforcement Act, the Volstead Act became void in 1933 following the ratification of the Twenty-first Amendment, which repealed Prohibition.

von Braun, Wernher (1912–77), German-born rocket engineer. A pioneer in the development of rockets for defense and space exploration, von Braun was a major force behind the idea of manned space flights and landing humans on the moon. After developing the German V-2 rocket used against the Allies during World War II, he came to the United States, where he helped develop the Jupiter-C rocket, which carried *Explorer I,* the first U.S. satellite, into orbit. In 1960 von Braun became director of the Marshall Space Flight Center of the NATIONAL AERONAUTICS AND SPACE ADMINISTRATION (NASA), where he developed the Saturn rockets used in the Apollo moon program.

Vote, The *See* SUFFRAGE.

Voting Rights Act (August 6, 1965), law expanding the powers of the federal government to eliminate discrimination in voting, especially against blacks. Supported and signed into law by President Lyndon B. Johnson, the act authorized the U.S. attorney general to send federal examiners to register black voters in areas where discrimination existed. It also eliminated all literacy tests and prohibited the use of poll taxes.

Waco Siege (April 19, 1993), raid on the Branch Davidian complex near Waco, Texas. In February 1993, agents from the Bureau of Alcohol, Tobacco, and Firearms (ATF) tried to enforce a search warrant for illegal weapons and explosives at the compound of the Branch Davidians (a schism of the Seventh-Day Adventist church) near Waco, Texas. Self-described messiah David Koresh and his followers resisted, killing four of the agents and injuring sixteen others. An undetermined number of Davidians were killed and wounded as well. The FBI became the lead agency for negotiations during the ensuing fifty-one-day standoff. On April 19, federal agents attacked the compound with armored vehicles and tear gas. Fires erupted, leaving seventy-six people, including twenty children, dead. The Justice Department was strongly criticized for its actions in the siege. Attorney General JANET RENO accepted full responsibility for the incident and defended the action of the federal agents. She appointed a special counsel, former Republican Senator John Danforth, to conduct an inquiry into the assault. After a ten-month investigation, Danforth cleared the government and its agents of any wrongdoing, blaming the group's leaders instead.

Wade, Benjamin (1800–78), abolitionist and politician. Wade served Ohio in the U.S. Senate from 1851 to 1869 as a Whig and Republican. He opposed the KANSAS-NEBRASKA ACT and coauthored the WADE-DAVIS BILL. A leader of the Radical Republicans, he favored stern RECONSTRUCTION policies after the CIVIL WAR. Wade opposed President Andrew Johnson, voting to remove him from office during the impeachment trial. Wade served as president pro tempore at the time, and had Johnson been removed from office, Wade would have succeeded him as president.

Wade-Davis Bill (July 4, 1864), measure passed by Congress during the Civil War assuring congressional power to set up a procedure for readmission of the Confederate states into the Union. Introduced by Ohio Senator BENJAMIN WADE and Maryland Representative Henry Davis, both RADICAL REPUBLICANS, the bill allowed a state to set up a new government and return to the Union when a majority of the white citizens took an oath of loyalty to the U.S. Constitution and agreed to black equality. Abraham Lincoln, favoring a more lenient plan, blocked the passage of the bill with a pocket veto. Wade and Davis responded with the Wade-Davis Manifesto, denouncing Lincoln for dictatorial actions.

Wagner, Honus (Johannes Peter; 1874–1955), baseball player. Wagner, known as the flying Dutchman, worked for the Pittsburgh Pirates for more than thirty-five years as player, coach, and manager. He was the first player to have his signature on a "Louisville Slugger" bat and is considered the greatest shortstop of all time, but he excelled at every position he ever played. He broke into the majors by hitting .344 in 1897 and batted seventeen consecutive .300 seasons with the Pirates. He was the National League (NL) batting champion for seven of those seasons, with a lifetime average of .329. One of the first five players inducted into the Baseball Hall of Fame, Wagner led the league in stolen bases on six occasions with a total of 722 steals. Wagner ended his career with more hits, runs, RBIs, doubles, triples, games, and steals than any other NL player.

Wagner, Robert (1877–1953), German-born politician. Wagner served as a Democratic senator from New York from 1927 to 1949 and as a loyal ally to

Franklin D. Roosevelt during the New Deal. A liberal social reformer, he sponsored the NATIONAL INDUSTRIAL RECOVERY ACT, the SOCIAL SECURITY ACT, the NATIONAL LABOR RELATIONS ACT, and the Wagner-Steagall Housing Act. His son, Robert Wagner, Jr. (1910–91), served three terms as mayor of New York City, from 1954 to 1965.

Wainwright, Jonathan (1883–1953), military leader. Wainwright was second in command to Gen. DOUGLAS MACARTHUR in the Philippines during WORLD WAR II. After MacArthur's departure to Australia he led the forces defending BATAAN and CORREGIDOR, but had to surrender to the Japanese on May 6, 1942. Wainwright was imprisoned for three years but was freed in time to attend the surrender ceremonies in Tokyo in September 1945. He received the Congressional Medal of Honor and became a full general after the war.

Waite, Morrison Remick (1816–88), seventh chief justice of the United States (1874–88). As chief consul for the American delegation at the Geneva Tribunal of Arbitration in 1871, Waite helped settle the ALABAMA CLAIMS. Selected chief justice by Ulysses S. Grant in 1874, he made his most influential decision in *Munn* v. *Illinois*, the most important of the GRANGER LAWS cases. Originally a Whig, Waite was one of the founders of the REPUBLICAN PARTY.

Walker, David (1785–1830), black abolitionist. Walker, a free man, became involved in the abolition movement in the North and spoke openly against slavery. He was the Boston agent for *Freedom's Journal*, the nation's first black newspaper. His antislavery pamphlet *Appeal to the Colored Citizens of the World* (1829) was an angry call for action and launched a militant ABOLITIONIST crusade in the United States. Banned in the South, the *Appeal* was smuggled to the southern states in the pockets of garments from Walker's secondhand clothing business. A price was put on his head, and on June 28, 1830, he was found dead in the doorway of his shop under mysterious circumstances. Walker influenced WILLIAM LLOYD GARRISON to shift from being a moderate abolitionist to a militant.

Walker, Jimmy (James John; 1881–1946), politician. Walker, with the support of TAMMANY HALL, served as mayor of New York City from 1926 to 1932. His classy style of dress and fun-loving attitude helped him become a celebrity symbolizing the spirit of the ROARING TWENTIES. Walker made improvements in sanitation, transit, and health care, but his administration was also marked by incompetence, corruption, and fraud. Unable to explain some large financial transactions, Walker resigned in 1932 and went to Europe, where he lived for several years.

Walker, Mary Edwards (1832–1919), writer, reformer, and physician during the CIVIL WAR. For her pioneering medical treatments as a surgeon with the Union army, Walker received the Medal of Honor in 1865. A controversy over her military status caused the award to be revoked in 1917, but the medal was restored in 1977. Walker wore trousers and was active in the women's rights movement of the late 1800s, campaigning for the right to vote and freedom of dress. Her books on women's role in society include *Hit* (1871) and *Unmasked, or the Science of Immorality* (1878).

Walker, William (1824–60), adventurer and filibusterer. Walker led a number of filibustering expeditions into Latin America. In 1853 he led a band of colonists in an attempt to seize Baja California, declaring himself president. Arrested for violating neutrality laws, he was acquitted. In 1855 Walker led a successful expedition against Nicaragua, where he set himself up as dictator for two years. Arousing the hostility of CORNELIUS VANDERBILT for seizing his ships, Walker was overthrown in a coup supported by Vanderbilt. In an attempt to gain control of Honduras in 1860, he was captured by Honduras authorities and executed.

Wallace, George C. (1919–98), politician. A candidate for president four times, Wallace served four terms as governor of Alabama (1963–67, 1971–79, 1983–87). Because Alabama law prohibited two terms in a row, Wallace ran his wife, Lurleen, for governor in 1966. She won the election, but died in office in 1968. An outspoken opponent of racial desegregation in the 1960s and an advocate of states' rights, Wallace gained national attention for his stands against school integration and later, busing. As the nominee of the American Independent party in the ELECTION OF 1968, he polled 10 million votes and carried five states. Wallace unsuccessfully sought the Democratic presidential nomination in 1964, 1972, and 1976, but drew strong primary support. While campaigning in Maryland's Democratic primary in 1972, Wallace was shot and paralyzed from the waist down by a would-be assassin. He retired from politics in 1987.

Wallace, Henry A. (1888–1965), vice president of the United States (1941–45) under Franklin D. Roosevelt. An agricultural expert and civil rights advocate, Wallace served as FDR's secretary of agriculture from 1933 to 1940, promoting New Deal farm programs such as the AGRICULTURAL ADJUSTMENT ACT. Roosevelt replaced Wallace with Harry S. Truman in the 1944 election, naming Wallace secretary of commerce in 1945. Roosevelt dropped Walace from the Democratic ticket because Wallace was widely criticized for his leaning toward the Soviet Union. His outspoken criticisms of President Truman's policy toward the Soviet Union resulted in a request for his resignation as commerce secretary. After cofounding the PROGRESSIVE PARTY in 1948, Wallace ran unsuccessfully as the party's presidential candidate, receiving over 1 million popular votes but no electoral votes.

Wallace, Mike (Myron; 1918–), television journalist. Mike Wallace's news experience began in the 1940s when he was a radio news writer and broadcaster in Chicago. He served as a communications officer during World War II and later narrated several radio and television programs. He is known for his tough, straightforward, and sometimes controversial interviews on

Nightbeat (1956–57), *The Mike Wallace Interview* (1957–60), and *60 Minutes* (1968–). From 1959 to 1961 he anchored *Biography*, which focused on a wide range of historical figures. Later he had several assignments in Vietnam. His memoir, *Close Encounters*, was published in 1984. Wallace's son, Chris Wallace, is also a television newsman.

Walters, Barbara (1931–), television journalist. In 1976 Walters became the first woman to anchor a network nightly news program when she accepted a seven-figure contract from ABC. She began at NBC's *Today* (1963–76), becoming the show's first female host (1974–76). In 1979 she became a correspondent for *20–20*, eventually becoming its cohost (1984–). Her other television work includes *The Barbara Walters Specials*, an occasional series of interviews with world newsmakers and celebrities that consistently top the ratings. Walters is co-owner, co-executive producer, and cohost of daily talk show *The View* (1997–). She wrote *How to Talk with Practically Anybody about Practically Anything* (1971).

Walton, Samuel (1918–92), founder of Wal-Mart. Walton graduated from the University of Missouri with a degree in economics. After serving in the army intelligence corps during World War II, he borrowed $20,000 from his father-in-law and bought a Ben Franklin department store. He achieved great success by experimenting with innovations such as discounts, self-service, and profit sharing. Believing that large discount stores could make a profit in small towns, Walton began his chain of Wal-Mart stores in Rogers, Arkansas, in 1962 and, by 1991 became the world's number one retailer, with more than two thousand stores in the United States alone. He revolutionized retailing in the United States by building large stores in rural areas and selling a wide variety of merchandise at low prices.

Wanghia, Treaty of (July 3, 1844), the first commercial treaty between the United States and China. The agreement opened five Chinese ports to American trade and provided that U.S. citizens living in China would be subject only to U.S. laws. The first U.S. commissioner to China, Caleb Cushing, negotiated the treaty for President John Tyler.

War between the States *See* CIVIL WAR.

War Hawks, name for southern and western leaders who favored war with Great Britain in 1810–12. The War Hawks, named by political adversary John Randolph of Virginia, were young Democratic-Republicans who gained significant power in Congress, such as Henry Clay of Kentucky, John C. Calhoun of South Carolina, Felix Grundy of Tennessee, and Richard M. Johnson of Kentucky.

Warhol, Andy (Andrew Warhola; 1928?–1987), artist and filmmaker. Warhol pioneered the POP ART movement of the 1960s. He became famous for his paintings of Campbell soup cans, Coke bottles, and Marilyn Monroe. Warhol used silk-screen printing techniques to present a style that looks mass-produced, repetitive, and impersonal. Later in the 1960s his innovative and lengthy films (*Sleep*, six hours, 1963; *Empire*, eight hours, 1964) experimented with "still" and "split-screen" techniques.

War of 1812 (1812–15), a conflict between Great Britain and the United States, sometimes called "the second war for independence" and "Mr. Madison's war." During the war between France and England starting in 1793, the British put blockades on European ports to restrict American merchant shipping with France. About 1807 the British stepped up IMPRESSMENT of American seamen into their navy. The United States passed the EMBARGO ACT, which banned all exports and limited American shipping to coastal trade. In 1810 a group of young Democratic-Republican congressmen from the West called WAR HAWKS urged that the United States defend itself against the British (who were inciting the Indians along the Great Lakes frontier) and invade Canada.

Despite the opposition of the FEDERALIST PARTY, centered in New England, Congress declared war against Great Britain on June 18, 1812. The United States invaded Canada on three fronts, but were unsuccessful. The American navy fared quite well, with USS *Constitution* defeating HMS *Guerrière*. In 1813 Capt. Oliver H. Perry won the Battle of Lake Erie and Gen. William Henry Harrison defeated the British and Indians at the Battle of the Thames. In 1814 the British invaded Washington, D.C., forcing President James Madison to flee the city; they burned the White House and other public buildings. The British failed in their attempt to capture Baltimore, and Thomas Macdonough defeated the British at the Battle of Plattsburg Bay on Lake Champlain.

After negotiations for peace, the TREATY OF GHENT was signed ending the war on December 24, 1814. Because communications were so slow at the time, American forces led by Gen. ANDREW JACKSON, unaware that the war had ended inflicted a crushing defeat on invading British forces at New Orleans on January 8, 1815, two weeks after the treaty was signed.

War on Terrorism (2001–), war against international terrorism launched by President GEORGE W. BUSH following the SEPTEMBER 11, 2001, TERRORIST ATTACKS. The strategy to combat terrorism consists of several steps, including denial of safe havens for terrorist training, eradicating funding for terrorist organizations, collapsing terrorist networks by defeating terrorist leaders, detention and interrogation of suspected and known terrorists, and the building of a united global front against the practice. U.S.-led military forces launched attacks against Osama bin Laden and the repressive Taliban in the AFGHANISTAN WAR in 2001, dismantling the Taliban and repressing al-Qaeda's safe haven. In 2002 Bush identified Iraq as the next battle in the war against terrorism, citing the possession of weapons of mass destruction, links to terrorism, and Saddam Hussein's dictatorial rule. With congressional approval but without support from the U.N., the IRAQ WAR began in March 2003 and defeated Saddam's regime and a state sponsor of terrorism. Several domestic initiatives emerged as part of the war on terrorism including a $40 million emergency spending bill and an additional $20 billion bailout of the airline industry. The Terrorist Threat Integration Center (TTIC) has been established, integrating and analyzing terrorism threat-related information, and the FEDERAL BUREAU OF INVESTIGATION (FBI) is being restructured into an agency dedicated to the prevention of terrorism. The U.S.A. PATRIOT ACT increased investigative powers of law enforcement agencies, and the creation of the DEPARTMENT OF HOMELAND SECURITY resulted in the largest reorganization of the federal government since the creation of the PENTAGON.

War Powers Act (November 7, 1973), law prescribing the balance of power between the president and Congress in declaring war. The act requires the president to inform Congress within forty-eight hours of military action in a hostile area. Forces must be removed within sixty to ninety days unless Congress approves of the action or declares war. The resolution, prompted by the aggressive actions of Presidents Lyndon B. Johnson and Richard M. Nixon without congressional approval or a declaration of war during the VIETNAM WAR, was passed over Nixon's veto.

Warren, Earl (1891–1974), fourteenth chief justice of the United States (1953–69). Warren's court was a people's court with civil and individual liberties most important. In 1954 school segregation was ended in the Court's *BROWN V. BOARD OF EDUCATION OF TOPEKA* decision, and its "one-person, one-vote" opinion (1964) transformed congressional representation. Warren headed the commission that investigated the assassination of President John F. Kennedy. Warren ran unsuccessfully as the vice-presidential candidate for the Republican party in the ELECTION OF 1948, with Thomas Dewey of New York and, again unsuccessfully, as a favorite son candidate for president in 1948 and 1952.

Warren, Gouverneur Kemble (1830–82), Union general and engineer during the Civil War. Warren was called "the savior of Gettysburg": when Gen. Dan Sickles left Little Round Top, Warren held the hill from Confederate attack until reinforcements arrived. Warren served as chief engineer, Army of the Potomac, and was engaged in the Battles of the Wilderness, Spotsylvania, and Cold Harbor.

Warren, Mercy Otis (1728–1814), colonial playwright and author. Warren ridiculed the British colonial government in such plays as *The Adulateur* (1773), *The Defeat* (1773), and *The Group* (1775). Her major work was the three-volume *History of the Rise, Progress, and Termination of the American Revolution* (1805). Politically knowledgeable and acquainted with leading Revolutionaries, she opposed the ratification of the U.S. Constitution because she felt that the federal government had too much power and because the document did not include a bill of rights. She was the sister of patriot lawyer JAMES OTIS.

Warren, Robert Penn (1905–89), novelist and poet. A three-time Pulitzer Prize winner, Warren served as the first poet laureate of the United States in 1986 and 1987. *All the King's Men* (1946), his 1947 prize-winning novel based on the rise and fall of Huey Long, was made into an Academy Award–winning movie. The Pulitzer Prizes for poetry went to *Promises: Poems, 1954–56* (1957) and *Now and Then: Poems, 1976–78* (1979). Many of Warren's works reflect social values and issues that trouble the South, where he made his home.

Warren Commission Report (September 27, 1964), controversial report of findings resulting from the investigation into the assassination of President JOHN F. KENNEDY. Issued by the Warren Commission, which was established in late November 1963 by President Lyndon B. Johnson, the report found no evidence of a conspiracy and concluded that LEE HARVEY OSWALD, the accused assassin, acted alone when he fired three shots from the sixth floor of the Texas School Book Depository Building, hitting Kennedy and Governor John Connally from behind. It also said that Jack Ruby, who shot and killed Oswald in a Dallas jail, had no prior contact with Oswald and acted alone. The report criticized the Federal Bureau of Investigation and Secret Service for inadequate protection of the president and also recommended that the killing of a president or vice president be made a federal crime. The panel, headed by Chief Justice Earl Warren, has been criticized by many for not probing deeply enough into the possibility of a conspiracy. A congressional committee during the late 1970s reexamined the evidence and came up with conclusions contradictory to those of the Warren Report.

Washington (Evergreen State) became the forty-second state in the Union on November 11, 1889, and the only state named for a U.S. president. (See maps, pages 540 and 541.) Separated by the Cascade Mountains, displaying the peaks of many inactive volcanoes, the state consists of lush, deep, evergreen forests in the west and dry grain land in the east. The 1980 volcanic explosion of Mount St. Helens blew away over one thousand feet of its height, leaving fifty-seven dead or missing and millions of dollars of damage to the surrounding area. The Columbia River, one of the longest in the nation, is the greatest source for hydroelectric water power in the United States and features Grand Coulee Dam, the largest concrete dam in the country. Seattle, the largest city and an important port, is home to the Boeing Company, a leading producer of aircraft and spacecraft. Seattle's 1962 World's Fair established the first monorail service in the United States and featured the Space Needle, a 605-foot observation tower and revolving restaurant that has become a symbol of the city. Other major cities include Bellevue, Spokane, and Tacoma; the capital is Olympia. Tourists are attracted to some of the best hunting and fishing in the nation. Washington is a leading producer of apples, pears, lumber, wheat, aluminum, fish, and flower bulbs. Noted Washingtonians include MARY MCCARTHY, JONATHAN WAINWRIGHT, WILLIAM GATES, and GARY LARSON.

Washington, Booker T. (1856–1915), black educator. A spokesman for his race, Washington was born a slave. He graduated from Hampton Institute in Virginia and founded Tuskegee Institute, a black vocational school, in Alabama. Washington advocated practical vocational education and self-improvement of blacks and opposed confrontation with whites to gain equality. Although his influence was widespread and he advised Presidents Theodore Roosevelt and William Howard Taft regarding black federal appointments, his passive philosophy and practices came under attack by others, particularly W.E.B. DU BOIS, who advocated academic education for blacks and direct challenge to racist laws and practices. The NATIONAL ASSOCIATION FOR THE ADVANCEMENT OF COLORED PEOPLE (NAACP) was formed as a result of a growing movement away from Washington's policies. Washington wrote several books including his best-selling autobiography, *Up from Slavery* (1901).

Washington, D.C., capital of the United States. The name honors President George Washington; *D.C.* stands for District of Columbia. The only American city not part of a state, Washington lies on a peninsula formed by the merging of the Potomac and Anacostia rivers between Virginia and Maryland on federally controlled land. President Washington selected the site in 1791 and hired French engineer PIERRE L'ENFANT to plan the city. Also involved in laying out the city were surveyor Andrew Ellicott and mathematician BENJAMIN BANNEKER. Washington replaced Philadelphia as the national capital in 1800. The White House, the U.S. Capitol, the Supreme Court Building, and numerous monuments, museums, and memorials are located there attracting millions of tourists each year.

Washington, Denzel (1954–), actor. Born in New York, Washington earned a degree in journalism from Fordham University before studying acting with the American Conservatory Theater. His national recognition came on television's *St. Elsewhere* (1982–88). Washington's early film credits include *Cry Freedom* (1987) and his Oscar-winning (best supporting actor) portrayal of a runaway slave in *Glory* (1989). Other important films include *Malcolm X* (1992), *Philadelphia* (1993), and *Antwone Fisher* (2002), in which he made his directorial debut. He won the Best Actor Oscar for his role in *Training Day* (2001), becoming the first African-American actor to receive the honor in forty years, since SIDNEY POITIER.

Washington, George (1732–99), military leader and first president of the United States (1789–97). Born in Westmoreland County, Virginia, Washington served in the Virginia militia in the FRENCH AND INDIAN WARS — a conflict sparked, in part, by his failed 1755 expedition into territory claimed by both Britain and France. He was a leader of the Virginia colonists who resisted British colonial policy in the 1760s and 1770s and a delegate to the

First and Second CONTINENTAL CONGRESSES. In 1775 the Second Continental Congress named him commander of the Continental army, a post he held throughout the AMERICAN REVOLUTION. Washington's steadiness, administrative and political ability, and symbolic importance made him indispensable to the cause of independence and union.

At the end of the war, he resigned his commission, determined to return to private life at his beloved plantation, MOUNT VERNON. Washington's hopes for the Union and his concern over the weaknesses of the ARTICLES OF CONFEDERATION led him to encourage a national reform movement; he hosted a key event of this movement, the 1785 Mount Vernon conference, and agreed to come out of retirement to attend the CONSTITUTIONAL CONVENTION in 1787. Elected president of that body, his support for the Constitution it proposed was vital to its ratification.

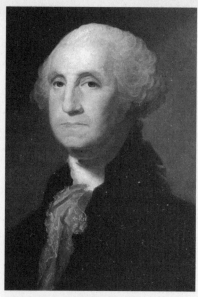

George Washington
A portrait by Gilbert Stuart.

Washington was the electoral college's unanimous choice for president in 1789. He is recognized (with Abraham Lincoln) as one of the nation's two greatest presidents. He invented the cabinet and assembled a first-rate team of advisers, including Secretary of the Treasury Alexander Hamilton, Secretary of State Thomas Jefferson, Secretary of War Henry Knox, and Attorney General Edmund Randolph. Washington supported the adoption of the BILL OF RIGHTS, the creation of executive departments of government, and the adoption of the JUDICIARY ACT OF 1789. He also chose the permanent site of the U.S. capital on the banks of the Potomac River, backed Hamilton's fiscal policies, and approved the establishment of the BANK OF THE UNITED STATES. An advocate of American neutrality, he issued the Proclamation of Neutrality (1793) and rebuffed the conspiracies of the GENET AFFAIR. He also supported the JAY TREATY and the PINCKNEY TREATY. A foe of political parties, Washington nonetheless was aligned with the FEDERALISTS. Reelected unanimously in 1792 to a second term, which he accepted only at the urging of Hamilton and Jefferson, he determined in 1796 to retire to private life.

His Farewell Address warned of the dangers of political parties, urged American neutrality in European politics, and established the two-term tradition. Retiring in 1797, he was called back into public life in 1798, when President John Adams named him commander in chief of the American army in preparation for the undeclared naval war with France resulting from the XYZ AFFAIR. He died of pneumonia at the age of sixty-seven.

Washington Naval Disarmament Conference (November 12, 1921–February 6, 1922), a post-World War I conference convened by President Warren G. Harding in Washington, D.C., to discuss reduction of the size of the world's major navies and security in the Pacific. The conference was attended by Belgium, China, France, Great Britain, Italy, Japan, the Netherlands, Portugal, and the United States. Three treaties resulted. The Five-Powers Treaty was adopted by France, Great Britain, Italy, Japan, and the United States. It established a ratio for the size of each navy, placed a ten-year ban on the building of warships, put restrictions on submarine warfare, and outlawed poisonous gas. France, Great Britain, Japan, and the United States signed the Four-Power Treaty, agreeing to respect each other's territories in the Pacific. China's territorial integrity became guaranteed in a Nine-Power Treaty, signed by all conference delegates and recognizing the OPEN DOOR POLICY. This conference was the first successful disarmament conference in American history.

Watergate (1972–74), series of political scandals involving President RICHARD M. NIXON and his administration, resulting in Nixon's resignation in 1974. On June 17, 1972, five men were arrested for breaking into the Democratic National Headquarters at the Watergate apartment and office complex in Washington, D.C. The intruders, who had been hired by the Committee to Re-elect the President (CREEP), were found guilty of conspiracy and burglary. Nixon steadily maintained he had no prior knowledge of the break-in and denied any White House connection. Investigative reporting by BOB WOODWARD and CARL BERNSTEIN of the *Washington Post* and testimony during the trial of the burglars led to televised Senate hearings headed by Senator Sam Ervin of North Carolina.

When Ervin learned of the existence of secret tapes of conversations in the president's Oval Office, he demanded that they be released. Nixon refused, claiming executive privilege. Special prosecutor ARCHIBALD COX petitioned the U.S. Court of Appeals, asking it to order Nixon to release the tapes to Judge JOHN J. SIRICA. Cox was fired by Solicitor General Robert Bork in the "Saturday Night Massacre." On June 24, 1974, the U.S. Supreme Court voted unanimously in *UNITED STATES V. NIXON* that Nixon had to turn over the tapes to the new special prosecutor, LEON JAWORSKI.

The House Judiciary Committee, headed by Peter Rodino, began IMPEACHMENT proceedings against Nixon on three charges, including obstruction of justice. Crucial evidence on the Watergate tapes proved that the president not only had known about the cover-up of the illegal actions but had ordered it. When the Judiciary Committee voted to recommend impeachment to the full House, Nixon decided to resign from office. On August 8, 1974, he announced in a televised address his resignation. GERALD FORD was sworn in as the new president the following day. On September 8, 1974, President Ford pardoned Nixon for any crimes he may have committed in the Watergate affair.

Waters, Ethel (1900?–77), black singer and actress. Gaining fame as a singer of blues and popular songs, Waters starred in Broadway musicals such as *Africana* (1927) and *At Home Abroad* (1935). Her hit songs include "Heat Wave," "Stormy Weather," and "Taking a Chance on Love," and she became the first woman entertainer to sing W. C. Handy's "St. Louis Blues" on stage. Her dramatic achievements include her performances in the film *Pinky* (1949) and in *Member of the Wedding* (1950; film, 1953). Her best-selling autobiography, *His Eye Is on the Sparrow,* was published in 1951.

Waters, Muddy (McKinley Morganfield; 1915–83), blues musician. Playing the guitar and harmonica, Waters became a primary influence in the development of the blues. During the 1950s he led the first electronic blues-rock band and made recordings that guided British and American groups. His songs include "Hoochie Coochie Man," "Got My Mojo Working," "Honey Bee," and "Rollin' Stone."

Watson, James (1928–), biochemist. Watson, Francis Crick, and Maurice Wilkins won the 1962 Nobel Prize for physiology and medicine for successfully deciphering the structure of DNA (deoxyribonucleic acid) in 1953. Their works, conducted at Cambridge University in England, revealed the chemical basis of heredity and generated massive interest in genetic research. Watson taught at Harvard University and also served as director of the Laboratory of Quantitative Biology at Cold Spring Harbor, New York, where he concentrated on cancer research. In 1988 he was selected by the National Institutes of Health as director of the Office of Human Genome Research, with the task of coordinating a project to map all genes in the human chromosomes. Funded by Congress, it is the largest biomedical project ever conducted in the United States. Watson's books include *The Double Helix* (1968), describing the discovery of the DNA structure, and *The Molecular Biology of the Gene* (1965).

Watts Riot (August 11–16, 1965), a six-day riot in Watts, a depressed black section of Los Angeles. Sparked by a drunken-driving arrest of a twenty-one-year-old black and by charges of police brutality, racial tensions exploded into a riot that led to thirty-four deaths, over one thousand injuries, and four thousand arrests. Some two hundred businesses were destroyed, and property damage was estimated at $200 million. Most of the damage was caused by blacks outraged by police brutality and their impoverished living conditions. The explosion of racial tensions had been building throughout the country for many years. Governor Edmund Brown called in twenty thousand National Guardsmen to bring the rioting under control.

Wayne, Anthony (1745–96), general during the AMERICAN REVOLUTION and Indian wars. Wayne served at BRANDYWINE and GERMANTOWN in 1777 and, after spending the winter at VALLEY FORGE, fought at MON-MOUTH, led a daring attack to recapture Stony Point, and took part in the siege of YORKTOWN. After the war Wayne served Georgia in the U.S. House of Representatives (1791–92). Known as "Mad Anthony" because of his daring heroics, Wayne, in command of American troops, won a decisive victory over the Indians in the Battle of FALLEN TIMBERS in 1795 and negotiated the TREATY OF GREENVILLE with the Indians in the same year, forcing them to abandon Ohio to white settlers.

Wayne, John (Marion Michael Morrison; 1907–79), actor. Known for his tough hero roles in westerns and war dramas, Wayne achieved stardom in John Ford's classic western, *Stagecoach* (1939). Known as "Duke," Wayne made over 250 movies, playing a leading role in all but 11, more than any other actor. He won an Academy Award for his performance in *True Grit* (1969). Other noted films include *Red River* (1948), *She Wore a Yellow Ribbon* (1949), *Sands of Iwo Jima* (1950), and *The Green Berets* (1968).

Weaver, James (1833–1912), politician. Weaver was the Greenback-Labor party nominee for president in 1880 and in 1892 won twenty-two electoral votes and over one million popular votes on the POPULIST PARTY ticket. He served in the House of Representatives from Iowa from 1879 to 1881 as a Greenbacker and again as a candidate of both the Democratic and Greenback-Labor parties from 1885 to 1889.

Weaver, Robert (1907–97), economist and political leader. Appointed by President Lyndon B. Johnson, Weaver, the first black to hold a cabinet position, was the first secretary of housing and urban development (HUD) when it came into existence in 1966. As an adviser to HAROLD ICKES, secretary of the interior in 1934, Weaver became involved in housing and slum clearance projects. He headed the Federal Housing and Home Finance Agency in 1961. In 1968 he resigned to become president of Baruch College in New York City. He received the SPIN-GARN MEDAL in 1962.

Webster, Daniel (1782–1852), lawyer, politician, and statesman. Webster was one of the foremost advocates of a strong national government,

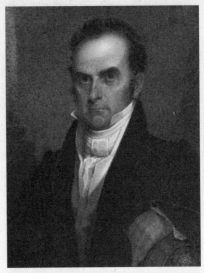

Daniel Webster
A portrait by James Barton Longacre, ca. 1850.

earning him the title, "Defender of the Constitution." A brilliant orator, he is remembered for his part in the WEBSTER-HAYNE DEBATES (1830) over states' rights and for his speech to the Senate supporting the COMPROMISE OF 1850 in order to preserve the Union. Webster served in the House of Representatives from New Hampshire and Massachusetts. As a lawyer, he argued a number of significant cases before the Supreme court, among them DARTMOUTH COLLEGE v. WOODWARD (1819), McCULLOCH v. MARYLAND (1819), and GIBBONS v. OGDEN. Webster served in the U.S. Senate from Massachusetts and supported the TARIFF OF ABOMINATIONS, opposed Andrew Jackson by supporting the Second BANK OF THE UNITED STATES, and opposed the Mexican War and the annexation of Texas. Webster served as secretary of state under Presidents William Henry Harrison, John Tyler, and Millard Fillmore, and negotiated the WEBSTER-ASHBURTON TREATY with England in 1842.

Webster, Noah (1758–1843), author, editor, and educator. Webster published the first dictionary that distinguished American usage from British, *American Dictionary of the English Language* (two volumes, 1828). His publication of *The American Spelling Book,* or the *Blue-Backed Speller* (1783), helped standardize American spelling as it became a best-selling school textbook. Webster helped found Amherst College in Massachusetts, serving as first president of its board of trustees. He compiled a *History of the U.S.* in 1832.

Webster-Ashburton Treaty (August 9, 1842), agreement between the United States and Great Britain fixing the Maine-New Brunswick border and ending a threat of war between the two countries. The United States obtained land that included the fertile Aroostook Valley and about two hundred square miles at the head of the Connecticut River. The negotiators of the treaty were Secretary of State DANIEL WEBSTER for the United States and Baron Ashburton for Great Britain.

Webster-Hayne Debates (January 19–27, 1830), series of debates in the U.S. Senate between Senators Robert Hayne of South Carolina and DANIEL WEBSTER of Massachusetts. The debates started over a resolution by Senator Samuel Foot of Connecticut to temporarily restrict the sale of federal public lands, but quickly turned into a verbal battle over the questions of nullification and states' rights. Hayne defended the southern position supporting states' rights; Webster upheld the doctrine of the supremacy of the national government over the states. His speech in defense of preservation of the Union ended with the famous words "Liberty and Union, now and forever, one and inseparable."

Welch, Joseph (1890–1960), lawyer. Welch won national attention for his role as special counsel for the army in the televised Army-McCarthy hearings. A noted Boston trial lawyer, Welch was outraged by McCarthy's mudslinging. His question, "Senator, have you no sense of decency?" helped discredit McCarthy, leading to the senator's censure by the U.S. Senate.

Weld, Theodore (1803–95), ABOLITIONIST and reformer. An evangelist in New York, Weld became a lecturer and effective organizer, bringing many prominent people into the antislavery movement. After marrying abolitionist ANGELINA GRIMKÉ in 1838, he wrote *American Slavery as It Is* (1839), which is said to have inspired *UNCLE TOM'S CABIN*. Weld also wrote *The Bible against Slavery* (1837) and helped found Oberlin College in Ohio.

Welles, Orson (George; 1915–85), actor, director, and writer. In a career that spanned nearly fifty years, Welles achieved his greatest fame for two controversial projects. The first, the 1938 radio adaptation of H. G. Wells's *War of the Worlds* on Halloween night, panicked many listeners, who had not heard the opening announcement that it was a play and thought they were hearing a news report that the United States had been invaded by Martians. The second was his first film — his masterpiece, *Citizen Kane* (1941), which he wrote, directed, and starred in. Inspired by the life of newspaper publisher WILLIAM RANDOLPH HEARST, the film won Academy Awards but led to legal battles with Hearst, who wanted it suppressed. Welles strongly influenced the art of film with his innovative camera, sound, and editing techniques. Other film credits include *The Magnificent Ambersons* (1942), *The Lady from Shanghai* (1948), and *Macbeth* (1948).

West, Benjamin (1738–1820), painter. Born to a Quaker family, West was noted for his paintings of historical subjects. After moving to Europe in 1760, he became the first American artist to achieve an international reputation. He settled in London and attracted many students, among them GILBERT STUART, JOHN SINGLETON COPLEY, and Thomas Sully. A founder of the Royal Academy of Arts in 1768, West became historical painter to King George III.

West, Jerry (1938–), basketball player, coach, and executive. Playing guard for the Los Angeles Lakers from 1960 to 1974, West is credited with 6,238 assists. He led the league in scoring in 1970 with a 31.2 average and ranked third in regular season scoring with 25,192 points. He served as coach of the Lakers from 1976 to 1979 and became general manager in 1979. He was inducted into the basketball Hall of Fame in 1979.

West, Mae (1893?–1980), actress. Beginning her career on Broadway and in vaudeville, West made her name as a sex symbol in Hollywood films. She became known for her humorous bawdy, suggestive performances and wisecracks, leading to efforts to regulate the content of movies. Many of her twelve films became embroiled in legal battles over censorship. West wrote the screenplays for many of her films, including *She Done Him Wrong* (1933), *I'm No Angel* (1933), *Goin' to Town* (1934), and *My Little Chickadee* (1940), with W. C. FIELDS.

Westinghouse, George (1846–1914), inventor and industrialist. Westinghouse obtained about four hundred patents during his lifetime, most concerning railways, electricity, and natural gas. He invented the air brake in 1868, leading to the formation of the Westinghouse Air Brake Company and his fortune. He also invented the gas meter and pioneered a control system of pipes to conduct natural gas into homes safely. In 1886 he formed the Westinghouse Electric Company and devised the use of alternating current for electric power transmission.

Westmoreland, William C. (1914–), military leader. Westmoreland commanded U.S. forces in the VIETNAM WAR from 1964 to 1968, during which U.S. involvement grew to more than 500,000 troops. In 1968 he was replaced as commander by Gen. Creighton Abrams. Westmoreland served as army chief of staff from 1968 to 1972. He took part in the invasion of NORMANDY during WORLD WAR II and served in the KOREAN WAR.

West Virginia (Mountain State) became the thirty-fifth state in the Union on June 20, 1863. (See maps, pages 540 and 541.) Originally part of the state of Virginia, the western counties broke away during the Civil War and became the state of West Virginia, which remained loyal to the Union. Its largest cities include Charleston (the capital), Huntington, and Wheeling. Most of the state is covered with rugged mountains and hills, part of the region called Appalachia. The beautiful mountain scenery attracts many tourists. Coal mining is the state's largest industry, and it is also a leader in tobacco, lumber, chemicals, glass, and steel. Notable Americans born in West Virginia include Thomas "STONEWALL" JACKSON, CHUCK YEAGER, and PEARL BUCK.

Whaling, the hunting and killing of whales for whalebone, oil, and meat. In colonial times whales were the principal source of fuel and tallow for lighting and cooking. Colonists used whalebone for such products as corsets, fishing poles, and umbrellas. New England served as the center of the whaling industry, with New Bedford and Nantucket, Massachusetts, the most important. The first whaling ship set sail from New Bedford in 1755. By 1850 there were more than seven hundred whaling ships afloat. San Francisco became the most important whaling port on the Pacific Coast and the port of Lahaina, Maui, in the Hawaiian Islands was an important whaling center in the Pacific. By the outbreak of World War I the growth of the petroleum industry virtually brought whaling to an end.

Wheatley, Phillis (1753?–84), poet. Wheatley was the first notable black author in the United States. A slave, she was sold to a wealthy Boston tailor who educated her, and she began writing poetry. In 1773 *Poems on Various Subjects, Religious and Moral* was published in London.

Wheeler, Burton K. (1882–1975), lawyer and politician. Wheeler won the nomination for vice president to run with ROBERT LA FOLLETTE in 1924 on the PROGRESSIVE PARTY ticket, but lost to Calvin Coolidge. Wheeler served in the U.S. Senate as a Republican from Montana from 1923 to 1947. He cosponsored the Wheeler-Howard Act (1934), which was aimed at improving the plight of the American Indians, the Wheeler-Lea Transportation Act (1940), and the Wheeler-Rayburn Act (1935) to eliminate abuses in public utilities. He helped expose the political corruption during Warren G. Harding's administration and became an extreme isolationist in the years before World War II.

Wheeler, William A. (1819–87), nineteenth vice president of the United States (1877–81). In 1860 Wheeler was elected to one term in the House of Representatives, and in 1867–68 he presided over the New York State constitutional convention. In 1868 he was reelected to the House in that year's Republican landslide and served until 1877. Known for his honesty and integrity, Wheeler opposed the "salary grab" of 1873 that increased the salaries of many government officials and refused to accept it after its passage. When Rutherford B. Hayes was chosen to run for president in the ELECTION OF 1876 at the end of Reconstruction, an image of integrity was important and thus Wheeler was chosen as the vice-presidential candidate. Hayes and Wheeler won the closest election in U.S. history, 185 to 184 electoral votes. Although their administrative record was impeccably honest, Wheeler and Hayes were not chosen to run for a second term. Wheeler retired to upstate New York.

Whig Party (1834–56), major political party formed to oppose ANDREW JACKSON, and the DEMOCRATIC PARTY. Led by HENRY CLAY and DANIEL WEBSTER, the Whigs supported the AMERICAN SYSTEM, a high protective tariff, a national bank, and federal aid for roads, canals, and bridges. The Whigs were victorious in 1840 by parading WILLIAM HENRY HARRISON as a humble "log cabin" candidate who drank hard cider, and they won again in 1848 with another war hero, Gen. ZACHARY TAYLOR. The slavery issue and the annexation of Texas destroyed the Whigs, and in 1856 many members joined either the KNOW-NOTHING PARTY or the new REPUBLICAN PARTY, which opposed the extension of slavery.

Whiskey Rebellion (1794), uprising of western Pennsylvania farmers against the 1791 federal tax on whiskey proposed by Secretary of the Treasury Alexander Hamilton and enacted by Congress. When farmers refused to pay an excise tax on corn liquor, the rebellion became the first serious test of the U.S. government's ability to enforce federal laws. On advice of Hamilton, President George Washington called out the militia, and the rebellion immediately collapsed. All those tried as participants were later acquitted or pardoned. The government's response to the rebellion confirmed its authority.

Whiskey Ring, a major scandal during President Ulysses S. Grant's second term (1873–77). Whiskey distillers, revenue collectors, and high federal officials conspired to avoid taxation through fraudulent reports on whiskey production. The association was formed in St. Louis, Missouri, and spread to the cities. Secretary of the Treasury Benjamin Bristow found evidence

against the lawbreakers in 1875, and many persons were convicted —
although most of the leaders escaped with light punishments.

White, Byron (1917–2002), jurist. White, an All-American running back
known as "the Whizzer," played professional football to finance his law
studies, went to England as a Rhodes Scholar, and later attended Yale Law
School. He was Robert Kennedy's deputy attorney general in 1961 before becoming associate justice as John F. Kennedy's first Supreme Court appointment 1962. White generally took moderate stands on cases before the Court.
White retired in 1993, after thirty-one years on the bench.

White, E. B. (Elwyn Brooks; 1899–1985), author and humorist. Awarded the
Presidential Medal of Freedom in 1963 and a special Pulitzer Prize in 1978,
White gained fame for his witty, satiric editorials and essays for the *New
Yorker* and *Harper's,* as well as for his light, humorous verse. His sensitive
children's books include *Stuart Little* (1945), *Charlotte's Web* (1952), and *The
Trumpet of the Swan* (1970). In 1959 White, noted for his stylistic excellence,
revised William Strunk Jr.'s classic *The Elements of Style* (1935). With James
Thurber, he wrote the spoof *Is Sex Necessary?* (1929).

White, Edward Douglass (1845–1921), ninth chief justice of the United
States (1911–21). After serving in the Confederate army during the Civil War
and representing Louisiana in the U.S. Senate (1891–94), White was appointed associate justice of the Court in 1894 by Grover Cleveland and later
(1910) chief justice by William Howard Taft. A conservative, White is best
known for his "rule of reason" statements in the antitrust cases against the
American Tobacco and Standard Oil companies in 1911.

White, Edward H., II (1930–67), astronaut. White, on June 3, 1965, during a
four-day flight with James McDivitt, became the first American to walk in
space. He maneuvered outside *Gemini* for a space walk lasting twenty-one
minutes. White and fellow astronauts Virgil Grissom and Roger Chafee
died on January 27, 1967, when a flash fire swept through their *Apollo* spacecraft during a test at Cape Kennedy in Florida.

White, Theodore (1915–86), journalist. White is known for his "Making of
the President" books about presidential campaigns between 1960 and 1972.
He won the Pulitzer Prize for *The Making of the President: 1960* (1960).
Other books include *Breach of Faith: The Fall of Richard Nixon* (1975),
America in Search of Itself: The Making of the President, 1956–80 (1982) and
his autobiography *In Search of History* (1982).

White House, the residence of the president of the United States, located at
1600 Pennsylvania Avenue, Washington, D.C. It was officially called the
White House when Congress titled it so in 1902 at the request of Theodore Roosevelt, though it had been painted white since 1817. In 1792 the
White House was the first public building started in Washington, D.C., and
in June 1800 John Adams became the first president to occupy it. The
British set the building on fire in 1814 during the War of 1812, but it was

rebuilt and expanded in 1818. During Harry S. Truman's administration, it was discovered that much of its structure had become dangerously weak. The entire interior was dismantled, stored, and then replaced after the walls and foundation had been strengthened and rebuilt.

Whitewater Scandal (1994–2000), political scandal during the first term of the Clinton administration. Named for a failed real estate development project on the Whitewater River in Arkansas during the 1970s, the scandal questioned then Arkansas Attorney General Bill Clinton and his wife Hillary Rodham Clinton's business partnership with Jim McDougal, the owner of Madison Guaranty, a failed savings and loan company in Little Rock. The partnership did poorly and finally dissolved, but led to charges that the Clintons lied about their partnership and exact losses in the land development deal and alleged improper campaign contributions, political and financial favors, and tax benefits. Independent federal counsels Robert Fisk, Kenneth Starr, and Robert Ray investigated the allegations for six years, searching for evidence of criminal activity. The investigation included testimony from Mrs. Clinton (the first time a first lady was subpoenaed by a grand jury) and videotaped testimony from the president. The case was closed in 2000 when no wrongdoing by the Clintons could be found. It was during the course of the Whitewater inquiry that Kenneth Starr uncovered Clinton's relationship with White House intern Monica Lewinsky, winning him the right to extend his investigation and eventually leading to the IMPEACHMENT OF BILL CLINTON.

Whitman, Marcus (1802–47), doctor, pioneer, and missionary. A Presbyterian missionary, Whitman and his wife, Narcissa, established missions in the Pacific Northwest. He encouraged settlement in Oregon, but the new settlers in 1847 brought with them diseases, particularly measles, that caused the deaths of many Indian children. In revenge, the Cayuse Indians massacred Whitman, his wife, and twelve others and burned their missionary buildings in what came to be known as the Whitman Massacre.

Whitman, Walt (1819–92), poet. Whitman's verse was characterized by remarkable freedom in form, rejection of rhyme, frank celebration of feeling and sensuality, and passionate enthusiasm for individualism and democracy. His masterpiece, *Leaves of Grass*, first appeared in 1855, and he spent the rest of his life revising and expanding it. In 1867 he published a moving elegy on the death of President Abraham Lincoln, "O Captain! My Captain!" His prose celebration of American democracy, *Democratic Vistas*, appeared in 1873. Always controversial because of his advanced views on sexual freedom, Whitman became known in his last years as "the good gray poet," a characterization that would have shocked his first reader.

Whitney, Eli (1765–1825), inventor. As inventor of the COTTON GIN (patented in 1794), which separated lint from cotton seeds, Whitney helped make cotton the principal money crop of the South. He obtained a government

---

★ Walt Whitman
I Hear America Singing (1860)

> I hear America singing, the varied carols I hear,
> Those of mechanics, each one singing his as it should be blithe and strong,
> The carpenter singing his as he measures his plank or beam,
> The mason singing his as he makes ready for work, or leaves off work,
> The boatman singing what belongs to him in his boat, the deckhand singing on the steamboat deck,
> The shoemaker singing as he sits on his bench, the hatter singing as he stands,
> The wood-cutter's song, the ploughboy's on his way in the morning, or at noon intermission or at sundown,
> The delicious singing of the mother, or of the young wife at work, or of the girl sewing or washing,
> Each singing what belongs to him or her and to none else,
> The day what belongs to the day — at night the party of young fellows, robust, friendly,
> Singing with open mouths their strong melodious songs.

---

contract for ten thousand muskets in 1798, and used interchangeable parts to manufacture the firearms in his New Haven, Connecticut, factory, becoming one of the first to use mass production methods. His manufacturing techniques influenced those of HENRY FORD, SAMUEL COLT, and others.

Whittier, John Greenleaf (1807–92), poet. Whittier's simple, direct style made him popular. He wrote against slavery and in praise of New England country life. A QUAKER and ABOLITIONIST, Whittier began as a journalist for William Lloyd Garrison. His political poem "Ichabod" (1850) attacks Daniel Webster's support of the Compromise of 1850. Popular works include "The Barefoot Boy" (1855), "Barbara Frietchie" (1863), and "Snowbound" (1866). Whittier, California, and Whittier College were named for him.

Wilder, L. Douglas (1931–), politician. A Democrat from Virginia, Wilder in 1989 became the first elected black governor in the United States. After success as a trial lawyer, in 1969 Wilder became the first black to be elected in the Virginia State Senate since 1877. He also won election as lieutenant governor in 1985.

Wilder, Laura Ingalls (1867–1957), author. Wilder wrote a series of nine autobiographical novels about growing up on the frontier in the 1870s and 1880s. Now considered classics, her "Little House" books began with *Little House in the Big Woods* (1932) and include *Little House on the Prairie* (1935),

On the Banks of Plum Creek (1937), and *The Long Winter* (1940). The books inspired a successful television series running for ten seasons from 1974 to 1983, which has never been out of syndication.

Wilder, Thornton (1897–1975), playwright and author. Wilder won three Pulitzer Prizes, one for his novel *The Bridge of San Luis Rey* (1927) and two for his plays *Our Town* (1938) and *The Skin of Our Teeth* (1942). Writing in a variety of styles, Wilder used clever plots, good-humored satire, and expressionistic fantasy to present characters in search of the meaning and beauty of daily life. Other works include the play *The Matchmaker* (1954), which became the Broadway musical hit and movie *Hello, Dolly!* (1964).

Wilderness, Battle of the (May 5–6, 1864), conflict between Union and Confederate forces in the latter part of the CIVIL WAR. Union troops numbering over 100,000 led by Gen. ULYSSES S. GRANT met about 65,000 Confederate troops under Gen. ROBERT E. LEE The dense, tangled forest northwest of Richmond, Virginia, made cavalry and artillery useless. After two days of infantry fighting and heavy losses on both sides, the battle remained undecided, and Grant pushed his forces on to Richmond.

Wilkins, Roy (1901–81), black civil rights leader. Wilkins headed the NATIONAL ASSOCIATION FOR THE ADVANCEMENT OF COLORED PEOPLE (NAACP) from 1955 to 1977. Although he led the organization into a more militant posture in the 1960s, he rejected the extremism of black-power advocates. He helped lead the legal challenge that ended in the landmark Supreme Court desegregation decision in BROWN V. BOARD OF EDUCATION OF TOPEKA (1954) and helped bring about the 1964 Civil Rights Act.

Willard, Emma (1787–1870), educator. Willard was the first American woman to promote higher education for women and furthered women's education worldwide. She opened her own school in 1814 and introduced mathematics and philosophy into the curriculum. With the support of De Witt Clinton, governor of New York, her *Plan for Improving Female Education* (1819) was backed by the New York legislature, which awarded her a grant to establish the Waterford Academy for Young Ladies, renamed the Emma Willard School after it moved to Troy, New York.

Willard, Frances (1839–98), educator and social reformer. Willard was an organizer in the temperance movement, serving as president of the Woman's Christian Temperance Union (WCTU) from 1879 until her death. She also became a strong advocate of woman suffrage and helped found the Prohibition party and the People's party. Willard became president of the World's Woman's Christian Temperance Union in 1891.

Williams, Hank, Sr. (Hiram; 1923–53), country western singer and composer. Although he could not read or write music, Williams at age thirteen formed his own band, the Drifting Cowboys, and eventually worked his way to Nashville, achieving great popularity at the "Grand Ole Opry."

Considered by many as the greatest country musician of all time, Williams turned out one hit after another, combining pop and country music. Some of his hits were "Cold, Cold Heart" (1951), "Jambalaya" (1952), and "Your Cheating Heart" (1953). Alcoholism and drug addiction led to his decline, and he died from a heart ailment at age twenty-nine. His son, Hank Williams, Jr. (1949–), continues the country western singing tradition.

Williams, Roger (1603?–83), English-born Puritan clergyman and dissenter. Williams founded the colony of Rhode Island following his banishment from MASSACHUSETTS BAY COLONY in 1635, and served as president of the colony from 1654 to 1657. He made friends with the Narragansett Indians and bought land from them. Believing that religion should be free of government control, he made the colony a haven for QUAKERS and other dissenters who were persecuted by the Puritan theocracies in Massachusetts and Connecticut.

Williams, Ted (1918–2002), baseball player. Williams compiled a lifetime batting average of .344, being the last baseball player to average over .400 (.406 in 1941). He won the American League's most valuable player award in 1946 and 1949 and also won six batting titles during his fourteen-year career with the Boston Red Sox. Williams won baseball's Triple Crown (most home runs, most runs batted in, and highest batting average) twice (1942 and 1947). He hit 521 career home runs and joined baseball's Hall of Fame in 1966.

Williams, Tennessee (Thomas; 1911–83), playwright. Williams's dramas portray the loneliness and isolation of life. His characters are often fragile, neurotic people who are helpless victims of their circumstances and passions. He won Pulitzer Prizes for *A Streetcar Named Desire* (1947) and *Cat on a Hot Tin Roof* (1955) and also won the New York Drama Critics' Circle Award in 1945 for *The Glass Menagerie* (1944). Some of his more than seventy plays include *Summer and Smoke* (1948), *The Rose Tattoo* (1948), *Sweet Bird of Youth* (1959), and *The Night of the Iguana* (1961).

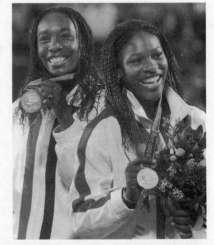

Venus and Serena Williams
Showing their 2000 Olympic Games gold medals.

Williams, Venus (1980–) and **Serena** (1981–), tennis players. The Williams sisters began their professional tennis careers as teenagers in the mid-1990s, quickly rising in the rankings in both women's singles and doubles competitions. Known for their powerful ground strokes and serves, the sisters have both been ranked number one in the world and have been credited with raising public awareness of women's tennis. When they won the 1999 French Open doubles title, they became the first pair of sisters to win a doubles title in the twentieth century. Serena won her first Grand Slam tournament in 1999 when she became the U.S. Open champion. She was the first African-American woman to win a Grand Slam singles title since ALTHEA GIBSON, in 1958. Venus won two straight Wimbledon championships (in 2000 against her sister and in 2001). Serena followed with back-to-back Wimbledon wins in 2002 and 2003, defeating her sister. As partners, they won the Wimbledon 2000 and 2002 doubles championships as well.

Willkie, Wendell L. (Lewis; 1892–1944), politician. Willkie won the Republican presidential nomination in 1940 and polled over 22 million votes, but lost to incumbent Franklin D. Roosevelt. Most of his adult life Willkie had been a loyal Democrat, but became a liberal Republican in the 1930s, opposing the New Deal. After the United States entered World War II, Willkie rallied his supporters in a program of national unity. His book *One World* (1943) outlined his ideas for international cooperation.

Wilmot Proviso (August 8, 1846), an amendment to President James K. Polk's $2 million appropriations bill to negotiate peace with Mexico during the MEXICAN WAR. The measure, introduced in the House of Representatives by antislavery Democrat David Wilmot of Pennsylvania, would have prohibited slavery in any newly acquired territory. The House approved the declaration in 1847, but it failed to pass in the southern-dominated Senate. The proviso was unsuccessfully attached to many subsequent bills and led to bitter debate over the issue of slavery in the territories, becoming a plank in the platforms of the FREE-SOIL and REPUBLICAN PARTIES.

Wilson, Henry (Jeremiah Colbath; 1812–75), vice president of the United States under Ulysses S. Grant (1873–75). Called the "Natick Cobbler," Wilson became a successful shoe manufacturer and antislavery leader. He served as a Republican senator from Massachusetts from 1855 to 1873, having helped found the REPUBLICAN PARTY. A RADICAL REPUBLICAN, he was a member of the Senate Military Affairs Committee during the Civil War and Reconstruction. He was implicated in the CRÉDIT MOBILIER scandal in 1872 and died while in office as vice president in 1875.

Wilson, James (1742–98), Scottish-born jurist and politician. Wilson, a prominent Pennsylvania lawyer, was one of only six people who signed both the Declaration of Independence and the U.S. Constitution. He spoke 168 times during the Constitutional Convention, arguing for a strong national government with the president and legislators elected directly by the people. George Washington appointed Wilson an associate justice on the U.S. Supreme Court in 1789, and in the 1793 case of *Chisholm* v. *Georgia*, he upheld federal over state authority.

Wilson, Teddy (1912–86), jazz pianist and composer. Wilson became the first black to publicly perform with a white group in 1935 when he played piano for the BENNY GOODMAN trio, along with GENE KRUPA on drums. This was the first interracial group of the swing era. Wilson had his own band in 1939 and 1940 and later taught at the Juilliard School of Music in New York City. After the swing era ended, Wilson continued to compose, broadcast, record, and tour the United States with small groups.

Wilson, (Thomas) Woodrow (1856–1924), twenty-eighth president of the United States (1913–21). Born in Staunton, Virginia, Wilson earned a Ph.D. from Johns Hopkins University and developed strong leadership abilities as a college teacher and as president of Princeton University. He published many books on government and political science. In 1910 Wilson was elected governor of New Jersey, and two years later he gained the Democratic nomination for president. A split in the Republican party between William Howard Taft and Theodore Roosevelt allowed Wilson to win the ELECTION OF 1912 with a minority of votes. Wilson won reelection in a close race with Republican Charles Evans Hughes in 1916.

During the Wilson administration Congress passed the FEDERAL RESERVE ACT (1913) and the CLAYTON ANTI-TRUST ACT (1914). It broadened the Constitution by passing the Seventeenth Amendment (1913) allowing the direct election of senators, the Eighteenth Amendment (1919) establishing PROHIBITION, and the Nineteenth Amendment (1920) giving women the right to vote. The PANAMA CANAL opened in 1914, the United States purchased the VIRGIN ISLANDS from Denmark in 1917, and the United States entered WORLD WAR I in 1917.

At war's end Wilson drew up his FOURTEEN POINTS (1918) and helped write the TREATY OF VERSAILLES (1919) and the Covenant of the LEAGUE OF NATIONS (1919) in an effort to bring about a lasting world peace. In 1919 he suffered a paralyzing stroke while campaigning for the peace treaty. The U.S. Senate did not ratify the treaty, but Wilson received the Nobel Peace Prize for his efforts. Although an idealistic and intelligent man, he tended to be arrogant and inflexible, which hurt him in the attainment of his goals, especially during the contest over the Treaty of Versailles.

Winchell, Walter (1897–1972), gossip columnist and broadcast journalist. Winchell was the country's best-known and most influential syndicated columnist and radio commentator who, at his peak, was published in two thousand newspapers and reached up to 20 million listeners with his weekly radio broadcast. He became a household word by 1929 when he pioneered the gossip column in the *New York Daily Mirror*. First covering only Broadway features, he later expanded his coverage to include show business, social, and political news. Throughout World War II, he backed President FRANKLIN D. ROOSEVELT. Often controversial, during the COLD WAR Winchell used his power to cause fear when he supported Senator JOSEPH

McCARTHY, distressing millions of readers and eventually leading to law-suits and loss of media support. His radio broadcasts ended in 1959; his column, after thirty-eight years, in 1967.

Winfrey, Oprah (1954–), talk show host, actress, producer, philanthropist. Born in Mississippi to unwed teenagers, Oprah rose from humble adversity to the highest level of success and influence. First raised by her grand-mother, Oprah moved to Milwaukee to live with her mother at age six. She spent her teenage years with her father, who taught her the importance of education and discipline. Earning a B.A. in speech and drama at Tennessee State, she became Nashville's first female and first black TV-news anchor. Her success as host of *AM Chicago* led to the show's name change to *The Oprah Winfrey Show,* which went into national syndication in 1986, eventu-ally gaining over 26 million viewers, the highest-rated talk show in syndica-tion history. Her on-air book club causes any book she chooses to become an instant bestseller. An accomplished actress, Oprah earned an Oscar nomination for *The Color Purple* (1985). She founded Harpo, Inc., joining MARY PICKFORD and LUCILLE BALL as the only women to own their own movie production studios and the first woman in history to own and pro-duce her own talk show. Abused herself as a child, Winfrey lent her support to the 1984 National Child Protection Act, designed to protect children from abuse. In 1988 she received the International Radio and Television So-ciety's Broadcaster of the Year Award, the youngest person and only the fifth woman to receive the honor. In 2000 she launched *O,* a women's magazine, which became one of the most successful new magazines in publishing his-tory. When *Forbes* magazine published its list of America's billionaires for 2003, it disclosed that Oprah Winfrey was the first African-American woman to join the ranks. Winfrey was named one of the one hundred most influential people of the twentieth century by *Time* magazine in 1998.

Winnemucca, Sarah (Thocmetony, or "Shell Flower"; 1844?–91), Paiute activist and author. Sarah's grandfather was Chief Truckee of the Northern Paiutes, a tribe in Nevada and California, who welcomed the white people and guided JOHN C. FRÉMONT during his mapmaking journey to Califor-nia. She attended a convent school and used her language skills to work as an army interpreter and scout. Through lecturing, writing, and founding a school for Indian children, she sought understanding between her people and the whites. She gained much attention for the plight of her people through her speaking engagements, particularly in the Northeast, where other prominent reformers joined her cause to enlist government action. In 1880 she spoke with President RUTHERFORD B. HAYES and Secretary of the Interior CARL SCHURZ, and in 1887 her work helped lead to passage of the DAWES SEVERALTY ACT, which promised improvements for her people. However, injustice and corruption among government agents continued. Sarah wrote *Life Among the Piutes* [sic]: *Their Wrongs and Claims* (1863), becoming the first Native American woman known to secure a copyright and publish in the English language.

Winslow, Edward (1595–1655), English-born founder of PLYMOUTH COLONY. Winslow came to Plymouth aboard the *Mayflower* and negotiated a treaty with Indian chief MASSASOIT. Winslow and Susanna White became the first couple to marry in the new colony. He served as an assistant to the governor for twenty years and governor for three years. Leaving Plymouth for England in 1646, he never returned but held several positions in Oliver Cromwell's government.

Winthrop, John (1588–1649), colonial leader. A founder of MASSACHUSETTS BAY COLONY, Winthrop left England for Salem in 1630, followed by about one thousand settlers. As PURITAN governor of the colony succeeding John Endecott, he was one of the founders of Boston. Winthrop helped the colony maintain some political independence. He established strict rules and played a leading role in the prosecution and banishment of both ANNE HUTCHINSON and ROGER WILLIAMS.

Wisconsin (Badger State) became the thirtieth state in the Union on May 29, 1848. (See maps, pages 540 and 541.) The largest cities include Madison (the capital), Milwaukee, and Green Bay. With over eight thousand lakes, Wisconsin has become a popular vacation spot for fishing and water skiing. It is the leading dairy state in the nation and is world-famous for its cheese. Milwaukee is known for its beer. Other major products are machinery, paper, furniture, and processed food. Famous people from Wisconsin include ROBERT LA FOLLETTE, THORNTON WILDER, and FRANK LLOYD WRIGHT.

Witherspoon, John (1723–94), Scottish-born educator, clergyman, and political leader. The only minister to sign the Declaration of Independence, Witherspoon served in the Continental Congress from New Jersey. In 1768 he became president of the College of New Jersey, later Princeton University, and played a role in organizing the Presbyterian church in America.

Wolfe, Thomas (1900–38), author. Wolfe won fame for his dramatic, detailed autobiographical novels. His first novel, *Look Homeward, Angel* (1929), edited by Maxwell Perkins, became a best-seller and was followed by a sequel, *Of Time and the River* (1935). After Wolfe's sudden death Edwin Aswell edited his two other novels, *The Web and the Rock* (1939) and *You Can't Go Home Again* (1940). The plots follow the narrator from his home in rural Carolina to his life as a writer in New York City.

Woman Suffrage, women's right to vote. The U.S. Constitution of 1787 did not specify who could or could not vote, leaving the matter to the states, which initially granted voting rights only to landowning white men. Although property qualifications were abolished during the 1820s and 1830s, women were still excluded. When the SENECA FALLS CONVENTION met in 1848, one of its demands was the enfranchisement of women. Many activists

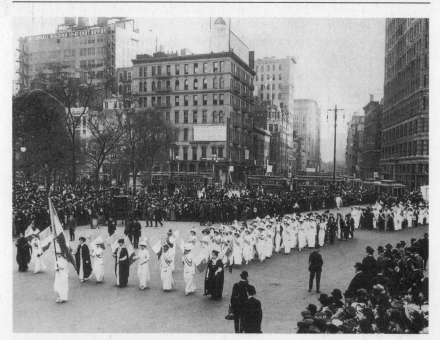

Woman Suffrage
Suffrage parade, New York, ca. 1912.

in the years thereafter engaged in the struggles both for abolition and for woman suffrage. When efforts to include woman suffrage in the Fourteenth Amendment failed, women intensified the campaign.

In 1869 ELIZABETH CADY STANTON and SUSAN B. ANTHONY formed the NATIONAL WOMAN SUFFRAGE ASSOCIATION (NWSA). The AMERICAN WOMAN SUFFRAGE ASSOCIATION (AWSA) was formed also in 1869 by LUCY STONE, JULIA WARD HOWE, and others to work for inclusion of women in the Fifteenth Amendment. That effort failed, too. In 1890 the two groups merged as the NATIONAL AMERICAN WOMAN SUFFRAGE ASSOCIATION (NAWSA) to continue the struggle.

In 1869 the territory of Wyoming had become the first to allow women to vote, and Colorado, Utah, and Idaho followed in the 1890s. But in the early 1900s, leaders such as CARRIE CHAPMAN CATT, president of NAWSA, and ALICE PAUL of the Congressional Union and the National Woman's party geared up to make the final drive for an amendment to the Constitution allowing all women in the United States to vote. During World War I, women's contributions to the war effort enhanced their demands for the suffrage, and President Woodrow Wilson, though initially reluctant, was induced to back the drive. The Nineteenth Amendment (called the Susan B. Anthony Amendment) became law in 1920.

Wood, Grant (1892–1942), artist. An American regionalist painter, Wood is best known for his midwestern farm painting *American Gothic* (1930) and *The Midnight Ride of Paul Revere* (1931). Noted for his paintings of the rural Midwest, Wood primarily portrayed the people and landscapes of Iowa. (Wood headed the art department at the State University of Iowa for many years.) His paintings are reminiscent of German and Flemish painters of the 1400s and 1500s in their realism and precise details.

Wood, Leonard (1860–1927), military leader. Wood commanded the ROUGH RIDERS, a volunteer regiment, in which Theodore Roosevelt also served during the SPANISH-AMERICAN WAR in 1898. He served as military governor of Cuba from 1899 to 1902, building roads and schools and eliminating yellow fever by cleaning up swamps and mosquito-ridden areas. Wood commanded the U.S. forces in the Philippines from 1906 to 1908, was chief of staff from 1910 to 1914, and served as governor general of the Philippines from 1921 until his death.

Wooden, John (1910–), college basketball coach. Wooden coached at the University of California at Los Angeles (UCLA) from 1948 to 1975. Between 1964 and 1975 he led them to a record ten national championships. Two of his championship teams won eighty-eight straight games between 1971 and 1974, a record. Wooden is the only man to win election to basketball's Hall of Fame as both a player and a coach. He also won the Basketball Writers' coach of the year award six times.

Woodhull, Victoria (1838–1927), social reformer. Woodhull, the first woman to run for president, was the candidate of the new Equal Rights party in 1872. She caused controversy with her outspoken support for equal rights and woman suffrage and was criticized for her support of "free love" and communal living. Woodhull became the first woman to address Congress. In 1870 she and her sister Tennessee Claflin established the first stock brokerage firm owned by women on Wall Street and founded *Woodhull and Claflin's Weekly,* devoted to controversial issues including an English translation of the *Communist Manifesto.* She moved to England in 1877 where she married a wealthy banker.

Woods, Tiger (Eldrick; 1975–), golfer. In 1994 at age eighteen, Woods became the youngest person and first minority to win the U.S. Amateur Open; he won it again in 1995 and 1996. Since becoming a professional golfer in 1996, his career has been unprecedented. Between 1996 and 2003 he won thirty-nine tournaments on the PGA Tour, including the 1997, 2001, and 2002 Masters, the 1999 and 2000 PGA Championships, the 2000 and 2002 U.S. Open Championships, and the 2000 British Open Championship. Woods became the first golfer ever to hold all four professional major championships of golf simultaneously. Nicknamed Tiger after his father's old army friend, he was noted at an early age for his long, accurate drives and competitive, determined demeanor. At the age of two he appeared on the *Mike Douglas Show* to putt against comedian BOB HOPE, and by age five he had appeared in *Golf Digest* and on television's *That's Incredible*. He is (as of 2004) the all-time career money leader on the PGA Tour. Woods won the PGA Tour Player of the Year Award for an unprecedented five straight seasons (1997 and 1999, 2000, 2001, 2002, 2003). The only professional athlete to win more consecutive player of the year awards is NHL great WAYNE GRETZKY.

Woodstock (August 15–17, 1969), rock music festival on a farm near Woodstock, New York. More than 400,000 people gathered at Bethel, New York, at the "Woodstock Nation" for a weekend of peace and "good vibrations." Max Yasgur

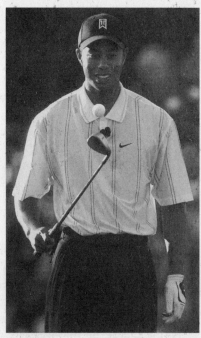
Tiger Woods

turned over his six-hundred-acre farm for the festival, which included the most famous rock music performers and bands of the time, including The Who, Jefferson Airplane, Country Joe and the Fish, JIMI HENDRIX, JANIS JOPLIN, The Band, and others. This event, central to the solidarity of HIPPIES, "flower children," and VIETNAM WAR protesters and marked by amplified music and drugs, was heavily covered by the media and depicted in the movie *Woodstock* (1970).

Woodward, Bob (1943–), and **Carl Bernstein** (1944–), reporters for the *Washington Post* whose investigative reporting implicated President RICHARD M. NIXON in the WATERGATE scandal and led to his resignation from the presidency. They won the 1973 Pulitzer Prize for their stories. The men wrote two best-sellers about the affair, *All the President's Men* (1974; made into a film, 1976) and *The Final Days* (1976). Woodward, who has been assistant managing editor of the *Post* since 1981, also wrote an exposé of the Supreme Court, *The Brethren: Inside the Supreme Court* (with Scott Armstrong, 1979), *The Man Who Would Be President — Dan Quayle* (with David Broder, 1992) and *Plan of Attack* (2004), a behind-the-scenes account of how and why President GEORGE W. BUSH decided to go to war against Iraq. Bernstein, after working as Washington bureau chief for ABC (1979–81) and as correspondent for ABC News, New York City (1981–84), spent two years writing for *Time* (1990–92), and then became a freelance writer.

World Series, annual series of championship baseball games between the pennant winners of the American League (AL) and the National League (NL), played after the end of the regular season in October. The first team to win four games becomes the U.S. champion. The 1919 series is the most notorious because after the heavily favored Chicago White Sox were upset by the Cincinnati Reds, it was proven that members of the White Sox team had conspired with gamblers to throw the series. In what became known as the Black Sox Scandal, eight players were eventually acquitted but banned from baseball for life by the game's first commissioner, KENESAW MOUNTAIN LANDIS. Played every year since 1903 (except 1904 and 1994), the World Series is a major sporting event. The team with the most World Series wins is the Yankees, with twenty-six. For individual record-setting performances in the series, YOGI BERRA and MICKEY MANTLE hold the best batting records and Whitey Ford dominates in pitching.

World Trade Center, a former building complex in lower Manhattan, New York City, which attracted about two hundred thousand visitors daily and was the workplace for some fifty thousand. It was the world's largest commercial complex, home to many businesses, government agencies, international trade organizations, and a hotel; it even had its own Zip Code. The site consisted of seven buildings and a shopping concourse constructed and operated by the Port Authority of New York and New Jersey. Most prominent were the 110-story twin towers, rising to over 1,350 feet, the tallest buildings in the world when they were dedicated in 1973. Because the towers were built on six acres of

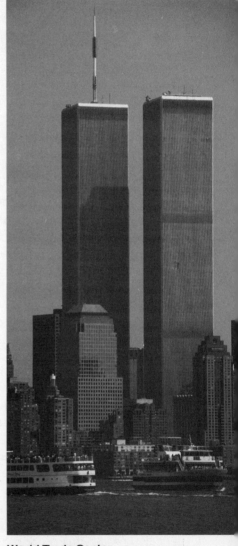

World Trade Center
The twin towers defined the New York City skyline until their destruction by terrorists in September 2001.

landfill, the foundation had to extend more than seventy feet below ground to rest on solid bedrock. When two hijacked commercial jetliners struck the towers on the morning of September 11, 2001, the resultant fires weakened the towers' central cores, collapsing the upper floors and creating too much load for the lower floors to bear. Both towers collapsed, killing 2,752 people. In 2003 a design was selected for the rebuilding of the site. It will feature a hanging garden, a memorial, a cultural center, and a spiraling tower reaching 1,776 feet, which will make it the tallest building in the world.

World Trade Center Attack 1 (February 26, 1993), first attack on the WORLD TRADE CENTER in New York City. Islamic terrorists detonated a rented van with more than one thousand pounds of explosives in the underground garage of the north tower of the WORLD TRADE CENTER in Manhattan, killing six and injuring more than one thousand others. Damage estimates totaled more than $500 million. Despite the extent of the destruction, the towers were repaired and reopened in less than a month. In 1995, militant Islamist Sheik Omar Abdel-Rahman and others were convicted of conspiracy charges in the attack and sentenced to life in prison. British-educated Islamic extremist Ramzi Yousef, believed to have been the mastermind, was convicted and sentenced to 240 years in solitary confinement in 1998. Al-Qaeda involvement is suspected.

World War I (1914–18), the first truly global conflict involving more countries than any war except World War II; also called "the war to end all wars" and "the Great War." The fighting took place mostly in Europe. The Allies included Great Britain, France, Russia (until 1917), Italy, and the United States (1917–18). The Central Powers consisted of Germany, Austria-Hungary, Turkey, and Bulgaria. Its causes included extreme nationalism among Europeans, a race for colonial possessions fueled by imperialism, and economic rivalries. Germany wanted to become the most powerful nation in Europe and challenge the naval superiority of Great Britain. The immediate cause of the war was the assassination on June 28, 1914, of Archduke Francis Ferdinand, heir apparent to the Austro-Hungarian throne, in Sarajevo by a Serbian nationalist. A month later, after Serbia refused Austria-Hungary's ultimatum, Austria-Hungary declared war on Serbia. Other war declarations followed quickly.

On the western front Germany advanced through Belgium and into France, almost to Paris. After the first BATTLE OF THE MARNE and Ypres, the Germans and Allies bogged down, and trench warfare dragged on for four long years. Poison gas was used and the battle lines became almost stationary. There were heavy casualties at Verdun and the Somme during 1916.

The Central Powers had more success on the eastern front, defeating the Russians at Tannenberg and the Masurian Lakes in 1914. Serbia and Montenegro surrendered in 1915, the Italian campaigns were indecisive, and an Allied attempt to force Turkey out of the war was a costly error.

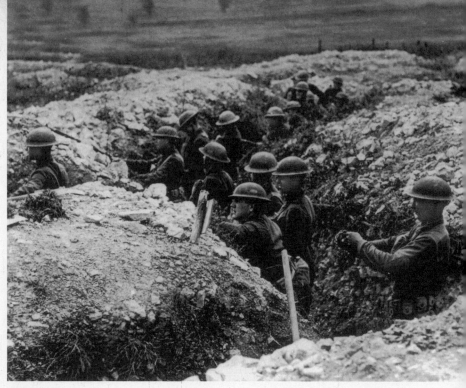

World War I
U.S. Army troops stand in the trenches in France.

The neutrality of the United States had been threatened by several German acts. These included the sinking of unarmed ships such as the LUSITANIA (1915) and the interception of the ZIMMERMANN NOTE (1917). In 1917, when the Germans resorted to unrestricted submarine warfare, the United States entered the war on the side of the Allies.

The American Expeditionary Force, led by Gen. JOHN J. PERSHING landed in France and became involved in the BATTLE OF CHÂTEAU-THIERRY in June 1917. The Bolsheviks of Russia signed the Peace Treaty of Brest-Litovsk with Germany in March 1918, giving up much territory including Finland, Poland, and the Ukraine. The Germans were stopped short of Paris in the second BATTLE OF THE MARNE, and American troops also fought in battles at the MEUSE-ARGONNE and ST. MIHIEL.

Turkey, Austria-Hungary, and Bulgaria, decaying from within, surrendered to the Allies and on November 11, 1918, Kaiser Wilhelm II of Germany also surrendered. Representatives at the Paris Peace Conference (1919) signed the TREATY OF VERSAILLES, officially ending hostilities. President WOODROW WILSON's efforts to form a LEAGUE OF NATIONS were rejected by the U.S. Senate, which refused to ratify the treaty or join the League. The United States and Germany signed a separate treaty in 1921.

The "Great War" was one of the bloodiest in history — an estimated eight to ten million troops were killed, including over 112,000

Americans. Nearly as many civilians died from disease, starvation, or other causes.

World War II (1939–45), global conflict involving every major power in the world. The Allies originally consisted of Great Britain, France, and China, but totaled fifty nations, including the United States and the Soviet Union, by the end of the war. The Axis powers of Germany, Italy, Japan, and (until 1941) the Soviet Union were eventually joined by six other nations. Causes of the war were the rise of imperialist and totalitarian dictatorships in Germany, Italy, and Japan after World War I and a worldwide economic collapse, the GREAT DEPRESSION.

Several aggressions led up to the war. In 1931 Japan invaded Manchuria. In 1936 the Fascist Benito Mussolini of Italy sent his troops to conquer Ethiopia. In 1938 Nazi Germany under Adolf Hitler annexed Austria, and the Munich Pact awarded part of Czechoslovakia to Germany, carrying out an Allied policy of appeasement in the hope of avoiding war (Germany annexed all of Czechoslovakia through invasion the next year). In 1939 Germany and the Soviet Union signed a ten-year nonaggression pact, and the two nations invaded Poland on September 1, 1939. World War II officially began when Great Britain and France immediately declared war.

After a quick victory in Poland, Germany occupied Denmark and Norway in 1940. In May, Germany conducted a blitzkrieg ("lightning") invasion of Holland, Belgium, and France, driving to the English Channel. With France's surrender, Great Britain was left to fight alone under the leadership of Prime Minister Winston Churchill. The Battle of Britain, Hitler's attempt to bomb England into surrendering, took place in August through October of 1940. London and other cities were bombed daily by the Nazis, but Royal Air Force fighter planes engaged in around-the-clock dogfights with the German planes, saving the country from invasion and prompting Churchill's famous statement, "Never have so many owed so much to so few."

Axis powers were active in North Africa and in the Balkans, where Germany occupied Greece and Yugoslavia in April 1941. Germany broke its nonaggression pact and invaded the Soviet Union on June 22, 1941, bringing that country, under its leader Joseph Stalin, into the war.

Meanwhile, in the United States, sentiment was divided about what course America should take regarding these events in Europe and those in the Far East, where Japan continued its aggression in China and Indochina. ISOLATIONISM was strong, with groups like the AMERICA FIRST COMMITTEE insisting that the United States stay out of "foreign" wars. Congress accordingly passed four NEUTRALITY ACTS in the late 1930s. President FRANKLIN D. ROOSEVELT, aware of the strength of this view, but also of the danger to the democracies posed by the Nazis and Fascists, steered a middle course. In response to that concern, Congress passed the LEND-LEASE ACT on March 11, 1941, which enabled Roosevelt to transfer war matériel to be-leaguered Britain and other countries without a cash payment as required by the Neutrality Act of 1939.

The question of whether the United States would enter the war was re-solved when, on December 7, 1941, Japan staged a surprise attack on the American base at PEARL HARBOR, Hawaii, and, on December 11, Germany and Italy declared war on the United States. America geared up for a war on two fronts, with Congress on December 19 extending military conscription to men between the ages of twenty and forty-four.

The attack on Pearl Harbor and Japanese advances in the Pacific (by 1942, Japan had captured the Philippines and many other Pacific islands) led to a wartime hysteria in the United States concerning a perceived threat of sabotage on the West Coast. In February 1942 the JAPANESE-AMERICAN INTERNMENT program started, and over 100,000 Americans of Japanese descent had been relocated to camps inland by September.

In Europe, German forces reached Stalingrad on August 22, 1942, and started a siege that ended when they entered the city on September 13. The harsh winter and lack of supplies caused thousands of German soldiers to starve or freeze to death, and on February 2, 1943, the last of these troops surrendered, halting Germany's eastward advance.

At the same time, German and Italian forces in North Africa led by Irwin Rommel, "the Desert Fox," were taking a beating. British general Bernard Montgomery's tank corps defeated Rommel at the Battle of El Alamein, again handing Hitler a setback. This was followed by an Allied invasion of French colonies in North Africa.

Gen. GEORGE C. MARSHALL chief of staff of the U.S. Army, led in plan-ning overall war strategy from his headquarters in Washington, D.C., and Lt. Gen. DWIGHT D. EISENHOWER was named commander of Allied forces organized to invade North Africa. Gen. GEORGE S. PATTON led the Allied West Task Force ashore in Morocco in the invasion of North Africa in No-vember 1942, which resulted in the recapture of the region from German and Italian forces. Promoted to four-star general, Eisenhower organized the Allied invasions of Sicily in July 1943 and of Italy in September 1943, led by Patton and later Gen. OMAR BRADLEY, who replaced Patton as commander of U.S. ground forces for the invasion of France.

The United States initially fared badly in the Pacific, as the Japanese quickly overran the Philippines, Guam, and Wake Island. Gen. DOUGLAS MACARTHUR, commander of the Southwest Pacific Allied Forces, led land forces of combined Philippine and American troops in defense of the Philippines in December 1941. Unable to defeat the Japanese, MacArthur abandoned Manila and withdrew to nearby Bataan Peninsula. President Roosevelt ordered MacArthur to Australia, where he became supreme com-mander of the Allied forces in the Pacific. As he left in March 1942, he promised the Filipinos, "I shall return." His exhausted troops surrendered to the Japanese and were forced to walk to prison camps in what came to be known as the Bataan Death March.

Adm. ERNEST J. KING, commander of the combined U.S. fleet and naval operations chief, recognized the importance of an air war and the superiority of aircraft carriers over battleships, and the tide began to turn in 1942. Under the direction of Adm. CHESTER W. NIMITZ, commander of the U.S. Pacific Fleet, the Battle of the CORAL SEA (May 4–8, 1942) was fought from aircraft carriers and temporarily halted the threat to Australia. The Battle of MIDWAY (June 4, 1942), led by Rear Adm. RAYMOND SPRUANCE, was the first notable victory of the war. Further efforts to stop Japanese expansion in the South Pacific included a series of sea battles and island landings in the Solomon Islands (1942–43), the Gilbert Islands (1943), the Marshalls, Marianas, Palaus, and the Philippines (1944), and Iwo Jima and Okinawa (1945). This, combined with MacArthur's offensive island-hopping operations, led to MacArthur's return to the Philippines in October 1944. The Philippines were liberated after battles in the Philippine Sea, LUZON LEYTE GULF, and CORREGIDOR.

A Russian counteroffensive between November 1942 and March 1943 led to the Russians lifting a seventeen-month siege of Leningrad on January 18, 1943, and retaking Stalingrad (February 2) and several other cities. The Russians then took the offensive, and by 1944 they had occupied Poland, Hungary, and the Balkans. The German submarine forces were destroyed.

Selected supreme commander of the Allied Expeditionary Force in Europe in December 1943, Eisenhower coordinated the plan to cross the English Channel in early June 1944 and invade Normandy on the coast of northern France. Called Operation Overlord, the invasion began June 6, 1944 (D-DAY), and resulted in capture of the beaches of Normandy. By late 1944 France and Belgium were freed and Allied troops were in Holland and Germany. Heavy Allied bombing hammered the industrial centers of Germany. On December 16–26, 1944, the Nazis tried a last desperate counteroffensive in the BATTLE OF THE BULGE, but it was thwarted, and the Allies swept into Germany. Hitler, trapped in a Berlin bunker between Russians advancing from the east and Americans and British from the west, committed suicide. The German provisional government announced his death on May 1, 1945, and on V-E DAY, May 8, Germany's unconditional surrender was celebrated. The Soviet Union then declared war on Japan and occupied Manchuria.

Allied planes had started bombing Tokyo in February 1945, and while U.S. troops were preparing to invade Japan, President HARRY S. TRUMAN, who had succeeded to the presidency upon Roosevelt's death April 12, 1945, ordered ATOMIC BOMBS (fruits of the Manhattan Project) to be dropped on Hiroshima on August 6, 1945, and on Nagasaki three days later, ushering in the nuclear age. Japan surrendered and on V-J DAY, August 15, 1945, World War II ended.

Military deaths in the worldwide conflict were predictably massive, totaling in excess of 17 million troops. The number of civilian deaths due to bombing raids, starvation, and disease was even greater. When the Allies liberated the death camps in Germany and Poland, they were horrified to discover the extent of the Holocaust that Germany had conducted during the war. Some 12 million people had been murdered, including 6 million Jews. The Soviet Union suffered the most deaths of any single country — about 20 million military personnel and civilians died. The United States lost more than 405,000 troops.

WorldCom Bankruptcy (2002), the largest corporate fraud and business failure in U.S. history. WorldCom was the nation's second-largest long distance and data services provider (after AT&T). In 2002, as a result of an internal audit of the company's accounting, the Securities and Exchange Commission (SEC) launched an investigation that resulted in charges of improper bookkeeping and fraudulent accounting dating back to 1999. It was eventually found that a handful of corporate executives allegedly overstated the company's financial statements by $11 billion. Shares, which previously had been as high as sixty-four dollars, plummeted, falling as low as twenty cents. WorldCom's bankruptcy was twice the size of ENRON's, and severely rocked investor confidence in the global financial markets. In 2003, under new management and renamed MCI, the company was controversially given a government contract to build a wireless telephone network in Iraq.

Wounded Knee, Battle of (December 29, 1890), massacre of 146 Sioux men, women, and children by U.S. soldiers at Wounded Knee, South Dakota, the last major clash between federal troops and American Indians. Sweeping through the western reservations was a religion centering on the Ghost Dance ritual, which predicted the coming of an Indian Messiah and the restoring of America to the Indians. Fearful that the religion would incite an uprising, authorities sent troops to arrest Sioux leaders. On December 14, SITTING BULL suffered fatal wounds while resisting arrest. The Sioux warriors were ordered to disarm; when they refused, federal troops opened fire, killing Chief Big Foot and most of his followers. Those who survived were pursued and butchered.

Wozniak, Stephen (1950–), inventor and computer executive. Wozniak helped launch the personal computer industry when he cofounded Apple Computer, Inc., with STEVE JOBS in 1976. He built the first Apple computer in his garage. When his employer at the time, Hewlett Packard, decided not to develop the product, Wozniak and Jobs produced it themselves. Disinterested in the management aspects of business, "Woz" left Apple in 1985 to pursue further creative interests.

Wright, Fanny (Frances; 1795–1852), reformer. Wright was born in Scotland but had an early interest in America. She was appalled by the practice of slavery, and in her efforts to see it abolished, she established Nashoba in Tennessee, a community where slaves (purchased by Wright) could be educated and work for their freedom. She became ill with malaria and went to Europe to recuperate, and without her leadership the colony failed. She eventually freed the slaves who had been members of the colony and paid for their transportation to Haiti. Wright's colorful accounts of her travels were published as *Views of Society and Manners in America* (1821). She also lobbied for equal rights for women, liberal divorce laws, birth control, and free love, which placed her on the fringes of society. However, she was recognized as one of the early reformers who influenced the beginnings of the woman suffrage movement.

Wright, Frank Lloyd (1867–1959), architect. One of the most innovative and influential figures in modern architecture, Wright championed the virtues of organic architecture, or buildings based on natural forms and reflecting their function and their surroundings. During his seventy-year career, he designed buildings in styles ranging from those of the late 1800s to ultra-modern. During his final years, Wright designed two of his most famous projects, the Guggenheim Museum in New York City and the Marin County Civic Center in California.

Wright, Richard (1908–60), black writer and social critic. Wright gained a reputation for artistic excellence and outspoken criticism of social injustice and the plight of blacks. His first novel, *Native Son* (1940), portrays a black Chicago youth victimized and enraged by whites. Wright's other works include his autobiographical *Black Boy* (1945) and its sequel *American Hunger* (1977), and *White Man, Listen!* (1957). He inspired other black writers including JAMES BALDWIN and RALPH ELLISON.

Wright, Wilbur (1867–1912), and **Orville Wright** (1871–1948), aviation pioneers. The Wright brothers achieved the first sustained, powered, controlled flight in a heavier-than-air machine. Beginning as bicycle manufacturers in Dayton, Ohio, in 1892, the brothers became interested in flight, first experimenting with gliders and kites. On December 17, 1903, near Kitty Hawk, North Carolina, they made history with four successful flights, the longest being 852 feet and lasting 59 seconds. The Wrights improved their machine and patented it in 1906. A series of exhibitions in the United States and Europe popularized flying and led to the formation of the Wright Company in 1909 to manufacture aircraft.

Writs of Assistance, general search warrants used in colonial times by British agents to find smuggled goods. The writs did not specify the places to be searched or the goods to be seized. JAMES OTIS strongly opposed the indiscriminate use of the writs of assistance by the British. The controversy over the writs eventually led to the Fourth Amendment in the Bill of Rights.

Wyeth, family of painters and illustrators. N. C. Wyeth (Newell Convers; 1882–1945), a distinguished illustrator of children's books, illustrated twenty-five juvenile classics, including *Treasure Island* and *Robinson Crusoe,* for Charles Scribner's Sons. Noted for his naturalistic style, he taught his disciplined drafting techniques to his son, Andrew Wyeth (1917–). Known for his realistic, almost photographic paintings of people and places in rural Pennsylvania and Maine, Andrew's works in watercolor and tempera present careful detail of old buildings and deserted beaches. His best-known work is *Christina's World* (1948). His son James Browning Wyeth (1946–) is also a painter.

Wyoming (Equality State) became the forty-fourth state in the Union on July 10, 1890. (See maps, pages 540 and 541.) The largest cities include Cheyenne (the capital), Casper, Laramie, and Rock Springs. Wyoming is called "the equality state" because it was the first to give women the right to vote. In 1872 Congress designated Yellowstone the first national park; its famous geyser, Old Faithful, spurts into the air every sixty-five minutes. Tourists are also attracted to the Grand Teton National Park and Jackson Hole National Monument. Wyoming is a leader in the production of wool, sheep, cattle, oil, uranium, and natural gas. JACKSON POLLOCK was born in the state.

Wythe, George (1726–1806), statesman, lawyer, and judge. Wythe, a well-known attorney and jurist, trained many of the leading lawyers of his time, including Thomas Jefferson, John Marshall, and Henry Clay, and signed the Declaration of Independence. As a member of the VIRGINIA HOUSE OF BURGESSES he had drafted Virginia's protest against the STAMP ACT. He later served in the Second CONTINENTAL CONGRESS. In 1779 Wythe received the nation's first law professorship at the College of William and Mary. He helped secure Virginia's ratification of the U.S. Constitution in 1788 and served as state chancellor from 1788 to 1801. In 1806 Wythe was poisoned by his grandnephew, who wanted to collect his inheritance. The murderer was acquitted, ironically, because the only witness was a slave, who was barred from testifying by a Virginia law that Wythe had drafted in the 1770s. Wythe, however, lived long enough to disinherit the young man.

XYZ Affair (1797–98), scandal caused by three French agents offering bribes to U.S. representatives who were attempting to negotiate a treaty with France. The incident almost led the two countries to war. ELBRIDGE GERRY, JOHN MARSHALL, and CHARLES C. PINCKNEY were sent to France by President JOHN ADAMS to negotiate difficulties resulting from JAY'S TREATY and French seizure of American ships. French agents, later identified by the American envoys only as X, Y, and Z, demanded a loan of $12 million and payment of a $250,000 bribe to French foreign minister Charles Maurice Talleyrand before discussions could take place. The terms were refused, and Adams reported the mission's failure to Congress. The publication of the correspondence regarding the affair led to anger in the United States and to two years of fighting between French and American ships, although there was no official declaration of war.

Y **Yalta Conference** (February 4–11, 1945), meeting between President FRANKLIN D. ROOSEVELT, British prime minister Winston Churchill, and Soviet premier Joseph Stalin at Yalta in the Russian Crimea during the last year of WORLD WAR II. The Allies agreed upon final plans for the defeat of Germany and the occupation and control of Germany after the war, including its division into four occupied zones. They also called for a conference at San Francisco to draw up a charter for the UNITED NATIONS. The Soviet Union agreed to join the war against Japan after Germany's defeat and to hold free elections in Eastern European countries under its sway. Because Stalin failed to keep the latter agreement and instead installed governments dominated by the Soviet Union, critics in the United States later charged that FDR had "sold out" American interests at Yalta, even though it was Stalin who broke the agreement.

Yamasaki, Minoru (1912–86), architect. Yamasaki was a chief designer of the WORLD TRADE CENTER complex in Manhattan. Born in Seattle, he worked for prominent architectural firms in New York City before forming his own company in 1949. Although he favored traditional Japanese design, he gained recognition for his sleek, modern design of many universities in the Midwest and numerous airports, including the Lambert–St. Louis

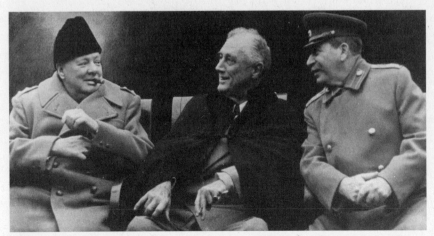

Yalta
Winston Churchill, Franklin D. Roosevelt, and Joseph Stalin at the Yalta conference, February 1945.

Municipal Airport. Yamasaki designed the U.S. Science Pavilion for the 1962 World's Fair in Seattle, famed for its soaring arches and Gothic influences, before preliminary work began on the World Trade Center in 1965. Despite the enormity of the explosion of the WORLD TRADE CENTER ATTACK in 1993, the foundation was unaffected by the blast. Yamasaki's engineering skill was credited at the time with thwarting the terrorist plan to topple the 110-story north tower.

"Yankee Doodle," song popularized from the 1750s through the years of the American Revolution. Although the tune probably originated during the Middle Ages, the American words were written, a common legend has it, by British army surgeon Dr. Richard Schuckburgh in 1775 to ridicule untrained American troops during the French and Indian War. The colonists nevertheless soon came to like the term and the song became popular, sung by troops throughout the course of the Revolution.

Yeager, Chuck (Charles; 1923–), World War II fighter pilot and test pilot. On October 14, 1947, Yeager became the first person to fly faster than the speed of sound, piloting the Bell X-1 rocket plane to a level flight speed of about 670 miles per hour. Yeager also set a world speed record when he flew the Air Force's Bell X-1A rocket plane at 1,650 miles per hour, or over 2½ times the speed of sound. He served on the presidential commission to investigate the CHALLENGER DISASTER in 1986.

Yellow Journalism, also called the *yellow press,* a term describing the use of extreme sensationalism and blaring headlines in newspapers and magazines to attract readers. The term was derived from an early comic strip character called the "Yellow Kid," which first appeared in JOSEPH PULITZER's *New York World* (1896). Yellow journalism reached its peak in 1898 when Pulitzer and WILLIAM RANDOLPH HEARST, editor of the *New York Journal,* were competing for circulation. Supporting the Cuban revolution, they exaggerated and falsified stories to attract readers and sell papers, contributing to U.S. involvement in the SPANISH-AMERICAN WAR.

York, Alvin (1887–1964), WORLD WAR I hero. Originally a conscientious objector, York enlisted in the army in 1917. On October 8, 1918, he and his men captured a German machine-gun nest in the Argonne Forest. Twenty-five German soldiers were killed, and York, acting mostly on his own, took 132 enemy prisoners. He was promoted to sergeant and given more than fifty decorations, including the Congressional Medal of Honor. A movie was made about his exploit.

Yorktown, Battle of (August 30–October 19, 1781), the last major battle of the AMERICAN REVOLUTION. Gen. George Washington and the Continental army, aided by French general Jean Rochambeau and French troops, surrounded British general CHARLES CORNWALLIS and British troops on the Yorktown, Virginia, peninsula. A French fleet under Adm. François de Grasse drove away the British fleet trying to bring help to Cornwallis.

Surrounded on land and blockaded by sea, Cornwallis surrendered his army of more than six thousand men to Washington, resulting in the decisive victory that earned independence for the United States.

Young, Andrew, Jr. (1932–), clergyman, civil rights leader, politician, and diplomat. During the 1960s, as a minister for the United Church of Christ, Young joined the SOUTHERN CHRISTIAN LEADERSHIP CONFERENCE (SCLC), serving as executive director from 1964 to 1970. Young served as a Democratic member of the House of Representatives from 1973 to 1977, becoming the first black elected to Congress from the South since 1901. Young was also the first black to serve as U.S. ambassador to the United Nations, a post he held from 1977 to 1979. In 1978 he received the SPINGARN MEDAL for his political work. In 1981 Young won election as mayor of Atlanta, Georgia, serving until 1989.

Young, Brigham (1801–77), Mormon leader and colonizer. After the murder of Mormon leader JOSEPH SMITH in 1844, Young assumed leadership, serving as president of the church until his death in 1877. Young in 1846 led the MORMONS on their westward migration from Illinois to the Great Salt Lake Valley in Utah, where they established a prosperous settlement. He also directed the colonization of several hundred other settlements in Utah, Idaho, Wyoming, Nevada, Arizona, and California. Young became the first territorial governor of Utah. He established telegraph lines and railroads to connect Mormon communities in Idaho, Utah, and Nevada. He built the Mormon Tabernacle in Salt Lake City and founded Brigham Young University and what is now the University of Utah. He was an energetic politician and leader for thirty-three years.

Young, Cy (Denton True; 1867–1955), baseball player. Playing twenty-two years in the major leagues, Young won (511) and lost (313) more games than any pitcher in the history of baseball. He also pitched the most completed games (751), the most innings (7,356), and the most consecutive hitless innings (23). The award given annually to the best pitcher from both the American and the National Leagues is named for him. He entered the Hall of Fame in 1937.

Yugoslav Crises, two U.S. military interventions during the 1990s, first in Bosnia-Herzegovina and later in Kosovo following the breakup of Yugoslavia. In February of 1992 the Croats and Muslims of Bosnia and Herzegovina declared independence from Yugoslavia. Recognized by the United States and what is now the European Union, it entered the United Nations, but Bosnian Serbs opposed the new republic and responded with armed resistance, leading to three years of interethnic civil war. Muslims were forced from their homes and thousands were killed or placed in detention camps as part of a Serbian "ethnic cleansing" policy. Although military intervention was rejected, the U.N. established "safe areas" where Muslims would be safe. Several attacks of the "safe areas" led to U.S. intervention, which eventually achieved a formal end to the war in November of 1995 when the leaders of Bosnia, Croatia, and Serbia met in Dayton, Ohio, to broker a peace accord (the Dayton Agreement). The accord provided for a 60,000-strong NATO-led force for peacekeeping purposes, and in December President BILL CLINTON sent the first 8,000 of 20,000 U.S. troops to Bosnia. Although the accord was implemented and conditions slowly improved, all provisions have not been realized, and traditional divisions among Serbs, Croats, and Muslims continue. U.S. forces have been reduced significantly, but NATO-led peacekeeping forces remain in the region.

By the summer of 1998, full-scale war had erupted in Kosovo between Kosovar Albanians seeking independence and the Serbian government, resulting in the killing and deportation of thousands of ethnic Albanians. When a NATO-brokered cease-fire and peace talks between the Serbs and the Albanians broke down, the United States and Britain took the lead when NATO forces (without U.N. support) waged an air campaign (March 24–June 10, 1999) against Serbia in an effort to end the atrocities of the practice of "ethnic cleansing" and allow the return of ethnic Albanian refugees to their homes. Serbia agreed to sign a U.N.-approved peace agreement with NATO, and an international peacekeeping force headed by NATO was delegated to monitor Kosovo and the return of the refugees. Although NATO reacted far more quickly in Kosovo than in the Bosnia crisis, it was still too late to prevent terrible human rights abuses. Several accidental civilian attacks and the destructive use of air power to cripple the economic and military capacity of the country clearly harmed its people, and NATO came under strong criticism over the legitimacy of its actions in Kosovo. Acceptance by the American public was cautious, due to the tragic loss of American soldiers in the SOMALIA INTERVENTION and the concurrent presence of troops in Bosnia.

Zaharias, Babe Didrikson (Mildred Ella; 1914–56), athlete. Although she became most famous for her performance in golf and track and field, Didrikson excelled at every sport she tried and is considered one of the twentieth century's greatest athletes. In the 1932 Olympics she won two gold medals and one silver medal in track and field events. After several successful years as an amateur golfer, she turned professional in 1948 and won the U.S. Women's Open title three times. Didrikson was an expert in pocket billiards, tennis, swimming, diving, rifle shooting, basketball, and baseball. She was called "Babe," after baseball player Babe Ruth, because of her success at baseball as a child. She died of cancer at age forty-two.

Zanuck, Darryl (1902–79), film executive. Zanuck wrote *Rin Tin Tin* and other scripts for silent films and produced the first talkie, *The Jazz Singer* (1927). In 1933, with Joseph Schenck, he founded Twentieth Century

Pictures, and in 1934 Twentieth Century-Fox. Zanuck produced *The Grapes of Wrath* (1940), *Gentleman's Agreement* (1947), *The Longest Day* (1962), and *The Sound of Music* (1965).

Zenger, John Peter (1697–1746), German-born printer and journalist. As printer of the *New-York Weekly Journal,* a publication backed by political opponents of the colonial government, Zenger was arrested and tried in 1735 for criminal libel for printing bitter attacks against the royal governor of New York. Defended by Philadelphia lawyer Andrew Hamilton (1676–1741), Zenger was acquitted on the grounds that he had printed the truth, and the truth cannot be defined as libelous. Zenger published an account of his trial, *A Brief Narrative of the Case and Tryal of John Peter Zenger* (1736). The Zenger case provided a major symbolic victory for freedom of the press in the American colonies.

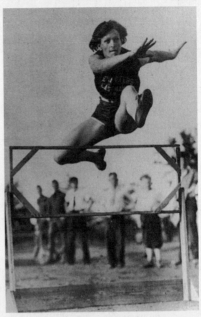

Babe Didrikson Zaharias

Ziegfeld, Florenz (1867–1932), theatrical producer. Ziegfeld produced a series of lavish Broadway musicals starring French actress Anna Held. His greatest success came with his *Follies of* 1907, popularizing a new form of sophisticated entertainment called the revue. Eventually named *The Ziegfeld Follies,* it was presented annually until 1931, with a few exceptions. Produced in a lavish style, the shows featured a sixty-woman chorus and the music of IRVING BERLIN, Jerome Kern, and Victor Herbert. Such talents as FANNY BRICE, W. C. FIELDS, EDDIE CANTOR, and Ed Wynn achieved stardom through the *Follies.*

Zimmermann Note (1917), a message from German foreign minister Alfred Zimmermann to the German ambassador to Mexico during World War I, instructing him to persuade Mexico to make war on the United States. In return, Mexico would be given financial aid and restoration of its lost territory of New Mexico, Texas, and Arizona. Intercepted and decoded by the British Secret Service, the telegram was turned over to the U.S. State Department and published by the Associated Press on March 1. It provided strong proof of German hostility toward the United States and helped persuade Congress to vote a declaration of war in April.

Suggested
Additional Reading

★   ★   ★   ★   ★   ★

The American Indian

Beal, Merrill D. *"I Will Fight No More Forever": Chief Joseph and the Nez Perce War.* New York: Ballantine, 1975.

Brown, Dee. *Bury My Heart at Wounded Knee: An Indian History of the American West.* New York: Holt, 1991.

Foreman, Grant. *Indian Removal: The Emigration of the Five Civilized Tribes of Indians.* Norman: University of Oklahoma Press, 1953.

Hoxie, Frederick E., ed. *Encyclopedia of North American Indians.* Boston: Houghton Mifflin, 1996.

Josephy, Alvin M., Jr. *The Indian Heritage of America.* Boston: Houghton Mifflin, 1991.

Josephy, Alvin M., Jr., ed. *America in 1492: The World of the Indian Peoples before the Arrival of Columbus.* New York: Knopf, 1992.

Antebellum Period, 1800–60

Peterson, Merrill D. *The Great Triumvirate: Webster, Clay, and Calhoun.* New York: Oxford University Press, 1987.

Potter, David M., and Don Fehrenbacher, *The Impending Crisis, 1848–1861.* New York: Harper and Row, 1976.

Schlesinger, Arthur M., Jr. *The Age of Jackson.* Boston: Little, Brown, 1953.

Stampp, Kenneth M. *The Peculiar Institution: Slavery in the Ante-Bellum South.* New York: Vintage, 1964.

Between the Wars

Allen, Frederick Lewis. *Only Yesterday and Since Yesterday: A Popular History of the '20s and '30s.* New York: Bonanza, 1986.

Brinkley, Alan. *Voices of Protest: Huey Long, Father Coughlin, and the Great Depression.* New York: Vintage, 1983.

Galbraith, John Kenneth. *The Great Crash, 1929.* Boston: Houghton Mifflin, 1988.

Garraty, John A. *The Great Depression.* New York: Doubleday, 1987.

Leuchtenburg, William E. *Franklin D. Roosevelt and the New Deal, 1932–1940.* New York: Harper and Row, 1963.

Biographies

Albright, Madeleine. *Madam Secretary.* New York: Miramax Books, 2003.

Berg, A. Scott. *Lindbergh.* New York: Putnam's, 1998.

Brands, H. W. *The First American: The Life and Times of Benjamin Franklin.* New York: Anchor Books, 2000.

Brookhiser, Richard. *America's First Dynasty: The Adamses.* New York: The Free Press, 2002.

Brookhiser, Richard. *Founding Father: Rediscovering George Washington.* New York: The Free Press, 1996.

Burns, James MacGregor. *Roosevelt: The Lion and the Fox.* Norwalk, CT: Easton Press, 1989.

Burns, James MacGregor. *Roosevelt: The Soldier of Freedom.* Norwalk, CT: Easton Press, 1989.

Cannon, Lori. *President Reagan: The Role of a Lifetime.* New York: Public Affairs, 2000.

Caro, Robert. *The Years of Lyndon Johnson: Master of the Senate.* New York: Knopf, 2002.

Clinton, Hillary Rodham. *Living History.* New York: Simon and Schuster, 2003.

Cunningham, Noble E., Jr. *In Pursuit of Reason: The Life of Thomas Jefferson.* Baton Rouge: Louisiana State University Press, 1987.

Dalleck, Robert. *An Unfinished Life: John F. Kennedy, 1917–1963.* Boston: Little, Brown and Co., 2003.

D'Este, Carlo. *Eisenhower.* New York: Henry Holt, 2002.

Diggins, John Patrick. *John Adams.* New York: Henry Holt, 2003.

Ferling, John. *John Adams.* New York: Henry Holt, 1992.

Freedman, Russell. *Lincoln: A Photobiography.* New York: Clarion, 1987.

Gordon-Reed, Annette. *Thomas Jefferson and Sally Hemmings: An American Controversy.* Charlottesville: University Press of Virginia, 1997.

Graham, Katharine. *Personal History.* New York: Random House, 1997.

Halberstam, David. *The Teammates.* New York: Hyperion Press, 2003.

Hamilton, Nigel. *Bill Clinton: An American Journey.* New York: Random House, 2003.

Isaacson, Walter. *Benjamin Franklin.* New York: Simon and Schuster, 2003.

Kennedy, John F. *Profiles in Courage.* New York: Harper and Row, 1991.

Levin, Phyllis Lee. *Abigail Adams: A Biography.* New York: St. Martins, 1987.

Maraniss, David. *First in His Class: The Biography of Bill Clinton.* New York: Simon and Schuster, 1995.

McCullough, David. *John Adams.* New York: Simon and Schuster, 2001.

McCullough, David. *Truman.* New York: Simon and Schuster, 1992.

McFeely, William S. *Grant: A Biography.* New York: Norton, 1981.

McFeely, William S. *Frederick Douglass.* New York: Norton, 1991.

Miller, Merle. *Lyndon: An Oral Biography.* New York: Putnam, 1980.

Miller, Merle. *Plain Speaking: An Oral Biography of Harry S. Truman.* New York: Greenwich House, 1985.

Morris, Edmund. *The Rise of Theodore Roosevelt.* New York: Modern Library, 2001.

Morris, Edmund. *Theodore Rex.* New York: Modern Library, 2002.

Oates, Stephen B. *With Malice Toward None: The Life of Abraham Lincoln.* New York: Harper and Row, 1977.

Remini, Robert V. *John Quincy Adams.* New York: Henry Holt, 2002.

Schlesinger, Arthur M., Jr. *A Thousand Days: John F. Kennedy in the White House.* New York: Greenwich House, 1983.

Van Doren, Carl. *Benjamin Franklin.* New York: Penguin, 1991.

Williams, T. Harry. *Huey Long*. New York: Vintage, 1981.

X, Malcolm. *The Autobiography of Malcolm X*. New York: Grove Press, 1965.

Black History

Branch, Taylor. *Parting the Waters: America in the King Years, 1954–1963*. New York: Simon and Schuster, 1988.

Franklin, John Hope. *From Slavery to Freedom: A History of Negro Americans*. New York: Knopf, 1988.

Franklin, John Hope. *Race and History: Selected Essays, 1938–1988*. Baton Rouge: Louisiana State University Press, 1989.

Jones, Jacqueline. *Labor of Love, Labor of Sorrow: Black Women, Work, and the Family, from Slavery to the Present*. New York: Vintage, 1986.

Kluger, Richard. *Simple Justice: The History of* Brown *v.* Board of Education *and Black America's Struggle for Equality*. New York: Vintage, 1977.

Low, W. Augustus, and Virgil A. Clift, eds. *Encyclopedia of Black America*. New York: Da Capo, 1984.

Oates, Stephen B. *Let the Trumpet Sound: The Life of Martin Luther King, Jr.* New York: New American Library, 1983.

Woodward, Bob. *Shadow*. New York: Simon and Schuster, 1999.

The Civil War

Donald, David. *Lincoln Reconsidered: Essays on the Civil War Era*. New York: Vintage, 1964.

Foote, Shelby. *The Civil War: A Narrative*. 3 vols. New York: Vintage, 1986.

Leech, Margaret. *Reveille in Washington, 1860–1865*. Alexandria, VA: Time-Life, 1980.

McPherson, James M. *Battle Cry of Freedom: The Civil War Era*. New York: Oxford University Press, 1988.

McPherson, James M. *Hallowed Ground: A Walk at Gettysburg*. New York: Crown, 2003.

Sears, Stephen W. *Gettysburg*. Boston: Houghton Mifflin, 2003.

Wills, Garry. *Lincoln at Gettysburg: The Words That Remade America*. New York: Simon and Schuster, 1992.

The Constitution

Bernstein, Richard B., and Kym S. Rice. *Are We to Be a Nation? The Making of the Constitution*. Cambridge, MA: Harvard University Press, 1987.

Kelly, Alfred H. *The American Constitution: Its Origins and Development*. Winfred A. Harbison, and Herman Belz. seventh ed. New York: Norton, 1991.

Rossiter, Clinton. *1787: The Grand Convention*. New York: Macmillan, 1966.

Sexton, John, and Nat Brandt. *How Free Are We? What the Constitution Says We Can and Cannot Do*. New York: Evans, 1986.

Van Doren, Carl. *The Great Rehearsal: The Story of the Making and Ratifying of the Constitution of the United States*. New York: Penguin, 1986.

Exploration, Colonization, and Revolution

Bakeless, John Edwin. *The Eyes of Discovery: The Pageant of North America as Seen by Its First Explorers*. New York: Dover, 1989.

Commager, Henry Steele, and Richard B. Morris. *The Spirit of 'Seventy-Six: The of the American Revolution as Told by Participants*. New York: Harper a 1975.

Draper, Theodore. *A Struggle for Power: The American Revolution.* New York: Times Books, 1996.

Ellis, Joseph J. *Founding Brothers: The Revolutionary Generation.* New York: Knopf, 2001.

Greene, Jack P., and J. R. Pole, eds. *The Blackwell Encyclopedia of the American Revolution.* Cambridge, MA: Blackwell Reference, 1991.

Hawke, David Freeman. *Everyday Life in Early America.* New York: Harper and Row, 1988.

Kerber, Linda K. *Women of the Republic: Intellect and Ideology in Revolutionary America.* New York: Norton, 1986.

Morris, Richard B. *The Peacemakers: The Great Powers and American Independence.* Boston: Northeastern University Press, 1983.

Scheer George F., and Hugh F. Rankin. *Rebels and Redcoats: The American Revolution through the Eyes of Those Who Fought and Lived It.* New York: Da Capo, 1987.

Simmons, R. C. *The American Colonies from Settlement to Independence.* New York: Norton, 1980.

From the Cold War to the Collapse of Communism

Dionne, E. J., Jr. *Why Americans Hate Politics.* New York: Simon and Schuster, 1991.

Goldman, Eric F. *The Crucial Decade — and After: America, 1945–1960.* New York: Knopf, 1966.

Griffith, Robert. *The Politics of Fear: Joseph R. McCarthy and the Senate.* Amherst: University of Massachusetts Press, 1987.

Lewis, Anthony. *Gideon's Trumpet.* New York: Vintage, 1989.

Lewis, Anthony. *Make No Law: The Sullivan Case and the First Amendment.* New York: Vintage, 1992.

Karnow, Stanley. *Vietnam: A History.* New York: Penguin, 1991.

Kennedy, Robert F. *Thirteen Days: A Memoir of the Cuban Missile Crisis.* New York: Norton, 1971.

Lukas, J. Anthony. *Nightmare: The Underside of the Nixon Years.* New York: Viking, 1976.

Manchester, William. *The Glory and the Dream: A Narrative History of America. 1932–1972.* New York: Bantam, 1990.

Patterson, James T. *Grand Expectations: The United States, 1945–1974.* New York: Oxford University Press, 1996.

Williams, William A., et al., eds. *America in Vietnam: A Documentary History.* New York: Norton, 1989.

Yergin, Daniel. *Shattered Peace: The Origins of the Cold War.* New York: Penguin, 1990.

General Histories

Boller, Paul F. *Not So Popular Myths about America's Past from Columbus to Clinton.* New York: ̷ ̷ ̷ ̷ sity Press, 1996.

̷ ̷ ̷ *American Heritage Encyclopedia of American History.* New York:

̷ ̷ ̷ Garraty, eds. *The Reader's Companion to American History.* ̷ ̷ flin, 1991.

̷ ̷ ̷ gs Everyone Should Know about American History. New York:

̷ ̷ ̷ rd Guide to United States Supreme Court Decisions. New York:

̷ ̷ ̷ New Encyclopedia of American Scandal. New York: Facts on

Morris, Richard B., ed. *Encyclopedia of American History*. sixth ed. New York: Harper and Row, 1982.

Nevins, Allan, Henry Steele Commager, and Jeffrey B. Morris. *A Pocket History of the United States*. New York: Washington Square Press, 1986.

Ravitch, Diane, ed. *The American Reader: Words That Moved a Nation*. New York: HarperCollins, 1990.

Shenkman, Richard. *Legends, Lies, and Cherished Myths of American History*. New York: Morrow, 1988.

The Gilded Age and the Progressive Era

Asinof, Eliot. *Eight Men Out: The Black Sox and the 1919 World Series*. New York: Holt, 1987.

Cashman, Sean Dennis. *America in the Gilded Age: From the Death of Lincoln to the Rise of Theodore Roosevelt*. New York: New York University Press, 1988.

Hofstadter, Richard. *The Age of Reform: From Bryan to F.D.R.* New York: Knopf, 1955.

Link, Arthur S. *Woodrow Wilson and the Progressive Era, 1910–1917*. Norwalk, CT: Easton Press, 1982.

Mowry, George E. *The Era of Theodore Roosevelt, 1900–1912*. New York: Harper and Row, 1958.

Historical Novels

Gingrich, Newt, and William Forstchen. *Gettysburg: A Novel of the Civil War*. New York: Thomas Dunne Books, 2003.

Haley, Alex. *Roots*. New York: Doubleday, 1976.

Sandburg, Carl. *Remembrance Rock*. San Diego: Harcourt Brace Jovanovich, 1991.

Shaara, Michael. *The Killer Angels*. New York: McKay, 1974.

Vidal, Gore. *Lincoln: A Novel*. New York: Random House, 1984.

Warren, Robert Penn. *All the King's Men*. San Diego: Harcourt Brace Jovanovich, 1946, 1982.

Immigration

Barton, Josef J. *Peasants and Strangers: Italians, Romanians, and Slovaks in an American City*. Cambridge, MA: Harvard University Press, 1975.

Daniels, Roger. *Coming to America: A History of Immigration and Ethnicity in American Life*. New York: HarperCollins, 1990.

Golab, Caroline. *Immigrant Destinations*. Philadelphia: Temple University Press, 1977.

Jones, Maldwyn Allen. *American Immigration*. second ed. Chicago: University of Chicago Press, 1992.

Mangione, Jerre, and Ben Morreale. *La Storia: Five Hundred Years of the Italian-American Experience, 1492–1992*. New York: HarperCollins, 1992.

The Presidency

Andrew, Christopher. *For the President's Eyes Only: Secret Intelligence and the American Presidency from Washington to Bush*. New York: Harper-Collins, 1995.

Bernstein, Carl, and Bob Woodward. *All the President's Men*. New York: Simon and Schuster, 1974.

Boller, Paul F., Jr. *Presidential Campaigns*. New York: Oxford University Press, 1984.

McGinniss, Joe. *The Selling of the President, 1968*. New York: Trident Press, 1969.

Rossiter, Clinton. *The American Presidency*. Baltimore: Johns Hopkins University Press, 1987.

Schlesinger, Arthur M., Jr. *The Imperial Presidency.* Boston: Houghton Mifflin, 1989.

White, Theodore H. *The Making of the President, 1960.* New York: Atheneum, 1988.

Wills, Garry. *Nixon Agonistes: The Crisis of the Self-Made Man.* Atlanta: Cherokee, 1990.

Woodward, Bob, and Carl Bernstein. *The Final Days.* New York: Simon and Schuster, 1976.

Reconstruction

Benedict, Michael L. *The Impeachment and Trial of Andrew Johnson.* New York: Norton, 1973.

Brodie, Fawn M. *Thaddeus Stevens, Scourge of the South.* New York: Norton, 1959.

Du Bois, W.E.B. *The Souls of Black Folk.* New York: Vintage, 1990.

Foner, Eric. *Reconstruction: America's Unfinished Revolution, 1863–1877.* New York: Harper and Row, 1989.

Foner, Eric. *A Short History of Reconstruction, 1863–1877.* New York: Harper and Row, 1990.

Lewis, David Levering. *W.E.B. DuBois: A Biography of a Race, 1868–1919.* New York: Henry Holt, 1993.

Women's History

Clinton, Catherine. *The Other Civil War: American Women in the Nineteenth Century.* New York: Hill and Wang, 1984.

Flexner, Eleanor. *Century of Struggle: The Woman's Rights Movement in the United States.* Cambridge, MA: Harvard University Press, 1975.

Hoff-Wilson, Joan. *Law, Gender, and Injustice: A Legal History of U.S. Women.* New York: New York University Press, 1991.

Lerner, Gerda. *The Majority Finds Its Past: Placing Women in History.* New York: Oxford University Press, 1979.

World War I

Coffman, Edward M. *The War to End All Wars: The American Military Experience in World War I.* Madison: University of Wisconsin Press, 1986.

Ferrell, Robert H. *Woodrow Wilson and World War I, 1917–1921.* New York: Harper and Row, 1985.

Tuchman, Barbara W. *The Zimmermann Telegram.* New York: Macmillan, 1966.

World War II

Brinkley, David. *Washington Goes to War.* New York: Knopf, 1988.

Brokaw, Tom. *The Greatest Generation.* New York: Random House, 1998.

Churchill, Winston S. *The Second World War.* 6 vols. Boston: Houghton Mifflin, 1985.

Fussell, Paul. *Wartime: Understanding and Behavior in the Second World War.* New York: Oxford University Press, 1989.

Goodwin, Doris Kearns. *No Ordinary Time: Franklin and Eleanor Roosevelt: The Home Front in World War II.* New York: Simon and Schuster, 1994.

Irons, Peter. *Justice at War.* New York: Oxford University Press, 1983.

Prange, Gordon W. *At Dawn We Slept: The Untold Story of Pearl Harbor.* New York: Viking, 1991.

Appendix

★ ★ ★ ★ ★ ★

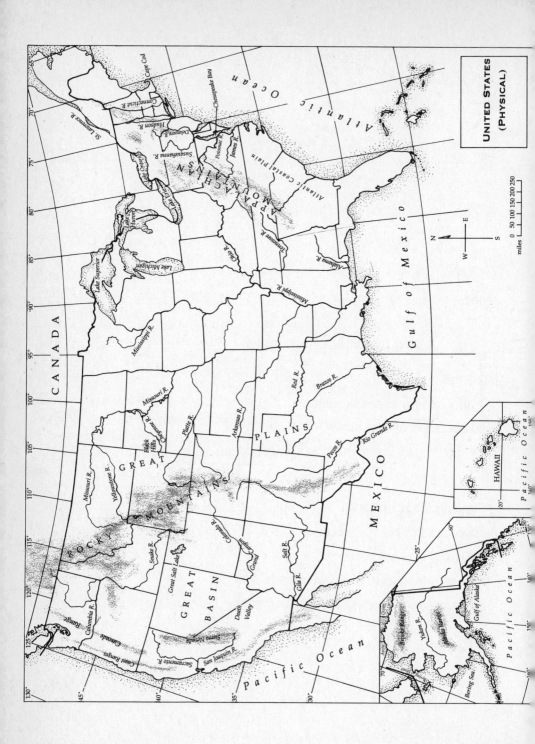

UNITED STATES (PHYSICAL)

N
W — E
S

miles
0 50 100 150 200 250

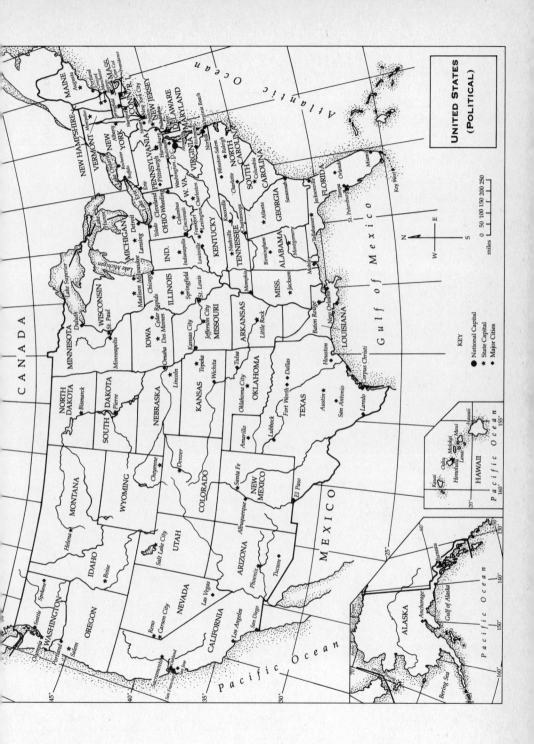

UNITED STATES
(POLITICAL)

KEY
● National Capital
★ State Capital
• Major Cities

Information About the States

(Including the District of Columbia)

State	Capital	Year of Statehood
Alabama	Montgomery	1819
Alaska	Juneau	1959
Arizona	Phoenix	1912
Arkansas	Little Rock	1836
California	Sacramento	1850
Colorado	Denver	1876
Connecticut	Hartford	1788
Delaware	Dover	1787
District of Columbia		
Florida	Tallahassee	1845
Georgia	Atlanta	1788
Hawaii	Honolulu	1959
Idaho	Boise	1890
Illinois	Springfield	1818
Indiana	Indianapolis	1816
Iowa	Des Moines	1846
Kansas	Topeka	1861
Kentucky	Frankfort	1792
Louisiana	Baton Rouge	1812
Maine	Augusta	1820
Maryland	Annapolis	1788
Massachusetts	Boston	1788
Michigan	Lansing	1837
Minnesota	St. Paul	1858
Mississippi	Jackson	1817
Missouri	Jefferson City	1821
Montana	Helena	1889
Nebraska	Lincoln	1867
Nevada	Carson City	1864
New Hampshire	Concord	1788
New Jersey	Trenton	1787
New Mexico	Santa Fe	1912
New York	Albany	1788
North Carolina	Raleigh	1789
North Dakota	Bismarck	1889

2000 Population	Reps. in Congress*	Total Area (Sq. mi.)
4,447,100	7	52,423
626,732	1	656,424
5,130,632	8	114,006
2,673,400	4	53,182
33,871,648	53	163,707
4,301,261	7	104,100
3,405,565	5	5,544
783,600	1	2,489
572,059	0	68
15,982,378	25	65,758
8,186,453	13	59,441
1,211,537	2	10,932
1,293,953	2	83,574
12,419,293	19	57,918
6,080,485	9	36,420
2,926,324	5	56,276
2,688,418	4	82,282
4,041,769	6	40,411
4,468,976	7	51,843
1,274,923	2	35,387
5,296,486	8	12,407
6,349,097	10	10,555
9,938,444	15	96,810
4,919,479	8	86,943
2,844,658	4	48,434
5,595,211	9	69,709
902,195	1	147,046
1,711,263	3	77,358
1,998,257	3	110,567
1,235,786	2	9,351
8,414,350	13	8,722
1,819,046	3	121,598
18,976,457	29	54,475
8,049,313	13	53,821
642,200	1	70,704

Information About the States (*continued*)

State	Capital	Year of Statehood
Ohio	Columbus	1803
Oklahoma	Oklahoma City	1907
Oregon	Salem	1859
Pennsylvania	Harrisburg	1787
Rhode Island	Providence	1790
South Carolina	Columbia	1788
South Dakota	Pierre	1889
Tennessee	Nashville	1796
Texas	Austin	1845
Utah	Salt Lake City	1896
Vermont	Montpelier	1791
Virginia	Richmond	1788
Washington	Olympia	1889
West Virginia	Charleston	1863
Wisconsin	Madison	1848
Wyoming	Cheyenne	1890

Population of the United States, 1790–2000

Census Year	Population	% Change from Last Census	Census Year	Population	% Change from Last Census
1790	3,929,214	—	1850	23,191,876	35.9
1800	5,308,483	35.1	1860	31,443,321	35.6
1810	7,239,881	36.4	1870	39,818,449	26.6
1820	9,638,453	33.1	1880	50,155,783	26.0
1830	12,866,020	33.5	1890	62,947,714	25.5
1840	17,069,453	32.7	1900	75,994,575	20.7

2000 Population	Reps. in Congress*	Total Area (Sq. mi.)
11,353,140	18	44,828
3,450,654	5	69,903
3,421,399	5	98,386
12,281,054	19	46,058
1,048,319	2	1,545
4,012,012	6	32,007
754,844	1	77,121
5,689,283	9	42,146
20,851,820	32	268,601
2,233,169	3	84,904
608,827	1	9,615
7,078,515	11	42,769
5,894,121	9	71,303
1,808,344	3	24,231
5,363,675	8	65,503
493,782	1	97,818

*This column lists the number of members of the House of Representatives for each state; as provided in the Constitution, each state has, in addition, two senators.

Census Year	Population	% Change from Last Census	Census Year	Population	% Change from Last Census
1910	91,972,266	21.0	1960	179,323,175	18.5
1920	105,710,620	14.9	1970	203,211,926	13.3
1930	122,775,046	16.1	1980	226,504,825	11.5
1940	131,669,275	7.2	1990	248,709,873	10.21
1950	151,325,798	14.5	2000	281,421,906	13.2

United States Presidents and Vice Presidents

No.	Name	Born–Died	Years in Office
1	George Washington	1732–99	1789–97
2	John Adams	1735–1826	1797–1801
3	Thomas Jefferson	1743–1826	1801–09
4	James Madison	1751–1836	1809–17
5	James Monroe	1758–1831	1817–25
6	John Quincy Adams	1767–1848	1825–29
7	Andrew Jackson	1767–1845	1829–37
8	Martin Van Buren	1782–1862	1837–41
9	William Henry Harrison	1773–1841	1841
10	John Tyler	1790–1862	1841–45
11	James K. Polk	1795–1849	1845–49
12	Zachary Taylor	1784–1850	1849–50
13	Millard Fillmore	1800–74	1850–53
14	Franklin Pierce	1804–69	1853–57
15	James Buchanan	1791–1868	1857–61
16	Abraham Lincoln	1809–65	1861–65
17	Andrew Johnson	1808–75	1865–69
18	Ulysses S. Grant	1822–85	1869–77
19	Rutherford B. Hayes	1822–93	1877–81
20	James A. Garfield	1831–81	1881
21	Chester A. Arthur	1830–86	1881–85
22	Grover Cleveland	1837–1908	1885–89
23	Benjamin Harrison	1833–1901	1889–93
24	Grover Cleveland	1837–1908	1893–97
25	William McKinley	1843–1901	1897–1901
26	Theodore Roosevelt	1858–1919	1901–09
27	William Howard Taft	1857–1930	1909–13
28	Woodrow Wilson	1856–1924	1913–21
29	Warren G. Harding	1865–1923	1921–23

Political Party	Home State	Vice President	Born–Died
None	Va.	John Adams	1735–1826
Federalist	Mass.	Thomas Jefferson	1743–1826
Republican[a]	Va.	Aaron Burr	1756–1836
		George Clinton	1739–1812
Republican	Va.	George Clinton	
		Elbridge Gerry	1744–1814
Republican	Va.	Daniel D. Tompkins	1774–1825
Republican	Mass.	John C. Calhoun	1782–1850
Democratic	Tenn.	John C. Calhoun	
		Martin Van Buren	1782–1862
Democratic	N.Y.	Richard M. Johnson	1780–1850
Whig	Ohio	John Tyler	1790–1862
Whig	Va.	—	
Democratic	Tenn.	George M. Dallas	1792–1864
Whig	La.	Millard Fillmore	1800–74
Whig	N.Y.	—	
Democratic	N.H.	William R. King	1786–1853
Democratic	Pa.	John C. Breckinridge	1821–75
Republican	Ill.	Hannibal Hamlin	1809–91
		Andrew Johnson	1808–75
Republican	Tenn.	—	
Republican	Ill.	Schuyler Colfax	1823–85
		Henry Wilson	1812–75
Republican	Ohio	William A. Wheeler	1819–87
Republican	Ohio	Chester A. Arthur	1829–86
Republican	N.Y.	—	
Democratic	N.Y.	Thomas A. Hendricks	1819–85
Republican	Ind.	Levi P. Morton	1824–1920
Democratic	N.Y.	Adlai E. Stevenson	1835–1914
Republican	Ohio	Garret A. Hobart	1844–99
		Theodore Roosevelt	1858–1919
Republican	N.Y.	—	
		Charles W. Fairbanks	1852–1918
Republican	Ohio	James S. Sherman	1855–1912
Democratic	N.J.	Thomas R. Marshall	1854–1925
Republican	Ohio	Calvin Coolidge	1872–1933

No.	Name	Born–Died	Years in Office
30	Calvin Coolidge	1872–1933	1923–29
31	Herbert Hoover	1874–1964	1929–33
32	Franklin D. Roosevelt	1882–1945	1933–45
33	Harry S. Truman	1884–1972	1945–53
34	Dwight D. Eisenhower	1890–1969	1953–61
35	John F. Kennedy	1917–63	1961–63
36	Lyndon B. Johnson	1908–73	1963–69
37	Richard M. Nixon	1913–94	1969–74
38	Gerald Ford	1913–	1974–77
39	Jimmy Carter	1924–	1977–81
40	Ronald Reagan	1911–2004	1981–89
41	George H. W. Bush	1924–	1989–93
42	Bill Clinton	1946–	1993–2000
43	George W. Bush	1941–	2000–

Political Party	Home State	Vice President	Born–Died
Republican	Mass.	—	
		Charles G. Dawes	1865–1951
Republican	Calif.	Charles Curtis	1860–1936
Democratic	N.Y.	John Nance Garner	1868–1967
		Henry Wallace	1888–1965
		Harry S. Truman	1884–1972
Democratic	Mo.	—	
		Alben W. Barkley	1877–1956
Republican	Kans.	Richard M. Nixon	1913–94
Democratic	Mass.	Lyndon B. Johnson	1908–73
Democratic	Tex.	—	
		Hubert H. Humphrey	1911–78
Republican	Calif.	Spiro T. Agnew	1918–96
		Gerald Ford	1913–
Republican	Mich.	Nelson A. Rockefeller	1908–79
Democratic	Ga.	Walter F. Mondale	1928–
Republican	Calif.	George H. W. Bush	1924–
Republican	Tex.	J. Danforth Quayle	1947–
Democratic	Ark.	Al Gore, Jr.	1948–
Republican	Tex.	Richard B. Cheney	1941–

[a] The Republican party of the third through sixth presidents was not the modern party, which was founded in 1854.

The Supreme Court

Chief Justices

Chief Justices	Term of Service[a]	Years of Service	Life Span
John Jay	1789–95	5	1745–1829
John Rutledge[b]	1795	—	1739–1800
Oliver Ellsworth	1796–1800	4	1745–1807
John Marshall	1801–35	34	1755–1835
Roger B. Taney	1836–64	28	1777–1864
Salmon P. Chase	1864–73	8	1808–73
Morrison R. Waite	1874–88	14	1816–88
Melville W. Fuller	1888–1910	21	1833–1910
Edward D. White	1910–21	11	1845–1921
William H. Taft	1921–30	8	1857–1930
Charles E. Hughes	1930–41	11	1862–1948
Harlan F. Stone	1941–46	5	1872–1946
Fred M. Vinson	1946–53	7	1890–1953
Earl Warren	1953–69	16	1891–1974
Warren E. Burger	1969–86	17	1907–95
William H. Rehnquist	1986–	—	1924–

[a] Term of service refers only to years as chief justice. Any previous service as associate justice appears below.
[b] Appointed and served one term, but not confirmed by the Senate.

Associate Justices

Associate Justices	Term of Service	Years of Service	Life Span
John Rutledge	1789–91	1	1739–1800
William Cushing	1789–1810	20	1732–1810
James Wilson	1789–98	8	1742–98
John Blair	1789–96	6	1732–1800
Robert H. Harrison	1789–90	—	1745–90
James Iredell	1790–99	9	1751–99
Thomas Johnson	1791–93	1	1732–1819
William Paterson	1793–1806	13	1745–1806
Samuel Chase	1796–1811	15	1741–1811
Bushrod Washington	1798–1829	31	1762–1829
Alfred Moore	1799–1804	4	1755–1810
William Johnson	1804–34	30	1771–1834
Henry Brockholst Livingston	1806–23	16	1757–1823
Thomas Todd	1807–26	18	1765–1826
Joseph Story	1811–45	33	1779–1845
Gabriel Duvall	1811–35	24	1752–1844

Associate Justices (*continued*)

Associate Justices	Term of Service	Years of Service	Life Span
Smith Thompson	1823–43	20	1768–1843
Robert Trimble	1826–28	2	1777–1828
John McLean	1829–61	32	1785–1861
Henry Baldwin	1830–44	14	1780–1844
James M. Wayne	1835–67	32	1790–1867
Philip P. Barbour	1836–41	4	1783–1841
John Catron	1837–65	28	1786–1865
John McKinley	1837–52	15	1780–1852
Peter V. Daniel	1841–60	19	1784–1860
Samuel Nelson	1845–72	27	1792–1873
Levi Woodbury	1845–51	5	1789–1851
Robert C. Grier	1846–70	23	1794–1870
Benjamin Curtis	1851–57	6	1809–74
John A. Campbell	1853–61	8	1811–89
Nathan Clifford	1858–81	23	1803–81
Noah H. Swayne	1862–81	18	1804–84
Samuel F. Miller	1862–90	28	1816–90
DAVID DAVIS	1862–77	14	1815–86
STEPHEN J. FIELD	1863–97	34	1816–99
William Strong	1870–80	10	1808–95
Joseph P. Bradley	1870–92	22	1813–92
Ward Hunt	1873–82	9	1810–86
JOHN M. HARLAN	1877–1911	34	1833–1911
William B. Woods	1880–87	7	1824–87
Stanley Matthews	1881–89	7	1824–89
Horace Gray	1882–1902	20	1828–1902
Samuel Blatchford	1882–93	11	1820–93
Lucius Q. C. Lamar	1888–93	5	1825–93
David J. Brewer	1890–1910	20	1837–1910
Henry B. Brown	1890–1906	16	1836–1913
George Shiras, Jr.	1892–1903	10	1832–1924
Howell E. Jackson	1893–95	2	1832–95
EDWARD D. WHITE	1894–1910	16	1845–1921
Rufus W. Peckham	1895–1909	14	1838–1909
Joseph McKenna	1898–1925	26	1843–1926
OLIVER W. HOLMES	1902–32	30	1841–1935
William R. Day	1903–22	19	1849–1923
William H. Moody	1906–10	3	1853–1917
Horace H. Lurton	1910–14	4	1844–1914
CHARLES E. HUGHES	1910–16	5	1862–1948
Willis Van Devanter	1911–37	26	1859–1941
Joseph R. Lamar	1911–16	5	1857–1916
Mahlon Pitney	1912–22	10	1858–1924

Associate Justices (*continued*)

Associate Justices	Term of Service	Years of Service	Life Span
James C. McReynolds	1914–41	26	1862–1946
LOUIS D. BRANDEIS	1916–39	22	1856–1941
John H. Clarke	1916–22	6	1857–1945
George Sutherland	1922–38	15	1862–1942
Pierce Butler	1923–39	16	1866–1939
Edward T. Sanford	1923–30	7	1865–1930
HARLAN F. STONE	1925–41	16	1872–1946
Owen J. Roberts	1930–45	15	1875–1955
BENJAMIN N. CARDOZO	1932–38	6	1870–1938
HUGO L. BLACK	1937–71	34	1886–1971
STANLEY F. REED	1938–57	19	1884–1980
FELIX FRANKFURTER	1939–62	23	1882–1965
WILLIAM O. DOUGLAS	1939–75	36	1898–1980
Frank Murphy	1940–49	9	1890–1949
JAMES F. BYRNES	1941–42	1	1879–1972
ROBERT H. JACKSON	1941–54	13	1892–1954
Wiley B. Rutledge	1943–49	6	1894–1949
Harold H. Burton	1945–58	13	1888–1964
Tom C. Clark	1949–67	18	1899–1977
Sherman Minton	1949–56	7	1890–1965
John Marshall Harlan	1955–71	16	1899–1971
WILLIAM J. BRENNAN, JR.	1956–90	34	1906–97
Charles E. Whittaker	1957–62	5	1901–73
Potter Stewart	1958–81	23	1915–85
BYRON R. WHITE	1962–1993	31	1917–2002
ARTHUR J. GOLDBERG	1962–65	3	1908–90
ABE FORTAS	1965–69	4	1910–82
THURGOOD MARSHALL	1967–91	24	1908–93
Harry A. Blackmun	1970–1994	24	1908–99
Lewis F. Powell, Jr.	1972–87	15	1907–98
WILLIAM H. REHNQUIST	1972–86	14	1924–
John P. Stevens III	1975–	—	1920–
SANDRA DAY O'CONNOR	1981–	—	1930–
Antonin Scalia	1986–	—	1936–
Anthony M. Kennedy	1988–	—	1936–
David Souter	1990–	—	1939–
Clarence Thomas	1991–	—	1948–
RUTH BADER GINSBURG	1993–	—	1933–
Stephen G. Breyer	1994–	—	1938–

Declaration of Independence

Philadelphia, Pennsylvania
July 4, 1776

The Unanimous Declaration of the Thirteen United States of America

When, in the course of human events, it becomes necessary for one people to dissolve the political bonds which have connected them with another, and to assume, among the powers of the earth, the separate and equal station to which the laws of nature and of nature's God entitle them, a decent respect to the opinions of mankind requires that they should declare the causes which impel them to the separation.

We hold these truths to be self-evident: That all men are created equal; that they are endowed by their Creator with certain unalienable rights; that among these are life, liberty, and the pursuit of happiness; that, to secure these rights, governments are instituted among men, deriving their just powers from the consent of the governed; that whenever any form of government becomes destructive of these ends, it is the right of the people to alter or to abolish it, and to institute new government, laying its foundation on such principles, and organizing its powers in such form, as to them shall seem most likely to effect their safety and happiness. Prudence, indeed, will dictate that governments long established should not be changed for light and transient causes; and accordingly all experience hath shown that mankind are more disposed to suffer, while evils are sufferable, than to right themselves by abolishing the forms to which they are accustomed. But when a long train of abuses and usurpations, pursuing invariably the same object, evinces a design to reduce them under absolute despotism, it is their right, it is their duty, to throw off such government, and to provide new guards for their future security. Such has been the patient sufferance of these colonies; and such is now the necessity which constrains them to alter their former systems of government. The history of the present King of Great Britain is a history of repeated injuries and usurpations, all having in direct object the establishment of an absolute tyranny over these states. To prove this, let facts be submitted to a candid world.

He has refused his assent to laws, the most wholesome and necessary for the public good.

He has forbidden his governors to pass laws of immediate and pressing importance, unless suspended in their operation till his assent should be obtained; and, when so suspended, he has utterly neglected to attend to them.

He has refused to pass other laws for the accommodation of large districts of people, unless those people would relinquish the right of representation in the legislature, a right inestimable to them, and formidable to tyrants only.

He has called together legislative bodies at places unusual, uncomfortable, and distant from the depository of their public records, for the sole purpose of fatiguing them into compliance with his measures.

He has dissolved representative houses repeatedly, for opposing, with manly firmness, his invasions on the rights of the people.

He has refused for a long time, after such dissolutions, to cause others to be elected; whereby the legislative powers, incapable of annihilation, have returned to the people at large for their exercise; the state remaining, in the mean time, exposed to all the dangers of invasions from without and convulsions within.

He has endeavored to prevent the population of these states; for that purpose obstructing the laws for naturalization of foreigners; refusing to pass others to encourage their migration hither, and raising the conditions of new appropriations of lands.

He has obstructed the administration of justice, by refusing his assent to laws for establishing judiciary powers.

He has made judges dependent on his will alone, for the tenure of their offices, and the amount and payment of their salaries.

He has erected a multitude of new offices, and sent hither swarms of officers to harass our people and eat out their substance.

He has kept among us, in times of peace, standing armies, without the consent of our legislatures.

He has affected to render the military independent of, and superior to, the civil power.

He has combined with others to subject us to a jurisdiction foreign to our constitution, and unacknowledged by our laws, giving his assent to their acts of pretended legislation:

For quartering large bodies of armed troops among us;

For protecting them, by a mock trial, from punishment for any murders which they should commit on the inhabitants of these states;

For cutting off our trade with all parts of the world;

For imposing taxes on us without our consent;

For depriving us, in many cases, of the benefits of trial by jury;

For transporting us beyond seas, to be tried for pretended offenses;

For abolishing the free system of English laws in a neighboring province, establishing therein an arbitrary government, and enlarging its boundaries, so as to render it at once an example and fit instrument for introducing the same absolute rule into these colonies;

For taking away our charters, abolishing our most valuable laws, and altering fundamentally the forms of our governments;

For suspending our own legislatures, and declaring themselves invested with power to legislate for us in all cases whatsoever.

He has abdicated government here, by declaring us out of his protection and waging war against us.

He has plundered our seas, ravaged our coasts, burned our towns, and destroyed the lives of our people.

He is at this time transporting large armies of foreign mercenaries to complete the works of death, desolation, and tyranny already begun with circumstances of cruelty and perfidy scarcely paralleled in the most barbarous ages, and totally unworthy the head of a civilized nation.

He has constrained our fellow-citizens, taken captive on the high seas, to bear arms against their country, to become the executioners of their friends and brethren, or to fall themselves by their hands.

He has excited domestic insurrection among us, and has endeavored to bring on the inhabitants of our frontiers the merciless Indian savages, whose known rule of warfare is an undistinguished destruction of all ages, sexes, and conditions.

In every stage of these oppressions we have petitioned for redress in the most humble terms; our repeated petitions have been answered only by repeated injury. A prince, whose character is thus marked by every act which may define a tyrant, is unfit to be the ruler of a free people.

Nor have we been wanting in our attentions to our British brethren. We have warned them, from time to time, of attempts by their legislature to extend an unwarrantable jurisdiction over us. We have reminded them of the circumstances of our emigration and settlement here. We have appealed to their native justice and magnanimity; and we have conjured them, by the ties of our common kindred, to disavow these usurpations, which would inevitably interrupt our connections and correspondence. They, too, have been deaf to the voice of justice and of consanguinity. We must, therefore, acquiesce in the necessity which denounces our separation, and hold them, as we hold the rest of mankind, enemies in war, in peace friends.

We, therefore, the representatives of the United States of America, in General Congress assembled, appealing to the Supreme Judge of the world for the rectitude of our intentions, do, in the name and by the authority of the good people of these colonies, solemnly publish and declare, that these United Colonies are, and of right ought to be, FREE AND INDEPENDENT STATES; that they are absolved from all allegiance to the British crown, and that all political connection between them and the state of Great Britain is, and ought to be, totally dissolved; and that, as free and independent states, they have full power to levy war, conclude peace, contract alliances, establish commerce, and do all other acts and things which independent states may of right do. And for the support of this declaration, with a firm reliance on the protection of Divine Providence, we mutually pledge to each other our lives, our fortunes, and our sacred honor.

John Hancock

New Hampshire
Josiah Bartlett
William Whipple
Matthew Thornton

Massachusetts
John Adams
Samuel Adams
Robert Treat Paine
Elbridge Gerry

New York
William Floyd
Philip Livingston
Francis Lewis
Lewis Morris

Rhode Island
Stephen Hopkins
William Ellery

New Jersey
Richard Stockton
John Witherspoon
Francis Hopkinson
John Hart
Abraham Clark

Pennsylvania
Robert Morris
Benjamin Rush
Benjamin Franklin
John Morton
George Clymer
James Smith
George Taylor
James Wilson
George Ross

Delaware
Caesar Rodney
George Read
Thomas McKean

Maryland
Samuel Chase
William Paca
Thomas Stone
Charles Carroll of Carrollton

North Carolina
William Hooper
Joseph Hewes
John Penn

Virginia
George Wythe
Richard Henry Lee
Thomas Jefferson
Benjamin Harrison
Thomas Nelson, Jr.
Francis Lightfoot Lee
Carter Braxton

South Carolina
Edward Rutledge
Thomas Heyward, Jr.
Thomas Lynch, Jr.
Arthur Middleton

Connecticut
Roger Sherman
Samuel Huntington
William Williams
Oliver Wolcott

Georgia
Button Gwinnett
Lyman Hall
George Walton

Articles of Confederation

To all to whom these Presents shall come, we the undersigned Delegates of the States affixed to our Names send greeting. Whereas the Delegates of the United States of America in Congress assembled did on the fifteenth day of November in the Year of our Lord One Thousand Seven Hundred and Seventy seven, and in the Second Year of the Independence of America agree to certain articles of Confederation and perpetual Union between the States of Newhampshire, Massachusetts-bay, Rhodeisland and Providence Plantations, Connecticut, New York, New Jersey, Pennsylvania, Delaware, Maryland, Virginia, North-Carolina, South-Carolina and Georgia in the Words following, viz. "Articles of Confederation and perpetual Union between the states of Newhampshire, Massachusetts-bay, Rhodeisland and Providence Plantations, Connecticut, New-York, New-Jersey, Pennsylvania, Delaware, Maryland, Virginia, North-Carolina, South-Carolina and Georgia.

Art. I. The Stile of this confederacy shall be "The United States of America."

Art. II. Each state retains its sovereignty, freedom and independence, and every Power, Jurisdiction and right, which is not by this confederation expressly delegated to the United States, in Congress assembled.

Art. III. The said states hereby severally enter into a firm league of friendship with each other, for their common defence, the security of their Liberties, and their mutual and general welfare, binding themselves to assist each other, against all force offered to, or attacks made upon them, or any of them, on account of religion, sovereignty, trade, or any other pretence whatever.

Art. IV. The better to secure and perpetuate mutual friendship and intercourse among the people of the different states in this union, the free inhabitants of each of these states, paupers, vagabonds and fugitives from Justice excepted, shall be entitled to all privileges and immunities of free citizens in the several states; and the people of each state shall have free ingress and regress to and from any other state, and shall enjoy therein all the privileges of trade and commerce, subject to the same duties, impositions and restrictions as the inhabitants thereof respectively, provided that such restriction shall not extend so far as to prevent the removal of property imported into any state, to any other state of which the Owner is an inhabitant; provided also that no imposition, duties or restriction shall be laid by any state, on the property of the united states, or either of them.

If any Person guilty of, or charged with treason, felony, or other high misdemeanor in any state, shall flee from Justice, and be found in any of the united states, he shall upon demand of the Governor or executive power, of the state from which he fled, be delivered up and removed to the state having jurisdiction of his offence.

Full faith and credit shall be given in each of these states to the records, acts and judicial proceedings of the courts and magistrates of every other state.

Art. V. For the more convenient management of the general interests of the united states, delegates shall be annually appointed in such manner as the legislature of each state shall direct, to meet in Congress on the first Monday in November, in every year, with a power reserved to each state, to recall its delegates, or any of them, at any time within the year, and to send others in their stead, for the remainder of the Year.

No state shall be represented in Congress by less than two, nor by more than seven Members; and no person shall be capable of being a delegate for more than three years in any term of six years;

nor shall any person, being a delegate, be capable of holding any office under the united states, for which he, or another for his benefit receives any salary, fees or emolument of any kind.

Each state shall maintain its own delegates in a meeting of the states, and while they act as members of the committee of the states.

In determining questions in the united states, in Congress assembled, each state shall have one vote.

Freedom of speech and debate in Congress shall not be impeached or questioned in any Court, or place out of Congress, and the members of congress shall be protected in their persons from arrests and imprisonments, during the time of their going to and from, and attendance on congress, except for treason, felony, or breach of the peace.

Art. VI. No state without the Consent of the united states in congress assembled, shall send any embassy to, or receive any embassy from, or enter into any conference, agreement, or alliance or treaty with any King, prince or state; nor shall any person holding any office of profit or trust under the united states, or any of them, accept of any present, emolument, office or title of any kind whatever from any king, prince or foreign state; nor shall the united states in congress assembled, or any of them, grant any title of nobility.

No two or more states shall enter into any treaty, confederation or alliance whatever between them, without the consent of the united states in congress assembled, specifying accurately the purposes for which the same is to be entered into, and how long it shall continue. ,

No state shall lay any imposts or duties, which may interfere with any stipulations in treaties, entered into by the united states in congress assembled, with any king, prince or state, in pursuance of any treaties already proposed by congress, to the courts of France and Spain.

No vessels of war shall be kept up in time of peace by any state, except such number only, as shall be deemed necessary by the united states in congress assembled, for the defence of such state, or its trade; nor shall any body of forces be kept up by any state, in time of peace, except such number only, as in the judgment of the united states, in congress assembled, shall be deemed requisite to garrison the forts necessary for the defence of such state; but every state shall always keep up a well regulated and disciplined militia, sufficiently armed and accoutred, and shall provide and constantly have ready for use, in public stores, a due number of field pieces and tents, and a proper quantity of arms, ammunition and camp equipage.

No state shall engage in any war without the consent of the united states in congress assembled, unless such state be actually invaded by enemies, or shall have received certain advice of a resolution being formed by some nation of Indians to invade such state, and the danger is so imminent as not to admit of a delay, till the united states in congress assembled can be consulted: nor shall any state grant commissions to any ships or vessels of war, not letters of marque or reprisal, except it be after a declaration of war by the united states in congress assembled, and then only against the kingdom or state and the subjects thereof, against which war has been so declared, and under such regulations as shall be established by the united states in congress assembled, unless such state be infested by pirates, in which case vessels of war may be fitted out for that occasion, and kept so long as the danger shall continue, or until the united states in congress assembled shall determine otherwise.

Art. VII. When land-forces are raised by any state for the common defence, all officers of or under the rank of colonel, shall be appointed by the legislature of each state respectively by whom such forces shall be raised, or in such manner as such state shall direct, and all vacancies shall be filled up by the state which first made the appointment.

Art. VIII. All charges of war, and all other expences that shall be incurred for the common defence or general welfare, and allowed by the united states in congress assembled, shall be defrayed out of a common treasury, which shall be supplied by the several states, in proportion to the value of all land within each state, granted to or surveyed for any Person, as such land and the buildings and improvements thereon shall be estimated according to such mode as the united states in congress assembled, shall from time to time direct and appoint. The taxes for paying that proportion shall be laid and levied by the authority and direction of the legislatures of the several states within the time agreed upon by the united states in congress assembled.

Art. IX. The united states in congress assembled, shall have the sole and exclusive right and power of determining on peace and war, except in the cases mentioned in the sixth article — of sending and receiving ambassadors — entering into treaties and alliances, provided that no treaty of commerce shall be made whereby the legislative power of the respective states shall be restrained from imposing such imposts and duties on foreigners, as their own people are subjected to, or from prohibiting the exportation or importation of any species of goods or commodities whatsoever — of establishing rules for deciding in all cases, what captures on land or water shall be legal, and in what manner prizes taken by land or naval forces in the service of the united states shall be divided or appropriated. — of granting letters of marque and reprisal in times of peace — appointing courts for the trial of piracies and felonies committed on the high seas and establishing courts for receiving and determining finally appeals in all cases of captures, provided that no member of congress shall be appointed a judge of any of the said courts.

The united states in congress assembled shall also be the last resort on appeal in all disputes and differences now subsisting or that hereafter may arise between two or more states concerning boundary, jurisdiction or any other cause whatever; which authority shall always be exercised in the manner following. Whenever the legislative or executive authority or lawful agent of any state in controversy with another shall present a petition to congress stating the matter in question and praying for a hearing, notice thereof shall be given by order of congress to the legislative or executive authority of the other state in controversy, and a day assigned for the appearance of the parties by their lawful agents, who shall then be directed to appoint by joint consent, commissioners or judges to constitute a court for hearing and determining the matter in question: but if they cannot agree, congress shall name three persons out of each of the united states, and from the list of such persons each party shall alternately strike out one, the petitioners beginning, until the number shall be reduced to thirteen; and from that number not less than seven, nor more than nine names as congress shall direct, shall in the presence of congress be drawn out by lot, and the persons whose names shall be so drawn or any five of them, shall be commissioners or judges, to hear and finally determine the controversy, so always as a major part of the judges who shall hear the cause shall agree in the determination: and if either party shall neglect to attend at the day appointed, without showing reasons, which congress shall judge sufficient, or being present shall refuse to strike, the congress shall proceed to nominate three persons out of each state, and the secretary of congress shall strike in behalf of such party absent or refusing; and the judgment and sentence of the court to be appointed, in the manner before prescribed, shall be final and conclusive; and if any of the parties shall refuse to submit to the authority of such court, or to appear to defend their claim or cause, the court shall nevertheless proceed to pronounce sentence, or judgment, which shall in like manner be final and decisive, the judgment or sentence and other proceedings being in either case transmitted to congress, and lodged among the acts of congress for the security of the parties concerned: provided that every commissioner, before he sits in judgment, shall take an oath to be administered by one of the judges of the supreme or superior court of the state, where the cause shall be tried, "well and truly to hear and determine the matter in question, according to the best of his judgment, without favour, affection or hope of reward:" provided also that no state shall be deprived of territory for the benefit of the united states.

All controversies concerning the private right of soil claimed under different grants of two or more states, whose jurisdictions as they may respect such lands, and the states which passed such grants are adjusted, the said grants or either of them being at the same time claimed to have originated antecedent to such settlement of jurisdiction, shall on the petition of either party to the congress of the united states, be finally determined as near as may be in the same manner as is before prescribed for deciding disputes respecting territorial jurisdiction between different states.

The united states in congress assembled shall also have the sole and exclusive right and power of regulating the alloy and value of coin struck by their own authority, or by that of the respective states — fixing the standard of weights and measures throughout the united states. — regulating the trade and managing all affairs with the Indians, not members of any of the states, provided that the legislative right of any state within its own limits be not infringed or violated — establishing and regulating post-offices from one state to another, throughout all the united states, and exacting such postage on the papers passing thro' the same as may be requisite to defray the expences of the said office — appointing all officers of the land forces, in the service of the united states, excepting regimental officers. — appointing all the officers of the naval forces, and commissioning all officers whatever in the service of the united states — making rules for the government and regulation of the said land and naval forces, and directing their operations.

The united states in congress assembled shall have authority to appoint a committee, to sit in the recess of congress, to be denominated "A Committee of the States," and to consist of one delegate from each state; and to appoint such other committees and civil officers as may be necessary for managing the general affairs of the united states under their direction — to appoint one of their number to preside, provided that no person be allowed to serve in the office of president more than one year in any term of three years; to ascertain the necessary sums of Money to be raised for the service of the united states, and to appropriate and apply the same for defraying the public expenses — to borrow money, or emit bills on the credit of the united states, transmitting every half year to the respective states an account of the sums of money so borrowed or emitted, — to build and equip a navy — to agree upon the number of land forces, and to make requisitions from each state for its quota, in proportion to the number of white inhabitants in such state; which requisition shall be binding, and thereupon the legislature of each state shall appoint the regimental officers, raise the men and cloath, arm and equip them in a soldier like manner, at the expence of the united states, and the officers and men so cloathed, armed and equipped shall march to the place appointed, and within the time agreed on by the united states in congress assembled: But if the united states in congress assembled shall, on consideration of circumstances judge proper that any state should not raise men, or should raise a smaller number than its quota, and that any other state should raise a greater number of men than the quota thereof, such extra number shall be raised, officered, cloathed, armed and equipped in the same manner as the quota of such state, unless the legislature of such state shall judge that such extra number cannot be safely spared out of the same, in which case they shall raise officer, cloath, arm and equip as many of such extra number as they judge can be safely spared. And the officers and men so cloathed, armed and equipped, shall march to the place appointed, and within the time agreed on by the united states in congress assembled.

The united states in congress assembled shall never engage in a war, nor grant letters of marque and reprisal in time of peace, nor enter into any treaties or alliances, nor coin money, nor regulate the value thereof, nor ascertain the sums and expences necessary for the defence and welfare of the united states, or any of them, nor emit bills, nor borrow money on the credit of the united states, nor appropriate money, nor agree upon the number of vessels of war, to be built or purchased, or the number of land or sea forces to be raised, nor appoint a commander in chief of the army or navy, unless nine states assent to the same: nor shall a question on any other point, except for adjourning from day to day be determined, unless by the votes of a majority of the united states in congress assembled.

The congress of the united states shall have power to adjourn to any time within the year, and to any place within the united states, so that no period of adjournment be for a longer duration than the space of six Months, and shall publish the Journal of their proceedings monthly, except such parts thereof relating to treaties, alliances or military operations as in their judgment require secresy; and the yeas and nays of the delegates of each state on any question shall be entered on the Journal, when it is desired by any delegate; and the delegates of a state, or any of them, at his or their request shall be furnished with a transcript of the said Journal, except such parts as are above excepted, to lay before the legislatures of the several states.

Art. X. The committee of the states, or any nine of them, shall be authorised to execute, in the recess of congress, such of the powers of congress as the united states in congress assembled, by the consent of nine states, shall from time to time think expedient to vest them with; provided that no power be delegated to the said committee, for the exercise of which, by the articles of confederation, the voice of nine states in the congress of the united states assembled is requisite.

Art. XI. Canada acceding to this confederation, and joining in the measures of the united states, shall be admitted into, and entitled to all the advantages of this union: but no other colony shall be admitted into the same, unless such admission be agreed to by nine states.

Art. XII. All bills of credit emitted, monies borrowed and debts contracted by, or under the authority of congress, before the assembling of the united states, in pursuance of the present confederation, shall be deemed and considered as a charge against the united states, for payment and satisfaction whereof the said united states, and the public faith are hereby solemnly pledged.

Art. XIII. Every state shall abide by the determinations of the united states in congress assembled, on all questions which by this confederation are submitted to them. And the Articles of this confederation shall be inviolably observed by every state, and the union shall be perpetual; nor shall any alteration at any time hereafter be made in any of them; unless such alteration be agreed to in a congress of the united states, and be afterwards confirmed by the legislatures of every state.

And WHEREAS it hath pleased the Great Governor of the World to incline the hearts of the legislatures we respectively represent in congress, to approve of, and to authorize us to ratify the said articles of confederation and perpetual union. Know Ye that we the undersigned delegates, by virtue of the power and authority to us given for that purpose, do by these presents, in the name and in behalf of our respective constituents, fully and entirely ratify and confirm each and every of the said articles of confederation and perpetual union, and all and singular the matters and things therein contained: And we do further solemnly plight and engage the faith of our respective constituents, that they shall abide by the determinations of the united states in congress assembled, on all questions, which by the said confederation are submitted to them. And that the articles thereof shall be inviolably observed by the states we respectively represent, and that the union shall be perpetual. In Witness whereof we have hereunto set our hands in Congress. Done at Philadelphia in the state of Pennsylvania the ninth Day of July in the Year of our Lord one Thousand seven Hundred and Seventy-eight, and in the third year of the independence of America.

Josiah Bartlett John Wentworth Junr August 8th 1778	On the part & behalf of the State of New Hampshire	Robt Morris Daniel Roberdeau Jon^a Bayard Smith William Clingan Joseph Reed 22^d July 1788	On the part and behalf of the State of Pennsylvania
John Hancock Samuel Adams Elbridge Gerry Francis Dana James Lovell Samuel Holten	On the part and behalf of The State of Massachusetts Bay	Tho M:Kean Feby 12 1779 John Dickinson May 5th 1779 Nicholas Van Dyke	On the part & behalf of the State of Delaware
William Ellery Henry Marchant John Collins	On the part and behalf of the State of Rhode-Island and Providence Plantations	John Hanson March 1 1781 Daniel Carroll d°	On the part and behalf of the State of Maryland
		Richard Henry Lee John Banister Thomas Adams Jn° Harvie Francis Lightfoot Lee	On the Part and Behalf of the State of Virginia
Roger Sherman Samuel Huntington Oliver Wolcott Titus Hosmer Andrew Adams	On the part and behalf of the State of Connecticut	John Penn July 21st 1778 Corn^s Harnett Jn° Williams	On the part and Behalf of the State of N° Carolina
Ja^s Duane Fra^s Lewis Wm Duer Gouv Morris	On the Part and Behalf of the State of New York	Henry Laurens William Henry Drayton Jn° Mathews Richd Hutson Thos Heyward Junr	On the part & behalf of the State of South-Carolina
Jno Witherspoon Nath^L Scudder	On the Part and in Behalf of the State of New Jersey. Novr 26, 1778. —	Jn° Walton 24th July 1778 Edwd Telfair Edwd Langworthy	On the part & behalf of the State of Georgia

Constitution of the United States of America

[Passages no longer in effect are printed in italic type.]

Preamble

We the people of the United States, in order to form a more perfect union, establish justice, insure domestic tranquility, provide for the common defense, promote the general welfare, and secure the blessings of liberty to ourselves and our posterity, do ordain and establish this Constitution for the United States of America.

Article I

Section 1 All legislative powers herein granted shall be vested in a Congress of the United States, which shall consist of a Senate and a House of Representatives.

Section 2 The House of Representatives shall be composed of members chosen every second year by the people of the several States, and the electors in each State shall have the qualifications requisite for electors of the most numerous branch of the State Legislature.

No person shall be a Representative who shall not have attained to the age of twenty-five years, and been seven years a citizen of the United States, and who shall not, when elected, be an inhabitant of that State in which he shall be chosen.

Representatives and direct taxes shall be apportioned among the several States which may be included within this Union, according to their respective numbers, *which shall be determined by adding to the whole number of free persons, including those bound to service for a term of years and excluding Indians not taxed, three-fifths of all other persons.* The actual enumeration shall be made within three years after the first meeting of the Congress of the United States, and within every subsequent term of ten years, in such manner as they shall by law direct. The number of Representatives shall not exceed one for every thirty thousand, but each State shall have at least one Representative; *and until such enumeration shall be made, the State of New Hampshire shall be entitled to choose three, Massachusetts eight, Rhode Island and Providence Plantations one, Connecticut five, New York six, New Jersey four, Pennsylvania eight, Delaware one, Maryland six, Virginia ten, North Carolina five, South Carolina five, and Georgia three.*

When vacancies happen in the representation from any State, the Executive authority thereof shall issue writs of election to fill such vacancies.

The House of Representatives shall choose their Speaker and other officers; and shall have the sole power of impeachment.

Section 3 The Senate of the United States shall be composed of two Senators from each State, *chosen by the legislature thereof,* for six years; and each Senator shall have one vote.

Immediately after they shall be assembled in consequence of the first election, they shall be divided as equally as may be into three classes. The seats of the Senators of the first class shall be vacated at the expiration of the second year, of the second class at the expiration of the fourth year, and of the third class at the expiration of the sixth year, so that one-third may be chosen every second year; *and if vacancies happen by resignation or otherwise, during the recess of the legislature of any State, the Executive thereof may make temporary appointments until the next meeting of the legislature, which shall then fill such vacancies.*

No person shall be a Senator who shall not have attained to the age of thirty years, and been nine years a citizen of the United States, and who shall not, when elected, be an inhabitant of that State for which he shall be chosen.

The Vice-President of the United States shall be President of the Senate, but shall have no vote, unless they be equally divided.

The Senate shall choose their other officers, and also President *pro tempore,* in the absence of the Vice-President, or when he shall exercise the office of President of the United States.

The Senate shall have the sole power to try all impeachments. When sitting for that purpose, they shall be on oath or affirmation. When the President of the United States is tried, the Chief Justice shall preside: and no person shall be convicted without the concurrence of two-thirds of the members present.

Judgment in cases of impeachment shall not extend further than to removal from the office, and disqualification to hold and enjoy any office of honor, trust or profit under the United States: but the party convicted shall nevertheless be liable and subject to indictment, trial, judgment and punishment, according to law.

Section 4 The times, places and manner of holding elections for Senators and Representatives shall be prescribed in each State by the legislature thereof; but the Congress may at any time by law make or alter such regulations, except as to the places of choosing Senators.

The Congress shall assemble at least once in every year, and such meeting *shall be on the first Monday in December, unless they shall by law appoint a different day.*

Section 5 Each house shall be the judge of the elections, returns and qualifications of its own members, and a majority of each shall constitute a quorum to do business; but a smaller number may adjourn from day to day, and may be authorized to compel the attendance of absent members, in such manner, and under such penalties, as each house may provide.

Each house may determine the rules of its proceedings, punish its members for disorderly behavior, and with the concurrence of two-thirds, expel a member.

Each house shall keep a journal of its proceedings, and from time to time publish the same, excepting such parts as may in their judgment require secrecy; and the yeas and nays of the members of either house on any question shall, at the desire of one-fifth of those present, be entered on the journal.

Neither house, during the session of Congress, shall, without the consent of the other, adjourn for more than three days, nor to any other place than that in which the two houses shall be sitting.

Section 6 The Senators and Representatives shall receive a compensation for their services, to be ascertained by law and paid out of the treasury of the United States. They shall in all cases except treason, felony and breach of the peace, be privileged from arrest during their attendance at the session of their respective houses, and in going to and returning from the same; and for any speech or debate in either house, they shall not be questioned in any other place.

No Senator or Representative shall, during the time for which he was elected, be appointed to any civil office under the authority of the United States, which shall have been created, or the emoluments whereof shall have been increased, during such time; and no person holding any office under the United States shall be a member of either house during his continuance in office.

Section 7 All bills for raising revenue shall originate in the House of Representatives; but the Senate may propose or concur with amendments as on other bills.

Every bill which shall have passed the House of Representatives and the Senate, shall, before it become a law, be presented to the President of the United States; if he approve he shall sign it, but if not he shall return it with objections to that house in which it originated, who shall enter the objections at large on their journal, and proceed to reconsider it. If after such reconsideration two-thirds of that house shall agree to pass the bill, it shall be sent, together with the objections, to the other house, by which it shall likewise be reconsidered, and, if approved by two-thirds of that house, it shall become a law. But in all such cases the votes of both houses shall be determined by yeas and nays, and the names of the persons voting for and against the bill shall be entered on the journal of each house respectively. If any bill shall not be returned by the President within ten days (Sundays excepted) after it shall have been presented to him, the same shall be a law, in like manner as if he had signed it, unless the Congress by their adjournment prevent its return, in which case it shall not be a law.

Every order, resolution, or vote to which the concurrence of the Senate and House of Representatives may be necessary (except on a question of adjournment) shall be presented to the President of the United States; and before the same shall take effect, shall be approved by him, or being disapproved by him, shall be repassed by two-thirds of the Senate and House of Representatives, according to the rules and limitations prescribed in the case of a bill.

Section 8 The Congress shall have power

To lay and collect taxes, duties, imposts, and excises, to pay the debts and provide for the common defense and general welfare of the United States; but all duties, imposts and excises shall be uniform throughout the United States;

To borrow money on the credit of the United States;

To regulate commerce with foreign nations, and among the several States, and with the Indian tribes;

To establish an uniform rule of naturalization, and uniform laws on the subject of bankruptcies throughout the United States;

To coin money, regulate the value thereof, and of foreign coin, and fix the standard of weights and measures;

To provide for the punishment of counterfeiting the securities and current coin of the United States;

To establish post offices and post roads;

To promote the progress of science and useful arts by securing for limited times to authors and inventors the exclusive right to their respective writings and discoveries;

To constitute tribunals inferior to the Supreme Court;

To define and punish piracies and felonies committed on the high seas and offenses against the law of nations;

To declare war, grant letters of marque and reprisal, and make rules concerning captures on land and water;

To raise and support armies, but no appropriation of money to that use shall be for a longer term than two years;

To provide and maintain a navy;

To make rules for the government and regulation of the land and naval forces;

To provide for calling forth the militia to execute the laws of the Union, suppress insurrections, and repel invasions;

To provide for organizing, arming, and disciplining the militia, and for governing such part of them as may be employed in the service of the United States, reserving to the States respectively the appointment of the officers, and the authority of training the militia according to the discipline prescribed by Congress;

To exercise exclusive legislation in all cases whatsoever, over such district (not exceeding ten miles square) as may, by cession of particular States, and the acceptance of Congress, become the seat of government of the United States, and to exercise like authority over all places purchased by the consent of the legislature of the State, in which the same shall be, for erection of forts, magazines, arsenals, dockyards, and other needful buildings; — and

To make all laws which shall be necessary and proper for carrying into execution the foregoing powers, and all other powers vested by this Constitution in the government of the United States, or in any department or officer thereof.

Section 9 The migration or importation of such persons as any of the States now existing shall think proper to admit shall not be prohibited by the Congress prior to the year 1808; but a tax or duty may be imposed on such importation, not exceeding $10 for each person.

The privilege of the writ of habeas corpus shall not be suspended, unless when in cases of rebellion or invasion the public safety may require it.

No bill of attainder or ex post facto law shall be passed.

No capitation, or other direct, tax shall be laid, unless in proportion to the census or enumeration herein before directed to be taken.

No tax or duty shall be laid on articles exported from any State.

No preference shall be given by any regulation of commerce or revenue to the ports of one State over those of another; nor shall vessels bound to, or from, one State, be obliged to enter, clear, or pay duties in another.

No money shall be drawn from the treasury, but in consequence of appropriations made by law; and a regular statement and account of the receipts and expenditures of all public money shall be published from time to time.

No title of nobility shall be granted by the United States: and no person holding any office of profit or trust under them, shall, without the consent of the Congress, accept of any present, emolument, office, or title, of any kind whatever, from any king, prince, or foreign state.

Section 10 No State shall enter into any treaty, alliance, or confederation; grant letters of marque and reprisal; coin money; emit bills of credit; make anything but gold and silver coin a tender in payment of debts; pass any bill of attainder, ex post facto law, or law impairing

the obligation of contracts, or grant any title of nobility.

No State shall, without the consent of Congress, lay any imposts or duties on imports or exports, except what may be absolutely necessary for executing its inspection laws: and the net produce of all duties and imposts, laid by any State on imports or exports, shall be for the use of the treasury of the United States; and all such laws shall be subject to the revision and control of the Congress.

No State shall, without the consent of Congress, lay any duty of tonnage, keep troops or ships of war in time of peace, enter into any agreement or compact with another State, or with a foreign power, or engage in war, unless actually invaded, or in such imminent danger as will not admit of delay.

Article II

Section 1 The executive power shall be vested in a President of the United States of America. He shall hold his office during the term of four years, and, together with the Vice-President, chosen for the same term, be elected as follows:

Each State shall appoint, in such manner as the legislature thereof may direct, a number of electors, equal to the whole number of Senators and Representatives to which the State may be entitled in the Congress; but no Senator or Representative, or person holding an office of trust or profit under the United States, shall be appointed an elector.

The electors shall meet in their respective States, and vote by ballot for two persons, of whom one at least shall not be an inhabitant of the same State with themselves. And they shall make a list of all the persons voted for, and of the number of votes for each; which list they shall sign and certify, and transmit sealed to the seat of government of the United States, directed to the President of the Senate. The President of the Senate shall, in the presence of the Senate and House of Representatives, open all the certificates, and the votes shall then be counted. The person having the greatest number of votes shall be the President, if such number be a majority of the whole number of electors appointed; and if there be more than one who have such majority, and have an equal number of votes, then the House of Representatives shall immediately choose by ballot one of them for President; and if no person have a majority, then from the five highest on the list said house shall in like manner choose the President. But in choosing the President the votes shall be taken by States, the representation from each State having one vote; a quorum for this purpose shall consist of a member or members from two-thirds of the States, and a majority of all the States shall be necessary to a choice. In every case, after the choice of the President, the person having the greatest number of votes of the electors shall be the Vice-President. But if there should remain two or more who have equal votes, the Senate shall choose from them by ballot the Vice-President.

The Congress may determine the time of choosing the electors and the day on which they shall give their votes; which day shall be the same throughout the United States.

No person except a natural-born citizen, or a citizen of the United States at the time of the adoption of this Constitution, shall be eligible to the office of President; neither shall any person be eligible to that office who shall not have attained to the age of thirty-five years, and been fourteen years a resident within the United States.

In case of the removal of the President from office or of his death, resignation, or inability to discharge the powers and duties of the said office, the same shall devolve on the Vice-President, and the Congress may by law provide for the case of removal, death, resignation, or inability, both of the President and Vice-President, declaring what officer shall then act as President, and such officer shall act accordingly, until the disability be removed, or a President shall be elected.

The President shall, at stated times, receive for his services a compensation, which shall neither be increased nor diminished during the period for which he shall have been elected, and he shall not receive within that period any other emolument from the United States, or any of them.

Before he enter on the execution of his office, he shall take the following oath or affirmation: — "I do solemnly swear (or affirm) that I will faithfully execute the office of the President of the United States, and will to the best of my ability preserve, protect and defend the Constitution of the United States."

Section 2 The President shall be commander in chief of the army and navy of the United States, and of the militia of the several States, when called into the actual service of the United States; he may require the opinion, in writing, of the principal officer in each of the executive departments, upon any subject relating to the duties of their respective offices, and he shall have power to grant reprieves and pardons for offenses against the United States, except in cases of impeachment.

He shall have power, by and with the advice and consent of the Senate, to make treaties, provided two-thirds of the Senators present concur; and he shall nominate, and by and with the advice and consent of the Senate, shall appoint ambassadors, other public ministers and consuls, judges of the Supreme Court, and all other officers of the United States, whose appointments are not herein otherwise provided for, and which shall be established by law: but Congress may by law vest the appointment of such inferior officers, as they think proper, in the President alone, in the courts of law, or in the heads of departments.

The President shall have power to fill up all vacancies that may happen during the recess of the Senate, by granting commissions which shall expire at the end of their next session.

Section 3 He shall from time to time give to the Congress information of the state of the Union, and recommend to their consideration such measures as he shall judge necessary and expedient; he may, on extraordinary occasions, convene both houses, or either of them, and in case of disagreement between them, with respect to the time of adjournment, he may adjourn them to such time as he shall think proper; he shall receive ambassadors and other public ministers; he shall take care that the laws be faithfully executed, and shall commission all the officers of the United States.

Section 4 The President, Vice-President and all civil officers of the United States shall be removed from office on impeachment for, and on conviction of, treason, bribery, or other high crimes and misdemeanors.

Article III

Section 1 The judicial power of the United States shall be vested in one Supreme Court, and in such inferior courts as the Congress may from time to time ordain and establish. The judges, both of the Supreme and inferior courts, shall hold their offices during good behavior, and shall, at stated times, receive for their services a compensation which shall not be diminished during their continuance in office.

Section 2 The judicial power shall extend to all cases, in law and equity, arising under this Constitution, the laws of the United States, and treaties made, or which shall be made, under their authority; — to all cases affecting ambassadors, other public ministers and consuls; — to all cases of admiralty and maritime jurisdiction; — to controversies to which the United States shall be a party; — to controversies between two or more States; — *between a State and citizens of another State;* — between citizens of different States; — between citizens of the same State claiming lands under grants of different States, and between a State, or the citizens thereof, and foreign states, citizens or subjects.

In all cases affecting ambassadors, other public ministers and consuls, and those in which a State shall be party, the Supreme Court shall have original jurisdiction. In all the other cases before mentioned, the Supreme Court shall have appellate jurisdiction, both as to law and fact, with such exceptions, and under such regulations, as the Congress shall make.

The trial of all crimes, except in cases of impeachment, shall be by jury; and such trial shall be held in the State where said crimes shall have been committed; but when not committed within any State, the trial shall be at such place or places as the Congress may by law have directed.

Section 3 Treason against the United States shall consist only in levying war against them, or in adhering to their enemies, giving them aid and comfort. No person shall be convicted of treason unless on the testimony of two witnesses to the same overt act, or on confession in open court.

The Congress shall have power to declare the punishment of treason, but no attainder of treason shall work corruption of blood, or forfeiture except during the life of the person attainted.

Article IV

Section 1 Full faith and credit shall be given in each State to the public acts, records, and judicial proceedings of every other State. And the Congress may by general laws prescribe the manner in which such acts, records, and proceedings shall be proved, and the effect thereof.

Section 2 The citizens of each State shall be entitled to all privileges and immunities of citizens in the several States.

A person charged in any State with treason, felony, or other crime, who shall flee from justice, and be found in another State, shall on demand of the executive authority of the State from which he fled, be delivered up, to be removed to the State having jurisdiction of the crime.

No person held to service or labor in one State, under the laws thereof, escaping into another, shall, in consequence of any law or regulation therein, be discharged from such service or labor, but shall be delivered up on claim of the party to whom such service or labor may be due.

Section 3 New States may be admitted by the Congress into this Union; but no new State shall be formed or erected within the jurisdiction of any other State; nor any State be formed by the junction of two or more States, or parts of States, without the consent of the legislatures of the States concerned as well as of the Congress.

The Congress shall have power to dispose of and make all needful rules and regulations respecting the territory or other property belonging to the United States; and nothing in this Constitution shall be so construed as to prejudice any claims of the United States, or of any particular State.

Section 4 The United States shall guarantee to every State in this Union a republican form of government, and shall protect each of them against invasion; and on application of the legislature, or of the executive (when the legislature cannot be convened), against domestic violence.

Article V

The Congress, whenever two-thirds of both houses shall deem it necessary, shall propose amendments to this Constitution, or, on the application of the legislatures of two-thirds of the several States, shall call a convention for proposing amendments, which, in either case, shall be valid to all intents and purposes, as part of this Constitution, when ratified by the legislatures of three-fourths of the several States, or by conventions in three-fourths thereof, as the one or the other mode of ratification may be proposed by the Congress; provided *that no amendments which may be made prior to the year one thousand eight hundred and eight shall in any manner affect the first and fourth*

clauses in the ninth section of the first article; and that no State, without its consent, shall be deprived of its equal suffrage in the Senate.

Article VI

All debts contracted and engagements entered into, before the adoption of this Constitution, shall be as valid against the United States under this Constitution, as under the Confederation.

This Constitution, and the laws of the United States which shall be made in pursuance thereof; and all treaties made, or which shall be made, under the authority of the United States, shall be the supreme law of the land; and the judges in every State shall be bound thereby, anything in the Constitution or laws of any State to the contrary notwithstanding.

The Senators and Representatives before mentioned, and the members of the several State legislatures, and all executive and judicial officers, both of the United States and of the several States, shall be bound by oath or affirmation to support this Constitution; but no religious test shall ever be required as a qualification to any office or public trust under the United States.

Article VII

The ratification of the conventions of nine States shall be sufficient for the establishment of this Constitution between the States so ratifying the same.

Done in Convention by the unanimous consent of the States present, the seventeenth day of September in the year of our Lord one thousand seven hundred and eighty-seven and of the Independence of the United States of America the twelfth. In witness whereof we have hereunto subscribed our names.

George Washington
and thirty-eight others*

*For a list of signers and non-signers of the original Constitution, SEE APPENDIX.

Amendments to the Constitution

[The first ten Amendments (the Bill of Rights) were adopted in 1791.]

Amendment I Congress shall make no law respecting an establishment of religion, or prohibiting the free exercise thereof; or abridging the freedom of speech, or of the press; or the right of the people peaceably to assemble, and to petition the government for a redress of grievances.

Amendment II A well-regulated militia being necessary to the security of a free state, the right of the people to keep and bear arms shall not be infringed.

Amendment III No soldier shall, in time of peace, be quartered in any house without the consent of the owner, not in time of war, but in a manner to be prescribed by law.

Amendment IV The right of the people to be secure in their persons, houses, papers, and effects, against unreasonable searches and seizures, shall not be violated, and no warrants shall issue but upon probable cause, supported by oath or affirmation, and particularly describing the place to be searched, and the persons or things to be seized.

Amendment V No person shall be held to answer for a capital, or otherwise infamous crime, unless on a presentment or indictment of a grand jury, except in cases arising in the land or naval forces, or in the militia, when in actual service in time of war or public danger; nor shall any person be subject for the same offense to be twice put in jeopardy of life or limb; nor shall be compelled in any criminal case to be a witness against himself, nor be deprived of life, liberty, or property, without due process of law; nor shall private property be taken for public use without just compensation.

Amendment VI In all criminal prosecutions, the accused shall enjoy the right to a speedy and public trial, by an impartial jury of the State and district wherein the crime shall have been committed, which district shall have been previously ascertained by law, and to be informed of the nature and cause of the accusation; to be confronted with the witnesses against him; to have compulsory process for obtaining witnesses in his favor, and to have the assistance of counsel for his defense.

Amendment VII In suits at common law, where the value in controversy shall exceed twenty dollars, the right of trial by jury shall be preserved, and no fact tried by a jury shall be otherwise reexamined in any court of the United States, than according to the rules of the common law.

Amendment VIII Excessive bail shall not be required, nor excessive fines imposed, nor cruel and unusual punishments inflicted.

Amendment IX The enumeration in the Constitution, of certain rights, shall not be construed to deny or disparage others retained by the people.

Amendment X The powers not delegated to the United States by the Constitution, nor prohibited by it to the States, are reserved to the States respectively, or to the people.

Amendment XI [Adopted 1798] The judicial power of the United States shall not be construed to extend to any suit in law or equity, commenced or prosecuted against one of the United States by citizens of another State, or by citizens or subjects of any foreign state.

Amendment XII [Adopted 1804] The electors shall meet in their respective States, and vote by ballot for President and Vice-President, one of whom, at least, shall not be an inhabitant of the same State with themselves; they shall name in their ballots the person voted for as President, and in distinct ballots the person voted for as Vice-President, and they shall make distinct lists of all persons voted for as President, and of all persons voted for as Vice-President, and of the number of votes for each, which lists they shall sign and certify, and transmit sealed to the seat of government of the United States, directed to the President of the Senate; — the President of the Senate shall, in the presence of the Senate and House of Representatives, open all the certificates and the votes shall then be counted; — the person having the greatest number of votes for President shall be the President, if such number be a majority of the whole number of electors appointed; and if no person have such majority, then from the persons having the highest numbers not exceeding three on the list of those voted for as President, the House of Representatives shall choose immediately, by ballot, the President. But in choosing the President, the votes shall be taken by States, the representation from each State having one vote; a quorum for this purpose shall consist of a member or members from two-thirds of the States, and a majority of all the States shall be necessary to a choice. And if the House of Representatives shall not choose a President whenever the right of choice shall devolve upon them, before *the fourth day of March* next following, then the Vice-President shall act as President, as in the case of the death or other constitutional disability of the President.

The person having the greatest number of votes as Vice-President shall be the Vice-President, if such number be a majority of the whole number of electors appointed; and if no person have a majority, then from the two highest numbers on the list the Senate shall choose the Vice-President; a quorum for the purpose shall consist of two-thirds of the whole number of Senators, and a majority of the whole number shall be necessary to a choice. But no person constitutionally ineligible to the office of President shall be eligible to that of Vice-President of the United States.

Amendment XIII [Adopted 1865]

Section 1 Neither slavery nor involuntary servitude, except as a punishment for crime whereof the party shall have been duly convicted, shall exist within the United States, or any place subject to their jurisdiction.

Section 2 Congress shall have power to enforce this article by appropriate legislation.

Amendment XIV [Adopted 1868]

Section 1 All persons born or naturalized in the United States, and subject to the jurisdiction thereof, are citizens of the United States and of the State wherein they reside. No State shall make or enforce any law which shall abridge the privileges or immunities of citizens of the United States; nor shall any State deprive any person of life, liberty, or property, without due process of law; nor deny to any person within its jurisdiction the equal protection of the laws.

Section 2 Representatives shall be apportioned among the several States according to their respective numbers, counting the whole number of persons in each State, excluding Indians not taxed. But when the right to vote at any election for the choice of Electors for President and Vice-President of the United States, Representatives in Congress, the executive and judicial officers of a State, or the members of the legislature thereof, is denied to any of the male inhabitants of such State, being twenty-one years of age and citizens of the United States, or in any way abridged, except for participation in rebellion, or other crime, the basis of representation therein shall be reduced in the proportion which the number of such male citizens shall bear to the whole number of male citizens twenty-one years of age in such State.

Section 3 No person shall be a Senator or Representative in Congress, or Elector of President and Vice-President, or hold any office, civil or military, under the United States, or under any State, who, having previously taken an oath, as a member of Congress, or as an officer of the United States, or as a member of any State legislature, or as an executive or judicial officer of any State, to support the Constitution of the United States, shall have engaged in insurrection or rebellion against the same, or given aid or comfort to the enemies thereof. Congress may, by a vote of two-thirds of each house, remove such disability.

Section 4 The validity of the public debt of the United States, authorized by law, including debts incurred for payment of pensions and bounties for services in suppressing insurrection or rebellion, shall not be questioned. But neither the United States nor any State shall assume or pay any debt or obligation incurred in aid of insurrection or rebellion against the United States, or any claim for the loss of emancipation of any slave; but all such debts, obligations, and claims shall be held illegal and void.

Section 5 The Congress shall have power to enforce, by appropriate legislation, the provisions of this article.

Amendment XV [Adopted 1870]

Section 1 The right of citizens of the United States to vote shall not be denied or abridged by the United States or by any State on account of race, color, or previous condition of servitude.

Section 2 The Congress shall have power to enforce this article by appropriate legislation.

Amendment XVI [Adopted 1913]

The Congress shall have power to lay and collect taxes on incomes, from whatever source derived, without apportionment among the several States, and without regard to any census or enumeration.

Amendment XVII [Adopted 1913]

Section 1 The Senate of the United States shall be composed of two Senators from each State, elected by the people thereof, for six years; and each Senator shall have one vote. The electors in each State shall have the qualifications requisite for electors of [voters for] the most numerous branch of the State legislatures.

Section 2 When vacancies happen in the representation of any State in the Senate, the executive authority of such State shall issue writs of election to fill such vacancies: Provided, that the Legislature of any State may empower the executive thereof to make temporary appointments until the people fill the vacancies by election as the Legislature may direct.

Section 3 This amendment shall not be so construed as to affect the election or term of any Senator chosen before it becomes valid as part of the Constitution.

Amendment XVIII [Adopted 1919; Repealed 1933]

Section 1 After one year from the ratification of this article the manufacture, sale, or transportation of intoxicating liquors within, the importation thereof into, or the exportation thereof from the United States and all territory subject to the jurisdiction thereof, for beverage purposes, is hereby prohibited.

Section 2 The Congress and the several States shall have concurrent power to enforce this article by appropriate legislation.

Section 3 This article shall be inoperative unless it shall have been ratified as an amendment to the Constitution by the legislatures of the several States, as provided by the Constitution, within seven years from the date of the submission thereof to the States by the Congress.

Amendment XIX [Adopted 1920]

Section 1 The right of citizens of the United States to vote shall not be denied or abridged by the United States or by any State on account of sex.

Section 2 The Congress shall have power to enforce this article by appropriate legislation.

Amendment XX [Adopted 1933]

Section 1 The terms of the President and Vice-President shall end at noon on the 20th day of January, and the terms of Senators and Representatives at noon on the 3d day of January, of the years in which such terms would have ended if this article had not been ratified; and the terms of their successors shall then begin.

Section 2 The Congress shall assemble at least once in every year, and such meeting shall begin at noon on the 3d day of January, unless they shall by law appoint a different day.

Section 3 If, at the time fixed for the beginning of the term of the President, the President-elect shall have died, the Vice-President-elect shall become President. If a President shall not have been chosen before the time fixed for the beginning of his term, or if the President-elect shall have failed to qualify, then the Vice-President-elect shall act as President until a President shall have qualified; and the Congress may by law provide for the case wherein neither a President-elect nor a Vice-President-elect shall have qualified, declaring who shall then act as President, or the manner in which one who is to act shall be selected, and such persons shall act accordingly until a President or Vice-President shall have qualified.

Section 4 The Congress may by law provide for the case of the death of any of the persons from whom the House of Representatives may choose a President whenever the right of choice shall have devolved upon them, and for the case of the death of any of the persons from whom the Senate may choose a Vice-President whenever the right of choice shall have devolved upon them.

Section 5 Sections 1 and 2 shall take effect on the 15th day of October following the ratification of this article.

Section 6 This article shall be inoperative unless it shall have been ratified as an amendment to the Constitution by the Legislatures of three-fourths of the several States within seven years from the date of its submission.

Amendment XXI [Adopted 1933]

Section 1 The eighteenth article of amendment to the Constitution of the United States is hereby repealed.

Section 2 The transportation or importation into any State, Territory, or Possession of the United States for delivery or use therein of intoxicating liquors, in violation of the laws thereof, is hereby prohibited.

Section 3 This article shall be inoperative unless it shall have been ratified as an amendment to the Constitution by conventions in the several States, as provided in the Constitution, within seven years from the date of submission thereof to the States by the Congress.

Amendment XXII [Adopted 1951]

Section 1 No person shall be elected to the office of President more than twice, and no person who has held the office of President, or acted as President, for more than two years of a term to which some other person was elected President shall be elected to the office of President more than once. But this article shall not apply to any person holding the office of President when this article was proposed by the Congress, and shall not prevent any person who may be holding the office of President, or acting as President, during the term within which this article becomes operative from holding the office of President or acting as President during the remainder of such term.

Section 2 This article shall be inoperative unless it shall have been ratified as an amendment to the Constitution by the legislatures of three-fourths of the several States within seven years from the date of its submission to the Senate by the Congress.

Amendment XXIII [Adopted 1961]

Section 1 The District constituting the seat of Government of the United States shall appoint in such manner as the Congress may direct:

A number of electors of President and Vice-President equal to the whole number of Senators and Representatives in Congress to which the District would be entitled if it were a State, but in no event more than the least populous State; they shall be in addition to those appointed by the States, but they shall be considered for the purposes of the election of President and Vice-President, to be electors appointed by a State; and they shall meet in the District and perform such duties as provided by the twelfth article of amendment.

Section 2 The Congress shall have the power to enforce this article by appropriate legislation.

Amendment XXIV [Adopted 1964]

Section 1 The right of citizens of the United States to vote in any primary or other election for President or Vice-President, for electors for President or Vice-President, or for Senator or Representative in Congress, shall not be denied or abridged by the United States or any State by reason of failure to pay any poll tax or other tax.

Section 2 The Congress shall have the power to enforce this article by appropriate legislation.

Amendment XXV [Adopted 1967]

Section 1 In case of the removal of the President from office or of his death or resignation, the Vice-President shall become President.

Section 2 Whenever there is a vacancy in the office of the Vice-President, the President shall nominate a Vice-President who shall take office upon confirmation by a majority vote of both Houses of Congress.

Section 3 Whenever the President transmits to the President pro tempore of the Senate and the Speaker of the House of Representatives his written declaration that he is unable to discharge the powers and duties of his office, and until he transmits to them a written declaration to the contrary, such powers and duties shall be discharged by the Vice-President as Acting President.

Section 4 Whenever the Vice-President and a majority of either the principal officers of the executive departments or of such other body as Congress may by law provide, transmit to the President pro tempore of the Senate and the Speaker of the House of Representatives their written declaration that the President is unable to discharge the powers and duties of his office, the Vice-President shall immediately assume the powers and duties of the office as Acting President.

Thereafter, when the President transmits to the President pro tempore of the Senate and the Speaker of the House of Representatives his written declaration that no inability exists, he shall resume the powers and duties of his office unless the Vice-President and a majority of either the principal officers of the executive department[s] or of such other body as Congress may by law provide, transmit within four days to the President pro tempore of the Senate and the Speaker of the House of Representatives their written declaration that the President is unable to discharge the powers and duties of his office. Thereupon Congress shall decide the issue, assembling within forty-eight hours for that purpose if not in session. If the Congress, within twenty-one days after receipt of the latter written declaration, or, if Congress is not in session, within twenty-one days after Congress is required to assemble, determines by two-thirds vote of both Houses that the President is unable to discharge the powers and duties of his office, the Vice-President shall continue to discharge the same as Acting President; otherwise, the

President shall resume the powers and duties of his office.

Amendment XXVI [Adopted 1971]

Section 1 The right of citizens of the United States, who are eighteen years of age or older, to vote shall not be denied or abridged by the United States or by any State on account of age.

Section 2 The Congress shall have power to enforce this article by appropriate legislation.

Amendment XXVII [Adopted 1992]

No law, varying the compensation for the services of the Senators and Representatives, shall take effect until an election of Representatives shall have intervened.

Signers of the Original Constitution

George Washington, *President and deputy from Virginia*

Delaware
George Read
Gunning Bedford, Junior
John Dickinson
Richard Bassett
Jacob Broom

Maryland
James McHenry
Daniel of St. Thomas Jenifer
Daniel Carroll

Virginia
John Blair
James Madison, Junior

North Carolina
William Blount
Richard Dobbs Spaight
Hugh Williamson

South Carolina
John Rutledge
Charles Cotesworth Pinckney
Charles Pinckney
Pierce Butler

Georgia
William Few
Abraham Baldwin

New Hampshire
John Langdon
Nicholas Gilman

Massachusetts
Nathaniel Gorham
Rufus King

Connecticut
William Samuel Johnson
Roger Sherman

New York
Alexander Hamilton

New Jersey
William Livingston
David Brearley
William Paterson
Jonathan Dayton

Pennsylvania
Benjamin Franklin
Thomas Mifflin
Robert Morris
George Clymer
Thomas FitzSimmons
Jared Ingersoll
James Wilson
Gouverneur Morris

Non-signing Delegates to the Constitutional Convention

Massachusetts
Caleb Strong
Elbridge Gerry

Connecticut
Oliver Ellsworth

New York
Robert Yates
John Lansing, Jr.

New Jersey
William Churchill Houston

Maryland
John Françis Mercer
Luther Martin

Virginia
George Mason
George Wythe
Edmund Randolph
James McClurg

North Carolina
Alexander Martin
William Richardson Davie

Georgia
William Houstoun
William Pierce

Gettysburg Address

Delivered by Abraham Lincoln, November 19, 1863, at the site of the battle of Gettysburg, July 1 through 3, 1863, Gettysburg, Pennsylvania

Four score and seven years ago our fathers brought forth on this continent, a new nation, conceived in Liberty, and dedicated to the proposition that all men are created equal.

Now we are engaged in a great civil war, testing whether that nation, or any nation so conceived and so dedicated, can long endure. We are met on a great battlefield of that war. We have come to dedicate a portion of that field, as a final resting place for those who here gave their lives that that nation might live. It is altogether fitting and proper that we should do this.

But, in a larger sense, we can not dedicate — we can not consecrate — we can not hallow — this ground. The brave men, living and dead, who struggled here, have consecrated it, far above our poor power to add or detract. The world will little note, not long remember what we say here, but it can never forget what they did here. It is for us the living, rather, to be dedicated here to the unfinished work which they who fought here have thus far so nobly advanced. It is rather for us to be here dedicated to the great task remaining before us — that from these honored dead we take increased devotion to that cause for which they gave the last full measure of devotion — that we here highly resolve that these dead shall not have died in vain — that this nation, under God, shall have a new birth of freedom — and that government of the people, by the people, for the people, shall not perish from the earth.

Index

Page numbers in italics are main entries.

Illustrations

Maps